BMW
COUPES AND SEDANS
1970-88 REPAIR MANUAL

CHILTON'S

President	Dean F. Morgantini, S.A.E.
Vice President–Finance	Barry L. Beck
Vice President–Sales	Glenn D. Potere
Executive Editor	Kevin M. G. Maher, A.S.E.
Manager–Consumer	Richard Schwartz, A.S.E.
Manager–Professional	George B. Heinrich III, A.S.E., S.A.E.
Manager–Marine/Recreation	James R. Marotta, A.S.E., S.T.S.
Manager–Production	Ben Greisler, S.A.E.
Production Assistant	Melinda Possinger
Project Managers	Will Kessler, A.S.E., S.A.E., Todd W. Stidham, A.S.E., Ron Webb
Schematics Editor	Christopher G. Ritchie, A.S.E.
Editor	Gordon Tobias, S.A.E.

CHILTON ™ *Automotive Books*

PUBLISHED BY **W. G. NICHOLS, INC.**

Manufactured in USA
© 1996 Chilton Book Company
1020 Andrew Drive
West Chester, PA 19380
ISBN 0-8019-8789-X
Library of Congress Catalog Card No. 96-83140
6789012345 8765432109

www.Chiltononline.com

Contents

Contents

DRIVE TRAIN 7

STEERING AND SUSPENSION 8

BRAKES 9

BODY AND TRIM 10

GLOSSARY

MASTER INDEX

See last page for information on additional titles

SAFETY NOTICE

Proper service and repair procedures are vital to the safe, reliable operation of all motor vehicles, as well as the personal safety of those performing repairs. This manual outlines procedures for servicing and repairing vehicles using safe, effective methods. The procedures contain many NOTES, CAUTIONS and WARNINGS which should be followed, along with standard procedures to eliminate the possibility of personal injury or improper service which could damage the vehicle or compromise its safety.

It is important to note that repair procedures and techniques, tools and parts for servicing motor vehicles, as well as the skill and experience of the individual performing the work vary widely. It is not possible to anticipate all of the conceivable ways or conditions under which vehicles may be serviced, or to provide cautions as to all possible hazards that may result. Standard and accepted safety precautions and equipment should be used when handling toxic or flammable fluids, and safety goggles or other protection should be used during cutting, grinding, chiseling, prying, or any other process that can cause material removal or projectiles.

Some procedures require the use of tools specially designed for a specific purpose. Before substituting another tool or procedure, you must be completely satisfied that neither your personal safety, nor the performance of the vehicle will be endangered.

Although information in this manual is based on industry sources and is complete as possible at the time of publication, the possibility exists that some car manufacturers made later changes which could not be included here. While striving for total accuracy, NP/Chilton cannot assume responsibility for any errors, changes or omissions that may occur in the compilation of this data.

PART NUMBERS

Part numbers listed in this reference are not recommendations by Chilton for any product brand name. They are references that can be used with interchange manuals and aftermarket supplier catalogs to locate each brand supplier's discrete part number.

SPECIAL TOOLS

Special tools are recommended by the vehicle manufacturer to perform their specific job. Use has been kept to a minimum, but where absolutely necessary, they are referred to in the text by the part number of the tool manufacturer. These tools can be purchased, under the appropriate part number, from your local dealer or regional distributor, or an equivalent tool can be purchased locally from a tool supplier or parts outlet. Before substituting any tool for the one recommended, read the SAFETY NOTICE at the top of this page.

ACKNOWLEDGMENTS

NP/Chilton expresses appreciation to BMW of North America for their generous assistance.

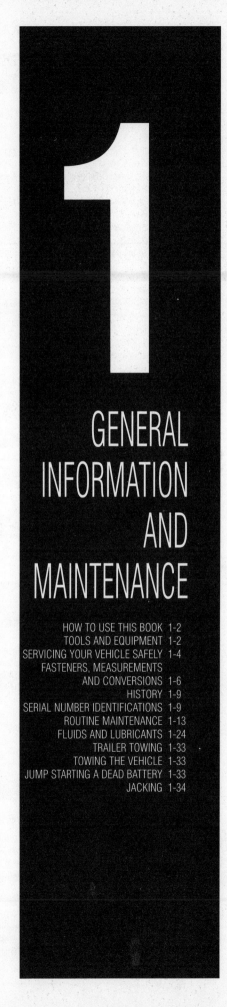

1

GENERAL INFORMATION AND MAINTENANCE

HOW TO USE THIS BOOK

This Chilton's Total Car Care manual for the BMW is intended to help you learn more about the inner workings of your vehicle while saving you money on its upkeep and operation.

The beginning of the book will likely be referred to the most, since that is where you will find information for maintenance and tune-up. The other sections deal with the more complex systems of your vehicle. Systems (from engine through brakes) are covered to the extent that the average do-it-yourselfer can attempt. This book will not explain such things as rebuilding a differential because the expertise required and the special tools necessary make this uneconomical. It will, however, give you detailed instructions to help you change your own brake pads and shoes, replace spark plugs, and perform many more jobs that can save you money and help avoid expensive problems.

A secondary purpose of this book is a reference for owners who want to understand their vehicle and/or their mechanics better.

Where to Begin

Before removing any bolts, read through the entire procedure. This will give you the overall view of what tools and supplies will be required. So read ahead and plan ahead. Each operation should be approached logically and all procedures thoroughly understood before attempting any work.

If repair of a component is not considered practical, we tell you how to remove the part and then how to install the new or rebuilt replacement. In this way, you at least save labor costs.

Avoiding Trouble

Many procedures in this book require you to "label and disconnect . . . " a group of lines, hoses or wires. Don't be think you can remember where everything goes—you won't. If you hook up vacuum or fuel lines incorrectly, the vehicle may run poorly, if at all. If you hook up electrical wiring incorrectly, you may instantly learn a very expensive lesson.

You don't need to know the proper name for each hose or line. A piece of masking tape on the hose and a piece on its fitting will allow you to assign your own label. As long as you remember your own code, the lines can be reconnected by matching your tags. Remember that tape will dissolve in gasoline or solvents; if a part is to be washed or cleaned, use another method of identification. A permanent felt-tipped marker or a metal scribe can be very handy for marking metal parts. Remove any tape or paper labels after assembly.

Maintenance or Repair?

Maintenance includes routine inspections, adjustments, and replacement of parts which show signs of normal wear. Maintenance compensates for wear or deterioration. Repair implies that something has broken or is not working. A need for a repair is often caused by lack of maintenance. for example: draining and refilling automatic transmission fluid is maintenance recommended at specific intervals. Failure to do this can shorten the life of the transmission/transaxle, requiring very expensive repairs. While no maintenance program can prevent items from eventually breaking or wearing out, a general rule is true: MAINTENANCE IS CHEAPER THAN REPAIR.

Two basic mechanic's rules should be mentioned here. First, whenever the left side of the vehicle or engine is referred to, it means the driver's side. Conversely, the right side of the vehicle means the passenger's side. Second, screws and bolts are removed by turning counterclockwise, and tightened by turning clockwise unless specifically noted.

Safety is always the most important rule. Constantly be aware of the dangers involved in working on an automobile and take the proper precautions. Please refer to the information in this section regarding SERVICING YOUR VEHICLE SAFELY and the SAFETY NOTICE on the acknowledgment page.

Avoiding the Most Common Mistakes

Pay attention to the instructions provided. There are 3 common mistakes in mechanical work:

1. Incorrect order of assembly, disassembly or adjustment. When taking something apart or putting it together, performing steps in the wrong order usually just costs you extra time; however, it CAN break something. Read the entire procedure before beginning. Perform everything in the order in which the instructions say you should, even if you can't see a reason for it. When you're taking apart something that is very intricate, you might want to draw a picture of how it looks when assembled in order to make sure you get everything back in its proper position. When making adjustments, perform them in the proper order. One adjustment possibly will affect another.

2. Overtorquing (or undertorquing). While it is more common for overtorquing to cause damage, undertorquing may allow a fastener to vibrate loose causing serious damage. Especially when dealing with aluminum parts, pay attention to torque specifications and utilize a torque wrench in assembly. If a torque figure is not available, remember that if you are using the right tool to perform the job, you will probably not have to strain yourself to get a fastener tight enough. The pitch of most threads is so slight that the tension you put on the wrench will be multiplied many times in actual force on what you are tightening.

There are many commercial products available for ensuring that fasteners won't come loose, even if they are not torqued just right (a very common brand is Loctite®). If you're worried about getting something together tight enough to hold, but loose enough to avoid mechanical damage during assembly, one of these products might offer substantial insurance. Before choosing a threadlocking compound, read the label on the package and make sure the product is compatible with the materials, fluids, etc. involved.

3. Crossthreading. This occurs when a part such as a bolt is screwed into a nut or casting at the wrong angle and forced. Crossthreading is more likely to occur if access is difficult. It helps to clean and lubricate fasteners, then to start threading the bolt, spark plug, etc. with your fingers. If you encounter resistance, unscrew the part and start over again at a different angle until it can be inserted and turned several times without much effort. Keep in mind that many parts have tapered threads, so that gentle turning will automatically bring the part you're threading to the proper angle. Don't put a wrench on the part until it's been tightened a couple of turns by hand. If you suddenly encounter resistance, and the part has not seated fully, don't force it. Pull it back out to make sure it's clean and threading properly.

Be sure to take your time and be patient, and always plan ahead. Allow yourself ample time to perform repairs and maintenance.

TOOLS AND EQUIPMENT

▶ **See Figures 1 thru 15**

Without the proper tools and equipment it is impossible to properly service your vehicle. It would be virtually impossible to catalog every tool that you would need to perform all of the operations in this book. It would be unwise for the amateur to rush out and buy an expensive set of tools on the theory that he/she may need one or more of them at some time.

The best approach is to proceed slowly, gathering a good quality set of those tools that are used most frequently. Don't be misled by the low cost of bargain tools. It is far better to spend a little more for better quality. Forged wrenches, 6 or 12-point sockets and fine tooth ratchets are by far preferable to their less expensive counterparts. As any good mechanic can tell you, there are few worse

experiences than trying to work on a vehicle with bad tools. Your monetary savings will be far outweighed by frustration and mangled knuckles.

Begin accumulating those tools that are used most frequently: those associated with routine maintenance and tune-up. In addition to the normal assortment of screwdrivers and pliers, you should have the following tools:

• Wrenches/sockets and combination open end/box end wrenches in sizes 1/8–3/4 in. and/or 3mm–19mm 13/16 in. or 5/8 in. spark plug socket (depending on plug type).

➡**If possible, buy various length socket drive extensions. Universal-joint and wobble extensions can be extremely useful, but be careful when using them, as they can change the amount of torque applied to the socket.**

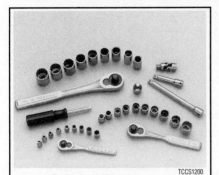

Fig. 1 All but the most basic procedures will require an assortment of ratchets and sockets

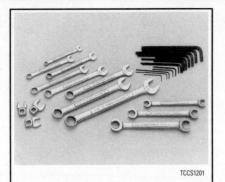

Fig. 2 In addition to ratchets, a good set of wrenches and hex keys will be necessary

Fig. 3 A hydraulic floor jack and a set of jackstands are essential for lifting and supporting the vehicle

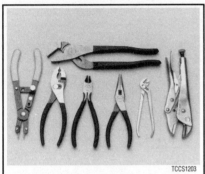

Fig. 4 An assortment of pliers, grippers and cutters will be handy for old rusted parts and stripped bolt heads

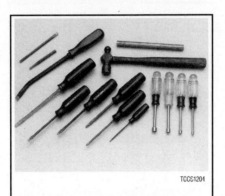

Fig. 5 Various drivers, chisels and prybars are great tools to have in your toolbox

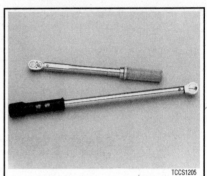

Fig. 6 Many repairs will require the use of a torque wrench to assure the components are properly fastened

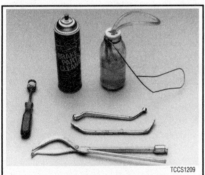

Fig. 7 Although not always necessary, using specialized brake tools will save time

Fig. 8 A few inexpensive lubrication tools will make maintenance easier

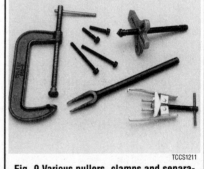

Fig. 9 Various pullers, clamps and separator tools are needed for many larger, more complicated repairs

- Jackstands for support.
- Oil filter wrench.
- Spout or funnel for pouring fluids.
- Grease gun for chassis lubrication (unless your vehicle is not equipped with any grease fittings)
- Hydrometer for checking the battery (unless equipped with a sealed, maintenance-free battery).
  - A container for draining oil and other fluids.
  - Rags for wiping up the inevitable mess.

In addition to the above items there are several others that are not absolutely necessary, but handy to have around. These include an equivalent oil absorbent gravel, like cat litter, and the usual supply of lubricants, antifreeze and fluids. This is a basic list for routine maintenance, but only your personal needs and desire can accurately determine your list of tools.

After performing a few projects on the vehicle, you'll be amazed at the other tools and non-tools on your workbench. Some useful household items are: a large turkey baster or siphon, empty coffee cans and ice trays (to store parts), a ball of twine, electrical tape for wiring, small rolls of colored tape for tagging lines or hoses, markers and pens, a note pad, golf tees (for plugging vacuum lines), metal coat hangers or a roll of mechanic's wire (to hold things out of the way), dental pick or similar long, pointed probe, a strong magnet, and a small mirror (to see into recesses and under manifolds).

A more advanced set of tools, suitable for tune-up work, can be drawn up easily. While the tools are slightly more sophisticated, they need not be outrageously expensive. There are several inexpensive tach/dwell meters on the market that are every bit as good for the average mechanic as a professional model. Just be sure that it goes to a least 1200–1500 rpm on the tach scale and that it works on 4, 6 and 8-cylinder engines. The key to these purchases is to make them with an eye towards adaptability and wide range. A basic list of tune-up tools could include:

- Tach/dwell meter.
- Spark plug wrench and gapping tool.

Fig. 10 A variety of tools and gauges should be used for spark plug gapping and installation

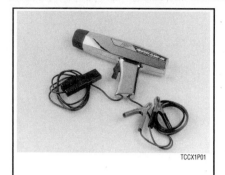

Fig. 11 Inductive type timing light

Fig. 12 A screw-in type compression gauge is recommended for compression testing

Fig. 13 A vacuum/pressure tester is necessary for many testing procedures

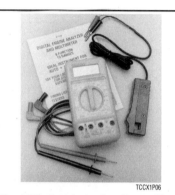

Fig. 14 Most modern automotive multimeters incorporate many helpful features

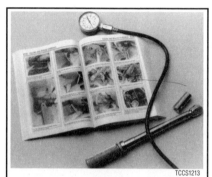

Fig. 15 Proper information is vital, so always have a Chilton Total Car Care manual handy

- Feeler gauges for valve adjustment.
- Timing light.

The choice of a timing light should be made carefully. A light which works on the DC current supplied by the vehicle's battery is the best choice; it should have a xenon tube for brightness. On any vehicle with an electronic ignition system, a timing light with an inductive pickup that clamps around the No. 1 spark plug cable is preferred.

In addition to these basic tools, there are several other tools and gauges you may find useful. These include:

- Compression gauge. The screw-in type is slower to use, but eliminates the possibility of a faulty reading due to escaping pressure.
- Manifold vacuum gauge.
- 12V test light.
- A combination volt/ohmmeter
- Induction Ammeter. This is used for determining whether or not there is current in a wire. These are handy for use if a wire is broken somewhere in a wiring harness.

As a final note, you will probably find a torque wrench necessary for all but the most basic work. The beam type models are perfectly adequate, although the newer click types (breakaway) are easier to use. The click type torque wrenches tend to be more expensive. Also keep in mind that all types of torque wrenches should be periodically checked and/or recalibrated. You will have to decide for yourself which better fits your pocketbook, and purpose.

Special Tools

Normally, the use of special factory tools is avoided for repair procedures, since these are not readily available for the do-it-yourself mechanic. When it is possible to perform the job with more commonly available tools, it will be pointed out, but occasionally, a special tool was designed to perform a specific function and should be used. Before substituting another tool, you should be convinced that neither your safety nor the performance of the vehicle will be compromised.

Special tools can usually be purchased from an automotive parts store or from your dealer. In some cases special tools may be available directly from the tool manufacturer.

SERVICING YOUR VEHICLE SAFELY

▶ See Figures 16, 17 and 18

It is virtually impossible to anticipate all of the hazards involved with automotive maintenance and service, but care and common sense will prevent most accidents.

The rules of safety for mechanics range from "don't smoke around gasoline," to "use the proper tool(s) for the job." The trick to avoiding injuries is to develop safe work habits and to take every possible precaution.

Do's

- Do keep a fire extinguisher and first aid kit handy.
- Do wear safety glasses or goggles when cutting, drilling, grinding or prying, even if you have 20–20 vision. If you wear glasses for the sake of vision, wear safety goggles over your regular glasses.

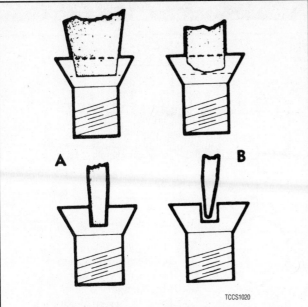

Fig. 16 Screwdrivers should be kept in good condition to prevent injury or damage which could result if the blade slips from the screw

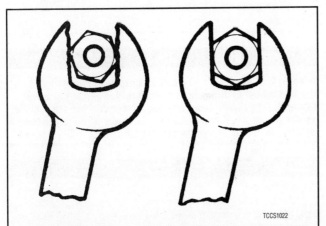

Fig. 17 Using the correct size wrench will help prevent the possibility of rounding off a nut

• Do shield your eyes whenever you work around the battery. Batteries contain sulfuric acid. In case of contact with, flush the area with water or a mixture of water and baking soda, then seek immediate medical attention.

• Do use safety stands (jackstands) for any undervehicle service. Jacks are for raising vehicles; jackstands are for making sure the vehicle stays raised until you want it to come down.

• Do use adequate ventilation when working with any chemicals or hazardous materials. Like carbon monoxide, the asbestos dust resulting from some brake lining wear can be hazardous in sufficient quantities.

• Do disconnect the negative battery cable when working on the electrical system. The secondary ignition system contains EXTREMELY HIGH VOLTAGE. In some cases it can even exceed 50,000 volts.

• Do follow manufacturer's directions whenever working with potentially hazardous materials. Most chemicals and fluids are poisonous.

• Do properly maintain your tools. Loose hammerheads, mushroomed punches and chisels, frayed or poorly grounded electrical cords, excessively worn screwdrivers, spread wrenches (open end), cracked sockets, slipping ratchets, or faulty droplight sockets can cause accidents.

• Likewise, keep your tools clean; a greasy wrench can slip off a bolt head, ruining the bolt and often harming your knuckles in the process.

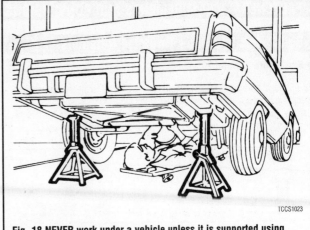

Fig. 18 NEVER work under a vehicle unless it is supported using safety stands (jackstands)

• Do use the proper size and type of tool for the job at hand. Do select a wrench or socket that fits the nut or bolt. The wrench or socket should sit straight, not cocked.

• Do, when possible, pull on a wrench handle rather than push on it, and adjust your stance to prevent a fall.

• Do be sure that adjustable wrenches are tightly closed on the nut or bolt and pulled so that the force is on the side of the fixed jaw.

• Do strike squarely with a hammer; avoid glancing blows.

• Do set the parking brake and block the drive wheels if the work requires a running engine.

Don'ts

• Don't run the engine in a garage or anywhere else without proper ventilation—EVER! Carbon monoxide is poisonous; it takes a long time to leave the human body and you can build up a deadly supply of it in your system by simply breathing in a little at a time. You may not realize you are slowly poisoning yourself. Always use power vents, windows, fans and/or open the garage door.

• Don't work around moving parts while wearing loose clothing. Short sleeves are much safer than long, loose sleeves. Hard-toed shoes with neoprene soles protect your toes and give a better grip on slippery surfaces. Watches and jewelry is not safe working around a vehicle. Long hair should be tied back under a hat or cap.

• Don't use pockets for toolboxes. A fall or bump can drive a screwdriver deep into your body. Even a rag hanging from your back pocket can wrap around a spinning shaft or fan.

• Don't smoke when working around gasoline, cleaning solvent or other flammable material.

• Don't smoke when working around the battery. When the battery is being charged, it gives off explosive hydrogen gas.

• Don't use gasoline to wash your hands; there are excellent soaps available. Gasoline contains dangerous additives which can enter the body through a cut or through your pores. Gasoline also removes all the natural oils from the skin so that bone dry hands will suck up oil and grease.

• Don't service the air conditioning system unless you are equipped with the necessary tools and training. When liquid or compressed gas refrigerant is released to atmospheric pressure it will absorb heat from whatever it contacts. This will chill or freeze anything it touches.

• Don't use screwdrivers for anything other than driving screws! A screwdriver used as an prying tool can snap when you least expect it, causing injuries. At the very least, you'll ruin a good screwdriver.

• Don't use an emergency jack (that little ratchet, scissors, or pantograph jack supplied with the vehicle) for anything other than changing a flat! These jacks are only intended for emergency use out on the road; they are NOT designed as a maintenance tool. If you are serious about maintaining your vehicle yourself, invest in a hydraulic floor jack of at least a 1½ ton capacity, and at least two sturdy jackstands.

FASTENERS, MEASUREMENTS AND CONVERSIONS

Bolts, Nuts and Other Threaded Retainers

♦ **See Figures 19 and 20**

Although there are a great variety of fasteners found in the modern car or truck, the most commonly used retainer is the threaded fastener (nuts, bolts, screws, studs, etc.). Most threaded retainers may be reused, provided that they are not damaged in use or during the repair. Some retainers (such as stretch

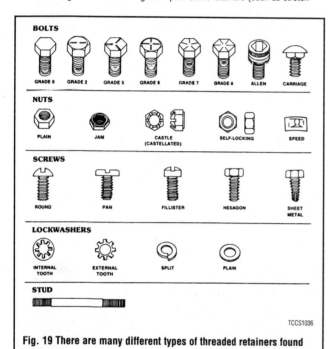

Fig. 19 There are many different types of threaded retainers found on vehicles

bolts or torque prevailing nuts) are designed to deform when tightened or in use and should not be reinstalled.

Whenever possible, we will note any special retainers which should be replaced during a procedure. But you should always inspect the condition of a retainer when it is removed and replace any that show signs of damage. Check all threads for rust or corrosion which can increase the torque necessary to achieve the desired clamp load for which that fastener was originally selected. Additionally, be sure that the driver surface of the fastener has not been compromised by rounding or other damage. In some cases a driver surface may become only partially rounded, allowing the driver to catch in only one direction. In many of these occurrences, a fastener may be installed and tightened, but the driver would not be able to grip and loosen the fastener again.

If you must replace a fastener, whether due to design or damage, you must ALWAYS be sure to use the proper replacement. In all cases, a retainer of the same design, material and strength should be used. Markings on the heads of most bolts will help determine the proper strength of the fastener. The same material, thread and pitch must be selected to assure proper installation and safe operation of the vehicle afterwards.

Thread gauges are available to help measure a bolt or stud's thread. Most automotive and hardware stores keep gauges available to help you select the proper size. In a pinch, you can use another nut or bolt for a thread gauge. If the bolt you are replacing is not too badly damaged, you can select a match by finding another bolt which will thread in its place. If you find a nut which threads properly onto the damaged bolt, then use that nut to help select the replacement bolt.

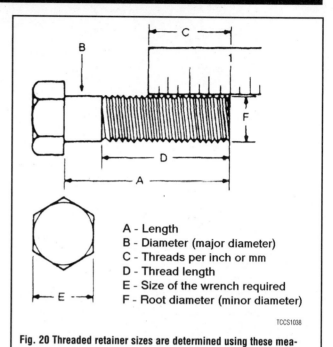

A - Length
B - Diameter (major diameter)
C - Threads per inch or mm
D - Thread length
E - Size of the wrench required
F - Root diameter (minor diameter)

TCCS1038

Fig. 20 Threaded retainer sizes are determined using these measurements

✳✳ WARNING

Be aware that when you find a bolt with damaged threads, you may also find the nut or drilled hole it was threaded into has also been damaged. If this is the case, you may have to drill and tap the hole, replace the nut or otherwise repair the threads. NEVER try to force a replacement bolt to fit into the damaged threads.

Torque

Torque is defined as the measurement of resistance to turning or rotating. It tends to twist a body about an axis of rotation. A common example of this would be tightening a threaded retainer such as a nut, bolt or screw. Measuring torque is one of the most common ways to help assure that a threaded retainer has been properly fastened.

When tightening a threaded fastener, torque is applied in three distinct areas, the head, the bearing surface and the clamp load. About 50 percent of the measured torque is used in overcoming bearing friction. This is the friction between the bearing surface of the bolt head, screw head or nut face and the base material or washer (the surface on which the fastener is rotating). Approximately 40 percent of the applied torque is used in overcoming thread friction. This leaves only about 10 percent of the applied torque to develop a useful clamp load (the force which holds a joint together). This means that friction can account for as much as 90 percent of the applied torque on a fastener.

TORQUE WRENCHES

♦ **See Figure 21**

In most applications, a torque wrench can be used to assure proper installation of a fastener. Torque wrenches come in various designs and most automotive supply stores will carry a variety to suit your needs. A torque wrench should be used any time we supply a specific torque value for a fastener. Again, the

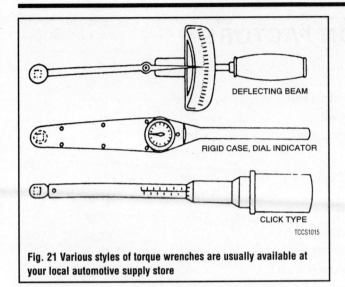

Fig. 21 Various styles of torque wrenches are usually available at your local automotive supply store

general rule of "if you are using the right tool for the job, you should not have to strain to tighten a fastener" applies here.

Beam Type

The beam type torque wrench is one of the most popular types. It consists of a pointer attached to the head that runs the length of the flexible beam (shaft) to a scale located near the handle. As the wrench is pulled, the beam bends and the pointer indicates the torque using the scale.

Click (Breakaway) Type

Another popular design of torque wrench is the click type. To use the click type wrench you pre-adjust it to a torque setting. Once the torque is reached, the wrench has a reflex signaling feature that causes a momentary breakaway of the torque wrench body, sending an impulse to the operator's hand.

Pivot Head Type

♦ **See Figure 22**

Some torque wrenches (usually of the click type) may be equipped with a pivot head which can allow it to be used in areas of limited access. BUT, it must be used properly. To hold a pivot head wrench, grasp the handle lightly, and as you pull on the handle, it should be floated on the pivot point. If the handle comes in contact with the yoke extension during the process of pulling, there is a very good chance the torque readings will be inaccurate because this could alter the wrench loading point. The design of the handle is usually such as to make it inconvenient to deliberately misuse the wrench.

➥**It should be mentioned that the use of any U-joint, wobble or extension will have an effect on the torque readings, no matter what type of wrench you are using. For the most accurate readings, install the socket directly on the wrench driver. If necessary, straight extensions (which hold a socket directly under the wrench driver) will have the least effect on the torque reading. Avoid any extension that alters the length of the wrench from the handle to the head/driving point (such as a crow's foot). U-joint or wobble extensions can greatly affect the readings; avoid their use at all times.**

Rigid Case (Direct Reading)

A rigid case or direct reading torque wrench is equipped with a dial indicator to show torque values. One advantage of these wrenches is that they can be held at any position on the wrench without affecting accuracy. These wrenches

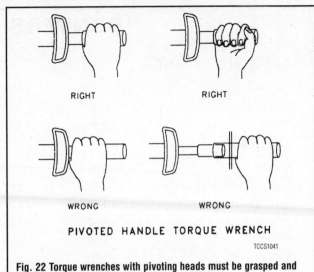

PIVOTED HANDLE TORQUE WRENCH

Fig. 22 Torque wrenches with pivoting heads must be grasped and used properly to prevent an incorrect reading

are often preferred because they tend to be compact, easy to read and have a great degree of accuracy.

TORQUE ANGLE METERS

Because the frictional characteristics of each fastener or threaded hole will vary, clamp loads which are based strictly on torque will vary as well. In most applications, this variance is not significant enough to cause worry. But, in certain applications, a manufacturer's engineers may determine that more precise clamp loads are necessary (such is the case with many aluminum cylinder heads). In these cases, a torque angle method of installation would be specified. When installing fasteners which are torque angle tightened, a predetermined seating torque and standard torque wrench are usually used first to remove any compliance from the joint. The fastener is then tightened the specified additional portion of a turn measured in degrees. A torque angle gauge (mechanical protractor) is used for these applications.

Standard and Metric Measurements

♦ **See Figure 23**

Throughout this manual, specifications are given to help you determine the condition of various components on your vehicle, or to assist you in their installation. Some of the most common measurements include length (in. or cm/mm), torque (ft. lbs., inch lbs. or Nm) and pressure (psi, in. Hg, kPa or mm Hg). In most cases, we strive to provide the proper measurement as determined by the manufacturer's engineers.

Though, in some cases, that value may not be conveniently measured with what is available in your toolbox. Luckily, many of the measuring devices which are available today will have two scales so the Standard or Metric measurements may easily be taken. If any of the various measuring tools which are available to you do not contain the same scale as listed in the specifications, use the accompanying conversion factors to determine the proper value.

The conversion factor chart is used by taking the given specification and multiplying it by the necessary conversion factor. For instance, looking at the first line, if you have a measurement in inches such as "free-play should be 2 in." but your ruler reads only in millimeters, multiply 2 in. by the conversion factor of 25.4 to get the metric equivalent of 50.8mm. Likewise, if the specification was given only in a Metric measurement, for example in Newton Meters (Nm), then look at the center column first. If the measurement is 100 Nm, multiply it by the conversion factor of 0.738 to get 73.8 ft. lbs.

CONVERSION FACTORS

LENGTH–DISTANCE

Inches (in.)	x 25.4	= Millimeters (mm)	x .0394	= Inches
Feet (ft.)	x .305	= Meters (m)	x 3.281	= Feet
Miles	x 1.609	= Kilometers (km)	x .0621	= Miles

VOLUME

Cubic Inches (in3)	x 16.387	= Cubic Centimeters	x .061	= in3
IMP Pints (IMP pt.)	x .568	= Liters (L)	x 1.76	− IMP pt.
IMP Quarts (IMP qt)	x 1.137	= Liters (L)	x .88	= IMP qt.
IMP Gallons (IMP gal.)	x 4.546	= Liters (L)	x .22	= IMP gal.
IMP Quarts (IMP qt.)	x 1.201	= US Quarts (US qt.)	x .833	= IMP qt.
IMP Gallons (IMP gal.)	x 1.201	= US Gallons (US gal.)	x .833	= IMP gal.
Fl. Ounces	x 29.573	= Milliliters	x .034	= Ounces
US Pints (US pt.)	x .473	= Liters (L)	x 2.113	= Pints
US Quarts (US qt.)	x .946	= Liters (L)	x 1.057	= Quarts
US Gallons (US gal.)	x 3.785	= Liters (L)	x .264	= Gallons

MASS–WEIGHT

Ounces (oz.)	x 28.35	= Grams (g)	x .035	= Ounces
Pounds (lb.)	x .454	= Kilograms (kg)	x 2.205	= Pounds

PRESSURE

Pounds Per Sq. In. (psi)	x 6.895	= Kilopascals (kPa)	x .145	= psi
Inches of Mercury (Hg)	x .4912	= psi	x 2.036	= Hg
Inches of Mercury (Hg)	x 3.377	= Kilopascals (kPa)	x .2961	= Hg
Inches of Water (H_2O)	x .07355	= Inches of Mercury	x 13.783	= H_2O
Inches of Water (H_2O)	x .03613	= psi	x 27.684	= H_2O
Inches of Water (H_2O)	x .248	= Kilopascals (kPa)	x 4.026	= H_2O

TORQUE

Pounds–Force Inches (in–lb)	x .113	= Newton Meters (N·m)	x 8.85	= in–lb
Pounds–Force Feet (ft–lb)	x 1.356	= Newton Meters (N·m)	x .738	= ft–lb

VELOCITY

Miles Per Hour (MPH)	x 1.609	= Kilometers Per Hour (KPH)	x .621	= MPH

POWER

Horsepower (Hp)	x .745	= Kilowatts	x 1.34	= Horsepower

FUEL CONSUMPTION*

Miles Per Gallon IMP (MPG)	x .354	= Kilometers Per Liter (Km/L)
Kilometers Per Liter (Km/L)	x 2.352	= IMP MPG
Miles Per Gallon US (MPG)	x .425	= Kilometers Per Liter (Km/L)
Kilometers Per Liter (Km/L)	x 2.352	= US MPG

*It is common to covert from miles per gallon (mpg) to liters/100 kilometers (1/100 km), where mpg (IMP) x 1/100 km = 282 and mpg (US) x 1/100 km = 235.

TEMPERATURE

Degree Fahrenheit (°F)	= (°C x 1.8) + 32
Degree Celsius (°C)	= (°F − 32) x .56

TCCS1044

Fig. 23 Standard and metric conversion factors chart

HISTORY

BMW (Bavarian Motor Works) began its life in 1916 as a builder of aircraft engines (called the "Bavarian Aircraft Works"), although the name was changed to the present one only a year later. The company logo which still appears several places on each car represents a propeller spinning against a blue sky. Thus, the high performance associated with BMW engines has its origin in the necessity to minimize weight in an aircraft. BMW's first car was a vehicle produced by the Dixi automobile works which BMW purchased in 1928.

In 1933, BMW produced its first in-house design, the BMW 303. This model series began two BMW traditions which are well known—the 6-cylinder engine and twin kidney grills. By the end of the 30s, BMW was making the 328, which featured an engine using a light allow head, with V-type overhead values and hemi-head combustion chambers.

BMW's history as a major manufacturer of performance cars was eclipsed by the destruction of the Munich plant in World War II. The '50s were dominated by the extremes—the too-large 501, and the Isetta with a BMW motorcycle engine propelling it. Neither brought much profit to the company.

In 1959 Dr. Herbert Quant invested heavily in the company to save it from a sale of assets. In 1961, the 1500 was introduced, in the tradition of the later models. This "new wave" of 4-cylinder sports sedans has become recognized for its high output, low displacement and fuel efficient engine and light and compact chassis-body, which offers excellent road holding and braking. With the introduction of the 530i in 1975, BMW began to be associated with luxury-performance cars as well as sports sedans.

SERIAL IDENTIFICATION NUMBER

Vehicle

▶ **See Figures 24, 25, 26, 27 and 28**

On 1970–74 models, this number is stamped on a plate attached to the upper steering column and on a Certification Label located on the edge of the driver's door. On most 1975–88 models, the number is located at the left end of the dashboard, visible through the windshield. The vehicle serial number and the vehicle identification plate are also found in various other locations in the engine compartment.

Engine

This serial number is stamped on the left, rear side of the engine itself, usually above the starter motor.

Transmission

The manual transmission number is on a label affixed to the upper portion of the bell housing. The label is located just behind the flat portion cast at the bell housing to engine block mounting face.

The automatic transmission number is on a label affixed to the side of the casing. The label is located between the shift lever and bracket.

Drive Axle

The drive axle ratio is stamped on a tag attached to the axle housing cover. Return this tag to its original location whenever the cover is removed and replaced.

Transfer Case

The transfer case of the 325iX has an identification label affixed to the upper side of the unit. The label is positioned on the case in front of the case vent.

Fig. 24 Steering column mounted identification label—early 2002 model

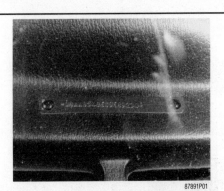

Fig. 25 Dashboard mounted identification plate—3 Series

Fig. 26 The door pillar tire and identification stickers—3 Series

Fig. 27 Engine compartment mounted emission and tire pressure sticker—early 2002 model

Fig. 28 Engine compartment mounted identification plate—early 2002 model

ENGINE IDENTIFICATION

Year	Model	Engine Displacement cu In. (cc)	Engine Displacement (liters)	Engine Code	Fuel System	No. of Cylinders	Engine Type
1980	320i	121(1990)	2.0L	M10/M92	K-JET	4	OHC
	528i	170(2788)	2.8L	M20/M86	L-JET	6	OHC
	633CSi	196(3210)	3.2L	M30/M69	L-JET	6	OHC
	733i	196(3210)	3.2L	M30/M69	L-JET	6	OHC
1981	320i	121(1990)	2.0L	M10/M92	K-JET	4	OHC
	528i	170(2788)	2.8L	M20/M86	L-JET	6	OHC
	633CSi	196(3210)	3.2L	M30/M69	L-JET	6	OHC
	733i	196(3210)	3.2L	M30/M69	L-JET	6	OHC
1982	320i	121(1990)	2.0L	M10/M69	K-JET	4	OHC
	325e	165(2693)	2.7L	M20	L-JET	6	OHC
	528e	165(2693)	2.7L	M20	L-JET	6	OHC
	533i	196(3210)	3.2L	M30	L-JET	6	OHC
	633CSi	196(3210)	3.2L	M30/M69	L-JET	6	OHC
	733i	196(3210)	3.2L	M30/M69	L-JET	6	OHC
1983	320i	121(1990)	2.0L	M10/M92	K-JET	4	OHC
	325e	165(2693)	2.7L	M20	L-JET	6	OHC
	528e	165(2693)	2.7L	M20	L-JET	6	OHC
	533i	196(3210)	3.2L	M30	L-JET	6	OHC
	633CSi	196(3210)	3.2L	M30/M69	L-JET	6	OHC
	733i	196(3210)	3.2L	M30/M69	L-JET	6	OHC
1984	318i	108(1766)	1.8L	M10	MOFI	4	OHC
	325e	152(2494)	2.5L	M20	MOFI	6	OHC
	533i	196(3210)	3.2L	M30	MOFI	6	OHC
	633CSi	196(3210)	3.2L	M30	MOFI	6	OHC
	733i	196(3210)	3.2L	M30	MOFI	6	OHC
1985	318i	108(1766)	1.8L	M10	MOFI	4	OHC
	325e	165(2693)	2.7L	M20	MOFI	6	OHC
	528e	165(2693)	2.7L	M20	MOFI	6	OHC
	524td	149(2443)	2.4L	M21	D	6	OHC
	533i	196(3210)	3.2L	M30	MOFI	6	OHC
	633CSi	196(3210)	3.2L	M30	MOFI	6	OHC
	733i	196(3210)	3.2L	M30	MOFI	6	OHC
1986	325e	152(2494)	2.5L	M20	MOFI	6	OHC
	528e	165(2693)	2.7L	M20	MOFI	6	OHC
	524td	149(2443)	2.4L	M21	D	6	OHC
	535i	196(3210)	3.2L	M30	MOFI	6	OHC
	633CSi	196(3210)	3.2L	M30	MOFI	6	OHC
	733i	196(3210)	3.2L	M30	MOFI	6	OHC

87891C02

ENGINE IDENTIFICATION

Year	Model	Engine Displacement cu in. (cc)	Engine Displacement (liters)	Engine Code	Fuel System	No. of Cylinders	Engine Type
1970	1600	96(1573)	1.6L	M10/M41	C	4	OHC
	2000, 2002Ti	121(1990)	2.0L	M10/M42	C	4	OHC
	2500	152(2493)	2.5L	M30/M68	C	6	OHC
	2800, CS	170(2788)	2.8L	M30/M68	C	6	OHC
	Bavaria	170(2788)	2.8L	M30/M68	C	6	OHC
1971	1600	96(1573)	1.6L	M10/M41	C	4	OHC
	2000, 2002Ti	121(1990)	2.0L	M10/M42	C	4	OHC
	2500	152(2493)	2.5L	M30/M68	C	6	OHC
	2800, CS	170(2788)	2.8L	M30/M68	C	6	OHC
	Bavaria	170(2788)	2.8L	M30/M68	C	6	OHC
1972	2000, 2002	121(1990)	2.0L	M10/M42	C	4	OHC
	2002Tii	121(1990)	2.0L	M10/M42	KFI	4	OHC
	2800,3000, CS	170(2788)	2.8L	M30/M68	C	6	OHC
	Bavaria	170(2788)	2.8L	M30/M68	C	6	OHC
1973	2000, 2002	121(1990)	2.0L	M10/M42	C	4	OHC
	2002Tii	121(1990)	2.0L	M10/M42	KFI	4	OHC
	2800,3000, CS	170(2788)	2.8L	M30/M68	C	6	OHC
	Bavaria	170(2788)	2.8L	M30/M68	C	6	OHC
1974	2002	121(1990)	2.0L	M10/M42	C	4	OHC
	2002Tii	121(1990)	2.0L	M10/M42	KFI	4	OHC
	Bavaria	170(2788)	2.8L	M30/M68	C	6	OHC
	3.0, CS, S, Si	182(2985)	3.0L	M30/M68	L-JET	6	OHC
1975	2002	121(1990)	2.0L	M10/M42	C	4	OHC
	3.0, CS, S	182(2985)	3.0L	M30/M68	L-JET	6	OHC
	530i	182(2985)	3.0L	M20	L-JET	6	OHC
1976	2002	121(1990)	2.0L	M10/M41	C	4	OHC
	3.0, CS, S	182(2985)	3.0L	M30/M68	L-JET	6	OHC
	530i	182(2985)	3.0L	M20	L-JET	6	OHC
	630CS	182(2985)	3.0L	M69	L-JET	6	OHC
1977	320i	107(1766)	1.8L	M10/M92	K-JET	4	OHC
	530i	182(2985)	3.0L	M20	L-JET	6	OHC
	630CSi	182(2985)	3.0L	M30/M69	L-JET	6	OHC
1978	320i	107(1766)	1.8L	M10/M92	K-JET	4	OHC
	530i	182(2985)	3.0L	M20	L-JET	6	OHC
	630CSi	182(2985)	3.0L	M30/M69	L-JET	6	OHC
	633CSi	196(3210)	3.2L	M30/M69	L-JET	6	OHC
	733i	196(3210)	3.2L	M30/M69	L-JET	6	OHC
1979	320i	107(1766)	1.8L	M10/M92	K-JET	4	OHC
	528i	170(2788)	2.8L	M20/M86	L-JET	6	OHC
	633CSi	196(3210)	3.2L	M30/M69	L-JET	6	OHC
	733i	196(3210)	3.2L	M30/M69	L-JET	6	OHC

87891C01

ENGINE IDENTIFICATION

Year	Model	Engine Displacement cu in. (cc)	Engine Displacement (liters)	Engine Code	Fuel System	No. of Cylinders	Engine Type
1987	325	152(2494)	2.5L	M20	MOFI	6	OHC
	325i	152(2494)	2.5L	M30	MOFI	6	OHC
	325iS	152(2494)	2.5L	M30	MOFI	6	OHC
	528e	165(2693)	2.7L	M20	MOFI	6	OHC
	535i	209(3428)	3.4L	M30	MOFI	6	OHC
	635CSi	209(3428)	3.4L	M30/M90	MOFI	6	OHC
	735i	209(3428)	3.4L	M30	MOFI	6	OHC
	M5	211(3453)	3.5L	S38	MOFI	6	DOHC
	M6	211(3453)	3.5L	S38	MOFI	6	DOHC
1988	325	152(2494)	2.5L	M20	MOFI	6	OHC
	325i	152(2494)	2.5L	M20	MOFI	6	OHC
	325iS	152(2494)	2.5L	M20	MOFI	6	OHC
	325iX	152(2494)	2.5L	M20	MOFI	6	OHC
	528e	165(2693)	2.7L	M20	MOFI	6	OHC
	535i	209(3428)	3.4L	M30	MOFI	6	OHC
	635i	209(3428)	3.4L	M30/M90	MOFI	6	OHC
	735i	209(3428)	3.4L	M30	MOFI	6	OHC
	M3	141(2302)	2.3L	S14	MOFI	4	DOHC
	M5	211(3453)	3.5L	S38	MOFI	6	DOHC
	M6	211(3453)	3.5L	S38	MOFI	6	DOHC
	L6	209(3428)	3.4L	M30	MOFI	6	OHC
	L7	209(3428)	3.4L	M30	MOFI	6	OHC

C: Carbureted

D: Diesel

KFI: Kugelfischer Fuel Injection

K-JET: K-Jetronic Fuel Injection

L-JET: L-Jetronic Fuel Injection

MOFI: Motronic Fuel Injection

87891C03

BMW BODY CODE CHART

BMW Code	Model	Coupe/Sedan
114	1600, 2002	2 dr Sedan
116	1600	4 dr Sedan
118	1800, 1800ti	4 dr Sedan
120	2000, 2000ti	4 dr Sedan
121	2000 C, 2000 CS	Coupe

BMW Code	Model	Coupe/Sedan
E3	2500,2800, 3.0Si, Bavaria	4 dr Sedan
E9	2800 CSi, 3.0CSi	Coupe
E10	2002, 2002tii	2 dr Sedan
E21	320i	3 Series until 1983
E30	318i, 325e,325is	3 Series after 1984
E30/16	325ix	3 Series all wheel drive
E12	528i, 530i	5 Series until 1981
E28	524td, 528e, 535i, M5	5 Series 1982-88
E24	633 CSi, 635CSi, L6, M6	6 Series until 1988
E23	733i, 735i, L7	7 Series until 1987
E32	735i	7 Series after 1988

87891C98

ROUTINE MAINTENANCE

See Figures 29 thru 38

Air Cleaner

All the dust present in the air is kept out of the engine by means of the air cleaner filter element. Proper maintenance is vital, as a clogged element not only restricts the airflow and thus the power, but can also cause premature engine wear.

The filter element should be cleaned or replaced every 15,000 miles (24,000 km), or more often if the car is driven in dusty areas. The condition of the element should be checked periodically; if it appears to be overly dirty or clogged, shake it; if this does not help, the element must be replaced.

➡The paper element should not be cleaned or soaked with gasoline, cleaning solvent or oil.

REMOVAL & INSTALLATION

Carbureted Engines

The air filter on these engines sits on top of the carburetor, usually towards the center of the engine compartment. To remove the filter element, simply unsnap the housing cover and lift out the element.

Clean the element by lightly shaking it against the palm of your hand (blowing with compressed air is also acceptable). If the filter element remains clogged after cleaning, replace it.

Fuel Injected Engines

▶ See Figures 39 thru 44

2002TII MODELS

This model utilizes a long cylindrical air cleaner housing with 2 separate filters in each end; it is located in the left side of the engine compartment. To remove, unsnap each end from the main body of the housing and lift out the filter elements. Clean in the same manner as described for carbureted engines.

318I AND 320I MODELS

This model utilizes a square air filter element and housing, located in the left, front side of the engine compartment.

To remove, loosen the clamp connecting the vacuum limiting valve to the air intake duct. Next, remove the 2 bolts fastening this valve and its companion valve, the cold start valve, to the bracket near the injection pump. Unsnap the over-center catches and, while holding the 2 valves out of the way, pull the filter

Fig. 29 Before beginning any work, review the placement of the engine compartment components

Fig. 30 The engine and transmission as viewed from underneath a 3 Series BMW

Fig. 31 The clean rear underside of a 1986 BMW 325

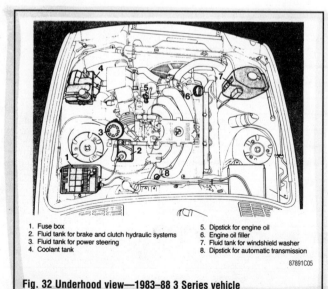

1. Fuse box
2. Fluid tank for brake and clutch hydraulic systems
3. Fluid tank for power steering
4. Coolant tank
5. Dipstick for engine oil
6. Engine oil filler
7. Fluid tank for windshield washer
8. Dipstick for automatic transmission

Fig. 32 Underhood view—1983–88 3 Series vehicle

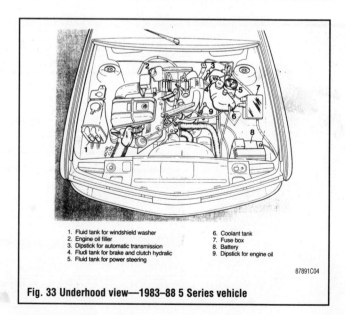

1. Fluid tank for windshield washer
2. Engine oil filler
3. Dipstick for automatic transmission
4. Fluid tank for brake and clutch hydraulic
5. Fluid tank for power steering
6. Coolant tank
7. Fuse box
8. Battery
9. Dipstick for engine oil

Fig. 33 Underhood view—1983–88 5 Series vehicle

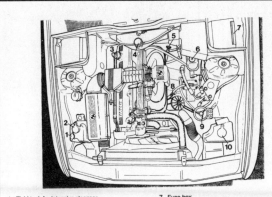

1. Fluid tank for intensive cleanser
2. Fluid tank for windshield washer
3. Engine oil filler
4. Coolant tank
5. Dipstick for automatic transmission
6. Fluid tank for brake and clutch hydraulic systems
7. Fuse box
8. Dipstick for engine oil
9. Fluid tank for brake booster servo and power steering
10. Fluid tank for fog and headlight washer

87891C07

Fig. 34 Underhood view—1983–88 7 Series vehicle

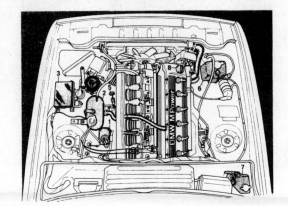

1. Fluid tank for brake and clutch hydraulic systems
2. Coolant tank
3. Fuse box
4. Fluid-tank for power steering
5. Dipstick for engine oil
6. Fluid tank for windshield washer
7. Fluid tank for intensive cleanser
8. Engine oil filler

87891C06

Fig. 35 Underhood view—1983–88 M6

87891P06

Fig. 36 Always read any warning labels such as this

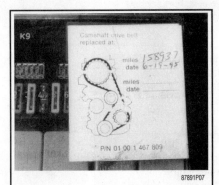

87891P07

Fig. 37 Some vehicles will have stickers indicating belt and other part replacement

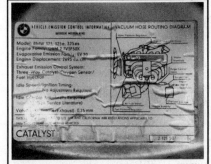

87891P08

Fig. 38 This vehicle emission sticker contains information on idle speed, idle CO and valve lash

element up and out of the air cleaner housing. Clean in the same manner as described for carbureted engines.

6-CYLINDER MODELS

▶ **See Figures 39 thru 44**

The air filter element on all 6-cylinder models is removed in basically the same manner. Unsnap the 2 over-center catches and split the 2 halves of the housing apart. Lift the element upward slightly to separate it from the lower half of the housing and then slide it out of the opening between the 2 halves.

➡When replacing the square type element used on most later models, always make sure that the arrow indicating airflow direction points toward the engine (or into the manifold) when positioning the filter. Also make sure that the rubber border on the element is properly positioned around the lower case half before closing the catches.

Clean in the same manner as described for carbureted engines.

87891P09

Fig. 39 Loosen the retaining hardware which secures the top of the air cleaner in place

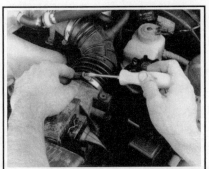

87891P10

Fig. 40 Loosen the hose clamp securing the hose between the intake manifold and air cleaner assembly

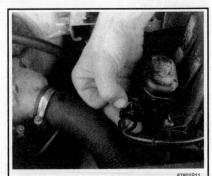

87891P11

Fig. 41 Unfasten any wire harnesses attached to the air cleaner assembly. If necessary, tag for identification

Fig. 42 Unclip the securing tabs surrounding the air filter

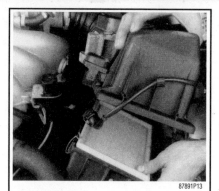

Fig. 43 Slowly lift the top of the air cleaner up to expose the filter element

Fig. 44 Lift the filter element out of the air filter base

Fuel Filter

SERVICE PRECAUTIONS

✳✳ CAUTION

Gasoline is extremely volatile and can easily be ignited. Work on fuel system parts only when the engine is cold. Keep all other sources of ignition away. Carefully observe all precautions given in the procedures as to clamping fuel lines, collecting fuel in a metal container, and disposing of it in a safe manner. Always relieve fuel system pressure before unclamping lines, as fuel injection systems maintain very high pressure, even when the engine is off.

The pressure in the fuel injected system is enough to cause the fuel to spray from the line that is being opened. If the fuel is allowed to spray from the line it could be ignited by a spark. Pressurized fuel spray could also squirt into your eyes and cause severe injury.

RELIEVING SYSTEM PRESSURE

To relieve the pressure in fuel injected systems, first find the fuel pump relay plug, located on the cowl in most vehicles. Unplug the relay, leaving it in a safe position where the connections cannot ground. If necessary, tape the plug in place or tape over the connector prongs with electrical tape. Then, start the engine and operate it until it stalls. Crank the engine for 10 seconds after it stalls to remove any residual pressure.

REMOVAL & INSTALLATION

Carbureted Version

▶ See Figure 45

1600, 2000, 2002, 2002TII, 2500, 2800, BAVARIA, 3000CS, 3.0CS AND 3.0S MODELS

On all carbureted models, the fine mesh filter screen in the fuel pump is removed at 8,000 mile (13,000 km) intervals for cleaning. On 1600 models, this is accomplished by removing the cover plate bolt. On all other models, this is accomplished by removing the filter sieve retaining bolt. Discard the old sealing ring and wash out the filter sieve in clean gasoline or kerosene. On 1600 models, clean the cover plate also. On all others, replace the filter sieve using a new sealing ring, and tighten the retaining bolt. At this time, check that the bolts on the fuel pump are evenly tightened using a screwdriver.

Fuel Injected Version

On many fuel injected models, a total of 4 fuel filters must be cleaned or replaced. Three are serviced at 40,000 mile (64,000 km) intervals. The fourth, or main filter should be serviced at least every 8,000 (13,000 km) miles.

Fig. 45 An example of a carbureted engine fuel filter

Each filter consists of a fine mesh which filters the fuel in the fuel tank pick-up, electric fuel pump, engine compartment and the mechanical fuel injection pump.

MAIN FILTER ELEMENT

▶ See Figures 46, 47 and 48

To replace the in-line main fuel filter, the following procedure is used:
1. Loosen the hose clamps and the filter retaining clamp. Mark the fuel line for reassembly.

➡ In some models, battery removal may facilitate better access to the fuel filter.

2. Disconnect and plug both fuel lines, remove and discard the old filter.
3. Install a new filter, taking care to note the prescribed direction of flow shown on the filter label.

INJECTION PUMP FILTER

To clean the fine mesh filter in the fuel injection pump, the following procedure is used:
1. Remove the 17mm hollow screw in the fuel inlet pipe.
2. Clean the thimble-sized fine mesh filter located in the hollow screw using clean gasoline or kerosene.
3. Reverse the above procedure to install.

FULL FLOW FILTER

These filters are located as follows:
• 318i, 320i, 325e, 325es, 325i, 325is, 325ix, M3—near the electric fuel pump on the left side of the rear axle

Fig. 46 Location of the main fuel filter in the engine compartment, above the steering column U-joint

Fig. 47 Fuel filter as viewed from the top of the engine

Fig. 48 Loosening the hose clamp at the base of the filter. During removal, some fuel will spill out of the filter, so place a container under the element

- 528e—above the rear suspension next to the fuel pump
- 528i, 530i, 630CSi, 633CSi, 635CSi, M6—above the rear suspension, left rear
- 3.0Si—left, front wheel arch, under the fusebox
- 535i, 535is, M5, 733i—above and slightly to the left of the rear axle
1. Loosen the hose clamps.
2. Remove the filter unit.
3. Replace it with a new filter, making sure the arrow indicating direction of flow is facing the same direction as with the old unit (away from the tank).

FUEL PUMP STRAINER (3.0SI MODELS ONLY)

1. Loosen the intake hose clamp on the fuel pump. This is located above the right rear halfshaft.
2. Remove the fine mesh basket type filter, located inside the hose connection.
3. Clean the filter in fresh gasoline or kerosene.

PCV Valve and Evaporative Canister

SERVICE

The BMW vehicles covered by this manual employ crankcase ventilation and evaporative canister systems which do not require fresh air for their operation. This eliminates the need for periodic replacement of the PCV valves and canister filters generally associated with other types of systems.

Battery

LOCATION

♦ **See Figures 49, 50 and 51**

The battery in your vehicle can be mounted in a variety of locations depending on the model, engine or chassis style, convertible or hardtop. The battery is located either in the engine compartment on the right side, under the rear seat, or mounted in the trunk on the right side, under the trunk liner.

When the battery is mounted under the rear seat cushion, the cushion can be removed by pulling up on the front edge and removing it from the vehicle. Be sure that the seat cushion is secure when it is replaced so it doesn't become dislodged in a sudden stop. Be sure the vent tube is not crimped when replacing the cushion.

PRECAUTIONS

Always use caution when working on or near the battery. Never allow a tool to bridge the gap between the negative and positive battery terminals. Also, be careful not to allow a tool to provide a ground between the positive cable/terminal and any metal component on the vehicle. Either of these conditions will cause a short circuit, leading to sparks and possible personal injury.

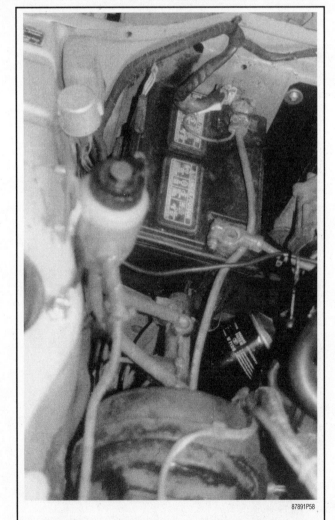

Fig. 49 Battery mounted in the engine compartment—2002 model

Do not smoke or all open flames/sparks near a battery; the gases contained in the battery are very explosive and, if ignited, could cause severe injury or death.

All batteries, regardless of type, should be carefully secured by a battery hold-down device. If not, the terminals or casing may crack from stress during vehicle operation. A battery which is not secured may allow acid to leak, making it discharge faster. The acid can also eat away at components under the hood.

Always inspect the battery case for cracks, leakage and corrosion. A white corrosive substance on the battery case or on nearby components would indi-

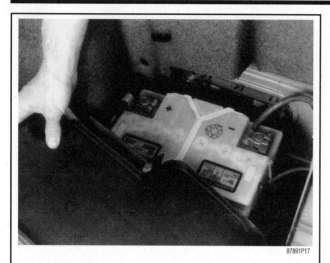

Fig. 50 Battery located in trunk compartment— 3 Series and 7 Series vehicles

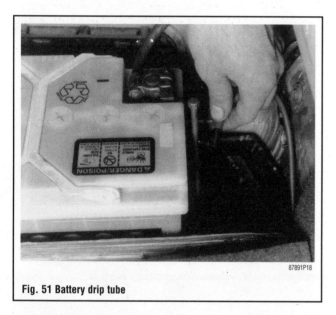

Fig. 51 Battery drip tube

cate a leaking or cracked battery. If the battery is cracked, it should be replaced immediately.

GENERAL MAINTENANCE

Always keep the battery cables and terminals free of corrosion. Check and clean these components about once a year.

Keep the top of the battery clean, as a film of dirt can help discharge a battery that is not used for long periods. A solution of baking soda and water may be used for cleaning, but be careful to flush this off with clear water. DO NOT let any of the solution into the filler holes. Baking soda neutralizes battery acid and will de-activate a battery cell.

Batteries in vehicles which are not operated on a regular basis can fall victim to parasitic loads (small current drains which are constantly drawing current from the battery). Normal parasitic loads may drain a battery on a vehicle that is in storage and not used for 6–8 weeks. Vehicles that have additional accessories such as a phone or an alarm system may discharge a battery sooner. If the vehicle is to be stored for longer periods in a secure area and the alarm system is not necessary, the negative battery cable should be disconnected to protect the battery.

Remember that constantly deep cycling a battery (completely discharging and recharging it) will shorten battery life.

BATTERY FLUID

▶ **See Figure 52**

Check the battery electrolyte level at least once a month, or more often in hot weather or during periods of extended vehicle operation. On non-sealed batteries, the level can be checked either through the case (if translucent) or by removing the cell caps. The electrolyte level in each cell should be kept filled to the split ring inside each cell, or the line marked on the outside of the case.

If the level is low, add only distilled water through the opening until the level is correct. Each cell must be checked and filled individually. Distilled water should be used, because the chemicals and minerals found in most drinking water are harmful to the battery and could significantly shorten its life.

If water is added in freezing weather, the vehicle should be driven several miles to allow the water to mix with the electrolyte. Otherwise, the battery could freeze.

Although some maintenance-free batteries have removable cell caps, the electrolyte condition and level on all sealed maintenance-free batteries must be checked using the built-in hydrometer "eye." The exact type of eye will vary. But, most battery manufacturers, apply a sticker to the battery itself explaining the readings.

➡**Although the readings from built-in hydrometers will vary, a green eye usually indicates a properly charged battery with sufficient fluid level. A dark eye is normally an indicator of a battery with sufficient fluid, but which is low in charge. A light or yellow eye usually indicates that electrolyte has dropped below the necessary level. In this last case, sealed batteries with an insufficient electrolyte must usually be discarded.**

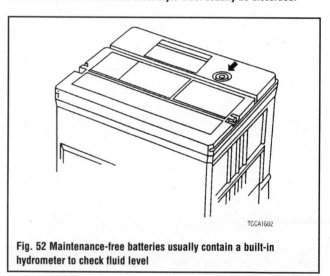

Fig. 52 Maintenance-free batteries usually contain a built-in hydrometer to check fluid level

Checking the Specific Gravity

▶ **See Figures 53, 54 and 55**

A hydrometer is required to check the specific gravity on all batteries that are not maintenance-free. On batteries that are maintenance-free, the specific gravity is checked by observing the built-in hydrometer "eye" on the top of the battery case.

❊❊ CAUTION

Battery electrolyte contains sulfuric acid. If you should splash any on your skin or in your eyes, flush the affected area with plenty of clear water. If it lands in your eyes, get medical help immediately.

The fluid (sulfuric acid solution) contained in the battery cells will tell you many things about the condition of the battery. Because the cell plates must be kept submerged below the fluid level in order to operate, the fluid level is extremely important. And, because the specific gravity of the acid is an indication of electrical charge, testing the fluid can be an aid in determining if the battery must be replaced. A battery in a vehicle with a properly operating charging system should require little maintenance, but careful, periodic inspection should reveal problems before they leave you stranded.

Fig. 53 On non-sealed batteries, the fluid level can be checked by removing the cell caps

Fig. 54 If the fluid level is low, add only distilled water until the level is correct

Fig. 55 Check the specific gravity of the battery's electrolyte with a hydrometer

At least once a year, check the specific gravity of the battery. It should be between 1.20 and 1.26 on the gravity scale. Most auto stores carry a variety of inexpensive battery hydrometers. These can be used on any non-sealed battery to test the specific gravity in each cell.

The battery testing hydrometer has a squeeze bulb at one end and a nozzle at the other. Battery electrolyte is sucked into the hydrometer until the float is lifted from its seat. The specific gravity is then read by noting the position of the float. If gravity is low in one or more cells, the battery should be slowly charged and checked again to see if the gravity has come up. Generally, if after charging, the specific gravity between any two cells varies more than 50 points (0.50), the battery should be replaced, as it can no longer produce sufficient voltage to guarantee proper operation.

CABLES

▶ **See Figures 56, 57, 58 and 59**

Once a year (or as necessary), the battery terminals and the cable clamps should be cleaned. Loosen the clamps and remove the cables, negative cable first. On top post batteries, the use of a puller specially made for this purpose is recommended. These are inexpensive and available in most parts stores. Side terminal battery cables are secured with a small bolt.

Clean the cable clamps and the battery terminal with a wire brush, until all corrosion, grease, etc., is removed and the metal is shiny. It is especially important to clean the inside of the clamp thoroughly (an old knife is useful here), since a small deposit of oxidation there will prevent a sound connection and inhibit starting or charging. Special tools are available for cleaning these parts, one type for conventional top post batteries and another type for side terminal batteries. It is also a good idea to apply some dielectric grease to the terminal, as this will aid in the prevention of corrosion.

After the clamps and terminals are clean, reinstall the cables, negative cable last; DO NOT hammer the clamps onto battery posts. Tighten the clamps securely, but do not distort them. Give the clamps and terminals a thin external coating of grease after installation, to retard corrosion.

Check the cables at the same time that the terminals are cleaned. If the cable insulation is cracked or broken, or if the ends are frayed, the cable should be replaced with a new cable of the same length and gauge.

CHARGING

✵✵ CAUTION

The chemical reaction which takes place in all batteries generates explosive hydrogen gas. A spark can cause the battery to explode

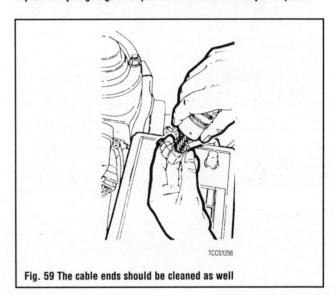

Fig. 59 The cable ends should be cleaned as well

Fig. 56 The underside of this special battery tool has a wire brush to clean post terminals

Fig. 57 Place the tool over the battery posts and twist to clean until the metal is shiny

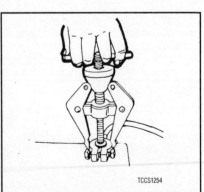

Fig. 58 A special tool is available to pull the clamp from the post

and splash acid. **To avoid personal injury, be sure there is proper ventilation and take appropriate fire safety precautions when working with or near a battery.**

A battery should be charged at a slow rate to keep the plates inside from getting too hot. However, if some maintenance-free batteries are allowed to discharge until they are almost "dead," they may have to be charged at a high rate to bring them back to "life." Always follow the charger manufacturer's instructions on charging the battery.

REPLACEMENT

When it becomes necessary to replace the battery, select one with an amperage rating equal to or greater than the battery originally installed. Deterioration and just plain aging of the battery cables, starter motor, and associated wires makes the battery's job harder in successive years. This makes it prudent to install a new battery with a greater capacity than the old.

Belts

INSPECTION

♦ See Figures 60, 61, 62, 63 and 64

Inspect the belts for signs of glazing or cracking. A glazed belt will be perfectly smooth from slippage, while a good belt will have a slight texture of fabric visible. Cracks will usually start at the inner edge of the belt and run outward. All worn or damaged drive belts should be replaced immediately. It is best to replace all drive belts at one time, as a preventive maintenance measure, during this service operation.

PRECAUTIONS

1. Replace belts with the proper part. A belt of the wrong length will have to be pried on if too short, a procedure that will seriously damage the belt even before it turns around once, or which may prevent sufficient tightening to compensate for wear long before the belt has really worn out. If you must use a belt that is just a little too short, you might be able to avoid stretching it during installation by completely dismounting the driven accessory, working the belt around the pulleys, and then remounting the accessory.

2. Replace the multiple belts in sets only, as work belts stretch and mixing stretched belts with new ones will prevent even division of the load.

3. Do not attempt to change belt tension or rotate an accessory for belt replacement without loosening both the adjustment bolt (the bolt which runs in a slotted bracket) and the pivot bolt. Do not pry belts on to avoid rotating the drive accessory.

4. Do not pry the driven accessory with a heavy metal bar if you can get sufficient belt tension by hand. This applies especially to aluminum castings or air/fluid pumps, where distortion of the housing can be a critical problem. If you must pry, do so on a substantial steel bracket only or, if none is present, on the part of the casting the adjusting bolt screws into. Some accessory mounting brackets are designed with a slit or square hole into which you can insert a socket drive for tensioning purposes.

REMOVAL & INSTALLATION

♦ See Figures 65 and 66

1. Locate the pivot bolt. This bolt holds the accessory to the engine block or to a bracket. If the pivot bolt does not use a nut welded onto the back of the accessory or the bracket, you will have to use wrenches at both ends to loosen the bolt. Loosen the bolt enough to allow the accessory to move.

2. Loosen the adjusting bolt. This passes through a long slot in a bracket and usually runs right into threads cut into the main body of the accessory. As the adjusting bolt is loosened, the belt will slacken.

3. Move the accessory until the belt can be removed. Position the new belt around the pulleys. Make sure it tracks in all the grooves.

4. To tension the belt, pull or pry the accessory away from the engine until the tension is correct, then tighten the adjusting bolt. Check the tension, and if correct, tighten the pivot bolt.

➡**When installing a new belt (one run less than 10 minutes) put a little extra tension on the belt to allow for stretch and seating in the pulley during break-in. About 30–40 percent extra tension will do. Check the tension of new belts several days after installation.**

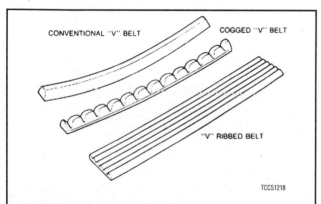

Fig. 60 There are typically 3 types of accessory drive belts found on vehicles today

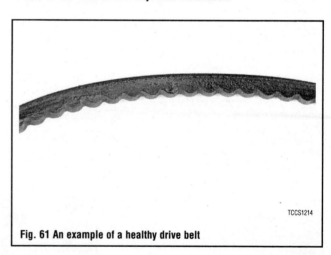

Fig. 61 An example of a healthy drive belt

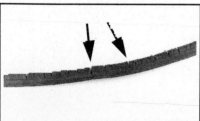

Fig. 62 Deep cracks in this belt will cause flex, building up heat that will eventually lead to belt failure

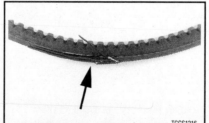

Fig. 63 The cover of this belt is worn, exposing the critical reinforcing cords to excessive wear

Fig. 64 Installing too wide a belt can result in serious belt wear and/or breakage

Fig. 65 Some early models like this 2002 have large fans and tight engine compartments which make belt changing and adjustment more difficult

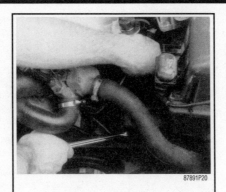

Fig. 66 An example of loosening a pivot bolt for belt replacement or adjustment

Fig. 67 Checking timing belt wear

Timing Belt

Timing belts are designed to last 60,000 miles (96,618 km). If the vehicle has been stored for an extended period (2 or more years), the timing belt should be changed before returning the vehicle to service.

INSPECTION

♦ See Figure 67

→Do not turn the engine with the timing belt removed. Because these engines are interference type engines, the pistons will contact the valves and cause internal engine damage.

Remove the timing belt cover from the engine and inspect the condition of the timing belt. The belt should have no excessive cracks tears or worn edges. Minor cracks on the face of the belt is normal and no reason for concern. If the belt shows any excessive wear, replace as soon as possible.

Carefully inspect the underside of the timing belt paying particular attention to any missing teeth from the belt. If for any reason one or more belt teeth are missing, the timing belt should be replaced immediately.

Finally, grasp the timing belt with the first two fingers of your hand at at the position between the camshaft and crankshaft pulleys and slowly twist the belt. The belt should be able to rotate 75–90°.

Hoses

♦ See Figures 68, 69, 70, 71 and 72

Worn hoses may feel spongy, brittle and discolored. The lower hose may be permanently narrowed at one point from suction, or may appear frayed or cracked. In contrast, new hoses will be springy and pliable yet firm. The rubber surface will be solid and smooth, and there will be no evidence of string reinforcements showing through.

REPLACEMENT

1. Put a bucket with at least a 2 gallon capacity under the radiator draincock, if equipped, or under the radiator end of the lower hose.
2. Open the draincock, or loosen the hose clamp and carefully slide the bottom hose off the radiator, and allow the coolant to flow out.

❄❄ CAUTION

When draining coolant, keep in mind that cats and dogs are attracted to ethylene glycol antifreeze, and could drink any that is left in an uncovered container or in puddles on the ground. This will prove fatal in sufficient quantity. Always drain the coolant into a sealable container. Coolant should be reused unless it is contaminated or several years old.

3. If a heater hose is being removed/replaced, turn the rotary heater control to **WARM** and allow any coolant contained in the heater core and hoses to drain out.
4. Loosen the clamps at both ends of the hose(s). Work the hose ends off the radiator or heater core and engine block connections.
5. Install the new hose in reverse order. If the hose has certain bends molded into it, make sure to position such that crimping is prevented. Install new hose clamps onto the hose from both ends before sliding hose ends onto the fittings. Make sure hoses slide all the way onto the connectors.
6. Tighten the clamps securely, then refill the cooling system as described later in this section.

Fig. 68 Cracks at the end of this hose indicate an old hose that has hardened. The reinforcing cords have most likely broken and will fail soon

Fig. 69 If a hose clamp is tightened too much, it can cause an older hose to weaken. This hose has torn and separated

Fig. 70 Hoses should be firm to the touch; a soft or spongy hose is a weak hose. Swollen ends are one indication of a soft, weakened hose

Fig. 71 Debris such as rust and scale can ruin a hose quickly. This is another reason why a regular coolant flush and change is important

CV-Boot

INSPECTION

▶ See Figures 73 and 74

The rear wheels on all BMW vehicles, and the front wheels on the 325ix are connected to the differentials by way of constant velocity joints. These swivel joints allow the wheels to rotate freely, while being able to move up and down independently of the opposite wheel.

The constant velocity joint is surrounded by a heavy moly-type grease which helps keep the parts cool, reducing wear, while enabling the components to move with ease. These joints are covered by rubber boots which need to be inspected regularly. In the event a boot tears, the grease inside will escape, allowing dirt any other foreign matter to enter, quickly destroying the entire joint.

To inspect a CV-boot, raise the vehicle and support it safely on jackstands. Using a light, inspect each boot for cracks or tears or missing retinning clamps. There should be no visible signs of grease on the exterior of the boot or the surrounding components, and the boot should feel firm when grasp, revealing that the joint has enough grease.

In the event the boot and/or CV-joint need replacing or other type of service, refer to the procedures in Section 8 of this manual.

Air Conditioning System

SYSTEM SERVICE & REPAIR

➡It is recommended that the A/C system be serviced by an EPA Section 609 certified automotive technician utilizing a refrigerant recovery/recycling machine.

The do-it-yourselfer should not service his/her own vehicle's A/C system for many reasons, including legal concerns, personal injury, environmental damage and cost.

According to the U.S. Clean Air Act, it is a federal crime to service or repair (involving the refrigerant) a Motor Vehicle Air Conditioning (MVAC) system for money without being EPA certified. It is also illegal to vent R-12 and R-134a refrigerants into the atmosphere. State and/or local laws may be more strict than the federal regulations, so be sure to check with your state and/or local authorities for further information.

➡**Federal law dictates that a fine of up to $25,000 may be levied on people convicted of venting refrigerant into the atmosphere.**

When servicing an A/C system you run the risk of handling or coming in contact with refrigerant, which may result in skin or eye irritation or frostbite. Although low in toxicity (due to chemical stability), inhalation of concentrated refrigerant fumes is dangerous and can result in death; cases of fatal cardiac arrhythmia have been reported in people accidentally subjected to high levels of refrigerant. Some early symptoms include loss of concentration and drowsiness.

➡**Generally, the limit for exposure is lower for R-134a than it is for R-12. Exceptional care must be practiced when handling R-134a.**

Also, some refrigerants can decompose at high temperatures (near gas heaters or open flame), which may result in hydrofluoric acid, hydrochloric acid and phosgene (a fatal nerve gas).

It is usually more economically feasible to have a certified MVAC automotive technician perform A/C system service on your vehicle.

R-12 Refrigerant Conversion

If your vehicle still uses R-12 refrigerant, one way to save A/C system costs down the road is to investigate the possibility of having your system converted to R-134a. The older R-12 systems can be easily converted to R-134a refrigerant by a certified automotive technician by installing a few new components and changing the system oil.

The cost of R-12 is steadily rising and will continue to increase, because it is no longer imported or manufactured in the United States. Therefore, it is often possible to have an R-12 system converted to R-134a and recharged for less than it would cost to just charge the system with R-12.

If you are interested in having your system converted, contact local automotive service stations for more details and information.

PREVENTIVE MAINTENANCE

Although the A/C system should not be serviced by the do-it-yourselfer, preventive maintenance should be practiced to help maintain the efficiency of the vehicle's A/C system. Be sure to perform the following:

• The easiest and most important preventive maintenance for your A/C system is to be sure that it is used on a regular basis. Running the system for five minutes each month (no matter what the season) will help ensure that the seals and all internal components remain lubricated.

➡**Some vehicles automatically operate the A/C system compressor whenever the windshield defroster is activated. Therefore, the A/C system would not need to be operated each month if the defroster was used.**

Fig. 72 Coolant hoses—2002 model

Fig. 73 Inspect each boot for tears, cracks or signs of grease

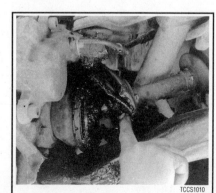

Fig. 74 Torn boots like this one need immediate attention

• In order to prevent heater core freeze-up during A/C operation, it is necessary to maintain proper antifreeze protection. Be sure to properly maintain the engine cooling system.

• Any obstruction of or damage to the condenser configuration will restrict air flow which is essential to its efficient operation. Keep this unit clean and in proper physical shape.

➡**Bug screens which are mounted in front of the condenser (unless they are original equipment) are regarded as obstructions.**

• The condensation drain tube expels any water which accumulates on the bottom of the evaporator housing into the engine compartment. If this tube is obstructed, the air conditioning performance can be restricted and condensation buildup can spill over onto the vehicle's floor.

SYSTEM INSPECTION

Although the A/C system should not be serviced by the do-it-yourselfer, system inspections should be performed to help maintain the efficiency of the vehicle's A/C system. Be sure to perform the following:

The easiest and often most important check for the air conditioning system consists of a visual inspection of the system components. Visually inspect the system for refrigerant leaks, damaged compressor clutch, abnormal compressor drive belt tension and/or condition, plugged evaporator drain tube, blocked condenser fins, disconnected or broken wires, blown fuses, corroded connections and poor insulation.

A refrigerant leak will usually appear as an oily residue at the leakage point in the system. The oily residue soon picks up dust or dirt particles from the surrounding air and appears greasy. Through time, this will build up and appear to be a heavy dirt impregnated grease.

For a thorough visual and operational inspection, check the following:

• Check the surface of the radiator and condenser for dirt, leaves or other material which might block air flow.

• Check for kinks in hoses and lines. Check the system for leaks.

• Make sure the drive belt is properly tensioned. During operation, make sure the belt is free of noise or slippage.

• Make sure the blower motor operates at all appropriate positions, then check for distribution of the air from all outlets.

➡**Remember that in high humidity, air discharged from the vents may not feel as cold as expected, even if the system is working properly. This is because moisture in humid air retains heat more effectively than dry air, thereby making humid air more difficult to cool.**

Windshield Wipers

ELEMENT (REFILL) CARE & REPLACEMENT

▶ **See Figures 75, 76 and 77**

For maximum effectiveness and longest element life, the windshield and wiper blades should be kept clean. Dirt, tree sap, road tar and so on will cause streaking, smearing and blade deterioration if left on the glass. It is advisable to wash the windshield carefully with a commercial glass cleaner at least once a month. Wipe off the rubber blades with the wet rag afterwards. Do not attempt to move wipers across the windshield by hand; damage to the motor and drive mechanism will result.

To inspect and/or replace the wiper blade elements, place the wiper switch in the **LOW** speed position and the ignition switch in the **ACC** position. When the wiper blades are approximately vertical on the windshield, turn the ignition switch to **OFF**.

Examine the wiper blade elements. If they are found to be cracked, broken or torn, they should be replaced immediately. Replacement intervals will vary with usage, although ozone deterioration usually limits element life to about one year. If the wiper pattern is smeared or streaked, or if the blade chatters across the glass, the elements should be replaced. It is easiest and most sensible to replace the elements in pairs.

If your vehicle is equipped with aftermarket blades, there are several different types of refills and your vehicle might have any kind. Aftermarket blades and arms rarely use the exact same type blade or refill as the original equipment.

Regardless of the type of refill used, be sure to follow the part manufacturer's instructions closely. Make sure that all of the frame jaws are engaged as the refill is pushed into place and locked. If the metal blade holder and frame are allowed to touch the glass during wiper operation, the glass will be scratched.

Tires and Wheels

Common sense and good driving habits will afford maximum tire life. Make sure that you don't overload the vehicle or run with incorrect pressure in the tires. Either of these will increase tread wear. Fast starts, sudden stops and sharp cornering are hard on tires and will shorten their useful life span.

➡**For optimum tire life, keep the tires properly inflated, rotate them often and have the wheel alignment checked periodically.**

Inspect your tires frequently. Be especially careful to watch for bubbles in the tread or sidewall, deep cuts or underinflation. Replace any tires with bubbles in the sidewall. If cuts are so deep that they penetrate to the cords, discard the tire. Any cut in the sidewall of a radial tire renders it unsafe. Also look for uneven tread wear patterns that may indicate the front end is out of alignment or that the tires are out of balance.

TIRE ROTATION

▶ **See Figure 78**

Tires must be rotated periodically to equalize wear patterns that vary with a tire's position on the vehicle. Tires will also wear in an uneven way as the front steering/suspension system wears to the point where the alignment should be reset.

Rotating the tires will ensure maximum life for the tires as a set, so you will not have to discard a tire early due to wear on only part of the tread. Regular rotation is required to equalize wear.

When rotating "unidirectional tires," make sure that they always roll in the same direction. This means that a tire used on the left side of the vehicle must not be switched to the right side and vice-versa. Such tires should only be rotated front-to-rear or rear-to-front, while always remaining on the same side of the vehicle. These tires are marked on the sidewall as to the direction of rotation; observe the marks when reinstalling the tire(s).

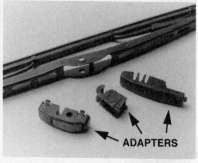

TCCS1223

Fig. 75 Most aftermarket blades are available with multiple adapters to fit different vehicles

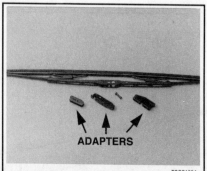

TCCS1224

Fig. 76 Choose a blade which will fit your vehicle, and that will be readily available next time you need blades

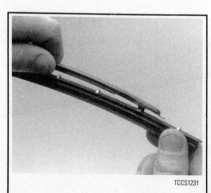

TCCS1231

Fig. 77 When installed, be certain the blade is fully inserted into the backing

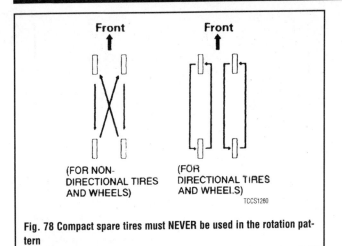

Fig. 78 Compact spare tires must NEVER be used in the rotation pattern

Some styled or "mag" wheels may have different offsets front to rear. In these cases, the rear wheels must not be used up front and vice-versa. Furthermore, if these wheels are equipped with unidirectional tires, they cannot be rotated unless the tire is remounted for the proper direction of rotation.

➡**The compact or space-saver spare is strictly for emergency use. It must never be included in the tire rotation or placed on the vehicle for everyday use.**

TIRE DESIGN

▶ **See Figure 79**

For maximum satisfaction, tires should be used in sets of four. Mixing of different brands or types (radial, bias-belted, fiberglass belted) should be avoided. In most cases, the vehicle manufacturer has designated a type of tire on which the vehicle will perform best. Your first choice when replacing tires should be to use the same type of tire that the manufacturer recommends.

When radial tires are used, tire sizes and wheel diameters should be selected to maintain ground clearance and tire load capacity equivalent to the original specified tire. Radial tires should always be used in sets of four.

✳✳ CAUTION

Radial tires should never be used on only the front axle.

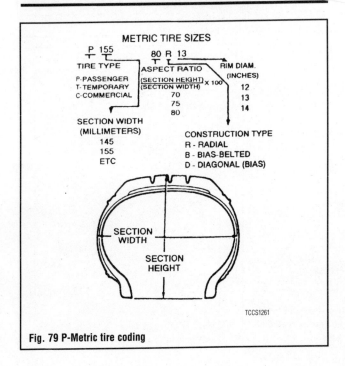

Fig. 79 P-Metric tire coding

When selecting tires, pay attention to the original size as marked on the tire. Most tires are described using an industry size code sometimes referred to as P-Metric. This allows the exact identification of the tire specifications, regardless of the manufacturer. If selecting a different tire size or brand, remember to check the installed tire for any sign of interference with the body or suspension while the vehicle is stopping, turning sharply or heavily loaded.

Snow Tires

Good radial tires can produce a big advantage in slippery weather, but in snow, a street radial tire does not have sufficient tread to provide traction and control. The small grooves of a street tire quickly pack with snow and the tire behaves like a billiard ball on a marble floor. The more open, chunky tread of a snow tire will self-clean as the tire turns, providing much better grip on snowy surfaces.

To satisfy municipalities requiring snow tires during weather emergencies, most snow tires carry either an M + S designation after the tire size stamped on the sidewall, or the designation "all-season." In general, no change in tire size is necessary when buying snow tires.

Most manufacturers strongly recommend the use of 4 snow tires on their vehicles for reasons of stability. If snow tires are fitted only to the drive wheels, the opposite end of the vehicle may become very unstable when braking or turning on slippery surfaces. This instability can lead to unpleasant endings if the driver can't counteract the slide in time.

Note that snow tires, whether 2 or 4, will affect vehicle handling in all non-snow situations. The stiffer, heavier snow tires will noticeably change the turning and braking characteristics of the vehicle. Once the snow tires are installed, you must re-learn the behavior of the vehicle and drive accordingly.

➡**Consider buying extra wheels on which to mount the snow tires. Once done, the "snow wheels" can be installed and removed as needed. This eliminates the potential damage to tires or wheels from seasonal removal and installation. Even if your vehicle has styled wheels, see if inexpensive steel wheels are available. Although the look of the vehicle will change, the expensive wheels will be protected from salt, curb hits and pothole damage.**

TIRE STORAGE

If they are mounted on wheels, store the tires at proper inflation pressure. All tires should be kept in a cool, dry place. If they are stored in the garage or basement, do not let them stand on a concrete floor; set them on strips of wood, a mat or a large stack of newspaper. Keeping them away from direct moisture is of paramount importance. Tires should not be stored upright, but in a flat position.

INFLATION & INSPECTION

▶ **See Figures 80 thru 85**

The importance of proper tire inflation cannot be overemphasized. A tire employs air as part of its structure. It is designed around the supporting strength of the air at a specified pressure. For this reason, improper inflation drastically reduces the tire's ability to perform as intended. A tire will lose some air in day-to-day use; having to add a few pounds of air periodically is not necessarily a sign of a leaking tire.

Two items should be a permanent fixture in every glove compartment: an accurate tire pressure gauge and a tread depth gauge. Check the tire pressure (including the spare) regularly with a pocket type gauge. Too often, the gauge on the end of the air hose at your corner garage is not accurate because it suffers too much abuse. Always check tire pressure when the tires are cold, as pressure increases with temperature. If you must move the vehicle to check the tire inflation, do not drive more than a mile before checking. A cold tire is generally one that has not been driven for more than three hours.

A plate or sticker is normally provided somewhere in the vehicle (door post, hood, tailgate or trunk lid) which shows the proper pressure for the tires. Never counteract excessive pressure build-up by bleeding off air pressure (letting some air out). This will cause the tire to run hotter and wear quicker.

✳✳ CAUTION

Never exceed the maximum tire pressure embossed on the tire! This is the pressure to be used when the tire is at maximum load-

ing, but it is rarely the correct pressure for everyday driving. Consult the owner's manual or the tire pressure sticker for the correct tire pressure.

Once you've maintained the correct tire pressures for several weeks, you'll be familiar with the vehicle's braking and handling personality. Slight adjustments in tire pressures can fine-tune these characteristics, but never change the cold pressure specification by more than 2 psi. A slightly softer tire pressure will give a softer ride but also yield lower fuel mileage. A slightly harder tire will give crisper dry road handling but can cause skidding on wet surfaces. Unless you're fully attuned to the vehicle, stick to the recommended inflation pressures.

All automotive tires have built-in tread wear indicator bars that show up as ½ in. (13mm) wide smooth bands across the tire when ¹⁄₁₆ in. (1.5mm) of tread remains. The appearance of tread wear indicators means that the tires should be replaced. In fact, many states have laws prohibiting the use of tires with less than this amount of tread.

You can check your own tread depth with an inexpensive gauge or by using a Lincoln head penny. Slip the Lincoln penny (with Lincoln's head upside-down) into several tread grooves. If you can see the top of Lincoln's head in 2 adjacent grooves, the tire has less than ¹⁄₁₆ in. (1.5mm) tread left and should be replaced. You can measure snow tires in the same manner by using the "tails" side of the Lincoln penny. If you can see the top of the Lincoln memorial, it's time to replace the snow tire(s).

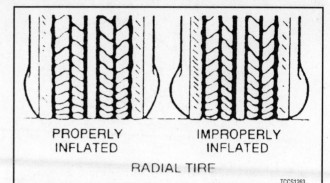

PROPERLY INFLATED   IMPROPERLY INFLATED

RADIAL TIRE

TCCS1263

Fig. 81 Radial tires have a characteristic sidewall bulge; don't try to measure pressure by looking at the tire. Use a quality air pressure gauge

TCCS1095

Fig. 80 Tires with deep cuts, or cuts which bulge, should be replaced immediately

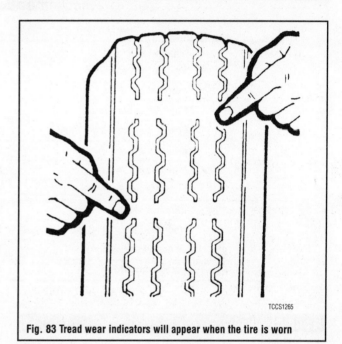

TCCS1265

Fig. 83 Tread wear indicators will appear when the tire is worn

CONDITION	RAPID WEAR AT SHOULDERS	RAPID WEAR AT CENTER	CRACKED TREADS	WEAR ON ONE SIDE	FEATHERED EDGE	BALD SPOTS	SCALLOPED WEAR
EFFECT							
CAUSE	UNDER-INFLATION OR LACK OF ROTATION	OVER-INFLATION OR LACK OF ROTATION	UNDER-INFLATION OR EXCESSIVE SPEED*	EXCESSIVE CAMBER	INCORRECT TOE	UNBALANCED WHEEL / OR TIRE DEFECT *	LACK OF ROTATION OF TIRES OR WORN OR OUT-OF-ALIGNMENT SUSPENSION.
CORRECTION	ADJUST PRESSURE TO SPECIFICATIONS WHEN TIRES ARE COOL ROTATE TIRES			ADJUST CAMBER TO SPECIFICATIONS	ADJUST TOE-IN TO SPECIFICATIONS	DYNAMIC OR STATIC BALANCE WHEELS	ROTATE TIRES AND INSPECT SUSPENSION

*HAVE TIRE INSPECTED FOR FURTHER USE.

TCCS1267

Fig. 82 Common tire wear patterns and causes

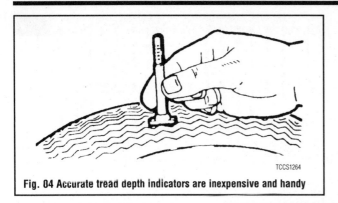

Fig. 04 Accurate tread depth indicators are inexpensive and handy

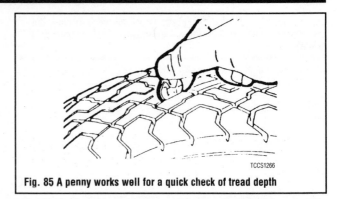

Fig. 85 A penny works well for a quick check of tread depth

FLUIDS AND LUBRICANTS

Recommended Lubricants

Item	Lubricant
Engine Oil	API "SE" or "SF"
Manual Transmission	SAE 80W or SAE 80W/90 (non-hypoid)
Automatic Transmission	DEXRON® or DEXRON® 11 ATF
Rear Axle–Standard	SAE 90W GL-5
Power Steering Reservoir	DEXRON® ATF
Brake Fluid	DOT 4
Antifreeze	Ethylene Glycol
Front Wheel Bearings	Wheel Bearing Grease
Clutch Linkage	Engine Oil
Hood and Door Hinges	Engine Oil
Chassis Lubrication	NLGI #1 or NLGI #2
Lock Cylinders	WD-40 or Powdered Graphite

87891C14

Fluid Disposal

Used fluids such as engine oil, transmission fluid, antifreeze and brake fluid are hazardous wastes and must be disposed of properly. Before draining any fluids, consult with the local authorities; in many areas, waste oil, etc. is being accepted as a part of recycling programs. A number of service stations and auto parts stores are also accepting waste fluids for recycling.

Be sure of the recycling center's policies before draining any fluids, as many will not accept different fluids that have been mixed together.

Fuel and Engine Oil Recommendations

FUEL

For the years 1970–74, premium grade fuel is recommended. The actual octane required varies with the year and vehicle model.

For the years 1975–79, octane requirements are standardized at 87 AKI (which means "Anti-Knock Index"), which is an average of "Motor" and "Research" octane ratings. All BMWs made in the 1975–79 model years, except the 528i, recommend the use of regular, leaded fuel. Since this type of fuel is no longer available, high octane unleaded fuel is suggested as a suitable alternative.

The 528i, and all 1980 and later models have been designed to run on unleaded fuel. In all cases, the minimum octane rating of the unleaded fuel being used must be at least 91 RON (87 CLC). Al unleaded fuels sold in the US are required to meet this minimum rating.

The use of a fuel too low in octane (a measurement of anti-knock quality) will result in spark knock. Since many factors such as altitude, terrain, air tempera-ture and humidity affect operating efficiency, knocking may result even though the recommended fuel is being used. If persistent knocking occurs, it may be necessary to switch to a high grade of fuel. Continuous or heavy knocking may result in engine damage.

➡️ **Your engine's fuel requirement can change with time, mainly due to carbon buildup, which will in turn change the compression ratio. If your engine pings, knocks, or runs on, switch to a higher grade of fuel. Sometimes just changing brands will cure the problem. If it becomes necessary to retard the timing from the specifications don't change it more than a few degrees. Retarded timing will reduce power output and fuel mileage, in addition to increasing the engine tempera-ture.**

OIL

▶ See Figure 86

The Society of Automotive Engineers(SAE) grade number indicates the vis-cosity of the engine oil and thus its ability to lubricate at a given temperature. The lower the SAE grade number, the lighter the oil; the lower the viscosity, the easier it is to crank the engine in cold weather.

Oil viscosities should be chosen from those oils recommended for the lowest anticipated temperature during the oil change interval.

Multi-viscosity oils (10W-30, 20W-50, etc.) offer the important advantage of being adaptable to temperature extremes. They allow easy starting at low tem-peratures, yet they give good protection at high speeds and engine tempera-tures. This is a decided advantage in changeable climates or in long distance touring.

The American Petroleum Institute(API) designation indicates the classification of engine oil used under certain given operating conditions. Only oils designated for use "Service SF" should be used. Oils of the SF type perform a variety of functions inside the engine in addition to their basic function as a lubricant. Through a balanced system of metallic detergents and polymeric dispersants, the oil prevents the formation of high and low temperature deposits and also keeps sludge and particles of dirt in suspension. Acids, particularly sulfuric acid, as well as other by-products of combustion, are neutralized. Both the SAE grade number and the API designation can be found on top of the oil can.

For recommended oil viscosities, refer to the chart.

✳✳ CAUTION

Non-detergent or straight mineral oils should not be used in your car.

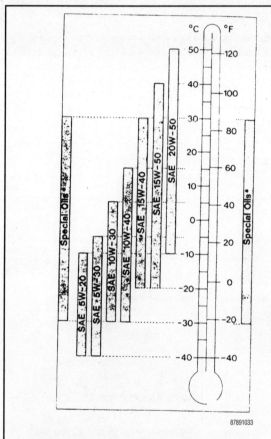

Fig. 86 Recommended oil viscosity for given temperatures

Engine

OIL LEVEL CHECK

▶ **See Figures 87, 88, 89 and 90**

Every time you stop for fuel, check the engine oil as follows:
1. Make sure the car is parked on level ground.
2. When checking the oil level it is best for the engine to be at normal operating temperature, although checking the oil immediately after stopping will lead to a false reading. Wait a few minutes after turning off the engine to allow the oil to drain back into the crankcase.
3. Open the hood and locate the dipstick on the left side of the engine compartment. Pull the dipstick from its tube, wipe it clean and then fully reinsert it.
4. Pull the dipstick out again and, holding it horizontally, read the oil level. The oil should be between the 2 marks on the dipstick. If the oil is below the upper mark, add oil of the proper viscosity through the capped opening in the top of the cylinder head cover.
5. Replace the dipstick and check the oil level again after adding any oil. Be careful not to overfill the crankcase. Approximately one quart of oil will raise the level from the lower mark to the upper mark. Excess oil will generally be consumed at an accelerated rate.

CHANGE INTERVAL

The oil should be changed every 3 months or 3,000 miles (4,831 km) in all models. It is recommended that you change the oil based on whichever interval comes first.

The oil drain plug is located on the lower right hand side of the oil pan (bottom of the engine, underneath the car). The oil filter is located on the left side of the engine.

➡**Certain operating conditions may warrant more frequent oil changes. If the vehicle is used for short trips, where the engine does not have a chance to fully warm up before it is shut off, water condensation and low temperature deposits may make it necessary to change the oil sooner. If the vehicle is used mostly in stop-and-go traffic, corrosive acids and high temperature deposits may necessitate shorter oil changing intervals. The shorter intervals also apply to industrial or rural areas where high concentrations of dust and other airborne particulate matter contaminate the oil. Finally, if the car is used for towing trailers (in spite of BMW's recommendation to the contrary), a severe load is placed on the engine causing the oil to thin out sooner, making necessary the shorter oil changing intervals.**

PRECAUTIONS

✳✳ CAUTION

Prolonged and repeated skin contact with used engine oil, with no effort to remove the oil, may be harmful. Always follows these simple precautions when handling used motor oil:

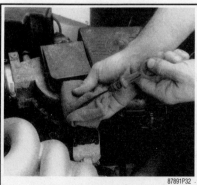

Fig. 87 After allowing the oil to drip into the oil pan, remove the dipstick

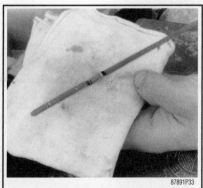

Fig. 88 The correct oil level is between the two hash marks

Fig. 89 To add engine oil, remove the filler cap . . .

1. Avoid prolonged skin contact with used motor oil.
2. Remove oil from skin by washing thoroughly with soap and water or - Waterless hand cleaner. Do not use gasoline, thinners or other solvents.
3. Avoid prolonged skin contact with oil-soaked clothing.

OIL AND FILTER CHANGE

▶ **See Figures 91, 92, 93, 94 and 95**

BMW cars are equipped with either of 2 styles of oil filter. One is the familiar spin-on cartridge type and the other is a housing enclosed full flow element. The types are easy to identify. If there is a cast aluminum housing with a bolt through the top center, towards the front of the engine, it is the full flow element type. The spin-on cartridge type is easy to recognize on the side of the engine block.

Use only a BMW approved filter or its commercial market equivalent. Use only a high grade filter as it is there to protect a high grade engine. Some low grade filters do not fit correctly and may cause the filter housing not to seal correctly. Always use new O-rings when changing the oil filter and replace the oil pan plug crush washer.

1. Run the engine until it reaches normal operating temperature.
2. Jack up the from of the car and support it safely on jackstands.
3. Slide a drain pan of at least 6 quarts (3.8l) capacity under the oil pan.
4. Loosen the drain plug with a suitable wrench. Once loosened, finish turning the plug out by hand.

➡ **By keeping an inward pressure on the plug as you unscrew it, oil won't escape past the threads and you can remove the plug without being burned by hot oil.**

5. Allow the oil to drain completely and then reinstall the drain plug, using a new sealing washer between the drain plug and oil pan. Do not overtighten the plug, or you may strip the threads on the oil pan.
6. Using a strap wrench or other suitable filter removal tool, remove the oil filter. Keep in mind that the oil filter holds about 1 quart oil, and some will spill out during removal.

7. Empty the old filter into the drain pan and dispose of the filter properly.
8. Using a clean rag, wipe off the filter adapter on the engine block. Be sure that the rag doesn't leave any lint which could clog an oil passage.
9. Coat the rubber gasket on the filter with fresh oil. Spin the filter onto the engine by hand; when the gasket touches the adapter surface, give it another ½–¾ turn. No more, or you'll squash the gasket and it will leak.
10. Refill the engine with the correct amount of fresh oil. See the Capacities chart at the end of this section.
11. Check the oil level on the dipstick. It is normal for the level to be a bit above the full mark. Start the engine and allow it to idle for a few minutes.

✳✳ CAUTION

Do not run the engine above idle speed until it has built up oil pressure, indicated when the oil light goes out.

12. Shut off the engine, allow the oil to drain for a minute, and check the oil level. Check around the filter and drain plug for any leaks, and correct as necessary.

Cooling System

BMW recommends that the coolant be changed every 2 years. Collect your used coolant in a clean pan, do not allow any other fluids to mix with it, and return it to a recycling facility or shop. Do not drain the coolant on the ground or pour it into a sewer.

FLUID RECOMMENDATIONS

BMW recommends that an ethylene glycol based antifreeze coolant be used. Stay with a name brand that is compatible with aluminum and is nitrate and amino free. The coolant should be a 50/50 mix to achieve protection to -35°F. (-37°C.). Any concentration in excess of 50/50 will actually reduce the effectiveness of the fluid as a heat transfer medium.

Fig. 90 . . . then add the oil in small amounts until the correct level is reached. Check the dipstick after each addition

Fig. 91 Loosen and remove the oil pan drain plug

Fig. 92 Allow the oil to drain into a suitable container

Fig. 93 Using a filter removal tool, remove the oil filter. This is a spin-type filter

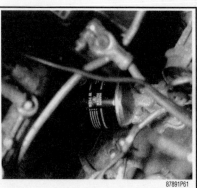

Fig. 94 The 2002 oil filter, mounted to the driver's side of the engine

Fig. 95 Always coat the new spin-on type oil filter gasket with clean oil

LEVEL CHECK

▶ **See Figures 96, 97, 98 and 99**

It is recommended that you check the coolant level every time you stop for fuel. If the engine is hot, let it cool for a few minutes before checking the coolant.

Check the freezing as well as the boilover protection rates at least once a year, preferably just before the winter and/or the summer. This can be done with an antifreeze tester (many service stations will have one on hand and will probably check it for you, if not, they are available at most automotive parts stores). Maintain a protection rating of at least -35°F (-37°C) to prevent engine damage as a result of freezing and to assure the proper engine operating temperature.

In addition to testing the coolant protection level, the cooling system should also be pressure tested at least once a year. To perform a pressure test, a coolant pressure tester is required. Although available at most automotive parts stores, this tool is fairly expensive; therefore, you may wish to have this service completed by a mechanic.

A pressure test runs an artificially high pressure level though the entire cooling system. This pressure level will show whether the cooling system can withstand this level, which it should, and if there are any weak hoses or components which may need replacement.

DRAIN AND REFILL

▶ **See Figures 100, 101, 102 and 103**

The cooling system should be drained, thoroughly flushed and then refilled at least every 30,000 miles (48,000 km). This should be done with the engine cold.

1. Remove the radiator cap, if equipped.

✳✳ CAUTION

Make sure the system is cool before removing the cap!

2. Turn the heater control to **WARM**.
3. Loosen the radiator end clamp on the lower radiator hose, and pull the hose off the radiator connector.
4. Remove the 19mm plug from the right rear of the engine block.
5. Allow the coolant to drain completely before installing the plug and radiator hose.
6. To refill the system, first replace the drain plug and reconnect the radiator hose and clamp it.
7. On 6-cylinder engines, loosen the bleeder screw on the thermostat housing. On all other engines, make sure the heater control is still in the **WARM** position.
8. Fill the cooling system with a 50/50 mixture of antifreeze and distilled water and then replace the filler cap, turning it to the second stop. Start the engine and run it at 2,500 rpm until normal operating temperature is reached, and then stop it. If equipped with a 6-cylinder engine, watch for water coming out at the bleed point, then close the bleeder screw. On other engines, when the engine is cool, check the coolant level in the radiator, or expansion tank and add antifreeze if needed.
9. Start the engine after a wait of at least 1 minute and then run it at 4,000 rpm for 30 seconds. Release the throttle and make sure heat comes from the heater at idle speed. Then, shut off the engine again.

SYSTEM BLEEDING

▶ **See Figure 104**

The cooling system must be bled to remove air from the coolant passages. If the system is not bled, hot spots can form leading to overheating and engine damage.

To bleed the cooling system, proceed as follows:
1. Fill the radiator and reservoir, if equipped, with coolant.
2. Run the engine at normal operating temperature.
3. Set the heater controls to **WARM**.
4. Bring the engine idle up to 2000 RPM.
5. Unscrew the bleeder bolt at the thermostat housing until the escaping coolant is free of air bubbles.

Fig. 96 Checking the cooling system freezing and boiling points with an antifreeze tester

TCCS1233

Fig. 97 An example of a coolant reservoir

87891P22

Fig. 98 Remove the cap slowly to relieve any system pressure

87891P23

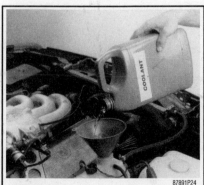

Fig. 99 Add coolant to the reservoir up to the MAX line

87891P24

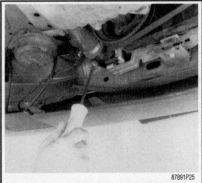

Fig. 100 Loosen the plastic draincock at the base of the radiator

87891P25

Fig. 101 Carefully remove the draincock. The coolant may be hot

87891P26

Fig. 102 Allow the coolant to drain into a suitable container

Fig. 103 A funnel may be used to control coolant spillage

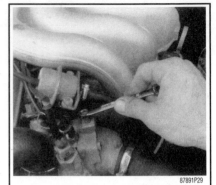

Fig. 104 Unscrew the bleeder bolt to allow trapped air to escape

6. After the system has been bled, tighten the bleeder bolt and check that the coolant level is correct.

Integral Expansion Tank Systems

These systems have the expansion tank as part of the radiator assembly. It is the vertically mounted, translucent tank on the side of the radiator.

1. With the expansion tank filled with coolant mix, run the engine to operating temperature. Set the heater controls to **WARM** and engine speed to fast idle.

2. Loosen the radiator mounted bleeder screw. Allow coolant to run out of the bleeder until a solid stream of coolant and no air is coming out. Keep the expansion tank full during this step. Tighten the bleeder screw.

3. Turn off the engine, but keep the ignition switch in the **ON** position. On vehicles with a thermostat housing bleeder screw, open the screw and allow coolant to run out of the bleeder until a solid stream of coolant and no air is coming out. Keep the expansion tank full during this step. Tighten the bleeder screw to 4.5–7.0 ft lbs. (6–10 Nm).

4. Start the engine and run at 2500 rpm. The coolant level will drop to the COLD mark on the expansion tank or close to it, indicating that residual air has been purged from the system.

5. Install the expansion tank cap.

Remote Expansion Tank Systems

EXCEPT M5 MODELS

1. With the expansion tank filled with coolant mix, run the engine to operating temperature. Set the heater controls to **WARM** and engine speed to fast idle.

2. Loosen the thermostat housing mounted bleeder screw. Allow coolant to run out of the bleeder until a solid stream of coolant and no air is coming out. Do not allow the expansion tank to run dry during this step. Tighten the bleeder screw to 4.5–7.0 ft lbs. (6–10 Nm).

3. Fill the expansion tank to the COLD mark, then install the tank cap.

M5 MODELS

1. Fill the expansion tank to the MAX marking.

2. Start the engine, then press the side and window defroster button on the climate control panel.

3. Loosen the cooling system bleeder valve located near the remote positive battery connection. Allow any air to escape, then tighten the valve.

4. Refill the expansion tank to the MAX mark and run the engine at 2500 rpm.

5. When the level in the expansion tank steadies itself at the MAX mark, replace the fill cap.

6. If the expansion tank is equipped with an air fill valve, use a tire pump to pressurize the cooling system at the fill valve on the expansion tank to 7 psi (0.5 bar).

❊❊ WARNING

If the system is not pressurized, engine damage will occur. The system is designed to be precisely pressurized. If the system cannot be pressurized at the moment, avoid driving the vehicle, or limit the engine speed to 3000 rpm or less until the first possible opportunity to restore pressure.

7. If the expansion tank is not equipped with an air fill valve, check the present coolant level, then allow the engine to cool for at least 6 hours and recheck the level. The coolant level should be between the COLD and MAX marks with the engine warm, and at the COLD mark when cold.

8. If the level has to be adjusted, remove the cap and add the required amount of coolant. If the amount was in excess of 1.1 quart (1 liter) repeat the bleeding procedure.

FLUSHING AND CLEANING THE SYSTEM

With the use of electrically actuated heater valves and bi-zone heater cores, it is not easy or advisable to cut hoses to mount a flushing tee. Drain the system, add clear water, bleed the system and run the engine to flush the system of old coolant. Drain the system, add fresh coolant and bleed the system. This will get rid of most of the old coolant and keep the cooling system in good shape. It is important to change the coolant on a regular basis, every 2 years, as this will prevent corrosion from building up and creating the need for cleaning the cooling system.

RADIATOR CAP INSPECTION

◆ **See Figure 105**

Allow the engine to cool sufficiently before attempting to remove the radiator cap. Use a rag to cover the cap, then remove by pressing down and turning counterclockwise to the first stop. If any hissing is noted (indicating the release of pressure), wait until the hissing stops completely, then press down again and turn counterclockwise until the cap can be removed.

❊❊ CAUTION

DO NOT attempt to remove the radiator cap while the engine is hot. Severe personal injury from steam burns can result.

Fig. 105 Radiator with traditional radiator cap—2002 model

Check the condition of the radiator cap gasket and seal inside of the cap. The radiator cap is designed to seal the cooling system under normal operating conditions which allows the build up of a certain amount of pressure (this pressure rating is stamped or printed on the cap). The pressure in the system raises the boiling point of the coolant to help prevent overheating. If the radiator cap does not seal, the boiling point of the coolant is lowered and overheating will occur. If the cap must be replaced, purchase the new cap according to the pressure rating which is specified for your vehicle.

Prior to installing the radiator cap, inspect and clean the filler neck. If you are reusing the old cap, clean it thoroughly with clear water. After turning the cap on, make sure the arrows align with the overflow hose.

Manual Transmission

FLUID RECOMMENDATIONS

BMW recommends the use of non-hypoid GL4 SAE 80 or SAE 80W/90 in all models.

➡ **Due to running production changes, the lubricant in your transmission may be a different type than what is listed here or in your owner's manual. The recommended fluid for the transmission installed in your vehicle will be specified on a tag on the transmission body.**

Synthetic oils can offer easier shifting in cold weather and greater protection from wear, but can sometimes cause noisier operation and they may not be compatible with all transmissions. If you wish to use a synthetic manual transmission lubricant, check with your BMW dealer for suggestions and details.

LEVEL CHECK

The oil in the manual transmission should be checked at least every 6,000–7,500 miles (9,600–12,000 km).

1. With the car parked on a level surface, remove the filler plug from the side of the transmission housing.
2. If the lubricant begins to trickle out of the hole, there is enough gear oil, and you need not go any further. Otherwise, carefully insert your finger (watch out for sharp threads) and check to see if the oil is up to the edge of the hole.
3. If not, add oil through the hole until the gear oil level is at the edge of the hole. Most gear lubricants come in a plastic squeeze-type bottle with a nozzle. You can also use a common kitchen baster. Use only standard non hypoid-type gear oil—SAE 80W or SAE 80W/90.
4. Replace the filler plug, run the engine and check for leaks.

DRAIN AND REFILL

▶ **See Figures 106, 107, 108 and 109**

1. The oil must be warm before it can be drained. Drive the car until the engine reaches normal operating temperature.
2. Raise and safely support the vehicle on jackstands.

3. Remove the side filler plug to provide a vent.
4. Place a large container underneath the transmission and then remove the drain plug.
5. Allow the oil to drain completely. Clean the magnetic drain plug of any excessive metal particles and install it, tightening it until it is just snug.
6. Fill the transmission with the proper lubricant as detailed earlier in this section. Refer to the Capacities chart for the correct amount of lubricant.
7. When the oil level is up to the edge of the filler hole, replace the filler plug. Drive the car for a few minutes, then stop and check for any leaks.

Automatic Transmission

FLUID RECOMMENDATION

BMW recommends the use of DEXRON®II or III Automatic Transmission Fluid (ATF).

FLUID LEVEL CHECK

▶ **See Figures 110 and 111**

Check the automatic transmission fluid level at least every 12,500 miles (20,000 km). The dipstick can be found at the rear of the engine compartment. The fluid level should be checked only when transmission is at normal operating temperature. The transmission is considered warm after about 20 miles (30 km) of highway driving.

1. Park the car on a level surface with the engine idling. Shift the transmission into **NEUTRAL** and set the parking brake.
2. Remove the dipstick, wipe it clean and then reinsert it firmly. Be sure that It has been pushed all the way in. Remove the dipstick again and check the fluid level while holding it horizontally. With the engine running, the fluid level should be between the 2 marks on the dipstick.
3. If the fluid level is below the second mark, add DEXRON®II or III automatic transmission fluid through the dipstick tube. This is easily done with the aid of a funnel. Check the level often as you are filling the transmission. Be extremely careful not to over fill it. Overfilling will cause slippage, seal damage and overheating. Approximately one pint of ATF will raise the fluid level from one mark to the other.

➡ **Always use DEXRON®II or III ATF. The use of Type F or any other fluid will cause severe damage to the transmission. The fluid on the dipstick should always be a red color. If it is discolored (brown or black) or smells burnt, serious transmission troubles, probably due to overheating, should be suspected. The transmission should be inspected by a qualified technician to locate the cause of the burnt fluid.**

DRAIN AND REFILL

The drain and refill procedures for an automatic transmission are detailed in Section 7.

Fig. 106 Loosen and remove the side filler plug, then loosen and remove the lower plug

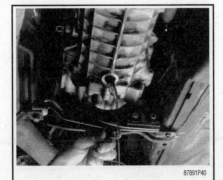

Fig. 107 Drain the oil into a suitable container

Fig. 108 Notice the lower drain plug has a magnetic insert to catch any metal particles in the oil

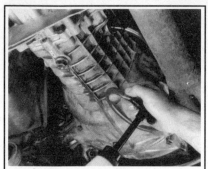

Fig. 109 When filling with new oil, it is easier to use containers equipped with a pump

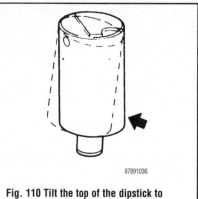
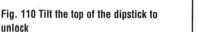

Fig. 110 Tilt the top of the dipstick to unlock

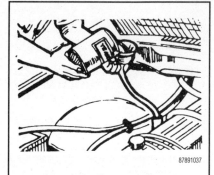

Fig. 111 Use a funnel to add ATF fluid through the dipstick hole

Transfer Case

FLUID RECOMMENDATION

325ix Models

This is the only 4-wheel drive available from BMW. The transfer case contains 1.1 pts. (0.6l)® II or III ATF. This is the factory recommended fluid to use in the transfer case.

LEVEL CHECK

Remove the filler plug on the side of the transfer case. The fluid should be level with the bottom of the filler plug hole. Torque the plug to 22–25 ft. lbs. (30–35 Nm).

DRAIN AND REFILL

The transfer case has a drain plug that is removed to drain the fluid. To fill the transfer case, open the filler plug located on the top edge of the case and add the fluid. The fluid should flow from the filler hole, this is how you know it is full.

Drive Axle

LEVEL CHECK

Rear Axle

➡**This procedure covers all models.**

The oil in the differential on models through 1974 should be checked at least every 8,000 miles (13,000 km); 12,500 miles (20,000 km) for 1975 and later models.

To check the fluid level, proceed as follows:

1. With the car parked on a level surface, remove the filler plug from the side of the rear differential.
2. If the oil begins to trickle out of the hole, the level is correct. Otherwise, carefully insert your finger (watch out for sharp threads) into the hole and check that the oils is up to the bottom edge of the filler hole.
3. If not, add oil through the hole until the level is at the edge of the hole. Most gear oils come in a plastic squeeze-type bottle with a nozzle. You can also use a common kitchen baster. Use only standard GL-5 hypoid-type gear oil, SAE 90W.

325iX Models

➡**This model comes equipped with front and rear axles**

1. With the car on a level surface, remove the filler plug from the side of the front differential or rear differential.
2. If the oil begins to trickle out of the hole, there is enough. Otherwise, carefully insert your finger (watch out for sharp threads) into the hole and check that the oil is up to the bottom edge of the filler hole.
3. If not, add oil through the hole until the level is at the edge of the hole. Most gear oils come in a plastic squeeze bottle with a nozzle; making additions is simple. You can also use a common kitchen baster. Use only standard GL-5 hypoid-type gear oil, SAE 90.

DRAIN AND REFILL

▶ **See Figures 112, 113 and 114**

There is not recommended change interval for the rear axle but it is always a good idea to change the fluid if you have purchased the car used or if it has been drive in water high enough to reach the axle.

1. Park the car on a level surface and set the parking brake.
2. Raise the rear and support safely on jackstands.
3. Remove the filler plug (10mm Allen wrench) at the side of the differential.
4. Place a large container underneath the rear axle. Remove the drain plug (10mm Allen wrench) at the bottom of the differential and allow all lubricant to drain into the pan.

Fig. 112 Remove the lower drain plug . . .

Fig. 113 . . . and allow the fluid to drain into a suitable container

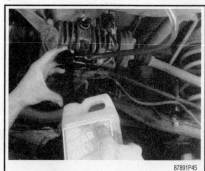

Fig. 114 Add new oil using a pump-equipped container

5. When all lubricant has drained out, clean and replace the drain plug.

6. Refill the differential using the proper grade and quantity of lubricant as detailed earlier in this section. Replace the filler plug, run the car, then check for any leaks.

Clutch and Brake Master Cylinder

FLUID RECOMMENDATION

Use only high quality, name brand DOT 4 brake fluid. Use tightly sealed small containers to refill the reservoir. Large containers offer a false economy. A large container that has been opened will absorb moisture and ruin the fluid. Only use large containers when performing major work on the brake or clutch hydraulic systems and the entire contents will be used at once.

Tightly cap any container to prevent moisture from being absorbed into the brake fluid.

LEVEL CHECK

▶ **See Figures 115, 116, 117 and 118**

On all but the 1600 models, the fluid reservoir services both he brake and clutch master cylinder. On the 1600, no fluid is involved in clutch operation. The fluid level should be checked at every oil change.

Wipe the reservoir cap and surrounding area clean. Make sure the level is up to the full marker located on the side of the reservoir. If necessary, add DOT 4 specification fluid that is brand new. Never attempt to reuse brake fluid). Be careful not to drop any dirt into the fluid, and avoid spilling fluid on the paint work, or wipe it up immediately if it spills. Make sure the vent hole used in earlier type reservoirs is clean. If it is not clean, blow air through the hole.

Power Steering Pump

FLUID RECOMMENDATIONS

All vehicles except the M5 use automatic transmission fluid (ATF) as the power steering fluid. Use DEXRON®II type ATF.

The M5 has a self-leveling suspension that shares a hydraulic fluid reservoir with the power steering system. Use the hydraulic fluid printed on the reservoir. DO NOT use ATF, brake fluid or engine oil.

➡**Those models requiring special power steering fluid will have a sticker on or around the reservoir.**

LEVEL CHECK

▶ **See Figures 119, 120, 121 and 122**

On 1970–74 models, at 8,000 mile (13,000 km) intervals, check the level of oil in the steering box. Carefully pry up the plastic cap on the steering gear cover and check to see that the oil level reaches the lower edge of the filler aperture. Top up as necessary with SAE 90 hypoid gear oil.

On 4-cylinder models build in 1975 and later years, the vehicle is equipped with a rack and pinion unit which requires only greasing. On 1975 and later 6-cylinder vehicles (with the exception of the 528e), check the power steering fluid as follows at every oil change:

Fig. 115 The 2002 brake fluid reservoir

Fig. 116 Brake fluid reservoir. Notice the MAX and MIN marks

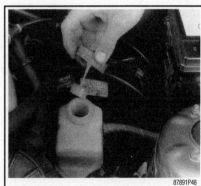

Fig. 117 Clean around the fill cap with a rag, then unscrew it

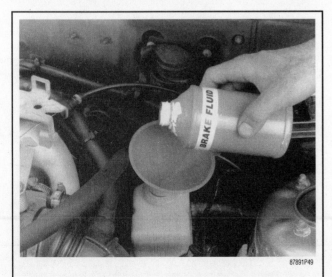

Fig. 118 Add DOT 3 or DOT 4 brake fluid to just below the MAX line

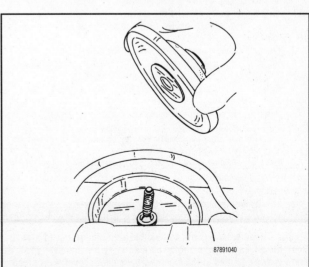

Fig. 119 Remove the wingnut and lift off the cap to check the steering fluid level

Fig. 120 Remove the power steering reservoir cap

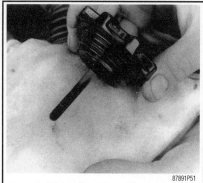

Fig. 121 The correct fluid level is between the two hash marks

Fig. 122 Add fluid if needed. Make sure you are adding the correct type of fluid

1. With the engine off, remove the wing nut located at the top of the reservoir. The oil level should be just above the mark on the reservoir. If necessary, refill with a DEXRON®II or III type automatic transmission fluid.

2. Start the engine and watch the fluid level. If the fluid drops below the line level, add fluid until the level just reaches the line. The, shut the engine off and observe that the fluid level rises to slightly above the line.

3. Reinstall the reservoir cover, making sure the seal seats properly. Check for any leaks in the steering box.

The 528e has a translucent plastic reservoir similar to a brake master cylinder reservoir. To check the fluid level in this reservoir, simply unscrew the cap and check that the level. The correct level is between the 2 marks on the reservoir. If the level is not correct, add fluid in the manner already described for previous models.

Chassis Greasing

The steering rods, suspension joints and ball joints of BMW suspension are maintenance-free. Therefore no regular greasing is needed on these components, although regular inspection is highly recommended.

Body Lubrication and Maintenance

FRONT WHEEL BEARINGS

Adjustment

The front wheels each rotate on a set of opposed, tapered roller bearings. The grease retainer at the inside of the hub prevents lubricant from leaking.

To check the condition of the grease, proceed as follows:

1. Raise and support the front of the vehicle on jackstands.

2. Remove the grease cap and remove any excess grease from the end of the spindle.

3. Remove the cotter pin and nut lock shown in the illustration.

4. Rotate the wheel, hub and drum assembly while tightening the adjusting nut to 17–25 ft. lbs. (22–32 Nm) in order to seat the bearings.

5. Back off the adjusting nut ½ rotation (180°), then retighten the nut to 10–15 ft.. lbs. (13–19 Nm).

6. Locate the nut lock on the adjusting nut so that the castellations on the lock are lined up with the cotter pin hole in the spindle.

7. Install the new cotter pin, bending the ends of the cotter pin around the castellated flange of the nut lock.

8. Check the wheel for proper rotation, then install the grease cap. If the wheel still does not rotate properly, inspect and clean or replace the wheel bearings and cups.

❋❋ WARNING

Sodium-based grease is not compatible with lithium-based grease. Read the package labels and be careful not to mix the two types. If there is any doubt as to the type of grease used, completely clean the old grease from the bearing and hub before replacing.

Repacking

1. Raise and support the front of the vehicle on jackstands.

2. Remove the wheel cover. Remove the wheel.

3. Remove the caliper from the disc and wire it to the underbody to prevent damage to the brake hose. See Section 9.

4. Remove the grease cap from the hub. Then, remove the cotter pin, nut lock, adjusting nut and flat washer from the spindle. Remove the outer bearing assembly from the hub.

5. Pull the hub and disc assembly off the wheel spindle.

6. Remove and discard the old grease retainer. Remove the inner bearing cone and roller assembly from the hub.

7. Clean all grease from the inner and outer bearing cups with solvent. Inspect the cups for pits, scratches, or excessive wear. If the cups are damaged, remove them with a drift.

8. Clean the inner and outer cone and roller assemblies with solvent and shake them dry. If the cone and roller assemblies show excessive wear or damage, replace them with the bearing cups as a unit.

9. Clean the spindle and the inside of the hub with solvent to thoroughly remove all old grease.

10. Covering the spindle with a clean cloth, brush all loose dirt and dust from the brake assembly. Remove the cloth carefully so as to not get dirt on the spindle.

11. If the inner and/or outer bearing cups were removed, install the replacement cups on the hub. Be sure that the cups seat properly in the hub.

12. It is imperative that all old grease be removed from the bearings and surrounding surfaces before repacking. The new lithium-based grease is not compatible with the sodium base grease used in the past.

13. Install the hub and disc on the wheel spindle. To prevent damage to the grease retainer and spindle threads, keep the hub centered on the spindle.

14. Install the outer bearing cone and roller assembly and the flat washer on the spindle. Install the adjusting nut.

15. Adjust the wheel bearings by torquing the adjusting nut to 17–25 ft. lbs. (22–32 Nm) with the wheel rotating to seat the bearing. Then back off the adjusting nut ½ rotation (180°). Retighten the adjusting nut to 10–15 ft. lbs. (13–19 Nm) Install the locknut so that the castellations are aligned with the cotter pin hole. Install the cotter pin. Bend the ends of the cotter pin around the castellations of the locknut to prevent interference with the radio static collector in the grease cap. Install the grease cap.

16. Install the wheels.

17. Install the wheel cover.

LOCK CYLINDERS

Apply graphite lubricant sparingly thought the key slot. Insert the key and operate the lock several times to be sure that the lubricant is worked into the lock cylinder.

DOOR HINGES AND HINGE CHECKS

Spray a silicone lubricant on the hinge pivot points to eliminate any binding conditions. Open and close the door several times to be sure that the lubricant is evenly and thoroughly distributed.

BODY DRAIN HOLES

Be sure that the drain holes in the doors and rocker panels are cleared of obstruction. A small screwdriver can be used to clear them of any debris.

WASHING AND WAXING

Wash the car either by hand or in an automatic car wash. Rinse the car first with a light stream of water to loosen any dirt on the painted surfaces. Soak any dead bugs with water and car washing solution, then wipe off. Wash the car out of direct sunlight as water spots can form if water is allowed to evaporate from the painted surfaces.

Use only waxes with carnauba or synthetic formulations. Keep a good coat of wax on the car to protect the surface from contaminants. Use only high quality paint care products as available through your dealer or specialty boutique.

Wash the car often in the winter months to keep road salt off the car. Touch up any paint damage with matching paint. Do not allow moisture to collect under a car cover if one is used.

UNDERHOOD

The engine compartment should be cleaned and treated once a year. This will clean away any accumulated dirt, grease and oil that may be hiding leaks or other problems. A clean engine runs cooler and makes routine maintenance more pleasurable.

GLASS CARE

Interior glass surfaces can be cleaned with a commercial cleaner or a one to one mixture of water and white vinegar. Do not use any cleaner containing an abrasive. Exterior glass and lenses can be cleaned with water and car washing solution or with the same mixture used for the interior glass.

RUBBER SEATS AND TRIM

Clean with water and treat with silicone spray. A commercial rubber treatment can also be used. Do not use harsh solvents as these will damage the rubber.

Interior Cleaning

SEATBELTS

Wash the seatbelts with soap and water. Keep the seatbelts fully extended until they dry completely. Never allow the seatbelts to retract while still wet.

UPHOLSTERY

Use a product designed for the seating surfaces your car has. If you have a cloth interior, brush the nap of the fabric after cleaning to restore the pile. Wipe down leather seats with a wool or cotton cloth that is slightly moist. Dry the leather and treat it with a leather care product.

TRAILER TOWING

BMW of North America does not recommend using your BMW to tow trailers. In Europe, towing equipment is made available for various BMW models, but due to regulatory and litigious matters, BMW NA has chosen not to recommend trailer towing.

TOWING THE VEHICLE

If your car needs to be towed, the best method is by flatbed. The risk of body damage or drive axle and transmission damage is reduced by using a flatbed. If a flatbed is not available, have the car towed by a wheel lift type tow truck. Do not tow the vehicle with a bumper lift type tow truck or severe damage to the bodywork will occur.

If the car is equipped with automatic transmission, a few special precautions must be taken to prevent the transmission from being damaged. The car must be towed with the selector lever in the **NEUTRAL** position. The car may be towed a maximum distance of 30 miles (50 km) at a maximum towing speed of 25–30 mph (40–48 km/h). If the car must be towed a greater distance then stated above, either the driveshaft must be disconnected or an additional 2.1 pts. of DEXRON®II or III must be added to the transmission (to be drained immediately after towing).

If the vehicle needs to be pulled out of mud or sand, use a nylon tow strap to pull the vehicle out. All vehicles are equipped with tow eyes or attachment points for screw-in tow eyes. The screw-in tow eye is located in the tool kit. The tow eyes or attachment points are located behind panels in the front and back of the vehicle. Pry the panel off to expose the tow eye or attachment point. Screw in the tow eye fully and tightly. Do not tow with the tow eye loose.

It is recommended not to push your BMW. Due to height differences in bumpers and the possibility of damaging the energy absorption bumper, do not push your car.

JUMP STARTING A DEAD BATTERY

▶ **See Figure 123**

Whenever a vehicle is jump started, precautions must be followed in order to prevent the possibility of personal injury. Remember that batteries contain a small amount of explosive hydrogen gas which is a by-product of battery charging. Sparks should always be avoided when working around batteries, especially when attaching jumper cables. To minimize the possibility of accidental sparks, follow the procedure carefully.

✳✳ CAUTION

NEVER hook the batteries up in a series circuit or the entire electrical system will go up in smoke, especially the starter!

Cars equipped with a diesel engine may utilize two 12 volt batteries. If so, the batteries are connected in a parallel circuit (positive terminal to positive terminal, negative terminal to negative terminal). Hooking the batteries up in parallel circuit increases battery cranking power without increasing total battery voltage output. Output remains at 12 volts. On the other hand, hooking two 12 volt batteries up in a series circuit (positive terminal to negative terminal, posi-

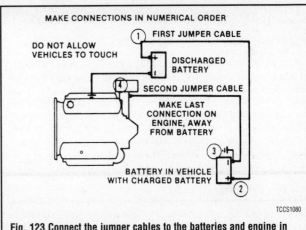

Fig. 123 Connect the jumper cables to the batteries and engine in the order shown

tive terminal to negative terminal) increases total battery output to 24 volts (12 volts plus 12 volts).

Jump Starting Precautions

• Be sure that both batteries are of the same voltage. Vehicles covered by this manual and most vehicles on the road today utilize a 12 volt charging system.

• Be sure that both batteries are of the same polarity (have the same terminal, in most cases NEGATIVE grounded).

• Be sure that the vehicles are not touching or a short could occur.

• On serviceable batteries, be sure the vent cap holes are not obstructed.

• Do not smoke or allow sparks anywhere near the batteries.

• In cold weather, make sure the battery electrolyte is not frozen. This can occur more readily in a battery that has been in a state of discharge.

• Do not allow electrolyte to contact your skin or clothing.

Jump Starting Procedure

▶ **See Figure 124**

1. Make sure that the voltages of the 2 batteries are the same. Most batteries and charging systems are of the 12 volt variety.

2. Pull the jumping vehicle (with the good battery) into a position so the jumper cables can reach the dead battery and that vehicle's engine. Make sure that the vehicles do NOT touch.

3. Place the transmissions of both vehicles in **NEUTRAL** or **PARK**, as applicable, then firmly set their parking brakes.

➡ **If necessary for safety reasons, the hazard lights on both vehicles may be operated throughout the entire procedure without significantly increasing the difficulty of jumping the dead battery.**

4. Turn all lights and accessories off on both vehicles. Make sure the ignition switches on both vehicles are turned to the **OFF** position.

5. Cover the battery cell caps with a rag, but do not cover the terminals.

6. Make sure the terminals on both batteries are clean and free of corrosion or proper electrical connection will be impeded. If necessary, clean the battery terminals before proceeding.

7. Identify the positive (+) and negative (-) terminals on both battery posts.

8. Connect the first jumper cable to the positive (+) terminal of the dead battery, then connect the other end of that cable to the positive (+) terminal of the booster (good) battery.

9. Connect one end of the other jumper cable to the negative (-) terminal on the booster battery and the other cable clamp to an engine bolt head, alternator bracket or other solid, metallic point on the engine with the dead battery. Try to pick a ground on the engine that is positioned away from the battery in order to minimize the possibility of the 2 clamps touching should one loosen during the procedure. DO NOT connect this clamp to the negative (–) terminal of the bad battery.

Fig. 124 Models equipped with trunk mounted batteries have a jumper module in the engine compartment. This module is located on the right firewall

✳✳ CAUTION

Be very careful to keep the jumper cables away from moving parts (cooling fan, belts, etc.) on both engines.

10. Check to make sure that the cables are routed away from any moving parts, then start the donor vehicle's engine. Run the engine at moderate speed for several minutes to allow the dead battery a chance to receive some initial charge.

11. With the donor vehicle's engine still running slightly above idle, try to start the vehicle with the dead battery. Crank the engine for no more than 10 seconds at a time and let the starter cool for at least 20 seconds between tries. If the vehicle does not start in 3 tries, it is likely that something else is also wrong or that the battery needs additional time to charge.

12. Once the vehicle is started, allow it to run at idle for a few seconds to make sure that it is operating properly operating.

13. Turn on the headlights, heater blower and, if equipped, the rear defroster of both vehicles in order to reduce the severity of voltage spikes and subsequent risk of damage to the vehicles' electrical systems when the cables are disconnected. This step is especially important to late model vehicles equipped with computer control modules.

14. Carefully disconnect the cables in the reverse order of connection. Start with the negative cable that is attached to the engine ground, then the negative cable on the donor battery. Disconnect the positive cable from the donor battery and finally, disconnect the positive cable from the formerly dead battery. Be careful when disconnecting the cables from the positive terminals not to allow the alligator clips to touch any metal on either vehicle or a short and sparks will occur.

JACKING

▶ **See Figures 125, 126, 127, 128 and 129**

Do not use the tire changing jack to work on the vehicle. Use a hydraulic floor jack rated for the weight of the vehicle. BMW supplies a wheel chock with each vehicle. Use the wheel chock whenever raising the car.

The vehicle should be jacked up only using the factory jacking points. The jacking points along the rocker panel are marked with indentations in the metal. Chock the wheel opposite the corner being raised. Pad the jack saddle with a rubber pad or a block of wood. Use jackstands to support the car. Do not go under the car with the car supported only by the jack.

On most BMW vehicles, the jacking points for a garage jack are located directly below the openings for the tire changing jack and are raised platforms on the underside of the body.

✳✳ CAUTION

The car must be secure on the jack and the jackstands at all times during the lifting phase or when stationary. If the car is not stable and secure, the car may fall, damaging the vehicle and causing personal injury or death.

Fig. 125 When jacking the front of the vehicle, lift from the center of the subframe. Do not jack from the oil pan

Fig. 128 When supporting the rear of the vehicle, position a block of wood between the jackstand and control arm mount

Fig. 126 When jacking the rear of the vehicle, lift the center of the frame section. Do not jack under the differential

Fig. 129 Closeup of correct rear jackstand positioning

Fig. 127 When supporting the front of the vehicle on jackstands, use the lift point behind the front wheel

Capacities

Year	Model	Engine Crankcase		Transmission (pts.)			Drive Axle (pts.)	Fuel Tank (gal.)	Cooling System (qts.)
		With Filter	Without Filter	4-Spd	5-Spd	Auto.			
1970	1600	4.5	4.25	2.1	—	3.6	1.7 ①	12.1	7.4
	2000	4.5	4.25	2.1	—	3.6	1.7 ①	12.1	7.4
	2002,Tii	4.5	4.25	2.1	—	3.6	1.7 ①	12.1	7.4
	2800,CS	6.1	5.3	2.5	—	3.2	2.6	19.8 ②	12.7
	2500	6.1	5.3	2.5	—	3.2	2.6	19.8	12.7
1971	1600	4.5	4.25	2.1	—	3.6	1.7 ①	12.1	7.4
	2000,2002,Tii	4.5	4.25	2.1	—	3.6	1.7 ①	12.1	7.4
	2500	6.1	5.3	2.5	—	3.2	2.6	19.8	12.7
	2800,CS	6.1	5.3	2.5	—	3.2	2.6	19.8 ②	12.7
	Bavaria	6.1	5.3	2.5	—	3.2	2.6	19.8	12.7
1972	2000,2002,Tii	4.5	4.25	2.1	—	3.6	1.7 ①	12.1	7.4
	Bavaria	6.1	5.3	2.5	—	3.2	2.6	19.8	12.7
	3000CS	6.1	5.3	2.5	—	3.2	2.6	15.4	12.7
1973	2000,2002,Tii	4.5	4.25	2.1	—	3.6	1.9	13.5	7.4
	3.0CS,S,Si	5.3	5.0	2.5	—	3.8	3.4	16.5	12.7
	Bavaria	6.1	5.3	2.5	—	3.2	2.6	19.8	12.7
1974	2002	4.5	4.25	2.1	—	3.6	1.9	13.5	7.4
	Bavaria	6.1	5.3	2.5	—	3.2	2.6	19.8	12.7
	3.0CS,S,Si	5.3	5.0	2.5	—	3.8	3.4	16.5	12.7
1975	2002	4.5	4.25	2.8	—	3.6	1.9	13.5	7.4
	3.0CS,S,Si	5.3	5.0	2.5	—	3.8	3.4	16.5	12.7
	530i	6.0	5.25	2.3	—	4.2	3.4	16.4	12.7
1976	2002	4.5	4.25	2.8	—	3.6	1.9	13.5	7.4
	3.0CS,S,Si	5.3	5.0	2.5	—	3.8	3.4	16.5	12.7
	530i	6.0	5.25	2.3	—	4.2	3.4	16.4	12.7
1977	320i	4.5	4.25	2.2	—	4.2	2.0	15.9	7.4
	530i	6.0	5.25	2.3	—	4.2	3.4	16.4	12.7
	630CSi	6.0	5.25	2.3	—	4.2	3.2	16.4	12.7
1978	320i	4.5	4.25	2.2	—	4.2	2.0	15.9	7.4
	530i	6.0	5.25	2.3	—	4.2	3.4	16.4	12.7
	633CSi	6.0	5.3	2.3	—	4.2	3.2	16.4	12.7
	733i	6.0	5.3	2.3	—	4.0	3.8	22.5	12.7
1979	320i	4.5	4.25	2.2	—	4.2	2.0	15.9	7.4
	528i	6.0	5.25	2.3	—	4.2	3.4	16.4	12.7
	633CSi	6.0	5.3	2.3	—	4.2	3.2	16.4	12.7
	733i	6.0	5.3	2.3	—	4.0	3.8	22.5	12.7
1980	320i	4.5 ③	4.25 ④	2.2	—	4.2	1.9	15.3	7.4
	528i	6.0	5.25	2.3	—	4.2	3.4	16.4	12.7
	633CSi	6.0	5.3	2.3	—	4.2	3.2	16.4	12.7

87891C11

Capacities (cont.)

| Year | Model | Engine Crankcase | | Transmission (pts.) | | | Drive Axle (pts.) | Fuel Tank (gal.) | Cooling System (qts.) |
		With Filter	Without Filter	4-Spd	5-Spd	Auto.			
1980	733i	6.0	5.3	2.3	—	4.0	3.8	22.5	12.7
1981	320i	4.5 ③	4.25 ④	2.2	—	4.2	1.9	15.3	7.4
	528i	6.0	5.25	2.3	—	4.2	3.4	16.4	12.7
	633CSi	6.0	5.3	2.3	—	4.2	3.2	16.4	12.7
	733i	6.0	5.3	2.3	—	4.0	3.8	22.5	12.7
1982	320i	4.5 ③	4.25 ④	2.2	—	4.2	1.9	15.3	7.4
	528e	4.5	4.2	3.4	—	4.2	3.8	16.6	12.7
	633CSi	6.0	5.25	2.4	—	4.2	3.2	16.5	12.7
	733i	6.0	5.25	2.4	—	4.0	3.8	22.5	12.7
1983	320i	4.5 ③	4.25 ④	2.2	—	4.2	1.9	15.3	7.4
	528e	4.5	4.2	—	3.4	4.2	3.8	16.6	12.7
	533i	6.0	5.3	—	2.65	6.3	3.6	16.6	12.7
	633CSi	6.0	5.25	2.4	—	4.2	3.2	16.5	12.7
	733i	6.0	5.25	—	2.4	4.0	3.8	22.5	12.7
1984	318i	4.5	4.2	—	2.4	6.3	1.9	14.5	7.4
	528e	4.5	4.2	—	3.4	4.2	3.8	16.6	12.7
	533i	6.0	5.3	—	2.65	6.3	3.6	16.6	12.7
	633CSi	6.0	5.25	2.4	—	4.2	3.2	16.5	12.7
	733i	6.0	5.25	—	2.4	4.0	3.8	22.5	12.7
1985	318i	4.5	4.2	—	2.4	6.3	1.9	14.5	7.4
	325e	4.5	4.2	—	2.4	6.3	3.4	14.5	7.4
	325es	4.5	4.2	—	2.4	6.3	3.4	14.5	7.4
	528e	4.5	4.2	—	3.4	4.2	3.8	16.6	12.7
	524td	6.1	5.3	—	3.4	6.4	4.0	16.6	12.7
	535i	6.1	5.3	—	3.4	6.4	4.0	16.6	12.7
	635CSi	6.1	5.3	—	3.4	6.4	4.0	16.6	12.7
	735i	6.1	5.3	—	3.4	6.4	4.0	22.5	12.7
1986	325e	4.5	4.2	—	2.4	6.3	3.4	14.5	7.4
	325es	4.5	4.2	—	2.4	6.3	3.4	14.5	7.4
	524td	6.1	5.3	—	3.4	6.4	4.0	16.6	12.7
	528e	4.5	4.2	—	3.4	4.2	3.8	16.6	12.7
	535i	6.1	5.3	—	3.4	6.4	4.0	16.6	12.7
	635CSi	6.1	5.3	—	3.4	6.4	4.0	16.6	12.7
	735i	6.1	5.3	—	3.4	6.4	4.0	22.5	12.7
1987	325	4.5	4.2	—	2.6	6.4	3.6	15.3	12.7
	528e	4.5	4.2	—	3.4	6.4	3.8	16.6	11.6
	535i	6.1	5.3	—	3.4	6.4	4.0	16.6	12.7
	635CSi	6.1	5.3	—	3.4	6.4	4.0	16.6	12.7
	735i	6.1	5.3	—	3.4	6.4	3.6	21.4	12.7

87891C12

Capacities (cont.)

Year	Model	Engine Crankcase		Transmission (pts.)			Drive Axle (pts.)	Fuel Tank (gal.)	Cooling System (qts.)
		With Filter	Without Filter	4-Spd	5-Spd	Auto.			
1987	M5	6.1	5.3	—	2.6	6.4	4.0	16.6	12.7
	M6	6.1	5.3	—	2.6	6.4	4.0	16.6	12.7
1988	325	4.5	4.2	—-	2.6	6.4	3.6	16.4	11.6
	325i	5.0	4.75	—	2.6	6.4 ⑤	3.6 ⑥	16.4	11.0
	325iS	5.0	4.75	—	2.6	6.4 ⑤	3.6 ⑥	16.4	11.0
	325iX	5.0	4.75	—	2.6	6.4 ⑤	3.6 ⑥	16.4	11.0
	528e	4.5	4.2	—	3.4	6.4	3.8	16.6	11.6
	535i	6.1	5.3	—	2.6	6.4	4.0	16.6	11.6
	535iS	6.1	5.3	—	2.6	6.4	4.0	16.6	12.7
	635CSi	6.1	5.3	—	3.4	6.4	4.0	16.6	12.7
	L6	6.1	5.3	—	3.4	6.4	4.0	16.6	12.7
	735i	6.1	5.3	—	2.6	6.4	4.0	21.4	12.7
	M3	5.0	4.75	—	2.6	6.4	3.6	16.4	NA
	M5	6.1	5.3	—	2.6	6.4	4.0	16.6	12.7
	M6	6.1	5.3	—	2.6	6.4	4.0	16.6	12.7

NA—Not available
① 1600-2 Short neck differential up to chassis no. 15678-45
  2002 Long neck differential up to chassis no. 1664750—capacity of 2.1 pts.
② 2800CS—15.4 gals
③ With chrome plated guide tube for dipstick—4.25
④ With chrome plated guide tube for dipstick—4.0
⑤ 325iX Transfer case—1.1
⑥ 325iX Front drive axle—1.5

87891C13

2

ENGINE PERFORMANCE AND TUNE-UP

TUNE-UP PROCEDURES

In order to extract the full measure of performance and economy from your engine it is essential; that it is properly tuned at regular intervals. A regular tune-up will keep your car's engine running smoothly and can prevent the annoying breakdowns and poor performance associated with an untuned engine.

➡**Except for the 633CSi and 733i, all models built before 1980 have a conventional breaker point ignition system. All models built after 1980 utilize a pointless, electronic ignition system.**

A complete tune-up should be performed on early models every 12 months or 12,000 miles (19,000 km), whichever comes first. On later models, the interval is 12 months or 15,000 (24,000 km), whichever comes first.

This interval should be halved if the car is operated under severe conditions such as trailer towing, prolonged idling, start-and-stop driving, or if starting or running problems are noticed. It is assumed that the routine maintenance described in Section 1 has been kept up, as this will have a decided effect on the results of a tune-up. All of the applicable steps of a tune-up should be followed in order, as the result is a cumulative one.

➡**If the specifications on the underhood tune-up sticker in the engine compartment of your car disagree with the Tune-Up Specifications chart in this section, the figures on the sticker must be used. The sticker often reflects changes made during the production run.**

Spark Plugs

A typical spark plug consists of a metal shell surrounding a ceramic insulator. A metal electrode extends downward through the center of the insulator and protrudes a small distance. Located at the end of the plug and attached to the side of the outer metal shell is the side electrode. The side electrode bends in at a 90° angle so that its tip is just past and parallel to the tip of the center electrode. The distance between these two electrodes (measured in thousandths of an inch or hundredths of a millimeter) is called the spark plug gap. The spark plug does not produce a spark but instead provides a gap across which the current can arc. The coil produces anywhere from 20,000 to 40,000 volts which travels through the wires to the spark plugs. The current passes along the center electrode and jumps the gap to the side electrode, and in doing so, ignites the fuel/air mixture in the combustion chamber.

SPARK PLUG HEAT RANGE

Spark plug heat range is the ability of the plug to dissipate heat. The longer the insulator (or the farther it extends into the engine), the hotter the plug will operate; the shorter the insulator (the closer the electrode is to the block's cooling passages) the cooler it will operate. A plug that absorbs little heat and remains too cool will quickly accumulate deposits of oil and carbon since it is not hot enough to burn them off. This leads to plug fouling and consequently to misfiring. A plug that absorbs too much heat will have no deposits but, due to the excessive heat, the electrodes will burn away quickly and possibly lead to preignition. Preignition takes place when plug tips get so hot that they glow suf-

ficiently to ignite the fuel/air mixture before the actual spark occurs. This early ignition will usually cause a pinging during low speeds and heavy loads.

The general rule of thumb for choosing the correct heat range when picking a spark plug is: if most of your driving is long distance, high speed travel, use a colder plug; if most of your driving is stop and go, use a hotter plug. Original equipment plugs are generally a good compromise between the 2 styles and most people never have the need to change their plugs from the factory-recommended heat range.

REMOVAL

▶ **See Figures 1, 2, 3 and 4**

➡**Depending on the engine type, some spark plug wires and plugs are covered by a decorative cover which must be removed prior to spark plug removal.**

When you're removing spark plugs, you should work on one plug at a time. Whenever possible, do not remove the plug wires all at once, unless you number them. On some models, it will be more convenient to remove all the wires before working on the plugs. If this is necessary, take a minute before you begin and number the wires with tape. The time you spend here will pay off later on.

To remove the spark plug, proceed as follows:

1. Twist the spark plug boot and remove the boot from the plug. You may also use a plug wire removal tool designed especially for this purpose. Do not pull on the wire itself. When the wire has been removed, take a wire brush and clean the area around the plug. Make sure that all the grime is removed so that none will enter the cylinder after the plug has been removed.

2. Remove the spark plug using the proper size socket. For most engines, a 13⁄16 in. spark plug socket is required.

➡**All BMW cylinder heads are made of aluminum. Extreme care should be used when removing the spark plugs so as not to strip the threads.**

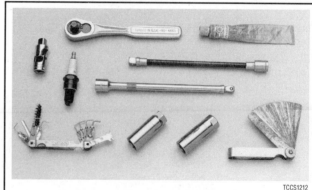

TCCS1212

Fig. 1 A variety of tools are needed for spark plug service

87892P01

Fig. 2 On early model 4-cylinder engines, the spark plugs are located on the passenger side of the engine

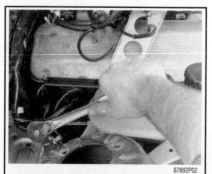

87892P02

Fig. 3 Using the proper sized socket, loosen the spark plug—6-cylinder engine shown

87892P03

Fig. 4 With the spark plug fully loosened, remove it from the engine

3. If a spark plug is difficult to remove, drip some penetrating oil on the plug threads and allow it to soak into the threads, then remove the plug. Also, be sure that the socket is straight on the plug, especially on those hard to reach plugs.

INSPECTION & GAPPING

▶ **See Figures 5, 6, 7 and 8**

Check the plugs for deposits and wear. If they are not going to be replaced, clean the plugs thoroughly. Remember that any kind of

deposit will decrease the efficiency of the plug. Plugs can be cleaned on a spark plug cleaning machine, which can sometimes be found in service stations, or you can do an acceptable job of cleaning with a stiff brush. If the plugs are cleaned, the electrodes must be filed flat. Use an ignition points file, not an emery board or the like, which will leave deposits. The electrodes must be filed perfectly flat with sharp edges; rounded edges reduce the spark plug voltage by as much as 50%.

Check spark plug gap before installation. The ground electrode (the L-shaped one connected to the body of the plug) must be parallel to the center

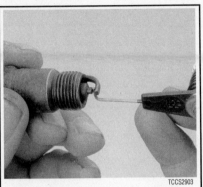
TCCS2903

Fig. 5 Checking the spark plug gap with a feeler gauge

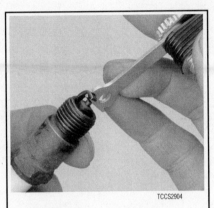
TCCS2904

Fig. 6 Adjusting the spark plug gap

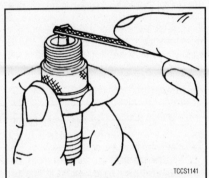
TCCS1141

Fig. 7 If the standard plug is in good condition, the electrode may be filed flat—WARNING: do not file platinum plugs

A **normally worn** spark plug should have light tan or gray deposits on the firing tip.

A **carbon fouled** plug, identified by soft, sooty, black deposits, may indicate an improperly tuned vehicle. Check the air cleaner, ignition components and engine control system.

This spark plug has been **left in the engine too long,** as evidenced by the extreme gap- Plugs with such an extreme gap can cause misfiring and stumbling accompanied by a noticeable lack of power.

An **oil fouled** spark plug indicates an engine with worn poston rings and/or bad valve seals allowing excessive oil to enter the chamber.

A **physically damaged** spark plug may be evidence of severe detonation in that cylinder. Watch that cylinder carefully between services, as a continued detonation will not only damage the plug, but could also damage the engine.

A **bridged or almost bridged** spark plug, identified by a build-up between the electrodes caused by excessive carbon or oil build-up on the plug.

TCCA1P40

Fig. 8 Inspect the spark plug to determine engine running conditions

electrode and the specified size wire gauge (please refer to the Tune-Up Specifications chart for details) must pass between the electrodes with a slight drag.

➡**NEVER adjust the gap on a used platinum type spark plug.**

Always check the gap on new plugs as they are not always set correctly at the factory. Do not use a flat feeler gauge when measuring the gap on a used plug, because the reading may be inaccurate. A round-wire type gapping tool is the best way to check the gap. The correct gauge should pass through the electrode gap with a slight drag. If you're in doubt, try one size smaller and one larger. The smaller gauge should go through easily, while the larger one shouldn't go through at all. Wire gapping tools usually have a bending tool attached. Use that to adjust the side electrode until the proper distance is obtained. Absolutely never attempt to bend the center electrode. Also, be careful not to bend the side electrode too far or too often as it may weaken and break off within the engine, requiring removal of the cylinder head to retrieve it.

INSTALLATION

1. With all plugs gapped, lubricate the threads of the spark plugs with a drop of oil or anti-seize paste. Install the plugs and tighten them hand-tight. Take care not to cross-thread them.
2. Tighten the spark plugs with the socket. Do not apply the same amount of force you would use for a bolt, just snug them in. If a torque wrench is available, tighten to 17–21 ft. lbs. (22–27 Nm).
3. Install the wires on their respective plugs. Make sure the wire are firmly connected. You should be able to feel them click into place.

RETHREADING

Should you encounter uneven or unduly stiff resistance when removing or installing a spark plugs into the cylinder head, the threads may be stripped or cross-threaded. This will necessitate either rethreading the existing threads or the installation of a Heli-Coil®. Consult the Engine Rebuilding portion of Section 3 for details on these procedures.

Spark Plug Wires

The spark plug wires are routed individually or in a tube or duct. The spark plug leads can be replaced as a unit with the tubing or individually. If necessary, unplug the spark plug wires at the distributor cap Original equipment wires and distributor caps are marked with the cylinder number, making the installation easy.

If installed in a tube or duct, unclip the spark plug wire duct or tube and remove the wire. Replace the wire in the same routing as the old wire. Be sure to match the wire number with the distributor cap number or coil pack number. Snap the ducting or tubing together.

INSPECTION

Every 15,000 miles (24,000 km), inspect the spark plug wires for burns, cuts, or breaks in the insulation. Check the boots and the nipples on the distributor cap. Replace any damaged wiring.

Every 45,000 miles (72,000 km) or so, the resistance of the wires should be checked with an ohmmeter. Wires with excessive resistance will cause misfiring, and may make the engine difficult to start in damp weather. Generally, the useful life of the cables is 45,000–60,000 miles (72,000–97,000 km).

To check resistance, remove the distributor cap, leaving the wires in place. Connect one lead of an ohmmeter to an electrode within the cap; connect the other lead to the corresponding spark plug terminal (remove it from the spark plug for this test). Replace any wire which shows a resistance over 30,000 ohms.

It should be remembered that resistance is also a function of length; the longer the wire, the greater the resistance. Thus, if the wires on your car are longer than the factory originals, resistance will be higher, quite possibly outside these limits.

REMOVAL & INSTALLATION

◆ **See Figures 9 and 10**

When removing or installing spark plug wires, replace them one at a time to avoid mixups. It is also a good idea to tag spark plug wires if you intend to reuse them. Start by replacing the longest one first. Install the boot firmly over the spark plug. Route the wire over the same path as the original. Insert the nipple firmly onto the tower on the distributor cap, then install the cap cover and latches to secure the wires.

➡**Never remove a spark plug wire by pulling on the wire. Remove by grasping with your fingers or a plug wire removal tool around the boot at the spark plug head or distributor cap.**

Fig. 9 Unclipping the spark plug wire from a side mounted distributor

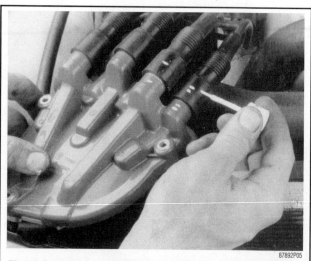

Fig. 10 If removing multiple spark plug wires, it is a good idea to first matchmark their positions

FIRING ORDERS

▶ **See Figures 11, 12, 13, 14 and 15**

➡**To avoid confusion, remove and tag the spark plug wires one at a time, for replacement.**

If a distributor is not keyed for installation with only one orientation, it could have been removed previously and rewired. The resultant wiring would hold the correct firing order, but could change the relative placement of the plug towers in relation to the engine. For this reason it is imperative that you label all wires before disconnecting any of them. Also, before removal, compare the current wiring with the accompanying illustrations. If the current wiring does not match, make notes in your book to reflect how your engine is wired.

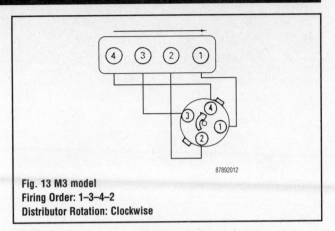

Fig. 13 M3 model
Firing Order: 1–3–4–2
Distributor Rotation: Clockwise

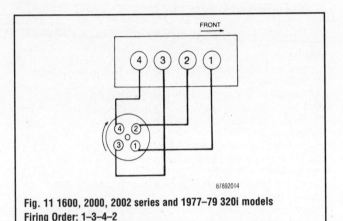

Fig. 11 1600, 2000, 2002 series and 1977–79 320i models
Firing Order: 1–3–4–2
Distributor Rotation: Clockwise

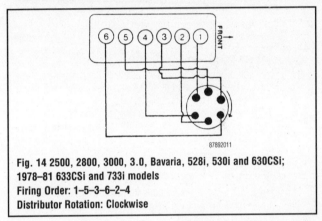

Fig. 14 2500, 2800, 3000, 3.0, Bavaria, 528i, 530i and 630CSi; 1978–81 633CSi and 733i models
Firing Order: 1–5–3–6–2–4
Distributor Rotation: Clockwise

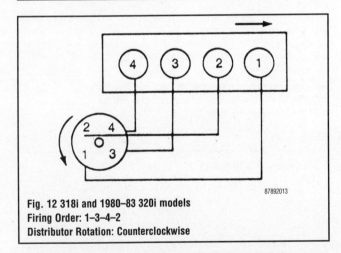

Fig. 12 318i and 1980–83 320i models
Firing Order: 1–3–4–2
Distributor Rotation: Counterclockwise

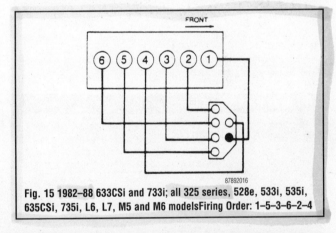

Fig. 15 1982–88 633CSi and 733i; all 325 series, 528e, 533i, 535i, 635CSi, 735i, L6, L7, M5 and M6 modelsFiring Order: 1–5–3–6–2–4

POINT-TYPE IGNITION

Rotor and Distributor Cap

REMOVAL & INSTALLATION

▶ **See Figure 16**

➡**To prevent scraping the skin off your knuckles, slide a thin piece of cardboard or equivalent down between the engine and firewall.**

1. Disconnect the high tension wire from the top of the distributor cap and place aside.
2. Unclip the two retaining clips which secure the distributor cap to the distributor body. Once unclip, lift the cap up.

3. If replacing the distributor cap, tag each individual wire as to its location on the cap. Then carefully remove the wires. Plug the wires, in their correct order, into the new distributor cap.

➡**Never remove a spark plug wire by pulling on the wire. Always remove a spark plug wire by grasping the boot.**

4. If you are not replacing the distributor cap at this time, carefully inspect the metal contact points on the inside of the cap. Some wear is acceptable, but excessive wear, in the form of grooves or burnt contacts, indicates that the cap should be replaced.
5. To remove the rotor cap, pull the rotor straight up. With the cap off, check the condition of the lubricating wick at the center of the rotor shaft. It should be moist with lubricating oil. If it is not, add several drops of oil to the pad.

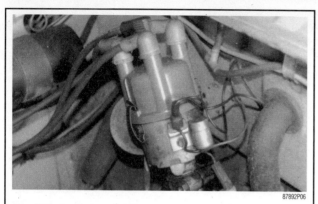
Fig. 16 Early clip-type distributor cap—2002 model

To install:

6. Align the tab on the rotor with the groove on the rotor shaft, then slide the rotor cap on to the shaft. Wiggle the rotor to make sure the alignment is correct. If it is not correct, the rotor will move from side to side.

7. If you are installing a new distributor cap, and have not already installed the spark plug wires into their correct locations, do this now. Leave the high tension wire to the coil off.

8. Position the distributor cap on to the distributor body making sure the tabs on the cap and body align correctly. In the event they do not align correctly, you will be unable to fasten both retainer clips.

9. With the cap positioned, secure by fastening the two clips.

10. Connect the high tension wire to the distributor cap. Start the vehicle and check for proper operation.

INSPECTION

Check the cap and rotor for signs of burning, carbon tracks or excessive corrosion on the terminals. Do not try to clean the terminals. The cap and rotor should be replaced at the same time.

1. Disconnect the high tension wire from the top of the distributor and the coil.

2. Remove the distributor cap by prying off the spring clips on the sides of the cap.

3. Examine the condition of the cap. If it is cracked or the metal tip is excessively worn or burned, it should be replaced.

Breaker Points and Condenser

The points function as a circuit breaker for the primary circuit of the ignition system. The ignition coil must boost the 12 volts of electrical pressure supplied by the battery to as much as 25,000 volts or higher in order to correctly fire the plugs. To do this, the coil depends on the points and the condenser to make a clean break in the primary circuit.

The coil has both primary and secondary circuits. When the ignition is

turned on, the battery supplies voltage through the coil and onto the points. The points are connected to ground, completing the primary circuit. As the current passes through the coil, a magnetic field is created in the iron center core of the coil. When the cam in the distributor turns, the points open, breaking the primary circuit.

The magnetic field in the primary circuit of the coil then collapses and cuts through the secondary circuit windings around the iron core. Because of the physical principle called "electromagnetic induction," the battery voltage is increased to a level sufficient to fire the spark plugs.

When the points open, the electrical charge in the primary circuit tries to jump the gap created between the two open contacts of the points. If this electrical charge were not transferred elsewhere, the metal contacts of the points would start to change rapidly.

The function of the condenser is to absorb excessive voltage from the points when they open and thus prevent the points from becoming pitted or burned

If you have ever wondered why it is necessary to tune-up your engine occasionally, consider the fact that the ignition system must complete the above cycle each time a spark plug fires. On a 4-cylinder, 4-cycle engine, two of the four plugs must fire once for every engine revolution. If the idle speed of your engine is 800 revolutions per minute (800 rpm), the breaker points open and close two times each revolution. For every minute your engine idles, your points open and close 1,600 times (2 x 800 = 1,600). And that is just at idle. What about at 60 mph?

There are two ways to check breaker point gap: with a feel gauge or with a dwell meter. Either way you set the points, you are adjusting the amount of time (in degrees of distributor rotation) that the points will remain open. If you adjust the points with a feeler gauge, you are setting the maximum amount the points will open when the rubbing block on the points is on a high point of the distributor cam. When you adjust the points with a dwell meter, you are measuring the number of degrees (of distributor cam rotation) that the points will remain closed before they start to open as a high point of the distributor cam approaches the rubbing block of the points.

If you still do not understand how the points function, take a friend, go outside, and remove the distributor cap from your engine. Have your friend operate the starter (make sure the transmission is not in gear) as you look at the exposed parts of the distributor.

There are two rules that should always be followed when adjusting or replacing points. The points and condenser are a matched set; never replace one without replacing the other. If you change the point gap or swell of the engine, you also change the ignition timing. Therefore, if you adjust the points, you must also adjust the timing.

➡️**Certain 1978–79 and virtually all 1980 and later BMWs are equipped with electronic, breakerless ignition systems. See the following section for maintenance procedures.**

INSPECTION

♦ **See Figures 17, 18 and 19**

1. Disconnect the high tension wire from the top of the distributor and the coil.

2. Remove the distributor cap by prying off the spring clips on the sides of the cap.

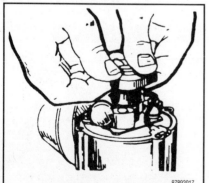
Fig. 17 To access the breaker points, the rotor must be lifted straight up

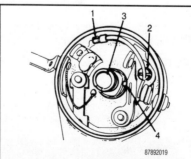
Fig. 18 Breaker point parts and lubrication points: (1) primary connection, (2) hold-down screw, (3) advance mechanism lubrication wick, (4) breaker arm rubbing block

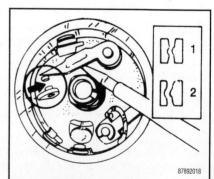
Fig. 19 Inspect the condition of the breaker points; (1) is acceptable, (2) is unacceptable

3. Remove the rotor from the distributor shaft by pulling it straight up. Examine the condition of the rotor. If it is cracked or the metal tip is excessively worn or burned, it should be replaced. Clean the top with fine emery paper.

4. Pry open the contacts of the points with a screwdriver and check the condition of the contacts. If they are excessively worn, burned or pitted, they should be replaced.

5. If the points are in good condition, adjust them and replace the rotor and the distributor cap. If the points need to be replaced, follow the replacement procedure given below.

REMOVAL & INSTALLATION

▶ **See Figures 17 and 20**

On 1970–74 cars, BMW recommends that the breaker points be inspected and adjusted every 6 months or 8,000 miles (13,000 km). If, upon inspection, the points prove to be faulty, they must be replaced with the condenser as a unit. On later models, replace the points every 12,500 miles (20,000 km), if the car is so equipped.

✷✷ CAUTION

Make sure that the ignition is OFF!

The usual procedure is to replace the condenser each time the point set is replaced. Although this is not always necessary, it is easy to do at this time and the cost is negligible. Every time you adjust or replace the breaker points, the ignition timing must be checked and, if necessary, adjusted. No special equipment other than a feeler gauge is required for point replacement or adjustment, but a dwell meter is strongly advised. A magnetic screwdriver is handy to prevent the small points and condenser screws from falling down into the distributor.

1. Disconnect the coil high tension wire from the top of the distributor cap. Remove the distributor cap and place it out of the way. Remove the rotor from the distributor shaft by pulling straight up.

87892020

Fig. 20 Install the points onto the locating dowel and secure with the retaining screw, then attach the primary wire

2. Disconnect the electrical lead to the condenser, loosen the condenser bracket retaining screw and slide out the condenser.

3. Disconnect the point set electrical lead.

4. Remove the points assembly attaching screws and then remove the points. A magnetic screwdriver or one with a holding mechanism will come in handy here, so that you don't drop a screw into the distributor and have to remove the entire distributor to retrieve it.

After the points are removed, wipe off the cam and apply new cam lubricant. If you don't, the points will wear out in a few thousand miles.

5. Slip the new set of points onto the locating dowel and install the screws that hold the assembly onto the plate. Don't tighten them all the way yet, since you'll only have to loosen them to set the point gap.

6. Install the new condenser and attach the condenser lead to the points.

7. Set the point gap and dwell, as described in the following procedures.

ADJUSTMENT

▶ **See Figures 21, 22 and 23**

1. If the contact points of the assembly are not parallel, bend the stationary contact so that they make contact across the entire surface of the contacts. Bend only the stationary bracket part of the point assembly; not the movable contact.

2. Turn the engine until the rubbing block of the points is on one of the high points of the distributor cam. You can do this by either turning the ignition switch to the start position and releasing it quickly ("bumping" the engine) or by using a wrench on the bolt which holds the crankshaft pulley to the crankshaft.

3. Place the correct size feeler gauge between the contacts (see the Tune-Up Specifications chart). Make sure that it is parallel with the contact surfaces.

4. With your free hand, insert a screwdriver into the eccentric adjusting slot, then twist the screwdriver to either increase and decrease the gap to the proper setting.

5. Tighten the adjustment lockscrew and recheck the contact gap to make sure that it didn't change when the lockscrew was tightened.

6. Replace the rotor and distributor cap, and the high tension wire which connects the top of the distributor and the coil. Make sure that the rotor is firmly seated all the way onto the distributor shaft and that the of the rotor is aligned with the notch in the shaft. Align the tab in the base of the distributor cap with the notch in the distributor body. Make sure that the end of the high tension wire is firmly placed in the top of the distributor and the coil.

DWELL ANGLE

▶ **See Figure 24**

The dwell angle or cam angle is the number of degrees that the distributor cam rotates while the points are closed. There is an inverse relationship between dwell angle and point gap. Increasing the point gap will decrease the swell angle and vice versa. Checking the swell angle with a meter is a far more accurate method of measuring point opening than the feeler gauge method.

After setting the point gap to specification with a feeler gauge as described above, check the dwell angle with a meter. Attach the dwell meter according to the manufacturer's instruction sheet. The negative lead is grounded and the positive lead is connected to the primary wire terminal which runs from the coil to

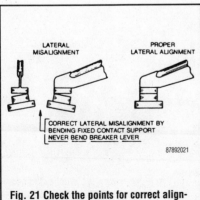
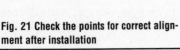

87892021

Fig. 21 Check the points for correct alignment after installation

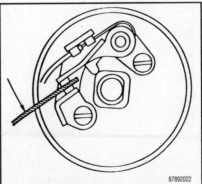

87892022

Fig. 22 Checking for proper point gap using a feeler gauge

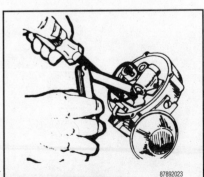

87892023

Fig. 23 Adjusting the point gap. Use a screwdriver inserted into the notch at the base of the points to adjust the gap

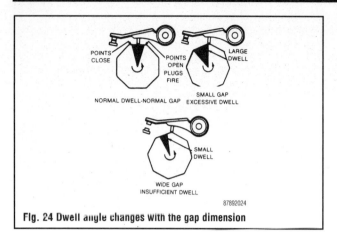

Fig. 24 Dwell angle changes with the gap dimension

the distributor. Start the engine, let it idle and reach operating temperature, and observe the dwell on the meter. The reading should fall within the allowable range. If it does not, the gap will have to be reset or the breaker points will have to be replaced.

Adjustment

Dwell can be checked with the engine running or cranking. Decrease dwell by increasing the point gap; increase by decreasing the gap. Dwell angle is simply the number of degrees of distributor shaft rotation during which the points stay closed. Theoretically, if the point gap is correct, the dwell should also be correct or nearly so. Adjustment with a dwell meter produces more exact, consistent results since it is a dynamic adjustment. If dwell varies more than 3° from idle speed to 1,750 engine rpm, the distributor is worn and will probably require adjustment.

1. Adjust the points with a feeler gauge as previously described.
2. Connect the dwell meter to the ignition circuit as per the manufacturer's instructions. One lead of the meter is connected to a ground and the other lead is connected to the distributor post on the coil. An adapter is usually provided for this purpose.
3. If the dwell meter has a set line on it. adjust the meter to zero the indicator.
4. Start the engine.

➡Be careful when working on any vehicle while the engine is running. Make sure that the transmission is in PARK or NEUTRAL and that the parking brake is applied. Keep hands, clothing, tools and the wires of the test instruments clear of the rotating fan blades.

5. Observe the reading on the dwell meter. If the reading is within the specified range, turn off the engine and remove the dwell meter.

➡If the meter does not have a scale for 4-cylinder engines, multiply the 8-cylinder reading by 2.

6. If the reading is above the specified range, the breaker point gap is too small. If the reading is below the specified range, the gap is too large. In either

case, the engine must be stopped and the gap adjusted in the manner previously covered.

After making the adjustment, start the engine and check the reading on the dwell meter. When the correct reading is obtained, disconnect the dwell meter.

7. Check the adjustment of the ignition timing.

Ignition Coil

◆ See Figure 25

✳✳ WARNING

Ignition coils for breaker type systems are not interchangeable with coils for transistorized models. Doing so could seriously damage the vehicle's ignition and electrical systems.

REMOVAL & INSTALLATION

◆ See Figures 26, 27, 28, 29 and 30

1. Disconnect the negative battery cable.
2. Access the ignition coil in the engine compartment and remove the high tension wire. If it is difficult to remove, use a twisting motion, then attempt to remove.

➡Do not remove the high tension wire by pulling on the wire. Remove by grasping only at the boot.

3. Tag the remaining wires connected to the coil. When properly tagged, remove and tuck out of the way.
4. Remove the retaining bolts securing the coil bracket to the vehicle body and remove the coil.
5. To install, reverse the procedures. Make sure the wire connections are correct and secure.

Fig. 25 Early 2002 ignition coil. Notice the ballast resistor above the coil

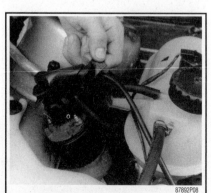

Fig. 26 Remove the high tension wire, and coil cover, if equipped

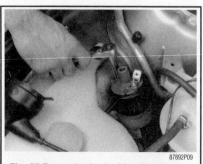

Fig. 27 Tag each wire for identification, then remove. Some wires are secured with nuts, while others have push-type connectors

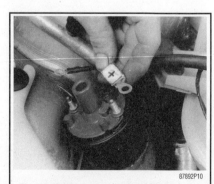

Fig. 28 Notice that on some coils, the connector ends are of different sizes to help ensure their correct installation

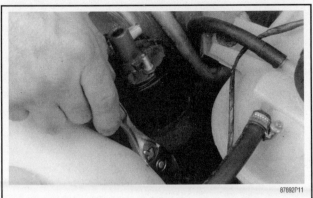

Fig. 29 Loosen the hardware securing the bracket to the coil

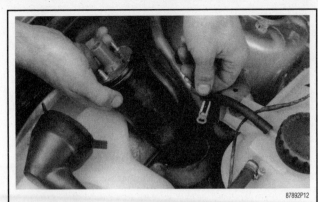

Fig. 30 When the bracket is loosened enough, slide the coil out

ELECTRONIC IGNITION

✳✳ CAUTION

The engine should be turned off or the battery cable disconnected when ignition system components are replaced or engine test equipment is connected to the ignition system, because of a dangerous current that can be present in the primary and secondary circuits. Personal injury could occur.

All 528i, 633CSI, 733i and 1980 and later 320i models are equipped with a Bosch® transistorized ignition system. The 528e and all 1982 and later models are all equipped with a Digital Motor Electronics (DME) engine control system. DME is basically an onboard computer. It is a microprocessor that controls many more engine related functions than would a conventional system.

Rotor and Distributor Cap

REMOVAL & INSTALLATION

▶ See Figures 31, 32, 33 and 34

1. Make sure the ignition is **OFF**. If easier, disconnect the negative battery cable.

➡ **To prevent scraping the skin off your knuckles on the radiator fins, slide a thin piece of cardboard or equivalent down between the radiator and the fan.**

2. Remove the ignition lead cover from the distributor cap. If not already marked, tag the ignition leads for later installation.
3. Pull off the ignition leads from the distributor cap.

4. Remove the screws from the distributor cap and remove the cap. Check the condition of the distributor cap seal and replace if necessary.
5. Unscrew the 3mm hexhead bolts holding the rotor and remove the rotor.
To install:
6. Place the new rotor on the shaft and tighten the hexhead bolts to 3–4 inch lbs. (0.3–0.4 Nm).
7. Replace the distributor cap and seal. Tighten the mounting screws.
8. Replace the ignition leads on the proper terminals and clip the cover into place. Remove the cardboard from between the radiator and fan.

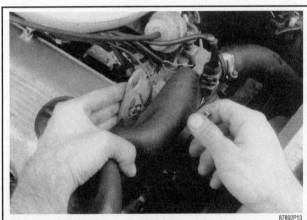

Fig. 31 On some models, you may need to move hoses aside to access the distributor cap

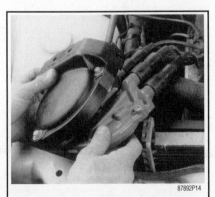

Fig. 32 With the cap removed, the protective cover can be detached

Fig. 33 Loosen, but do not completely remove, the Allen head bolts securing the rotor

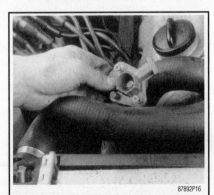

Fig. 34 Remove the rotor from the distributor

INSPECTION

Check the cap and rotor for signs of burning, carbon tracks or excessive corrosion on the terminals. Do not try to clean the terminals. The cap and rotor should be replaced at the same time.

Distributor Air Gap

◆ See Figure 35

Although no adjustment is possible, the air gap on 1980–84 models with the electronic distributors can and should be checked periodically.

➡ **On all 1984–88 models there is no adjustment possible.**

This is the gap between the rotor wheel (NOT the one directly underneath the distributor cap) and the stator. It should be measured when a tooth of each is lined up and should be in the range of 0.01–0.03 inches (0.30–0.70mm). If not within specifications, the distributor or certain components will require replacement.

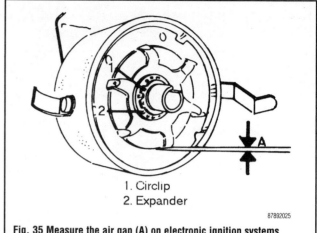
1. Circlip
2. Expander

87892025

Fig. 35 Measure the air gap (A) on electronic ignition systems

IGNITION TIMING

Ignition timing is the measurement, in degrees of crankshaft rotation, of the point at which the spark plugs fire in each of the cylinders. It is measure in degrees before or after Top Dead Center (TDC) of the compression stroke.

Because it takes a fraction of a second for the spark plug to ignite the mixture in the cylinder, the spark plug must fire slightly before the piston reaches TDC. Otherwise, the mixture will not be completely ignited as the piston passes TDC and the full power of the explosion will not be used by the engine.

The timing measurement is given in degrees of crankshaft rotation before the piston reaches TDC (BTDC). If the setting for the ignition timing is 5° BTDC, the spark plug must fire 5° before each piston reaches TDC. This only holds true, however, when the engine is at idle speed.

As the engine speed increases, the pistons move faster. The spark plugs have to ignite the fuel even sooner if it is to be completely ignited when the piston reaches TDC. To do this, the distributor has two means to advance the timing of the spark as the engine sped increases: a set of centrifugal weights within the distributor, and a vacuum diaphragm, mounted on the side of the distributor.

If the ignition is set too far advanced (BTDC), the ignition and expansion of the fuel in the cylinder will occur too soon and tend to force the piston down while it is still traveling up. This causes engine ping. If the ignition spark is set too far retarded, After TDC (ATDC), the piston will have already passed TDC and started on its way down when the fuel is ignited. This will cause the piston to be forced down for only a portion of its travel. This will result in poor engine performance and lack of power.

Timing

INSPECTION AND ADJUSTMENT

Distributor Not Removed

EXCEPT MOTRONIC MODELS

◆ See Figure 36

➡**Ignition timing on late model vehicles is constantly being adjusted by the Digital Motor Electronics (DME) engine control system. No manual timing adjustment is necessary or possible.**

In order to adjust the ignition timing dynamically, the engine must be at operating temperature and running at a specified rpm (see the Tune-Up Specifications chart). A stroboscopic timing light and tachometer are needed for this operation.

1. Disconnect and plug the vacuum line(s) at the distributor.
2. Attach a timing light and tachometer according to the manufacturer's instructions.
3. Raise the idle speed to that listed in the Tune-Up Specifications chart under Ignition Timing.

4. With the idle speed adjusted to the proper rpm direct the stroboscopic timing light beam straight down through the opening in the flywheel housing flange adjacent to the starter, and align the steel ball pressed into the flywheel with the timing mark on the flywheel housing.
5. Loosen the distributor hold-down bolt and rotate the distributor as necessary.
6. After the adjustment has been made, tighten the hold-down bolt and recheck the timing at the specified rpm to make sure that the setting was not disturbed during tightening.

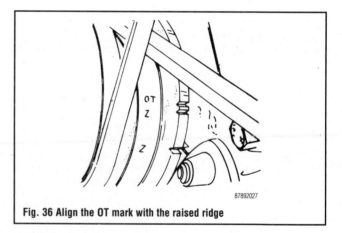

87892027

Fig. 36 Align the OT mark with the raised ridge

MOTRONIC MODELS

◆ See Figure 37

Although the timing on vehicles equipped with the Motronic control unit cannot be adjusted, the timing can still be checked.

On cars with the Motronic control unit, the only cure for improper timing is to replace the control unit. Also, timing must be within a certain range, as the computer changes the timing slightly to allow for various changes in operating condition. In other words, the timing does not have to be right on the mark, but anywhere in the specified range.

To check the timing, proceed as follows:

1. Look up the control unit number found on the casing of the assembly. If you vehicle is a 3, 5 and 6 series vehicles, the control unit unit is located in the glove box. If your vehicle is a 7 series, the control unit is in the right side speaker cutout. Find the unit number on the underside of the assembly and then cross reference the number to the corresponding number on the Computer Controlled Ignition Timing Chart.
2. The engine should be at normal operating temperature. The rpm level should be within the specified range as well.

Computer Controlled Ignition Timing Chart

Car/Model	Unit Number	RPM	Timing BTDC
325e	0261200021	650–750	4-12
325e	0261100007	650–750	6-12
528e	0261200007	650–750	4-12
528e	0261200021	650–750	6-12
	0261200027		
533i	0261200008	650–750	6-14
535i	0261200059	750–850	10-16
M5	0261200079	800–900	−3-3 ①
633CSi	0261200008	650–750	10-16
635CSi	0261200059	750–850	10-16
M6	0261200079	800–900	−3-3 ①
733i	0261200008	600–700	6-14
735i	0261200059	700–800	10-6

① That is − 3° after top dead center to 3° before top dead center

87892C02

Fig. 37 Computer Controlled Ignition Timing Chart

3. Connect a tachometer and a timing light to the engine. Start the engine and check the rpm. If it is not correct see the appropriate checks under Idle Speed and Mixture Adjustment. Operate the timing light to see if the timing is within the range specified on the chart. If it is significantly outside of the specified range, the control unit must be replaced.

Distributor Removed

ALIGNMENT METHOD

▶ See Figures 36 and 38

If the distributor has been removed for any reason, and the timing has been disturbed, the engine may be timed statically to obtain an initial setting. This will ensure that the dynamic timing adjustment will be an easier operation.

1. Crank the engine until the No. 1 cylinder is at the Top Dead Center (TDC) position. At this point both intake and exhaust valves for that cylinder should be closed (clearance at rocker arm). In addition, the engraved notch in the distributor rotor should align with the notch in the distributor housing (cap removed), the notch in the camshaft flange will align with the notch in the cylinder head (valve cover removed), and the OT mark or the first notch in the crankshaft pulley will align with the raised ridge in the center of the timing case cover.

2. If necessary, loosen the distributor clamp bolt and rotate the distributor housing so that the two marks coincide. This will at least guarantee that the engine will start so that a dynamic timing adjustment may be performed.

TEST LIGHT METHOD

Another means for adjusting static timing is the 12 volt test light method.

1. Connect a test light between the distributor primary connection and ground.

2. With the point gap correctly set and the timing marks aligned, rotate the distributor housing counterclockwise slightly until the breaker points just start to open. With the ignition switch turned on, the test light will light the moment the points open.

3. Tighten the distributor hold-down clamp slightly in this position and proceed to the dynamic timing adjustment.

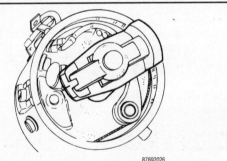

87892026

Fig. 38 Align the notch on the rotor with the groove on the distributor body

VALVE LASH

Adjustment

PROCEDURE

Except M3, M5 and M6 Models

▶ See Figures 39 thru 50

All BMW gasoline engines except for the 1987–88 M series, dual overhead camshaft designs are equipped with an overhead camshaft which operate the intake and exhaust valves through rocker arm linkage.

Valve lash on these engines should be adjusted at 8,000–12,500 mile (13,000–20,000 km) intervals, depending on the year of the car. See the owner's manual for exact intervals. It is important to adjust the lash to make up for wear in the valve train, which will cause noisy valve operation and reduced power, or, in some cases, excessive tightness in the valve train, which can cause the valves to burn and may even reduce compression. The BMW engine features a unique adjuster design that makes it easy to hold the required dimension while tightening the locknut; thus, valve adjustment is unusually easy.

1. Make sure the engine is as cold as possible. It need not actually sit overnight, but must be cool to the touch. Under 95°F (35°C) is the minimum. Several hours should be allowed for cooling if the engine was recently at operating temperature.

2. Remove the valve cover. This may require the removal of the air cleaner or main air intake hose.

➡ Note that the valve cover is secured to the cylinder head by cap nuts, while bolts attach it to the timing cover on the front of the engine. make sure you remove all the fasteners. Then, lift the cover straight off.

3. Disconnect the Positive Crankcase Ventilation (PCV) line or other vacuum lines. If unfastening multiple vacuum lines is needed, tag each line prior to removal.

4. The engine crankshaft must be rotated to a position that will ensure that there will be no closing effect from the camshaft when the valves are adjusted. This requests a different position for the adjustment of each cylinder.

The accompanying chart lists the cylinder to be adjusted in the first (left-hand) column, and the cylinder whose valves must be watched while positioning the engine in the right-hand column. Cylinders are numbered from front to rear, 1 through 4 or 1 through 6.

4 Cylinder Engines

To Adjust Cylinder:	Put This Cylinder at Overlap Position
1	4
3	2
4	1
2	3

6 Cylinder Engines

To Adjust Cylinder:	Put This Cylinder at Overlap Position
1	6
5	2
3	4
6	1
2	5
4	3

87892C01

Fig. 39 Valve adjustment order based upon cylinder

5. The engine may be rotated by rolling the car in third gear (if it is equipped with a manual transmission) or by installing a socket wrench on the bolt which attaches the front pulley and rotating the ring with the wrench. The valve of the cylinder to be adjusted (left hand column) will be in the fully closed position, so that you can wiggle the rockers up and down slightly. At this position, both valves will be slightly open. For example, to position the engine for adjustment of the valves on No. 1 cylinder, watch cylinder No. 4 on 4-cylinder engines, and cylinder No. 6 on 6-cylinder engines. As you rotate the engine in the direction of normal rotation, you'll note a point at which the valve on the right side of the engine (the exhaust valve) begins closing (moving upward). If you crank very slowly, you'll note that, just before the exhaust valve has closed, the intake begins opening. You want to stop rotating the engine when the valves are both open about the same amount. Now, you are ready to adjust cylinder No. 1.

6. Check the clearances on one of the valves with a feeler gauge that falls within the limits given in the Tune-Up Specifications chart. For example, if the dimension is 0.010–0.011 inches (0.25–0.30mm), use a 0.28mm gauge. The gauge should pass through between the valve and the outer end of the rocker with slight resistance (don't check between the camshaft and rocker, at the center of the engine). If there is any doubt about the clearance, try both the minimum and maximum specifications. For example, the specification is 0.010–0.011 inches (0.25–0.30mm), and the 0.25mm gauge passes through, but the 0.30mm gauge will not, the valve meets specification and will not need adjustment.

7. If the clearance is not correct, insert the bent wire tool supplied with the car (these may also be purchased at an automotive supply store or you can make one yourself with a piece of coat hanger) into the small hole in the adjusting cam located in the outer end of the rocker arm. Then, use a 10mm wrench to loosen the adjusting locknut, also located on the end of the rocker.

8. Rotate the adjusting cam with the wire, as you slide the gauge between the cam and valve. When the gauge will go in between the valve and adjusting cam and can be slid back and forth with just a slight resistance, hold the position of the cam with the adjusting wire and tighten the locknut.

9. Recheck the clearance to make sure it has not changed.

10. Repeat the adjustment for the other valve on cylinder No. 1, located directly across from the one you've already adjusted.

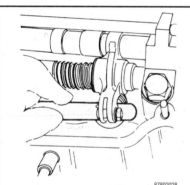

87892028

Fig. 40 Checking the valve clearance with a feeler gauge

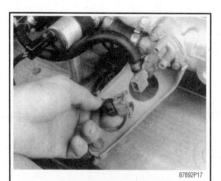

87892P17

Fig. 41 Tag for identification, then unfasten any wire connectors which may interfere with removal of the valve cover

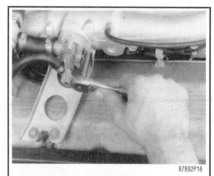

87892P18

Fig. 42 Remove any hardware securing brackets, such as this intake manifold bracket to the valve cover

87892P19

Fig. 43 Many of these brackets are secured with multiple pieces of hardware, so be patient and remove all the hardware first

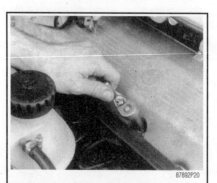

87892P20

Fig. 44 Remove the nuts which secure the lower portion of the valve cover and, in some cases, the spark plug tube

87892P21

Fig. 45 With all the nuts removed, lift the spark plug tube up and out of the way.

Fig. 46 Before removing the cover, make sure all breather hoses are unfastened

Fig. 47 With all hardware, hoses and connectors removed, slowly lift the cover out of the way

Fig. 48 With the cover removed, the adjusters are clearly visible

Fig. 49 After loosening the nut, use a suitable sized hex wrench and a feeler gauge to properly adjust the lifter

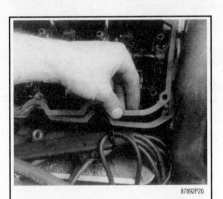

Fig. 50 When installing the valve cover, be sure to use a new valve cover gasket

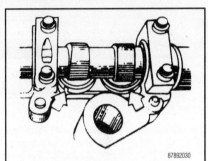

Fig. 51 On Dual Overhead Cam (DOHC) engines, rotate the valve tappet so the machined grooves in the tops are facing the 5 and 7 o'clock position

11. Then, rotate the engine to the next cylinder listed in the left hand column of the appropriate chart above, watching the valve of the cylinder listed in the right hand column. When the engine is positioned for this cylinder, adjust the valves for it as described. Then, proceed with the next cylinder in the left hand column in the same way, until all 4 or 6-cylinders have had their valves adjusted.

12. Replace the valve cover using a new gasket. Tighten the cover cap nuts or bolts in small increments and alternately in order to bring the cam cover down onto the gasket evenly in all areas. Be careful not to overtighten the cover cap nuts/bolts.

13. Fasten all disconnected hoses and, if necessary, replace the air cleaner.

14. Start the engine.

M3, M5 and M6 Models

♦ See Figure 51

➡ To perform this procedure, a special tool is needed to depress the valves against spring pressure to gain access to the valve adjusting discs. Use BMW Tool 11 3 170 or equivalent. Also needed are: compressed air to lift valve adjusting discs that must be removed and replaced out of the valve tappet; an assortment of adjusting discs of various thicknesses and a precise outside micrometer.

1. Make sure the engine is overnight cold. Remove the rocker cover.

2. Turn the engine until the No. 1 cylinder intake valve cams are both straight up. The intake cam is labeled A on the cylinder head.

3. Slide a flat feeler gauge in between each of the cams and the adjacent valve tappet. Check to see if the clearance is within the specified range. If not, switch gauges and measure the actual clearance. When actual clearance is achieved, proceed to the next step.

4. Turn the valve tappets so the grooves machined into the edges are

aligned. Looking at the valves from the center of the engine, the right hand tappet's groove should be at about the 5 o'clock position and the left hand tappet's groove should be at about the 7 o'clock position. Use the special tool with the end mark corresponding to the proper valve. In this case use the A end of the tool for the valve marked A. Use the E end of the tool for the E valve. (A is intake, E is exhaust). Slide the proper end of the tool, going from the center of the engine outward, under the cam, with the heel of the tool pivoting on the inner side of the camshaft valley. Force the handle downward until the handle rests on the protrusion on the center of the cylinder head.

5. Use compressed air to pop the disc out of the tappet. Read the thickness dimension on the disc.

6. Determine the thickness required as follows:

   a. If the valve clearance is too tight, try the next thinner diameter.

   b. If the valve clearance is too loose, try the next thicker disc.

7. Slip the thinner or thicker disc into the tappet with the letter facing downward.

8. Rock the valve spring depressing tool out and remove it.

9. Recheck the clearance. Change the disc again, if necessary, until the clearance falls within the specified range.

10. Turn the engine in firing order sequence (1–5–3–6–2–4 for the 6-cylinder engines or, for the M3 1–3–4–2), turning the crankshaft forward ⅓ of a turn each time to get the intake cams to the upward position for each cylinder. Measure the valve clearance and, if it is outside the specified range, follow the steps outlined earlier for all the intake valves.

11. Follow the same sequence for all the exhaust valves, going through the firing order.

➡ It is necessary to use the opposite end of the special tool, the end marked E to depress the exhaust valves.

12. When all the clearances are in the specified range, replace the cam cover, start the engine, and check for leaks.

IDLE SPEED AND MIXTURE ADJUSTMENTS

With the advent of emission control legislation on the Federal level, as well as state emission inspection legislation, it has become increasingly important that idle adjustments do not violate the letter of the law. The only way to make sure that the idle mixture setting remains at a legal level is to have it checked with an exhaust gas analyzer of known accuracy. This is an extremely expensive electronic device which your BMW dealer or a reputable independent garage is required to have on hand to make these adjustments. Therefore, it is recommended that the mixture adjustment be referred to them.

➡**The idle speed and mixture can be adjusted ONLY with the aid of a CO meter. If this tool is not available, do not attempt any of the following procedures. The idle mixture can be adjusted ONLY with the aid of a CO meter on most models; on the 318i, it can be adjusted ONLY with a BMW digital mixture adjustment unit 12 6 400. Idle speed is not adjustable on any model with the Motronic control unit except the M5 and M6. If idle speed is incorrect, either the idle valve or the idle control unit must be replaced.**

Carburetors

SOLEX 38 PDSI, 40 PDSI, AND 40 PDSIT

▶ **See Figure 52**

➡**Before checking or adjusting the engine idle, make sure the vehicle is in a well ventilated area, and the transmission is in NEUTRAL or PARK with the wheels securely blocked for your protection.**

1. Run the engine until it reaches normal operating temperature. Disconnect the air pump outlet hose (leading from the air pump to the exhaust manifold) at the air pump.
2. Adjust the idle speed to 1000 rpm with the idle speed screw.
3. With a CO meter attached to the exhaust pipe of the car, turn the idle mixture adjustment screw to obtain a reading of 0.6–8% CO.
4. Reset idle to 1000 rpm, as necessary, and reconnect the air pump outlet hose.

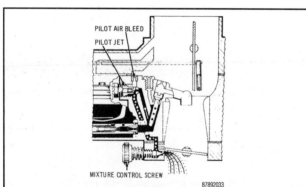

PILOT AIR BLEED
PILOT JET
MIXTURE CONTROL SCREW
87892033

Fig. 52 Turn the mixture control screw to adjust the idle—Solex PDSI and PDSIT type carburetors

SOLEX 32/32 DIDTA

▶ **See Figure 53**

➡**Before checking or adjusting the engine idle, make sure the vehicle is in a well ventilated area, and the transmission is in NEUTRAL or PARK with the wheels securely blocked for your protection.**

1. Run the engine until it reaches normal operating temperature.
2. Adjust the idle speed by turning the idle air by-pass control screw until the reading is 850–950 rpm.
3. With a CO meter attached to the exhaust pipe of the car, turn idle mixture control screw to obtain a reading of 0.8–1.2% CO.

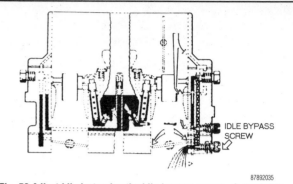

IDLE BYPASS
SCREW
87892035

Fig. 53 Adjust idle by turning the idle by-pass screw—Solex DIDTA type carburetor

4. Refer to the engine specification sticker in the engine compartment and adjust the idle if not within factory range.

ZENITH 35/40 INAT TWIN CARBURETORS

➡**Before checking or adjusting the engine idle, make sure the vehicle is in a well ventilated area, and the transmission is in NEUTRAL or PARK with the wheels securely blocked for your protection.**

1. Run the engine until it reaches normal operating temperature. Remove the plugs from the exhaust manifolds and insert the test probes.
2. Remove the air cleaner. You will notice doing this will cause the engine rpm to decrease by about 100 rpm.
3. Disconnect the throttle linkage rod at the ball stud (2) near the rear carburetor. Mark the position of the rod to ease reinstallation.

➡**This adjustment requires a carburetor synchronizing meter with 2 caps which replace the effect of the air cleaner on each carburetor, and a CO meter with taps designed to connect with the BMW exhaust manifolds.**

4. Install the 2 caps over the carburetor tops, and connect them to the synchronizer. Now, adjust the 2 idle screws to get an idle rpm between 900–1000, and a reading of 0 on the synchronizing meter. These are the larger screws near the base of each carburetor . If the synchronizing meter shows greater vacuum on one carburetor than on another, adjust the large screws in opposite directions of each other in equal amounts, adjusting the screw of the carburetor with the higher vacuum in the clockwise direction.
5. Adjust the idle mixture screws in or out to bring the CO content in the exhaust under each carburetor to 1.95–2.05% CO. These screws are the small ones next to the large idle screws.
6. If this changes the idle speed, reset the idle screws as described. Then, read the CO meter and, if necessary, readjust the mixture screws as necessary. Continue in this manner until both idle speed (including balance) and mixture are within specification.
7. With the engine off, reinstall the air cleaner, disconnect the exhaust probes and reinstall the plugs. Reconnect the throttle linkage. When reconnecting the throttle linkage, if needed, adjust the length of the connecting rod with the knurled nut so that the rod can be connected without changing the idle speed.

Fuel Injection Systems

KUGELFISCHER MECHANICAL SYSTEM

2002Tii Models

➡**Before checking or adjusting the engine idle, make sure the vehicle is in a well ventilated area, and the transmission is in NEUTRAL or PARK with the wheels securely blocked for your protection.**

1. Run the engine until it reaches normal operating temperature. Remove the cap from the top of the throttle butterfly port.

2. Adjust the idle speed by turning the idling speed screw to obtain an idle of 850–950 rpm.

3. With a CO meter attached to the exhaust pipe of the car, turn the throttle butterfly air adjustment screw to obtain a reading of 2.0–3.0% CO. Turning the screw in clockwise direction will lean the mixture, while turning counterclockwise will richen the mixture. Refer to the engine compartment sticker for idle and CO specifications.

4. With the vehicle still in NEUTRAL or PARK, apply throttle several times to increase the rpm, and check to see if the idle returns to normal. If necessary, readjust each screw until the CO reading and idle speed remain constant.

ELECTRONIC SYSTEMS

320i Models

➡️All 320i models are equipped with the Bosch® K-Jetronic continuous fuel injection system.

❋❋ CAUTION

Before checking or adjusting the engine idle, make sure the vehicle is in a well ventilated area, and the transmission is in NEUTRAL or PARK with the wheels securely blocked for your protection.

1. Run the engine until it reaches normal operating temperature.
2. Adjust the engine idle speed. The adjustment screw is located near the throttle valve linkage.
3. Detach the exhaust check valve and plug the hose.
4. To adjust the CO, remove the plug from the fuel distributor with BMW special wrench. Adjust the CO level to a maximum of 2.0% for the 49 state vehicles or 3.5% for the California cars.
5. Reconnect the exhaust check valve hose and check the idle speed.

530i Models

▶ **See Figure 54**

➡️All 530i models are equipped with the Bosch® L-Jetronic fuel injection system.

❋❋ CAUTION

Before checking or adjusting the engine idle, make sure the vehicle is in a well ventilated area, and the transmission is in NEUTRAL or PARK with the wheels securely blocked for your protection.

1. Run the engine until it reaches normal operating temperature.
2. Disconnect the hose from the collector to the charcoal filter. Do not plug the line.

➡️**The hose is located between the first and second air induction tubes.**

3. Disconnect the air pump hose at the air pump and plug the line.

4. Adjust the idle speed by turning the adjusting screw on the side of the throttle housing.
5. Turn the screw until the the CO level is between 1.5–3.0% at idle.
6. If necessary, adjust the CO with the idle air screw located on the air volume control.
7. Reconnect the hoses when complete.

528e Models

➡️**All 528e models are equipped with the Bosch® L-Jetronic fuel injection system.**

❋❋ CAUTION

Before checking or adjusting the engine idle, make sure the vehicle is in a well ventilated area, and the transmission is in NEUTRAL or PARK with the wheels securely blocked for your protection.

1. Pull the canister purge hose off the solenoid, leaving the connections unplugged.
2. Fasten the CO meter 13 0 070 or equivalent to the manifold using BMW nipple 13 0 100.
3. With the engine valve clearances correctly adjusted, ignition timing correct and the engine at normal operating temperature, measure the CO percentage at idle. the CO nominal value is 0.2–1.2%.
4. If the CO level is within the specified range, disconnect the test unit, replace the plug in the exhaust manifold, and conclude the test. If not, adjust the CO as described below:

a. Turn **OFF** the engine and unplug the oxygen sensor. Remove the anti-tamper plug in the throttle body with special tool No. 13 1 092 or equivalent. Then screw the special extractor tool No. 13 1 094 or equivalent into the hole and draw the plug out with a slide hammer or suitable tool.

b. With the engine running and at normal operating temperature, use adjustment tool 13 1 060, 13 1 100 or equivalent to fine tune the CO level.

c. When the adjustment is complete, install a new anti-tamper plug, and reconnect the oxygen sensor plug and the carbon canister hose. Also, remove the nipple in the exhaust manifold and replace the plug. d. Reinstall the exhaust manifold bolts.

528i Models

▶ **See Figure 55**

➡️All 528i models are equipped with the Bosch® L-Jetronic fuel injection system.

❋❋ CAUTION

Before checking or adjusting the engine idle, make sure the vehicle is in a well ventilated area, and the transmission is in NEUTRAL or PARK with the wheels securely blocked for your protection.

1. Adjust the idle speed if needed. The idle screw is on the side of the throttle body housing. Turning it clockwise will decrease the idle and counterclockwise will increase it.

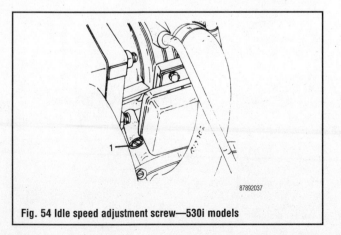

87892037

Fig. 54 Idle speed adjustment screw—530i models

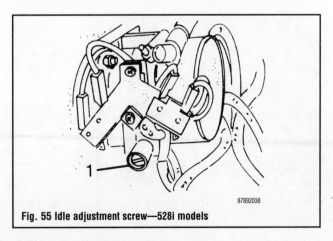

87892038

Fig. 55 Idle adjustment screw—528i models

2. Remove the CO test plug at the rear of the exhaust manifold and connect a CO meter. Start the engine and run it until operating temperature is reached, if not unready done. Measure the CO reading and adjust to 0.2–0.8% CO.

3. Unfasten the connector for the oxygen sensor on the right side of the firewall in the engine compartment. When disconnected, the CO valve should not change.

4. If CO is not to specification, adjust the mixture by turning the adjusting screw, located low on the airflow meter. Adjust for 0.5% CO.

5. Reconnect the oxygen sensor and check CO again. If CO does not meet specification, the vehicle should be taken to a professionally trained injection system specialist.

6. When complete, disconnect the test probe and reinstall the test plug into the exhaust manifold.

7. Recheck the idle speed.

318i Models

▶ See Figures 56, 57 and 58

➡All 318i models are equipped with the Bosch® L-Jetronic fuel injection system.

✳✳ CAUTION

Before checking or adjusting the engine idle, make sure the vehicle is in a well ventilated area, and the transmission is in NEUTRAL or PARK with the wheels securely blocked for your protection.

1. The engine must be run until it is at normal operating temperature. Ignition timing and valve clearances must be to specification. Connect the BMW digital mixture measurement tool 12 6 400 or equivalent according to the instrument instructions. Disconnect the hose going to the active carbon filter on the throttle housing. Do not plug the open connections.

2. Operate the engine at 3000 rpm for 30 seconds to ensure that the oxygen sensor is at operating temperature.

3. Disconnect the oxygen sensor wire, and fasten it where it cannot touch a ground. Read the display on the gauge and note the reading. This reading will be the nominal value.

4. Reconnect the oxygen sensor into the test unit. The actual value will appear in the display. If the actual value is within 0.3 volts of the original value, the CO is within tolerance. If not, proceed as follows.

➡Several special tools are required to remove the anti-tamper plug for the adjustment screw and to turn the adjustment screw. Get a new anti-tamper plug before beginning work.

   a. Use special tool 13 1 092 or equivalent to remove the anti-tamper plug. If you do not have access to the correct tool, the plug can be removed by drilling it out.

   b. When the anti-taper plug is removed,. Then screw special tool 13 1 094 or equivalent into the plug, and use the slide hammer on the tool to draw the plug out.

   c. Use a special tool 13 1 060 to turn the adjusting screw to bring the actual valve to within 0.3 volt of the nominal value. Turn **OFF** the engine, then disconnect the test unit and reconnect the oxygen sensor wire to the oxygen sensor. Replace the anti-tamper plug with a new one.

325, 325e, 325i, 325iS and 325iX Models

▶ See Figures 36, 57 and 58

➡All 325, 325e, 325i, 325iS and 325iX models are equipped with the Bosch® L-Jetronic fuel injection system.

✳✳ CAUTION

Before checking or adjusting the engine idle, make sure the vehicle is in a well ventilated area, and the transmission is in NEUTRAL or PARK with the wheels securely blocked for your protection.

1. Disconnect the hose leading from the throttle housing to the carbon canister. Do not plug the openings.

2. Remove the bolts on either side of the exhaust manifold plug.

3. Remove the plug in the exhaust manifold and install test nipple 13 0 100 or equivalent and connect the CO tester 13 0 070 or equivalent into the open nipple.

4. With the engine valve clearances correctly adjusted, ignition timing correct and the engine at normal operating temperature, measure the CO percentage at idle. the CO nominal value is 0.2–1.2%.

5. If the CO level is within the specified range, disconnect the test unit, replace the plug in the exhaust manifold, and conclude the test. If not, adjust the CO as described below:

   a. Turn **OFF** the engine and unplug the oxygen sensor. Remove the anti-tamper plug in the throttle body with special tool No. 13 1 092 or equivalent. Then screw the special extractor tool No. 13 1 094 or equivalent into the hole and draw the plug out with a slide hammer or suitable tool.

   b. With the engine running and at normal operating temperature, use adjustment tool 13 1 060, 13 1 100 or equivalent to fine tune the CO level.

   c. When the adjustment is complete, install a new anti-tamper plug, and reconnect the oxygen sensor plug and the carbon canister hose. Also, remove the nipple in the exhaust manifold and replace the plug. d. Reinstall the exhaust manifold bolts.

633CSi and 733i Models

1982 VEHICLES

➡All 1982 633CSi and 733i models are equipped with the Bosch® L-Jetronic fuel injection system.

✳✳ CAUTION

Before checking or adjusting the engine idle, make sure the vehicle is in a well ventilated area, and the transmission is in NEUTRAL or PARK with the wheels securely blocked for your protection.

1. Run the engine until at normal operating temperature.

2. Disconnect the throttle housing-to-activated carbon filter hose. Unfasten and plug the air hose at the air pump.

3. Adjust the idle speed, if needed using the idle adjusting screw, located in the side of the throttle housing.

4. Adjust the CO to 1.5–3.0% at idle. If adjustment is needed, remove the

Fig. 56 Anti-tamper plug in the air filter assembly

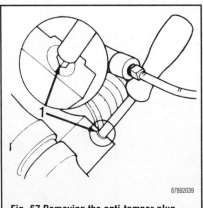

Fig. 57 Removing the anti-tamper plug

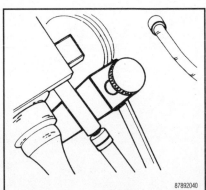

Fig. 58 Special tool installed to adjust the CO level

cap from the air flow sensor and use either the BMW adjustment tool, or a short screwdriver, turn the bypass air screw located in the air flow sensor.

5. When complete, reconnect the hoses.

533i, 535i, 633CSi, 635CSi,733i and 735i Models

1983–88 VEHICLES

➡All 1983–88 533i, 535i, 633CSi, 733i and 735i models are equipped with the Bosch® L-Jetronic fuel injection system.

✳✳ CAUTION

Before checking or adjusting the engine idle, make sure the vehicle is in a well ventilated area, and the transmission is in NEUTRAL or PARK with the wheels securely blocked for your protection.

1. Check and adjust the idle speed, if needed, to specification.
2. Disconnect the evaporative canister purge hose at the bottom of the solenoid mounted on the firewall. Leave the openings unplugged.
3. Unscrew the bolts on the exhaust manifold and install a BMW nipple No. 13 0 100 or equivalent, then connect the CO test unit 13 0 070 or equivalent. Check to see if the CO level is between 0.2–1.2%. If the CO is not within limits, adjust it as followed:
  a. Turn off the engine and unplug the oxygen sensor plug.
  b. Remove the air flow sensor by unfastening the air cleaner and remove the 3 mounting bolts to separate the airflow sensor.
  c. Use special tool 13 1 092 or equivalent to remove the anti-tamper plug. Use tool 13 1 094 or equivalent and slide hammer the remaining plug.
  d. Once the plug is removed, install the air flow sensor back onto the air cleaner and reinstall the air cleaner. With the engine at normal operating temperature and the oxygen sensor plug still disconnected, measure the CO and adjust it with Tool 13 1 060 or 13 1 100 or equivalent. The CO level should meet the nominal value of 0.2–1.2%.
  e. Once the level is adjusted, stop the engine and reconnect the oxygen sensor plug. Then, remove the air flow sensor, put it on a bench, and install a new anti-tamper plug. Reinstall the airflow sensor and air cleaner. Reconnect the canister purge hose to the solenoid.

M5 and M6 Models

▶ **See Figure 59**

➡All M5 and M6 models are equipped with the Bosch® L-Jetronic fuel injection system.

✳✳ CAUTION

Before checking or adjusting the engine idle, make sure the vehicle is in a well ventilated area, and the transmission is in NEUTRAL or PARK with the wheels securely blocked for your protection.

1. Make sure the engine is at normal operating temperature, and that the air cleaner is in reasonably clean condition. All basic engine tuning factors (spark plug condition and gap, valve adjustment, ignition timing, etc.) must be correct.
2. Adjust the idle speed by turning the screw shown in the illustration.

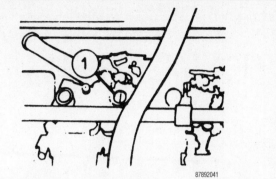

Fig. 59 To adjust the idle speed, turn the screw (1) in small increments

3. To adjust CO, remove the cap located at the center of the top surface of the airflow sensor. Use special tool 13 1 100 to turn the airflow control screw in the airflow sensor. To access this the anti-tamper cap must be removed.
4. Adjust the CO content until CO is between 0.4–1.2%.
5. Install a new cap when CO meets specification.

M3 Models

➡All M3 models are equipped with the Bosch® L-Jetronic fuel injection system.

✳✳ CAUTION

Before checking or adjusting the engine idle, make sure the vehicle is in a well ventilated area, and the transmission is in NEUTRAL or PARK with the wheels securely blocked for your protection.

➡This test must be performed at essentially sea level altitude. In an area well above sea level, it will be necessary to use a BMW Service Tester (or equivalent device from another source) and run the test with the system's altitude correction box connected.

1. Make sure the engine is at operating temperature, and that the air cleaner is clean. All basic engine tuning factors (spark plug condition and gap, valve adjustment, ignition timing, etc.) must be correct.
2. Make sure all accessories are **OFF**.
3. A special electrical fitting (BMW special tool 13 4 010 or equivalent) is required to disable the Motronic control system's throttle valve switch. Pull off the electrical connector leading to the throttle valve switch. Then, plug the special tool into the open end of the connector.
4. Adjust the idle speed to specification by turning the screw located just above the **M** on the valve cover. Make sure to restore the throttle valve switch when the idle speed is correct.
5. To adjust CO, remove the cap located at the center of the top surface of the airflow sensor. Use special tool 13 1 100 to turn the airflow control screw in the airflow sensor. To access this the anti-tamper cap must be removed.
6. Adjust the CO content until CO is between 0.4–1.2%.
7. Install a new cap when CO meets specification.

Gasoline Engine Tune-Up Specifications (cont.)

Year	Model	Engine Displacement cu. in. (cc)	Spark Plugs Type	Gap (in.)	Distributor Dwell Angle (deg)	Point Gap (in.)	Ignition Timing Δ (deg) BTDC MT	AT	Compression Pressure (psi)	Fuel Pump (psi)	Idle Speed (rpm) MT	AT	Valve Clearance In.	Ex.
1977	320i	121 (1990)	W145T30	.024	59-65	.014	25B @ 2200 (2400)		128	67-74	950	950	.006-.008	.010-.012
	530i	182 (2985)	W145T30	.024	35-41	.014	22B @ 1700 (2700)		149	35	950	950	.010-.012	.010-.012
	630CSi	182 (2985)	W145T30	.024	35-41	.014	22B @ 1700 (2700)		114	35	950	950	.010-.012	.010-.012
1978	320i	121 (1990)	W145T30	.024	59-65	.014	25B @ 2200 (2400)		128	67-74	950	950	.006-.008	.010-.012
	530i	182 (2985)	W145T30	.024	35-41	.014	22B @ 1700 (2700)		149	35	950	950	.010-.012	.010-.012
	633CSi	196 (3210)	W145T30	.025	Electronic	③	22B @ 3400 (2750)		114	37	950	950	.010-.012	.010-.012
	733i	196 (3210)	W145T30	.025	Electronic	③	22B @ 2400 (2750)		114	37	950	950	.010-.012	.010-.012
1979	320i	121 (1990)	W125T30	.027	59-65	.014	25B @ 2200 (2400)		128	67-74	950	950	.006-.008	.010-.012
	528i	170 (2788)	W125T30	.024	Electronic	③	22B @ 2100		142	35	900	900	.010-.012	.010-.012
	633CSi	196 (3210)	W145T30	.025	Electronic	③	22B @ 2400 (2750)		114	37	950	950	.010-.012	.010-.012
	733i	196 (3210)	W145T30	.025	Electronic	③	22B @ 2400 (2750)		114	37	950	950	.010-.012	.010-.012
1980	320i	107 (1766)	WR9DS	.024	Electronic	③	25B @ 2200		128	67-74	850	900	.006-.008	.010-.012
	528i	170 (2788)	WR9DS	.024	Electronic	③	22B @ 2100		142	35	900	900	.010-.012	.010-.012
	633CSi	196 (3210)	WR9DS	.024	Electronic	③	22B @ 1650		114	35	950	950	.010-.012	.010-.012
	733i	196 (3210)	WR9DS	.024	Electronic	③	22B @ 650		114	35	900	900	.010-.012	.010-.012
1981	320i	107 (1766)	WR9DS	.024	Electronic	③	25B @ 2200		128	67-74	850	900	.006-.008	.010-.012
	528i	170 (2788)	WR9DS	.024	Electronic	③	22B @ 2100		142	35	900	900	.010-.012	.010-.012
	633CSi	196 (3210)	WR9DS	.024	Electronic	③	22B @ 350		114	35	900	900	.010-.012	.010-.012
	733i	196 (3210)	WR9DS	.024	Electronic	③	22B @ 650		114	35	900	900	.010-.012	.010-.012
1982	320i	108 (1766)	WR9DS	0.024	Electronic	③	25B @ 2200	25B @ 2200	128	64-74	850	900	.006-.008	0.007
	325e	165 (2693)	WR9LS	0.024	Electronic	④	④		142	33-38	④	④	.010-.012	0.010
	528e	165 (2693)	WR9LS	0.024	Electronic	④	④		142	33-38	④	④	.010-.012	0.010
	533i	196 (3210)	WR9LS	0.024	Electronic	④	④		114	35	④	④	.011	0.011
	633CSi	196 (3210)	WR9LS	0.024	Electronic	④	④		114	35	④	④	.011	0.011
	733i	196 (3210)	WR9LS	0.024	Electronic	④	④		114	35	④	④	.011	0.011

87892C09

Gasoline Engine Tune-Up Specifications

Year	Model	Engine Displacement cu. in. (cc)	Spark Plugs Type	Gap (in.)	Distributor Dwell Angle (deg)	Point Gap (in.)	Ignition Timing Δ (deg) BTDC MT	AT	Compression Pressure (psi)	Fuel Pump (psi)	Idle Speed (rpm) MT	AT	Valve Clearance In.	Ex.
1970	1600	96 (1573)	①	.024	61-66	.016	25B @ 1400		142	3.0-3.6	1000	1000	.0059-.0079	.0059-.0079
	2000,2002,Tii	121 (1990)	W145T30	.024	59-66	.016	25B @ 1400		142	3.0-3.6	900	900	.006-.008	.006-.008
	2500	152 (2493)	W175T2	.024	35-41	.016	22B @ 1700		142	2.8-3.5	900	900	.010-.012	.010-.012
	2800,CS	170 (2788)	WG160T30	.024	35-41	.015	22B @ 1700		149	2.8-3.5	900	900	.010-.012	.010-.012
	Bavaria	170 (2788)	WG160T30	.024	35-41	.015	22B @ 1700		149	2.8-3.5	900	900	.010-.012	.010-.012
1971	1600	96 (1573)	①	.024	61-66	.016	25B @ 1400		142	3.0-3.6	1000	1000	.0059-.0079	.0059-.0079
	2000,2002	121 (1990)	W145T30	.024	59-66	.016	25B @ 1400		142	3.0-3.6	900	900	.006-.008	.006-.008
	2500	152 (2493)	W175T2	.024	35-41	.016	22B @ 1700		149	2.8-3.5	900	900	.010-.012	.010-.012
	Bavaria	170 (2788)	WG160T30	.024	35-41	.015	22B @ 1700		149	2.8-3.5	900	900	.010-.012	.010-.012
1972	2000,2002Tii	121 (1990)	W175T30	.024	59-66	.016	25B @ 1400		142	3.0-3.6	900	900	.006-.008	.006-.008
	Bavaria	170 (2788)	WG160T30	.024	35-41	.015	22B @ 1700		149	2.8-3.5	900	900	.010-.012	.010-.012
1973	3000CS	170 (2788)	WG160T30	.024	35-41	.015	22B @ 1700		149	2.8-3.5	900	900	.010-.012	.010-.012
	2000,2002Tii	121 (1990)	W175T30	.024	59-66	.016	25B @ 1400		142	3.0-3.6②	900	900	.006-.008	.006-.008
	3.0CS,S,Si	182 (2985)	W145T30	.024	35-41	.015	22B @ 1700		149	2.8-3.5	900	900	.010-.012	.010-.012
	Bavaria	170 (2788)	WG160T30	.024	35-41	.015	22B @ 1700		149	2.8-3.5	900	900	.010-.012	.010-.012
1974	2000,2002,Tii	121 (1990)	W175T30	.024	59-66	.016	25B @ 1400		142	3.0-3.6②	900	900	.006-.008	.006-.008
	Bavaria	170 (2788)	WG160T30	.024	35-41	.015	22B @ 1700		149	2.8-3.5	900	900	.010-.012	.010-.012
	3.0CS,S,Si	182 (2985)	W145T30	.024	35-41	.015	22B @ 1700		149	2.8-3.5	900	900	.010-.012	.010-.012
1975	2002,Tii	121 (1990)	W175T30	.024	59-66	.016	25B @ 1400		142	3.0-36②	900	900	.006-.008	.006-.008
	3.0CS,S,Si	182 (2985)	W145T30	.024	35-41	.015	22B @ 1700		149	29-31	950	950	.010-.012	.010-.012
	530i	182 (2985)	W145T30	.024	35-41	.014	22B @ 1700 (2700)		149	35	950	950	.010-.012	.010-.012
1976	2002,Tii	121 (1990)	W175T30	.024	59-66	.016	25B @ 1400		142	3.0-3.6②	900	900	.006-.008	.006-.008
	3.0CS,S,Si	182 (2985)	W145T30	.024	35-41	.015	22B @ 1700		149	29-31	900	900	.010-.012	.010-.012
	630CS 530i	182 (2985)	W145T30	.024	35-41	.014	22B @ 1700 (2700)		149	35	950	950	.010-.012	.010-.012

87892C08

Gasoline Engine Tune-Up Specifications (cont.)

Year	Model	Engine Displacement cu. in. (cc)	Spark Plugs Type	Gap (in.)	Distributor Dwell Angle (deg)	Point Gap (in.)	Ignition Timing ▲ (deg.)■● MT	AT	Compression Pressure (psi)*	Fuel Pump (psi)	Idle Speed (rpm) MT	AT	Valve Clearance In.	Ex.
1983	320i	10B (1766)	WR9DS	0.024	Electronic ③		25B @ 2200	25B @ 2200	128	64–74	850	900	0.007	0.007
	325e	165 (2693)	WR9LS	0.024	Electronic ③		④	④	149	33–38	④	④	0.010	0.010
	528e	165 (2693)	WR9LS	0.024	Electronic ③		④	④	149	33–38	④	④	0.010	0.010
	533i	196 (3210)	WR9LS	0.024	Electronic ③		④	④	149	35	④	④	0.012	0.012
	633CSi	196 (3210)	WR9LS	0.024	Electronic ③		④	④	149	35	④	④	0.012	0.012
	733i	196 (3210)	WR9LS	0.024	Electronic ③		④	④	149	35	④	④	0.012	0.012
1984	318i	108 (1766)	WR9DS	0.024	Electronic ③		④	④	149	43	750	750	0.008	0.008
	325e	165 (2693)	WR9LS	0.024	Electronic ③		④	④	149	33–38	700	700	0.010	0.010
	528e	165 (2693)	WR9LS	0.024	Electronic ③		④	④	149	33–38	700	700	0.010	0.010
	533i	196 (3210)	WR9LS	0.024	Electronic ③		④	④	149	35	700	700	0.012	0.012
	633CSi	196 (3210)	WR9LS	0.024	Electronic ③		④	④	149	35	700	700	0.012	0.012
	733i	196 (3210)	WR9LS	0.024	Electronic ③		④	④	149	35	700	700	0.012	0.012
1985	318i	108 (1766)	WR9DS	0.033	Electronic ③		④	④	149	43	750	750	0.008	0.008
	325e	165 (2693)	WR9LS	0.029	Electronic ③		④	④	149	33–38	700	700	0.010	0.010
	528e	165 (2693)	WR9LS	0.029	Electronic ③		④	④	149	33–38	700	700	0.010	0.010
	533i	196 (3210)	WR9LS	0.024	Electronic ③		④	④	149	35	700	700	0.012	0.012
	633CSi	196 (3210)	WR9LS	0.024	Electronic ③		④	④	149	35	700	700	0.012	0.012
	535i	209 (3428)	WR9LS	0.029	Electronic ③		④	④	149	43	800	800	0.012	0.012
	635CSi	209 (3428)	WR9LS	0.029	Electronic ③		④	④	149	43	800	800	0.012	0.012
	733i	196 (3210)	WR9LS	0.024	Electronic ③		④	④	149	35	700	700	0.012	0.012
	735i	209 (3428)	WR9DS	0.029	Electronic ③		④	④	149	43	800	800	0.012	0.012
1986	325e	165 (2693)	WR9LS	0.029	Electronic ③		④	④	149	33–38	700	700	0.010	0.010
	528e	165 (2693)	WR9LS	0.029	Electronic ③		④	④	149	33–38	700	700	0.010	0.010
	535i	209 (3428)	WR9LS	0.029	Electronic ③		④	④	149	43	800	800	0.012	0.012
	635CSi	209 (3428)	WR9LS	0.029	Electronic ③		④	④	149	43	800	800	0.012	0.012
	535i	209 (3428)	WR9LS	0.029	Electronic ③		④	④	149	43	800	800	0.012	0.012
1987	325	165 (2693)	WR9LS	0.029	Electronic ③		④	④	149	33–38	700	700	0.010	0.010
	528e	165 (2693)	WR9LS	0.029	Electronic ③		④	④	149	33–38	700	700	0.010	0.010
	325i	152 (2494)	W8LCR	0.029	Electronic ③		④	④	149	43	720	720	0.010	0.010
	325iS	152 (2494)	W8LCR	0.029	Electronic ③		④	④	149	43	720	720	0.010	0.010
	535i	209 (3428)	WR9LS	0.029	Electronic ③		④	④	149	43	800	800	0.012	0.012
	635CSi	209 (3428)	WR9LS	0.029	Electronic ③		④	④	149	43	800	800	0.012	0.012
	735i	209 (3428)	WR9DS	0.029	Electronic ③		④	④	149	43	800	800	0.012	0.012
	M5	210.6 (3453)	X5DC	0.029	Electronic ③		④	④	149	43	800	—	0.013	0.013
	M6	210.6 (3453)	X5DC	0.029	Electronic ③		④	④	149	43	800	—	0.013	0.013

87892C10

Gasoline Engine Tune-Up Specifications (cont.)

Year	Model	Engine Displacement cu. in. (cc)	Spark Plugs Type	Spark Plugs Gap (in.)	Distributor Dwell Angle (deg)	Distributor Point Gap (in.)	Ignition Timing ▲(deg.)■● MT	Ignition Timing ▲(deg.)■● AT	Compression Pressure (psi)*	Fuel Pump (psi)	Idle Speed (rpm) MT	Idle Speed (rpm) AT	Valve Clearance In.	Valve Clearance Ex.
1988	325	165 (2693)	WR9LS	0.027	Electronic ③		④	④	149	36	720	720	0.010	0.010
	528e	165 (2693)	WR9LS	0.027	Electronic ③		④	④	149	36	720	720	0.010	0.010
	325i	152 (2494)	WR9LS	0.027	Electronic ③		④	④	149	43	760	760	0.010	0.010
	325iS	152 (2494)	WR9LS	0.027	Electronic ③		④	④	149	43	760	760	0.010	0.010
	325iX	152 (2494)	WR9LS	0.027	Electronic ③		④	④	149	43	760	760	0.010	0.010
	535i	209 (3428)	WR9LS	0.027	Electronic ①		④	④	149	43	800	800	0.012	0.012
	635CSi	209 (3428)	WR9LS	0.027	Electronic ③		④	④	149	43	800	800	0.012	0.012
	L6	209 (3428)	WR9LS	0.027	Electronic ③		④	④	149	43	800	800	0.012	0.012
	M3	140.4 (2302)	WR9LS	0.027	Electronic ③		④	④	149	43	880	—	0.012	0.012
	M5	210.6 (3453)	WR9LS	0.027	Electronic ③		④	④	149	43	850	—	0.013	0.013
	M6	210.6 (3453)	WR9LS	0.027	Electronic ③		④	④	149	43	850	—	0.013	0.013
	735iL	209 (3428)	W8LCR	0.027	Electronic ③		④	④	149	43	④	④	0.012	0.012

NOTE: The underhood specifications sticker often reflects tune-up specification changes made in production. Sticker figures must be used if they disagree with those in this chart.
NA Not available
B Before Top Dead Center
*When analyzing compression figures, look for uniformity between cylinders
▲ See text for procedures
● Figures in parenthesis are for California
■ All figures are Before Top Dead Center
① Bosch W200T30 or WG190T30
② 2002Tii—21–29 psi.
③ Although not adjustable the air gap should be checked periodically. The gap should be .012–.028, if not within specification the unit should be replaced.
④ Motronic injection system—controlled by computer, please refer to the underhood sticker for specifications

87892C11

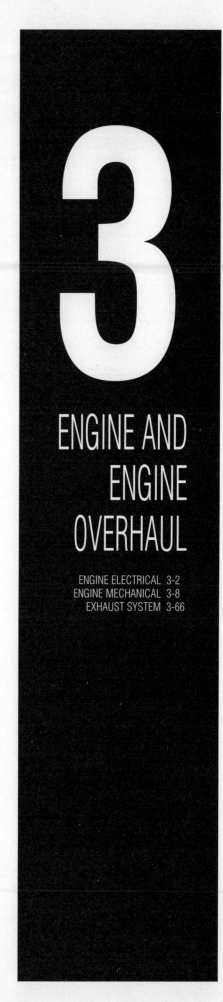

3

ENGINE AND ENGINE OVERHAUL

ENGINE ELECTRICAL

Battery

REMOVAL & INSTALLATION

From Engine Compartment

▶ **See Figure 1**

1. Disconnect the negative battery cable.
2. Disconnect the positive battery cable.
3. Loosen and remove the bolt which secures the battery bracket the vehicle.
4. Remove the battery by grasping at both sides and lifting out. Note the position and direction of the terminal posts for reinstallation.

To install:

5. Clean both the positive and negative battery terminal posts with a terminal cleaner.
6. Place the battery into the engine compartment with the posts positioned correctly.
7. Secure the battery into position by installing the battery bracket and securing with the bolt.

➡**Make sure that no hoses, vacuum lines or wires are caught between the battery or bracket when securing in place.**

8. Connect the positive terminal to the battery.
9. Connect the negative cable to the battery.
10. Apply a small amount of grease on and around the cable ends and battery posts to protect and prevent corrosion.

Under Rear Seat

▶ **See Figures 1 and 2**

1. Grasp the bottom of the lower seat cushion and lift up to release to clips securing the seat into position.

2. If equipped with a protective cover over the battery, remove and place aside.
3. Disconnect the negative battery cable.
4. Disconnect the positive battery cable.
5. Remove the overflow hose attached to the top of the battery, if equipped.
6. Loosen and remove the bolt which secures the battery bracket to the vehicle.
7. Remove the battery by grasping at both sides and lifting out. Note the position and direction of the terminal posts for reinstallation.

To install:

8. Clean both the positive and negative battery terminal posts with a terminal cleaner.
9. Place the battery into position with the posts positioned correctly.
10. Secure the battery into position by installing the battery bracket and securing with the bolt.

➡**Make sure that no hoses, vacuum lines or wires are caught between the battery or bracket when securing in place.**

11. Connect the positive terminal to the battery.
12. Connect the negative cable to the battery.
13. Apply a small amount of grease on and around the cable ends and battery posts to protect and prevent corrosion.
14. Install the overflow hose and protective cover, if equipped.
15. Install the rear sear cushion, making sure the clips lock into position.

Trunk Compartment

▶ **See Figures 2 thru 8**

1. Remove the plastic screws from right side trim panel cover.
2. Lift the plastic cover up and place aside.
3. Disconnect the negative battery cable.
4. Disconnect the positive battery cable.

Fig. 1 Use a terminal cleaner to clean each post of the battery

Fig. 2 There is a jumper block on the right side firewall to make jump starting easier

Fig. 3 Remove the plastic trim cover over the battery

Fig. 4 Disconnect the negative battery cable

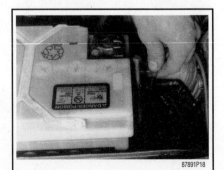

Fig. 5 Some batteries have an overflow hose attached to the top of the battery

Fig. 6 Remove the battery retaining bolt and bracket

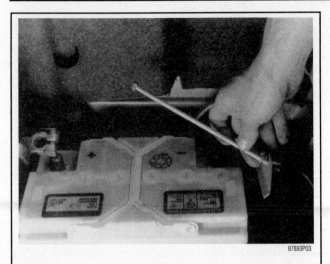

Fig. 7 Battery retaining bolt and bracket removed. Notice the length of the bolt

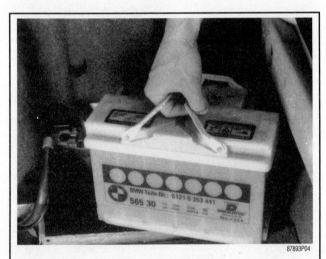

Fig. 8 Most batteries are removed by grasping the sides, but some have handles to make this easier

5. Unfasten the overflow hose attached to the top of the battery, if equipped.

6. Loosen and remove the bolt which secures the battery bracket the vehicle.

7. Remove the battery by grasping at both sides and lifting out. Note the position and direction of the terminal posts for reinstallation.

To install:

8. Clean both the positive and negative battery terminal posts with a terminal cleaner.

9. Place the battery into position with the posts positioned correctly.

10. Secure the battery into position by installing the battery bracket and securing with the bolt.

➡**Make sure that no hoses, vacuum lines or wires are caught between the battery or bracket when securing in place.**

11. Connect the positive terminal to the battery.

12. Connect the negative cable to the battery.

13. Apply a small amount of grease on and around the cable ends and battery posts to protect and prevent corrosion.

14: Attach the overflow hose to the top of the battery, if equipped.

15. Slide the trim cover over the battery and secure using the plastic screws.

Alternator

PRECAUTIONS

Several precautions must be observed with alternator equipped vehicles to avoid damaging the unit. They are as follows:

• If the battery is removed for any reason, make sure that it is reconnected with the correct polarity. Reversing the battery connections may result in damage to the one-way rectifiers.

• When utilizing a booster battery as a starting aid, always connect it as follows: positive to positive, and negative (booster battery) to a good ground on the engine of the car being started. Note that on the 1982 733i, the No. 5 fuse must be pulled out of the fuse panel before using a booster battery, or the inboard computer may be damaged.

• Never use a fast charger as a booster to start cars with alternating-current (AC) circuits.

• When servicing the battery with a fast charger, always disconnect the battery cables.

• Never attempt to polarize an alternator.

• Avoid long soldering times when replacing diodes or transistors. Prolonged heat is damaging to alternators.

• Do not use test lamps of more than 12 volts for checking diode continuity.

• Do not short across or ground any of the terminals on the alternator.

• The polarity of the battery, alternator, and regulator must be matched and considered before making any electrical connections within the system.

• Never operate the alternator on an open circuit. Make sure that all connections within the circuit are clean and tight.

• Turn **OFF** the ignition switch and then disconnect the battery terminals when performing any service on the electrical system or charging the battery.

• Disconnect the battery ground cable if arc welding is to be done on any part of the car.

CHARGING SYSTEM TROUBLESHOOTING

There are many possible ways in which the charging system can malfunction. Often the source of a problem is difficult to diagnose, requiring special equipment and a good deal of experience. This is usually not the case, however, where the charging system fails completely and causes the dash board warning light to come on or the battery to become dead. To troubleshoot a complete system failure only two pieces of equipment are needed: a test light, to determine that current is reaching a certain point; and a current indicator (ammeter), to determine the direction of the current flow and its measurement in amps.

This test works under three assumptions:

1. The battery is known to be good and fully charged.

2. The alternator belt is in good condition and adjusted to the proper tension.

3. All connections in the system are clean and tight.

➡**In order for the current indicator to give a valid reading, the car must be equipped with battery cables which are of the same gauge size and quality as original equipment battery cables.**

4. Turn **OFF** all electrical components in the car. Make sure the doors of the car are closed. If the car is equipped with a clock, disconnect the clock by removing the lead wire from the rear of the clock. Disconnect the positive battery cable from the battery and connect the ground wire on a test light to the disconnected positive battery cable. Touch the probe end of the test light to the positive battery post. The test light should not light. If the test light does light, there is a short or open circuit on the car.

5. Unfasten the voltage regulator wiring harness connector at the voltage regulator. Turn **ON** the ignition. Connect the wire on a test light to a good ground (engine bolt). Touch the probe end of a test light to the ignition wire connector into the voltage regulator wiring connector. This wire corresponds to the **I** terminal on the regulator. If the test light goes on, the charging system warning light circuit is complete. If the test light does not come on and the warning light on the instrument panel is on, either the resistor wire, which is parallel with the warning light, or the wiring to the voltage regulator, is defective. If the test light does not come on and the warning light is not on, either the bulb is defective or the power supply wire form the battery through the ignition switch to the bulb has an open circuit. Connect the wiring harness to the regulator.

6. Examine the fuse link wire in the wiring harness from the starter relay to the alternator. If the insulation on the wire is cracked or split, the fuse link may be melted. Connect a test light to the fuse link by attaching the ground wire on the test light to an engine bolt and touching the probe end of the light to the bottom of the fuse link wire where it splices into the alternator output wire. If the bulb in the test light does not light, the fuse link is melted.

7. Start the engine and place a current indicator on the positive battery cable. Turn off all electrical accessories and make sure the doors are closed. If the charging system is working properly, the gauge will show a draw of less than 5 amps. If the system is not working properly, the gauge will show a draw of more than 5 amps. A charge moves the needle toward the battery, a draw moves the needle away from the battery. Turn the engine **OFF**.

8. Disconnect the wiring harness from the voltage regulator at the regulator at the regulator connector. Connect a male spade terminal (solderless connector) to each end of a jumper wire. Insert one end of the wire into the wiring harness connector which corresponds to the **A** terminal on the regulator. Insert the other end of the wire into the wiring harness connector which corresponds to the **F** terminal on the regulator. Position the connector with the jumper wire installed so that it cannot contact any metal surface under the hood. Position a current indicator gauge on the positive battery cable. Have an assistant start the engine. Observe the reading on the current indicator. Have your assistant slowly raise the speed of the engine to about 2,000 rpm or until the current indicator needle stops moving, whichever comes first. Do not run the engine for more than a short period of time in this condition. If the wiring harness connector or jumper wire becomes excessively hot during this test, turn **OFF** the engine and check for a grounded wire in the regulator wiring harness. If the current indicator shows a charge of about three amps less than the output of the alternator, the alternator is working properly. If the previous tests showed a draw, the voltage regulator is defective. If the gauge does not show the proper charging rate, the alternator is defective.

REMOVAL & INSTALLATION

1970–81 Models

▶ See Figure 9

1. Disconnect the negative battery cable, then the positive battery cable. On some models, it may be necessary to remove the battery for alternator removal clearance.

2. Remove the stabilizer bar, if necessary on 2002Tii models.

3. Mark any individual electrical leads that could be installed to the wrong terminal during reinstallation. Then, pull off any multiple connectors, To disconnect individual leads, remove the rubber covers, then the attaching nuts, and pull the leads off.

4. Remove the bolt which runs in the slotted adjusting bar and loosen the mounting bolt. Slide the unit toward the engine, remove the adjusting bolt and the main mounting bolt and detach the alternator from the engine.

To install:

5. Locate the alternator in its normal position and install the main mounting bolt loosely.

6. Install the fan belt onto the alternator pulley. Position the sliding bracket appropriately and install the mounting bolt for that bracket. Finally, tension the fan belt.

7. Fasten all electrical connections.

8. Install the stabilizer bar and/or battery if removed. Reconnect the battery cable(s).

1982–88 Models

▶ See Figures 10, 11 and 12

1. Disconnect the negative battery cable followed by the positive cable.

2. Disconnect the wires from the rear of the alternator, marking them for later installation. Note that there is a ground wire attached to the alternator on some models.

3. Unscrew the nut and loosen the hose clamp around the airflow sensor. Unfasten the plug attached to the sensor. Then, lift out the air cleaner and airflow sensor as a unit.

4. Loosen the adjusting and pivot bolts, and remove the V-belt.

➡If the alternator has a star tensioning bolt, loosen the lockbolt, turn the tensioning bolt so as to eliminate belt tension and then remove the belt.

5. Remove the bolts and remove the alternator. On 633CSi, 635CSi, 733i and 735i models, it may be necessary to loosen the fan cowl to get at the mounting bolts. On 535i models, it may be necessary to disconnect a power steering line that runs near the alternator.

To install:

6. Position the alternator into position and install the mounting bolts. Install the nuts, and tighten by hand.

7. Install the necessary wires to the alternator. Do not forget to install the ground wire to the alternator body, if equipped.

8. Adjust the belt tension to approximately 0.4 inches (9mm), measured between the balancer and the alternator pulley.

9. On some 1984–88 models, a star bolt is used to adjust the belt tension. The tensioning bolt on the front of the alternator must be turned to tension the belt. Use a torque wrench, until the torque is approximately 5 ft. lbs. (6 Nm). Then, hold the star bolt with a wrench while tightening the locknut at the rear of the unit.

10. When the belt is tensioned to specification, tighten the remaining retainer bolts

11. Install the air cleaner and airflow sensor if removed. If the power steering line had to be disconnected, reconnect it securely, refill, and bleed the system.

12. Connect the negative battery cable followed by the positive.

Voltage Regulator

REMOVAL & INSTALLATION

Depending on the year of the vehicle and the model of alternator used, the voltage regulator will be either an internal type unit where it is attached to the alternator, or an external regulator, in which case it is mounted to the side of one of the fenders in the engine compartment.

Fig. 9 An alternator as installed on a 2002

Fig. 10 Loosen the bracket bolt from the engine block to the upper portion of the alternator

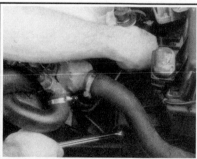

Fig. 11 On star bolts, after the locknut has been loosened, use two wrenches to remove the bolt

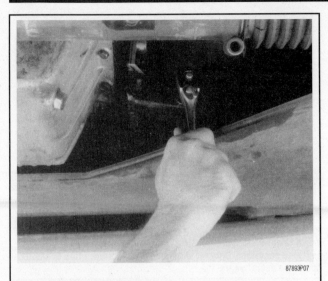

Fig. 12 Remove the bolt from the lower portion of the alternator

External Regulator

1. Disconnect the negative battery cable.
2. Disconnect the multiple connector from the bottom of the regulator.
3. Remove the retaining screws from the regulator.

➡**On some regulator installations, there are ground wires attached to the screws securing the regulator in place. When removing the screws, the ground wires will have to be tucked aside.**

4. Lift off the regulator. If you are replacing it with another unit, make sure that the color coding is the same. Regulators with yellow tape or paint contain no radio suppression circuitry, while units with white or green tape or paint contain radio suppression circuitry.

To install:

5. Position the regulator and install the retaining screws. If there were ground wires attached to one or more screws, do not forget to install them.
6. Connect the multiple connector.
7. Connect the negative battery cable.

VOLTAGE ADJUSTMENT

➡**The voltage regulators used on most BMW's are non-adjustable. This procedure applies to external voltage regulators installed on 4-cylinder models built through 1975.**

Tools required include a voltmeter, an ohmmeter, a tachometer, and test equipment which will permit you to isolate the battery and alternator from the rest of the vehicle's electrical system and a load rheostat to permit loading the system a set the correct voltage amount.

1. Install a battery post adapter on the positive post of the battery according to the manufacture specifications. Connect the voltmeter across the battery.

Hook up the tachometer using instructions provided with the unit. With all electrical accessories turned **OFF**, and the battery post adaptor switch closed, start the engine.

2. Open the post adapter switch.
3. Adjust the engine speed to 2500 rpm, and load the system with a ¼ ohm resistance. With the voltage reading stabilized, any figure between 13.5 and 14.8 volts is acceptable.
4. If the reading is not within this range, remove the regulator cover and adjust the armature spring tension until the voltmeter reads 14.0 volts.
5. Install the cover and disconnect any equipment used.

Integral Regulator

▶ **See Figures 13, 14 and 15**

On these models, the regulator and carbon brushes are an integral assembly, and the regulator cannot be adjusted.

1. Disconnect the negative battery cable.
2. Access the regulator assembly from the rear of the alternator.

➡**On these type models, the alternator does not have to be detached to remove and install a voltage regulator.**

3. Remove the mounting screws, one located at either end of the unit and slide out the regulator/brush assembly.

To install:

4. Position the regulator/brush assembly into position and secure with the retainer screws.

➡**During installation, make sure the brushes are located flat on the slip rings.**

5. Connect the negative battery cable.

Starter

REMOVAL & INSTALLATION

1970–82 Models

1. Disconnect the negative battery cable.
2. Disconnect the starter power cable at the solenoid by removing the nut and washer, and pulling the connection off the terminal.
3. On fuel injected 4-cylinder models, remove the intake cowl from the mixture control unit. On 6-cylinder fuel injected models, remove No. 6 intake tube.
4. Pull off the 2 solenoid connectors, tagging each as it is being removed.
5. On 4-cylinder models, disconnect the mounting bracket at the engine block by removing the 2 bolts.
6. On 528e models, remove the front Allen screw from the rear of the starter.
7. Remove the starter mounting bolts from the transmission and remove the unit.

Fig. 13 Remove the retaining screws from the rear of the voltage regulator

Fig. 14 Carefully lift the regulator out of the alternator

Fig. 15 Remove the regulator from the engine compartment

To install:

8. Position the starter into place and secure with the mounting bolts.

9. Install the terminal wires and main power cable and tighten. Before completing the procedure, check and make sure none of the wires are rubbing on any part of the engine or starter. This could cause the wire insulation to rub off and cause a short circuit.

10. Connect the negative battery cable.

1983–88 Models

♦ **See Figure 16**

1. Disconnect the negative battery cable.

2. On 6-cylinder models with 6 identical intake tubes, it may be necessary to remove the No. 6 intake tube for clearance. On 4-cylinder models, remove the intake cowl from the mixture control unit.

3. On 318i models, remove the wire holding bracket.

4. On 1983–87 325 models;

a. Remove the air cleaner with the airflow sensor.

b. Make sure the engine is cool and then drain the coolant into a clean container. Disconnect the heater hose that runs near the starter. Remove the coolant pipe if necessary for added clearance.

✳✳ CAUTION

When draining coolant, keep in mind that cats and dogs are attracted to ethylene glycol antifreeze, and could drink any that is left in an uncovered container or in puddles on the ground. This will prove fatal in sufficient quantity. Always drain the coolant into a sealable container. Coolant should be reused unless it is contaminated or several years old.

5. On the 1988 325 and the M3 models;

a. remove the air cleaner and airflow sensor. Then, remove the mounting bolts for the bracket for the air collector and remove it.

6. On the 528e models;

a. Remove the air cleaner and airflow sensor.

b. Disconnect and tag the electrical leads. Remove the bolts and remove the mounting bracket attached to the starter.

7. On the 533i and 535i models;

a. Make sure the engine is cool. Drain some coolant from the cooling system and then remove the expansion tank.

✳✳ CAUTION

When draining coolant, keep in mind that cats and dogs are attracted to ethylene glycol antifreeze, and could drink any that is left in an uncovered container or in puddles on the ground. This will prove fatal in sufficient quantity. Always drain the coolant into a sealable container. Coolant should be reused unless it is contaminated or several years old.

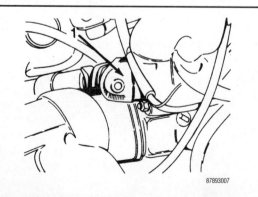

87893007

Fig. 16 On 318i models, remove the nut and bracket from the starter

8. On 633CSi and 635CSi models;

a. Make sure the engine is cool and drain some coolant out. Disconnect the heater hose that is near the starter.

b. Depress the brake pedal hard 20 times. Disconnect the power steering line that would otherwise prevent access to the starter.

c. Cut off the straps and remove the solenoid switch insulating cover.

9. On the M5 and M6 models;

a. Remove the exhaust manifold as described in this section.

b. Cut off the straps and remove the solenoid switch insulating cover.

10. Remove the starter solenoid wire leads, tagging them for later installation.

11. On 4-cylinder models, disconnect the mounting bracket at the block.

✳✳ CAUTION

When draining coolant, keep in mind that cats and dogs are attracted to ethylene glycol antifreeze, and could drink any that is left in an uncovered container or in puddles on the ground. This will prove fatal in sufficient quantity. Always drain the coolant into a sealable container. Coolant should be reused unless it is contaminated or several years old.

12. Remove the accelerator cable holder on automatic transmission equipped vehicles.

13. Unbolt and remove the starter from the engine. On the 325 models the lower nut can be removed more easily from underneath. On late model 5, 7 Series, M5 and M6 models, it may be necessary to use a box wrench with an angled handle to unscrew the main starter mounting bolts. On the 528e, 633CSi and 635CSi, the final mounting bolt must be removed from underneath. On the 1988 325 and the M3, the starter must be pulled out from above.

To install:

14. Install the starter into position and secure with the mounting bolts.

15. Attached any brackets and hoses removed earlier.

16. Connect all wires and secure tightly.

17. Refill and bleed the cooling system and power steering system if any fluid was removed.

18. Where the solenoid switch cover has been unstrapped, reinstall it using new straps.

19. Inspect all wires and make sure none will rub against the body or engine and create an electrical short circuit.

20. Connect the negative battery cable.

SOLENOID REPLACEMENT

➡**This procedure is best done with the starter removed from the vehicle.**

1. With the starter out of the car, disconnect the field coil connection located at the bottom of the solenoid assembly.

2. Unscrew the solenoid mounting screws from the front of the housing. Then, pull the solenoid unit upward to disengage the solenoid plunger from the shift lever, and pull the unit off the starter.

3. Install in the reverse order of removal.

Ignition Coil

REMOVAL & INSTALLATION

1. Disconnect the negative battery cable.

2. Tag each wire attached to the coil. once marked, remove the nuts securing the wires in place, or unplug each wire from the connection on the coil.

3. Disconnect the high tension wire from the coil.

4. Loosen the screw retaining the ignition coil in its bracket. Slide the coil from the bracket and remove it.

To install:

5. Slide the coil into position and tighten the bracket screw.

6. Connect the ignition lead wires and the high tension coil wire.

7. Connect the negative battery cable.

Distributor

REMOVAL & INSTALLATION

Timing Undisturbed

1970–83 4-CYLINDER ENGINES

▶ **See Figures 17 and 18**

➡**These distributors are vertically mounted at the rear of the engine.**

1. Prior to removal, use paint or chalk to scribe alignment marks showing the relative position of the distributor body to its mount on the cylinder head. Put marks on both the cylinder head and distributor body.

2. Mark each spark plug wire at the spark plug, with a dab of paint or chalk noting its respective cylinder position. Remove the plug wire from the spark plug. Continue this until all the spark plug wire are removed.

➡**It will be easier to install the distributor cap if you leave the plug wires attached in the cap.**

3. Disconnect the high tension cable leading front the coil to the center of the distributor cap.

4. If equipped, remove the spark plug loom retaining nut(s) from the cylinder head cover.

5. Tag then disconnect the vacuum line(s) from the vacuum capsule on the distributor.

6. Unsnap the distributor cap retaining clasps and lift off the cap and wire assembly.

7. With the aid of a remote starter switch or a friend, "bump" the starter a few times until the No. 1 piston is at Top Dead Center (TDC) of its compression stroke, If aligned correctly, the notch scribed on the metal tip of the distributor rotor will be aligned with a corresponding notch scribed on the distributor case. Before removing the distributor, make sure that these 2 marks are in correct alignment.

8. Loosen the clamp bolt at the base of the distributor and lift the distributor up and out. You will notice that the rotor turns clockwise as the distributor is removed.

To install:

9. Slide the distributor into position, rotating the rotor approximately 1.4 inches (35mm) counterclockwise from the notch scribed in the distributor body. This will ensure that when the distributor is fully seated in its mount, the rotor and distributor marks will coincide. When the scribe marks on the parts align as well as the painted/chalked marks also align, tighten the hold-down bolt by hand so the distributor will not move while installing the remaining parts.

10. Position the distributor cap and spark plug wires on the distributor body and secure the clips. If the clip will not engage, it most likely means the tab on the cap is not aligned correctly with the tab in the distributor. Remove and try again.

11. Connect each spark plug to its respective spark plug. If equipped with a loom or bracket for the spark plug wires on the cylinder head cover, secure using the retainer nuts removed earlier.

12. Connect the vacuum line(s) to the distributor.

13. Connect the high tension wire and battery negative cable.

14. Adjust the ignition timing as described in Section 2. Tighten the hold-down bolt to 8 ft. lbs. (10 Nm).

1970–83 6-CYLINDER ENGINES

▶ **See Figures 19 and 20**

1. Disconnect the negative battery cable.

2. Tag and remove the vacuum hoses for advance and retard from the distributor.

3. With chalk or paint, mark the relationship between the distributor body and the cylinder head. Paint/chalk marks on both the cylinder head and distributor body.

4. With the aid of a remote starter switch or a friend, "bump" the starter a few times until the No. 1 piston is at Top Dead Center (TDC) of its compression stroke, If aligned correctly, the notch scribed on the metal tip of the distributor rotor will be aligned with a corresponding notch scribed on the distributor case. Before removing the distributor, make sure that these 2 marks are correctly aligned. Also make sure that the TDC timing marks on the flywheel or balancer pulley are in line.

5. Loose the clamp bolt at the bottom of the distributor.

6. Unscrew the mounting bracket screw for the electrical connector on the distributor body, pull the mounting bracket off, and unplug the connector.

7. Pull the distributor out of the cylinder head.

To install:

8. Position the rotor 1.0–1.4 inches (25–38mm) counterclockwise from the notch in the distributor housing.

9. Position the distributor body into the cylinder head so the alignment marks you made in Step 1 are aligned.

10. When the distributor is fully seated, reconnect the electrical harness, vacuum lines and install the cap.

11. Connect the negative battery cable.

12. Adjust the ignition timing as described in Section 2.

1984–88 MODELS

Engines produced in model year 1984 and later are equipped with the Digital Motor Electronics (DME) control system. The distributor on these models is contained within the engine itself. Other than distributor cap and rotor removal and installation, no general service is possible.

Timing Disturbed

If the engine is accidentally turned while the distributor is removed, it will be necessary to find the TDC position for No. 1 cylinder before installing the distributor.

1. Remove the cylinder head cover by unfastening the retaining nuts. Depending on the model, certain brackets and hoses will also have to be removed.

2. With the cylinder head cover removed, and the valves clearly visible, rotate the engine crank by either placing the vehicle in gear (manual transmission equipped models only), and rocking the vehicle back and forth,

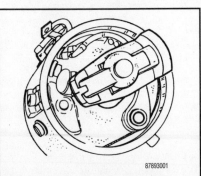

Fig. 17 Before removing the distributor, align the marks on the rotor with the marks on the distributor body

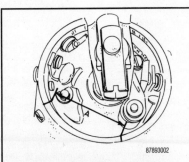

Fig. 18 Before installing the distributor into the hole, turn the rotor 1.4 inches (35mm) counterclockwise to properly align the gears during installation

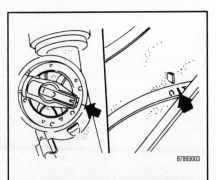

Fig. 19 Align the scribe marks on the rotor and distributor body, as well as the flywheel

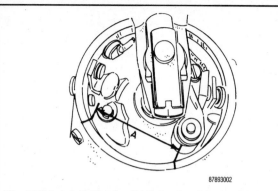

Fig. 20 Before installing the distributor, turn the rotor 1.0–1.5 inches (25–38mm) counterclockwise to properly align the gears

or rotating the crack with a socket and breaker bar attached to the nut on the crank pulley. Rotate the engine in the direction of normal rotation until the last cylinder's valves are open the same amount. For a 4-cylinder model, watch cylinder No. 4 valves, for a 6-cylinder model, watch cylinder No. 6.

3. When both valves are open the same amount, proceed to install the distributor.

ENGINE MECHANICAL

Engine Overhaul Tips

Most engine overhaul procedures are fairly standard. In addition to specific parts replacement procedures and complete specifications for your individual engine, this section also is a guide to engine rebuilding procedures. Examples of standard rebuilding practices are shown and should be used along with specific details concerning your particular engine.

Competent and accurate machine shop services will ensure maximum performance, reliability and engine life.

In most instances it is more profitable for the do-it-yourself mechanic to remove, clean and inspect the component, buy the necessary parts and deliver these to a shop for actual machine work.

TOOLS

The tools required for an engine overhaul or parts replacement will depend on the depth of your involvement. With a few exceptions, they will be the tools found in a mechanic's tool kit (see Section 1). More in-depth work will require any or all of the following:

- A dial indicator (reading in thousandths) mounted on a universal base
- Micrometers and telescope gauges
- Jaw and screw-type pullers
- Scraper
- Valve spring compressor
- Ring groove cleaner
- Piston ring expander and compressor
- Ridge reamer
- Cylinder hone or glaze breaker
- Plastigage®
- Engine stand

The use of most of these tools is illustrated in this section. Many can be rented for a one-time use from a local parts jobber or tool supply house specializing in automotive work.

Occasionally, the use of special tools is called for. See the information on Special Tools and Safety Notice in the front of this book before substituting another tool.

INSPECTION TECHNIQUES

Procedures and specifications are given in this section for inspecting, cleaning and assessing the wear limits of most major components. Other procedures such as Magnaflux® and Zyglo® can be used to locate material flaws and stress cracks. Magnaflux® is a magnetic process applicable only to ferrous materials. The Zyglo® process coats the material with a fluorescent dye penetrant and can be used on any material. Checks for suspected surface cracks can be more readily made using spot check dye. The dye is sprayed onto the suspected area, wiped off and area sprayed with a developer. Cracks will show up brightly.

OVERHAUL TIPS

Aluminum has become extremely popular for use in engines, due to its low weight. Observe the following precautions when handling aluminum parts:

Never hot tank aluminum parts (the caustic hot-tank solution will eat the aluminum).

Remove all aluminum parts (identification tag, etc.) from engine parts prior to hot-tanking.

Always coat threads lightly with engine oil or anti-seize compounds before installation, to prevent seizure.

Never over-tighten bolts or spark plugs, especially in aluminum threads. Stripped threads can usually be repaired using any of several commercial repair kits (Heli-Coil®, Microdot®, Keenserts®, etc.)

When assembling the engine, any parts that will be in frictional contact must be prelubed to provide lubrication at initial start-up.

When semi-permanent (locked, but removable) installation of bolts or nuts is desired, threads should be cleaned and coated with Loctite® or other similar, commercial non-hardening sealant.

To determine whether a particular engine or component is constructed of aluminium, use a magnet. If the magnet attaches to the item, it is not made of aluminium, but a metal with a high iron content. If the magnet does not attach to the item, it is most likely made of aluminium.

REPAIRING DAMAGED THREADS

▶ See Figures 21, 22, 23, 24 and 25

Several methods of repairing damaged threads are available. Heli-Coil®, Keenserts® and Microdot® are among the most widely used. All involve basically the same principle—drilling out the stripped threads, tapping the hole and installing a prewound insert—making welding, plugging and oversize fasteners unnecessary.

Two types of thread repair inserts are usually supplied: a standard type for most Inch Coarse, Inch Fine, Metric Coarse and Metric Fine thread sizes and a spark plug type to fit most spark plug port sizes. Consult the individual manufacturer's catalog to determine exact applications. Typical thread repair kits will contain a selection of prewound threaded inserts, a tap (corresponding to the outside diameter threads of the insert) and an installation tool. Spark plug inserts usually differ because they require a tap equipped with pilot threads and combined reamer/tap section. Most manufacturers also supply blister-packed thread repair inserts separately in addition to a master kit containing a variety of taps and inserts plus installation tools.

Before repairing a threaded hole, remove any snapped, broken or damaged bolts or studs. Penetrating oil can be used to free frozen threads; the offending item can be removed with locking pliers or with a screw or stud extractor. After the hole is clear, the thread can be repaired, as shown in the figures.

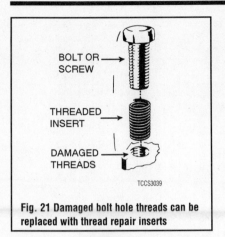

Fig. 21 Damaged bolt hole threads can be replaced with thread repair inserts

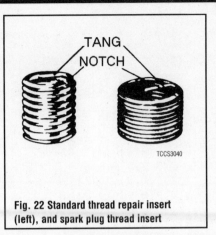

Fig. 22 Standard thread repair insert (left), and spark plug thread insert

Fig. 23 Drill out the damaged threads with the specified drill. Drill completely through the hole or to the bottom of a blind hole

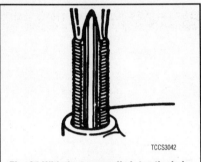

Fig. 24 With the tap supplied, tap the hole to receive the thread insert. Keep the tap well oiled and back it out frequently to avoid clogging the threads

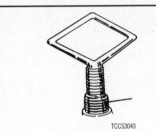

Fig. 25 Screw the threaded insert onto the installer tool until the tang engages the slot. Screw the insert into the tapped hole until it is ¼ or ½ turn below the top surface. After installation, break off the tang with a hammer and punch

Fig. 26 A screw-in type compression gauge is more accurate and easier to use

CHECKING ENGINE COMPRESSION

▶ **See Figure 26**

A noticeable lack of engine power, excessive oil consumption and/or poor fuel mileage measured over an extended period of time are all indicators of internal engine wear. Worn piston rings, scored or worn cylinder bores, blown head gaskets, sticking or burnt valves and worn valve seats are all possible culprits here. A check of each cylinder's compression will help you locate the problems.

As mentioned earlier, a screw-in type compression gauge is more accurate than the type you simply hold against the spark plug hole, although it takes slightly longer to use. It's worth it to obtain a more accurate reading. Check engine compression as follows:

1. Warm up the engine to normal operating temperature.
2. Remove all spark plugs.
3. Disconnect the high tension lead from the ignition coil.
4. Fully open the throttle either by operating the carburetor throttle linkage by hand or by having an assistant floor the accelerator pedal.
5. Screw the compression gauge into the No. 1 spark plug hole until the fitting is snug.

➡ **Be careful not to crossthread the plug hole. On aluminum cylinder heads use extra care, as the threads in these heads are easily ruined.**

6. Ask an assistant to depress the accelerator pedal fully on both carbureted and fuel injected models. Then, while you read the compression gauge, ask the assistant to crank the engine two or three times in short bursts.
7. Read the compression gauge at the end of each series of cranks, and record the highest of these readings. Repeat this procedure for each of the engine's cylinders. Compare the highest reading of each cylinder to the compression pressure specification in the Tune-Up Specifications chart in Section 2. The specs in this chart are maximum values.

A cylinder's compression pressure is usually acceptable if it is not less than 80% of maximum. The difference between each cylinder should be no more than 12–14 pounds.

8. If a cylinder is unusually low, pour a tablespoon of clean engine oil into the cylinder through the spark plug hole and repeat the compression test. If the compression comes up after adding the oil, it appears that the cylinder's piston rings or bore are damaged or worn. If the pressure remains low, the valves may not be seating properly (a valve job is needed), or the head gasket may be blown near that cylinder. If compression in any two adjacent cylinders is low, and if the addition of oil doesn't help the compression, there is leakage past the head gasket. Oil and coolant in the combustion chamber can result from this problem. There may be evidence of water droplets on the engine dipstick when a head gasket has blown.

General Engine Specifications

Year	Model	Engine Displacement cu. in. (cc)	Fuel System Type	Net Horsepower @ rpm	Net Torque @ rpm (ft. lbs.)	Bore x Stroke (in.)	Compression Ratio	Oil Pressure @ rpm
1970	1600	96 (1573)	Solex 38 PDSI	105 @ 5500	91 @ 3000	3.307 x 2.795	8.6:1	57 @ 4000
	2000,2002	121 (1990)	Solex 38 PDSI	113 @ 5800	116 @ 3000	3.504 x 3.130	8.5:1	57 @ 4000
	2500	152.1 (2493)	Zenith 35 INAT	170 @ 6000	176 @ 3700	3.386 x 2.820	9.0:1	71 @ 6400
	2800,CS Bavaria	170.1 (2788)	Zenith 35 INAT	192 @ 6000	174 @ 3700	3.386 x 3.150	9.0:1	71 @ 6400
1971	1600	96 (1573)	Solex 38 PDSI	105 @ 5500	91 @ 3000	3.307 x 2.795	8.6:1	57 @ 4000
	2000,2002	121 (1990)	Solex 38 PDSI	113 @ 5800	116 @ 3000	3.504 x 3.130	8.5:1	57 @ 4000
	2500	152.1 (2493)	Zenith 35 INAT	170 @ 6000	176 @ 3700	3.386 x 2.820	9.0:1	71 @ 6400
	2800,CS Bavaria	170.1 (2788)	Zenith 35 INAT	192 @ 6000	174 @ 3700	3.386 x 3.150	9.0:1	71 @ 6400
1972	2000,2002	121 (1990)	Solex 38 PDSI	113 @ 5800	116 @ 3000	3.504 x 3.130	8.5:1	57 @ 4000
	2002Tii	121 (1990)	Kugel Fisher Inj.	125 @ 5500	127 @ 4000	3.504 x 3.130	9.0:1	57 @ 4000
	2800,3000CS Bavaria	170.1 (2788)	Zenith 35 INAT	192 @ 6000	174 @ 3700	3.386 x 3.150	9.0:1	71 @ 6400
1973	2000,2002	121 (1990)	Solex 32 DIPTA	98 @ 5500	100 @ 3500	3.504 x 3.130	8.3:1	57 @ 4000
	2002Tii	121 (1990)	Kugel Fisher Inj.	125 @ 5500	127 @ 4000	3.504 x 3.130	9.0:1	57 @ 4000
	3.0	182 (2985)	Zenith 35 INAT	180 @ 6000	188 @ 3700	3.504 x 3.149	9.0:1	71 @ 6000
1974	2000,2002	121 (1990)	Solex 32 DIPTA	98 @ 5500	100 @ 3500	3.504 x 3.130	8.3:1	57 @ 4000
	2002Tii	121 (1990)	Kugel Fisher Inj.	125 @ 5500	127 @ 4000	3.504 x 3.130	9.0:1	57 @ 4000
	3.0	182 (2985)	Zenith 35 INAT	180 @ 6000	188 @ 3700	3.504 x 3.149	9.0:1	71 @ 6000
1975	2002,Tii	121 (1990)	Solex 32 DIPTA	98 @ 5500	100 @ 3500	3.504 x 3.149	8.3:1	57 @ 4000
	3.0	182 (2985)	EFI ①	200 @ 5500	200 @ 4000	3.504 x 3.150	9.0:1	71 @ 6000
	530i, 630CSi	182 (2985)	EFI ②	176 @ 5500	188 @ 4500	3.504 x 3.150	8.1:1	71 @ 6000
1976	2002,Tii	121 (1990)	Solex 32 DIPTA	98 @ 5500	100 @ 3500	3.504 x 3.130	8.3:1	57 @ 4000
	3.0	182 (2985)	EFI ①	200 @ 5500	200 @ 4000	3.504 x 3.149	9.0:1	71 @ 6000
	530i, 630CSi	182 (2985)	EFI ②	176 @ 5500	188 @ 4500	3.504 x 3.150	8.1:1	71 @ 6000
1977	320i	121 (1990)	EFI ②	110 @ 5800	112 @ 3750	3.504 x 3.150	8.2:1	57 @ 4000
	530i, 630CSi	182 (2985)	EFI ②	176 @ 5500	188 @ 4500	3.504 x 3.150	8.1:1	71 @ 6000
1978	320i	121 (1990)	EFI ②	110 @ 5800	112 @ 3750	3.504 x 3.150	8.2:1	57 @ 4000
	530i, 630CSi	182 (2985)	EFI ②	176 @ 5500	188 @ 4500	3.504 x 3.150	8.1:1	71 @ 6000
	633CSi, 733i	196 (3210)	EFI ③	176 @ 5500	192 @ 4000	3.504 x 3.386	8.0:1	71 @ 6000

General Engine Specifications (cont.)

Year	Model	Engine Displacement cu. in. (cc)	Fuel System Type	Net Horsepower @ rpm	Net Torque @ rpm (ft. lbs.)	Bore x Stroke (in.)	Compression Ratio	Oil Pressure @ rpm
1979	320i	121 (1990)	EFI ②	110 @ 5800	112 @ 3750	3.504 x 3.150	8.2:1	57 @ 4000
	528i	170.1 (2788)	EFI ③	169 @ 5500	166 @ 4500	3.386 x 3.150	8.2:1	71 @ 6000
	633CSi, 733i	196 (3210)	EFI ③	176 @ 5500	192 @ 4000	3.504 x 3.386	8.0:1	71 @ 6000
1980	320i	107 (1766)	EFI ②	101 @ 5800	100 @ 4500	3.504 x 2.793	8.8:1	57 @ 4000
	528i	170.1 (2788)	EFI ③	169 @ 5500	166 @ 4500	3.386 x 3.150	8.2:1	71 @ 6000
	633CSi, 733i	196 (3210)	EFI ③	174 @ 5200	184 @ 4200	3.504 x 3.386	8.0:1	71 @ 6000
1981	320i	107 (1766)	EFI ②	101 @ 5800	100 @ 4500	3.504 x 2.793	8.8:1	57 @ 4000
	528i	170.1 (2788)	EFI ③	169 @ 5500	166 @ 4500	3.386 x 3.150	8.2:1	71 @ 6000
	633CSi, 733i	196 (3210)	EFI ③	174 @ 5200	184 @ 4200	3.504 x 3.386	8.0:1	71 @ 6000
1982	320i	108 (1766)	EFI ②	101 @ 5800	100 @ 4500	3.504 x 2.793	8.8:1	57 @ 4000
	325e	165 (2693)	EFI ④	121 @ 4250	170 @ 3250	3.307 x 3.189	9.0:1	71 @ 5000
	528e	165 (2693)	EFI ④	121 @ 4250	170 @ 3250	3.307 x 3.189	9.0:1	71 @ 5000
	533i	196 (3210)	EFI ④	181 @ 6000	195 @ 4000	3.504 x 3.386	8.8:1	64 @ 4000
	633CSi	196 (3210)	EFI ④	181 @ 6000	195 @ 4000	3.504 x 3.386	8.8:1	64 @ 4000
	733i	196 (3210)	EFI ④	181 @ 6000	195 @ 4000	3.504 x 3.386	8.8:1	64 @ 4000
1983	320i	108 (1766)	EFI ④	101 @ 5800	100 @ 4500	3.504 x 2.793	8.8:1	57 @ 4000
	325e	165 (2693)	EFI ④	121 @ 4250	170 @ 3250	3.307 x 3.189	9.0:1	71 @ 5000
	528e	165 (2693)	EFI ④	121 @ 4250	170 @ 3250	3.307 x 3.189	9.0:1	71 @ 5000
	533i	196 (3210)	EFI ④	181 @ 6000	195 @ 4000	3.504 x 3.386	8.8:1	64 @ 6000
	633CSi	196 (3210)	EFI ④	181 @ 6000	195 @ 4000	3.504 x 3.386	8.8:1	64 @ 6000
	733i	196 (3210)	EFI ④	181 @ 6000	195 @ 4000	3.504 x 3.386	8.8:1	64 @ 6000
1984	318i	108 (1766)	EFI ④	101 @ 5800	103 @ 4500	3.504 x 2.793	9.0:1	64 @ 4000
	325e	165 (2693)	EFI ④	121 @ 4250	170 @ 3250	3.307 x 3.189	9.0:1	71 @ 5000
	528e	165 (2693)	EFI ④	121 @ 4250	170 @ 3250	3.307 x 3.189	9.0:1	71 @ 5000
	533i	196 (3210)	EFI ④	181 @ 6000	195 @ 4000	3.504 x 3.386	8.8:1	64 @ 6000
	633CSi	196 (3210)	EFI ④	181 @ 6000	195 @ 4000	3.504 x 3.386	8.8:1	64 @ 6000
	733i	196 (3210)	EFI ④	181 @ 6000	195 @ 4000	3.504 x 3.386	8.8:1	64 @ 6000
1985	318i	103 (1766)	EFI ④	101 @ 5800	103 @ 4500	3.504 x 2.793	9.0:1	64 @ 4000
	325e	165 (2693)	EFI ④	121 @ 4250	170 @ 3250	3.307 x 3.189	9.0:1	71 @ 5000
	528e	165 (2693)	EFI ④	121 @ 4250	170 @ 3250	3.307 x 3.189	9.0:1	71 @ 5000
	524td	149 (2443)	DFI	114 @ 4800	155 @ 2400	3.15 x 3.19	22:1	71 @ 6000
	533i	196 (3210)	EFI ④	181 @ 6000	195 @ 4000	3.504 x 3.386	8.8:1	64 @ 6000
	633CSi	196 (3210)	EFI ④	181 @ 6000	195 @ 4000	3.504 x 3.386	8.8:1	64 @ 6000
	733i	196 (3210)	EFI ④	181 @ 6000	195 @ 4000	3.504 x 3.386	8.8:1	64 @ 6000
1986	535i	209 (3428)	EFI ④	182 @ 5400	213 @ 4000	3.62 x 3.38	8.0:1	71 @ 6000
	635CSi	209 (3428)	EFI ④	182 @ 5400	213 @ 4000	3.62 x 3.38	8.0:1	71 @ 6000
	735i	209 (3428)	EFI ④	182 @ 5400	213 @ 4000	3.62 x 3.38	8.0:1	71 @ 6000
	325e	165 (2693)	EFI ④	121 @ 4250	170 @ 3250	3.307 x 3.189	9.0:1	71 @ 5000
	528e	165 (2693)	EFI ④	121 @ 4250	170 @ 3250	3.307 x 3.189	9.0:1	71 @ 5000
	524td	149 (2443)	DFI	114 @ 4800	155 @ 2400	3.15 x 3.19	22:1	71 @ 6000

87893C05

87893C04

Valve Specifications

Year	Engine Displacement cu. in. (cc)	Seat Angle (deg.)	Face Angle (deg.)	Spring Test Pressure (lbs.)	Spring Installed Height (in.)	Stem-to-Guide Clearance (in.) Intake	Exhaust	Stem Diameter (in.) Intake	Exhaust
1970–72	96 (1573)	45	45.5	64 @ 1.48	1.171 (1)	0.0010–0.0020	0.0015–0.0030	0.3149	0.3149
	121 (1990)	45	45.5	64 @ 1.48	1.171 (1)	0.0010–0.0020	0.0015–0.0030	0.3149	0.3149
	152.1 (2493)	45	45.5	64 @ 1.48	1.171 (1)	0.0010–0.0020	0.0015–0.0030	0.3149	0.3149
	170.1 (2788)	45	45.5	64 @ 1.48	1.171 (1)	0.0010–0.0020	0.0015–0.0030	0.3149	0.3149
1973–76	121 (1990)	45	45.5	64 @ 1.48	1.171 (1)	0.0010–0.0020	0.0015–0.0030	0.3149	0.3149
	170.1 (2788)	45	45.5	64 @ 1.48	1.171 (1)	0.0010–0.0020	0.0015–0.0030	0.3149	0.3149
	182 (2985)	45	45.5	64 @ 1.48	1.171 (1)	0.0010–0.0020	0.0015–0.0030	0.3149	0.3149
1977–81	121 (1990)	45	45.5	64 @ 1.48	1.171 (1)	0.0010–0.0020	0.0015–0.0030	0.3149	0.3149
	107 (1766)	45	45.5	64 @ 1.48	1.171 (1)	0.0010–0.0020	0.0015–0.0030	0.3149	0.3149
	182 (2985)	45	45.5	64 @ 1.48	1.171 (1)	0.0010–0.0020	0.0015–0.0030	0.3149	0.3149
	170.1 (2788)	45	45.5	64 @ 1.48	1.171 (1)	0.0010–0.0020	0.0015–0.0030	0.3149	0.3149
	196 (3210)	45	45.5	64 @ 1.48	1.171 (1)	0.0010–0.0020	0.0015–0.0030	0.3149	0.3149
1982	108 (1766)	45	45.5	64 @ 1.48	1.171 (1)	0.0010–0.0020 (2)	0.0010–0.0020 (2)	0.3149	0.3149
1983	108 (1766)	45	45.5	64 @ 1.48	1.71 (1)	0.0010–0.0020	0.0010–0.0020	0.3149	0.3149
1984	165 (2693)	45	45	NA	NA	0.031 (3)	0.031 (3)	0.3149	0.3149
	196 (3210)	45	45.5	64 @ 1.48	1.71 (1)	0.031 (3)	0.031 (3)	0.3149	0.3149
	108 (1766)	45	45.5	64 @ 1.48	1.71 (1)	0.031 (3)	0.031 (3)	0.275	0.275
	165 (2693)	45	45	NA	NA	0.031 (3)	0.031 (3)	0.3149	0.3149
1985	196 (3210)	45	45.5	64 @ 1.48	1.71 (1)	0.031 (3)	0.031 (3)	0.3149	0.3149
	108 (1766)	45	45.5	64 @ 1.48	1.71 (1)	0.031 (3)	0.031 (3)	0.3149	0.3149
	149 (2443)	45	NA	NA	NA	0.031 (3)	0.031 (3)	0.275	0.275
	165 (2693)	45	45	NA	NA	0.031 (3)	0.031 (3)	0.275	0.275
1986	209 (3428)	45	45.5	64 @ 1.48	1.71 (1)	0.031 (3)	0.031 (3)	0.3149	0.3149
	149 (2443)	45	NA	NA	NA	0.031 (3)	0.031 (3)	0.275	0.275
	165 (2693)	45	45	NA	NA	0.031 (3)	0.031 (3)	0.275	0.275
	209 (3428)	45	45.5	64 @ 1.48	1.71 (1)	0.031 (3)	0.031 (3)	0.3149	0.3149

87893C07

General Engine Specifications (cont.)

Year	Model	Engine Displacement cu. in. (cc)	Fuel System Type	Net Horsepower @ rpm	Net Torque @ rpm (ft. lbs.)	Bore x Stroke (in.)	Compression Ratio	Oil Pressure @ rpm
1986	535i	209 (3428)	EFI (4)	182 @ 5400	213 @ 4000	3.62 x 3.38	8.0:1	71 @ 6000
	635CSi	209 (3428)	EFI (4)	182 @ 5400	213 @ 4000	3.62 x 3.38	8.0:1	71 @ 6000
	735i	209 (3428)	EFI (4)	182 @ 5400	213 @ 4000	3.62 x 3.38	8.0:1	71 @ 6000
1987	325	165 (2693)	EFI (4)	121 @ 4250	170 @ 3250	3.307 x 3.189	9.0:1	71 @ 5000
	528e	165 (2693)	EFI (4)	121 @ 4250	170 @ 3250	3.307 x 3.189	9.0:1	71 @ 5000
	325iS	152 (2494)	EFI (4)	167 @ 5800	164 @ 4300	3.307 x 2.953	8.8:1	71 @ 5000
	325iS	152 (2494)	EFI (4)	167 @ 5800	164 @ 4300	3.307 x 2.953	8.8:1	71 @ 5000
	535i	209 (3428)	EFI (4)	182 @ 5400	213 @ 4000	3.62 x 3.38	8.0:1	71 @ 6000
	635CSi	209 (3428)	EFI (4)	208 @ 5700	225 @ 4000	3.62 x 3.38	9.0:1	64 @ 6200
	735i	209 (3428)	EFI (4)	208 @ 5700	225 @ 4000	3.62 x 3.38	9.0:1	64 @ 6200
	M5	210.6 (3453)	EFI (4)	256 @ 6500	239 @ 4500	3.67 x 3.30	9.8:1	71 @ 6900
	M6	210.6 (3453)	EFI (4)	256 @ 6500	239 @ 4500	3.67 x 3.30	9.8:1	71 @ 6900
1988	325	165 (2693)	EFI (4)	121 @ 4250	170 @ 3250	3.307 x 3.189	9.0:1	71 @ 5000
	528e	165 (2693)	EFI (4)	121 @ 4250	170 @ 3250	3.307 x 3.189	9.0:1	71 @ 5000
	325i	152 (2494)	EFI (4)	167 @ 5800	164 @ 4300	3.307 x 2.953	8.8:1	71 @ 6000
	325iS	152 (2494)	EFI (4)	167 @ 5800	164 @ 4300	3.307 x 2.953	8.8:1	71 @ 6000
	325iX	152 (2494)	EFI (4)	167 @ 5800	164 @ 4300	3.307 x 2.953	8.8:1	71 @ 6000
	535i	209 (3428)	EFI (4)	182 @ 5400	213 @ 4000	3.62 x 3.38	8.0:1	71 @ 6000
	635CSi	209 (3428)	EFI (4)	208 @ 5700	225 @ 4000	3.62 x 3.38	9.0:1	64 @ 6200
	L6	209 (3428)	EFI (4)	208 @ 5700	225 @ 4000	3.62 x 3.38	9.0:1	64 @ 6200
	735i	209 (3428)	EFI (4)	208 @ 5700	225 @ 4000	3.62 x 3.38	9.0:1	64 @ 6200
	M3	104.4 (2302)	EFI (4)	194 @ 6750	166 @ 4750	3.67 x 3.30	10.5:1	71 @ 7250
	M5	210.6 (3453)	EFI (4)	256 @ 6500	239 @ 4500	3.67 x 3.30	9.8:1	71 @ 6800
	M6	210.6 (3453)	EFI (4)	256 @ 6500	239 @ 4500	3.67 x 3.30	9.8:1	71 @ 6800

EFI Electronic Fuel Injection
DFI Diesel Fuel Injection
(1) EFI—Bosch Electronic Injection
(2) EFI—Bosch K-Jetronic Fuel Injection
(3) EFI—Bosch L-Jetronic Fuel Injection
(4) EFI—Bosch Motronic Injection

87893C06

Crankshaft and Connecting Rod Specifications

All measurements are given in inches.

Year	Engine Displacement cu. in. (cc)	Crankshaft				Connecting Rod		
		Main Brg. Journal Dia.	Main Brg. Oil Clearance	Shaft End-play	Thrust on No.	Journal Diameter	Oil Clearance	Side Clearance
1970–72	96 (1573)	2.3622③	0.0012–0.0027	0.003–0.007	④	1.8898	0.0009–0.0027	0.0016
	121 (1990)	2.3622③	0.0012–0.0027	0.003–0.007	④	1.8898	0.0009–0.0027	0.0016
	152.1 (2493)	2.3622③	0.0012–0.0027	0.003–0.007	④	1.8898	0.0013–0.0027	0.0016
	170.1 (2788)	2.3622③	0.0012–0.0027	0.003–0.07	④	1.8898	0.0013–0.0027	0.0016
1973–76	121 (1990)	2.3622③	0.0012–0.0027	0.003–0.007	④	1.8898	0.0009–0.0031	0.0016
	170.1 (2788)	2.3622③	0.0012–0.0027	0.003–0.007	④	1.8898	0.0013–0.0027	0.0016
	182 (2985)	2.3622③	0.0012–0.0077	0.003–0.007	④	1.8898	0.0013–0.0027	0.0016
1977–81	121 (1990)	2.3622③	0.0012–0.0027	0.003–0.007	④	1.8898	0.0009–0.0027	0.0016
	107 (1766)	2.3622③	0.0012–0.0027	0.003–0.007	④	1.8898	0.0009–0.0031	0.0016
	182 (2985)	2.3622③	0.0012–0.0027	0.003–0.007	④	1.8898	0.0013–0.0027	0.0016
	170.1 (2788)	2.3622③	0.0012–0.0027	0.003–0.007	④	1.8898	0.0009–0.0027	0.0016
	196 (3210)	2.3622③	0.0012–0.0027	0.003–0.007	④	1.8898	0.0009–0.0031	0.0016
1982	108 (1766)	2.3622	0.0012–0.0027	0.003–0.007	3	1.8898	①	0.0016
	165 (2693)	2.3622	0.0012–0.0027	0.003–0.007	4	1.8898	①	0.0016
	196 (3210)	2.3622	0.0012–0.0027	0.003–0.007	4	1.8898	①	0.0016
1983	108 (1766)	2.3622	0.0012–0.0027	0.003–0.007	3	1.8898	0.0012–0.0028	0.0016
	165 (2693)	2.3622	0.0012–0.0027	0.003–0.007	4	1.7717	0.0012–0.0028	0.0016

87893C08

Valve Specifications (cont.)

Year	Engine Displacement cu. in. (cc)	Seat Angle (deg.)	Face Angle (deg.)	Spring Test Pressure (lbs.)	Spring Installed Height (in.)	Stem-to-Guide Clearance (in.)		Stem Diameter (in.)	
						Intake	Exhaust	Intake	Exhaust
1987	152 (2494)	45	45.5	64 @ 1.48	1.71①	0.031③	0.031③	0.3149	0.3149
	165 (2693)	45	45	NA	NA	0.031③	0.031③	0.275	0.275
	209 (3428)	45	45.5	64 @ 1.48	1.71①	0.031③	0.031③	0.3149	0.3149
	210.6 (3453)	45	NA	NA	NA	0.025③	0.031③	0.276	0.276
1988	140.4 (2302)	45	NA	NA	NA	0.025③	0.031③	0.276	0.276
	152 (2494)	45	NA	NA	NA	0.025③	0.031③	0.276	0.276
	165 (2693)	45	NA	NA	NA	0.031③	0.031③	0.275	0.275
	209 (3428)	45	NA	NA	NA	0.031③	0.031③	0.275	0.275
	210.6 (3453)	45	NA	NA	NA	0.025③	0.031③	0.276	0.276

① A dimension of 1.8110 applies to some springs, depending upon manufacturer. Figure given is free height
② Wear limit: .006 in.
③ Tilt clearance

87893C09

Piston and Ring Specifications

All measurements are given in inches.

Year	Engine Displacement cu. in. (cc)	Piston Clearance	Ring Gap Top Compression	Ring Gap Bottom Compression	Ring Gap Oil Control	Ring Side Clearance Top Compression	Ring Side Clearance Bottom Compression	Ring Side Clearance Oil Control
1970	96 (1573)	0.0018	0.008-0.020	0.008-0.016	0.010-0.016	0.002-0.003	0.001-0.002	0.001-0.002
	121 (1990)	0.0018	0.012-0.018	0.008-0.016	0.010-0.020	0.002-0.004	0.002-0.003	0.001-0.002
	152.1 (2493)	0.0016	0.012-0.018	0.012-0.018	0.010-0.016	0.0006-0.0011	0.0005-0.0009	0.0004-0.001
	170.1 (2788)	0.0016	0.012-0.018	0.012-0.018	0.010-0.016	0.0006-0.0011	0.0005-0.0009	0.0004-0.001
1971	96 (1573)	0.0018	0.008-0.020	0.008-0.016	0.010-0.016	0.002-0.003	0.001-0.002	0.001-0.002
	121 (1990)	0.0018	0.012-0.018	0.008-0.016	0.010-0.020	0.002-0.004	0.002-0.003	0.001-0.002
	152.1 (2493)	0.0016	0.012-0.018	0.012-0.018	0.010-0.016	0.0006-0.0011	0.0005-0.0009	0.0004-0.001
	170.1 (2788)	0.0016	0.012-0.018	0.012-0.018	0.010-0.016	0.0006-0.0011	0.0005-0.0009	0.0004-0.001
1972	121 (1990)	0.0018	0.012-0.018	0.008-0.016	0.010-0.020	0.002-0.004	0.002-0.003	0.001-0.002
	170.1 (2788)	0.0016	0.012-0.018	0.012-0.018	0.010-0.016	0.0006-0.0011	0.0005-0.0009	0.0004-0.001
1973	121 (1990)	0.0018	0.012-0.018	0.008-0.016	0.010-0.020	0.002-0.004	0.002-0.003	0.001-0.002
	152.1 (2493)	0.0016	0.012-0.018	0.012-0.018	0.010-0.016	0.0006-0.0011	0.0005-0.0009	0.0004-0.001
	170.1 (2788)	0.0016	0.012-0.018	0.012-0.018	0.010-0.016	0.0006-0.0011	0.0005-0.0009	0.0004-0.001
1974	121 (1990)	0.0018	0.012-0.018	0.008-0.016	0.010-0.020	0.002-0.004	0.002-0.003	0.001-0.002
	170.1 (2788)	0.0016	0.012-0.018	0.012-0.018	0.010-0.016	0.0006-0.0011	0.0005-0.0009	0.0004-0.001
	182 (2985)	0.0016	0.012-0.018	0.008-0.016	0.010-0.016	0.0024-0.0036	0.0012-0.0024	0.001-0.002
1975	121 (1990)	0.0018	0.012-0.018	0.008-0.016	0.010-0.020	0.002-0.004	0.002-0.003	0.001-0.002
	182 (2985)	0.0016	0.012-0.018	0.008-0.016	0.010-0.016	0.0024-0.0036	0.0012-0.0024	0.001-0.002
1976	121 (1990)	0.0018	0.012-0.018	0.008-0.016	0.010-0.020	0.002-0.004	0.002-0.003	0.001-0.002
	182 (2985)	0.0016	0.012-0.018	0.008-0.016	0.010-0.016	0.0024-0.0036	0.0012-0.0024	0.001-0.002
1977	121 (1990)	0.0018	0.012-0.018	0.008-0.016	0.010-0.020	0.002-0.004	0.002-0.003	0.001-0.002
	182 (2985)	0.0016	0.012-0.018	0.008-0.016	0.010-0.016	0.0024-0.0036	0.0012-0.0024	0.001-0.002
1978	121 (1990)	0.0018	0.012-0.018	0.008-0.016	0.010-0.020	0.0024-0.0036	0.002-0.003	0.001-0.002
	182 (2985)	0.0016	0.012-0.018	0.008-0.018	0.010-0.016	0.0024-0.0036	0.0012-0.0024	0.001-0.002

87893C11

Crankshaft and Connecting Rod Specifications (cont.)

All measurements are given in inches.

Year	Engine Displacement cu. in. (cc)	Main Brg. Journal Dia.	Crankshaft Main Brg. Oil Clearance	Crankshaft Shaft End-play	Crankshaft Thrust on No.	Connecting Rod Journal Diameter	Connecting Rod Oil Clearance	Connecting Rod Side Clearance
1983	196 (3210)	2.3622	0.0012-0.0027	0.003-0.007	4	1.8898	0.0012-0.0028	0.0016
1984	108 (1766)	2.1654	0.0012-0.0027	0.003-0.007	3	1.8898	0.0012-0.0028	0.0016
	165 (2693)	2.3622	0.0012-0.0027	0.003-0.007	4	1.7717	0.0012-0.0028	0.0016
	196 (3210)	2.3622	0.0012-0.0027	0.003-0.007	4	1.8898	0.0012-0.0028	0.0016
1985	108 (1766)	2.1654	0.0012-0.0027	0.003-0.007	3	1.8898	0.0012-0.0028	0.0016
	149 (2443)	②	0.0008-0.0018	0.0031-0.0064	4	1.7707-1.7713	0.0008-0.0022	—
	165 (2693)	2.3622	0.0012-0.0027	0.003-0.007	4	1.7717	0.0012-0.0028	0.0016
	209 (3428)	2.3622	0.0012-0.0027	0.003-0.007	4	1.8898	0.0012-0.0028	0.0016
1986	149 (2443)	②	0.0008-0.0018	0.0031-0.0064	4	1.7707-1.7713	0.0008-0.0022	0.0016
	165 (2693)	2.3622	0.0012-0.0027	0.003-0.007	4	1.7717	0.0012-0.0028	0.0016
	209 (3428)	2.3622	0.0012-0.0027	0.003-0.007	4	1.8898	0.0012-0.0028	0.0016
	210.6 (3453)	2.3622	0.0012-0.0027	0.003-0.007	4	1.88877-1.88940	0.0012-0.0028	0.0016
1987	152 (2494)	2.1653	0.0012-0.0028	0.030-0.007	4	1.7717	0.0012-0.0028	0.0016
	165 (2693)	2.3622	0.0012-0.0027	0.003-0.007	4	1.7717	0.0012-0.0028	0.0016
	209 (3428)	2.3622	0.0012-0.0027	0.003-0.007	4	1.8898	0.0012-0.0028	0.0016
	210.6 (3453)	2.3622	0.0012-0.0027	0.003-0.007	4	1.88877-1.88940	0.0012-0.0028	0.0016
1988	140.4 (2302)	2.1653	0.0012-0.0028	0.0033-0.0068	3	1.88877-1.88940	0.0012-0.0028	0.0016
	152 (2494)	2.3622	0.0012-0.0027	0.0033-0.0068	4	1.7717	0.0012-0.0028	0.0016
	165 (2693)	2.3622	0.0012-0.0027	0.0033-0.0068	4	1.7717	0.0012-0.0028	0.0016
	209 (3428)	2.3622	0.0012-0.0027	0.0033-0.0068	4	1.8898	0.0012-0.0028	0.0016
	210.6 (3453)	2.3622	0.0012-0.0027	0.0033-0.0068	4	1.88877-1.88940	0.0012-0.0028	0.0016

NOTE: BMW does not specify side clearance. The figure given expresses maximum permissible deviation from parallel of connecting rod bearing bores, with the shells 150mm or 5.905 in. apart
① 528i, 530i, 533i, 630CSi—0.0009-0.0027
320i, 733i—0.0009-0.0031
528e—0.0013-0.0027
Yellow—2.3616-2.3618
Green—2.3613-2.3615

② White—2.3611-2.3613
③ 1970-76 four cylinder models: 2.1654
④ Four cylinder models: 3
Six cylinder models: 4

87893C10

Piston and Ring Specifications (cont.)

All measurements are given in inches.

Year	Engine Displacement cu. in. (cc)	Piston Clearance	Ring Gap Top Compression	Ring Gap Bottom Compression	Ring Gap Oil Control	Ring Side Clearance Top Compression	Ring Side Clearance Bottom Compression	Ring Side Clearance Oil Control
1986	165 (2693)	0.0004–0.0016	0.0120–0.0200	0.0120–0.0200	0.0100–0.0200	0.0016–0.0028	0.0012–0.0024	0.0008–0.0017
	209 (3428)	0.0008–0.0020	0.0120–0.0020	0.0080–0.0160	0.0100–0.0200	0.020–0.032	0.0016–0.0028	0.0008–0.0020
1987	152 (2494)	0.0004–0.0016	0.0120–0.0200	0.0120–0.0200	0.0100–0.0200	0.0016–0.0028	0.0012–0.0024	0.0008–0.0017
	165 (2693)	0.0004–0.0016	0.0120–0.0200	0.0120–0.0200	0.0100–0.0200	0.0016–0.0028	0.0012–0.0024	0.0008–0.0017
	209 (3428)	0.0008–0.0020	0.0120–0.0200	0.0080–0.0160	0.0100–0.0200	0.020–0.032	0.0016–0.0028	0.0008–0.0020
	210.6 (3453)	0.0012–0.0024	0.0120–0.0220	0.0120–0.0220	0.0100–0.0200	0.0024–0.0035	0.0024–0.0035	0.0008–0.0020
1988	140 (2302)	0.0012–0.0024	0.0120–0.0220	0.0120–0.0220	0.0100–0.0200	0.0024–0.0035	0.0024–0.0035	0.0008–0.0020
	152 (2494)	0.0004–0.0016	0.0120–0.0200	0.0120–0.0200	0.0100–0.0200	0.0016–0.0028	0.0012–0.0024	0.0008–0.0017
	165 (2693)	0.0004–0.0016	0.0120–0.0200	0.0120–0.0200	0.0100–0.0200	0.0016–0.0028	0.0012–0.0024	0.0008–0.0017
	209 (3428) ③	0.0008–0.0020	0.0120–0.0200	0.0080–0.0160	0.0100–0.0200	0.020–0.032	0.0016–0.0028	0.0008–0.0020
	209 (3428) ④	0.0008–0.0020	0.008–0.018	0.016–0.026	0.016–0.024	0.0016–0.0028	0.0012–0.0024	0.0008–0.0022
	210.6 (3453)	0.0012–0.0024	0.0120–0.0220	0.0120–0.0220	0.0100–0.0200	0.0024–0.0035	0.0024–0.0035	0.0008–0.0020

① Mahle: .0008–.0020
KS: .0012–.0024
② Mahle: .0020–.0032
KS: .0016–.0028
③ B34 used in 535i
④ B35 used in 6 and 7 series cars

87893C13

Piston and Ring Specifications (cont.)

All measurements are given in inches.

Year	Engine Displacement cu. in. (cc)	Piston Clearance	Ring Gap Top Compression	Ring Gap Bottom Compression	Ring Gap Oil Control	Ring Side Clearance Top Compression	Ring Side Clearance Bottom Compression	Ring Side Clearance Oil Control
1978	196 (3210)	0.0018	0.012–0.020	0.008–0.016	0.010–0.016	0.0024–0.0036	0.0012–0.0024	0.0008–0.0028
1979	121 (1990)	0.0018	0.012–0.018	0.008–0.016	0.010–0.020	0.002–0.004	0.002–0.003	0.001–0.002
	170.1 (2788)	0.0016	0.012–0.018	0.012–0.018	0.010–0.016	0.0006–0.0011	0.0005–0.0009	0.0004–0.001
	196 (3210)	0.0018	0.012–0.020	0.008–0.016	0.010–0.016	0.0024–0.0036	0.0012–0.0024	0.0008–0.0020
1980	107 (1766)	0.0018	0.012–0.018	0.008–0.016	0.010–0.020	0.002–0.008	0.002–0.003	0.001–0.002
	170.1 (2788)	0.0016	0.012–0.018	0.012–0.018	0.010–0.016	0.0006–0.0011	0.0005–0.0009	0.0004–0.001
	196 (3210)	0.0018	0.012–0.020	0.008–0.016	0.010–0.016	0.0024–0.0036	0.0012–0.0024	0.0008–0.0020
1981	107 (1766)	0.0018	0.012–0.018	0.008–0.016	0.010–0.020	0.002–0.004	0.002–0.003	0.001–0.002
	170.1 (2788)	0.0016	0.012–0.018	0.012–0.018	0.010–0.016	0.0006–0.0011	0.0005–0.0009	0.0004–0.001
	196 (3210)	0.0018	0.012–0.020	0.008–0.016	0.010–0.016	0.0024–0.0036	0.0012–0.0024	0.0008–0.0020
1982	108 (1766)	0.0018	0.0120–0.0180	0.0080–0.0160	0.0100–0.0200	0.002–0.004	0.002–0.003	0.001–0.002
	165 (2693)	0.0004–0.0016	0.0120–0.0200	0.0120–0.0200	0.0100–0.0200	0.0016–0.0028	0.0012–0.0024	0.0008–0.0017
	196 (3210)	0.0018	0.0120–0.0200	0.0080–0.0160	0.0024–0.0036	②	①	—
1983	108 (1766)	0.0018	0.0120–0.0180	0.0080–0.0160	0.0100–0.0200	0.002–0.004	0.002–0.003	0.001–0.002
	165 (2693)	0.0004–0.0016	0.0120–0.0200	0.0080–0.0160	0.0100–0.0200	0.0016–0.0028	0.0012–0.0024	0.0008–0.0017
	196 (3210)	0.0008–0.0020	0.0120–0.0200	0.0080–0.0160	0.0100–0.0200	0.0020–0.0032	0.0016–0.0028	0.0008–0.0028
1984	108 (1766)	0.0008–0.0020	0.0120–0.0280	0.0080–0.0160	0.0100–0.0200	0.0024–0.0035	0.0012–0.0028	0.0008–0.0028
	165 (2693)	0.0004–0.0016	0.0120–0.0200	0.0120–0.0200	0.0100–0.0200	0.0016–0.0028	0.0012–0.0024	0.0008–0.0017
	196 (3210)	0.0008–0.0020	0.0120–0.0200	0.0080–0.0160	0.0100–0.0200	0.0020–0.0032	0.0016–0.0028	0.0008–0.0028
1985	108 (1766)	0.0008–0.0020	0.0120–0.0280	0.0080–0.0160	0.0100–0.0200	0.0024–0.0035	0.0012–0.0028	0.0008–0.0024
	149 (2443)	0.0010–0.0013	0.0008–0.0016	0.0080–0.0160	0.0100–0.0200	0.0024–0.0025	0.0020–0.0031	0.0012–0.0024
	165 (2693)	0.0004–0.0016	0.0120–0.0200	0.0120–0.0200	0.0100–0.0200	0.0016–0.0028	0.0012–0.0024	0.0008–0.0017
	209 (3428)	0.0008–0.0020	0.0120–0.0020	0.0080–0.0160	0.0100–0.0200	0.020–0.032	0.0016–0.0028	0.0008–0.0020
1986	149 (2443)	0.0008–0.0020	0.0120–0.0200	0.0080–0.0160	0.0100–0.0200	0.020–0.032	0.0016–0.0028	0.0008–0.0020

87893C12

Engine

Most engine repair work may be performed with the engine installed in the car. The only operations that should require removal of the engine is camshaft removal, or any extensive cylinder block overhaul.

➡ On all 1600, 2000 and 2002 models, the engine and transmission should be removed as a unit.

Before setting out to tear out your engine, and tying up both yourself and your BMW, there are a few preliminary steps that should be taken. Write down those engine and chassis numbers (see Section 1) and make a trip to your parts dealer to order all those gaskets, hoses, belts, filters, etc. (such as the exhaust manifold-to-head pipe flange gasket) that are in need of replacement. This will help avoid last minute or weekend parts dashes that can tie up a car even longer. Also, have enough oil, antifreeze, transmission fluid, etc. (see the Capacities chart) on hand for the job. If the car is still running, have the engine, engine compartment, and underbody steam cleaned. The less dirt, the better. Have all of the necessary tools together. These should include a sturdy hydraulic jack and a pair of jackstands of sufficient capacity, a chain/pulley engine hoist of sufficient test strength, a wooden block and small jack to support the oil pan or transmission, a can of penetrating fluid to help loosen rusty nuts and bolts, a few jars and plastic containers to store and identify used engine hardware, and a punch or bottle of brush paint to matchmark adjacent parts, to aid in reassembly. Once you have all of your parts, tools, and fluids together, proceed with the task.

REMOVAL & INSTALLATION

1600, 2000 and 2002 Models

▶ See Figures 27, 28, 29 and 30

➡ On all 1600, 2000 and 2002 models, the engine and transmission should be removed as a unit.

1. Open the hood and trace the outline of the hood hinge mounts on the hood.
2. Cover the fenders with protective aprons. With the help of an assistant, remove the hood hinge bolts and lift off the hood. Place the hood away from the work area.
3. Open the draincocks at the bottom of the radiator and the right rear side of the engine block. Drain the cooling system into a suitable container.

✳✳ CAUTION

When draining coolant, keep in mind that cats and dogs are attracted to ethylene glycol antifreeze, and could drink any that is left in an uncovered container or in puddles on the ground. This will prove fatal in sufficient quantity. Always drain the coolant into a sealable container. Coolant should be reused unless it is contaminated or several years old.

4. From under the vehicle, remove the oil pan drain plug, and allow the crankcase oil to drain into a suitable container.

✳✳ CAUTION

The EPA warns that prolonged contact with used engine oil may cause a number of skin disorders, including cancer! You should make every effort to minimize your exposure to used engine oil. Protective gloves should be worn when changing the oil. Wash your hands and any other exposed skin areas as soon as possible after exposure to used engine oil. Soap and water, or waterless hand cleaner should be used.

5. From under the vehicle, remove the transmission drain plug, and allow the gear oil or transmission fluid, depending on transmission type to drain into a suitable container.
6. Disconnect the negative battery cable followed by the positive battery cable. Remove the retaining bolt and bracket, and lift the battery out of the engine compartment. Place it aside.
7. Access the air cleaner assembly and tag each hose or vacuum line. Remove the cleaner assembly mounting bolts, vacuum control hose(s), breather hoses and tubes. Lift the air cleaner off and out of the engine compartment.
8. On carburetor equipped models, remove the preheating air regulation housing and hose assembly attached to the front panel.
9. Disconnect the radiator hoses at the thermostat and water pump, tagging each hose as it is being unfastened. On some 2002 models a transmission cooler is incorporated into the radiator. Tag and remove these lines at their radiator connections.
10. Remove the radiator retaining bolts and carefully lift out the radiator.
11. Disconnect the multiple plug from the alternator and tag, and remove the battery main power cable from the alternator and starter. Mark them for reassembly. Tag and disconnect the coolant temperature sensor.
12. Disconnect and tag the throttle linkage.
13. On 2002 models equipped with an automatic choke, disconnect the cable from the choke and the thermo-start valve. Detach the plug from the starter lock and pull the cable loom out of the retainer at the transmission. Detach the coolant hoses from the automatic choke housing.
14. On manual choke equipped models, disconnect the choke cable from the lever and the cable sleeve from the cable clamp and pull out the cable.
15. On all 2002 models equipped with the Solex 32 DIPTA model carburetor, disconnect and tag the wire for the electric choke, and the leads for the EGR system. If equipped with downshift linkage, disconnect the downshift linkage by detaching the clamp spring and return spring, then lifting out the wire retainer and disconnecting the linkage ball. Finally, pull the torsion shaft towards the front of the vehicle.
16. Disconnect and plug the fuel line at the tank side of the fuel pump.
17. On 2002Tii models, disconnect the fuel hose at the injection pump. Remove the main fuel filter from its mount on the front panel. Disconnect the fuel reflow hose. Tag all hoses prior to removal
18. On models equipped with the emission control air pump, disconnect the vacuum line from the check (non-return) valve at the intake manifold.
19. Disconnect the heater hoses at the return flow connection and cylinder head connection.
20. Disconnect and label the wire connector from the oil pressure switch, the distributor primary connection, and the ground strap at the engine transmission flange.

Fig. 27 When removing nuts, bolts and other parts, place them in a tray or other container

Fig. 28 An example of marked wires using reusable plastic tags

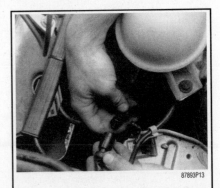

Fig. 29 Some wires are disconnected by separating sections of the harness . . .

Fig. 30 . . . while other wires are disconnected at the electrical device

21. On 2002Tii models, disconnect the cable from the thermo-time switch. Disconnect and label the vacuum hose from the air container and the cable from the start valve. Release the cable from the cable clamps on the cam cover.

22. Disconnect the coil high tension lead from the center of the distributor cap.

23. On 2002Tii models, pull out the induction transmitter from the coil.

24. On manual transmission equipped models, remove the shifter by accessing from inside the vehicle the shifter and sliding the boot up along with the foam rubber ring and inner sealing boot. Lift the leaf spring out of the selector head. On models with a pivot-ball on the shift lever end, pull up the rubber boot and gasket to access and remove the snapring and shift lever.

25. On automatic transmission equipped models, Remove the shifter plate retaining screws and lift the plate up and unfasten the shift rod snapring from the transmission assembly. Disconnect the reverse light neutral start switch lead.

26. Using a hydraulic floor jack of sufficient weight capacity, raise the front of the car, and position jackstands beneath the reinforced box members adjacent to the 2 front jacking points.

✳✳ CAUTION

Before climbing under the car, make sure that the jackstands are secure.

27. Disconnect the head pipe from the exhaust manifold. Disconnect the head pipe support and the front muffler mounting hardware.

28. Disconnect the driveshaft from the transmission flange by releasing the self-locking nuts and bolts from the giubo coupler. Tie up the drive shaft so that it does not fall on you as you work.

29. Disconnect the reverse light wires from their terminals, and the speedometer cable from the transmission.

30. On 2002 models, remove the hydraulic line bracket from the clutch housing, but do not disconnect the line from the slave cylinder. Disconnect the return spring from the throwout lever. Pull back the dust cover and remove the snap-ring from the slave cylinder. Then pull the slave cylinder forward and remove the pushrod.

31. On 1600 models, detach the pullrod on the intermediate shaft. Detach the bearing support from the engine support. Then remove the intermediate shaft.

32. Support the weight of the transmission with a floor jack and a block or wood. Attach lifting eyes to strong mounting points at the front and rear of the engine. Hook up an engine hoist to the eyelets and take the slack out of the host chain.

33. Remove the left and right-hand engine mount bolts. Remove the bolts retaining the driveshaft center support bearing to the body. Remove the C-bolts for the transmission support crossmember.

34. The engine/transmission unit should now be free. Check to make sure that all wires, hoses, etc. are disconnected. Remove the windshield washer reservoir for additional removal clearance.

35. Carefully, tilt the transmission down and the front of the engine up. Lift the engine out with the front raised higher than the transmission. With the engine raised above the top of the fenders, lower the car, and push back from under the engine. With the engine/transmission clear of the car, lower the engine onto a stand, workbench, or other suitable sturdy work surface.

To install:

36. Reverse the above procedure to install using the following installation notes:

a. When bolting the engine of the 1600, 2002, and 2002 models with an automatic transmission, make sure that the right engine mount support stop is adjusted so that a 0.11 inches (3mm) clearance exists.

b. When installing the center driveshaft support bearing mount, preload the bearing mount by adjusting it forward 0.08 inches (2mm) in its eccentric bolt holes. Make sure that the driveshaft bolts are tightened to 22 ft. lbs. (29 Nm).

c. When connecting the pullrod to the intermediate shaft, make sure that the bearing support is aligned at a 90° angle to the engine before tightening the mounting screws.

d. When hooking up the exhaust system, make sure to follow this sequence: first connect the head pipe to the manifold, then loosen the head pipe support mount on the transmission so that it rests tension-free against the pipe, then tighten the support mount on the transmission and finally tighten the support bracket on the head pipe.

e. Adjust the clutch free-play while the car is up in the air. Refer to Section 7 for details.

f. When installing the shift lever, make sure that the gearshift pin is installed in its lever with the bolt positioned in the centering recess of the pin. Also make sure that the breather holes in the shifter dust boot face downward.

g. When filling the radiator, make sure that the heater control is set to the **HOT** position.

h. When hooking up the choke on 1970–71 1600, 2000 and 2002 models, make sure that the choke handle on the dash is at its bottom notch. Then press the fast idle lever against the stop, and tighten the clamp screw. The sleeve must project exactly 0.6 inches (15mm) for the choke flap to close fully.

i. Before starting the car, make sure all hoses, vacuum lines and wires are connected securely, and will not rub against other parts of the engine or body and short circuit.

2500, 2800, Bavaria and 3000 Carbureted Models

➡**The transmission should be separated from the block prior to engine removal.**

1. Scribe alignment marks on the hood hinges, then remove the hood.
2. Disconnect and remove the battery.
3. Remove the air cleaner and hoses.
4. Drain the cooling system, disconnect and tag the hoses. Remove the radiator from the vehicle.

✳✳ CAUTION

When draining coolant, keep in mind that cats and dogs are attracted to ethylene glycol antifreeze, and could drink any that is left in an uncovered container or in puddles on the ground. This will prove fatal in sufficient quantity. Always drain the coolant into a sealable container. Coolant should be reused unless it is contaminated or several years old.

5. Remove the windshield washer reservoir and blower fan fan. Tag all connections

6. Disconnect and tag the wiring from all engine electrical devices including electric choke and control sensor units.

7. Unfasten the main power wires to the alternator and starter. Tag and remove the control harness from each.

8. Disconnect the accelerator linkage.

9. Unbolt the exhaust pipe from the exhaust manifold.

10. Remove the front lower apron and loosen both engine mounting retaining nuts.

11. On vehicles equipped with power steering, remove the pump from the mounting brackets and move the pump out of the way. Tie the pump to the vehicle body using a piece of wire. Do not kink the hoses.

12. Raise and support the vehicle safely on jackstands

13. Remove the locknuts and bolts securing the flexible giubo coupler to the

transmission and driveshaft. Separate the driveshaft on tie out of the way using a piece of wire.

14. On manual transmission cars, remove the slave cylinder from the clutch housing, leaving the hose attached.

15. From underneath the vehicle, remove the transmission retaining hardware and free the transmission from the engine. Lower the transmission down and move aside. Refer to Section 7 for transmission removal procedures.

16. Lower the car and attach a lifting sling to the engine.

17. Be sure that all wires, hoses and linkages are disconnected and out of the way.

18. To remove the engine, begin by angling the engine up towards the front of the vehicle, then out of the engine compartment.

19. Place the engine on a strong surface to perform any needed work.

To install:

20. Install the engine assembly into the vehicle. Be careful to position the engine correctly in the engine mount locations.

21. Once the engine is securely in its mounts, loosely install the mount retaining nuts.

22. Raise and safely support the vehicle on jackstands.

23. Install the transmission giubo coupler and driveshaft on the engine, being careful to align it with the engine. Refer to Section 7 for installation details.

24. After the transmission and driveshaft assemblies are secured to the engine, tighten the engine mount nuts. Remove the lifting device from the engine and lower the vehicle to the ground.

25. On manual transmission equipped vehicles, install the clutch slave cylinder to the transmission housing.

26. Install the power steering pump to the brackets, if equipped.

27. Reconnect the exhaust pipe to the exhaust manifold.

28. Install the accelerator linkage and all electrical wiring and hoses to the engine.

29. Install the windshield reservoir and the cooling fan.

30. Position and fasten the air cleaner assembly and hoses.

31. Install the front lower apron.

32. Connect the battery cables, positive first then negative.

33. Install the hood, aligning the scribe marks made during disassembly.

3.0 Models

➡ **When removing the engine from this model, automatic transmission assemblies should be remove prior to engine removal. Manual transmission assemblies can be removed with the engine.**

1. Open the hood and trace the outline of the hood hinge mounts on the hood.

2. Cover the fenders with protective aprons. With the help of an assistant, remove the hood hinge bolts and lift off the hood. Place the hood away from the work area.

3. Disconnect the negative battery cable followed by the positive cable.

4. Open the draincocks at the bottom of the radiator and the right rear side of the engine block. Drain the cooling system into a suitable container.

✲✲ CAUTION

When draining coolant, keep in mind that cats and dogs are attracted to ethylene glycol antifreeze, and could drink any that is left in an uncovered container or in puddles on the ground. This will prove fatal in sufficient quantity. Always drain the coolant into a sealable container. Coolant should be reused unless it is contaminated or several years old.

5. From under the vehicle, remove the oil pan drain plug, and allow the crankcase oil to drain into a suitable container.

✲✲ CAUTION

The EPA warns that prolonged contact with used engine oil may cause a number of skin disorders, including cancer! You should make every effort to minimize your exposure to used engine oil. Protective gloves should be worn when changing the oil. Wash your hands and any other exposed skin areas as soon as possible after exposure to used engine oil. Soap and water, or waterless hand cleaner should be used.

6. From under the vehicle, remove the transmission drain plug, and allow the gear oil or transmission fluid, depending on transmission type to drain into a suitable container.

7. Disconnect the main power wires from the battery to the alternator and starter. Unfasten the multiple wire connectors at each unit. Tag prior to removal.

8. Access the air cleaner assembly and tag each hose or vacuum line. Remove the cleaner assembly mounting bolts, vacuum control hose(s), breather hoses and tubes. Lift the air cleaner off and out of the engine compartment.

9. Disconnect the radiator hoses at the thermostat and water pump, tagging each hose as it is being unfastened. On some models a transmission cooler is incorporated into the radiator. Tag and remove these lines at their radiator connections.

10. Remove the radiator retaining bolts and carefully lift out the radiator.

11. Disconnect the multiple plug from the alternator and tag, and remove the battery main power cable from the alternator and starter. Mark them for reassembly. Tag and disconnect the coolant temperature sensor.

12. Separate the electrical connection for the fuel injection wire loom by removing the 3 retaining screws.

13. Remove the wire leads from the relays, sensors, and switches. Mark the wire connections for installation.

14. Disconnect and tag the throttle linkage.

15. On models equipped with the emission control air pump, disconnect the vacuum line from the check (non-return) valve at the intake manifold.

16. Disconnect the heater hoses at the return flow connection and cylinder head connection.

17. Disconnect and label the wire connector from the oil pressure switch, the distributor primary connection, and the ground strap at the engine transmission flange.

18. Disconnect the cable from the thermo-time switch. Disconnect and label the vacuum hose from the air container and the cable from the start valve. Release the cable from the cable clamps on the cam cover.

19. Disconnect the coil high tension lead from the center of the distributor cap.

20. Pull out the induction transmitter from the coil.

21. On manual transmission equipped models, remove the shifter by accessing it from inside the vehicle. Slide the shifter and sliding the boot up along with the foam rubber ring and inner sealing boot. Lift the leaf spring out of the selector head. On models with a pivot-ball on the shift lever end, pull up the rubber boot and gasket to access and remove the snapring and shift lever.

22. On automatic transmission equipped models, Remove the shifter plate retaining screws and lift the plate up and unfasten the shift rod snapring from the transmission assembly. Disconnect the reverse/neutral start switch lead.

23. Using a hydraulic floor jack of sufficient weight capacity, raise the front of the car, and position jackstands beneath the reinforced box members adjacent to the 2 front jacking points.

✲✲ CAUTION

Before climbing under the car, make sure that the jackstands are secure.

24. Disconnect the head pipe from the exhaust manifold. Disconnect the head pipe support and the front muffler mounting hardware.

25. Disconnect the driveshaft from the transmission flange by releasing the self-locking nuts and bolts from the giubo coupler. Tie up the drive shaft so that it does not fall on you as you work.

26. Disconnect the speedometer cable from the transmission.

27. Remove the hydraulic line bracket from the clutch housing, but do not disconnect the line from the slave cylinder. Disconnect the return spring from the throwout lever. Pull back the dust cover and remove the snap-ring from the slave cylinder. Then pull the slave cylinder forward and remove the pushrod.

28. Support the weight of the transmission with a floor jack and a block of wood. Attach lifting eyes to strong mounting points at the front and rear of the engine. Hook up an engine hoist to the eyelets and take the slack out of the host chain.

29. On automatic equipped models, remove all retaining hardware securing the transmission to the engine. Refer to Section 7 for details. Lower the automatic transmission down and away from the vehicle.

30. Remove the left and right-hand engine mount bolts.

31. The engine and transmission unit, if equipped with a manual transmission, should now be free. Check to make sure that all wires, hoses, etc. are disconnected. Remove the windshield washer reservoir for additional removal clearance.

32. Carefully, tilt the transmission down and the front of the engine up. Lift the engine out with the front raised higher than the transmission. With the engine raised above the top of the fenders, lower the car, and push back from under the engine. With the engine/transmission clear of the car, lower the engine onto a stand, workbench, or other suitable sturdy work surface.

To install:

33. Install the engine assembly into the vehicle. Be careful to position the engine correctly in the engine mount locations.

34. Once the engine is securely in its mounts, loosely install the mount retaining nuts.

35. Raise and safely support the vehicle on jackstands.

36. Install the transmission engine, being careful to align it with the engine. Refer to Section 7 for installation details.

37. When installing the center driveshaft support bearing mount, preload the bearing mount by adjusting it forward 0.08 inches (2mm) in its eccentric bolt holes. Make sure that the driveshaft bolts are tightened to 22 ft. lbs. (29 Nm).

38. Install the shift lever making sure that the gearshift pin is installed in its lever with the bolt positioned in the centering recess of the pin. Also make sure that the breather holes in the shifter dust boot face downward.

39. After the transmission and driveshaft assemblies are secured to the engine, tighten the engine mount nuts. Remove the lifting device from the engine and lower the vehicle to the ground.

40. On manual transmission equipped vehicles, install the clutch slave cylinder to the transmission housing.

41. Reconnect the exhaust pipe to the exhaust manifold.

42. Install the accelerator linkage and all electrical wiring and hoses to the engine.

43. Position and fasten the air cleaner assembly and hoses.

44. Connect the battery cables positive first, then negative.

45. Install the hood, aligning the scribe marks made during disassembly.

46. Before starting the car, make sure all hoses, vacuum lines and wires are connected securely, and will not rub against other parts of the engine or body and short circuit.

318i Models

▶ **See Figures 31, 32 and 33**

➡**The transmission must be separated from the block prior to engine removal.**

1. Scribe hood hinge locations on the hood, and then remove.
2. Disconnect the negative battery cable, followed by the positive cable.
3. Raise and safely support the vehicle on jackstand.
4. Remove the transmission assembly as detailed in Section 7.
5. Detach the 2 mounting bolts and remove the power steering pump with the hoses attached. Suspend the pump securely with a piece of wire so that hoses will not be damaged.
6. Looking at the top of the air conditioning compressor, loosen the 2 outer bolts (bolts screwed into the compressor) and remove the 2 bolts fastening the mounting bracket to the engine. Then, support the unit and remove the hinge nut and bolt form the bottom of the unit. Finally, pull the unit away from the engine and support it with wire to avoid putting strain on refrigerant hoses.

➡**Do not disconnect any air conditioning hoses!**

7. Remove the radiator cap and drain the coolant. Detach and tag the radiator hoses. On air conditioned equipped models, disconnect the wires at the temperature switches. Unscrew and remove the cover located at the left side of the radiator (driver's side). Unscrew and disconnect transmission oil cooler lines at the radiator (automatic only), and plug the openings. Finally, remove the mounting bolt located at the top of the radiator and lift the radiator upward until it clears the rubber mounts on the bottom, and remove it.

❋❋ CAUTION

When draining coolant, keep in mind that cats and dogs are attracted to ethylene glycol antifreeze, and could drink any that is left in an uncovered container or in puddles on the ground. This will prove fatal in sufficient quantity. Always drain the coolant into a sealable container. Coolant should be reused unless it is contaminated or several years old.

8. Disconnect the battery-to-alternator and stater wires, as well as the control harness for each. Disconnect the engine ground strap.

9. Open the clips that hold the wiring harness running along the fender just behind the battery. Disconnect the plugs from the temperature sensor and oxygen sensor. Tag prior to removal.

10. Remove the glovebox liner. Unplug the connectors at the idle control and L-Jetronic units. Unplug the connector that also comes out of this harness. Then, pull the harness through the rubber grommet into the engine compartment.

11. Tag and disconnect the coil wires and wire to the electronic ignition unit. Take the wires out of the clips mounted nearby.

12. At the air cleaner, disconnect the wire mounted on the side of the air cleaner housing, and disconnect the plug. Lift off the L-shaped cap for the relay mounted nearby, then remove the relay. Loosen the strap and disconnect the inlet hose.

13. Loosen the 2 mounting nuts and remove the air cleaner assembly.

14. Access the relay box mounted in between the cowl and suspension strut on the driver's side. Remove the top of the box and lift out and disconnect the plug on the outboard side. Remove the rubber guard for the control unit nearby and pull off the plug connected to it.

15. From the rear of the intake manifold, unscrew the clamp and pull off the large vacuum hose. Label and then disconnect the small vacuum hoses running to the distributor and intake manifold.

16. Disconnect the throttle cable. Remove the hose clamp and hose nearby.

17. Detach the fuel hoses at the injection system. Capture any spilled fuel with a rag or in a metal pan.

18. Attach a suitable hoist to the engine hooks at the front and rear of the engine and support the engine securely.

19. Detach both engine mounts.

20. Unbolts the locknuts and bolts securing the giubo coupler and driveshaft. Separate the driveshaft from the transmission and secure in place with wire.

21. Remove the transmission retaining bolts and separate the transmission from the engine. Lower and place aside. Refer to Section 7 for details.

22. Lift out the engine, taking care not to permit the engine to shift and hit anything on the way out.

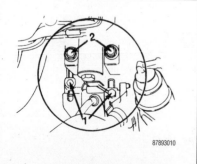

Fig. 31 To remove the A/C compressor, remove bolts 1 and 2. Then unfasten the bolts at the base of the compressor

Fig. 32 Tag and disconnect wires 3 and 5, then tag and unplug wires 6 and 7

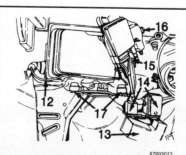

Fig. 33 Disconnect wire 12, then lift off cap 13 and remove the relay 14. Unfasten plug 15, open the hose clamp 16 and loosen the nuts 17

To install:

23. Lower the engine into place making sure the locating mandrel on the front of the engine is guided into the front suspension carrier. Install the engine mount retainer nuts and tighten to 31–35 ft. lbs. (40–47 Nm) .

24. Position the transmission under the vehicle and lift into place. Secure with retaining hardware. Refer to Section 7 for details.

25. Attach the giubo coupler and driveshaft to the transmission.

26. Connect the fuel lines using new hose clamps to connect the fuel lines to the fuel filter. Connect all of the multi-prong plugs and all vacuum hoses.

27. Connect the accelerator cable and adjust.

28. Install the radiator hoses using new hose clamps if needed.

29. Install the air cleaner and reconnect all electrical plugs. Connect and install the relays in the relay box.

30. Reconnect the wiring to the main control unit and install the idle control unit running the harnesses into the interior of the vehicle. Make sure the rubber grommet is seated correctly.

31. Install the air conditioning compressor and power steering pump.

32. Connect the alternator and starter wires.

33. Connect the battery cables, positive first, then negative.

34. Install the hood and align if needed.

35. Make sure all fluid levels are correct before starting the engine. Bleed air from the cooling system.

1977–79 320i Models

➡**The transmission must be separated from the block prior to engine removal.**

1. Disconnect the negative battery cable, followed by the positive cable.

2. Raise and support the vehicle on jackstands.

3. Remove the transmission, Refer to Section 7 for details. Disconnect the exhaust pipe from the exhaust manifold.

4. Remove the hood, after scribing the hinge locations.

5. Drain the cooling system, disconnect the hoses and remove the radiator. Remove the intake air panel.

> **⁑ CAUTION**
>
> **When draining coolant, keep in mind that cats and dogs are attracted to ethylene glycol antifreeze, and could drink any that is left in an uncovered container or in puddles on the ground. This will prove fatal in sufficient quantity. Always drain the coolant into a sealable container. Coolant should be reused unless it is contaminated or several years old.**

6. Tag and disconnect the lines to the injector valves.

7. Disconnect all electrical wires from the engine, marking them for installation.

8. Disconnect the main wires and control wires for both the starter and alternator. Mark prior to removal.

9. Disconnect all fuel and vacuum lines and mark them for installation.

10. Disconnect the accelerator cable.

11. Attach a lifting sling to the engine lifting eyes. Remove the retaining nuts from the left and right engine mounts and the upper engine damper.

12. Carefully raise and remove the engine from the vehicle.

To install:

13. Install the engine into the engine compartment, aligning the motor mounts in their appropriate position. Install the motor mount retaining nuts and install the upper engine damper.

14. Connect all of the electrical wiring, including starter and alternator.

15. Connect the fuel lines and vacuum hoses.

16. Install the radiator and connect all hoses.

17. Install the air intake panel.

18. Connect the exhaust pipe to the exhaust manifold.

19. Raise and safely support the vehicle and install the transmission, carefully aligning it with the engine.

20. Connect the battery cables positive first, then negative.

21. With the aid of a helper, install the hood aligning the scribe marks made before removing the engine.

22. Before starting the vehicle, add anti-freeze and bleed the cooling system. Check all fluids to make sure their levels are satisfactory.

1980–83 320i Models

➡**The transmission must be separated from the block prior to engine removal.**

1. Remove the transmission as detailed in Section 7.

2. Scribe lines around the hood hinges and remove the hood.

3. Disconnect the upper and lower radiator hoses and then remove the radiator.

> **⁑ CAUTION**
>
> **When draining coolant, keep in mind that cats and dogs are attracted to ethylene glycol antifreeze, and could drink any that is left in an uncovered container or in puddles on the ground. This will prove fatal in sufficient quantity. Always drain the coolant into a sealable container. Coolant should be reused unless it is contaminated or several years old.**

4. Unscrew and remove the air filter housing from the engine compartment.

5. On models equipped with air conditioning, detach the compressor and position it out of the way with the wires attached. Do not disconnect the refrigerant lines. Use a piece of wire to secure the compressor so the lines do not bend.

6. Disconnect the battery cables (negative cable first) and remove the battery.

7. Disconnect all fuel lines at the fuel distributor. Pull the hose off the charcoal canister.

8. Disconnect the ground wire form the front axle carrier.

9. Unscrew the retaining nut and lift the accelerator cable from the holders toward the side. Push the nipple out toward the rear and then disconnect the cable.

10. Tag and disconnect all remaining wires and hoses which may interfere with engine removal.

11. Lift out the relay socket and then pull out the 2 relays to the side of the housing. Disconnect the plug underneath and then lift out the wire harness from the holder on the wheel arch.

12. Open the glove box and disconnect the control unit plug on the left-hand side. Pull the harness out through the hole in the firewall (into the engine compartment) Pull the harness out of its holders.

13. Attach an engine hoist to the front and rear of the engine.

14. Unbolt the left engine mount and the upper engine damper.

15. Unbolt the right engine mount and lift out the engine.

To install:

16. Install the engine into the engine compartment and install the motor mount nuts.

17. Slide the electrical harness in through the firewall and connect it to the control unit.

18. Connect all the wires and hoses to the engine components, making sure to properly route the wiring.

19. Install the accelerator cable and its retaining nut. When installing the accelerator cable, push the cable through the eye on the lever, attach it and then press the nipple into the eye. Attach the cable to the holder.

20. Connect the fuel lines and the vacuum lines. Install the radiator and connect the hoses.

21. On models equipped with air conditioning install the compressor and connect the wiring.

22. Install the air filter housing.

23. Connect the wires to the starter and alternator.

24. Fill the coolant system with clean anti-freeze and bleed. Check the other fluid levels and adjust if needed.

25. Connect the battery cables, positive fist, then negative.

26. With the aid of an assistant, install the hood, aligning the scribe marks made on the hood.

1983–87 325, 325e, 325i, 325iS and 1988 325iX Models

◆ **See Figures 34 thru 54**

➡**The transmission must be separated from the block prior to engine removal.**

1. Disconnect the battery ground cable. Remove the transmission. refer to Section 7 for details. Unfasten the engine splash guard at the front bottom of the engine.

Fig. 34 Remove the fan shroud from the book of the radiator

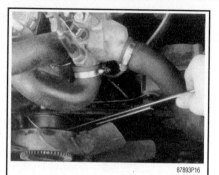

Fig. 35 Remove the fan from the pulley—remember the fan retainers use left-hand threads

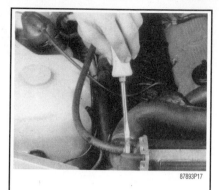

Fig. 36 Remove the radiator expansion tank hose

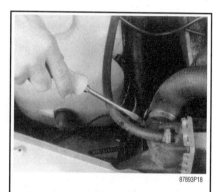

Fig. 37 Loosen the clamp for both radiator hoses and remove—top hose shown

Fig. 38 Disconnect any wires or harnesses attached to the radiator

Fig. 39 With all connections and hardware removed, lift the radiator out of the engine compartment

Fig. 40 Unplug the air-flow sensor harness

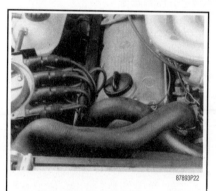

Fig. 41 Disconnect the distributor cap and place on top of the engine

Fig. 42 If equipped with a crank sensor, unclip and place aside

Fig. 43 Unfasten the idle control plug

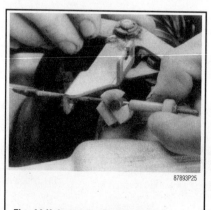

Fig. 44 Unfasten the throttle linkage

Fig. 45 Remove the air intake hose attached to the throttle body

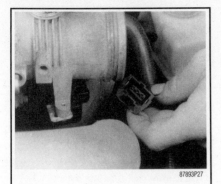

Fig. 46 Disconnect the throttle sensor harness

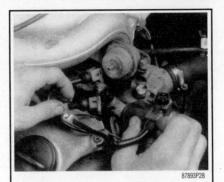

Fig. 47 Unfasten any remaining harnesses including coolant and fuel sensor

Fig. 48 To remove some hoses, the clamps securing them in place will have to be cut off

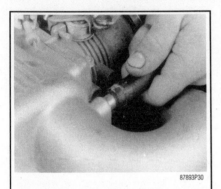

Fig. 49 With the clamp removed, slide the hose off

Fig. 50 When removing numerous hoses from a given area, tag each hose

Fig. 51 Remove the clutch cover plate from the lower portion of the engine/transmission

Fig. 52 With the bolts removed, the cover plate can be slid down and away from the engine

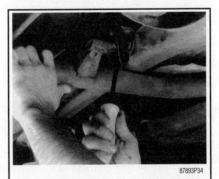

Fig. 53 Removing the exhaust hanger will allow play in the exhaust—this will aid component removal

Fig. 54 Loosen the front engine mount from under the engine

2. Disconnect the gas spring and prop rod and support hood safely in the fully open position.

3. Remove the fan cowl by turning the expansion rivets on the left and right sides. Lift the cowl up and out of the engine compartment.

4. Hold the fan pulley while unscrewing the fan nut from the shaft. The shaft uses left hand threads; turn the nut counterclockwise to unscrew.

5. Drain the coolant from the engine block. Disconnect the bottom hose from the radiator expansion tank, the engine coolant hoses and finally the heater hoses from the splash wall. When empty, remove the radiator from the vehicle.

✳✳ CAUTION

When draining coolant, keep in mind that cats and dogs are attracted to ethylene glycol antifreeze, and could drink any that is left in an uncovered container or in puddles on the ground. This will prove fatal in sufficient quantity. Always drain the coolant into a

sealable container. Coolant should be reused unless it is contaminated or several years old.

6. Disconnect the air flow meter electrical plug and loosen the hose clamp and mounting screws. Lift the air sensor with the air cleaner up and out of the engine compartment.

7. Unclip the throttle cable and pull the cable out with the rubber holder.

8. Disconnect the fuel lines taking note of their positions. Pull off the vent hose to the filter for tank venting.

9. Disconnect the vacuum fitting at the brake booster.

10. Remove the distributor cap and ignition leads from the coil.

11. Unscrew the connections at the alternator and starter. Disconnect the 2 plugs from the electrical duct.

12. Remove the plug from the throttle valve potentiometer located at the throttle neck. Pull off the tank venting valve plug located next to the air cleaner.

13. Disconnect the fuel injector plug located at the end of the electrical duct

near to the fuel pipes. Pull off the idle speed control connector at the rear of the intake manifold. Unfasten the oil pressure switch electrical connection.

14. Unscrew the front and rear intake manifold supports.

15. Remove the electrical duct from the engine. Disconnect the coolant temperature senders for the gauge and the DME control unit, if equipped.

16. Disconnect the electrical duct and wiring harness on the engine and lay it off to the side.

17. Use a suitable lifting tool and attach to the engine lifting eyes. Unscrew the motor mounts and the engine ground strap. Lift out the engine.

To Install:

18. Lower the engine into the engine compartment. Fasten the motor mounts and the ground strap.

19. Attach the engine wiring harness and electrical duct. Make sure that the rubber grommets on the duct are clipped in correctly. Connect the leads to the 2 coolant sensors and the oil pressure switch.

20. Fasten the front and rear intake manifold supports.

21. Connect the idle speed control plug, the fuel injector plug, the tank venting valve plug, the throttle valve potentiometer plug and the electrical lead duct plugs.

22. Reconnect the starter and the alternator wiring. Attach the ignition leads to the coil and install the distributor cap.

23. Refit the vacuum connection to the brake booster. Reconnect the tank vent hose and the fuel hoses.

➡**The upper fuel hose is the return line and the bottom is the feed line.**

24. Attach the throttle cable and its holder.

25. Replace the air cleaner and air flow meter assembly. Attach the electrical connector to the air flow meter.

26. Connect the heater hoses, engine coolant hoses and the radiator expansion tank hose.

27. Install the fan tightening the nut to 29 ft. lbs. (40 Nm).

28. Replace the fan cowl taking care to engage the tabs at the right and left.

29. Replace the splash guard and the transmission. Reconnect the hood prop rod and gas spring.

30. Add the proper coolant mixture and bleed the cooling system. Check all other fluid levels and adjust if needed.

31. Connect the battery leads and check all fluid levels before starting the engine.

1988 325, 325e, 325i and 325iS Models

➡**The transmission must be separated from the block prior to engine removal.**

1. Disconnect the battery ground cable.
2. Remove the transmission as outlined in Section 7.
3. Remove the engine splash guard below the front bumper.
4. Support hood safely in the fully open position.

※※ **CAUTION**

The hood must be propped in a secure manner! If it falls during work serious injury could result.

5. Remove the fan cowl by turning the expansion rivets on the left and right sides. Lift the cowl up and out of the engine compartment.

6. Disconnect the air conditioner compressor without removing the lines. Secure to the vehicle body with a piece of wire.

7. Hold the fan pulley while unscrewing the fan nut from the shaft. The shaft uses left hand threads. Turn the nut counterclockwise to unscrew.

8. Drain the coolant from the engine block. Disconnect the bottom hose from the radiator expansion tank, the engine coolant hoses and the heater hoses from the splash wall.

※※ **CAUTION**

When draining coolant, keep in mind that cats and dogs are attracted to ethylene glycol antifreeze, and could drink any that is left in an uncovered container or in puddles on the ground. This will prove fatal in sufficient quantity. Always drain the coolant into a sealable container. Coolant should be reused unless it is contaminated or several years old.

9. Disconnect the air flow meter electrical plug and loosen the hose clamp and mounting screws. Lift the air sensor with the air cleaner up and out of the engine compartment.

10. Remove the air intake duct and disconnect the idle speed control hose. Disconnect the wire holders from the duct.

11. Unbolt the power steering reservoir. Unbolt the power steering pump and support with a piece of wire. Do not bend or kink the hoses.

12. Unscrew the throttle body holder bracket and disconnect the cable from the linkage.

13. Mark the locations of the fuel feed and return hoses. The upper hose is the return line. Disconnect the hoses and plug.

14. Disconnect the vacuum line from the brake booster. Plug the opening to prevent dirt from entering.

15. Remove the grille from the air intake cowl at the base of the windshield. Remove the electrical lead tray. Remove the screws on the right side cowl holder bracket and the screw on the left side. Remove the cowl from the engine compartment.

16. Disconnect the wiring from the alternator and the starter.

17. Disconnect the cylinder ID sensor and the pulse sender located just behind the oil filter housing.

18. Disconnect the idle speed control and remove from the holder.

19. Disconnect the throttle position sensor lead, oil pressure sender and the tank venting valve connector.

20. Unbolt the fuel line holder and the intake manifold support. Loosen the clamp holding the pipe to the intake support.

21. Unscrew the intake support from the electrical lead duct. Disconnect the temperature sensors under the intake manifold. Unplug the fuel injectors and disconnect the electric lead duct from the engine.

22. Disconnect the coolant hose from the transfer pipe on the side of the engine.

23. Connect an engine lifting tool to the lifting tabs at the front and rear of the engine and take up any slack.

24. Disconnect the ground strap and motor mounts.

25. Remove the engine.

To install:

26. Install the engine in the vehicle. Connect the ground strap and tighten the engine mounts to 30 ft. lbs. (42 Nm).

27. Connect the coolant hose to the transfer pipe.

28. Replace the injector electrical lead duct and connect the injectors.

29. Replace the electric lead duct on the intake support and install the intake support.

30. Connect the temperature sensors under the intake manifold.

31. Attach the fuel line holder.

32. Connect the tank venting valve, the throttle position sender, the oil pressure switch and the idle speed control.

33. Install the idle speed control in its holder. Connect the cylinder ID sender and the pulse sender.

34. Connect the starter and alternator.

35. Install the air cowl, bracket and grill.

36. Connect the brake booster vacuum line and the fuel hoses.

➡**The upper hose is the fuel return line.**

37. Connect the throttle cable and holder bracket.

38. Install the power steering pump and reservoir.

39. Install the air intake duct and the air cleaner assembly. Connect the idle speed line and the electrical leads. Connect the air flow sensor.

40. Connect the coolant hoses. Install the fan, fan cowl and the air conditioner compressor.

41. Install the hood.

42. Install and transmission referring to Section 7 for details.

43. Install the splash guard and fill the engine fluids.

44. Connect the battery, start the car, bleed the coolant system and check for any fluid leaks.

M3 Models

◆ **See Figure 55**

➡**The transmission must be separated from the block prior to engine removal.**

1. Disconnect the negative battery cable.
2. Remove the transmission as outlined in Section 7.

3. Remove the splash guard from underneath the engine.

4. Put a drain pan underneath and then drain coolant from both the radiator and engine block.

✳✳ CAUTION

When draining coolant, keep in mind that cats and dogs are attracted to ethylene glycol antifreeze, and could drink any that is left in an uncovered container or in puddles on the ground. This will prove fatal in sufficient quantity. Always drain the coolant into a sealable container. Coolant should be reused unless it is contaminated or several years old.

5. Loosen the hose clamps at either end of the air intake hose leading to the air intake sensor. Pull off the hose. Then, pull both electrical connectors off the air cleaner/airflow sensor unit. Remove both mounting nuts and remove the assembly.

6. Disconnect the accelerator and cruise control cables. Unscrew the nuts mounting the cable housing mounting bracket and set the housings and bracket aside.

7. Loosen the clamp and disconnect the brake booster vacuum hose.

8. Loosen the clamp and disconnect the other end of the booster vacuum hose at the manifold. Remove the nut from the intake manifold brace.

9. Loosen the hose clamp and disconnect the air intake hose at the manifold. Then, remove all the nuts attaching the manifold assembly to the outer ends of the intake throttle necks and remove the intake assembly.

10. Place a drain pan underneath and loosen the hose clamps and disconnect the coolant expansion tank hoses.

11. Disconnect the engine ground strap.

12. Disconnect the ignition coil high tension lead.

13. Label and disconnect the plugs from the rear of the alternator.

14. Remove the cover for the electrical connectors from the starter. Label the leads and then remove the attaching nuts and disconnect them.

15. There is a wire running to a connector on the oil pan to warn of low oil level. Pull off the connector, unscrew the carrier for the lead, and then pull the lead out from above.

16. Find the vacuum hose leading to the fuel pressure regulator. Pull it off. Label and then disconnect the plugs. Unscrew the mounting screw for the electrical lead connecting with the top of the block and remove the lead and its carrier.

17. There is a vacuum hose connected to the throttle neck. Disconnect it and pull it out of the intake manifold bracket. Pull off the electrical harness. Pull out the rubber retainer, and then remove the idle speed control.

18. All the fuel injectors are plugged into a common plate. Carefully and evenly pull the plate off the injectors, pull it out past the pressure regulator, and lay it aside.

19. Loosen the clamp, then disconnect the PCV hose.

20. Label and then disconnect the fuel lines connecting the injector circuit.

21. Put a drain pan underneath then disconnect the heater hose from the cylinder head.

22. Loosen the clamp near the throttle necks and then pull the engine wiring harness out and put aside.

Fig. 55 Loosen the 3 arrowed nuts to remove the A/C compressor

87893A15

23. Loosen the mounting clamp for the carbon canister, slide it out of the clamp, and place it aside with the hoses still connected.

24. Note the routing of the oil cooler lines where they connect at the base of the oil filter. Label them if necessary. Put a drain pan underneath and unscrew the flared connectors for the lines.

25. Unbolt and remove the fan. Remove the radiator from the engine compartment.

26. Support the power steering pump. Remove the adjusting bolt, and secure it with a piece of wire. Do not kink the hoses.

27. Remove the adjusting bolt for the air conditioning compressor, then, remove the nut at one end of the hinge bolt and pull the bolt out, suspending the compressor. Secure the compressor to the vehicle body using a piece of wire.

28. Suspend the engine with a suitable lifting device. Then, remove the nuts for the engine mounting bolts. The mounts are on the axle carrier and left and bottom right. Then, carefully lift the engine out of the compartment, avoiding contact between the engine and the components remaining in the vehicle.

To install:

29. Keep these points in mind during installation:

   a. Tighten the engine mounting bolts to 32 ft. lbs. (44 Nm).

   b. Adjust the belt tension for the air conditioning compressor and power steering pump drive belts to give 0.5–0.7 inch (13–18mm) deflection.

   c. Tighten the oil cooler line flare nuts to 25 ft. lbs. (34 Nm).

   d. When reconnecting the intake manifold to the throttle necks, inspect and, if necessary, replace the O-rings. Tighten the mounting nuts to 6 ft. lbs. (9 Nm).

30. Reverse the procedures used for removal.

31. Lower the engine into the engine compartment. When the engine is positioned, the guide pin must fit in the bore of the axle carrier. Tighten the mounting bolts on the front axle carrier (small bolt) to 18–20 ft. lbs. (25–27 Nm), the larger bolt to 31–35 ft. lbs. (40–47 Nm).

32. Install the intake manifold assembly and connect the fuel lines, using new hose clamps, if needed, to connect the fuel lines to the fuel filter.

33. Connect all of the multi-prong plugs and vacuum hoses.

34. Connect the accelerator cable and cruise control cable to the throttle body and adjust.

35. Install the coolant recovery tank, using a new hose clamp on the coolant expansion tank.

36. Install the air cleaner and reconnect all electrical plugs.

37. Connect and install the relays in the relay box.

38. Reconnect the wiring to the main control unit and install the idle control unit.

39. Install the air conditioning compressor and power steering pump. Properly route the accessory drive belt. Adjust the belt tension.

40. Install the radiator and connect the hoses.

41. Install the transmission referring to Section 7 for details.

42. Make sure all fluid levels are correct before starting the engine. Bleed air from the cooling system.

528i and 530i Models

➡**The transmission must be separated from the block prior to engine removal.**

1. Raise and support the vehicle on jackstands.

2. Remove the transmission as outlined in Section 7.

3. Disconnect the exhaust pipe at the exhaust manifold.

4. Remove the power steering pump and place it out of the way along the inner fender panel using a piece of wire.

5. Lower the vehicle and scribe the hood hinge location. Remove the hood and place aside.

6. Remove the air cleaner with the duct work attached. Disconnect and remove the air volume control.

7. Disconnect and remove the battery.

8. Disconnect all electrical wires and connectors. Mark the wires and connector for installation.

9. Disconnect all vacuum hoses, marking them for installation.

10. Drain the cooling system, then disconnect the hoses and remove the radiator.

11. Disconnect the accelerator linkage.
12. Install a lifting sling on the engine and remove any slack.
13. Remove the left and right engine mount retainer nuts and washers.
14. Carefully lift the engine from the engine compartment.

To install:

15. Lower the engine into the engine compartment. When the engine is positioned, the guide pin must fit in the bore of the axle carrier. Tighten the mounting bolts on the front axle carrier (small bolt) to 18–20 ft. lbs. (23;26 Nm), the larger bolt to 31–35 ft. lbs. (40–45 Nm). The mount-to-bracket bolts are tightened to 31–35 ft. lbs. (40–45 Nm).
16. Connect the fuel lines, using new hose clamps where needed to connect the fuel lines to the fuel filter. Connect all of the multi-prong plugs and all vacuum hoses.
17. Install the air conditioning compressor and power steering pump. Properly route the accessory drive belt. Adjust the belt tension.
18. Install the radiator and connect the hoses.
19. Install the transmission as outlined in Section 7.
20. Install the hood support and lower the hood.
21. Make sure all fluid levels are correct before starting the engine. Bleed air from the cooling system.

528e Models

➡The transmission must be separated from the block prior to engine removal.

1. Remove the transmission as detailed in Section 7.
2. Disconnect the exhaust pipe from the exhaust manifold.
3. With the hoses attached, remove the power steering pump and position it out of the way using a piece of wire.
4. Unscrew the drain plug on the engine block, remove the upper and lower radiator hoses and drain the cooling system. After draining, remove the radiator.

5. With the refrigerant hoses still connected, remove the air conditioning compressor and position it out of the way using a piece of wire.
6. Disconnect the gas pressure hood springs, then scribe around the hinges and then remove the hood.
7. Disconnect the battery cables (negative first) and remove the battery.
8. Disconnect the accelerator and cruise control cables. Disconnect all hoses from the throttle housing (make sure you tag them all).
9. Disconnect the air duct.
10. Remove the air filter housing along with the air flow sensor.
11. Tag and disconnect all remaining lines, hoses and wires which may interfere with engine removal.
12. Tag and disconnect all plugs and wires attached to the control unit in the glove box. Unscrew the straps on the firewall and pull the wire harness through to the engine compartment.
13. Disconnect the engine ground strap.
14. Loosen both engine mounts.
15. Attach an engine lifting hoist to the front and rear of the engine, remove the engine mount bolts and then lift out the engine.

To install:

16. Lower the engine into the engine compartment. When the engine is positioned, the guide pin must fit in the bore of the axle carrier. Tighten the

mounting bolts on the front axle carrier (small bolt) to 18–20 ft. lbs. (23–26 Nm), the larger bolt to 31–35 ft. lbs. (40–45 Nm).
17. Connect all of the electrical wiring and all vacuum hoses.
18. Connect the accelerator cable and cruise control cable to the throttle body and adjust.
19. Install the air cleaner and reconnect all electrical plugs.
20. Reconnect the wiring to the main control unit in the interior of the vehicle.
21. Install the air conditioning compressor and power steering pump. Properly route the accessory drive belt. Adjust the belt tension.
22. Install the radiator and connect the hoses.
23. Install the transmission as described in Section 7.
24. Install the hood support and lower the hood.
25. Make sure all fluid levels are correct before starting the engine. Bleed the air from the cooling system.

630CSi Models

➡The transmission must be separated from the block prior to engine removal.

1. Raise and support the vehicle on jackstands.
2. Remove the transmission as outlined in Section 7.
3. Disconnect the exhaust pipe at the manifold.
4. Remove the power steering pump and place it out of the way using a piece of wire. Leave the hoses attached.
5. If equipped with air conditioning, remove the compressor and place it aside securing with wire. Do not remove the hoses.
6. Scribe the hood hinge locations and remove the hood.
7. Drain the cooling system, disconnect the hoses and remove the radiator.

8. Remove the air cleaner housing at the wheel housing.
9. Remove the electrical wires and connectors from the engine components. Tag the wires and connectors.

➡The fuel injection control box is located either above the glove box or behind the right side kick panel. Remove the plug and thread the wire and connector through the hole in the firewall into the engine compartment.

10. Tag and disconnect all plugs and wires attached to the control unit in the glove box. Unscrew the straps on the firewall and pull the wire harness through to the engine compartment.
11. Disconnect the engine ground strap.
12. Loosen both engine mounts.
13. Attach an engine lifting hoist to the front and rear of the engine and take up any slack.
14. Remove the engine mount bolts.
15. Lift out the engine.

To install:

16. Lower the engine into the engine compartment. When the engine is positioned, the guide pin must fit in the bore of the axle carrier. Tighten the mounting bolts on the front axle carrier (small bolt) to 18–20 ft. lbs. (23;26 Nm), the larger bolt to 31–35 ft. lbs. (40–45 Nm).
17. Connect all of the electrical wiring and all vacuum hoses.
18. Connect the accelerator cable and cruise control cable to the throttle body and adjust.
19. Install the air cleaner and reconnect all electrical plugs.
20. Reconnect the wiring to the main control unit.
21. Install the air conditioning compressor and power steering pump. Properly route the accessory drive belt. Adjust the belt tension.
22. Install the radiator and connect the hoses.
23. Install the transmission as outlined in Section 7.
24. Install the hood support and lower the hood.

25. Make sure all fluid levels are correct before starting the engine. Bleed the air from the cooling system.

533i, 535i, 633CSi and 635CSi Models

➡ **The transmission must be separated from the block prior to engine removal.**

1. Disconnect the battery cable from the battery, negative side first. Open the hood to the widest position possible and secure in place.

❊❊ CAUTION

The hood must be propped in a secure manner! If it falls during work, serious injury could result.

---

2. Remove the splash shield from under the vehicle.
3. Drain the coolant and remove the fan and radiator.

❊❊ CAUTION

When draining coolant, keep in mind that cats and dogs are attracted to ethylene glycol antifreeze, and could drink any that is left in an uncovered container or in puddles on the ground. This will prove fatal in sufficient quantity. Always drain the coolant into a sealable container. Coolant should be reused unless it is contaminated or several years old.

---

4. Remove the transmission as outlined in Section 7.
5. Disconnect the throttle cable and the cruise control cable. Disconnect the cable brackets from the intake manifold.
6. Loosen and remove the connections to the air cleaner assembly. Remove the air cleaner assembly and airflow meter from the engine.
7. Disconnect the coolant hoses from the engine.
8. Mark the feed and return fuel line connections. Remove the fuel lines, catching any excess fuel with a rag or suitable container placed underneath.
9. Disconnect the idle speed control.
10. Remove the brake booster vacuum line and plug the opening.
11. Disconnect the heater hoses and the vacuum line going into the passenger compartment. Disconnect the heater coolant pipe.
12. Disconnect the leads from the ignition coil and the oil pressure switch. Place the electrical lead duct from under the distributor to the left side of the engine.
13. If equipped, disconnect the oil cooler lines from the engine and place to the side. Plug the lines to prevent oil from leaking out.
14. Disconnect the starter and the alternator wiring. Disconnect the plug located behind the alternator.
15. Disconnect the engine harness and place off to the side.
16. Disconnect the ground strap.
17. Connect an engine lifting sling to the engine.
18. Disconnect the left engine mount from above and the right side mount from under the vehicle.
19. Lift the engine out of the car.

To install:
20. Install the engine and tighten the motor mounts to 32 ft. lbs. (45 Nm).
21. Install the ground strap.
22. Install the engine wiring harness and connect the sensors and hoses.
23. Connect the alternator and starter. Connect the plug located behind the alternator.
24. Install the oil cooler lines, if equipped. Tighten to 22–29 ft. lbs. (30–40 Nm).
25. Connect the ignition coil.
26. Connect the coolant lines and pipes.
27. Connect the vacuum line going into the passenger compartment.
28. Install the idle speed control and the brake booster vacuum line. Connect the radiator hoses and the fuel lines to the previously marked locations.
29. Install the air cleaner and the air flow meter.
30. Connect the air ducts and the electrical connections.
31. Install the throttle cables and the bracket.
32. Install the air conditioner compressor and the power steering pump. Tension the belts.
33. Install the radiator and connect the hoses.
34. Install the transmission.

35. Install the hood support.
36. Make sure all fluid levels are correct before starting the engine. Bleed air from the cooling system.

M5 and M6 Models

➡ **The transmission must be separated from the block prior to engine removal.**

1. Disconnect the battery terminals, negative side first, and remove the battery, if mounted in engine compartment. Unscrew and remove the battery tray.
2. Remove the transmission as outlined in Section 7.
3. Loosen the clamp on the cooling duct to the alternator and remove the duct.
4. Disconnect the plug to the air flow meter and loosen the clamps to the air cleaner duct. Unscrew the mounting bolts and remove the air cleaner assembly.
5. Hold the fan pulley while unscrewing the fan nut from the shaft. The shaft uses left hand threads, turn the nut clockwise to unscrew.
6. Drain the coolant from the engine block and radiator. The drain plug on the block is located between the exhaust manifolds. Disconnect the coolant hoses from the radiator and remove the coolant level switch plug.

❊❊ CAUTION

When draining coolant, keep in mind that cats and dogs are attracted to ethylene glycol antifreeze, and could drink any that is left in an uncovered container or in puddles on the ground. This will prove fatal in sufficient quantity. Always drain the coolant into a sealable container. Coolant should be reused unless it is contaminated or several years old.

---

7. On automatic transmission equipped vehicles, remove the cooler lines at the radiator and plug.
8. Disconnect the bottom radiator hose and remove the trim panel from the right side of the engine compartment to expose the side of the radiator and the air conditioner condenser.
9. Pull the plug off of the air conditioner temperature switch.
10. Remove the radiator supporting clips by inserting a small prybar down from above into the slot and pulling back. Pull the radiator free from the clip. Remove the radiator from the vehicle.
11. Disconnect the heater hoses from the heater valve and the heater.
12. Unscrew the fastener from the throttle cable cover and pull the cover forward and off. Unclip the cable and pull the cable out with the rubber holder.
13. Pull the vacuum fitting from the brake booster and plug the openings.
14. Unscrew the bolt holding the ground strap on the front lifting eye. Replace the bolt before lifting the engine out of the vehicle.
15. Unscrew the 2 bolts holding the plug plate and pull off the plug plate. Be careful not to damage the rubber seals. Take off the ignition coil electrical plugs. Remove the plug plate complete with the electrical leads.
16. Remove the cylinder head vent hose and pull off the air temperature sensor plug. Remove the throttle valve switch plug. Unclip the idle speed control valve mounted on the manifold. Disconnect the fuel hoses from the pipes.
17. Disconnect the plugs from the temperature sensor, temperature gauge, the oil pressure switch and the idle speed control valve. Disconnect the cylinder identifying sender plug (black) and the pulse sender plug (gray)for the DME. Unscrew the oxygen sensor and plug the hole.
18. Remove the electric leads from the alternator and the starter. Unscrew the electrical lead tray and place the engine wiring harness to the side.
19. Loosen the drive belt for the power steering pump and the air conditioner compressor by turning their respective tensioners. Release the tension on the belt and allow the belt to be removed.
20. Unbolt the power steering pump and secure to the side with a piece of wire. Unbolt the air conditioner compressor and place to the side with a piece of wire.
21. Attach a lifting tool to the engine hooks taking up any excess slack. Unscrew the engine mounts and ground strap.
22. Lift the engine out of the vehicle being careful of the front radiator mount.

To install:
23. Lower the engine into the vehicle and attach the motor mounts and ground strap.

24. Install the power steering pump and the air conditioner compressor. Install the drive belts.

25. Replace the wiring harness and electrical lead tray on the engine. Connect the leads to the starter and alternator. Screw in the oxygen sensor.

26. Connect the leads for the cylinder identifying sender, the DME pulse sender, the temperature sensor, the temperature gauge sender, the oil pressure switch and the idle speed control valve.

27. Attach the fuel lines. The upper line is the return and the lower is the feed.

28. Attach the idle speed control valve hose located on the manifold.

29. Connect the throttle valve switch plug, the throttle valve heating lines and the tank vent line.

30. Connect the air temperature sensor plug and attach the cylinder head venting hoses.

31. Reconnect the plugs for the ignition coils and mount the plug plate. Attach the ground strap to the front lifting eye.

32. Connect the line to the brake booster.

33. Reconnect the throttle cable and cover.

34. Connect the heater hoses to the valve and inlet.

35. Remount the radiator by pressing down on the mounting clips to fasten. Check that the lower mounts are in place. Connect the temperature switch plug for the air conditioner and replace the trim panel. Connect the cooling system hoses and the automatic transmission lines.

36. Install the fan and tighten the nut to 29 ft. lbs. (40 Nm). Replace the radiator cowling.

37. Replace the air cleaner assembly and connect the electrical plug.

38. Install the transmission as outlined in section 7.

39. Fill and bleed the cooling system.

40. Install the battery tray and battery. Check all fluids before starting engine.

1982 733i Models

➡ **The transmission must be separated from the block prior to engine removal.**

1. Raise and support the vehicle on jackstands.

2. Remove the transmission as outlined in Section 7.

3. Disconnect the exhaust pipe at the exhaust manifold or thermal reactor.

4. Remove the clutch housing from the engine.

5. Remove the power steering pump and place it out of the way using a piece of wire to secure it to the vehicle body. Do not disconnect the hoses.

6. If equipped with air conditioning, remove the compressor and place it out of the way using a piece of wire. Do not disconnect the hoses.

7. Remove the damper bracket from the crankcase and lower the vehicle.

8. Scribe the hood hinge locations and remove the hood.

9. Drain the cooling system, disconnect the hoses and remove the radiator.

✳✳ CAUTION

When draining coolant, keep in mind that cats and dogs are attracted to ethylene glycol antifreeze, and could drink any that is left in an uncovered container or in puddles on the ground. This will prove fatal in sufficient quantity. Always drain the coolant into a sealable container. Coolant should be reused unless it is contaminated or several years old.

10. Remove the windshield washer reservoir and the air filter housing located on the inner fender panel.

11. Remove the electrical wiring from the engine components. Tag all wires.

12. Disconnect and remove the battery.

13. Remove and tag all vacuum hoses.

➡ **Some vacuum hoses are color coded.**

14. Disconnect the throttle linkage.

15. Remove the right kick panel from the passenger compartment. Remove the fuel injection control unit wire connector and thread the connector and wire through the hole in the firewall.

16. Attach a lifting sling to the engine.

17. Remove the left and right engine mount retaining nuts and washers.

18. Lift the engine from the engine compartment.

To install:

19. Lower the engine into the engine compartment. When the engine is positioned, the guide pin must fit in the bore of the axle carrier. Tighten the mounting bolts on the front axle carrier (small bolt) to 18–20 ft. lbs. (23;26 Nm), the larger bolt to 31–35 ft. lbs. (40–45 Nm).

20. Connect all of the electrical wiring and all vacuum hoses.

21. Connect the accelerator cable and cruise control cable to the throttle body and adjust.

22. Install the air cleaner and reconnect all electrical plugs.

23. Reconnect the wiring to the main control unit.

24. Install the air conditioning compressor and power steering pump. Properly route the accessory drive belt. Adjust the belt tension.

25. Install the radiator and connect the hoses.

26. Install the transmission as described in Section 7.

27. Install the hood support and lower the hood.

28. Make sure all fluid levels are correct before starting the engine. Bleed the air from the cooling system.

733i and 735i

1983–86 MODELS

➡ **The transmission must be separated from the block prior to engine removal.**

1. Disconnect the cables from the battery, negative side first.

2. Open the hood to the widest position possible and secure in place.

✳✳ CAUTION

The hood must be propped in a secure manner! If it falls during work serious injury could result.

3. Remove the splash shield from under the car.

4. Drain the coolant and remove the radiator

✳✳ CAUTION

When draining coolant, keep in mind that cats and dogs are attracted to ethylene glycol antifreeze, and could drink any that is left in an uncovered container or in puddles on the ground. This will prove fatal in sufficient quantity. Always drain the coolant into a sealable container. Coolant should be reused unless it is contaminated or several years old.

5. Remove the transmission as outlined in Section 7.

6. Remove the nut holding the transmission oil cooler lines to the engine oil pan.

7. Loosen and remove the drive belts to the power steering pump and the air conditioner compressor. Remove the bolts holding the pump and compressor to the engine and remove them from the engine, keeping the lines connected. Wire the pump and compressor out of the way without any tension on the hoses.

8. Disconnect the hoses from the coolant expansion tank. Remove the screws on the side of the expansion tank and the expansion tank from the engine compartment.

9. Disconnect the heater hoses from the heater control valve and the heater inlet pipe.

10. Pull off the connections to the ignition coil.

11. Remove the air cleaner assembly.

12. Disconnect and remove the idle speed control from the intake duct.

13. Disconnect the harness to the airflow meter. Disconnect the ducting to the air flow meter and remove along with the crankcase breather vacuum line.

14. Disconnect the cruise control cable and the throttle cable at the throttle. Remove the cable mounting bracket.

15. Disconnect the leads to the starter. Disconnect the 2 electrical connectors in the starter area.

16. Disconnect the oil level sender leads and the alternator connections. Remove the air duct to the alternator.

17. Disconnect the tank venting valve and the hose to the carbon canister.

18. Mark the feed and return fuel lines. Disconnect the lines and catch any spilled fuel with a rag or suitable container placed underneath.

19. Disconnect the vacuum line from the brake booster and plug the opening.

20. Disconnect the ground strap and make a check for any remaining lines or electrical leads still attached.

21. Attach a lifting sling to the engine and take up any slack.

22. Remove the engine mount nuts and bolts and lift the engine from the engine bay.

To install:

23. Install the engine into the engine compartment. Tighten the engine mounts to 32 ft. lbs. (45 Nm). Connect the ground strap.

24. Connect the brake booster vacuum line.

25. Connect the fuel lines to their proper locations as previously marked.

26. Connect the tank venting valve and the carbon canister line.

27. Attach the alternator leads and the cooling duct.

28. Connect the starter leads and the electrical connector in the starter area.

29. Connect the oil level sender leads.

30. Connect the throttle cable and the cruise control cable and bracket.

31. Install the airflow sensor and the crankcase breather line.

32. Install the idle speed control to the air intake duct. Install the air cleaner assembly.

33. Connect the heater lines to the heater control valve and the heater inlet pipe. Install the coolant expansion tank and connect the lines.

34. Install the air conditioner compressor and power steering pump. Adjust the belt tensions.

35. Connect the transmission oil cooling lines to the bracket on the engine oil pan.

36. Install the transmission as outlined in Section 7.

37. Install the radiator. Fill the cooling system.

38. Check all other engine fluids levels and adjust if needed.

39. Install the splash shield.

40. Connect the battery cables, positive, then negative.

41. Run the engine and check for leaks. Bleed the cooling system.

1987–88 735I MODELS

1. Disconnect first the negative battery cable and then the positive.

2. Remove the transmission as described in Section 7.

3. Scribe hinge locations and remove the hood, or remove the support struts and prop it securely.

> **✳✳ CAUTION**
>
> **In lifting up the hood, the hood must be propped in a secure manner! If it falls during work serious injury could result.**

4. Remove the splash guard from underneath the engine.

5. Remove the drain plugs in the radiator and engine block and drain the engine coolant.

> **✳✳ CAUTION**
>
> **When draining coolant, keep in mind that cats and dogs are attracted to ethylene glycol antifreeze, and could drink any that is left in an uncovered container or in puddles on the ground. This will prove fatal in sufficient quantity. Always drain the coolant into a sealable container. Coolant should be reused unless it is contaminated or several years old.**

6. Loosen the power steering pump bolts from underneath. Turn the adjusting pinion to loosen the belt and remove. Then, remove the mounting bolts and remove the power steering pump without disconnecting the hoses. Support the pump out of the way with wire.

7. Remove the air conditioner compressor. This unit does not have the belt adjusting pinion. It is necessary, only to loosen all the bolts and push the compressor toward the engine to remove the belt. Use wire to secure the compressor to the vehicle body.

8. Loosen the air intake hose clamp and disconnect the hose. Remove the mounting nut and then remove the air cleaner assembly.

9. The unit on the opposite side of the intake hose from the air cleaner contains the idle speed control valve, which must be removed. Loosen the hose clamps and pull off the hoses. Disconnect the electrical connector. Remove the mounting nut and then pull the idle speed control out of the air intake hose.

10. Pull off the 3 retainers for the airflow sensor, and then pull the unit off

its mounting, disconnecting the vacuum hose from the PCV system at the same time.

11. Working on the coolant expansion tank, unfasten the electrical connector. Remove the nuts on both sides. Loosen the clamps and disconnect all 3 hoses and remove the tank.

12. Disconnect the heater hoses at both the control valve and at the heater core.

13. Disconnect the throttle and cruise control cables at the throttle lever. Unbolt the cable housing retainer and remove the housing and cables.

14. Pull off the low amperage starter connectors and disconnect the high amperage connector coming from the battery.

15. Unfasten the connecting plug for the oxygen sensor.

16. Loosen the clamps and then disconnect the fuel supply and return pipes, draining fuel into a metal container for safe disposal.

17. Disconnect the fuel pipe at the injector supply manifold.

18. Unfasten the electrical connector at the throttle body. Lift off the protective caps and remove the attaching nuts for the protective cover for the wiring harness for the injectors and remove.

19. Disconnect the ground strap at the block.

20. Remove the upper engine mount nuts from both sides of the engine.

21. Attach a lifting sling to the engine and support the assembly with a crane or other equivalent lifting device.

22. Disconnect the ground lead.

23. Carefully lift the engine out of the compartment, tilting the front of the engine upward for clearance.

Then, carefully lift the engine out of the compartment, avoiding contact between it and the components remaining in the car.

To install:

24. Keep these points in mind during installation:

   a. Tighten the engine mounting bolts to 32 ft. lbs. (42 Nm).

   b. Adjust the belt tension for the air conditioning compressor and power steering pump drive belts to give 0.5–0.75 inches (13–19 Nm) deflection.

   c. Tighten the oil cooler line flare nuts to 25 ft. lbs. (32 Nm).

   d. When reconnecting the intake manifold to the throttle necks, inspect and, if necessary, replace the O-rings. Tighten the mounting nuts to 78 in. lbs. (9 Nm).

25. To install, reverse the procedures used for removal.

26. Lower the engine into the engine compartment. When the engine is positioned, the guide pin must fit in the bore of the axle carrier. Tighten the mounting bolts on the front axle carrier (small bolt) to 18–20 ft. lbs. (23;26 Nm), the larger bolt to 31–35 ft. lbs. (40–45 Nm).

27. Connect the fuel lines, using new hose clamps to connect the fuel lines to the fuel filter.

28. Connect all of the multi-prong plugs and all vacuum hoses.

29. Connect the accelerator cable and cruise control cable to the throttle body and adjust.

30. Install the coolant recovery tank, using a new hose clamp on the coolant expansion tank.

31. Install the air cleaner and reconnect all electrical plugs. Connect and install the relays in the relay box.

32. Reconnect the wiring to the main control unit and install the idle control unit.

33. Install the air conditioning compressor and power steering pump. Properly route the accessory drive belt. Adjust the belt tension.

34. Install the radiator and connect the hoses.

35. Install the transmission as described in Section 7.

36. Install the hood support and lower the hood.

37. Make sure all fluid levels are correct before starting the engine. Bleed air from the cooling system.

Cylinder Head (Valve) Cover

REMOVAL & INSTALLATION

▶ **See Figures 56, 57 and 58**

Cylinder head cover removal and installation is basically a straightforward procedure on all models covered in this manual. Disconnect any hoses or lines which are in the way, the remove the retaining bolts or nuts and lift off the cover. It is always a good idea to remove and install the bolts/nuts in a cross-wise manner starting in the center to prevent gasket and valve cover warpage. Snug

Fig. 56 Some engine compartments are tighter than others— you may have to maneuver the cover off

Fig. 57 Some valve covers are installed with rubber insulators between the bolt head and valve cover. When tightening, make sure you do not tear the rubber

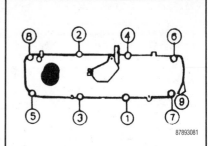

Fig. 58 Always remove and tighten the valve cover by starting in the middle and working outward in a crisscross pattern

all bolts/nuts finger tight and then tighten in the same order. Cylinder head cover removal will almost always require the replacement of the gasket upon installation, therefore purchase a new gasket prior to removing the valve.

Rocker Arm Shafts/Rocker Arms

INSPECTION

Check the rocker shafts for scoring and wear at the rocker arm pivot points. Check the shaft oiling holes for clogging and varnish. Check the bushing in the rocker arm for wear. Check the adjuster eccentric for flatspots. Check the iron pad for wear and looseness. If the iron pad is loose, it will make a ticking or tapping noise when the engine is running.

REMOVAL & INSTALLATION

Except 325, 325e, 325i, 325iS, 325iX and 528e

▶ **See Figures 59 and 60**

1. Remove the cylinder head cover.
2. Remove the cylinder head from the engine as outlined in this section. Place on a clean secure work surface
3. Remove the camshaft as outlined in this section.
4. On 6-cylinder engines, remove the retaining bolts and remove the end cover from the rear of the cylinder head. Slide the thrust rings and rocker arms rearward and remove the circlips from the rocker arm shafts.
5. On 4-cylinder engines:
   a. Remove the distributor flange from the rear of the cylinder head.
   b. Using a long punch, drive the rocker arm shaft from the rear toward the front of the cylinder head.
   c. Be sure all circlips are off the shaft before attempting to drive the shaft from the cylinder head.
   d. The intake rocker shaft is not plugged at the rear, while the exhaust rocker shaft must be plugged. Renew the plug if necessary, during the installation.
6. On 6-cylinder engines:
   a. Install dowel pins BMW part No. 11 1 063 or equivalent to keep the

rocker shafts from turning. Then, remove the rocker shaft retaining plugs from the front of the cylinder head. These require a hex head wrench. Then, back the rocker arms against the spring pressure and remove the circlips retaining the shafts. Remove the dowel pins. If the rocker shafts have welded plugs, the shafts will have to be pressed out of the head with a tool such as 11 3 050 or equivalent.

✳✳ CAUTION

There is considerable force on the springs positioning the rockers. They may pop out! Be cautious and wear safety glasses.

   b. Install a threaded slide hammer into the ends of the rear rocker shafts and remove.
7. The rocker arms, springs, washers, thrust rings and shafts should be examined and worn parts replaced. Special attention should be given to the rocker arm cam followers. If these are loose, replace the arm assembly. The valves can be removed, repaired or replaced, as necessary, while the shafts and rocker arms are out of the cylinder head.

To install:
8. Install noting the following procedures:
   a. Design changes of the rocker arms and shafts have occurred with the installation of a bushing in the rocker arm and the use of 2 horizontal oil flow holes drilled into the rocker shaft for improved oil supply. Do not mix the previously designed parts with the later design.
   b. When installing the rocker arms and components to the rocker shafts, install locating pins in the cylinder head bolt bores to properly align the rocker arm shafts. Note that on 6-cylinder engines, the longer rocker shafts go on the chain end of the engine. The openings face the bores for the cylinder head bolts. The plug threads face outward. The order of installation is: spring, washer, rocker arm, thrust washer, circlip. Note also that newer, short springs may be used with the older design.
   c. Install sealer on the rocker arm shaft retaining plugs and rear cover.
   d. On the 4-cylinder engines, position the rocker shafts so that the camshaft retaining plate ends can be engaged in the slots of shafts during camshaft installation.
   e. Adjust the valve clearance.

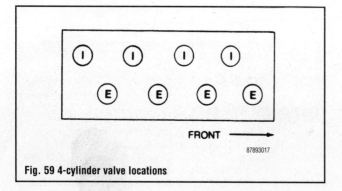

Fig. 59 4-cylinder valve locations

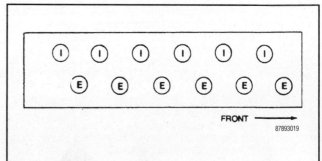

Fig. 60 6-cylinder valve locations

325, 325e, 325i, 325iS, 325iX and 528e Models

♦ See Figure 61

➡ **The cylinder head must be removed before the rocker arm shafts can be removed.**

1. Disconnect the negative battery cable. Remove the cylinder head.
2. Mount the head on a suitable holding fixture.
3. Remove the camshaft sprocket bolt and remove the camshaft distributor adapter and sprocket. Reinstall the adapter on the camshaft.
4. Adjust the valve clearance to the maximum allowable on all valves.
5. Remove the front and rear rocker shaft plugs and lift out the thrust plate.
6. Remove the spring-clips from the rocker arms by lifting them off.
7. Remove the exhaust side rocker arm shaft:
   a. Set the No. 6 cylinder rocker arms at the valve overlap position (rocker arms parallel), by rotating the camshaft through the firing order.
   b. Push in on the front cylinder rocker arm and then turn the camshaft in the direction of the intake rocker shaft, using a ½ inch drive breaker bar and a deep well socket to fit over the camshaft adapter. Slide each rocker arm to one side as it develops sufficient clearance away from its actuating camshaft and the valve it actuates. Rotate the camshaft until all of the rocker arms are relaxed.
   c. Remove the rocker arm shaft by driving it out or pulling it out.
8. Remove the intake side rocker arm shaft:
   a. Turn the camshaft in the direction of the exhaust rocker arm.
   b. Use a deep well socket and a ½ inch drive breaker bar on the camshaft adapter to turn the camshaft. Slide each rocker arm to one side as it

develops sufficient clearance away from its actuating camshaft and the valve it actuates. Rotate the camshaft until all of the rocker arms are relaxed.
   c. Remove the rocker arm shaft.

To install:

9. Install the rocker arm shafts by reversing the removal procedure. Keep the following points in mind:
   a. The large oil bores in the rocker shafts must be installed downward, toward the valve guides and the small oil bores and grooves for the guide plate face inward toward the center of the head.
   b. The straight sections of the spring clamps must fit into the grooves in the rocker arm shafts.
   c. The guide plate must fit into the grooves in the rocker arm shafts.
   d. Adjust the valve clearance.

Thermostat

REMOVAL & INSTALLATION

♦ **See Figures 62, 63, 64 and 65**

The thermostat is located near the water pump, either on the cylinder head, intake manifold or between 2 coolant hose sections. On the diesel engine, it is located directly above the water pump.

1. Remove the fan to gain access. See the water pump removal procedure in this section for special procedures required to remove the fan.
2. Drain enough coolant out to lower the coolant level below the thermostat.

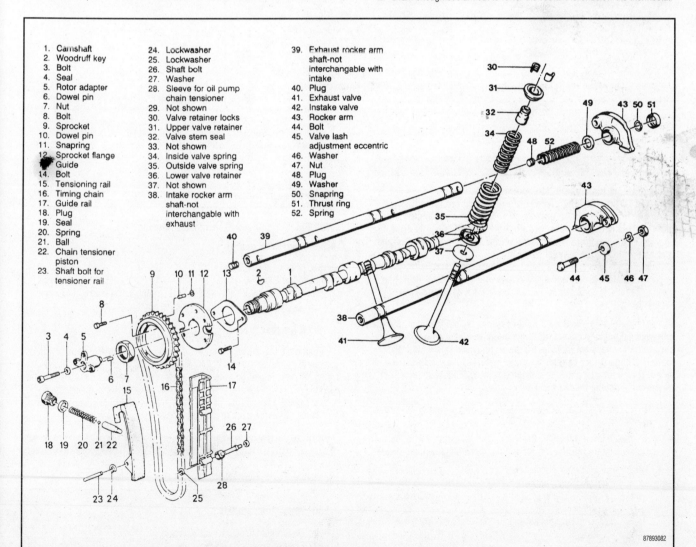

1. Camshaft	24. Lockwasher	39. Exhaust rocker arm shaft-not interchangable with intake
2. Woodruff key	25. Lockwasher	40. Plug
3. Bolt	26. Shaft bolt	41. Exhaust valve
4. Seal	27. Washer	42. Instake valve
5. Rotor adapter	28. Sleeve for oil pump chain tensioner	43. Rocker arm
6. Dowel pin	29. Not shown	44. Bolt
7. Nut	30. Valve retainer locks	45. Valve lash adjustment eccentric
8. Bolt	31. Upper valve retainer	46. Washer
9. Sprocket	32. Valve stem seal	47. Nut
10. Dowel pin	33. Not shown	48. Plug
11. Snapring	34. Inside valve spring	49. Washer
12. Sprocket flange	35. Outside valve spring	50. Snapring
13. Guide	36. Lower valve retainer	51. Thrust ring
14. Bolt	37. Not shown	52. Spring
15. Tensioning rail	38. Intake rocker arm shaft-not interchangable with exhaust	
16. Timing chain		
17. Guide rail		
18. Plug		
19. Seal		
20. Spring		
21. Ball		
22. Chain tensioner piston		
23. Shaft bolt for tensioner rail		

Fig. 61 Exploded view of valve train assembly—325 and 528e models

87893082

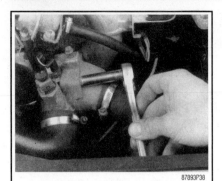

Fig. 62 Loose and remove the thermostat housing retainer bolts . . .

Fig. 63 . . . then remove the housing from the cylinder head

Fig. 64 When you remove the thermostat, note the positioning for installation purposes

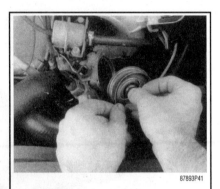

Fig. 65 Remove the seal(s) from the thermostat and housing

Fig. 66 Loosen the bleeder bolt until air comes out. NEVER remove the bolt entirely

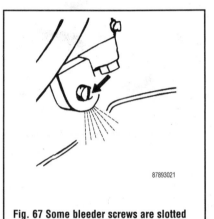

Fig. 67 Some bleeder screws are slotted

If reusing the coolant, save it in a clean container before removing the thermostat.

✳✳ CAUTION

When draining the coolant, keep in mind that cats and dogs are attracted by the ethylene glycol antifreeze, and are quite likely to drink any that is left in an uncovered container or in puddles on the ground. This will prove fatal in sufficient quantity. Always drain the coolant into a sealable container. Coolant should be reused unless it is contaminated or several years old.

3. On the M5, M6 engine, the forward (removable) portion of the thermostat housing has a hose connected to it. The hose need not be disconnected to remove the housing.

➡On the 1983–87 3.2 and all 3.5 liter engines including diesel, there is a thermostat housing gasket, and also an inner rubber seal to keep the closed thermostat from leaking. On the engine used in the M5, M6, there is a large O-ring seal for the main portion of the housing and a small, O-ring located above in a small passage. Replaced the seal(s) whenever removing the thermostat.

Note that thermostats for 3.5L engines built in 1986–88 carry an **A** designation. This thermostat is a smaller in diameter.

➡On all models except the M3, the thermostat is installed with the thermostatic sensing unit facing inward and the cross-band facing outward.

4. Remove the bolts securing the thermostat housing in place. Once removed, tap the housing lightly with the palm of your hand to break the seal.
5. Remove the thermostat and seal(s) from the housing. Remember the direction in which the thermostat faced.
6. Inspect the housing mating surface and remove any seals or gasket material which may be attached.

➡No gasket material is needed to install the thermostat.

7. Install the seal(s) around the thermostat and position in the housing.
8. Align the thermostat housing to the engine and secure with the retainer bolts. Tighten the bolts to 6–7 ft. lbs. (8–10 Nm).
9. Refill and bleed the cooling system.

BLEEDING THE COOLING SYSTEM

With Bleeder Screw on Thermostat Housing

▶ See Figures 66 and 67

Set the heat valve in the **WARM** position, start the engine and bring to normal operating temperature. Run the engine at fast idle and open the venting screw on the thermostat housing until the coolant comes out free of air bubbles. Close the bleeder screw and refill the cooling system.

Without Bleeder Screw

Fill the cooling system, place the heater valve in the **WARM** position, close the pressure cap to the second (fully closed) position. Start the engine and bring to normal operating temperature. Carefully release the pressure cap to the first position and squeeze the upper and lower radiator hoses in a pumping action to allow trapped air to escape through the cap. Recheck the coolant level and close the pressure cap to its second position.

Intake Manifold

REMOVAL & INSTALLATION

1600, 2000, 2002 Models

1. Disconnect the negative battery cable.
2. Remove the air cleaner assembly.

3. Remove and tag the fuel lines, vacuum lines and electrical wiring attached to the carburetor.

4. Drain the cooling system.

※※ CAUTION

When draining coolant, keep in mind that cats and dogs are attracted to ethylene glycol antifreeze, and could drink any that is left in an uncovered container or in puddles on the ground. This will prove fatal in sufficient quantity. Always drain the coolant into a sealable container. Coolant should be reused unless it is contaminated or several years old.

5. Disconnect the manual choke control cable. On automatic transmission equipped models, disconnect the wire connected to the choke cover.

6. Disconnect the accelerator linkage. On automatic transmission equipped models, disconnect the linkage at the ball socket.

7. Disconnect the coolant lines at the manifold.

8. Disconnect the dipstick support.

9. Remove the intake manifold by removing the retainer nuts securing the manifold in place. During removal, some of the studs may be removed with the retainer nuts. In this case replace both the stud and nut.

10. Remove the gasket between the manifold and cylinder head.

To install:

11. Position the manifold on the cylinder head studs, with a new gasket between the cylinder head and manifold. Tighten the retainer nuts to 15–17 ft. lbs. (20–24 Nm).

12. Connect the dipstick support and coolant lines to the manifold.

13. Connect the accelerator linkage, vacuum lines, electrical wiring and fuel lines removed earlier.

14. Connect the negative battery cable.

15. Fill the cooling system and bleed.

2002Tii Models

➡To remove the complete manifold system, first remove the resonator pipes, then remove the intake pipe.

INDUCTION RESONATOR PIPES (SECURED WITH CLAMPS)

◆ **See Figure 68**

1. Disconnect the negative battery cable.

2. Remove the air filter assembly.

3. Remove and tag the fuel lines, starter valve cable, vacuum hoses, and all induction resonator pipes.

4. Disconnect the throttle return spring and remove the injection pipe from No. 1 cylinder. Remove the injector valve.

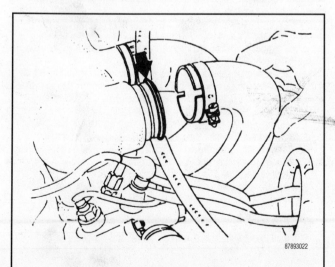

87893022

Fig. 68 The early 2002Tii induction pipes were secured with clamps

5. Remove the bracket bolts at the throttle housing.

6. Remove the vacuum hose, auxiliary air hose and injection pipe from the No. 4 cylinder.

7. Loosen the clamp(s) around the induction pipe(s), then remove the retaining nuts at the base.

8. Remove the air collector from the cylinder head.

9. Installation is the reverse of the removal procedure.

INDUCTION MANIFOLDS (SECURED WITH NUTS AND WASHERS)

1. Disconnect the negative battery cable.

2. Remove the air filter.

3. Remove the fuel line, fuel return line starter valve cable and vacuum hose from the air tube assembly.

4. Remove the bracket bolts on the throttle housing.

5. Remove the air collector support bolts at the top engine cover area.

6. Remove the nuts and washers from the bottom of the induction manifold.

7. Remove the air collector together with the induction manifolds and the throttle housing.

8. Installation is the reverse of the removal procedure.

INTAKE PIPE

1. Disconnect the negative battery cable.

2. After removing the air collector/induction resonator pipes as earlier in this section, remove the remaining injection pipes from the injection valves.

3. Disconnect the coolant hoses and electrical harness(s) at the thermostat housing and switches.

4. Remove the retaining nuts and washers from the cylinder head studs and remove the intake pipe.

5. Installation is the reverse of removal. Use new gaskets and place them on the intake opening properly so as not to interfere with the air flow.

2500, 2800, 3000 and Bavaria Models

FRONT INTAKE MANIFOLD

1. Drain the cooling system.

※※ CAUTION

When draining coolant, keep in mind that cats and dogs are attracted to ethylene glycol antifreeze, and could drink any that is left in an uncovered container or in puddles on the ground. This will prove fatal in sufficient quantity. Always drain the coolant into a sealable container. Coolant should be reused unless it is contaminated or several years old.

2. Remove the air filter assembly.

3. Disconnect and tag all fuel and vacuum lines.

4. Disconnect the throttle linkage and connecting bars and remove the bearing block.

5. Disconnect the manual choke cable.

6. Remove the coolant hoses to the manifold or carburetor.

7. Remove the dipstick support.

8. Remove the intake manifold with the carburetor attached by unfastening the retainer nuts. Discard the manifold gasket.

9. Installation is the reverse of the removal procedure using new gaskets. Tighten the nuts to 15–17 ft. lbs. (20–24 Nm).

REAR INTAKE MANIFOLD

1. Drain the cooling system.

※※ CAUTION

When draining coolant, keep in mind that cats and dogs are attracted to ethylene glycol antifreeze, and could drink any that is left in an uncovered container or in puddles on the ground. This will prove fatal in sufficient quantity. Always drain the coolant into a sealable container. Coolant should be reused unless it is contaminated or several years old.

2. Disconnect the negative battery cable.

3. Remove the air filter assembly.

4. Disconnect and tag all fuel and vacuum lines.
5. Disconnect the accelerator thrust bar and bearing block.
6. Disconnect the electrical wire from the choke cover. Remove the choke cover with the coolant lines attached.
7. Disconnect the heater hoses from the manifold base.
8. Remove the intake manifold with the carburetor attached, by unfastening the retainer nuts. Discard the manifold gasket.
9. Installation is the reverse of the removal procedure. Use new gaskets when installing the manifold. Tighten the nuts to 15–17 ft. lbs. (20–24 Nm).

3.0 CSi Models

➡**Combine the next 2 operations to remove both the front and rear intake manifolds.**

FRONT INTAKE MANIFOLD

1. Remove the air cleaner assembly.
2. Drain the cooling system.

❊❊ CAUTION

When draining coolant, keep in mind that cats and dogs are attracted to ethylene glycol antifreeze, and could drink any that is left in an uncovered container or in puddles on the ground. This will prove fatal in sufficient quantity. Always drain the coolant into a sealable container. Coolant should be reused unless it is contaminated or several years old.

3. Remove the intake air collector and the front intake pipes.
4. Remove the pressure regulator and support from the intake manifold.
5. Disconnect the coolant hoses from the thermostat housing and the wiring from the coolant switches.
6. Remove the flat plugs from the injection valves by carefully pulling upward.
7. Remove the first 3 injection valves from the manifold.

➡**Leave the circular pipe connected.**

8. Remove the retaining bolts from the intake manifold and remove from the cylinder head.
9. Installation is the reverse of removal. Install the manifold using a new gasket. Tighten the nuts to 15–17 ft. lbs. (20–24 Nm). Use new injection valve sealing rings.

REAR INTAKE MANIFOLD

1. Disconnect the negative battery cable.
2. Remove the air cleaner assembly.
3. Remove the intake air collector and the rear intake pipes.
4. Remove the pressure regulator and support from the intake manifold.
5. Remove the flat plugs from the injection valves by carefully pulling upwards.
6. Remove the 3 rear injector valves.

➡**Leave the circular pipe connected.**

7. Remove and tag the electrical plugs and harness from the end of the wire loom routed through the intake manifold.
8. Carefully pull the wire loom upward through the hole in the intake manifold.
9. Remove the intake manifold from the cylinder head by removing the retainer nuts. Once removed, discard the gasket.
10. Installation is the reverse of removal. Install the manifold using a new gasket. Tighten the nuts to 15–17 ft. lbs. (20–24 Nm). Always renew the injection valve sealing rings.

318i and 320i Models

1. Disconnect the negative battery cable.
2. Remove the air cleaner and drain the cooling system.

❊❊ CAUTION

When draining coolant, keep in mind that cats and dogs are attracted to ethylene glycol antifreeze, and could drink any that is

left in an uncovered container or in puddles on the ground. This will prove fatal in sufficient quantity. Always drain the coolant into a sealable container. Coolant should be reused unless it is contaminated or several years old.**

3. Disconnect the accelerator cable, then tag and remove the vacuum hoses from the air collector.
4. Remove the injection line holder from the No. 4 intake tube.
5. Remove the No. 3 intake tube and disconnect the vacuum and coolant lines from the throttle housing.
6. Disconnect the hoses at the EGR valve and remove the plugs at the temperature timing switch.
7. Remove the cold start valve from the air collector.
8. Disconnect the vacuum hose and electrical harness at the timing valve.
9. Disconnect the remaining intake tubes at the collector. Unfasten the collector brackets at the engine and remove the collector.
10. Remove the air intake tubes from the manifold and remove the injector valves.
11. Remove the intake manifold by removing the manifold retainer nuts.
To install:
12. Use new gaskets and install the manifold to the engine. Tighten the nuts to 16–18 ft. lbs. (22–25 Nm).
13. Install the air intake tubes and the injector valves. Install the collector and bracket.
14. Connect the vacuum line and electrical harness(s) to the timing valve. Install the cold start valve.
15. Connect the line at the EGR valve and the electrical plugs at the temperature timing switch.
16. Connect all vacuum, cooling and fuel lines at the throttle housing. Install the accelerator cable and vacuum hoses to the air collector.
17. Install the air cleaner and fill the cooling system. Check all hose connections and fluid levels before operating the engine.
18. Connect the negative battery cable.

All 6-Cylinder Engines

EXCEPT M5 AND M6 MODELS

➡**Slight variations may exist among models due to model changes and updating, but the basic removal and installation remains the same.**

1. Disconnect the negative battery cable and drain the cooling system.

❊❊ CAUTION

When draining coolant, keep in mind that cats and dogs are attracted to ethylene glycol antifreeze, and could drink any that is left in an uncovered container or in puddles on the ground. This will prove fatal in sufficient quantity. Always drain the coolant into a sealable container. Coolant should be reused unless it is contaminated or several years old.

2. Disconnect the wire harness at the airflow sensor. Remove the airflow sensor as an assembly. Disconnect the air intake hose running from the airflow sensor to the manifold.
3. Remove and tag the vacuum hoses and electrical plugs. Disconnect the accelerator linkage (and cruise control linkage, if so-equipped) from the throttle housing. Disconnect the throttle position sensor harness.
4. Disconnect the coolant hoses from the throttle housing.
5. Working from the rear of the manifold, disconnect the vacuum lines and the electrical harness. Tag the connectors and lines for ease of assembly.
6. Disconnect the fuel injector electrical plugs. Disconnect the injector harness loom from the manifold and pull out of the way.
7. Disconnect the fuel lines from the injector rail.
8. Disconnect the intake manifold support from the intake manifold at the bottom. Remove the nuts holding the intake manifold and remove the intake manifold.
To install:
9. Install the intake manifold with new gaskets and tighten the nuts to 16–18 ft. lbs. (22–25 Nm). Install the support and tighten to 15–17 ft. lbs. (20–24 Nm).
10. Install the fuel lines to the fuel rail. Install the injector harness loom and connect the fuel injector plugs.

11. Connect all lines and harness(s). Connect the coolant lines, the throttle position sensor and the throttle cables.

12. Connect the ducting from the airflow sensor to the throttle and the airflow sensor.

13. Fill the cooling system and connect the negative battery terminal.

M3 Models

➡**A Torx® nut driver is needed to perform this operation.**

1. Disconnect the negative battery cable.

2. Remove the cap nuts at the outer ends of the 4 throttle necks. Then remove the mounting nuts underneath.

3. Make sure the engine has cooled off. Loosen the hose clamps for the air intake lines and for the fuel lines where they connect with the injection pipe. Collect fuel in a metal container.

4. Disconnect the throttle cable.

5. Pull off the intake manifold. Cut off the crankcase ventilation hose running to it from the crankcase. Then, remove the manifold and place it aside.

6. Pull off the throttle valve switch plug. Carefully pull the injector plate evenly off all 4 injectors.

7. Pull the fuel pressure regulator vacuum hose off the pressure regulator.

8. Remove the 2 mounting bolts for the injector pipe. Then, carefully lift off the pipe and injectors.

9. Unscrew the nut attaching the ball joint at the end of the throttle actuating rod to the throttle linkage. Supply a new self-locking nut.

10. Remove the nuts attaching the throttle necks to the cylinder head. Then, remove the 4 throttle necks as an assembly.

11. Separate the throttle neck assemblies by pulling them apart at the connecting pipe.

12. Inspect the O-rings in the connecting pipe and at the outer ends of the throttle necks. Replace as necessary

To install:

13. Reverse the removal procedure to install. Use the new throttle linkage self-locking nut and the new crankcase ventilation hose.

14. Tighten the nuts attaching the throttle necks to the head and the intake manifold to the throttle necks to 6–8 ft. lbs. (9–11 Nm). Adjust the throttle cable.

M5 and M6 Models

The M5 and M6 employ a manifold chamber in combination with 6 throttle necks (one for each cylinder), each of which contains its own throttle. The throttle necks are divided into 3 assemblies each containing the necks for 2 adjacent cylinders.

1. Disconnect the negative battery terminal.

2. Disconnect the throttle cable. Remove the air intake hose. Remove the screws on each throttle valve assembly.

3. Disconnect the hose for the idle speed control, the venting hose and the oil return hose. Remove the nuts for the oil trap and pull off the air intake assembly.

4. Pull off the plug plate from the fuel injectors. Disconnect the fuel lines from the fuel rail. Pull of the intermediate plug for the idle speed control.

5. Remove the fuel rail with the fuel injectors.

6. Disconnect the vacuum hoses, after noting the routing pattern. Remove the 10mm nuts and the 13mm nuts. Remove the shaft connection nut. Disconnect the throttle linkage and remove the throttle bodies.

7. Separate the throttle bodies by detaching the connecting pipes. Check the O-rings on the pipe. Clean the throttle shafts before pulling out of the bores and do not use tools on the shaft or it may be damaged.

To install:

8. Install the throttle bodies together using new O-rings on the connecting pipes. Install the throttle bodies to the engine using new gaskets. Tighten the 10mm nuts to 6–8 ft. lbs. (9–11 Nm) and the 13mm nuts to 14–17 ft. lbs. (20–24 Nm).

9. Route and connect the vacuum hoses. Install the shaft connection nut and the throttle linkage. Install the fuel rail and the fuel connections. Connect the intermediate plug and the injector plug plate.

10. Check the O-rings on the air intake assembly and attach the pins at the bottom of the assembly. Install the air intake assembly.

11. Connect the oil return hose, the idle speed hose and the venting hose. Install the air intake duct and install the screws at each throttle. Connect the negative battery terminal.

Exhaust Manifold

REMOVAL & INSTALLATION

1600, 2000, and 2002 Models

1. Loosen the exhaust system supports.

2. Separate the exhaust pipe from the exhaust manifold and remove the hot air guide sleeve.

3. Remove the retaining nuts and washers from the exhaust manifold studs and remove the manifold from the cylinder head. Discard the manifold gasket

4. Installation is the reverse of removal. Install new manifold gasket(s). Tighten the retaining nuts to 16–18 ft. lbs. (22–25 Nm). Tighten the clamps holding the exhaust pipes last to avoid having an exhaust system vibration during operation.

2500, 2800, 3000, Bavaria and 3.0 Models

➡**Each exhaust manifold can be removed separately, after the exhaust pipes are disconnected.**

1. Remove the air cleaner and manifold cover plate.

2. On automatic transmission equipped vehicles, detach the oil filler pipe at the rear of the cover plate.

3. Disconnect the CO tap connector at the exhaust manifold. Disconnect the exhaust pipe from the manifold sections.

4. Remove the retaining nuts and washers and remove the exhaust manifolds from the cylinder head. Discard the manifold gaskets(s).

5. Installation is the reverse of removal. Use new manifold gaskets. Tighten retainer nuts to 16–18 ft. lbs. (22–25 Nm).

1977–88 Models

EXCEPT M3, M5 AND M6 MODELS

The exhaust manifolds can be referred to as exhaust gas recirculation reactors.

The removal and installation procedures are basically the same for all models. The 4-cylinder manifold, is a one piece, one outlet unit, while the 6-cylinder manifold assembly consists of a 2 piece, double outlet unit to the exhaust pipe. One piece can be replaced independently of the other.

1. Remove the air volume control and if necessary, air cleaner assembly.

2. Disconnect the exhaust pipe at the manifold/reactor outlet(s).

3. Remove the guard plate from the manifold/reactor(s), if equipped.

4. Disconnect the air injection pipe fitting, the EGR counter pressure line, EGR pressure line and any supports.

➡**An exhaust filter is used between the reactor and the EGR valve and must be disconnected. Replace the filter if found to be defective.**

5. Remove the retaining bolts or nuts at the reactor and remove it from the cylinder head.

6. Installation is the reverse of removal. Use new gaskets. Tighten the manifold/reactor nuts to 16–18 ft. lbs. (22–25 Nm).

M3 MODELS

1. Disconnect the negative battery cable.

2. With the engine cool, remove the coolant drain plug from the block, and allow the coolant to drain into a suitable container.

✳✳ CAUTION

When draining coolant, keep in mind that cats and dogs are attracted to ethylene glycol antifreeze, and could drink any that is left in an uncovered container or in puddles on the ground. This will prove fatal in sufficient quantity. Always drain the coolant into a sealable container. Coolant should be reused unless it is contaminated or several years old.

3. Remove the 2 electrical connectors from the front of the coolant manifold that runs along the exhaust side of the engine. Disconnect the radiator hose from the front of this pipe. Then, remove all the mounting bolts for this pipe and remove it. Inspect the O-rings and replace any that are worn or damaged.

4. Disconnect the exhaust pipe at the manifold flange. Remove the heat-shields from under the engine.

5. Remove the mounting nuts at the cylinder head and remove the manifold.

6. Clean all gasket material from the surfaces of the manifold and head and replace the gaskets.

To install:

7. Position the manifold on the head, tightening the manifold bolts to 6.5–7.0 ft. lbs. (9 Nm) and the coolant pipe mounting bolts to 7.5–8.5 ft. lbs. (11 Nm). Tighten the bolts at the flange attaching manifold and exhaust pipe first to 22–25 ft. lbs. (30–34 Nm) and then to 36–40 ft. lbs. (48–54 Nm). Make sure to refill the cooling system with fresh anti-freeze/water mix and bleed the cooling system.

M5 AND M6 MODELS

1. Disconnect the negative battery cable.
2. Remove the exhaust system.
3. Drain the coolant below the level of the head.

☀☀ CAUTION

When draining coolant, keep in mind that cats and dogs are attracted to ethylene glycol antifreeze, and could drink any that is left in an uncovered container or in puddles on the ground. This will prove fatal in sufficient quantity. Always drain the coolant into a sealable container. Coolant should be reused unless it is contaminated or several years old.

4. Disconnect the right side engine mount and ground strap.

5. Disconnect the air injection pipe and the heatshield. Remove the fan cowl and coolant expansion tank. Remove the air pump air filter housing.

6. Lift the right side of the engine as far as possible without damaging any connections.

7. Remove the heat shield holder and the air injection pipe. It may be necessary to use an universal joint on an extension. There is a mounting tab at cylinder No. 1.

8. Disconnect the sensor plugs on the coolant pipe. Remove the coolant pipe.

9. Remove the exhaust manifold nuts and pull of the studs. Push the rear manifold back and pull the front manifold. Remove the rear manifold.

To install:

10. Clean the manifold mounting surfaces of the manifold and cylinder head. Install new gaskets with the graphite surface facing towards the cylinder head.

11. Install the manifolds. Place the manifolds in the reverse order of removal. Tighten the nuts 6–8 ft. lbs. (9–11 Nm).

12. Replace the O-rings and install the coolant pipe. Tighten to 8.0–8.5 ft. lbs. (11–12 Nm). Replace the air injection pipe gaskets and the air injection pipe. Tighten to 25–33 ft. lbs. (35–45 Nm).

13. Install the heat shield. Lower the engine. Install the air pump filter, coolant expansion tank and the fan cowl. Connect the air injection pipe and tighten to 25–33 ft. lbs. (35–45 Nm). Install the heat shield holder.

14. Connect the ground strap and the engine mount. Tighten to 30 ft. lbs. (42 Nm). Install the exhaust system and fill the cooling system. Connect the negative battery terminal.

Radiator

REMOVAL & INSTALLATION

♦ **See Figures 69 thru 79**

1. Disconnect the negative battery cable.
2. Drain the cooling system.

☀☀ CAUTION

When draining coolant, keep in mind that cats and dogs are attracted to ethylene glycol antifreeze, and could drink any that is left in an uncovered container or in puddles on the ground. This will prove fatal in sufficient quantity. Always drain the coolant into a sealable container. Coolant should be reused unless it is contaminated or several years old.

3. If the car has a coolant expansion tank, remove the cap, disconnect the hose at the radiator, and drain the coolant into a clean container, if reusing the coolant. If the car has a splash guard, remove it.

4. Disconnect and remove the coolant hoses.

5. Disconnect the automatic transmission oil cooler lines and plug all ther openings.

6. Unfasten any of the temperature switch wire connectors (used in many applications, especially if the car has air conditioning).

7. Remove the shroud from the radiator, if equipped. On some models, this is done by simply pressing the plugs toward the rear of the car. On others, there are metal slips that must be pulled upward and off to free the shroud from the radiator..

8. On 735i models, remove the fan and shroud together. The fan must be held stationary with some sort of flat blade cut to fit over the hub and drilled to fit over 2 of the studs on the front of the pulley (or it is possible to use BMW special tool 11 5 020). Then, unscrew the retaining nut at the center of the fluid drive hub turning it clockwise to remove it because it has left hand threads.

9. On 318i models, remove the cover from the left side of the radiator.

10. On late model vehicle equipped with an oil cooler, spread the retaining clip and pull the oil cooler out to the right.

11. Remove the radiator retaining bolts (or single bolt on some models) and lift the radiator from the vehicle.

➡ **On 1983–88 vehicle equipped with the 3.3L or 3.5L engine, there are 2 bolts at the top/rear of the radiator and 2 bolts at the bottom rear which must be removed.**

To install:

12. Position the radiator into the vehicle, Some radiators slide into rubber mounts at the base. Install the retaining bolts where needed.

13. Install the oil cooler, if equipped. Tighten the fittings to 18–21 ft. lbs. (23–27 Nm).

14. Connect the radiator hoses, including transmission cooler lines, if equipped. Tighten the transmission line to 13–15 ft. lbs. (17–19 Nm).

Fig. 69 Example of an early BMW radiator. Notice there is no fan shroud on these early models—2002 shown

87891P60

Fig. 70 Remove the metal clips securing the fan shroud to the radiator—3 Series model

87893P43

Fig. 71 Remove the fan shroud from the engine compartment

87893P15

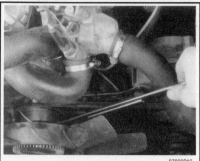

Fig. 72 Remove the fan by turning clockwise because the thread pattern is reversed

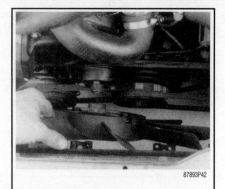

Fig. 73 Remove the fan from the engine compartment

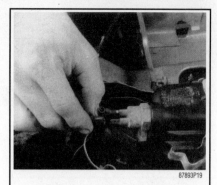

Fig. 74 Remove the wires from the side of the radiator

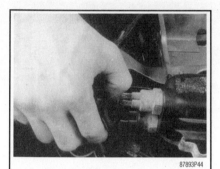

Fig. 75 Some late model vehicles have multiple plugs attached to the radiator—3 Series shown

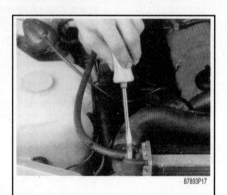

Fig. 76 Remove the expansion tank hose

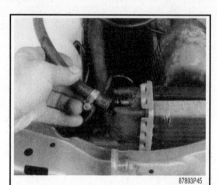

Fig. 77 With the clamp loosened, the hose can be slid off

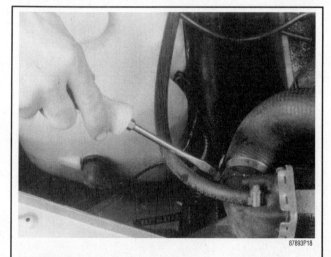

Fig. 78 Loosen the hose clamps securing the radiator inlet and outlet hoses and remove

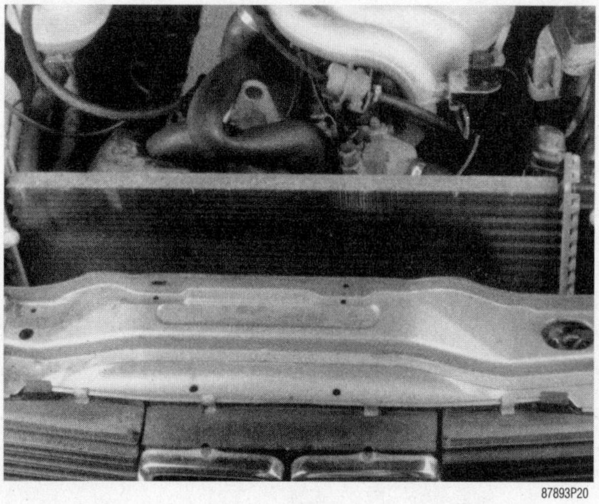

15. Connect the expansion tank hose, if equipped.
16. Fasten all electrical wires removed earlier.
17. Install the fan and/or shroud if removed.
18. Connect the negative battery cable.
19. Fill and bleed the cooling system.

Engine Fan

The engine cooling fan is driven by a belt and is bolted to the water pump. A temperature and engine speed sensitive clutch is used to limit the drag imposed on the engine by the fan.

Fig. 79 Remove the radiator from the engine compartment

REMOVAL & INSTALLATION

1. Disconnect the negative battery cable.
2. Determine whether the fan and clutch are secured with multiple bolts, a single viscous type coupler or a single reverse thread nut. Most early models up to 1982 are either viscous coupler or multiple bolts, whereas models after 1983 are a reverse thread nut.
3. To remove and early style fan, lift the tabs over the multiple bolts and remove the bolts from the pump pulley. To remove a viscous type fan, remove the center bolt from the fan, then remove the screws attaching the fan to the viscous coupler.

4. To remove late models fans, unscrew the fan clockwise. Remove the fan. The fan cowl may need to be removed. Be careful of the radiator fins.

5. Remove the fan from the fan clutch. Install the fan clutch bolts and tighten to 6–7 ft. lbs. (8–10 Nm).

6. To install reverse the above procedure.

Auxiliary Cooling Fan

REMOVAL & INSTALLATION

Some late model vehicles are equipped with an electric auxiliary fan to run when the air conditioning is turned on in the vehicle.

1. Disconnect the negative battery cable.

2. Remove the radiator. Remove the front grille.

3. Loosen and remove the bolts holding the air conditioning condenser. Do not disconnect the refrigerant lines.

4. Remove the trim panel behind the left side headlight. Disconnect the fan plug and remove the mounting nuts.

5. Pull back the condenser and remove the fan from above.

To install:

6. Install the cooling fan and tighten the nuts. Plug in the connector.

7. Install the trim panel behind the headlight. Install the condenser mounting bolts.

8. Install the radiator and the grilles.

9. Connect the negative battery terminal.

10. Fill and bleed the cooling system.

Water Pump

REMOVAL & INSTALLATION

Except 3 Series and 528e Models

1. Drain the cooling system and remove the radiator.

✳✳ CAUTION

When draining coolant, keep in mind that cats and dogs are attracted to ethylene glycol antifreeze, and could drink any that is left in an uncovered container or in puddles on the ground. This will prove fatal in sufficient quantity. Always drain the coolant into a sealable container. Coolant should be reused unless it is contaminated or several years old.

2. Remove the fan blade and any pulley attached to the water pump.

3. Remove the engine lifting hook that's in the way before removing any water pump retaining bolts.

4. Remove the retaining bolts securing the water pump to the engine.

5. Place a pan below the water pump to catch any coolant which may spill out when the pump is removed.

6. To remove the water pump, tap the water pump body with the palm of

your hand to break the seal and remove from the engine.

7. If reinstalling the pump, clean any gasket material from the water pump. Purchase a new water pump gasket.

8. Clean any gasket material from the engine mating surface.

To install:

9. Position the water pump up to the engine with a the gasket placed between the pump and the engine. Secure the pump in place with the retaining bolts. Tighten the bolts in a crisscross pattern to 16–17 ft. lbs. 20–24 Nm).

10. Attach the pulley, belt and fan.

11. Tension the belt. Connect the negative battery cable. Fill and bleed the cooling system.

3 Series Models

♦ See Figures 80 thru 85

1. Disconnect the negative battery cable.

2. Drain the cooling system.

✳✳ CAUTION

When draining coolant, keep in mind that cats and dogs are attracted to ethylene glycol antifreeze, and could drink any that is left in an uncovered container or in puddles on the ground. This will prove fatal in sufficient quantity. Always drain the coolant into a sealable container. Coolant should be reused unless it is contaminated or several years old.

3. Remove the distributor cap and rotor. Remove the rotor adapter, the dust shield and the distributor housing.

4. Remove the fan by removing the fan coupling nut. Remember the nut is left hand thread, therefore turn clockwise to remove.

5. Remove the belt and pulley.

6. Remove the rubber guard and distributor and or upper timing belt cover.

7. Compress the timing tensioner spring and clamp pin with the proper tool.

➡Observe the installed position of the tensioner spring pin on the water pump housing for reinstallation purposes.

8. Remove the water hoses.

9. Remove the 3 water pump bolts and remove the pump.

To install:

10. Clean the gasket surfaces and use a new gasket.

11. Install the water pump in position. Note the position of the tensioner spring pin. Tighten the grade M8 bolts to 16–17 ft. lbs. (20–24 Nm) and grade M6 bolts to 6–7 ft. lbs. (8–10 Nm).

12. Connect the hoses.

13. Release the tensioner from the holding pin. Install the upper timing cover. Install the pulley and tighten the bolts to 6–7 ft. lbs. (8–10 Nm). Install the belt and tighten.

14. Install the fan, distributor housing and dust shield. Tighten the rotor adapter to 39–47 ft. lbs. (55–65 Nm). Install the rotor, O-ring and cap.

15. Add coolant and bleed the cooling system. Connect the negative battery cable.

Fig. 80 Loosen the bolts on the water pump pulley—once loosened, remove the V-belt

Fig. 81 Remove the water pump pulley

Fig. 82 Loosen and remove the water pump retainer bolts

Fig. 83 With the water pump removed, you can easily see the attached tensioner

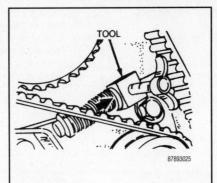

Fig. 84 Compressing the timing tensioner spring

Fig. 85 If reinstalling the water pump, clean all gasket material from the pump surface

528e Models

1. Disconnect the negative battery cable.
2. Drain the cooling system.

✷✷ CAUTION

When draining coolant, keep in mind that cats and dogs are attracted to ethylene glycol antifreeze, and could drink any that is left in an uncovered container or in puddles on the ground. This will prove fatal in sufficient quantity. Always drain the coolant into a sealable container. Coolant should be reused unless it is contaminated or several years old.

3. Remove the fan. Remove the drive belt and the water pump pulley.
4. Remove the pump mounting bolts.
5. Screw 2 bolts into the tapered bores and press the water pump out of the cover uniformly.

To install:

6. Lubricate and install a new O-ring.
7. Install the water pump and tighten the bolts to 6.5 ft. lbs. (9 Nm).
8. Install the pulley and tighten the bolts to 6.5 ft. lbs. (9 Nm). Install the belt and fan.
9. Fill and bleed the cooling system.
10. Connect the negative battery terminal.

Cylinder Head

REMOVAL & INSTALLATION

1600, 2000 and 2002 Models

♦ See Figures 86 and 87

➡ To prevent warpage of the aluminum head, the engine must be cold. This means a coolant temperature of less than 96°F (36°C).

1. Remove the air cleaner and disconnect the breather tube. On fuel injected engines, remove the intake manifold as detailed earlier.
2. Disconnect the negative battery cable and drain the cooling system.

✷✷ CAUTION

When draining coolant, keep in mind that cats and dogs are attracted to ethylene glycol antifreeze, and could drink any that is left in an uncovered container or in puddles on the ground. This will prove fatal in sufficient quantity. Always drain the coolant into a sealable container. Coolant should be reused unless it is contaminated or several years old.

3. Remove the choke cable, if equipped.
4. Disconnect the throttle linkage. On automatic transmission equipped models, disconnect the downshift linkage. On models equipped with the Solex 32 DIDTA type carburetor, disconnect and mark all electrical leads.

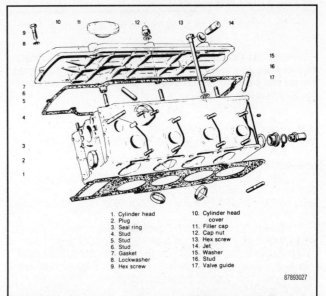

1. Cylinder head
2. Plug
3. Seal ring
4. Stud
5. Stud
6. Stud
7. Gasket
8. Lockwasher
9. Hex screw
10. Cylinder head cover
11. Filler cap
12. Cap nut
13. Hex screw
14. Jet
15. Washer
16. Stud
17. Valve guide

Fig. 86 An example of a 4-cylinder engine cylinder head and associated parts

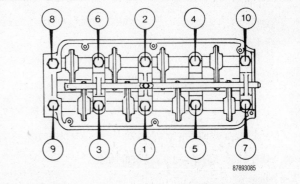

Fig. 87 Cylinder head torque sequence—1600, 2000 and 2002 models

5. On 2002Tii models, disconnect the throttle butterfly linkage, and all electrical leads, marking each lead as it is being removed. Pull the torsion shaft towards the firewall until the ball is free of the torsion shaft.
6. Remove and tag the vacuum hoses. On models equipped with the emission control air pump, disconnect the vacuum hose with the non-return valve from its fitting on the intake manifold.
7. Disconnect the coolant hoses from the cylinder head. Disconnect intake manifold water hoses, if so equipped.

8. Tag and disconnect the electrical wiring and connectors from the cylinder head and engine components.

9. On carbureted models, disconnect and plug the fuel line on the tank side of the fuel pump.

10. On 1975 models, disconnect and plug the fuel and reflow hose.

11. On the fuel injected models, disconnect the fuel line at the injection pump and all lines at the injectors.

12. Remove the cylinder head cover and the front upper timing case cover.

13. Rotate the engine until the distributor rotor points to the notch on the distributor body edge and the timing indicator points to the second notch on the pulley

14. On 2002 models. No. 1 piston should now be at TDC on its firing stroke.

15. Remove the timing chain tensioner piston by removing the plug in the side of the block.

✳✳✳ CAUTION

The plug is under heavy spring tension.

16. Open the lockplates, remove the retaining bolts and remove the timing chain sprocket from the camshaft.

➡**The dowel pin hole on the camshaft flange should be in the 6 o'clock position while the notch at the top for the cam flange should be aligned with the cast projection on the cylinder head and in the 12 o'clock position for proper installation.**

17. Remove the exhaust pipe from the exhaust manifold.
18. Remove the dipstick holder.
19. Unscrew the cylinder head bolts in the reverse of the tightening sequence and remove the cylinder head.

To install:

20. Clean the new head bolts and the bores of the cylinder block. Do not allow oil or contaminants to fill the bores. Use a 0.012 inch (0.3mm) thicker gasket if the head was machined. Install a new gasket for the timing case at the front of the cylinder head.

21. Install a new head gasket in the proper orientation as marked on the gasket. Check the condition of the guide dowels in the cylinder deck.

22. Tighten the new head bolts in a crisscross pattern starting at the center of the head and working towards the ends. Tighten to 24 ft. lbs. (33 Nm), then turn 93 degrees, then finish with a final turn of 93 degrees.

23. Install the timing chain, timing guide bolt on the right side and the upper chain guide.

24. If not installing a new tensioner piston, knock the outer sleeve of the tensioner piston so the piston is released from the sleeve. Assemble the tensioner with the spring, the piston and the snaprings in position. Place in a vice and press together until both snaprings engage. If the piston starts to extend, the procedure must be done again. The compressed tensioner will be 2.7 inches (68.5mm).

25. Install the tensioner into its bore and tighten the plug to 17–19 ft. lbs. (23–27 Nm). Push the tensioner rail against the tensioner to release the tensioner piston.

26. Install the front timing upper cover with new gaskets and fill the gaps with non hardening sealer. Press down on the cover to align it with the cylinder head. Install the bolts and tighten to 6–7 ft. lbs. (8–10 Nm) for grade M6 bolts and 15–17 ft. lbs. (20–22 Nm) for grade M8 bolts.

27. Install the remaining components in the reverse order of removal.

2500, 2800, 3000, Bavaria, 3.0 and 630i Models

♦ See Figure 88

1. Disconnect the battery ground cable. Drain the cooling system.

✳✳✳ CAUTION

When draining coolant, keep in mind that cats and dogs are attracted to ethylene glycol antifreeze, and could drink any that is left in an uncovered container or in puddles on the ground. This will prove fatal in sufficient quantity. Always drain the coolant into a sealable container. Coolant should be reused unless it is contaminated or several years old.

2. Disconnect throttle linkage rods running between the carburetors.

3. Disconnect the water temperature sensor at the thermostat and the electrically heated choke wires.

4. Remove the power brake hose from the base of the front carburetor. Remove the dipstick support.

5. Disconnect the heater and water hoses to the intake manifold.

6. Disconnect and remove the air cleaner assembly and hoses.

7. Remove the ignition high tension wire tube.

8. Disconnect the inductive switch and cable off the coil. Remove the distributor cap and disconnect the primary wire and vacuum line from the distributor.

9. Disconnect the 2 vacuum hoses at the rear of the intake manifold, and the 2 fuel lines at the fuel manifold.

10. Disconnect the water hoses for the heater at the firewall and disconnect the equalizing reservoir hose at the reservoir. Disconnect the oil pressure switch linc at the plug.

11. Disconnect and remove the air volume control assembly. Disconnect the ignition cable tube and wires and remove it, and disconnect the cam cover vent hose.

   a. Mark locations and then disconnect the 3 coil connections.

   b. Disconnect all 6 injection valve plugs, and the plug at the throttle switch. Disconnect the throttle linkage rod at the top and bottom.

   c. Disconnect the vacuum hose from the throttle housing and disconnect the temperature sensor wire at the front of the head.

   d. Disconnect the water hose at the throttle housing and the oil pressure switch wire.

   e. Disconnect water hoses at the thermostat housing. Disconnect the hose going to the charcoal filter. Disconnect the fuel feed line at the filter.

   f. On 630i models only, remove the connector from between No. 2 and 3 cylinder intake tubes.

   g. Disconnect the 4 vacuum sensing hoses from the EGR valve and collector/vacuum valve, noting color coding and locations. Disconnect the brake booster vacuum hoses at the manifold.

   h. Disconnect heater hoses at the firewall, noting locations. Disconnect the 2 air hoses at the auxiliary air valve; disconnect the 2 electrical connectors at the auxiliary air valve. Then, remove the auxiliary air valve wiring harness through the opening in the intake manifold.

   i. Disconnect and remove the EGR filter.

12. Remove the cylinder head cover.

13. Rotate the engine so that the distributor rotor points to the notch on the distributor body edge and the timing indicator points to the notch on the belt pulley. This will place number one piston at TDC on its firing stroke.

14. Remove the upper timing housing cover after removing the distributor and thermostat housing.

15. Remove the timing chain tensioner piston.

16. Open the camshaft sprocket bolt lockplates and remove the bolts. Remove the sprocket.

➡**For installation purposes, the sprocket dowel pin should be located at the lower left, between 7 and 8 o'clock, while the upper bolt bore must align with the threaded bore of the camshaft and the cylinder head cast tab, visible through the 2 bores, when at the 12 o'clock position.**

17. Disconnect the exhaust system at the exhaust manifold. Remove the exhaust filter, if equipped.

18. Remove the cylinder head bolts in the reverse order of the tightening

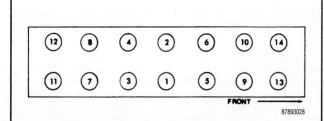

Fig. 88 Cylinder head torque sequence—2500, 2800, 3000, Bavaria and 630i models

sequence and install locating pins in 4 head bolt bores to prevent the rocker shafts from turning.

19. Remove the cylinder head.

To install:

20. Apply a very light coating of oil to the head bolts. Don't let oil get into the bolt holes or apply excessive amounts of oil, or torque specifications could be incorrect and the block could crack.

21. Tighten bolts 1–6 in the correct torque order to 42–44 ft. lbs. (57–60 Nm). Remove the pins holding the rocker shafts in place. Now, complete the first stage of torquing by tightening bolts 7–14 in the correct order, to the same specification.

22. Wait 20 minutes. Then tighten to 57–59 ft. lbs. (78–82 Nm).

23. Once the procedure is completed, run the engine for 25 minutes. Tighten the bolts, in the correct order, with a torque angle gauge 30–40 degrees.

24. Reinstall the timing sprocket to the camshaft. Make sure the camshaft is in proper time, and that new lock plates are used, and that nuts are properly tighten.

25. Install the tensioner piston.

26. When reinstalling the timing cover, make sure to apply a liquid sealer to the joints between the upper and lower timing covers.

27. The remainder of installation is the reverse of removal. Note these points:

    a. Adjust throttle, speed control, and accelerator cables.

    b. Inspect and if necessary replace the exhaust manifold gasket.

    c. When reinstalling the cylinder block coolant plug, coat it with sealer.

    d. Install the timing chain so the down pin on the camshaft sprocket is at the 8 o'clock position when its tapered bores are at right angles to the engine. Tighten the sprocket bolts to 6.5–7.5 ft. lbs. (8–10 Nm).

    e. Check the camshaft cover gasket, replacing, as necessary. Tighten camshaft cover bolts in the order shown. Tighten the bolts to 6.5–7.5 ft. lbs. (8–10 Nm).

    f. Make sure to refill the cooling system and bleed it.

    g. Make sure to refill the oil pan with the correct amount of oil.

318i and 320i Models

▶ See Figure 89

1. Disconnect the exhaust pipes at the exhaust manifold and remove the pipe clamp on the transmission.

2. Disconnect the negative battery cable. Remove the drain plug and drain coolant.

> **✳✳ CAUTION**
>
> **When draining the coolant, keep in mind that cats and dogs are attracted by the ethylene glycol antifreeze, and are quite likely to drink any that is left in an uncovered container or in puddles on the ground. This will prove fatal in sufficient quantity. Always drain the coolant into a sealable container. Coolant should be reused unless it is contaminated or several years old.**

3. Disconnect the wires and plug on the air cleaner. Loosen the clamp and disconnect the air intake hose. Then unscrew the nuts and remove the air cleaner.

4. Disconnect the throttle cable. Remove the dipstick tube locating bracket.

5. Disconnect the throttle position electronic plug. Disconnect the coolant and vacuum hoses nearby. Unscrew the support for the throttle body nearby.

6. Detach the fuel supply and return hoses as well as the hose mounting clamp.

7. Disconnect the intake manifold, distributor, and power brake unit vacuum hoses.

8. Disconnect the diagnosis plug, alternator wiring, and other plugs (2) nearby. Disconnect the coolant hoses at the cylinder head.

9. Disconnect any electrical plugs on the starter and injection system. This includes pulling off each injection plug and opening up the wiring straps.

10. Remove the distributor cap, wiring harness, and all plug wires.

11. Disconnect the coolant hoses going into the firewall.

12. Remove the cylinder head cover. Remove the bracket near the upper timing case over. Then, remove the bolts and remove the upper timing case cover.

13. Rotate the engine until the TDC mark on the front pulley is aligned with

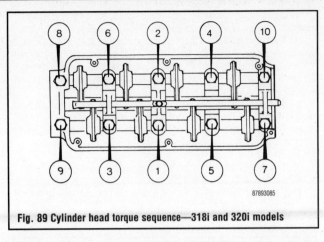

Fig. 89 Cylinder head torque sequence—318i and 320i models

the mark on the front cover and the distributor rotor is aligned with the mark on the side of the distributor (No. 1 cylinder is at TDC). Then, remove the distributor.

14. Remove the timing chain tensioner piston as described in this section.

15. Remove the retaining bolts and pull off the upper timing chain sprocket.

➡ Do not rotate the crankshaft while the sprocket is off.

16. Loosen the cylinder head bolts in reverse order of the torquing sequence and remove. Lift off the cylinder head.

To install:

17. Install in reverse order, noting these points:

    a. Use a new head gasket. Install the head gasket in the proper orientation as marked on the gasket. Check the condition of the guide dowels in the cylinder deck.

    b. Lightly oil all head bolts, keeping oil out of the threaded holes in the block.

    c. Tighten in the sequence shown in 3 stages. Tighten the new head bolts in a crisscross pattern starting at the center of the head and working towards the ends. Tighten to 24 ft. lbs. (33 Nm), then turn 93 degrees, then finish with a final turn of 93 degrees.

18. Install the timing chain, timing guide bolt on the right side and the upper chain guide.

19. Assemble the tensioner with the spring, piston and the snaprings in position. Place in a vice and press together until both snaprings engage. If the piston starts to extend, the procedure must be done again. The compressed tensioner will be 2.7 inches (68.5mm).

20. Install the tensioner into its bore and tighten the plug to 17–19 ft. lbs. (23–27 Nm). Push the tensioner rail against the tensioner to release the tensioner piston.

21. Install the front timing upper cover with new gaskets and fill the gaps with non hardening sealer. Press down on the cover to align it with the cylinder head. Install the bolts and tighten to 6–7 ft. lbs. (8–10 Nm) for grade M6 bolts and 15–17 ft. lbs. (20–22 Nm) for grade M8 bolts.

22. Install the remaining components in the reverse order of removal.

1982–87 325, 325e, 325i, 325iS, 325iX and 528e Models

▶ See Figures 90 thru 104

1. Disconnect the negative battery cable.

2. Disconnect the exhaust pipes at the manifold and at the transmission clamp.

3. Remove the drain plug at the bottom of the radiator and drain the coolant.

> **✳✳ CAUTION**
>
> **When draining the coolant, keep in mind that cats and dogs are attracted by the ethylene glycol antifreeze, and are quite likely to drink any that is left in an uncovered container or in puddles on the ground. This will prove fatal in sufficient quantity. Always drain the coolant into a sealable container. Coolant should be reused unless it is contaminated or several years old.**

4. Disconnect the accelerator and cruise control cables. If the vehicle has automatic transmission, disconnect the throttle cable that goes to the transmission.

5. Working at the front of the block, disconnect the upper radiator hose, the bypass water hose, and smaller water hoses. Remove the diagnosis plug located at the front corner of the manifold. Remove the bracket located just underneath. Disconnect the fuel line and drain the contents into a metal container for safe disposal.

6. Working on the air cleaner/airflow sensor, disconnect the vacuum hoses, labeling them if necessary. Unfasten all electrical connectors and unclip and remove the wiring harness. There is a relay located in an L-shaped box near the strut tower. Disconnect and remove it. Unclamp and remove the air hose. Remove the mounting nuts and remove the assembly.

7. Disconnect the hose at the coolant overflow tank. Disconnect the idle speed positioner vacuum hose and then remove the positioner from the manifold.

8. If equipped with 4-wheel drive, disconnect the vacuum hose from the servo mounted on the manifold.

9. Place a drain pan underneath and then unfasten the water connections at the front of the intake manifold. Unfasten the electrical connector.

10. Unbolt the dipstick tube bracket at the manifold. Remove the fuel hose bracket at the cylinder head. Make sure the engine is cold. Then, place a metal container under the connection and unfasten the fuel hose at the connection.

11. Unfasten the fuel injector connectors at all 6 injectors, as well as the 2 additional electrical connectors to the sensors on the head.

12. Unfasten the oil pressure sending unit connector. Then, unfasten the carriers and remove this wiring.

13. Unfasten the coil high tension wire and unfasten the high tension wires at the spark plugs. Then, disconnect the tube in which the wires run above the valve cover. Disconnect the PCV hose. Then, remove the retaining nuts and remove the valve cover.

14. Turn the crankshaft so the TDC line is aligned with the indicator and the valves of No. 6 cylinder are overlapping in the slightly open position.

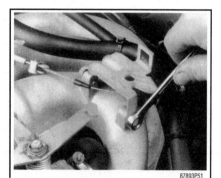

Fig. 90 Remove the accelerator cable and bracket—3 Series

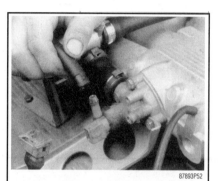

Fig. 91 Disconnect the vacuum hoses attached to the intake manifold including the cold start valve hose

Fig. 92 Unfasten the clip securing the diagnostic harness attached to the intake manifold

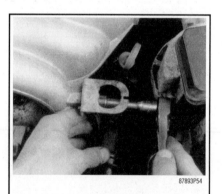

Fig. 93 Remove the bracket for the diagnostic harness

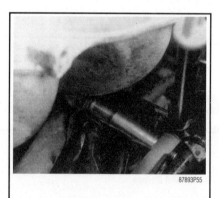

Fig. 94 Detach the dipstick tube bracket

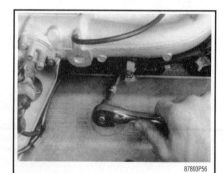

Fig. 95 Remove the fuel supply rail bolts. Be careful not to drop any of the bolts after removing them

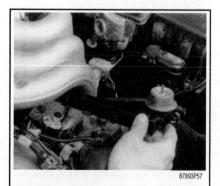

Fig. 96 Slide the rail out from under the intake manifold

Fig. 97 Remove the protective cover over the distributor cap, then remove the distributor cap

Fig. 98 With the distributor cap removed, unfasten the bolts securing the upper timing belt cover

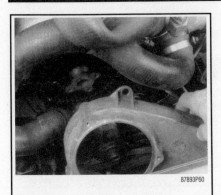

Fig. 99 Remove the upper timing belt cover

Fig. 100 The lower timing belt cover can also be removed for more access

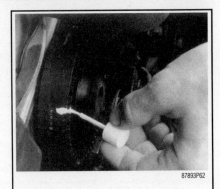

Fig. 101 Paint alignment marks on the timing belt and pulleys

Fig. 102 Loosen the timing belt tensioner

Fig. 103 Slide the timing belt off without moving the pulleys

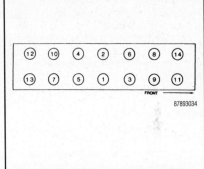

Fig. 104 Cylinder head torque sequence— 3 Series and 528e models

15. Remove the distributor cap. Then, unscrew and remove the rotor. Unscrew and remove the adapter just underneath the rotor. Remove the cover underneath the adapter. Check its O-ring and replace it, if necessary.

16. Remove the distributor mounting bolts and the protective cover.

17. These engines are equipped with a rubber timing belt. Remove the belt covers. To loosen the belt tension, loosen the tension roller bracket pivot bolt and adjusting slot bolt. Push the roller and bracket away from the belt to release the tension, hold the bracket in this position, and tighten the adjusting slot bolt to retain the bracket it this position.

18. Remove the timing belt.

➡**Make sure to avoid rotating both the engine and camshaft from this point onward.**

19. Remove the cylinder head mounting bolts in exact reverse order of the proper tightening sequence. Then, remove the cylinder head.

To install:

20. Clean both cylinder head and block sealing surfaces thoroughly with a hardwood scraper. Inspect the surfaces for flatness.

21. Install the head with a new gasket. Check that all passages line up with the gasket holes. Clean the threads on the head bolts and coat with a light coating of oil. Keep oil out of the bolt cavities in the head or the head could be cracked or proper tightening affected.

22. Tighten the bolts in a crisscross pattern staring at the center of the head and working towards the end. If equipped with hex head bolts, tighten to 29–34 ft. lbs. (40–45 Nm). Wait 15 minutes, then tighten to 43–47 ft. lbs. (60–65 Nm). After the installation is completed, run the engine for 25 minutes and give the bolts a final turn of 25–30 degrees. If equipped with Torx bolts, tighten to 22 ft. lbs. (30 Nm), turn 90 degrees, then complete with an additional 90 degrees. Do not wait or run engine.

23. Adjust the valves.

24. Complete the installation by reversing the removal procedures.

25. Replace the gaskets for the exhaust system connections, if necessary. Coat the studs with the proper sealant. Note that the plugs for the DME reference mark and speed signals should be connected so the gray plug goes to the socket with a ring underneath.

➡**Align the timing marks when installing the timing belt. The crankshaft sprocket mark must point at the notch in the flange of the front engine cover. The camshaft sprocket arrow must point at the alignment mark on the cylinder head. Also, the No. 1 piston must be at TDC of the compression stroke. BMW recommends that the timing belt be replaced every time the cylinder head is removed and the belt is disturbed as a consequence. Tension the belt. when complete.**

26. Make sure to refill the engine oil pan and cooling system with proper fluids and to bleed the cooling system.

1988 325, 325e, 325i, 325iS, 325iX and 528e Models

▸ **See Figure 104**

1. Unbolt the exhaust pipe connections at the manifold and at the transmission pipe clamp.

2. Disconnect the negative battery cable.

3. Remove the splash shield from under the engine.

4. Remove the drain plugs from the bottom of the radiator and engine block.

✳✳ CAUTION

When draining the coolant, keep in mind that cats and dogs are attracted by the ethylene glycol antifreeze, and are quite likely to drink any that is left in an uncovered container or in puddles on the ground. This will prove fatal in sufficient quantity. Always drain the coolant into a sealable container. Coolant should be reused unless it is contaminated or several years old.

5. Drain the engine oil.

6. Disconnect the throttle and cruise control cables at the throttle lever. Unbolt the cable housing retainer and remove the housing and cables.

7. Loosen the hose clamp and disconnect the air inlet hose from the air-flow sensor.

8. The unit on the opposite side of the intake hose from the air cleaner contains the idle speed control valve, which must be removed next. Loosen the hose clamps and pull off the hoses. Unfasten the electrical connector. Remove the mounting nut and then pull the idle speed control out of the air intake hose.

9. Disconnect and plug the brake booster vacuum line.

10. Unfasten the radiator hoses, the heater hoses and the fuel lines. Mark the lines for ease of installation.

11. Unfasten the venting valve vacuum line and electrical connector from under the intake manifold. Unfasten the connections on the plug plate located under the intake manifold and remove the plug plate.

12. Remove the fan. Lift out the expansion rivets on either side and remove the fan shroud.

13. Disconnect the throttle body coolant hoses. Loosen the mount for the engine oil dipstick.

14. Disconnect the plugs near the thermostat housing. Loosen the hose clamps and pull off the coolant hoses.

15. Disconnect the plug in the line leading to the oxygen sensor. Disconnect the other plugs.

16. Disconnect the fuel supply and return lines, collecting fuel in a metal container for safe disposal.

17. Unfasten the fuel pipe running along the cylinder head, near the manifold. Pull off the electrical connector at the throttle body. Remove the caps, then remove the attaching bolts and remove the wiring harness carrier and harness for the fuel injectors.

18. Disconnect the coil high tension lead. Disconnect the high tension wires at the plugs. Then, remove the mounting nuts and remove the carrier for the high tension wires from the head.

19. Remove the timing belt. The timing belt must be replaced anytime it is removed or the tensioner loosened.

20. Remove the heater hose from the cylinder head. Press down on the venting pipe collar and lock into position. Remove the valve cover. Check for any remaining connections that may have been missed.

21. Remove the head bolts in a crisscross pattern starting at the center and working out toward the ends. Lift off the head.

To install:

22. Make checks of the lower cylinder head and block deck surface to make sure they are true. Install a new head gasket, making sure all bolt, oil, and coolant holes line up. Use a 0.3mm thicker gasket, if the head has been machined.

23. Apply a very light coating of oil to the head bolts. Don't let oil get into the bolt holes or apply excessive amounts of oil, or tightening amounts could be incorrect and the block could crack.

24. Use the type of bolt without a collar. Install the bolts, finger tight.

25. Tighten the bolts in a crisscross pattern staring at the center of the head and working towards the end. If equipped with hex head bolts, tighten to 29–34 ft. lbs. (40–45 Nm). Wait 15 minutes then tighten to 43–47 ft. lbs. (60–65 Nm). After the installation is completed, run the engine for 25 minutes and give the bolts a final turn of 25–30 degrees.

➡ **If equipped with Torx® bolts, tighten to 22 ft. lbs. (30 Nm), turn 90 degrees, then complete with an additional 90 degrees.**

26. Adjust the valves.

27. Connect the venting pipe and release the collar. Connect the heater hose on the cylinder head.

28. Connect the throttle body coolant hoses and install the wiring harnesses and injector plugs.

29. Connect the sensors and vacuum lines.

30. Install a new timing belt. Never reuse a timing belt.

31. Install the fan and cowl.

32. Connect the fuel lines, air intake hoses, vacuum lines, idle air control and throttle cables.

33. Fill the engine with fluids and bleed the coolant system. Connect the exhaust system and the negative battery terminal.

530i, 533i, 633CSi and 733i Models

▶ **See Figure 105**

1. Unbolt the exhaust pipes at the exhaust manifold. Unclamp the exhaust pipe at the transmission.

2. Disconnect the battery negative then positive cables.

3. Drain the coolant by removing the plugs from the radiator and engine block.

✳✳ CAUTION

When draining coolant, keep in mind that cats and dogs are attracted to ethylene glycol antifreeze, and could drink any that is left in an uncovered container or in puddles on the ground. This will prove fatal in sufficient quantity. Always drain the coolant into a sealable container. Coolant should be reused unless it is contaminated or several years old.

4. Disconnect the throttle, accelerator, and cruise control cables at the throttle body.

5. These engines are all virtually identical, but wiring harnesses vary from model to model. Systematically unfasten all wiring that goes to the cylinder head, or would obstruct head removal. This includes wiring to the airflow sensor, ignition wiring and, wires to the fuel injectors, and on some models it may be necessary to unfasten the alternator wiring.

6. Disconnect the fuel lines, vacuum lines, and heater and coolant hoses that are in the way. Unfasten the DME plugs on models so equipped. Note that the gray plug connects to the sleeve with a ring underneath, for proper installation.

7. Remove the air cleaner and the windshield washer tank.

8. Remove the valve cover.

9. Disconnect the ground lead. Then, complete unfastening the engine wiring harness by disconnecting the oil pressure sending unit and set the harness aside.

10. Remove the upper timing case cover, tensioner piston, and then open the lockplates and remove the timing chain upper sprocket. Make sure to suspend the sprocket so the timing chain position isn't lost.

11. Loosen the cylinder head bolts following the illustration in reverse order. Install 4 special pins BMW part No. 11 1 063 or equivalent. This is necessary to keep the rocker arm shafts from moving. Then, lift off the head.

To install:

12. Make checks of the lower cylinder head and block deck surface to make sure they are true.

13. Install a new head gasket, making sure that all bolt, oil, and coolant holes line up. Use a 0.3mm thicker gasket if the head has been machined.

14. Apply a very light coating of oil to the head bolts. Don't let oil get into the bolt holes or the tighten rate could be incorrect and the block could crack. Use the newer type of bolt without a collar. Install the bolts, finger-tight.

15. Tighten bolts 1–6 in the order to 42–44 ft. lbs. (57–60 Nm). Remove the pins holding the rocker shafts in place. Now, complete the first stage of tightening by torquing bolts 7–14 in the correct order, to the same specification.

16. Wait 20 minutes. Tighten the bolts to 57–59 ft. lbs. (78–82 Nm). Once the procedure is completed, run the engine for 25 minutes. Tighten the bolts, in the correct order, with a torque angle gauge 30–40 degrees.

17. Reinstall the timing sprocket to the camshaft. Make sure the cam is in proper time, that new lockplates are used, and that nuts are properly tightened.

18. When reinstalling the timing cover, make sure to apply a liquid sealer to the joints between upper and lower timing covers. The remainder of installation is the reverse of removal. Note these points.

a. Adjust throttle, speed control, and accelerator cables. Inspect and if necessary replace the exhaust manifold gasket.

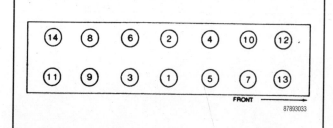

Fig. 105 Cylinder head torque sequence—530i, 533i, 633CSi and 733i models

   b. When reinstalling the cylinder block coolant plug, coat it with sealer. Make sure to refill the cooling system and bleed it (see the Cooling System procedure below).

535i, 635CSi and 735i Models

♦ See Figure 106

   1. Unbolt the exhaust pipe connections at the manifold and at the transmission pipe clamp. Disconnect the negative battery cable.

   2. Remove the splash shield from under the engine. With the engine cool, remove the drain plugs from the bottom of the radiator and block.

✳✳ CAUTION

When draining coolant, keep in mind that cats and dogs are attracted to ethylene glycol antifreeze, and could drink any that is left in an uncovered container or in puddles on the ground. This will prove fatal in sufficient quantity. Always drain the coolant into a sealable container. Coolant should be reused unless it is contaminated or several years old.

   3. Drain the engine oil.

✳✳ CAUTION

The EPA warns that prolonged contact with used engine oil may cause a number of skin disorders, including cancer! You should make every effort to minimize your exposure to used engine oil. Protective gloves should be worn when changing the oil. Wash your hands and any other exposed skin areas as soon as possible after exposure to used engine oil. Soap and water, or waterless hand cleaner should be used.

   4. Remove the fan. Lift out the expansion rivets on either side and remove the fan shroud.

   5. Loosen the hose clamp and unfasten the air inlet hose. Remove the mounting nut and remove the air cleaner.

   6. The unit on the opposite side of the intake hose from the air cleaner contains the idle speed control valve, which must be removed next. Loosen the hose clamps and pull off the hoses. Unfasten the electrical connector. Remove the mounting nut and then pull the idle speed control unit out of the air intake hose.

   7. Pull off the 3 retainers for the airflow sensor, and then pull the unit off its mounting, disconnecting the vacuum hose from the PCV system at the same time.

   8. Working on the coolant expansion tank, unfasten the electrical connector. Remove the nuts on both sides. Loosen their clamps and then disconnect all 3 hoses and remove the tank.

   9. Unfasten the heater hoses at both the control valve and at the heater core.

   10. Disconnect the throttle and cruise control cables at the throttle lever. Unbolt the cable housing retainer and remove the housing and cables.

   11. Disconnect the 4 plugs near the thermostat housing. Loosen the hose clamps and pull off the 2 coolant hoses.

   12. Disconnect the plug in the line leading to the oxygen sensor. Unfasten the other 2 plugs nearby.

   13. Disconnect the fuel supply and return lines, collecting fuel in a metal container for safe disposal.

   14. Disconnect the fuel pipe running along the cylinder head, near the manifold. Pull off the electrical connector at the throttle body. Remove the caps, then remove the attaching bolts and remove the wiring harness carrier and harness for the fuel injectors.

   15. Unfasten the coil high tension lead. Disconnect the high tension wires at the plugs. Then, remove the mounting nuts and remove the carrier for the high tension wires from the head.

   16. Remove the attaching nuts for the valve cover and remove it.

   17. Turn the engine until the timing marks are at TDC and the No. 6 valves are at overlap (both slightly open) position.

   18. Remove the upper timing case cover. Remove the timing chain tensioner piston.

   19. Remove the 4 upper timing chain sprocket bolts and pull the sprocket off, holding it upward and then support it securely so the relationship between the chain and sprocket top and bottom will not be lost.

   20. Disconnect the upper radiator hose at the thermostat housing. Remove the 3 bolts and remove the support for the intake manifold.

   21. Remove the cylinder head bolts in the opposite order of the torquing sequence. Then, install 4 special pins BMW part No. 11 1 063 or equivalent. This is necessary to keep the rocker arm shafts from moving. Then, lift off the head.

To install:

   22. Make checks of the lower cylinder head and block deck surface to make sure they are true.

   23. Install a new head gasket, making sure that all bolt, oil, and coolant holes line up. Use a 0.3mm thicker gasket if the head has been machined.

   24. Apply a very light coating of oil to the head bolts. Don't let oil get into the bolt holes or the tightening rate could be incorrect and the block could crack. Use the newer type of bolt without a collar. Install the bolts, finger tight.

   25. Tighten bolts 1–6 in the correct order to 42–44 ft. lbs. (57–60 Nm). Remove the pins holding the rocker shafts in place. Now, complete the first stage of tightening by torquing bolts 7–14 in the correct order, to the same specification.

   26. Wait 20 minutes. Tighten the bolts to 57–59 ft. lbs. (78–82 Nm). Once the procedure is completed, run the engine for 25 minutes. Tighten the bolts, in the correct order, with a torque angle gauge 30–40 degrees.

   27. Reinstall the timing sprocket to the camshaft. Make sure the cam is in proper time, and that new lockplates are used.

   28. When reinstalling the timing cover, make sure to apply a liquid sealer to the joints between upper and lower timing covers. The remainder of installation is the reverse of removal. Note these points.

   a. Adjust throttle, speed control, and accelerator cables. Inspect and if necessary replace the exhaust manifold gasket.

   b. When reinstalling the cylinder block coolant plug, coat it with sealer. Make sure to refill the cooling system and bleed it.

M3 Model

♦ See Figure 107

➡**This is an extremely difficult operation involving the use of a number of special tools. It is necessary to remove both of the camshafts to complete it. Refer to the camshaft removal and installation procedure below for information on those special tools required for that part of the job. It is also necessary to have a set of metric hex wrenches.**

   1. Disconnect the negative battery cable.

   2. Remove the splash guard from under the engine. Put drain pans underneath and remove the drain plugs from both the radiator and engine block to drain all coolant.

✳✳ CAUTION

When draining coolant, keep in mind that cats and dogs are attracted to ethylene glycol antifreeze, and could drink any that is left in an uncovered container or in puddles on the ground. This will prove fatal in sufficient quantity. Always drain the coolant into a sealable container. Coolant should be reused unless it is contaminated or several years old.

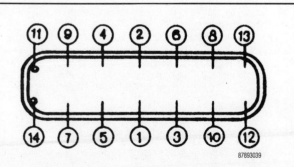

Fig. 106 Cylinder head torque sequence—535i, 635i and 735i models

3. Loosen the hose clamps for the air intake hose located next to the radiator and then remove the hose.

4. Unfasten the electrical connectors for the airflow sensor. Then, remove the attaching nuts and remove the air cleaner/ airflow sensor assembly.

5. Disconnect the accelerator and cruise control cables, if equipped. Unbolt the cable mounting bracket and move the cables and bracket aside.

6. Remove the attaching nut, pull off the clamp, and then detach the vacuum hose from the brake booster.

7. Loosen the hose clamp and remove the air intake hose from the intake manifold. Remove the nut from the manifold brace.

8. Loosen the clamp and disconnect the other end of the booster vacuum hose at the manifold. Remove the nut from the intake manifold brace.

9. Loosen the hose clamp and disconnect the air intake hose at the manifold. Then, remove the nuts attaching the manifold assembly to the outer ends of the intake throttle necks and remove the assembly.

10. Put a drain pan underneath and loosen the hose clamps and disconnect the coolant expansion tank hoses. Disconnect the engine ground strap.

11. Unfasten the ignition coil high tension lead. Label and then disconnect the plugs on the front of the block.

12. All the fuel injectors are plugged into a common plate. Carefully and evenly pull the plate off the injectors, pull it out past the pressure regulator, and lay it aside.

13. Loosen the clamp and then disconnect the PCV hose. Label and then unfasten the fuel lines connecting with the injector circuit. Put a drain pan underneath and then unfasten the heater hose from the cylinder head.

14. Loosen the clamp near the throttle necks and then pull the engine wiring harness out and put it aside.

15. Put a drain pan underneath and then disconnect the heater hose that connects to the block.

16. Remove the bolts from the flanges connecting the exhaust pipes to the exhaust manifold. Provide new gaskets and self-locking nuts. Disconnect the oxygen sensor plug.

17. Put a drain pan underneath and then unfasten the radiator hoses from the pipe at the front of the block.

18. Pull off the spark plug connectors. Remove the nuts from the valve cover, located just to one side of the row of spark plugs. Remove the ignition lead tube. Remove the remaining nuts and remove the valve cover. Provide new gaskets.

19. It is not necessary to remove the timing chain completely, but it is necessary to remove the valve cover, front covers for the camshaft drive sprockets, the upper guide rail for the timing chain and then turn the engine to TDC firing position for cylinder No. 1. Remove the timing chain tensioner. Note the relationship between the chain and both the crankshaft and camshaft sprockets, and then remove both camshaft drive sprockets. Leave the chain in a position that will not interfere with removal of the head and which will minimize the alignment position.

20. Remove the camshafts.

21. Remove the camshaft followers one at a time, keeping them in exact order for installation in the same positions.

22. Remove the bolts that retain the timing case to the head at the front of the engine assembly.

23. Remove the coolant pipe that runs along the left/rear of the block. Remove one bolt at the left/front of the block that is located outside the valve cover. Then, go along in the area under the valve cover and remove all the remaining bolts for the timing case. Remove the timing case.

24. Remove the hex bolts fastening the head to the block at the front. These are located outside the valve cover and just behind the water pump drive belt.

Then, remove the head bolts located under the valve cover in reverse order of the cylinder head tighten sequence.

To install:

➡ **BMW does not recommend machining the head.**

25. Make checks of the lower cylinder head and block deck surface to make sure they are true. Clean both cylinder head and block sealing surfaces thoroughly. Lubricate the head bolts with a light coating of engine oil. Make sure there is no oil or dirt in the bolt holes in the block.

26. Install a new head gasket, making sure all bolt, oil, and coolant holes line up. Install the bolts as follows:

   a. Tighten them in the correct order to 35–37 ft. lbs. (47–50 Nm).

   b. Then tighten them in order to 57–59 ft. lbs. (80–82 Nm).

   c. Wait 15 minutes.

   d. Tighten them, in order, to 71–73 ft. lbs. (96–100 Nm).

   e. Remember to reinstall the bolts that go outside the cylinder head cover and fasten the front of the head to the block at front and rear.

27. BMW recommends checking the fit of each tappet in the timing case, by performing the following procedure:

   a. Measure a tappet's outside diameter with a micrometer. Then, zero an inside micrometer at this exact dimension.

   b. Then, use the inside micrometer to measure the tappet bore that corresponds to this particular tappet. If the resulting measurement is 0.0001–0.0026 inches (0.002–0.07mm) the tappet may be reused. If it is worn past this dimension, replace it with a new one. If the tappet is being replaced, repeat Steps A and B to make sure it will now meet specifications. If the bore(s) are so worn that even a new tappet would not restore clearance to specification, it would be necessary to replace the timing case.

   c. Repeat for all the remaining tappets. Make sure to measure each tappet and its corresponding bore only.

28. The remaining steps of installation are the reverse of the removal procedure. Note the following:

   a. Before remounting the timing case, replace the O-ring in the oil passage located at the left/front of the block. Also, check the O-rings in the tops of the spark plug bores and replace these as necessary.

   b. Install the timing case and tighten the bolts in several stages. The smaller grade M7 bolts are tightened to 10–12 ft. lbs. (14–16 Nm); the larger grade M8 bolts are tightened to 14.5–15.5 ft. lbs. (19–21 Nm). Install each tappet back into the same bore.

   c. When bolting the exhaust pipes to the flange at the manifold, use new gaskets and self-locking nuts and tighten the nuts to 36 ft. lbs. (48 Nm).

   d. Then reinstall the intake manifold, check and, if necessary, replace the O-rings where the manifold tubes connect to the throttle necks. Tighten the nuts to 6.5 ft. lbs. (8 Nm).

   e. Make sure to refill the radiator and bleed the cooling system.

M5 and M6 Models

♦ See Figure 108

➡ **This is an extremely difficult operation involving the use of a number of special tools. It is necessary to remove both of the camshafts to complete it. Refer to the camshaft removal and installation procedure for information on those special tools.**

1. Mount the engine on a secure engine stand and have the intake and exhaust manifolds removed.

2. Remove the camshafts. Remove the tappets and store them in the order in which they were removed.

3. Remove the pipe that runs along the front of the engine and remove the bolts at the front of the camshaft case.

4. Remove the bolts in and along the camshaft case.

5. Remove the bolts at the front of the cylinder head. Remove the cylinder head bolts starting at the ends of the head and working towards the center in a crisscross fashion.

To install

➡ **BMW does not recommend having the head machined.**

6. Make checks of the lower cylinder head and block deck surface to make sure they are true.

7. Lubricate the head bolts with a light coating of engine oil. Make sure there is no oil or dirt in the bolt holes in the block.

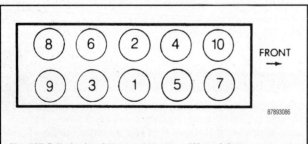

FRONT
→

87893086

Fig. 107 Cylinder head torque sequence—M3 models

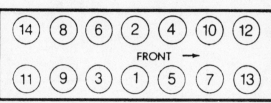

Fig. 108 Cylinder head torque sequence—M5 and M6 models

8. Install a new head gasket, making sure all bolt, oil, and coolant holes line up correctly.

9. Replace the O-ring in the head at the right/rear where the coolant pipe comes up from the block. Coat the pipe with a suitable sealer.

10. Install the head onto the block. Install the head bolts and tighten in a crisscross fashion starting in the center and working towards the ends. Tighten first to 34.5–37.5 ft. lbs. (48–52 Nm), then to 56.5–59.5 ft. lbs. (78–82 Nm). Wait 15 minutes then tighten to 71–73 ft. lbs. (98–102 Nm).

11. When installing the timing case, replace the O-rings in the small oil passages in the ends of the head. Inspect the O-rings in the center of the block and replace them if necessary. Coat all sealing surfaces with a sealer. Tighten the bolts evenly, torquing the smaller grade M7 bolts to 10–12 ft. lbs. (14–17 Nm) and the larger grade M8 bolts to 14.5–15.5 ft. lbs. (19–21 Nm).

12. Install all lifters back into the same bores.

13. Install the camshafts.

14. Reroute the timing chain, as necessary, and remount the drive sprockets for the camshaft. Install the tensioning rail that goes at the top of the timing chain.

15. Install the front cover.

16. Continue to reverse the removal procedure. Note these points:

   a. When reinstalling the intake manifold, inspect the O-rings and replace, as necessary.

   b. Refill the cooling system with an appropriate anti-freeze/water mix and bleed the cooling system.

CLEANING AND INSPECTION

♦ **See Figures 109, 110, 111 and 112**

Chip carbon away from the valve heads, combustion chambers and ports by using a chisel made of hardwood. Remove the remaining deposits with a stiff brush or a brush attachment for a hand drill.

➡**Aluminum is very soft and is easily damaged. Be very careful not to damage the head. Make sure that the deposits are actually removed, rather than just burnished.**

Clean the remaining cylinder head components in an engine cleaning solvent. Do not remove the protective coating from the valve springs.

NEVER "hot tank" a BMW cylinder head, since this process will damage aluminum heads.

Place a straightedge across the gasket surface of the cylinder head. On double overhead camshaft engines, check the camshaft bearing housing surfaces in addition to the gasket surface. Using feeler gauges, determine the clearance at the center of the straightedge. If warpage exceeds 0.0012 inches (0.03mm) over the total length, the cylinder head will require resurfacing. BMW does not recommend resurfacing the M3, M5 or M6 engines cylinder heads. It is acceptable to clean the surface with a whetstone, but the heads should not be ground.

The maximum amount of material removed must not exceed 0.012 inch (0.3mm). The head must be replaced if more material must be removed. Head gaskets with an additional thickness of 0.012 inch (0.3mm) are available to restore the compression ration to standard after the head has been reground.

➡**If warpage exceeds the manufacturer's tolerance for material removal, the cylinder head must be replaced.**

Cylinder head resurfacing should be performed by a reputable machine shop in your area. You will need to give the machine shop the stripped head and the front cover. The front cover needs to be machined at the same time as the cylinder head to keep the heights consistent.

Valves and Springs

➡**Never use old valves as punches or any other type of tool. The valve may crack and break if struck causing personal injury. Some exhaust valves, such as those installed in the late models 4 and 6-cylinder BMW engines are sodium filled. Do not cut the valve stems or throw them into a standard waste container for disposal. Take the old valves to a BMW dealer or machine shop for proper disposal. Sodium is extremely reactive and can be an explosive hazard if exposed to air and water.**

REMOVAL & INSTALLATION

♦ **See Figures 113, 114, 115 and 116**

It is understood that the cylinder head has been removed before performing valve removal. On all engines the camshafts must be removed. The rocker shafts and rocker arms must be removed on 2.5, 2.8L, 3.0L and 3.2L engine

1. The factory BMW valve spring compressor and removal tool mounts the cylinder head on a support tray with projections that fit into the combustion chamber. This supports the valves as the springs are compressed and the retainers removed. The BMW tool number for the spring compressor is 11 1 060. There is a different number for the support tray for each engine. Consult with your dealer if you wish to use the factory tools.

2. If an aftermarket tool is used, safely and securely support the head while placing the valve spring compressor. Compress the spring.

3. Remove the valve spring retainers and carefully release the tension on the spring. Use a magnet to retrieve hard to pick up retainers.

Fig. 109 Use a gasket scraper to remove the bulk of the old gasket from the cylinder head surface

Fig. 110 An electric drill equipped with a wire wheel will speed up complete gasket removal

Fig. 111 Check the cylinder head for warpage along the center using a straightedge and a feeler gauge

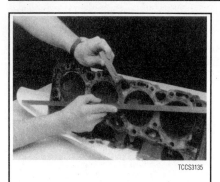

Fig. 112 Be sure to check for warpage across the cylinder head at diagonal points

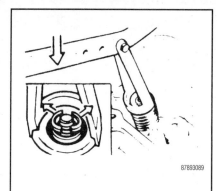

Fig. 113 Using a BMW spring compressor to remove a valve spring retainer lock

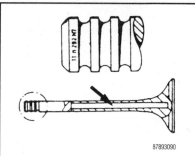

Fig. 114 Because sodium filled valves are extremely dangerous, they should be returned to BMW for proper disposal when they are no longer useful

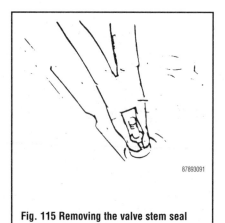

Fig. 115 Removing the valve stem seal

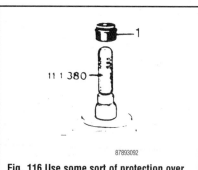

Fig. 116 Use some sort of protection over valve stem seals when sliding over the valve stem assembly. Use BMW tool or an equivalent

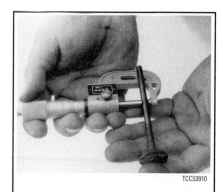

Fig. 117 Use a micrometer to measure the valve stem diameter

4. Remove the spring and upper retainer. Remove the valve from the combustion chamber side of the head.

5. Remove the valve stem seal with a removal pliers or equivalent. Remove the lower spring washer or retainer.

To install:

6. Lubricate the valve guide and stem. Place the valve in the valve guide. Put the lower retainer into place. Wrap the end of the valve stem with thin tape or use BMW tool 11 1 340, 11 1 350, 11 1 360, 11 1 380 depending on the engine to protect the valve stem seal as it is slid over the retainer grooves in the valve stem.

7. Press the new valve stem seal into place with tool 11 1 200 or equivalent. The tool fits over the valve stem and provides even pressure to the seal as it is pressed down.

8. Install the valve springs. If the valve springs are replaced, the inner and outer springs are replaced as a set. Do not mix new and used inner and outer springs. The color codes must match.

9. Place the upper retainer on the springs and compress with the valve spring compressor. Place the retainer locks into the grooves. Release the compressor slowly to make sure the retainers are in place.

INSPECTION

♦ **See Figures 117 and 118**

Inspect the valve faces and seats (in the cylinder head) for pits, burn spots and other evidence of poor seating. If the valve face or seat is in such bad shape that the head of the valve must be ground in order to true up the face, discard the valve because the sharp edge will run too hot. Check the edge thickness of the valve. Valve wear will cause this thickness to reduce. It is recommended that any reaming or resurfacing (grinding) be performed by a reputable machine shop.

Check the valve stem for scoring and/or burned spots. Check the stem lock retainer grooves for wear. Check the end of the stem for wear. If not noticeably scored or damaged, clean the valve stem with a suitable solvent to remove all gum and varnish. Clean the valve guides using a suitable solvent

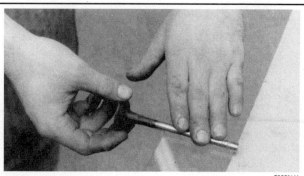

Fig. 118 Valve stems may be rolled on a flat surface to check for bends

Check the valve for signs of bending or piston contact. If a valve has contacted a piston, there will be a telltale mark on the piston crown, if the engine is still operational. If there has been piston contact, it is a good bet that the valve is bent. Replace the valve and guide.

Clean the valve face and valve seat in the head. Invert the head and place the valves into the guides. Fill the combustion chamber with gasoline and check for leakage into the ports. If leakage exists, the valve seat and valve face should be refaced to ensure seating.

STEM-TO-GUIDE CLEARANCE CHECKING

♦ **See Figure 119**

1. The head should be disassembled so the valve can be moved by hand. Remove the valve spring.

Fig. 119 Checking the stem to guide clearance with a dial indicator

Fig. 120 Check the valve spring for squareness on a flat surface. A carpenter's square can serve as a gauge

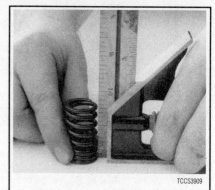

Fig. 121 The spring should be straight up and down when placed on a flat surface

2. Clean the valve guide and the valve stem. Lightly lubricate the valve stem and insert it into the valve guide.

3. Install a dial indicator with the push rod parallel with the cylinder head deck.

4. Place the end of the valve stem flush with the end of the valve guide on the cam side of the head.

5. Place the tip of the dial indicator on the edge of the valve and measure the distance the valve can move back and forth. This is the guide rocking measurement as BMW calls.

6. If the measurement is greater than recommended, have the valve guides replaced and reamed for the existing valves or have the guides reamed oversized to match new valves with oversized valve stems. The valve guides on the M3 and 5 and 7 Series engine typically are not replaced if they are worn, though they can be if necessary. These guides are reamed for an oversized valve stem and a replacement valve used with the appropriately oversized stem.

REFACING

If the valves need to be refaced, replacing the valves is the best bet. If the valves are to be refaced, refer the job to a reputable machine shop. The valves and the valve seats should be machined at the same time so the proper relationship of the seats can be maintained.

If after refacing the seats leak gasoline as tested above, lap the valves.

1. Clean the valve face and seat. Lubricate the valve stem and insert in the head.

2. Place a fine lapping compound on the valve seat and place the lapping tool on the valve head. The lapping tool is a stick with a suction cup to attach to the valve. The valve is rotated with the stick.

3. Rotate the valve back and forth, lifting the valve of its seat every so often.

4. Once a fine finish is achieved, remove the valve and clean all traces of lapping compound off. Clean the cylinder head of all traces of lapping compound. Check for leakage.

➡**All compound must be cleaned and removed as the lapping compound is extremely abrasive and will quickly wear any moving parts it contacts.**

Valve Springs

INSPECTION

▸ **See Figures 120 and 121**

The valve springs on BMW engines are of high quality and are capable of operating at high engine speeds. They should be replaced with original equipment units or specially made aftermarket units.

Line all the springs up. Check that they are all the same height. Place the springs against a straight edge. Check that they are straight and aren't twisted or bent.

Replace the inner and outer springs as a set. The springs must be a matched set and have the same color code.

Valve Lifters and Rocker Arms

REMOVAL & INSTALLATION

The single overhead camshaft engines use rocker arms that are removed in the process of removing the rocker shafts. To remove the rocker shafts, it is impossible not to remove the rocker arms. See rockershaft/arm removal in this section.

The double overhead camshaft engines use a direct valve actuation through a bucket and shim as on the M3 and M5 engines or a hydraulic lash adjuster as on the 5 Series engines.

The bucket and shim lifters on the M Series engines are removed after the camshafts have been removed. Mark their locations and lift them from their bores. The lifters must be replaced in the original positions. Measure the lifter bore with an inside micrometer and the outside diameter of the lifter with an outside micrometer. The difference should be 0.0010–0.0026 inches (0.025–0.066mm).

The hydraulic lifters on equipped engines are kept in the bearing plates for most operations. They can be held in place using BMW tool 11 3 250 or equivalent. Check the lifters for scoring and wear.

Oil Pan

REMOVAL & INSTALLATION

1600, 2000 and 2002 Models

1. Raise and support the vehicle. Drain the engine oil.

✳✳ CAUTION

The EPA warns that prolonged contact with used engine oil may cause a number of skin disorders, including cancer! You should make every effort to minimize your exposure to used engine oil. Protective gloves should be worn when changing the oil. Wash your hands and any other exposed skin areas as soon as possible after exposure to used engine oil. Soap and water, or waterless hand cleaner should be used.

2. Remove the front stabilizer bar, if equipped.

3. Remove the oil pan retaining bolts and loosen the pan from the engine block.

4. Disconnect the left and right engine supports.

5. Lower the vehicle and attach a lifting sling and raise the engine slightly.

6. Rotate the crankshaft so the the No. 4 piston is at TDC.

7. Remove the oil pan toward the front of the vehicle.

To install:

8. To install the oil pan, use a new gasket. Put sealer on the joints formed where the end cover and timing cover butt up against the block.

9. Slide the oil pan carefully into position and install the retaining bolts. Tighten the bolts to 7 ft. lbs. (9 Nm).

10. Lower the engine back into position.

11. Connect the left and right engine mounts. Install the front stabilizer bar, if removed.

12. Fill the crankcase to the correct level with clean engine oil.

2500, 2800, Bavaria, 3000, 3.0, 528i and 530i Models

1. Raise and support the vehicle. Drain the engine oil.

> **⁂ CAUTION**
>
> **The EPA warns that prolonged contact with used engine oil may cause a number of skin disorders, including cancer! You should make every effort to minimize your exposure to used engine oil. Protective gloves should be worn when changing the oil. Wash your hands and any other exposed skin areas as soon as possible after exposure to used engine oil. Soap and water, or waterless hand cleaner should be used.**

2. Remove the front lower apron (3.0 models) and remove the stabilizer bar.

3. Loosen the alternator (remove the alternator on 528i and 530i models) and remove the power steering pump, but do not disconnect the hoses. Support the power steering pump with a piece of wire.

4. Remove the lower power steering bracket bolt and loosen the remaining bolts (remove the remaining bolts on 528i and 530i models) enough to remove the oil pan retaining bolts.

5. Loosen the engine support bracket.

6. Remove the oil pan bolts and loosen the oil pan from the engine block.

7. Rotate the crankshaft until the No. 6 crankpin is above the bottom of the engine block.

8. Lower the front of the oil pan, turn the rear of the pan towards the support bracket and remove the pan.

To install:

9. To install the oil pan, use new gaskets. Put the sealer on the joints formed where the end cover and timing cover butt up against the block.

10. Move the oil pan carefully into position and install the retaining bolts. Tighten to bolts to 7 ft. lbs. (9 Nm).

11. Reinstall the alternator and power steering pump

12. Connect the left and right engine mounts. Install the front stabilizer bar, and the install the front lower apron.

13. Fill the crankcase to the correct level with clean engine oil.

318i Models

1. Remove the dipstick. Remove the lower pan by draining the oil, removing the pan bolts, and removing the lower pan.

> **⁂ CAUTION**
>
> **The EPA warns that prolonged contact with used engine oil may cause a number of skin disorders, including cancer! You should make every effort to minimize your exposure to used engine oil. Protective gloves should be worn when changing the oil. Wash your hands and any other exposed skin areas as soon as possible after exposure to used engine oil. Soap and water, or waterless hand cleaner should be used.**

2. Remove the oil pump.

3. Unscrew the ground strap, located at the right rear of the upper pan.

4. Remove the bottom 3 flywheel housing bolts, and 2 reinforcement plate bolts, and remove the reinforcement plate.

5. Remove upper pan bolts, and remove the upper pan.

6. Clean all 4 sealing surfaces. Replace both gaskets. Coat the mating surfaces on the timing case and end covers with sealer.

7. Install in reverse order, tightening the pan bolts to 7–8 ft. lbs. (9 Nm).

320i Models

1. Raise and support the vehicle. Drain the engine oil.

> **⁂ CAUTION**
>
> **The EPA warns that prolonged contact with used engine oil may cause a number of skin disorders, including cancer! You should make every effort to minimize your exposure to used engine oil. Protective gloves should be worn when changing the oil. Wash your hands and any other exposed skin areas as soon as possible after exposure to used engine oil. Soap and water, or waterless hand cleaner should be used.**

2. Loosen the steering gear bolts and pull the steering box off the front axle carrier.

3. Remove the oil pan bolts and separate the pan from the engine block.

4. Swing the oil pan downward while rotating the crankshaft to allow the pan to clear the crankpin and remove the pan toward the front.

5. Reverse the procedure to install the oil pan, using new gaskets.

6. Tighten the bolts to 7 ft. lbs. (9 Nm).

325, 325e, 325i, 325iS, 325iX and 528e Models

▶ **See Figures 122 thru 132**

1. Raise the vehicle and support it. Drain the engine oil.

> **⁂ CAUTION**
>
> **The EPA warns that prolonged contact with used engine oil may cause a number of skin disorders, including cancer! You should make every effort to minimize your exposure to used engine oil. Protective gloves should be worn when changing the oil. Wash your hands and any other exposed skin areas as soon as possible after exposure to used engine oil. Soap and water, or waterless hand cleaner should be used.**

2. Remove the front lower splash guard. This may not be necessary for access on 1988 models.

3. Unfasten the electrical terminal from the oil sending unit.

4. On 1987 and earlier models, skip to Step 5. On 1988 models, remove the power steering gear from the front axle carrier.

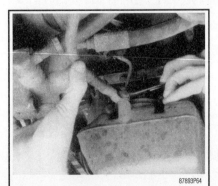

Fig. 122 Remove the ground strap attached to the front left part of the oil pan

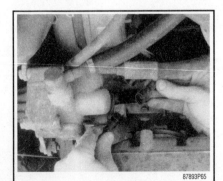

Fig. 123 Unplug the oil sender harness

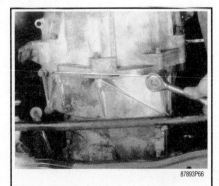

Fig. 124 Remove the bolts from the flywheel cover over the oil pan

Fig. 125 With the flywheel cover removed, inspect the gasket and replace if needed

Fig. 126 Remove the bolts from the front of the oil pan

Fig. 127 Remove the bolts from the side of the oil pan

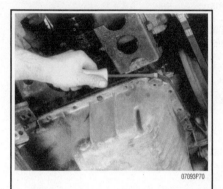

Fig. 128 Carefully pry the oil pan off

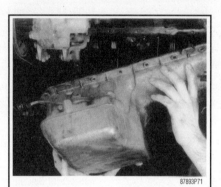

Fig. 129 Lower the oil pan until it catches the oil pump

Fig. 130 Remove the bolts securing the oil pump to the engine block

Fig. 131 Lower the oil pan and pump away from the engine block

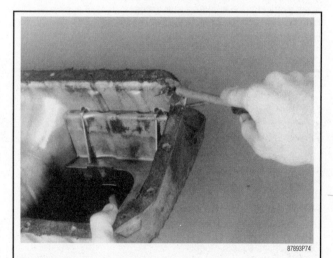

Fig. 132 Clean all gasket material from the oil pan and pan mating surfaces

5. Remove the flywheel cover.

6. Remove the oil pan bolts and lower the oil pan. Remove the oil pump bolts and take out the oil pump and oil pan.

To install:

7. Installation is the reverse of removal. Follow these installation notes:

  a. Clean the gasket surfaces and use a new gasket on the oil pan.

  b. Coat the joints on the ends of the front engine cover with a universal sealing compound.

  c. Tighten the bolts to 7 ft. lbs. (9 Nm).

  d. Install the sending unit wire and the engine oil. If the power steering gear was removed, make sure to refill and bleed this system.

M3 Models

1. Remove the dipstick. Remove the splash guard from underneath the engine.

2. Remove the drain plug and drain the oil. Unscrew all the bolts for the lower oil pan and remove it.

3. Remove the oil pan.

4. Remove the lower flywheel housing cover by removing the 3 bolts at the bottom of the flywheel housing and the 2 bolts in the cover just ahead of the flywheel housing.

5. Disconnect the oil pressure sending unit plug. Unbolt the oil pan bracket. Disconnect the ground lead. Loosen its clamp and unfasten the crankcase ventilation hose.

6. Remove the oil pan bolts and remove the upper oil pan.

To install:

7. Clean all sealing surfaces. Supply a new gasket and the coat the joints where the timing case cover and block meet with a brush-on sealant. Install the pan and tighten the bolts evenly to 7 ft. lbs. (9 Nm).

8. Reverse the remaining removal procedures to install, cleaning all sealing surfaces and using a new gasket on the lower pan, also. Tighten the lower pan bolts, also, to 7 ft. lbs. (9 Nm).

9. Install the oil pan drain plug, tightening to 24 ft. lbs. (31 Nm). Refill the oil pan with the required amount of approved oil. Start the engine and check for leaks.

530i Models

1. Raise the vehicle and support it. Drain the engine oil.

2. Remove the front lower splash guard.

3. Unfasten the electrical terminal from the oil sending unit.

4. Remove the flywheel cover.

5. Remove the oil pan bolts and lower the oil pan. Remove the oil pump bolts and take out the oil pump and oil pan.

6. Installation is the reverse of removal:

    a. Clean the gasket surfaces and use a new gasket on the oil pan.

    b. Tighten the pan bolts to 7 ft. lbs. (9 Nm).

    c. Coat the joints on the ends of the front engine cover with a universal sealing compound.

    d. Tighten the bolts to 7 ft. lbs. (9 Nm).

    e. Install the sending unit wire and the engine oil.

1982 533i and 633CSi Models

1. Raise and support the vehicle. Drain the engine oil.

2. Remove the front stabilizer bar.

3. Disconnect the wire terminal at the oil level switch.

4. Unfasten the power steering pump, but do not disconnect the hoses. Loosen all the power steering bracket bolts, and remove the bottom bolt.

5. Remove the engine oil pan bolts, separate the oil pan from the engine block and lower the front of the pan.

6. Rotate the crankshaft until the No. 6 crankpin is above the bottom of the engine block.

7. Lift the engine slightly at the clutch housing while removing the pan to the right side.

To install:

8. To install the oil pan, use new gaskets. Put the sealer on the joints formed where the end cover and timing cover butt up against the block.

9. Move the oil pan carefully into position and install the retaining bolts. Tighten the bolts to 7 ft. lbs. (9 Nm).

10. Reinstall the alternator and power steering pump

11. Connect the left and right engine mounts. Install the front stabilizer bar, and the install the front lower apron.

12. Fill the crankcase to the correct level with clean engine oil.

1983–84 533i and 633CSi; 535i, 635CSi, M5 and M6 Models

1. Disconnect the negative battery cable. Unfasten the electrical connector and separate the leads from the air cleaner/airflow sensor. Loosen the hose clamp and disconnect the air intake hose. Remove the mounting nut and remove the air cleaner and the airflow sensor as a unit. Remove the fan shroud.

2. Drain the engine oil.

3. Loosen the belt tensioner and remove the alternator drive belt. Loosen the upper front mounting bolt for the alternator and the 2 bolts on the side of the block that mount to the rear. Remove the lower front mounting bolt. Then, swing the alternator to the side.

4. Loosen the power steering pump mounts and remove the drive belt. Then, remove the mounting bolts and remove the pump and pump mounting bracket. Make sure to retain spacers. If the car has air conditioning, remove the nuts and bolts that fasten the compressor to the hinge type mounting bracket. Make sure the compressor is suspended so there is no tension on the hoses. Unbolt the hinge type mounting bracket and remove it.

5. Remove the brace plate located under the oil pan. Remove those oil pan bolts that can be reached.

6. Remove the engine ground strap. Remove the engine mount through-bolts. Attach a lifting sling to the hooks on top of the engine. Lift the engine slightly for clearance.

7. Shift the power steering pump out of the way and support it so no tension will be placed on the hoses.

8. Remove the remaining oil pan mounting bolts. Turn the crankshaft so the rods for cylinders 5 and 6 are as high as possible. Then, remove the pan.

To install:

9. Clean all sealing surfaces and supply a new gasket. Apply a liquid sealer to the joints between the block and the timing cover on the front and the rear main seal cover at the rear.

10. Install the oil pan in reverse order. Tighten the pan bolts to 6.5–7.5 ft. lbs. (8–10 Nm). Make sure to refill the pan with the required amount of the correct oil. Mount all accessories securely and adjust the drive belts.

630CSi Models

1. Raise and support the vehicle. Drain the engine oil.

Protective gloves should be worn when changing the oil. Wash your hands and any other exposed skin areas as soon as possible after exposure to used engine oil. Soap and water, or waterless hand cleaner should be used.

2. Remove the front stabilizer bar.
3. Unfasten the wire terminal at he oil level switch.
4. Disconnect the power steering pump, but do not disconnect the hoses. Loosen all the power steering bracket bolts, and remove the bottom bolt.
5. Remove the engine oil pan bolts, separate the oil pan from the engine block and lower the front of the pan.
6. Rotate the crankshaft until the No. 6 crankpin is above the bottom of the engine block.
7. Lift the engine slightly at the clutch housing while removing the pan to the right side.

To install:
8. To install the oil pan, use new gaskets. Put sealer on the joints where the end cover and timing cover butt up against the block.
9. Move the oil pan carefully into position and install the retaining bolts. Tighten the bolts to 7 ft. lbs. (9 Nm).
10. Reinstall the alternator and power steering pump
11. Connect the left and right engine mounts. Install the front stabilizer bar, and the install the front lower apron.
12. Fill the crankcase to the correct level with clean engine oil.

1982 733i Models

1. Raise and support the vehicle. Drain the engine oil.

> ❄❄ **CAUTION**
>
> **The EPA warns that prolonged contact with used engine oil may cause a number of skin disorders, including cancer! You should make every effort to minimize your exposure to used engine oil. Protective gloves should be worn when changing the oil. Wash your hands and any other exposed skin areas as soon as possible after exposure to used engine oil. Soap and water, or waterless hand cleaner should be used.**

2. Remove the power steering pump, but do not disconnect the hoses.
3. Remove the lower power steering bracket bolt. Loosen the upper bracket bolts to move the bracket away from the oil pan.
4. Unfasten the oil level switch wire terminal.
5. Remove the oil pan bolts and separate the oil pan from the engine block.
6. Disconnect the left and right engine mounts.
7. Remove the engine vibration damper.
8. Lower the vehicle and remove the fan housing from the radiator.
9. Attach a lifting sling and raise the engine until the oil pan can be removed.

To install:
10. To install the oil pan, use new gaskets. Put the sealer on the joints formed where the end cover and timing cover butt up against the block.
11. Move the oil pan carefully into position and install the retaining bolts. Tighten the bolts to 7 ft. lbs. (9 Nm).
12. Reinstall the alternator and power steering pump.
13. Connect the left and right engine mounts. Install the front stabilizer bar, and the install the front lower apron.
14. Fill the crankcase to the correct level with clean engine oil.

1983–86 733i Models

1. Remove the alternator drive belt, remove the alternator mounting bolts and move it aside.
2. Loosen the adjusting and mounting bolts and remove the power steering pump belt. Remove the power steering pump hinge bolt and nut. Remove the 2 bolts shown, keeping any shims that may have been used in assembly together with the bolt they were on.

> ❄❄ **CAUTION**
>
> **When draining coolant, keep in mind that cats and dogs are attracted to ethylene glycol antifreeze, and could drink any that is left in an uncovered container or in puddles on the ground. This will**

prove fatal in sufficient quantity. Always drain the coolant into a sealable container. Coolant should be reused unless it is contaminated or several years old.

3. Drain coolant out of the block. Drain the oil pan. Remove the plug from the block and drain the engine of coolant.

> ❄❄ **CAUTION**
>
> **The EPA warns that prolonged contact with used engine oil may cause a number of skin disorders, including cancer! You should make every effort to minimize your exposure to used engine oil. Protective gloves should be worn when changing the oil. Wash your hands and any other exposed skin areas as soon as possible after exposure to used engine oil. Soap and water, or waterless hand cleaner should be used.**

4. Remove the 2 attachments fastening the stabilizer bar to the body.
5. Remove the 2 bolts and nuts shown and move this bracket away from the engine.
6. Remove the bolts and remove the clutch housing cover. Remove all the oil pan bolts that can be reached.
7. Disconnect the oil level sending unit wire. Then, unfasten both engine mounts by removing the nuts from the ends of the bolts.
8. Unfasten the radiator hoses that's near one of the lifting hooks, and securely connect a lifting sling to the engine. Raise the engine.
9. Swing out and tie down the power steering bracket. Then, unscrew the remaining oil pan bolts.
10. Pull the oil pan down. Turn the crankshaft so the rods for cylinders 5 and 6 are in the highest position, pull the stabilizer bar away, and then remove the pan.

To install:
11. Install in reverse order, paying attention to these points:
   a. Clean all gasket surfaces thoroughly. Use a new gasket and coat all mating surfaces on the timing cover and clutch housing cover with a liquid sealer.
   b. Tighten the oil pan bolts to 7 ft. lbs. (9 Nm).
   c. Tighten the stabilizer bar attachment bolts to 16 ft. lbs. (21 Nm).
   d. Make sure spacers are used on the power steering pump brace so there will not be any tighten on the bracket due to misalignment.

1987–88 735i Models

1. Loosen the hose clamp for the air intake hose. Remove the mounting nut for the air cleaner, and remove the air cleaner. Remove the fan and shroud.
2. Unfasten the electrical plug and overflow hose from the coolant expansion tank. Be careful not to kink the hose. Remove the mounting nuts and remove the tank.
3. Remove the splash guard for the power steering pump. Loosen the locknut for the pump adjustment and remove the through bolt that mounts the pump lower bracket (which contains the adjustment mechanism) to the block. Swing the bracket aside. Unscrew the bolt attaching the power steering pump lines to the block and shift them aside too.
4. Unfasten the electrical plug for the suspension leveling switch on the left side engine mounting bracket. Remove the oil pan drain plug and drain the oil.

> ❄❄ **CAUTION**
>
> **The EPA warns that prolonged contact with used engine oil may cause a number of skin disorders, including cancer! You should make every effort to minimize your exposure to used engine oil. Protective gloves should be worn when changing the oil. Wash your hands and any other exposed skin areas as soon as possible after exposure to used engine oil. Soap and water, or waterless hand cleaner should be used.**

5. Remove the bracket for the exhaust pipes located near the oil pan.
6. Disconnect the ground strap from the engine. Remove the nuts and washers attaching the engine to the mounts on both sides.
7. Attach an engine lifting sling to the hooks at either end of the cylinder head. Lift the engine as necessary for clearance.
8. Remove all oil pan mounting bolts and remove the pan.

To install:

9. Clean both sealing surfaces and supply a new gasket. Coat the 4 joints (between the block and timing case cover at the front and the block and rear main seal housing cover at the rear) with a sealer such as 3M Bond Silicone Sealer®.

10. Install the oil pan bolts and tighten them to 6.5–7.5 ft. lbs. (8–10 Nm).

11. Reverse the remaining procedures to install the oil pan. Tighten the engine mount nuts to 31–34 ft. lbs. (40–44 Nm). Refill the oil pan with the required amount and type of oil.

Oil Pump

REMOVAL & INSTALLATION

Except 325 Series, 528e,1600, 2000, 2002 and M3 Models

1. Remove the oil pan. On the 318i and M3, only the lower section of the pan need be removed.

2. Remove the bolts retaining the sprocket to the oil pump shaft and remove the sprocket.

3. On 4-cylinder engines:

a. Remove the oil pump retaining bolts and lower the oil pump from the engine block.

b. Check the installed location of the O-ring seal, between the housing and the pressure safety line and make sure it is installed so it will seal properly.

c. Tighten the sprocket retaining nut to 18–22 ft. lbs. (23–29 Nm).

d. Be sure that the oil bore in the shim(s) is correctly positioned during the oil pump installation. If there is a lot of play in the drive chain, add one or more shims. The drive chain should give slightly under light thumb pressure.

4. On 6-cylinder engines:

a. Remove the oil pump retaining bolts and lower the oil pump from the engine block. On 6-cylinder. engines, there are 3 bolts at the front and 2 bolts attaching the rear of the oil pickup to the lower end of a support bracket. It is necessary to remove all 5 bolts.

b. Do not loosen the chain adjusting shims from the 2 mounting locations.

c. Add or subtract shims between the oil pump body and the engine block to obtain a slight movement of the chain under light thumb pressure.

5. Install the oil pump in the reverse order of removal. Tighten the bolts to 16 ft. lbs. (21 Nm).

✽✽ CAUTION

When used, the 2 shim thicknesses must be the same. Tighten the pump holder at the pick-up end after shimming is completed to avoid stress on the pump.

6. On 6-cylinder engines, after the main pump mounting bolts are tightened, loosen the bolts at the bracket on the rear of the pick-up, allowing the pick-up to assume its most natural position. This will relieve tension on the bracket. Tighten the oil pump mounting bolts to 16 ft. lbs. (21 Nm) and the sprocket bolts to 19 ft. lbs.

1600, 2000, and 2002 Models

1. Remove the oil pan as outlined in this section.

2. Remove the 3 retaining bolts for the oil pump drive sprocket and pull off the sprocket.

3. Open the lockplates for the pickup tube mounting bolts at the main bearing cap. Remove the 2 bolts for the support mount and the 2 oil pump retaining bolts. Lower the oil pump down and out of the car, taking care not to lose the O-ring in the oil pump housing.

To install:

4. Reverse the above procedure to install, observing the following installation notes:

a. Adjust the oil pump drive chain tension so that the chain may be depressed under light thumb pressure. If the proper tension cannot be achieved with either of the replacement lengths of chain, shims (compensating plates) may be installed between the pump housing and the block to take

up the slack. When installing shims, always make sure that the oil hole is not blocked. Use a new O-ring when possible.

b. After tightening the pump mounting bolts to 16 ft. lbs. (21 Nm), loosen the pickup tube support bracket and retighten the bracket bolts so that the bracket is tension-free.

325, 325e, 325i, 325iS, 325iX, 528e and M3 Models

1. Raise the vehicle and support it. Drain the engine oil.

✽✽ CAUTION

The EPA warns that prolonged contact with used engine oil may cause a number of skin disorders, including cancer! You should make every effort to minimize your exposure to used engine oil. Protective gloves should be worn when changing the oil. Wash your hands and any other exposed skin areas as soon as possible after exposure to used engine oil. Soap and water, or waterless hand cleaner should be used.

2. Remove the front lower splash guard.

3. Unfasten the electrical terminal from the oil sending unit.

4. Remove the flywheel cover.

5. Remove the 3 oil pan bolts: one on one side and 2 on the other and lower the oil pan. Remove the oil pump bolts and take out the oil pump and oil pan.

To install:

6. Installation is the reverse of removal. Installation notes:

a. Clean the gasket surfaces and use a new gasket on the oil pan.

b. Positioning the pump for installation of its mounting bolts, guide the pump driveshaft into the hole in the center of the drive gear. Tighten the bolts to 16 ft. lbs. (21 Nm).

c. Coat the joints on the ends of the front engine cover with a universal sealing compound.

d. Install the sending unit wire and the engine oil.

Timing Chain (Front) Cover

REMOVAL & INSTALLATION

1600, 2000, 2002, 318i and 320i Models

There are 2 timing chain covers, one upper and one lower, which must be removed to service the timing chain and sprocket assemblies.

1. Remove the cylinder head cover. Disconnect the negative battery cable. Disconnect the air injection line at the front of the thermal reactor (if so equipped).

2. On the 318i, unfasten the bracket located on the driver's side of the upper cover.

3. Remove the bolts which retain the upper timing gear cover to the cylinder head and lower timing gear cover. remove the upper cover, taking note of the placement of the alternator ground wire.

4. Drain the cooling system and remove the radiator, preheater intake air assembly (carburetor equipped cars only) and radiator hoses as outlined in this section.

✽✽ CAUTION

When draining coolant, keep in mind that cats and dogs are attracted to ethylene glycol antifreeze, and could drink any that is left in an uncovered container or in puddles on the ground. This will prove fatal in sufficient quantity. Always drain the coolant into a sealable container. Coolant should be reused unless it is contaminated or several years old.

5. Bend back the lockplates for the fan retaining bolts. Remove the bolts and lift off the fan.

6. Loosen the alternator retaining bolts. Push the alternator toward the engine and remove the fan pulley and the alternator drive (fan) belt.

7. On 318i models, remove the alternator and tensioning bar. remove the 4 mounting bolts from the air pump bracket (where it attaches to the block), and

remove the pump and bracket; then remove the bolt attaching the tensioning bar to the block and remove the tensioning bar.

8. Unfasten the coolant hoses from the water pump. Remove the 6 retaining bolts and copper sealing washers and lift off the water pump.

9. Unscrew the plug and remove the spring from the cam chain tensioner assembly, taking care to cushion the sudden release of spring tension. Remove the plunger (piston).

10. On 320i models, unfasten the multiple plug and cable lead from the alternator. Remove the alternator with its bearing block and clamping strap.

11. Remove the flywheel inspection plate and block the ring gear from turning with a small prybar.

12. Unscrew the crankshaft pulley nut and pull off the belt pulley.

13. Remove the bolts which retain the lower cover to the cylinder black and oil pan. On 318i models, remove the bolts retaining the brace plate and remove it. Also on the 318i, loosen the oil pan lower retaining bolts not directly involved with the lower cover. With a sharp knife, carefully separate the lower edge of the timing covr from the upper edge of the oil pan gasket at the front.

14. Remove the lower timing cover. At this time, it is advisable to replace the timing cover seal (sealing ring) with a new one. The sealing ring is a press fit into the cover.

To install:

15. Clean the mating surfaces of the timing covers, oil pan, cylinder head, and cylinder block. Replace all gaskets (except the oil pan gasket), and seal them at the corners with sealing compound such as Permatex® No. 2 or equivalent. If the oil pan gasket has been damaged, remove the oil pan and replace the gasket.

16. Reverse the above procedure to install, taking care to tighten the upper timing gear cover retaining bolts to 6–8 ft. lbs. (8–10 Nm). Note that on the 318i, the mounting web for the tensioning piston must be in the oil pocket. On 318i models, also make sure to pack the bores between the lower cover (at the top) and block with sealer.

6-Cylinder Models

EXCEPT M3, M5 AND M6 MODELS

➡On 530i, 533, 535, 633/635 CS Series, and 700 Series engines, this procedure requires the use of a special gauge, to be made to a certain dimension.

1. Remove the cylinder head cover. Remove the distributor. On all 3.2 liter models, detach the distributor guard and the air line going to the thermal reactor. On late model cars with Digital Motor Electronics (DME), follow this procedure to remove the distributor:

   a. Remove the distributor cap, which screws onto the cover directly in front of the camshaft.

   b. Then, if the rotor is of the slide-on type, simply pull the rotor off and then remove the cover underneath it.

   c. If the rotor is of the screw-on type, unscrew it from the distributor shaft, then unscrew the adapter underneath and, finally remove the cover underneath the adapter.

2. Drain the coolant to below the level of the thermostat and remove the thermostat housing cover.

✳✳ CAUTION

When draining coolant, keep in mind that cats and dogs are attracted to ethylene glycol antifreeze, and could drink any that is left in an uncovered container or in puddles on the ground. This will prove fatal in sufficient quantity. Always drain the coolant into a sealable container. Coolant should be reused unless it is contaminated or several years old.

3. Remove the bolts and remove the upper timing case cover with the worm drive which drives the distributor (pre DME cars only).

4. Remove the piston which tensions the timing chain, working carefully because of very high spring pressure.

5. Remove the cooling fan and all drive belts. On late model 600 Series cars, the alternator must be swung aside by loosing the front bolt and removing the 2 side bolts. On all cars with the 2.5L, 2.8L 3.0L and 3.2L engines, remove the attaching bolts and then remove the drive pulley from the water pump. The power steering pump must be removed, leaving the pump hoses connected and supporting the pump out of the way but so that the hoses are not stressed.

6. Remove the flywheel housing cover and lock the flywheel in position with an appropriate special tool.

7. Unscrew the nut from the center of the pulley and pull the pulley/vibration damper off the crankshaft.

8. Detach the TDC position transmitter on 600CS Series, 700 Series, and certain 528i models.

9. Loosen all the oil pan bolts, and then unscrew all the bolts from the lower timing case cover, noting their lengths for reinstallation in the same positions. Carefully use a knife to separate the gasket at the base of the lower timing cover. Then, remove the cover.

To install:

10. To install the lower cover, first coat the surfaces of the oil pan and block with sealer. Put it into position on the block, making sure the tensioning piston holding web (cast into the block) is in the oil pocket. Install all bolts; then tighten the lower front cover bolts evenly; finally, tighten the oil pan bolts evenly.

11. Inspect the hub of the vibration damper. If the hub is scored, install the radial seal so the sealing lip is in front of or to the rear of the scored area. Pack the seal with grease and install it with a sealer installer.

12. Install the pulley/damper and tighten the bolt to specifications. When installing, make sure the key and keyway are properly aligned.

13. Remove the flywheel locking tool and reinstall the cover. Reinstall and tension all belts.

14. Before installing the upper cover, use sealer to seal the joint between the back of the lower timing cover and block at the top. On some models, there are sealer wells which are to be filled with sealer. If these are present, fill them carefully. Check the cork seal at the distributor drive coupling, and replace it if necessary.

15. Just before installing the upper timing case cover, check the condition of that area of the head gasket. It will usually be in good condition. If it should show damage, it must be replaced.

16. If the car has the DME type dIstributor, inspect the sealing O-rings and replace as necessary. If it uses the DME distributor with the screw-off type rotor, make sure the bolt at the center of the rotor has its seal in place and that it is installed with a sealer designed to prevent the bolt from backing out.

17. Reverse the remaining portions of the removal procedures, making sure to bleed the cooling system.

M3 MODELS

1. Disconnect the negative battery cable. Drain the cooling system through the bottom of the radiator. Remove the radiator and fan.

✳✳ CAUTION

When draining coolant, keep in mind that cats and dogs are attracted to ethylene glycol antifreeze, and could drink any that is left in an uncovered container or in puddles on the ground. This will prove fatal in sufficient quantity. Always drain the coolant into a sealable container. Coolant should be reused unless it is contaminated or several years old.

2. Unfasten all electrical plugs, remove the attaching nuts, and remove the air cleaner and airflow sensor.

3. Note and if necessary mark the wiring connections. Then, unfasten all alternator wiring. Unbolt the alternator and remove it and the drive belt.

4. Unbolt the power steering pump. Remove the belt and then move the pump aside, supporting it out of the way but in a position where the hoses will not be stressed.

5. Remove the 3 bolts from the bottom of the bell housing and the 2 bolts below it which fasten the reinforcement plate in place.

6. Remove the drain plug and drain the oil from the lower oil pan. Then, remove the lower oil pan bolts and remove the lower pan.

✳✳ CAUTION

The EPA warns that prolonged contact with used engine oil may cause a number of skin disorders, including cancer! You should make every effort to minimize your exposure to used engine oil. Protective gloves should be worn when changing the oil. Wash your hands and any other exposed skin areas as soon as possible after exposure to used engine oil. Soap and water, or waterless hand cleaner should be used.

7. Remove the 3 bolts fastening the bottom of the front cover to the front of the oil pan. Loosen all the remaining oil pan bolts so the pan may be shifted downward just slightly to separate the gasket surfaces.

8. Remove the water pump as described in this section. Remove the center bolt and use a puller to remove the crankshaft pulley.

9. Remove the piston for the timing chain tensioner.

10. Remove the 2 bolts attaching the top of the front cover to the cylinder head. Then, remove all the bolts fastening the cover to the block.

11. Run a knife carefully between the upper surface of the oil pan gasket and the lower surface of the front cover to separate them without tearing the gasket. If the gasket is damaged, remove the oil pan and replace it, as described in this section.

To install:

12. Before reinstalling the cover, use a file to break or file off flashing at the top rear of the casting on either side so the corner is smooth. Replace all gaskets, coating them with silicone sealer. Where gasket ends extend too far, trim them off. Apply sealer to the area where the oil pan gasket passes the front of the block.

13. Slide the cover straight on to avoid damaging the seal. Install all bolts in their proper positions. Coat the 3 bolts fastening the front cover to the upper oil pan with a sealer such as Loctite® 270® or equivalent. Tighten the bolts at the top, fastening the lower cover to the upper cover first. Then, tighten the remaining front cover bolts and, finally, the oil pan bolts to 7 ft. lbs. (9 Nm). If the car has the DME type distributor, inspect the sealing O-rings and replace as necessary. If it uses the DME distributor with the screw-off type rotor, make sure the bolt at the center of the rotor has its seal in place and that it is installed with a sealer designed to prevent the bolt from backing out.

14. Reverse the remaining portions of the removal procedures, making sure to fill and bleed the cooling system and to refill the oil pan with the correct oil. Tighten the oil drain plug to 24 ft. lbs. (31 Nm) and both upper and lower oil pan bolts to 7 ft. lbs. (9 Nm).

M5 AND M6 MODELS

1. Disconnect the battery ground cable. Pull out the plug and remove the wiring leading to the airflow sensor. Loosen the hose clamp and disconnect the air intake hose. Remove the mounting nut and remove the air cleaner and airflow sensor as an assembly.

2. Remove the radiator and fan. Remove the flywheel housing cover and install a lock to lock the position of the flywheel. Remove the mounting nut for the vibration damper with a deepwell socket. Pull the damper off with a puller.

3. Remove the pipe that runs across in front of the front cover. Remove the mounting bolts and remove the water pump pulley.

4. Loosen the top front mounting bolt for the alternator. Remove the lower front bolt. Loosen the 2 side bolts. Swing the alternator aside.

5. Remove the power steering pump mounting bolts. Make sure to retain the spacer that goes between the pump and oil pan. Swing the pump aside and support it so the hoses will not be under stress.

6. Remove the flywheel housing cover and lock the flywheel in position with an appropriate special tool.

7. Unscrew the nut from the center of the pulley and pull the pulley/vibration damper off the crankshaft.

8. Remove the bolts at the top, fastening the lower front cover to the upper front cover. Remove the bolts at the bottom, fastening the lower cover to the oil pan. Loosen the remaining oil pan mounting bolts.

9. Run a knife carefully between the upper surface of the oil pan gasket and the lower surface of the front cover to separate them without tearing the gasket.

10. Loosen and then remove the remaining front cover mounting bolts, noting the locations of the TDC sending unit on the upper right side of the engine and the suspension position sending unit on the upper left. Also, keep track of the bolts that mount these accessories, as their lengths are slightly different. If necessary, lay the bolts out in a clean area in a pattern similar to that in which they are positioned on the engine. Remove the timing cover, pulling it off squarely.

To install:

11. Before reinstalling the cover, use a file to break or file off flashing at the top rear of the casting on either side so the corner is smooth. Replace all gaskets, coating them with silicone sealer. Where gasket ends extend too far, trim them off. Apply sealer to the area where the oil pan gasket passes the front of the block.

12. Slide the cover straight on to avoid damaging the seal. Install all bolts in their proper positions. Tighten the bolts at the top, fastening the lower cover

to the upper cover first. Then, tighten the remaining front cover bolts and, finally, the oil pan bolts. If the car has the DME type distributor, inspect the sealing O-rings and replace as necessary. If it uses the DME distributor with the screw-off type rotor, make sure the bolt at the center of the rotor has its seal in place and that it is installed with a sealer designed to prevent the bolt from backing out.

13. Reverse the remaining portions of the removal procedures, making sure to refill and bleed the cooling system.

Timing Chain and Tensioner

REMOVAL & INSTALLATION

Except M3, M5 and M6 Models

1. Rotate the crankshaft to set the No. 1 piston at TDC, at the beginning of its compression stroke.

2. Remove the distributor (6-cylinder engines only).

3. Remove the cylinder head cover, air injection pipe and guard plate.

4. Drain the cooling system and remove the thermostat housing.

❋❋ CAUTION

When draining coolant, keep in mind that cats and dogs are attracted to ethylene glycol antifreeze, and could drink any that is left in an uncovered container or in puddles on the ground. This will prove fatal in sufficient quantity. Always drain the coolant into a sealable container. Coolant should be reused unless it is contaminated or several years old.

5. Remove the upper timing housing cover.

6. Remove the timing chain tensioner piston by unscrewing the cap cautiously.

➡**The piston is under heavy spring tension.**

7. Remove the drive belts and fan.

8. Remove the flywheel guard and lock the flywheel with a locking tool.

9. Remove the vibration damper assembly.

➡**The crankshaft Woodruff key should be in the 12 o'clock position.**

10. Remove upper and lower timing covers as described above.

11. Turn the crankshaft so that the No. 1 cylinder is at firing position. Open the camshaft lockplates if so equipped, remove the bolts and remove the camshaft sprocket.

12. On 4-cylinder engines:

    a. Remove the bottom circlip holding the chain guide rail to the block. Loosen the upper pivot pin until the guide rail rests against the forward part of the cylinder head gasket.

    b. Remove the timing chain from the sprockets and remove the guide rail by pulling downward and swinging the rail to the right.

    c. Remove the chain from the guide rail and remove it from the engine.

    d. On the 4-cylinder engine, take the timing chain off top and bottom sprockets and remove carefully from the guide rail.

13. On 6-cylinder engines:

    a. Remove the chain from the lower sprocket, swing the chain to the right front and out of the guide rail and remove the chain from the engine.

14. Installation is the reverse of removal, but note the following:

15. Be sure that No. 1 piston remains at the top of its firing stroke and the key on the crankshaft is in the 12 o'clock position.

16. On 4-cylinder engines:

    a. Position the camshaft flange so that the dowel pin bore is located at the 6 o'clock position and the notch in the top of the flange aligns with the cast tab on the cylinder head.

    b. Position the chain in the chain guide rail and move the rail upward and to the left, engaging the lower locating pivot pin and threading the upper pivot pin into the block. Install the circlip on the lower guide pin. On the 318i, simply locate the chain carefully in the guide rail.

    c. Engage the chain on the crankshaft sprocket and fit the camshaft sprocket into the chain.

    d. Align the gear dowel pin to the camshaft flange and bolt the sprocket into place. Use new lockplates (where so equipped), and secure the bolt heads.

17. On 6-cylinder engines:

a. Position the camshaft flange so that the dowel pin bore is between the 7 and 8 o'clock position and the upper flange bolt hole is aligned with the cast tab on the cylinder head.

b. Position the chain on the guide rail and swing the chain inward and to the left.

c. Engage the chain on the crankshaft gear and install the camshaft sprocket into the chain.

d. Align the gear dowel pin to the camshaft flange and bolt and sprocket into place. Tighten the sprocket bolts to 6.5–7.5 (8–10 Nm).

18. Install the chain tensioner piston, spring and cap plug, but do not tighten.

19. To bleed the chain tensioner, fill the oil pocket, located on the upper timing housing cover, with engine oil and move the tensioner back and forth with a screwdriver until oil is expelled at the cap plug. Tighten the cap plug securely.

20. Complete the assembly in the reverse order of removal. Check the ignition timing and the idle speed. Be sure the flywheel holder is removed before any attempt is made to start the engine.

M3 Model

1. Remove the timing case cover.

2. Refer to the camshaft removal procedure below. Follow the procedure to the point where the 2 camshaft drive sprockets are unbolted and remove them. It is not necessary to remove the cover from the rear of the head.

3. Make sure to catch the washer and lockwashers which will be released at the front as the rest of this step is performed. Now, remove the 2 mounting bolts for the guide rail, which is located on the left (driver's) side of the engine. These are accessible from the rear.

4. Pull the guide rail forward and then turn it clockwise on its axis, looking at it from above, to free it from the chain.

5. Note the relationships between timing chain and sprocket marks. Remove the chain by separating it from the sprockets at top and bottom.

6. Engage the timing chain with the crankshaft sprocket so marks line up. Route the chain up through where the guide rail will go. Install the guide rail in reverse of the removal procedure.

7. Then engage the chain with the driver's side ("E") sprocket with the marks lined up. Bolt this sprocket and the lockplate onto the front end of the intake camshaft. Use the adapter to keep the sprocket from turning, and tighten the bolts to 6–7 ft. lbs. (8–9 Nm). Turn this camshaft in the direction opposite to normal rotation to tension the timing chain on that side.

8. Now, engage the timing marks with the mark on the passenger's side ("A") sprocket and then install the sprocket and lockplate onto the front end of the exhaust camshaft. Again, use the adapter to keep the sprocket from turning, and tighten the bolts to 6–7 ft. lbs. (8–9 Nm). Make sure the timing chain has stayed in time.

9. Slide the chain tensioner piston into its cylinder. Install a new seal. Now install the spring with the conical end out. Install the cap which retains the spring and tighten it to 29 ft. lbs. (38 Nm).

10. Turn the engine one revolution in the normal direction of rotation. Recheck the timing. With the crankshaft at TDC, one groove on each camshaft faces inward and another on each faces the cast boss on the nearby bearing cap.

11. Perform the remaining procedures for camshaft installation, including installing and centering the top chain guide rail and centering it.

12. Install the timing case cover as described above.

M5 and M6 Models

1. Remove the fan shroud and the fan. Remove the cylinder head cover. Remove the timing cover as described above.

2. Refer to the camshaft removal procedure below. Follow the procedure to the point where the 2 camshaft drive sprockets are unbolted and remove them. It is not necessary to perform Step 4 to remove the cover from the rear of the head.

3. Refer to the appropriate procedure and remove the water pump.

4. Remove the 2 mounting bolts for the guide rail, which is located on the left (driver's) side of the engine. These are accessible from the rear. Turn the guide rail counterclockwise on its axis, looking at it from above to clear the chain and block and remove it. Be careful to retain all washers.

5. Note the relationships between timing chain and sprocket marks. Remove the timing chain.

To install:

6. Install the timing chain with the marks on all 3 sprockets aligned with marked links on the chain. Make sure the chain runs on the inside of the guide sprocket on the left side of the engine and along the groove in the lower tensioning rail. Install the chain onto the camshaft drive sprockets and then install the sprockets onto the camshafts (note that the exhaust side sprocket is marked A and the intake sprocket is marked E. Then, install the guide rail with all washers and lockwashers by rotating it into position in reverse of the removal procedure.

7. Tighten the camshaft drive sprockets, install the chain tensioner, and install the upper guide rail as described in the camshaft removal and installation procedure. Reverse the remaining removal steps to complete the procedure. Make sure to refill the cooling system with an appropriate antifreeze/water mix and to bleed the cooling system.

Timing Belt and Front Cover

REMOVAL & INSTALLATION

325, 325e, 325i, 325iS, 325iX and 528e Models

▶ See Figures 133, 134, 135 and 136

The 325 and 528e are equipped with a rubber drive and timing belt and the distributor guard plate is actually the upper timing belt cover.

A timing belt has the advantage of being a quieter method of driving the camshaft as compared to the timing chain. The disadvantage is that the timing belt must be changed on a regular basis, or risk having the belt break and causing severe engine damage. If the belt breaks, the valve timing will be off compared to the piston timing. This will cause the valves to hang open and contact the pistons on the next engine revolution. Bent valves, damaged pistons and major engine repair is the result of ignoring timing belt changes.

BMW recommends that the timing belt be changed every second Inspection II, or every 4 years on cars that have low mileage. Most of the rest of the industry has timing belt changing intervals ranging from 40,000–60,000 miles (65,000–95,000 km). It is better to change the belt at a lower mileage than at a higher number.

The timing belt must be replaced every time the belt tensioner is loosened. Do not reinstall a used belt. Reusing a timing belt, even one with low mileage, is not worth the chance of having a belt break and damaging the engine.

1. Disconnect the negative battery cable. Remove the distributor cap and rotor. Remove the inner distributor cover and seal.

2. Remove the 2 distributor guard plate attaching bolts and one nut. Remove the rubber guard and take out the guard plate (upper timing belt cover).

3. Rotate the crankshaft to set No. 1 piston at TDC of its compression stroke.

➡**At TDC of No. 1 piston compression stroke, the camshaft sprocket arrow should align directly with the mark on the cylinder head.**

4. Remove the radiator.

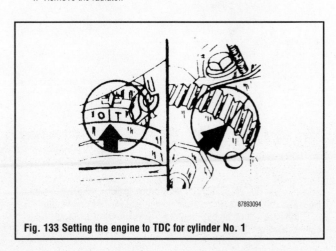

Fig. 133 Setting the engine to TDC for cylinder No. 1

87893094

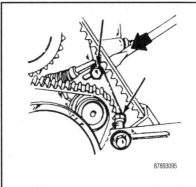

Fig. 134 Release the tension on the spring for the timing belt roller

Fig. 135 Check the alignment of the timing marks before installing the belt

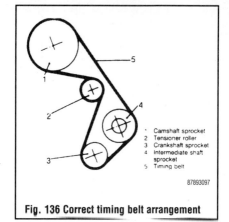

1. Camshaft sprocket
2. Tensioner roller
3. Crankshaft sprocket
4. Intermediate shaft sprocket
5. Timing belt

Fig. 136 Correct timing belt arrangement

✳✳ CAUTION

When draining coolant, keep in mind that cats and dogs are attracted to ethylene glycol antifreeze, and could drink any that is left in an uncovered container or in puddles on the ground. This will prove fatal in sufficient quantity. Always drain the coolant into a sealable container. Coolant should be reused unless it is contaminated or several years old.

5. Remove the lower splash guard and take off the alternator, power steering and air conditioning belts.

6. Remove the crankshaft pulley and vibration damper.

7. If equipped with a 2 piece hub, hold the crankshaft hub from rotating with the proper tool. Remove the crankshaft hub bolt.

8. Install the hub bolt into the crankshaft about 3 turns and use the proper gear puller, to remove the crankshaft hub.

9. Remove the bolt from the engine end of the alternator bracket. Loosen the alternator adjusting bolt and swing the bracket out of the way.

10. Lift out the TDC transmitter and set aside.

11. Remove the remaining bolt and lift off the lower timing belt protective cover.

12. Loosen the timing belt tensioner roller bolts and push the roller. Tighten the upper bolt with the roller pushed in. Remove the belt.

To install:

13. Check the alignment of the mark on the camshaft sprocket with the mark on the cylinder head. Check that the crankshaft sprocket mark aligns with the notch in the timing case.

14. Install the new timing belt by starting at the crankshaft sprocket and continuing in reverse direction of engine rotation.

15. Loosen the upper timing belt tensioner roller bolt. The spring tension should be enough to move the roller. Turn the engine 1 revolution in the direction of rotation using the crankshaft bolt to tension the belt. Check that the timing marks align exactly at the camshaft sprocket and the crankshaft sprocket. Tighten the roller bolts, top bolt first, then the bottom bolt.

16. Install the lower timing protective cover and tighten the bolt. Install the TDC sender.

17. Replace the alternator bracket. Install the crankshaft hub and tighten the nut to 281–309 ft. lbs. (390–430 Nm).

18. Install the vibration damper and pulley. Tighten the bolts to 17 ft. lbs. (23 Nm).

19. Install the upper cover and nut. Install the rubber guard. Check the condition of the O-ring and install the upper cover. Install the rotor and distributor cap.

20. Install the accessories and belts. Install the splash shield and fill the cooling system with coolant mixture. Bleed the cooling system.

21. Apply a sticker showing the date and mileage of the belt change on the engine.

528e Models

➡To perform this procedure, it is necessary to have a means to hold the camshaft stationary such as BMW special tool 11 3 090 and a pin to hold the injection pump gear stationary such as BMW 13 5 340. The engine must be cold.

1. Turn the engine to No. 1 cylinder at TDC, valves of No. 6 overlapping. Remove the timing belt cover and front pulley. Loosen the camshaft pulley bolt, and the bolt and nut mounting the tensioner.

2. Mark the direction the belt rotates and remove it.

3. Position the camshaft at TDC No. 6 valves overlapping and lock it there. Lock the injection pump in position with the pin 13 5 340.

To install:

4. Install the new belt with the timing marks on the sprockets and belt lined up. Turn the camshaft sprocket so as to begin tensioning the belt and seat it in the grooves. When the belt is in its normal, installed position, remove the pin holding the injection pump sprocket.

5. Insert a 2.5mm thick feeler gauge under the exhaust side of the jig holding the camshaft if the belt is new or had been used less than 10,000 miles (16,000 km).

6. Tighten the nut which rotates the tensioner. For belts with 10,000 miles (16,000 km) or less on them, tighten to 30–32 ft. lbs. (39–42 Nm). For belts with more mileage, tighten to 22–25 ft. lbs. (29–32 Nm).

7. Tighten the locknut for the tensioner and then tighten the camshaft sprocket bolt. Remove the camshaft-holding jig.

8. Rotate the engine in the forward direction one full turn and then recheck that timing marks are all lined up.

9. Adjust the static timing of the injection pump as described below. Reinstall the timing belt cover and front pulley in the reverse of removal.

Camshaft

♦ **See Figure 137**

REMOVAL & INSTALLATION

Except 325 Series, 528e, M3, M5 and M6 Models

1. Remove the oil line from the top of the cylinder head.

➡**Observe the location of the seals when removing the hollow oil line studs. Install new seals in the same position.**

2. Remove the cylinder head. Support the head in such a way that the valves can be opened during camshaft removal.

3. Adjust the valve clearance to the maximum clearance on all rocker arms.

4. Remove the fuel pump and pushrod on carbureted engines.

5. On 4-cylinder engines: Special tools are used to hold the rocker arms away from the camshaft lobes. On the 320i, use tool 11 1 040; on the 318i, use 11 0 040. Use these numbers to shop for tools from independent sources also.

➡**The proper tool or its equivalent, must be used on fuel injection engines to avoid distorting the valve heads.**

6. On the 320i and 318i, the clamping bolt for the special tool is off-center. The clamp must be mounted so the shorter end faces the exhaust side of the engine, or the valve heads may contact each other. On the 318i, install 2 dowel pins in the head.

7. On 6-cylinder engines: A special tool set (11 1 060 and 00 1 490) or its equivalent, is used to hold the rocker arms away from the camshaft lobes. When

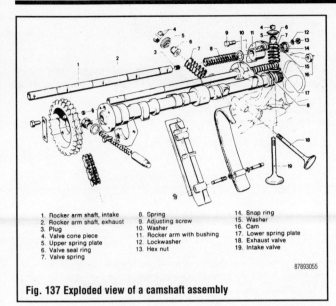

1. Rocker arm shaft, intake
2. Rocker arm shaft, exhaust
3. Plug
4. Valve cone piece
5. Upper spring plate
6. Valve seal ring
7. Valve spring
8. Spring
9. Adjusting screw
10. Washer
11. Rocker arm with bushing
12. Lockwasher
13. Hex nut
14. Snap ring
15. Washer
16. Cam
17. Lower spring plate
18. Exhaust valve
19. Intake valve

87893055

Fig. 137 Exploded view of a camshaft assembly

installing the tool, move the intake rocker arms of No. 2 and 4 cylinders forward approximately 0.25 inches (0.01mm) and tighten the intake side nuts to avoid contact between the valve heads. On 6-cylinder engines, turn the camshaft 15° clockwise to install the tool. On these engines, to avoid contact between the valve heads, first tighten the tool mounting nuts on the exhaust side to the stop and then tighten the intake side nuts slightly. Reverse this exactly during removal.

8. To remove the camshaft on 4-cylinder engines:

a. Turn the camshaft until the flange is aligned with the cylinder head boss. Remove the guide plate retaining bolts and move the plate downward and out of the slots on the rocker arm shafts.

b. Carefully remove the camshaft from the cylinder head.

c. Remove the 2 plugs behind the guide plate (at top), coat with Loctite® No. 270® or equivalent, and replace them.

9. To remove the camshaft on 6-cylinder engines:

a. Rotate the camshaft so that the 2 cutout areas of the camshaft flange are horizontal and remove the retaining plate bolts.

b. Carefully remove the camshaft from the cylinder head.

c. The flange and guide plate can be removed from the camshaft by removing the lockplate and nut from the camshaft end.

To install:

10. Install the camshaft and associated components in the reverse order of removal, but observe the following:

a. After installing the camshaft guide plate, the camshaft should turn easily. Measure and correct the camshaft end-play.

b. The camshaft flange must be properly aligned with the cylinder head before the sprocket is installed. Refer to the disassembly procedure.

c. Install the oil tube hollow stud washer seals properly, one above and one below the oil pipe. On 6-cylinder engines, the arrow on the oil line must face forward.

d. Install the cylinder head. Adjust the valves.

325, 325e, 325i, 325iS and 528e Models

➡The cylinder head and the rocker arm shafts must be removed before the camshaft can be removed.

1. Remove the cylinder head.

2. Mount the cylinder head on a stand. Secure the head to the stand with one head bolt.

3. Remove the camshaft sprocket bolt and remove the camshaft distributor adapter and sprocket. Reinstall the distributor adapter on the camshaft.

4. Adjust the valve clearance to the maximum allowable on all valves.

5. Remove the front and rear rocker shaft plugs and lift out the thrust plate.

6. Remove the clips from the rocker arms by lifting them off.

7. Remove the exhaust side rocker arm shaft:

a. Set the No. 6 cylinder rocker arm to the valve overlap position (both rocker arms parallel).

b. Push in on the rocker arm on the front cylinder and turn the camshaft in the direction of the intake rocker shaft, using a ½ inch breaker bar and a deep well socket to fit over the camshaft adapter. Rotate the camshaft until all of the rocker arms are relaxed.

8. Remove the rocker arm shaft.

9. Remove the intake side rocker arm shaft:

a. Turn the camshaft in the direction of the exhaust valves.

b. Use a deep well socket and ½ inch breaker bar on the camshaft adapter to turn the camshaft until all of the rocker arms are relaxed.

10. Pull out the rocker arm shaft.

11. Remove the camshaft thrust bearing cover. Check the radial oil seal and round cord seal and replace them if needed.

12. Pull out the camshaft.

To install:

13. Installation is the reverse of removal. Installation notes:

a. Use BMW tool 11 2 212 or equivalent over the end of the camshaft during installation of the thrust bearing cover; this will protect the oil seals and guide the cover on.

b. The rocker arm thrust plate must be fit into the grooves in the rocker shafts.

c. The straight side of the springclip must be installed in the groove of the rocker arm shafts.

d. The large oil bores in the rocker shafts must be installed down to the valve guides and the small oil bores must face inward toward the center of the head.

e. Adjust the valve clearance.

M3, M5 and M6 Models

➡Note that to perform this operation it is necessary to have an expensive jig, special tool No. 11 3 010 or equivalent. This is necessary to permit safe removal of the camshaft bearing caps and then safe release of the tension the valve springs put on the camshafts. The job also requires an adapter to keep the camshaft sprockets from turning while loosening and tightening their mounting bolts.

1. Remove the cylinder head cover. Remove the fan cowl and the fan.

2. Remove the mounting bolts and remove the distributor cap. Remove the mounting screws and remove the rotor. Unscrew the distributor adapter and the protective cover underneath. Inspect the O-ring that runs around the protective cover and replace it, if necessary.

3. Remove the 2 bolts and remove the protective cover from in front of the right side (intake) camshaft. Remove the bolts and remove the distributor housing from in front of the left (exhaust) side cam. Inspect the O-rings, and replace them if necessary.

4. Remove the mounting bolts from the cover at the rear end of the cylinder head and remove it. Replace the gasket. Note that on the M3, 2 of these bolts are longer. These fit into the 2 holes that are sleeved.

5. Remove the 2 nuts, located at the front of the head, which mount the upper timing chain guide rail. Then, remove the upper guide rail.

6. Turn the crankshaft to set the engine at No. 1 TDC. On the 6-cylinder engine, valves for No. 6 will be at overlap position: both valves just slightly open with timing marks at TDC. On the 4-cylinder engine, valves for No. 4 cylinder will be at overlap position: both valves just slightly open with timing marks, of course, at TDC.

7. Remove the cap for the timing chain tensioner, located on the right side of the front timing cover. Then, slide off the damper housing. Remove the seal, discard it, and supply a new one for reassembly.

✳✳ CAUTION

The next item to be removed is a plug which keeps the tensioner piston inside its hydraulic cylinder against considerable spring pressure. Use a socket wrench and keep pressure against the outer end of the plug, pushing inward, so that spring pressure can be released very gradually once the plug's threads are free of the block.

8. Remove the plug, and then release spring tension. Remove the spring and then the piston. Check the length of the spring. It must be 6.18–6.22 inches (158.5–159.5mm) in length; otherwise, replace it to maintain stable timing chain tension.

→The timing chain should remain engaged with the crankshaft sprocket while removing the camshafts. Otherwise, it will be necessary to do additional work to restore proper timing. Devise a way to keep the timing chain under slight tension by supporting it at the top while removing the camshaft sprockets in the next step.

9. Pry open the lockplates for the camshaft sprocket mounting bolts. Install an adapter to hold the sprockets still and remove the mounting bolts.

10. Using an adapter to keep the sprockets from turning and putting tension on the timing chain, loosen and remove the sprocket mounting bolts, keeping the chain supported.

11. Mount the special jig on the timing case (which mounts to the top of the head). Then, tighten the jig's shaft to the stop. This will hold both camshafts down against their lower bearings. On the 4-cylinder engine, mark the camshafts as to which side they are on; intake on the driver's side and exhaust on the passenger's side. Also, mark the camshafts as to which end faces forward.

12. Remove the mounting bolts and remove the camshaft bearing caps. It is possible to save time by keeping the caps in order, although they are marked for installation in the same positions.

13. Once all bearing caps are removed, slowly crank backwards on the jig shaft to gradually release the tension on the camshafts. Once all tension is released, remove the camshafts.

14. Carefully remove the camshafts in such a way as to avoid nicking any bearing surfaces or cams.
   To install:

15. Oil all bearing and cam surfaces with clean engine oil. Carefully install the camshafts (marked E for intake and A for exhaust) so as to avoid nicking any wear surfaces. The camshafts should be turned so that the groove between the front cam and sprocket mounting flange faces straight up. Install the special jig and tighten down on the shaft to seat the camshafts.

16. Install all bearing caps in order (or as marked). Tighten the attaching bolts to 15–17 ft. lbs. (19–22 Nm). Then, release the tension provided by the jig by turning the bolt and remove the jig.

17. Install the intake sprocket (marked E), install the lockplate, and install the mounting bolts. Use the adapter to keep the sprocket from turning, and tighten the bolts to 6–7 ft. lbs. (8–9 Nm). Do the same for the exhaust side sprocket. Make sure the timing chain stays in time.

18. Now, slide the timing chain tensioner piston into the opening in the cylinder in the block. Install the spring with the conically wound end facing the plug (or outward). Install the plug into the end of the sprocket and then install it over the spring and use the socket wrench to depress the spring until the plug's threads engage with those in the block. Start the threads in carefully and then tighten the plug to 27–31 ft. lbs. (35–40 Nm). Install a new seal, connector, damper housing, and the outside cap with a new cap seal. Tighten the outside cap to 16–20 ft. lbs. (21–26 Nm) on the engine used in the M5 and M6 and 29 ft. lbs. (38 Nm) on the M3 engine.

19. Crank the engine forward just one turn in normal direction of rotation. Now, one camshaft groove on each side should face toward the center of the head and one on each side should face the case boss on the front bearing cap. Lock the sprocket mounting bolts with the tabs on the lockplates.

20. Reverse the remaining removal procedures to complete the installation. Before final tightening of the mounting nuts for the guide rail for the top of the timing chain, go back and forth, measuring the clearance between the sprockets and the center of the guide rail to center it. Then, tighten the mounting nuts.

CHECKING CAMSHAFT

Camshaft End-Play

→On engines with an aluminum or nylon camshaft sprocket, prying against the sprocket, with the valve train load on the camshaft, can break or damage the sprocket. Therefore, the rocker arm adjusting nuts must be backed off, or the rocker arm and shaft assembly must be loosened sufficiently to free the camshaft. After checking the camshaft end-play, check the valve clearance and adjust if required. Refer to the procedure in Section 2.

1. Push the camshaft toward the rear of the engine. Install a dial indicator so that the indicator point is on the camshaft sprocket attaching screw.

2. Zero the dial indicator. Position a prybar between the camshaft gear and the engine. Pull the camshaft forward and release it. Compare the dial indicator reading with the specifications.

3. If the end-play is excessive, check the spacer for correct installation before it is removed. If the spacer is correctly installed, replace the thrust plate.

4. Remove the dial indicator.

Intermediate Shaft

REMOVAL & INSTALLATION

325, 325e, 325i, 325iS and 528e Models

1. Remove the front cover.
2. Remove the intermediate shaft sprocket.
3. Loosen and remove the 2 retaining screws and then remove the intermediate shaft guide plate.
4. Carefully slide the intermediate shaft out of the block. Turn the crankshaft if necessary to remove it. Inspect the gear on the intermediate shaft, replacing it if necessary.
5. Installation is in the reverse order of removal.

Pistons and Connecting Rods

♦ See Figure 138

GENERAL INFORMATION

Keep all of the following points in mind when rebuilding a BMW engine:
• The pistons and connecting rods may be removed from the engine after the cylinder head, oil pan and oil pump are removed. It may be necessary to first remove a ridge worn into the cylinder above the top ring. See the engine rebuilding section. The connecting rods and caps are marked for each cylinder with No. 1 cylinder at the sprocket end of the engine. Codes pairing the connecting rods with the matching cap are located on the exhaust side of the engine. However, it is a good idea to mark the exact relationship between each rod and the crankshaft to ensure replacement in the exact same position, in case the bearings can be re-used.
• To disassemble rods and pistons, remove the circlip and press out the piston pin. Note that pistons and piston pins come as a matched set. Do not mix them up.
• A piston pin must always slide through the connecting rod under light pressure.
• If replacing pistons, make sure all are of the same make and weight class written on the crown.
• Piston installed clearance must meet specifications. On the 318i, check installed clearance at a point measured up from the lower skirt edge, depending on the piston manufacturer: Mahle-14mm; KS-31mm; Alcan-15.5mm.
• On the engines used in 325e and 528e models, check piston diameter according to total height and manufacturer. On pistons 68.7mm high manufactured by Mahle, check the diameter at a point 8mm above the low point on the skirt; on those of this height manufactured by KS, check diameter 14mm above

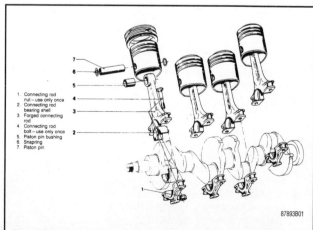

1. Connecting rod nut – use only once
2. Connecting rod bearing shell
3. Forged connecting rod
4. Connecting rod bolt – use only once
5. Piston pin bushing
6. Snapring
7. Piston pin

87893B01

Fig. 138 Exploded view of piston and connecting rod assembly

the low point of the skirt. If the total height is 77.7mm, check the diameter of both Mahle and KS pistons 23mm above the low point of the skirt. On the engines used in 325i, check the diameter 9mm above the low point of the skirt.

• On the 3.3 liter engine, measure Mahle pistons 26mm up from the lower skirt edge, and KS pistons 34mm up from the skirt edge. On the 3.5 liter engine, measure 14mm up from the skirt edge.

• On the 3.5 liter, engine, measure the Mahle pistons at a point 14mm up from the bottom of the skirt.

• On the engines used in the M3, M5, and M6, measure the piston at a point 6mm below the deepest part of the skirt.

• Lubricate the piston and rings with engine oil prior to installation. Offset ring gaps 120° apart. Install circlips facing downward.

• The side of rings marked TOP must face upward. 2.7, 2.5, 3.3 and 3.5 liter engines and the M3 engine use a plain compression ring at top, tapered or beveled second compression ring, and an oil control ring at the bottom. The 524td uses a keystone ring at the top, a taper face lower compression ring, and a beveled oil control ring with a rubber-lined expander at the bottom.

REMOVAL

▶ **See Figures 139 thru 144**

While the pistons and connecting rods can be removed from the engine with the engine installed in the vehicle most of the time, it is better to remove the engine to do this procedure. With the engine removed, it is easier to inspect the engine and to manipulate the tool and parts.

Before removing the pistons and connecting rods, mark the pistons, rod bearing caps and the rods with the cylinder number and orientation. This will ensure replacement of the pistons and bearing into the correct positions.

Before removing the pistons, the top of the cylinder bore must be examined for a ridge. A ridge at the top of the bore is the result of normal cylinder wear; caused by the piston rings only traveling so far up the bore in the cause of the piston stroke.

BMW uses a very high quality material to cast the cylinder blocks and cylinder ridges tend to be slight. If the ridge can be felt by hand, it must be removed before the pistons are removed. This is to prevent the rings from breaking while the piston is pushed past the ridge.

A ridge reamer is necessary for this operation. Place the piston at the bottom of its stroke, and cover it with a rag. Cut the ridge away with the ridge reamer, using extreme care to avoid cutting too deeply. Remove the rag, and remove the cuttings that remain on the piston with a magnet and a rag soaked in clean oil. Make sure the piston top and cylinder bore are absolutely clean before moving the piston.

1. Remove the cylinder head.
2. Remove the oil pan.
3. Remove the oil pump or oil pump pickup.
4. Matchmark the connecting rod cap to the connecting rod with a scribe; each cap must be reinstalled on its proper rod in the proper direction. Remove the connecting rod bearing cap and the rod bearing. It may be necessary to rock the cap back and forth to free it. Number the top of each piston with silver paint or a felt-tip pen for later assembly.
5. Cut lengths of ⅜ inch diameter rubber hose to use as rod bolt guides. Install the hose over the threads of the rod bolts, to prevent the bolt threads from damaging the crankshaft journals and cylinder walls when the piston is removed.
6. Squirt some clean engine oil onto the cylinder wall from above until the wall is coated. Carefully push the piston and rod assembly up and out of the cylinder by tapping on the bottom of the connecting rod with a wooden hammer handle.
7. Place the rod bearing and cap back on the connecting rod, and install the nuts temporarily. Using a number stamp or punch, stamp the cylinder number on the side of the connecting rod and cap this will help keep the proper piston and rod assembly on the proper cylinder. Do not stamp in the web area of the rod.

➡ **On all BMW engines, the cylinders are numbered 1–4 or 1–6 from front to back.**

8. Remove the remaining pistons in a similar manner.
9. When ready for reassembly, please not the following:
   a. Connecting rods/caps must be reinstalled in the same cylinder and are so marked. Make sure markings on rod and cap are on the same side when reassembling.

b. The piston pins are matched to the pistons and are not interchangeable.

c. The arrow on top of the piston must face forward (toward the timing chain). Pistons are also marked as to manufacturer and weight class. All pistons must be of the same manufacturer and weight class.

d. Offset each ring gap 120 degrees from each other. Do not align any of the gaps with the piston pin bore. This reduces blowby of combustion gases.

TCCS3916

Fig. 139 Remove the ridge from the cylinder bore using a ridge cutter

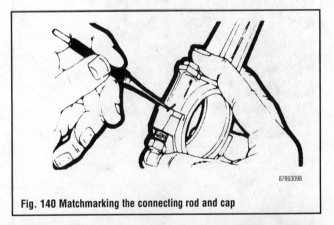

87893098

Fig. 140 Matchmarking the connecting rod and cap

87893P75

Fig. 141 With the engine installed in the vehicle, use a breaker bar and socket to loosen the bearing cap.

Fig. 142 Bearing cap removed

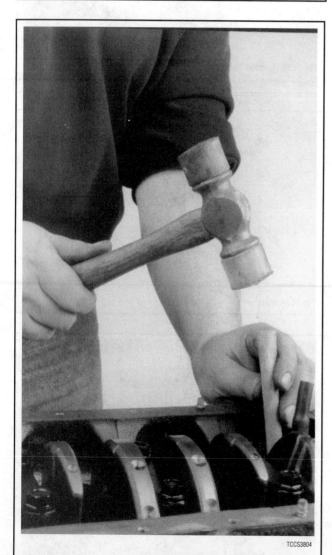

Fig. 143 With the engine inverted on a workstand, the pistons can be more easily removed by tapping them out with a piece of wood and a hammer

Fig. 144 If the pistons you are removing have studs attached to the connecting rods, place rubber hoses over the ends prior to removal

CLEANING & INSPECTION

▶ **See Figures 145, 146 and 147**

Before any kind of inspection is done to the piston, cylinder or piston pin, it is imperative that they be clean. All traces of varnish, carbon or build-up be removed. Measurements will be inaccurate and signs of wear hidden on a dirty part.

Clean the piston with solvents and chip off any carbon build-up with a hard-wood chisel. Do not hot tank aluminum pistons. Clean the cylinder bore with solvent, then wipe down with clean engine oil.

Inspect the piston for signs of scoring, scuffing, cracks, pitting or burning. Check the piston for mechanical damage such as valve strikes or denting due to ingested objects. Measure the piston diameter with a micrometer. Measure at points 90 degrees to the piston pin bore. Measure down from the edge of the piston skirt the proper distance from the piston skirt edge.

Measure the inside diameter of the cylinder at 3 points; top, middle and bottom. Measure at points which are contacted by the piston rings. If the cylinder walls are found to be tapered, scored or otherwise damaged, the cylinder will need to be honed or bored oversized.

Subtract the diameter of the piston from the diameter of the cylinder to find the piston clearance. Check that the clearance does not exceed the maximum permitted. If the clearance is too great, the cylinders will need to be bored over sized for the next available sized piston

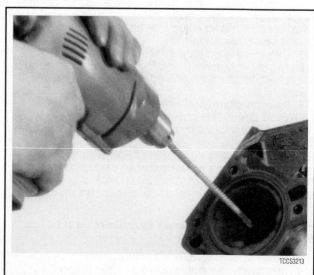

Fig. 145 Use a flexible honer to remove any cylinder glazing

Fig. 146 Use a telescopic gauge to measure the cylinder bore

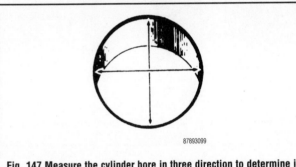

Fig. 147 Measure the cylinder bore in three direction to determine if it is out of round

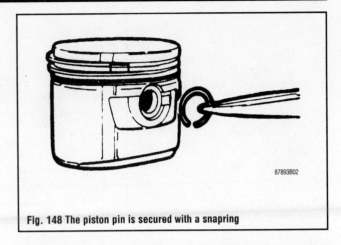

Fig. 148 The piston pin is secured with a snapring

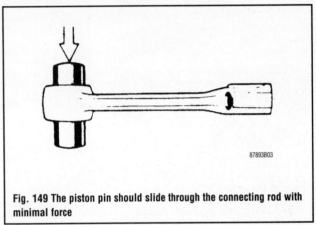

Fig. 149 The piston pin should slide through the connecting rod with minimal force

BORING & HONING

There are 2 basic machining operations that are done to a cylinder wall, boring and honing. Both procedures remove metal from the cylinder walls. The major difference is that boring removes a larger amount of metal than honing does. Boring is used to enlarge the cylinder so a larger diameter piston can be used. Honing is a finer process that gives the cylinder wall the correct machined finish for proper operation and sealing of the piston rings.

If the cylinders are out of round or tapered beyond allowable limits, the cylinders will need to be bored to the next standard oversize. Boring is done by a qualified machine shop. Provide the machine shop with the new oversized pistons. The machine shop will match the bore of the cylinder to diameter of the new piston, taking into account the piston clearance required. The machine shop will return the block and piston marked as to which piston goes to which cylinder.

Honing should be done by a machine shop to guarantee the proper cylinder wall finish. Honing can be accomplished with a hand held honing tool available from most automotive shops, but a machine shop can provide the best result. Honing is done to prepare the cylinder wall with the proper machined finish. The finish is a crosshatch pattern that catches and holds oil for the piston rings to ride on. Honing can be used without boring the cylinder when only new rings are being installed, or after the cylinder has been bored for a new piston and the proper finish is required.

PISTON PIN REPLACEMENT

▶ See Figures 148 and 149

The piston pins are matched to the pistons and must not be interchanged. The piston pins run in bushings pressed into the small end of the connecting rod. The pins are retained by snaprings.

Remove the snaprings with a snapring removal tool. The piston pin should slide out of the bore with some finger pressure. If the pin resists being pushed out, check that varnish or carbon hasn't collected at the end of the pin bore. Clean the bore and the pin should slide freely out.

Clean the pin and connecting rod bushing. Lightly lubricate the pin and slide it into the connecting rod. The pin should slide in with only hand pressure. There should be no discernible play with the pin installed in the rod. Check the pin bushing for scoring or damage. A sign of worn bushing is a knocking sound during engine acceleration.

Have new bushing pressed into the rod if the old bushing are found to be worn or damaged. The new bushing will be drilled for the oil lubrication hole at the top of the rod.

The piston pin is installed in the piston and connecting rod, making sure the orientation of the rod and piston is correct. Check the marks previously made on the rod during removal and the arrow on the piston top. The arrow should face the timing chain or belt. Replace the snapring if the old ring was damaged, though it is a good idea to always use new snaprings. Place the gap in the snapring opposite the groove cut into the piston used for snapring removal.

PISTON RING REPLACEMENT

▶ See Figures 150 thru 155

Piston rings provide the seal between the combustion gases and the crankcase. The rings do a tremendous job of separating the extreme pressure of the combustion chamber and the semi-vacuum of the crankcase. If the piston rings can not do the job properly, there will be leakage of oil into the combustion chamber and the resulting blue oil smoke from the tailpipe. There will be a reduction in compression resulting in a loss of performance.

The piston rings are located in grooves, called lands, machined into the pistons. As the piston moves up and down, the rings slowly rotate in the lands. This allows the rings to seal against the cylinder wall and the piston. If the ring lands get filled with carbon or varnish, the rings will stick and not be allowed to move. This will reduce the ability of the rings to seal. If the rings stick, the rings need to be removed, the lands cleaned and the rings replaced.

Fig. 150 Use a ring expander to remove the piston rings

Fig. 151 Clean the piston grooves with a ring groove cleaner

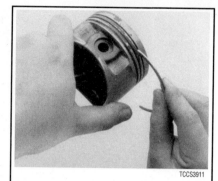

Fig. 152 Also part of an old piston ring can be used to clean the piston grooves

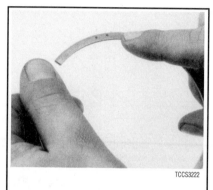

Fig. 153 Most new rings are marked as to which side faces upward

Fig. 154 Check the ring-to-ring groove (ring side) clearance

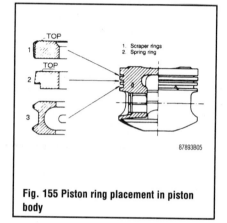

Fig. 155 Piston ring placement in piston body

The piston rings should be removed with a ring remover tool. The tool will grasp the ends of the ring at the gap and spread the ring enough to remove it from the piston. Do not use screwdrivers, pliers or any other tool not designed to do the job. The piston rings can break into sharp edged pieces of stretched too far.

With the piston rings removed, inspect the lands for carbon and varnish buildup. Clean the lands with solvent if varnish is found. Clean the lands with a mechanical cleaning tool if carbon is found. A piece of old ring can be used to remove light deposits. Check the bottom of the lands for wear. The pistons will need to be replaced if the lands are damaged or worn.

Piston ring end gap should be checked while the rings are removed from the pistons. Incorrect end gap indicates that the wrong size rings are being used; ring breakage could occur. Compress the piston rings to be used in a cylinder, one at a time, into that cylinder. Squirt clean oil into the cylinder, so that the rings and the top half of cylinder wall are coated. Using an inverted piston, press the rings approximately 1 inch below the deck of the block. Measure the ring end gap with a feeler gauge, and compare to the specifications chart in this section. Carefully pull the ring out of the cylinder and file the ends squarely with a fine file to obtain the proper clearance.

Install the rings on the piston, lowest ring first, using a piston ring expander. There is a high risk of breaking or distorting the rings, or scratching the piston, if the rings are installed by hand or other means. When installing new rings, refer to the installation diagram furnished with new parts.

Check the pistons to see that the ring grooves and oil return holes have been properly cleaned. Slide a piston ring into its groove, and check the side clearance with a feeler gauge. Make sure that you insert the gauge between the ring and its lower land (lower edge of the groove), because any wear that occurs, forms a step at the inner portion of the lower land. If the piston grooves have worn to the extent that relatively high steps exist on the lower land, the piston should be replaced, because these will interfere with the operation of the new rings and ring clearances will be excessive. Piston rings are not furnished in oversize widths to compensate for ring groove wear.

ROD BEARING REPLACEMENT

♦ See Figures 156 and 157

Connecting rod bearings for the engines covered in this guide consist of 2 halves or shells which are interchangeable in the rod and cap. When the shells are placed in position, the ends extend slightly beyond the rod and cap surfaces so that when the rod bolts are tightened, the shells will be clamped tightly in place to insure positive seating and to prevent turning. A tang holds the shells in place. Place one end of the bearing into the journal and press the other end down. Squeeze the bearing shell a bit while pressing down. The bearing shell will snap into place.

➡The ends of the bearing shells must never be filed flush with the mating surface of the rod and cap.

If a rod bearing becomes noisy or is worn so that its clearance on the crank journal is sloppy, a new bearing of the correct size must be selected and installed since there is no provision for adjustment.

✳✳ WARNING

Under no circumstances should the rod end or cap be filed to adjust the bearing clearance, nor should shims of any kind be used.

Inspect the rod bearings while the rod assemblies are out to the engine. If the shells are scored or show flaking, they should be replaced. If they are in good shape check for proper clearance on the crank journal. Any scoring or ridges on the crank journal means the crankshaft must be replaced.

The crankshaft is surface hardened at the factory and it must not be reground without the proper surface treatment being done to the reground crankshaft. It is recommended to use a factory reground or new crankshaft if the crankshaft must be replaced. Use the proper sized undersized bearings if a reground crankshaft is used.

Connecting rod-to-crankshaft bearing clearance is checked using Plastigage® having a range of 0.0005–0.0030 inches.

1. Remove the rod cap with the bearing shell. Completely clean the bearing shell and crank journal, and blow any oil from the oil hole in the crankshaft; Plastigage® is soluble in oil.

2. Place a piece of Plastigage® lengthwise along the bottom center of the lower bearing shell, then install the cap with shell and tighten to specification. DO NOT turn the crankshaft with the Plastigage® in the bearing.

3. Remove the bearing cap with the shell. The flattened Plastigage will be found sticking to either the bearing shell or crank journal. Do not remove it yet.

4. Use the scale printed on the Plastigage® envelope to measure the flattened material at its widest point. The number within the scale which most closely corresponds to the width of the Plastigage® indicates bearing clearance in thousandths of a inch.

5. Check the specifications chart in this section for the desired clearance.

➡**With the proper bearing clearance and the nuts tightened, It should be possible to move the connecting rod back and forth freely on the crank journal slightly. If the rod cannot be moved, either the rod bearing is too far undersize or the rod is misaligned.**

INSTALLATION

◆ **See Figures 158, 159 and 160**

Before installing the pistons and rods, but after checking bearing clearances, it is recommended to replace the connecting rod bolts. BMW uses forged steel rods which are very strong and will last an extremely long time. The rod bolts should be replaced after they have been tightened and released once. It is acceptable to used the old bolts during the bearing clearance checking procedure, but they should be replaced before the final assembly and installation is completed. The bolts are pressed into the rods. A machine shop can do this for a nominal fee. The bolts have to pressed in while supporting the rod to prevent any damage to either the rod or the bolt.

Install the connecting rod to the piston, making sure piston installation notches and any marks on the rod are in proper relation to one another. Lubricate the wrist pin with clean engine oil, and install the pin into the rod and piston assembly. Install snaprings and rotate them in their grooves to make sure they are seated. Position the snaprings with the ends opposite of the removal groove. To install the piston and connecting rod assembly:

1. Make sure that the connecting rod big-ends bearings (including end cap) are of the correct size and properly installed.

2. Fit rubber hoses over the connecting rod bolts to protect the crankshaft journals, as in the Piston Removal procedure. Coat the rod bearings with clean oil.

3. Using the proper ring compressor, insert the piston assembly into the cylinder so that the word TOP faces the front of the engine (this assumes that the dimple(s) or other markings on the connecting rods are in the correct relationship.

4. From beneath the engine, coat each crank journal with clean oil. Pull the connecting rod, with the bearing shell in place, into position against the crank journal.

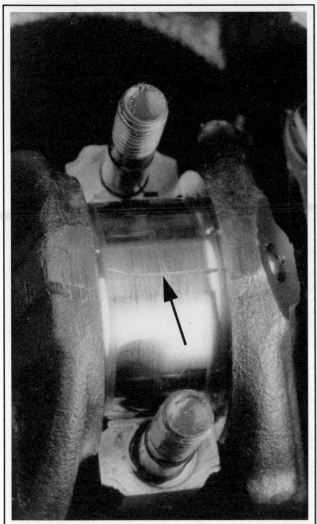

TCCS3243

Fig. 156 Place a strip of gauging material to the bearing journal, then install and tighten down

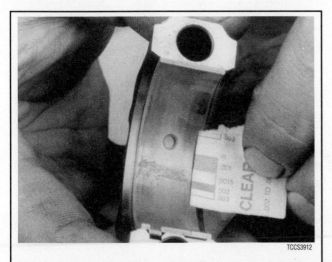

TCCS3912

Fig. 157 After the bearing cap has been removed, use the gauge supplied with the gauging material to check the bearing clearance

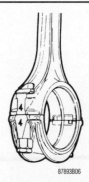

87893B06

Fig. 158 Check to make sure the marks on the connecting rod and rod cap match

5. Remove the rubber hoses. Install the bearing cap and cap nuts and tighten to the proper specifications.

6. If more than one rod and piston assembly is being installed, the connecting rod cap attaching nuts should only be tightened enough to keep each rod in position until all have been installed. This will ease the installation of the remaining piston assemblies as the crankshaft is rotated.

7. Replace the oil pump if removed and the oil pan.

8. Install the cylinder head.

Rear Main Seal

REMOVAL & INSTALLATION

▶ See Figure 161

The rear main bearing oil seal can be replaced after the transmission, and clutch/flywheel or the converter/flywheel has been removed from the engine.

Removal and installation, after the seal is exposed, is as follows.

1. Drain the engine oil and loosen the oil pan bolts. Carefully use a knife to separate the oil pan gasket from the lower surface of the end cover housing.

☀ CAUTION

The EPA warns that prolonged contact with used engine oil may cause a number of skin disorders, including cancer! You should make every effort to minimize your exposure to used engine oil. Protective gloves should be worn when changing the oil. Wash your hands and any other exposed skin areas as soon as possible after exposure to used engine oil. Soap and water, or waterless hand cleaner should be used.

2. Remove the 2 rear oil pan bolts.

3. Remove the bolts around the outside of the cover housing and remove the end cover housing from the engine block. Remove the gasket from the block surface.

4. Remove the seal from the housing. Coat the sealing lips of the new seal with oil. Install a new seal into the end cover housing with a special seal installer BMW Tool No. 11 1 260 backed up by a mandrel, Tool No. 00 5 500 or equivalent. Press the seal in until it is about 0.039–0.079 inches (1.00–2.00mm) deeper than the standard seal, which was installed flush.

5. While the cover is off, check the plug in the rear end of the main oil gallery. If the plug shows signs of leakage, replace it with another, coating it with Loctite® 270® or equivalent to keep it in place.

6. Coat the mating surface between the oil pan and end cover with sealer. Using a new gasket, install the end cover on the engine block and bolt it into place. Be careful to protect the lips of the seal from sharp edges while placing it over the end of the crankshaft. Tighten the grade M6 bolts to 6–7 ft. lbs. (8–0 Nm) and the grade M8 bolts to 15–17 ft. lbs. (20–24 Nm).

7. Reverse the removal procedure to complete the installation. If the oil pan gasket has been damaged, replace it.

Crankshaft and Main Bearings

REMOVAL

1. Drain the engine oil and remove the engine from the car. Mount the engine on a workstand in a suitable working area. Invert the engine, so the oil pan is facing up.

☀ CAUTION

The EPA warns that prolonged contact with used engine oil may cause a number of skin disorders, including cancer! You should make every effort to minimize your exposure to used engine oil. Protective gloves should be worn when changing the oil. Wash your hands and any other exposed skin areas as soon as possible after exposure to used engine oil. Soap and water, or waterless hand cleaner should be used.

2. Remove the engine front (timing) cover.

3. Remove the timing chain/belt and gears.

4. Remove the oil pan.

5. Remove the oil pump.

6. Stamp the cylinder number on the machined surfaces of the bolt bosses of the connecting rods and caps for identification when reinstalling. If the pistons are to be removed eventually from the connecting rod, mark the cylinder number on the pistons with silver paint or felt-tip pen for proper cylinder identification and cap-to-rod location.

7. Remove the connecting rod caps. Install lengths of rubber hose on each of the connecting rod bolts, to protect the crank journals when the crank is removed.

8. Mark the main bearings caps with a number punch or punch so that they can be reinstalled in their original positions.

9. Remove all main bearing caps.

10. Carefully lift the crankshaft out of the engine block.

MAIN BEARING INSPECTION

Like connecting rod big-end bearings, the crankshaft main bearings are shell-type inserts that do not utilize shims and cannot be adjusted. The bearings are available in various standard sizes; if main bearing clearance is found to be too sloppy, a new bearing (both upper and lower halves) is required.

Checking Clearance

▶ See Figures 162, 163 and 164

➡ Crankshaft bearing caps and bearing shells should NEVER be filed flush with the cap-to-block mating surface to adjust for wear in the old bearings. Always install new bearings.

1. Remove the bearing cap. Wipe all oil from the crank journal and bearing cap.

Fig. 159 Most pistons are marked on the top to indicate their relative position

Fig. 160 Use a ring compressor and a piece of wood to carefully install the piston into the cylinder bore

Fig. 161 Remove the retaining bolts on the rear main seal—3 Series model

Fig. 162 A dial indicator can be used to check crankshaft end-play

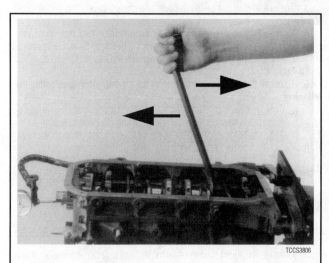

Fig. 163 Using a prytool and great care, pry back and forth to for end-play

2.　Place a strip of Plastigage® the full width of the bearing, (parallel to the crankshaft), on the journal.

➡**Do not rotate the crankshaft while the gaging material is between the bearing and the journal.**

3.　Install the bearing cap and evenly tighten the cap bolts to specification.

4.　Remove the bearing cap. The flattened Plastigage® will be sticking to either the bearing shell or the crank journal.

5.　Use the graduated scale on the Plastigage® envelope to measure the material at its widest point.

➡**If the flattened Plastigage® tapers towards the middle or ends, there is a difference in clearance indicating the bearing or journal has a taper, low spot or other irregularity. If this is indicated, measure the crank journal with a micrometer.**

6.　If bearing clearance is within specifications, the bearing insert is in good shape. Replace the insert if the clearance is not within specifications or show signs of damage. Always replace both upper and lower inserts as a unit.

7.　Standard, 0.010 inch or 0.020 inch (0.025mm or 0.050mm) undersize bearings should produce the proper clearance. If these sizes still produce a sloppy fit, the crankshaft must be replaced. Recheck all clearances after installing new bearings.

Fig. 164 Crankshaft run-out is measured using a dial gauge

8.　Replace the rest of the bearings in the same manner. After all bearings have been checked, rotate the crankshaft to make sure there is no excessive drag.

INSTALLATION

If the crankshaft is being replaced with factory reground unit, it will be supplied with matching bearings. Check the bearing clearance if the original crankshaft is being reused. It is a good idea to check the bearing clearances on both new and used crankshafts.

heck the crankshaft for scoring or burn marks. The crankshaft is surface hardened at the factory and can not be reground without the surface treatment being completed.

1.　Remove and inspect the crankshaft.

2.　Remove the main bearings from the bearing saddles in the cylinder block and main bearing caps.

3.　Coat the bearing surfaces of the new, correct size main bearings with clean engine oil and install them in the bearing saddles in the block and in the main bearing caps

4.　Inspect the oil spray jets in the bearing webs on equipped engines. Install the crankshaft and bearing caps.

5.　Clean and lubricate the bolts with oil. Tighten the bolts on the 2.5L , 2.7L, 2.8L, 3.0L and 3.2L engines to 42–46 ft. lbs. (58–63 Nm). On the 1.8L 16 valve, M3 and M5 engines, tighten the bolts to 14–18 ft. lbs. (20–25 Nm), then turn the bolts an additional 47–53 degrees.

6.　Check the end-play of the crankshaft by prying in one direction, then to the other side. Insert a feeler gauge between the crankshaft and a main bearing cap to measure the play. A dial indicator can also be used to measure the end-play. If the end-play is not correct, loosen the thrust bearing, tap the crankshaft in both directions and retighten. Recheck the end-play.

7.　Install a new pilot shaft bearing in the end of the crankshaft.

Flywheel/Flexplate and Ring Gear

REMOVAL & INSTALLATION

1. Remove the transmission. Remove the clutch cover and plate on manual transmission equipped vehicles.
2. Install a flywheel lock to hold the flywheel stationary.
3. Remove the bolts and pull the flywheel off.

EXHAUST SYSTEM

Safety Precautions

Exhaust system work can be the most dangerous type of work you can do on your car. Always observe the following precautions:

• Support the car securely. Not only will you often be working directly under it, but you'll frequently be using a lot of force, (heavy hammer blows, to dislodge rusted parts.) This can cause a car that's improperly supported to shift and possibly fall.

• Wear goggles. Exhaust system parts are always rusty. Metal chips can be dislodged, even when you're only turning rusted bolts. Attempting to pry pipes apart with a chisel makes the chips fly even more frequently.

• If you're using a cutting torch, keep it a great distance from the fuel tank or lines. Feel the temperature of the fuel pipes on the tank frequently. Even slight heat can expand and/or vaporize fuel, resulting in accumulated vapor, or even a liquid leak, near your torch.

• Watch where your hammer blows fall and make sure you hit squarely. You could easily tap a brake or fuel line when you hit an exhaust system part with a glancing blow. Inspect all lines and hoses in the area where you've been working.

✳✳ CAUTION

Be very careful when working on or near the catalytic converter! External temperatures can reach 1500°F (816°C) and more, causing severe burns. Removal or installation should be performed only on a cold exhaust system.

Special Tools

A number of special exhaust system tools can be rented from auto supply houses or local stores that rent special equipment. A common one is a tail pipe expander, designed to enable you to join pipes of identical diameter.

It may also be quite helpful to use solvents designed to loosen rusted bolts or flanges. Soaking rusted parts the night before you do the job can speed the work of freeing rusted parts considerably. Remember that these solvents are often flammable. Apply only to parts after they are cool!

To install:
4. Clean the mounting area of the crankshaft. Check the condition of the rear main seal and replace if necessary. Clean out the bolt holes.
5. Install the flywheel. Apply Loctite 270® or equivalent sealer to the new bolts.

➡**Use only new bolts when installing the flywheel. The bolts are not designed to be used more than once.**

6. Tighten the bolts to 82–94 ft. lbs. (113–130 Nm).
7. Replace the clutch, if equipped and transmission.

System Components

REMOVAL & INSTALLATION

1970–79 Models

1. Raise and safely support the vehicle on jackstands. Remove the 3 nuts retaining the header pipe to the exhaust manifold.
2. Loosen the exhaust holder at the rear of the header pipe, then remove the nuts attaching the rear muffler to the intermediate pipe.
3. The rear muffler can be left in place or removed, depending on the repair to be made.
4. Remove the bolt at the exhaust holder, while holding the intermediate and header pipes with your hand. Remove them from the vehicle. On models equipped with a front muffler (resonator), it will come out with the intermediate pipe.
   To install:
5. To install the exhaust system, reverse the removal procedures noting the following:
   a. Coat the header pipe bolts with Molykote® or equivalent and tighten.
   b. Align the system correctly before tightening the exhaust holder.
   c. Align the tailpipe at the back of the vehicle before tightening the rear muffler-to-intermediate pipe bolts.

1980–88 Models

1. Raise and safely support the vehicle on jackstands.
2. Remove the oxygen sensor from the exhaust system.
3. Unfasten the catalytic converter at the exhaust manifold.
4. Loosen the exhaust holder. Unbolt the catalytic converter shield and disconnect the catalytic converter at the flange.
5. Unfasten the shield from the final muffler and unfasten the final muffler at the flange.
6. Disconnect the final muffler and remove it from its hangers.
   To install:
7. To install the exhaust system, reverse the removal procedures noting the following:
   a. Coat the catalytic converter-to-exhaust manifold bolts with Molykote® or equivalent and tighten.
   b. Align the system correctly before tightening the exhaust holder.
   c. Align the tailpipe at the back of the vehicle before tightening the rear muffler-to-intermediate pipe bolts.

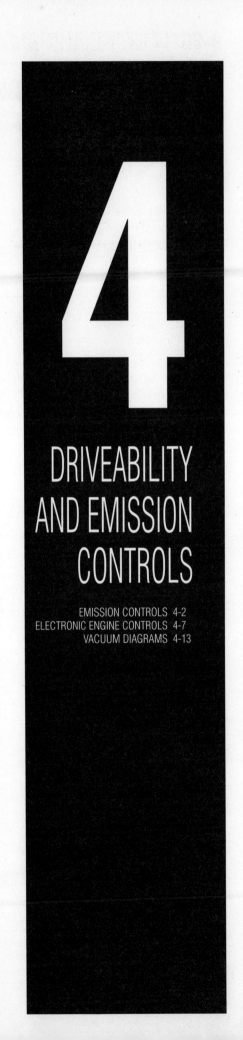

4

DRIVEABILITY AND EMISSION CONTROLS

EMISSION CONTROLS

Crankcase Ventilation System

OPERATION

The BMW crankcase emission control system is considered a sealed system. Rather than purging the crankcase of blow-by vapors with fresh air is done conventionally, the blow-by emissions are routed directly to the air cleaner or air collector with crankcase pressure behind them. Since the purpose of the PCV valve in conventional systems is to regulate the volume of purging air even with varying intake vacuum, this valve and the maintenance associated with it are eliminated.

TESTING

The Crankcase Emission Control System is virtually maintenance-free. The connecting tube from the top engine cover to the air cleaner or air collector should be inspected during the routine maintenance services and replaced if cracked, distorted or plugged.

With the engine operating and the connecting tube disconnected, a vacuum should be noted at the air cleaner or air collector side of the hose. If vacuum is not present, an air leak or plugged air induction system may be the cause.

Evaporative Emissions Control System

OPERATION

▶ **See Figure 1**

This system stores gasoline vapors which collect above liquid fuel in the fuel tank and, on carbureted engines, in the float bowl. The system stores the vapors while the engine is off, and then allows the vacuum created in the intake manifold to draw them off and burn them when the engine is started.

Fuel tank vapors are collected by a storage tank located in the trunk. Vapor which cannot be held there, as well as float bowl vapors, are stored in a charcoal canister located in the front of the engine compartment. The charcoal has the effect of keeping the vapors in liquid form so they can be held in a minimal space. As in the case of the crankcase ventilation system, no fresh air is used in purging, eliminating the need to change an air filter in the canister.

MAINTENANCE

Inspect the hoses and hose clamps occasionally or if raw fuel odor is noticed. Tighten clamps as necessary or replace hoses which have cracked.

Under certain operating conditions, contamination or excessive vapor collection may cause the vapor canister to become saturated with liquid fuel. Under these conditions, the unit should be replaced, even though replacement on a routine basis is not necessary.

Automatic Air Intake Preheating Valve

CHECKING

▶ **See Figure 2**

The automatic air induction pre-heat valve is located in a housing to the right of the radiator, on vehicles so equipped. Every 8000 miles (13,000 km), the lever should be placed in the winter (W) position and the valve's freedom of movement checked. If necessary, oil the valve. In the "W" position air drawn in at the front of the car is mixed with air preheated around the exhaust manifold in a ratio dependent on outside and engine temperatures, until it reaches approximately 86°F (30°C). At approximately this same outside temperature, the preheat supply hose is completely closed and the car obtains all its induction air supply from the fresh air hose. In summer, the lever should be used to set the valve to the "S" position. The cover plate can be removed for inspection purposes.

ADJUSTMENT

▶ **See Figure 2**

1. Remove the cover.
2. Adjust the butterfly valve by loosening the nuts.
3. The butterfly valve is correctly set when the distance is 2.3 inches (60mm).

Air Injection System

OPERATION

The Air Injection system is used to add oxygen to the hot exhaust gases in the Thermal Reactor or exhaust manifold. The introduction of fresh air (oxygen) aids in more complete combustion of the air/fuel mixture lessening the hydrocarbons and the carbon monoxide emissions. A belt driven air pump is used to force air into the exhaust system, through a series of valves and tubing.

87894P01

Fig. 1 Carbon canister in 2002 engine compartment

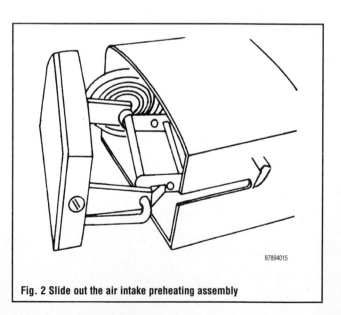

87894015

Fig. 2 Slide out the air intake preheating assembly

TESTING

2002 and 3.0 Models

AIR PUMP

Remove the air return pipe and hold the palm of the hand over the pressure regulating valve unit while increasing the engine speed. The excess pressure valve must open between 1700 and 200 rpm. If the valve opens early, replace the valve. If the valve opens at a higher rpm, replace the air pump.

BELT ADJUSTMENT

The air pump drive belt should have a deflection of no more than 0.38 inches (10mm) measured in the middle of its longest span, when properly adjusted.

CONTROL VALVE

▶ See Figure 3

The control valve should be replaced if the carburetors are difficult to adjust or if the engine back-fires when the throttle is released.

CHECK VALVE

The check valve should be replaced if air can be blown through the valve in both directions. Air should move towards the manifold only.

BLOW-IN PIPES

The exhaust manifold must be removed to expose the blow-in pipes. The pipes can be replaced by unscrewing them from the manifold and screwing in new ones.

3, 5, 6 and 7 Series Models

AIR PUMP

Disconnect the outlet hose and start the engine. The air velocity should increase as the engine speed increases. If not, the air pump drive belt could be slipping, the check valve or the air pump may be defective and would have to be adjusted or replaced.

BLOW-OFF VALVE

If backfiring occurs when releasing the accelerator or the air pump seems to be overloading, the blow-off valve may be defective.

The valve must release and blow-off during a coasting condition and the internal safety valve must open at 5 psi (34 kPa). The vacuum line must have suction when the engine is running and must allow the air to be blown off when reattached to the valve at idle.

ELECTRIC CONTROL VALVE

This control valve governs the blow-off valve and must be open at temperatures below 113°F (45°C) and closed above 113°F (45°C) of the coolant.

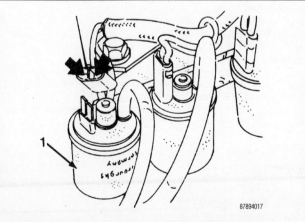

Fig. 3 Control valve assembly (1) and test connection points (arrows)

With the coolant temperatures above 113°F (45°C), the ignition switch on and the engine off, disconnect both vacuum hoses, attach a test hose to one nipple and blow air into the valve. The valve is functioning properly if air cannot flow through the valve. Turn the ignition switch **OFF** and blow into the valve again. Air should flow through the valve.

CHECK VALVE

The check valve must be replaced if air can be blown through the valve in both directions. Air should move towards the reactors only.

BLOW-IN PIPES

The air enters above the reactors, directly into the exhaust ports, behind the exhaust valves. The pipes can be replaced by removing the distribution tube assembly.

THERMAL REACTOR

The reactors have a double casing and has internally vented flame deflector plates. Spontaneous combustion, due to high temperatures, and the introduction of oxygen into the exhaust gas flow maintains the after-burning of the gases.

A warning light marked "Reactor" alerts the driver to have the unit inspected for external heat damage every 25,000 miles (40,000 km). A triggering device, located behind the dash and operated by the speedometer cable, can be reset to open the electrical contacts and extinguish the warning light.

➡ **Two different sized buttons are mounted side by side on the triggering device. The small button is for the reactor and the large button is for the EGR valve. Press the button to reset.**

REMOVAL & INSTALLATION

Air Pump

1600, 2002 AND 3.0 MODELS

1. Disconnect inlet and outlet hoses.
2. Remove the adjusting bolt. Then, loosen and remove the front and rear mounting bolts. Note that nuts will remain in the grooved portion of the housing.
3. Inspect the rubber bushings inside the mounting bracket and replace if necessary.
4. Install in reverse order; do not pry on the pump when adjusting the belt.

318I AND 320I MODELS

1. Disconnect the hose at the back of the pump.
2. Remove the adjusting bolt and disengage the belt. Then, remove the through bolt which passes through front and rear pump brackets, being careful to retain the nut and spacer located at the rear.
3. Pull the rubber bushings out of either end of the air pump mount. If the bushings are worn or cracked replace them. When reinstalling, make sure inside diameters of bushings fit over the inner spacer and outside diameters fit snugly into the mount.
4. Install in reverse order.

5, 6 AND 7 SERIES MODELS

1. Loosen the adjusting bolt, which is located at the top of the upper pump bracket. Pull off the belt.
2. Loosen the clamp and detach the air hose at the rear.
3. Remove the the mounting bolts from the bracket. Remove the single bolt from the front bracket and remove the pump.
4. Pull the rubber bushings out of the lower pump mount and inspect them. Replace them if they are worn or cracked, making sure the inside diameters fit around the inner (metal) bushing and outside diameters fit inside the mount.
5. Install the pump in reverse order.

Ignition Timing Controls

✳✳ CAUTION

Transistorized ignition systems utilize voltages that can be fatal if accidental contact is made with "live" parts or connections. When-

ever working on electronic ignition systems, always disconnect the battery and make sure the ignition switch is OFF before removing or installing any connections at the distributor, coil, spark plugs or control unit.

TESTING

Distributor Advance/Retard Units

▶ **See Figure 4**

A vacuum advance and retard unit is attached to the distributor and is controlled by engine vacuum. The advance can be checked with a strobe light by observing the action of the timing mark during the increase in engine speed. The retard side can be checked at idle by removing the retard vacuum line and noting the increase in engine speed of at least 300 rpm.

➡**Some models built for California and high altitude applications and equipped with manual transmissions, have the vacuum advance in operation only when the high gear is engaged. This controlled by an electrical switch connected to the shifting linkage. Automatic transmission 633CSi for California and high altitude, have the vacuum advance inoperative. Late model 530i and 630CSi vehicles are equipped with a vacuum retard unit only. The 528i has both advance and retard.**

Electric Control Valve (Black Cap)

CALIFORNIA MODELS

This control valve stops the retard distributor control over speeds of 3000 rpm.

Remove the outer hose (to distributor) and start engine. At engine rpm lower than 3000 rpm, vacuum should be present in the distributor retard unit hose and not present when the engine speed is increased above 3000 rpm.

Disconnect the wire terminal end at the control valve and have the engine operating at idle. Connect a test lamp to the terminal and check for the presence of current. If current is present, the speed switch is defective.

Increase the engine speed to 300 rpm or above, and the test lamp should light. If the test lamp does not light, the speed switch is defective.

Timing Valve

The timing valve is shut off when the engine is cold or in the warm up phase of operation. Turning on the ignition heats the timing valve continuously. To test the timing valve on a cold engine, detach the hose to the distributor vacuum advance unit and check that no vacuum is felt from the valve connection. When the engine reaches operating temperature, disconnect the hose to the throttle

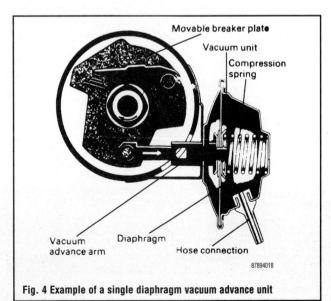

Fig. 4 Example of a single diaphragm vacuum advance unit

housing and check that the engine speed increases about 200 rpm. Any results other than these, replace the timing valve.

Speed Controlled Spark System

The Speed Controlled Spark (SCS) system allows either ignition advance or retard depending on vehicle speed. Generally, this system reduces advance during low speed operation but allows full advance at higher speeds. This system operates on the vacuum advance or retard unit. The SCS vacuum solenoid valve is controlled by a temperature sensor mounted in the intake manifold water passage and by an engine speed switch. When coolant temperature is below 133°F (56°C), or if the engine speed is over 3000 rpm, the solenoid valve closed vacuum flow to vacuum control valve and to first stage of the EGR valve. This prevents the EGR system from operating when the engine is cold, improving driveability and cold response.

TESTING THE SPEED SWITCH

With the engine running and at operating temperature, connect a test lamp to the disconnected plug of the solenoid valve. The test lamp should be on at engine speeds over 3000 rpm. If not, replace the speed switch.

Exhaust Gas Recirculation (EGR) System

OPERATION

The EGR valve is vacuum operated by the position of the carburetor or injection system throttle plate in the throttle bore during vehicle operation. A metered amount of exhaust gas enters the combustion chamber to be mixed with the air/fuel blend. The effect is to reduce the peak combustion temperatures, which in turn reduces the amount of nitrous oxides (NO_2), formed during the combustion process.

TESTING

EGR Valve

2002 AND 3.0 MODELS

Remove the air filter and adjust the engine idle to 900 rpm. Remove the vacuum line from the valve and using an engine vacuum source, attach the hose to the vacuum nipple. The engine speed should drop 500–600 rpm if the valve is operating properly. If little or no change of engine speed is noted, the recirculation pipes, the cyclone filter or the EGR valve may be plugged or defective.

318I AND 320I MODELS

1. Start the engine and let it idle. Disconnect the blue hose at the EGR valve, and leave both ends open. The engine speed should remain the same. If the engine speed changes, the throttle blade opens too far at idle or the EGR valve is sticking open.

2. Leave the blue hose detached and disconnect the black hose at the intake header. Detach the red hose at the throttle housing and connect it to the open port on the intake header. The engine speed should drop considerably, or the EGR valve is defective and must be replaced.

3. Detach the black hose the header. Detach the red hose at the temperature sensing valve and connect it to the open port on the intake header. If the engine speed drops, the EGR valve is sticking open or the pressure converter is defective. To check the pressure converter, detach red and blue hoses and check for vacuum at the open converter ports (engine running). If there is no vacuum at the ports, but the white hose to the converter has vacuum, the converter is defective.

5 SERIES MODELS

1. With the engine idling and hot, disconnect the black hose at the tee leading into the vacuum control valve.

2. Disconnect the hose at the vacuum limiter, and connect its open end with the open end of the black hose. The engine speed should drop about 100 rpm. Reconnect the black hose to the tee.

3. Disconnect the blue hose at the vacuum control valve and connect its

open end to the open end of the hose disconnected from the vacuum limiter in Step 2.The engine speed should now drop about 200 rpm. If either test is failed, replace the EGR valve.

6 AND 7 SERIES MODELS

1. Bring the engine to operating temperature at idle speed. Detach the blue hose at the EGR valve, do not plug either the open end or the hose or the fitting on the valve. The engine speed should stay the same. If the engine speed should stay the same. If the engine speed drops, check the red hose from the throttle housing for vacuum. If there is vacuum there, adjust the idle position of the throttle. If there is no vacuum, the EGR valve is defective.

2. Detach the blue hose at the EGR valve. On 6 Series models, remove the plug from the intake collector, On the 733i, disconnect the white hose at the collector. Pull the red hose off the throttle housing and attach it to the open fitting on the intake collector. If the engine speed does not drop considerably, the EGR valve, coolant temperature switch, or red electric switching valve is defective. If the engine speed does drop, go to Step 5.

3. To test the coolant temperature switch, turn on the engine with the engine stopped and cold _ temperature below 113°F (45°C). Pull the connector plug off the red magnetic valve and connect the test lamp between the 2 open terminals on the valve. The test lamp should not come on. If the test lamp does come on, test the speed switch as described in the next step.

4. To test speed switch, remove the electrical connector from the blue switching valve with the engine idling. Connect a test lamp between the 2 leads. If not, make sure the valve is properly grounded and, if so, replace the speed switch. If the engine speed did not drop in Step 2, and you have made tests described in Steps 3 and 4, test the red cap electric control valve (see below) before condemning the EGR valve.

5. Connect the blue hose back to the EGR valve. Leave the red hose connected as in Step 2. Engine speed should have dropped slightly from normal idle. If the idle speed drops considerably from the normal idle, there are leaking hoses, a defective pressure converter, or a bad EGR valve. Restore all hoses to their normal positions. Check for leaks. If there are no leaks, detach the red hose at the pressure converter with the engine idling and hot. There should be back pressure. Then, detach the white hose to make sure there is intake vacuum. Repair broken or loose red or white hoses, if necessary. Then, reinstall the white hose, pull off the blue hose, and check for vacuum at the blue pressure converter connection. If there is no vacuum, replace the pressure converter; otherwise, replace the EGR valve.

REMOVAL & INSTALLATION

EGR Valve

1. Note the color coding of vacuum hoses and disconnect them.

2. On 320i models, loosen the clamp and disconnect the hose running into the side of the valve.

3. Unscrew the nut at the bottom of the valve with a spanner wrench. On 6 cylinder engines, remove the 2 mounting bolts for the EGR valve holding bracket, from the intake pipes, and pull the valve free of the recirculation hose.

To install:

4. Install the valve to the hose and install the retaining bolts.

5. Screw in the nut at the bottom of the valve and connect the vacuum hoses. On 320i models, connect the hose to the side of the valve and tighten the clamp.

Electric Control Valve

5, 6 AND 7 SERIES MODELS

On models equipped, the electric control valve should stop the EGR valve operation at coolant temperatures below 113°F (45°C), and speeds above 3000 rpm. Tag and disconnect both vacuum hoses at the control valve with the engine off and the coolant temperature below 113°F (45°C). Connect a test hose to one of the nipples and blow through the hose. The valve is functioning properly when there is air flowing through the valve with the ignition **OFF** and no air flow through the valve with the ignition **ON**.

Connect the vacuum hoses to the valve and operate the engine until the coolant is heated over 113°F (45°C). Disconnect the hoses and check for air flow through the valve. Air should now flow through the valve.

Coolant Temperature Switch and Control Relay

1. With the coolant temperature below 113°F (45°C), turn the ignition **ON**, but do not start the engine. Remove the wire plug at the control valve and connect a test lamp to the plug.

   a. The test lamp should light. If the test lamp does not light, connect the test lamp to ground. If the lamp now operates, the ground wire to the control valve has an open circuit.

   b. If the test lamp still does not light, disconnect the wire terminal at the coolant temperature switch and connect it to ground. If the test lamp still does not light, replace the control valve.

2. With the coolant temperature above 113°F (45°C), turn the ignition switch **ON** but do not start the engine. Disconnect the wire terminal plug at the control valve and connect a test lamp. The lamp should be off. If the lamp is on, the coolant temperature switch or control relay is defective.

3. With the engine running at temperatures above 113°F (45°C), connect the test light to the disconnected plug of the control light to the disconnected plug of the control valve. The test lamp should be on over an engine speed of 3000 rpm. If the test lamp does not light, the speed switch is defective.

REMOVAL & INSTALLATION

EGR Filter

▶ See Figure 5

➡**The EGR filter should be replaced every 25,000 miles (40,000). The exhaust system should be cool before replacing.**

1. Detach all lines.
2. Loosen the hold-down bolts.
3. Remove the bolts and filter.
4. Installation is the reverse of removal.

EGR Warning Light

▶ See Figure 6

A warning light marked EGR is triggered at 25,000 miles (40,000 km) intervals, to alert the driver to service the exhaust gas recirculation system filter.

A triggering device, located under the dash and driven by the speedometer cable, can be reset to open the electrical contracts and extinguish the EGR warning light.

➡**Two different sized buttons are mounted side-by-side on the triggering device. The small button is for the reactor light and the large button is for the EGR light. Press the button to reset.**

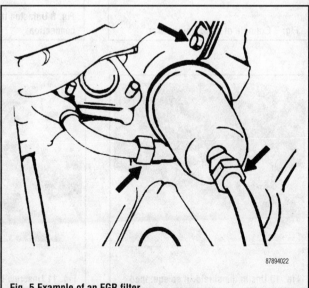

87894022

Fig. 5 Example of an EGR filter

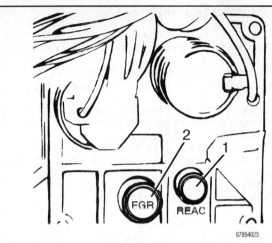

Fig. 6 EGR and thermal reactor triggering box, mounted in the engine compartment. The thermal reactor reset button (1) and EGR reset button (2) can be pressed with the eraser end of a pencil

Oxygen Sensor System

▶ See Figure 7

An oxygen (lambda) sensor system is used on all models equipped with a 3-way catalyst. No exhaust gas recirculation is required. Completely burned fuel in the form of carbon monoxide is used, within the catalyst, to remove oxygen from the nitrogen oxide emissions, leaving them in their normal state as nitrogen. This process can only be accomplished if the fuel/air ratio is kept precisely at the optimum level with no excess air or oxygen. A sensor located in the exhaust gas stream constantly regulates the fuel/air mixture provided by the injection system according to the amount of air (oxygen) in the exhaust.

MAINTENANCE

Every 30,000 miles (48,000 km) an oxygen sensor warning light will indicate the need to change the oxygen sensor. The warning light must be reset when the sensor is replaced by pushing the reset button on the mileage switch under the hood.

REMOVAL & INSTALLATION

▶ See Figures 8, 9, 10, 11 and 12

1. Disconnect the electrical sensor lead.

➡On some models the connection is beneath the vehicle, next to the exhaust system. On other models, the connection is in the engine compartment.

✳✳ CAUTION

Severe burns can result from a hot exhaust system. Be sure that the exhaust system is cold before proceeding.

2. Unscrew the oxygen sensor from the exhaust manifold.
To install:
3. Coat the replacement sensor threads with anti-seize compound.

➡Do not get any anti-seize compound on the sensor body, as it will ruin the sensor.

4. Thread the new sensor into the exhaust manifold and tighten to 3.5 ft. lbs. (5 Nm).

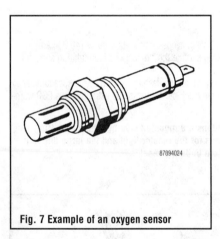

Fig. 7 Example of an oxygen sensor

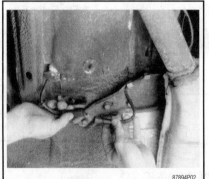

Fig. 8 Unfasten the oxygen sensor wire connection

Fig. 9 An oxygen sensor mounted in the exhaust pipe. Some models are equipped with a protective shield around the sensor

Fig. 10 Unclip the shield, if so equipped

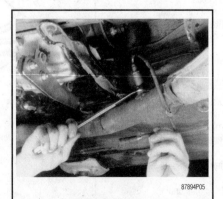

Fig. 11 Unscrew the oxygen sensor

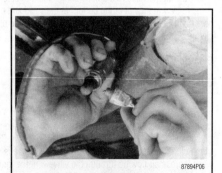

Fig. 12 Before installing the oxygen sensor, apply anti-seize compound to the threads

5. Reset the service interval switch and make sure the dash warning light is out.

6. Retest the CO level using an exhaust analyzer with the oxygen sensor disconnected. If the CO level fails to drop when the sensor is reconnected, there is a fault in the system.

Catalytic Converter System

A 3-way catalyst is installed in the exhaust system to reduce HC and CO emissions by a chemical reaction which finishes the combustion process on fuel that is not completely burned. The catalyst turns HC and CO emissions into carbon dioxide and water vapor (steam).

ELECTRONIC ENGINE CONTROLS

Motronic Emission Control System

▶ **See Figures 13, 14 and 15**

➡**The Motronic engine control system is an extremely complex, electrical control system. Most testing and repair on the system requires the use of very expensive, factory only, test equipment. The test procedures and explanations explained here, are to be used ONLY as a guide to basic system operation and testing. For any major problems, you should take the vehicle to an authorized factory shop for repair.**

GENERAL INFORMATION

The Motronic Emission Control system is an electronically controlled, computerized engine system which controls the fuel injection and ignition timing as well as air/fuel ratio.

The system uses this information to determine engine operating conditions, and adjusts timing and fuel ratio accordingly. The Motronic control unit is located behind the speaker in the right kick panel of 635CSi and 735i models and in the glove compartment of the 3 and 5 series vehicles.

The Motronic control unit is the brain of the system. Various engine sensors supply the unit with operating information air flow, air temperature, throttle position, coolant temperature, engine speed, piston position and oxygen content of exhaust gases.

The system receives electronic input signals from several engine sensors.

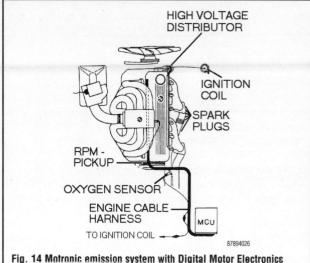

Fig. 14 Motronic emission system with Digital Motor Electronics (DME) controls—528e models

Information supplied by these sensors is used to determine optimum ignition and fuel injection timing under various engine operating conditions.

An ideal air/fuel ratio of 14:1 is maintained under most driving conditions. This is the ratio at which the catalytic converter operates most efficiently to reduce exhaust emissions.

The main components that make up the Motronic control system are: oxygen sensor, air flow sensor, 3 coolant temperature sensors, reference point pickup, engine speed sensor and the throttle position sensor.

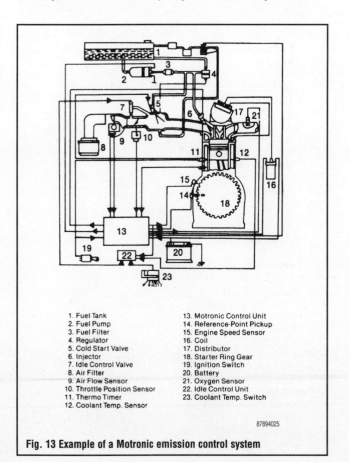

1. Fuel Tank	13. Motronic Control Unit
2. Fuel Pump	14. Reference-Point Pickup
3. Fuel Filter	15. Engine Speed Sensor
4. Regulator	16. Coil
5. Cold Start Valve	17. Distributor
6. Injector	18. Starter Ring Gear
7. Idle Control Valve	19. Ignition Switch
8. Air Filter	20. Battery
9. Air Flow Sensor	21. Oxygen Sensor
10. Throttle Position Sensor	22. Idle Control Unit
11. Thermo Timer	23. Coolant Temp. Switch
12. Coolant Temp. Sensor	

Fig. 13 Example of a Motronic emission control system

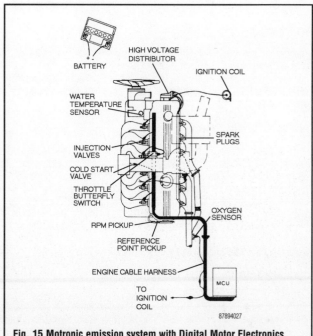

Fig. 15 Motronic emission system with Digital Motor Electronics (DME) controls—535i models

SYSTEM SENSORS

Coolant Temperature

There are 3 components that supply temperature information to the Motronic control unit. They are the coolant temperature sensor, coolant temperature switch and the thermo timer. All 3 devices are located in the water jacket of the engine block. They supply the temperature information to the control unit in the form of electrical signals.

The system interprets these signals as cold or normal operating temperatures. During cold operating conditions, the air/fuel mixture is enriched by the cold start valve. This valve is located in the intake manifold, downstream from the butterfly valve. It supplies additional fuel to the inlet charge when signaled by the control unit. Extra rich conditions are maintenance until the normal operating temperature is reached.

Throttle Position

The throttle position sensor is located in the throttle linkage at the intake butterfly valve, where it detects the position of the throttle valve. This data is converted into an electrical impulse and sent to the control unit. The control unit interprets the signal as either full throttle, idle or normal operating condition and adjusts accordingly.

Engine Speed

The engine speed sensor is located on the bell housing, next to the starter ring gear. A steel ball, embedded in the ring gear, causes an electronic pulse in the speed sensor, with each engine revolution. These pulses are transmitted to the control unit to be used as the rpm reading.

Reference-Point Pickup

This sensor is located in the bell housing next to the engine speed sensor. It supplies the control unit with piston position information. When the control unit has determined optimum ignition timing data, the reference-point pickup is used to signal ignition firing.

Oxygen

Oxygen content of the exhaust gas is measured by the oxygen sensor, which is located in the exhaust manifold. This sensor measures the amount of oxygen present in the exhaust and sends the data to the control unit as an electrical impulse. The control unit uses this input to keep the air/fuel mixture at the optimum ratio for optimum engine performance.

Air Flow

Intake air flow is detected by the air flow sensor. It is located in the intake passage between the air filter and the intake manifold and informs the control unit of the rate of air intake. Incorporated into the air flow sensor is the air temperature sensor. This sensor informs the control unit of the ambient temperature of incoming air.

Idle Speed Control System

This system uses an electrically governed idle rpm control valve to keep the idle speed stable under the various engine operating conditions. Measured intake air from the air flow sensor bypasses the throttle plate through the idle rpm control valve and subsequently calls for additional fuel injection. The amount of bypassed air is determined by the variable orifice of the control valve.

An additional electronic control unit, the Idle Speed Control Unit, controls the orifice opening according to the engine speed and the engine operating conditions as related to the engine coolant temperature, transmission, air conditioning and heater intake air temperature.

TROUBLESHOOTING THE MOTRONIC SYSTEM

The following is a list of conditions and causes that can be used as a helpful guide in determining any problems with the Motronic system. This guide should be referred to before testing the Motronic system.

Cold engine will not start:

The possible causes are as follows:
- Air flow sensor
- Cold Start valve
- Fuel injector
- Fuel pressure
- Ignition coil
- Motronic control unit
- Reference mark transmitter
- Speed transmitter
- Wire connections and plugs

Cold engine will start, but stalls immediately:

The possible causes are as follows:
- Fuel injector
- Motronic control unit
- Wire connections and plugs

Cold engine is hard to start:

The possible causes are as follows:
- Cold start injector
- Fuel pressure
- High voltage distributor
- Motronic control unit
- Spark plugs
- Temperature time switch

Warm engine will not start:

The possible causes are as follows:
- Fuel injector
- Fuel pressure
- Ignition coil
- Motronic control unit
- Reference mark transmitter
- Secondary air of the engine
- Speed transmitter
- Wire connections and plugs

Erratic idle during the warm-up stage:

The possible causes are as follows:
- Air temperature sensor
- Coolant
- Coolant temperature sensor
- High voltage distributor
- Idle control unit
- Idle valve
- Ignition circuit
- Ignition system
- Motronic control unit
- Spark plugs
- Temperature switch (112°F/44°C)
- Throttle switch
- Wire connections and plugs

The engine is backfiring:

The possible causes are as follows:
- Exhaust system
- Fuel injector
- High voltage distributor
- Ignition circuit
- Motronic control unit
- Spark plugs

The engine idle speed is incorrect:

The possible causes are as follows:
- Cold start injector
- Coolant temperature switch
- Fuel injector
- High voltage distributor
- Intake system
- Motronic control unit
- Temperature switch
- Throttle switch

The engine has a hesitation during acceleration:

The possible causes are as follows:
- Fuel injector
- High voltage distributor
- Ignition circuit

- Motronic control unit
- Spark plugs
- Wire connections and plugs

The engine is knocking during acceleration:

The possible causes are as follows:

- Ignition circuit
- Motronic control unit
- Spark plugs
- Wire connections and plugs

The engine has a coasting hesitation:

The possible causes are as follows:

- Fuel injector
- Motronic control unit
- Wire connections and plugs

The engine is misfiring under all conditions:

The possible causes are as follows:

- Air flow sensor
- Air temperature sensor
- Coolant
- Coolant temperature switch
- Exhaust system
- Fuel injector
- Fuel pressure
- Ignition circuit
- Intake system
- Insufficient engine power
- Motronic control unit
- Secondary air of the engine
- Throttle switch
- Wire connections and plugs

The engine has high fuel consumption:

The possible causes are as follows:

- Air temperature sensor
- Cold start injector
- Coolant temperature sensor
- Fuel injector
- Motronic control unit
- Temperature time switch
- Throttle switch

The engine CO level is incorrect:

The possible causes are as follows:

- Cold start injector
- Intake system
- Oxygen sensor
- Secondary air of the engine
- Wire connections and plugs

The HC and NOx levels are excessive:

The possible causes are as follows:

- Cold start injector
- Fuel injector
- Intake system
- Motronic control unit
- Oxygen sensor
- Secondary air of the engine
- Wire connections and plugs

TESTING

➡**The Motronic engine control system is an extremely complex, electrical control system. Most testing and repair on the system requires the use of very expensive, factory only, test equipment. The test procedures and explanations explained here, are to be used ONLY as a guide to basic system operation and testing. For any major problems, you should take the vehicle to an authorized factory shop for repair.**

Before suspecting the Motronic control system to be at fault, be sure that all other systems are in proper working order. Any engine system that would normally be checked in a vehicle not equipped with the Motronic control system, should be checked first.

If the Motronic control unit has been found to be causing the problem, determined which component or area is the most probable source of performance

difficulty and begin testing there. Many component failures may be traced to faults in the wiring circuit. Before beginning other diagnostic procedures, check the appropriate circuit for breaks or shorts and be sure that all electrical connections are clean and tight.

In order to properly diagnose and repair any defects in the Motronic control system the following test equipment will be necessary. The BMW service test kit, Bosch L-Jetronic fuel injection test kit and service procedures, BMW test meter 22 13 100 and a standard volt/ohm meter. Failure to use the proper test equipment may result in unnecessary replacement of good components or damage to the system. These special tools are expensive and designed for factory authorized and trained technicians. They are listed here only to give you a reference to the tools used.

Cold Start Valve

VALVE DOES NOT OPEN

1. Remove valve, leaving fuel lines connected. Supply battery voltage to valve with jumper wire and be sure valve is properly grounded. Pull off relay 1. Apply battery voltage to connector 87 in the relay plug and check that the fuel pump runs. The cold start valve should deliver fuel. If not, replace the valve.

2. If the valve functions properly, check power supply to the valve: Pull plug off the valve and connect a voltmeter between the plug wires. Start the engine. The meter should read battery voltage while cranking the engine. If not, trace the circuit and repair the wiring.

3. Check the thermo timer and replace if resistance values are not correct.

VALVE LEAKS

Check valve operation as in first cold start valve test. If valve operates properly (fuel is delivered), remove jumper wire to battery voltage and check that fuel delivery stops. If fuel is still delivered, or leaks, or seeps out, replace valve.

Idle Control Valve

◗ **See Figure 16**

1. Valve should be open when vehicle is at rest (no voltage to valve). When voltage is applied to valve (engine on), valve should close. Remove 2 valve hoses and observe valve operation. If valve does not operate as described, replace valve.

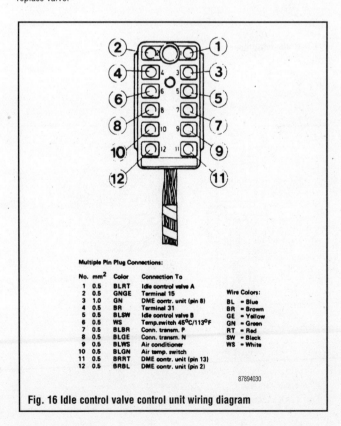

Multiple Pin Plug Connections:

No.	mm²	Color	Connection To
1	0.5	BLRT	Idle control valve A
2	0.5	GNGE	Terminal 15
3	1.0	GN	DME contr. unit (pin 8)
4	0.5	BR	Terminal 31
5	0.5	BLSW	Idle control valve B
6	0.5	WS	Temp.switch 45°C/113°F
7	0.5	BLBR	Conn. transm. P
8	0.5	BLGE	Conn. transm. N
9	0.5	BLWS	Air conditioner
10	0.5	BLGN	Air temp. switch
11	0.5	BRRT	DME contr. unit (pin 13)
12	0.5	BRBL	DME contr. unit (pin 2)

Wire Colors:

BL = Blue
BR = Brown
GE = Yellow
GN = Green
RT = Red
SW = Black
WS = White

87894030

Fig. 16 Idle control valve control unit wiring diagram

2. If valve operates properly, pull of connector plug and connect voltmeter between the 2 wires in plug. Start the engine and turn the A/C on. Voltmeter should read battery voltage. If it does not, see idle control diagnosis test.

Coolant Temperature Sensor

Check that sensor is properly installed and firmly seated. Check that cooling system is full. Bleed system. Check resistance between switch connections. If resistance is incorrect, replace sensor. If resistance is correct, trace sensor circuit and repair wiring.

Coolant Temperature Switch

Switch must be tightly installed. Check that cooling system is full. Bleed system. Check resistance between switch contacts. Resistance below 106°F (41°C) should be zero. At higher temperatures, resistance should be infinite. If values are correct, trace circuit and repair wiring. If values are incorrect, replace switch.

Thermo Timer

▶ See Figure 17

1. Check that the timer is properly installed and firmly seated. Check the radiator for correct coolant level. Bleed the cooling system.
2. Disconnect the timer and check resistance values between plug terminals G and W, G and ground, and W and ground. If values are correct, trace timer circuit and repair the wiring. If values are incorrect, replace the timer. Specifications are as follows:
    a. G to ground is 40–70 ohms.
    b. G to W & W to ground is infinite when the temperature is above 60°F (15°C).
    c. G to W & W to ground is zero when the temperature is below 60°F (15°C).

Oxygen Sensor

The oxygen sensor light on the dash will light the first time the mileage reaches 30,000 (48,000 km). Replace the oxygen sensor and remove the light bulb from the dash. The bulb lights the first time only. However, the sensor must be changed every 30,000 miles (48,000 km).

REMOVAL & INSTALLATION

All Models Through 1984

1. Disconnect the oxygen sensor wire connector and remove the wires from the clip.
2. Pull off the sensor protective plate.

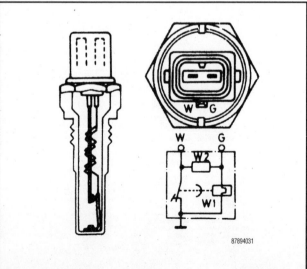

Fig. 17 Cut-away view of thermo timer and schematic of the switch

87894031

3. Unscrew the oxygen sensor.
4. Before installation, coat the threads of the new sensor with a suitable anti-seize compound.
5. Install the sensor unit.
6. Remove the call unit from the dash by unscrewing the bolt, push the unit to the right and remove the oxygen sensor display bulb. On some models, the bulb must be broken to remove it.

1985–88 Models

This heated type oxygen sensor needs to be replaced only at 50,000 mile (80,000 km) intervals. The sensor is located on the engine exhaust pipe, just in front of the catalytic convertor.

To replace it, unscrew the protective plate and disconnect the plug in the wire leading to the sensor. Then, unscrew the oxygen sensor. Replace in reverse order, coating the threads of the new sensor with an anti-seize compound.

➡ **A special tool (Special Service Indicator Resetter 62 1 100), only available through BMW sources, must be used to reset certain electronic type emission or oxygen sensor indicator light controls.**

Digital Motor Electronics (DME) System

OPERATION

Some BMW models are equipped with the Bosch Digital Motor Electronics (DME) system. This system incorporates various data sensors that monitor the air intake volume, engine speed, crankshaft position, coolant temperature, intake air temperature and throttle position. Signals from these sensors, as well as the oxygen sensor signal and the start sensor signal, are sent to the electronic control unit. The electronic control unit is a microcomputer and the brain of the DME system. It uses the information obtained from the data sensors in order to determine the correct amount of fuel and the optimum ignition timing.

The DME system also has the capability of switching from an open loop system to a closed loop system when the coolant temperature is above 113°F (45°C) and when the oxygen sensor temperature is above 480°F (249°C). The digital engine control system consists of 4 main sub-systems: spark timing, fuel control, electronic control unit, and various data sensors.

SUB-SYSTEMS

Spark Control

The spark control system allows the electronic control unit to determine the exact instant that ignition is required to operate the vehicle properly, based upon the information provided from the data sensors. At the proper time the electronic control unit breaks the primary circuit of the ignition coil and this in turn produces a high voltage spark at the coil center tower. This voltage surge fires the spark plug at the proper time for most efficient combustion, eliminating the need for vacuum and/or centrifugal advance.

Fuel Control

The vehicle is equipped with the Bosch air flow controlled fuel injection system. The system is electronically controlled by the electronic control unit, which is programmed to regulate fuel injection based upon data received from the various data sensors. The electronic control unit generates control signals for the fuel pump relay, auxiliary air valve, cold start injector coil and the cylinder port injector coils. These components control the curb idle speed and mixture, cold idle, air/fuel ratio and the fuel supply.

Electronic Control Unit

The electronic control unit monitors and controls all digital engine control functions. The electronic control unit consists of input and output devices, a central processing unit, a power supply and various memory banks. The input and output devices of the electronic control unit convert electrical signals received by the data sensors and switches to the digital signals that are used by the central processing unit. The central processing unit receives digital signals that are used to perform all mathematical computations and logic functions necessary to deliver proper air/fuel mixture. The central processing unit is also responsible for calculating spark timing information. The main source of power that allows the electronic control unit to function is generated from the battery of the vehicle and transported through the ignition system. The memory bank of the electronic control unit is programmed with exact information that is used by the electronic control unit during the open loop mode. This data is also used when a sensor of other component fails, allowing the vehicle to be driven to a repair facility.

Data Sensors

The digital engine control system consists of 6 data sensors. They are an oxygen sensor, reference mark sensor, speed sensor, coolant temperature sensor, air intake temperature sensor and the air flow sensor. Each sensor supplies electronic data to the electronic control unit, which in turn computes spark timing and the correct amount of fuel that is necessary to maintain proper engine operation. The system also uses a throttle switch, a high altitude switch, an auxiliary air valve, a fuel pressure regulator and a pressure damper.

The oxygen sensor is mounted in line with the exhaust system directly in front of the catalytic converter. The oxygen sensor supplies voltage under one half volt when the fuel mixture is lean and up to one volt when the fuel mixture is rich. The sensor must be hot to function properly and to allow the electronic control unit to accept its power signals. The function of the oxygen sensor measures the amount of oxygen. Most vehicles are equipped with a special electrically heated oxygen sensor which aids the system so that it will begin to function earlier. The heated oxygen sensor has 3 wires, 2 for the heater element and one for the sensor signal. The heating function begins as soon as the ignition is turned on. The plugs from the sensor to the wiring harness are located near the flywheel sensor plugs.

➡**No attempt should be made to measure oxygen sensor voltage output. Current drain on the voltmeter could permanently damage the sensor, shift sensor calibration range and/or render sensor unusable. Do not connect jumper wire, test leads or other electrical connectors to sensor. Use these devices only on the electronic control unit side of the harness after disconnecting sensor.**

The reference mark sensor is located on the engine crankcase flange. Its function is to detect crankshaft position in relation to top dead center and then to send the proper signal to the electronic control unit. It is triggered by a bolt which is fastened to the engine flywheel.

The speed sensor is mounted on an adjustable bracket along with the reference mark sensor. This sensor measures engine speed by counting the teeth on the starter ring gear. The speed sensor sends voltage surges to the electronic control unit for each tooth that passes.

The coolant temperature sensor is located on the intake manifold. Its function is to supply coolant temperature information to the electronic control unit. This generated data effects the air/fuel ratio, the spark timing and the engine temperature light.

The air intake temperature sensor is located in the air stream of the air flow meter. The main function of this sensor is to supply incoming air temperature information to the electronic control unit. The electronic control unit uses this data along with other important data to regulate the fuel injection rate.

The air flow sensor functions the same as the air intake temperature sensor, except that the air flow sensor incorporates a measuring flap that opens against the pressure of a spiral spring which is connected to a potentiometer. The potentiometer transmits an electrical signal which is determined by a position on the measuring flap to tell the electronic control unit the vehicle engine load.

A contact type throttle link switch, which is located on the throttle body, convert throttle position into electrical signals. These signals are used to inform the electronic control unit of throttle position. The potentiometer within the air flow meter prevents the loss of engine power during sudden acceleration or deceleration by signaling the electronic control unit for the necessary fuel requirements.

The high altitude switch is mounted under the dashboard on the driver's side of the vehicle. In altitudes higher than 3300 feet the switch closes, signaling the electronic control unit to lean out the fuel mixture so that the vehicle will continue to function properly.

The function of the auxiliary air valve is to provide additional air during engine warm up. The valve is located next to the throttle body. It consists of an electrically heated bi-metallic strip, a movable disc and an air by-pass channel. The heating coil on the bi-metallic strip is energized by the fuel pump relay.

Control of the auxiliary valve is governed by engine temperature. The air by-pass channel is open when the engine is cold and gradually closes as the

engine warms up. At predetermined temperature the air by-pass channel in the valve is blocked and additional air flow is cut off.

The fuel pressure regulator is located at the end of the fuel injection collection line. The function of the pressure regulator is to maintain constant fuel pressure to the fuel injectors.

The pressure damper is located at the inlet of the fuel injection collector tube. The pressure damper absorbs fuel pressure oscillation caused by the fuel injection cycle.

TESTING

DME Control Unit

1. Check the electrical power supply. Turn the ignition switch **ON** and disconnect the DME control unit electrical connector.
2. With a suitable voltmeter, check connection 18 and 35 of the DME control unit. There should be approximately 12 volts.
3. Connections 5, 16, 17 and 19 are all connected in with the ground.
4. Pull off relay number 2 and jump terminals 87 and 30. This will supply voltage to the control unit.
5. If necessary, check activation or replace relay number 2. Turn on the ignition and check the voltage on terminals 85 and 86. There should be 12 volts present.
6. To be sure that the source of defect is only in the control unit, it is recommended to replace the DME unit for comparison.
7. In addition, carry out the various L-Jetronic test with a suitable BMW service test unit first, depending on the type of complaint.

Adaptive Pilot Control

The adaptive pilot control has been integrated in the DME control unit since 1985.

1. Remove the adaptive pilot control screw from the exhaust manifold and mount exhaust tester 13 0 090 or equivalent with adapter 13 0 100 or equivalent into the exhaust manifold.
2. Connect the BMW service test unit or equivalent. Remove the anti-tamper lock.
3. Remove the air cleaner assembly and the air flow sensor.
4. Drill a hole in the anti-tamper lock with special tool 13 1 092 or equivalent.
5. Knock the tool with the anti-tamper lock out of the air flow sensor with suitable impact. Re-install the air flow sensor and air cleaner assembly.
6. Start the engine and let it run at idle to reach normal operating temperature. Pull off and plug the vacuum hose on the fuel pressure regulator.
7. The oxygen sensor must regulate the CO level back to nominal valve after a brief rise.
8. Tighten the air control screw in the air flow sensor completely with special tool 13 1 100 or equivalent for a richer mixture.
9. Run the engine at idle speed and the CO level will be regulated back to its nominal value.
10. Disconnect the oxygen sensor plug. The CO level will rise approximately 2.0% by volume. Also note the instantaneous actual value.
11. Stop the engine. Disconnect the negative battery so as to cancel the value stored in the memory of the DME control unit.
12. Start the engine. If the actual CO level value is considerably higher, the adaptive control pilot is working. Reconnect the vacuum hose.
13. Adjust the CO level to its nominal value (0.2–2.0%) with tool 13 1 100 or equivalent.
14. Connect the oxygen sensor plug and remove the exhaust tester. Remove the air cleaner and the air flow sensor (if necessary). Install a new anti-tamper lock in the air-flow sensor.
15. Reinstall the air flow sensor and air cleaner assembly. Remove all test equipment.

DME CHIP REPLACEMENT

◆ **See Figures 18 thru 23**

Inside the DME control unit is a removable computer chip which governs many of the function of the unit. In the event the control unit is found to be defective, this chip may well be the source of the problem.

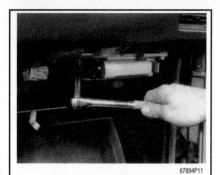

Fig. 18 Remove the DME control unit; it is mounted above the glove box on 3 Series models such as this

Fig. 19 Unplug the harness from the control unit

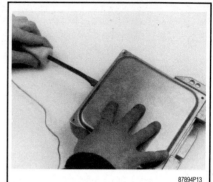

Fig. 20 Carefully pry off the control unit cover

Fig. 21 Unfasten the screws securing the circuit board in place

Fig. 22 Lift the circuit board up to access the DME chip

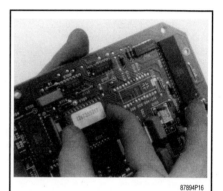

Fig. 23 Carefully lift out the DME chip

In recent years, many companies have offered replacement control unit chips which can be installed to improve engine performance and driveability. Although these chips are not original BMW parts, many work with excellent results and reliability.

➡️If you are replacing a DME chip with a non-BMW chip, make sure the new chip conforms to all state and federal emission regulations. Most chips available will clearly state on the package whether the product meets these government standards.

To replace a DME chip, proceed as follows:
1. Access the DME control unit. Depending on the model, this unit can be found above the glove box, or under the rear seat.
2. Disconnect the negative battery cable.
3. Remove the DME control unit from the vehicle.
4. Unplug the harness from the DME unit, and place on a clean, well lit surface.

✳️ WARNING

Before working on any electronic control unit, make sure your body is properly grounded to prevent the risk of any static electricity from your body damaging the control unit. Many electronic parts stores offer ground straps which attach to your wrist and neutralize any static electricity on your body.

5. With your body properly grounded, remove the screws from the DME control unit cover, and place aside.
6. Using a prytool with the end taped to protect the control unit, carefully pry off the cover.
7. Remove the screws from the back of the circuit board.
8. Lift the circuit board up to access the chip.
9. Locate the chip with a sticker on its top. Before attempting to remove the chip, make sure it is installed into holes and is not permanently installed with solder. In the event the chip is soldered in place, you have picked the wrong chip.
10. Once the correct chip has been located, carefully unplug the chip.

To install:
11. Install the chip in the same direction as the chip just removed. Do not attempt to force a chip into place. Make sure that each contact spider on the chip aligns with a hole in the circuit board.
12. Install the circuit board and secure with the screws.
13. Install the control unit cover making sure the seal is positioned correctly. Install the retaining screws.
14. Plug in the control unit and install it into the vehicle.
15. Connect the negative battery cable.

VACUUM DIAGRAMS

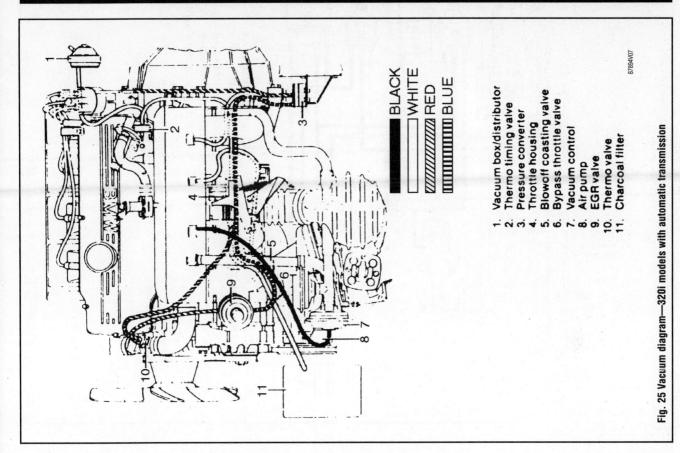

BLACK
WHITE
RED
BLUE

1. Vacuum box/distributor
2. Thermo timing valve
3. Pressure converter
4. Throttle housing
5. Blowoff coasting valve
6. Bypass throttle valve
7. Vacuum control
8. Air pump
9. EGR valve
10. Thermo valve
11. Charcoal filter

87894V07

Fig. 25 Vacuum diagram—320i models with automatic transmission

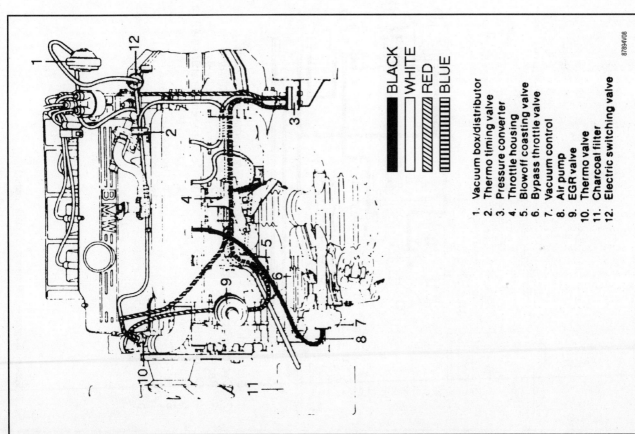

BLACK
WHITE
RED
BLUE

1. Vacuum box/distributor
2. Thermo timing valve
3. Pressure converter
4. Throttle housing
5. Blowoff coasting valve
6. Bypass throttle valve
7. Vacuum control
8. Air pump
9. EGR valve
10. Thermo valve
11. Charcoal filter
12. Electric switching valve

87894V08

Fig. 24 Vacuum diagram—320i models with manual transmission

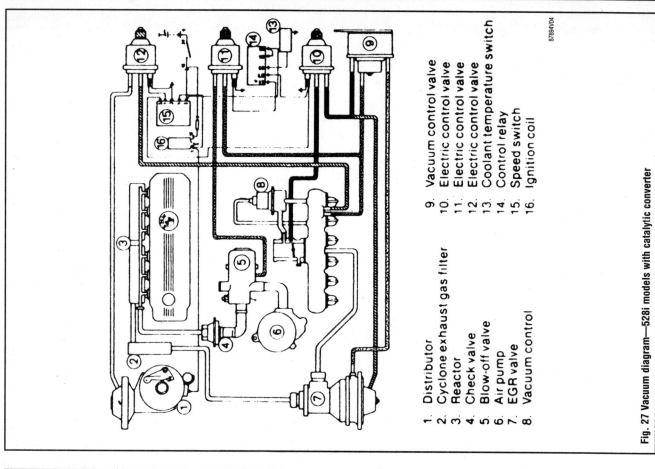

1. Distributor
2. Cyclone exhaust gas filter
3. Reactor
4. Check valve
5. Blow-off valve
6. Air pump
7. EGR valve
8. Vacuum control

9. Vacuum control valve
10. Electric control valve
11. Electric control valve
12. Electric control valve
13. Coolant temperature switch
14. Control relay
15. Speed switch
16. Ignition coil

Fig. 27 Vacuum diagram—528i models with catalytic converter

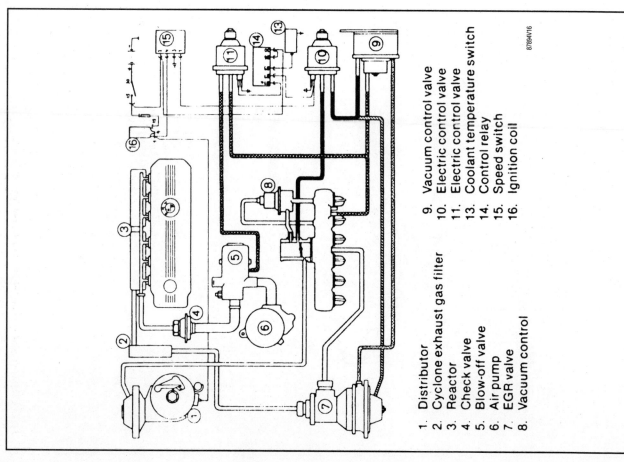

1. Distributor
2. Cyclone exhaust gas filter
3. Reactor
4. Check valve
5. Blow-off valve
6. Air pump
7. EGR valve
8. Vacuum control

9. Vacuum control valve
10. Electric control valve
11. Electric control valve
13. Coolant temperature switch
14. Control relay
15. Speed switch
16. Ignition coil

Fig. 26 Vacuum diagram—528i models (49 state version)

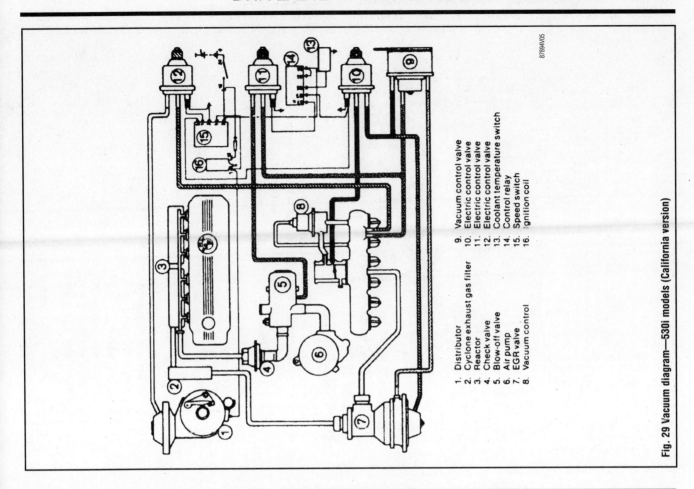

1. Distributor
2. Cyclone exhaust gas filter
3. Reactor
4. Check valve
5. Blow-off valve
6. Air pump
7. EGR valve
8. Vacuum control
9. Vacuum control valve
10. Electric control valve
11. Electric control valve
12. Electric control valve
13. Coolant temperature switch
14. Control relay
15. Speed switch
16. Ignition coil

Fig. 29 Vacuum diagram—530i models (California version)

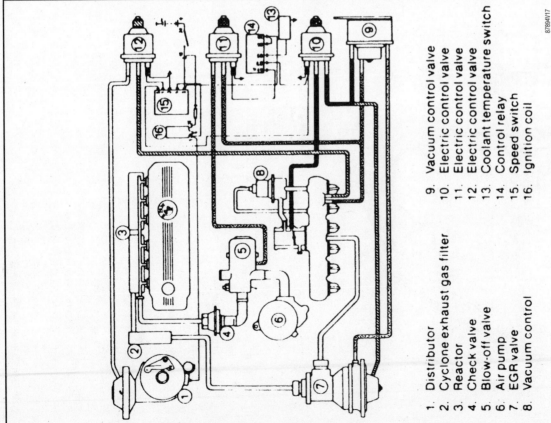

1. Distributor
2. Cyclone exhaust gas filter
3. Reactor
4. Check valve
5. Blow-off valve
6. Air pump
7. EGR valve
8. Vacuum control
9. Vacuum control valve
10. Electric control valve
11. Electric control valve
12. Electric control valve
13. Coolant temperature switch
14. Control relay
15. Speed switch
16. Ignition coil

Fig. 28 Vacuum diagram—530i models (49 state version)

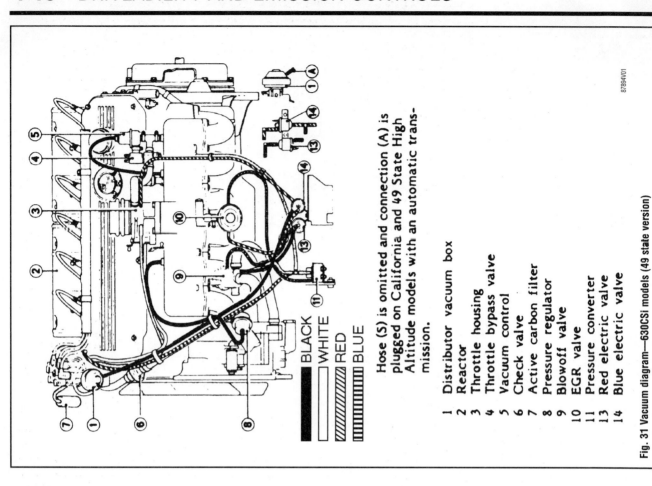

BLACK
WHITE
RED
BLUE

Hose (S) is omitted and connection (A) is plugged on California and 49 State High Altitude models with an automatic transmission.

1 Distributor vacuum box
2 Reactor
3 Throttle housing
4 Throttle bypass valve
5 Vacuum control
6 Check valve
7 Active carbon filter
8 Pressure regulator
9 Blowoff valve
10 EGR valve
11 Pressure converter
13 Red electric valve
14 Blue electric valve

Fig. 31 Vacuum diagram—630CSi models (49 state version)

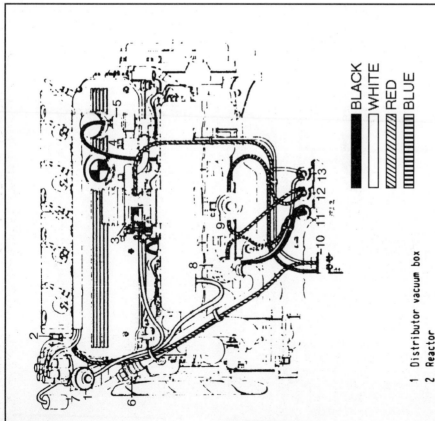

BLACK
WHITE
RED
BLUE

1 Distributor vacuum box
2 Reactor
3 Throttle housing
4 Auxiliary air valve
  (n/a to 1977 models)
5 Vacuum control
6 Check valve
7 Carbon filter
8 Booster blowoff valve
9 EGR valve
10 Pressure converter
11 Black electric switching valve
12 Red electric switching valve
13 White electric switching valve

Fig. 30 Vacuum diagram—630CSi models

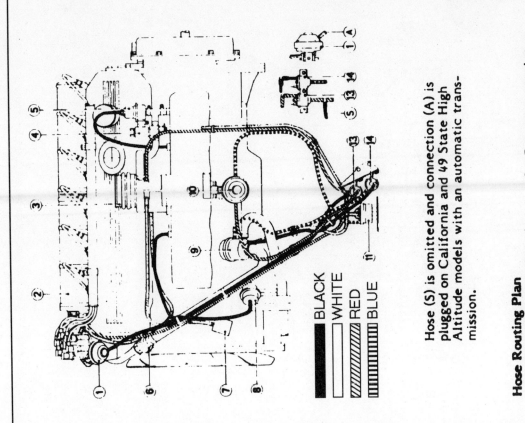

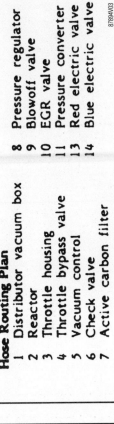

Hose (S) is omitted and connection (A) is plugged on California and 49 State High Altitude models with an automatic transmission.

Hose Routing Plan

1 Distributor vacuum box
2 Reactor
3 Throttle housing
4 Throttle bypass valve
5 Vacuum control
6 Check valve
7 Active carbon filter
8 Pressure regulator
9 Blowoff valve
10 EGR valve
11 Pressure converter
13 Red electric valve
14 Blue electric valve

Fig. 33 Vacuum diagram—733i models (49 state version)

BLACK
WHITE
RED
BLUE

1 Distributor vacuum box
2 Reactor
3 Throttle housing
4 Throttle bypass valve
5 Vacuum control
6 Check valve
7 Active carbon filter
8 Pressure regulator
9 Blowoff valve
10 EGR valve
11 Pressure converter
12 Black electric valve
13 Red electric valve
14 Blue electric valve

Fig. 32 Vacuum diagram—633CSi models (California version)

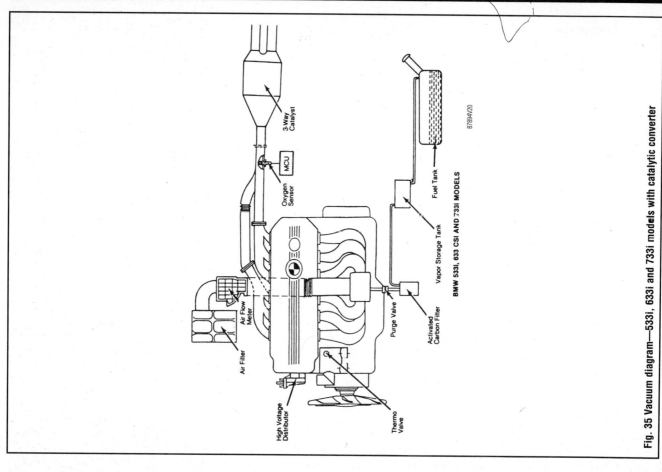

87894V20

Fig. 35 Vacuum diagram—533i, 633i and 733i models with catalytic converter

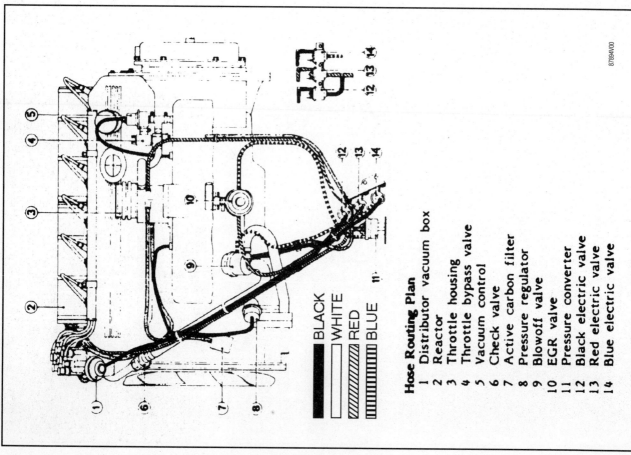

87894V00

Hose Routing Plan

1 Distributor vacuum box
2 Reactor
3 Throttle housing
4 Throttle bypass valve
5 Vacuum control
6 Check valve
7 Active carbon filter
8 Pressure regulator
9 Blowoff valve
10 EGR valve
11 Pressure converter
12 Black electric valve
13 Red electric valve
14 Blue electric valve

BLACK
WHITE
RED
BLUE

Fig. 34 Vacuum diagram—733i models (California version)

5

FUEL
SYSTEM

BASIC FUEL SYSTEM DIAGNOSIS

When there is a problem starting or driving a vehicle, two of the most important checks involve the ignition and the fuel systems. The questions most mechanics attempt to answer first, "is there spark?" and "is there fuel?" will often lead to solving most basic problems. For ignition system diagnosis and testing, please refer to the information on engine electrical components and ignition systems found earlier in this manual. If the ignition system checks out (there is spark), then you must determine if the fuel system is operating properly (is there fuel?).

CARBURETED FUEL SYSTEM

Mechanical Fuel Pump

▶ See Figures 1 and 2

TESTING

Insert a tee in the fuel pump discharge line where it enters the carburetor. Connect a gauge rated at about 10 psi (68 kPa) to the open end of the tee. Run the engine at 4,000 rpm. The pressure should be 3.0–3.5 psi (20–24.0 kPa).

REMOVAL & INSTALLATION

1. Remove the air cleaner. Disconnect and plug the 2 fuel lines.
2. Remove the 2 retaining nuts and pull the pump off the cylinder head. Pull the insulator block off and the pushrod out.
3. If there is any evidence of wear, check the length of the pushrod. It should be 3.4 inches (88mm) on 4-cylinder models and 4.7 inches (119mm) on 6-cylinder vehicles.
4. Install in reverse order. Do not use sealer on the insulator block, as this will change the effective length of the pushrod.

Carburetor

APPLICATIONS

The 1970–71 1600 and 2000 use a single barrel downdraft Solex 38 PDSI carburetor. This unit has a manual choke. The 1970–71 2002, (up to chassis no. 2 583 405) uses a Solex 40 PDSI, which also has a manual choke. The 1970–71 2002 with automatic transmission (up to chassis no. 2 532 752) uses a Solex 40PDSIT unit with a water heated automatic choke.

Later 2002 models use a Solex 32/32 DIDTA carburetor with the water heated choke, to which was added an electric heating element in 1974. Later models also incorporate a float bowl return valve to reduce vapor lock. The 2002Ti uses

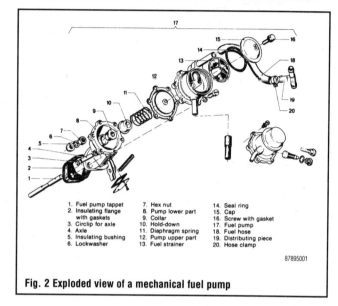

1. Fuel pump tappet
2. Insulating flange with gaskets
3. Circlip for axle
4. Axle
5. Insulating bushing
6. Lockwasher
7. Hex nut
8. Pump lower part
9. Collar
10. Hold-down
11. Diaphragm spring
12. Pump upper part
13. Fuel strainer
14. Seal ring
15. Cap
16. Screw with gasket
17. Fuel pump
18. Fuel hose
19. Distributing piece
20. Hose clamp

87895001

Fig. 2 Exploded view of a mechanical fuel pump

2 separate Solex 40 PHH carburetors, which have 2 progressively activated barrels each.

The 2500, 2800, Bavaria, 3000 and 3.0 use 2 Zenith 35/40 2 stage carburetors.

ADJUSTMENTS

Throttle Linkage

Throttle linkage adjustments are generally not necessary except that, if synchronization of the Zenith 35/40 units proves difficult, the adjustable link connecting the 2 throttle linkages should be adjusted to a center-to-center length of 1.5 inches (40mm).

Float Level

38 PDSI, 40 PDSI AND 40 PDSIT

1. Run the engine until it reaches normal operating temperature. Shut the engine off.
2. Disconnect the fuel feed line from the carburetor.
3. Remove the carburetor top cover and seal.
4. Using a depth gauge, the level of fuel in the bowl should be 0.7–0.8 inches (18–19mm).
5. Adjust, as necessary, by varying the number of or thickness of the seals underneath the float needle valve.

SOLEX 38 PDSI AND SOLEX 32/32 DIDTA

The float level cannot be adjusted without the carburetor completely disassembled. Therefore, this adjustment cannot be accomplished without a special sight glass and equipment for adjusting the amount of fuel in the bowl.

ZENITH 35/40

Although the float level is not adjustable, it does depend upon the condition of various parts of the carburetor, especially the gasket used under the float valve. This gasket must be 0.039 inches (1mm) thick.

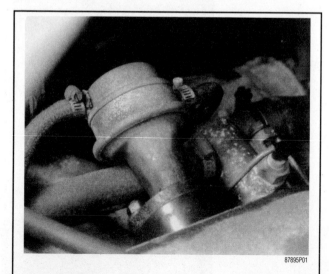

87895P01

Fig. 1 An example of a mechanical fuel pump—2002 model

Fast Idle

2002 MODELS WITH AUTOMATIC CHOKE

1. Start the engine and allow to reach normal operating temperature.
2. Operate the accelerator rod until the choke plate can be closed by hand. Then, close the choke plate until only 0.25 inches (6.5mm) clearance exists between the plate and the carburetor air horn. This will bring the stop lever into the fast idling speed position. Once this clearance is set, do not disturb the accelerator rod.
3. Using the adjusting nuts at the choke connector rod, adjust the fast idle speed to 2100 rpm. To increase engine speed, increase the rod length. To decrease engine speed, decrease rod length.

2500, 2800, BAVARIA, 3000 AND 3.0 MODELS

1. Make sure the engine is hot, the air cleaner is removed, the carburetors are synchronized, and that the idle speed is 900 rpm.
2. At the distributor there are 2 hoses going to the diaphragm, one advance, and one retard, remove the retard hose which is connected on the distributor side of the diaphragm.
3. Switch **OFF** the engine and disconnect the choke rod at the rear carburetor.
4. Using a drill bit with a 0.09 inch (2.4mm) diameter, insert it between the lower edge of the choke butterfly and the throttle bore. Open the throttle slightly then close the choke to touch the drill, and pin it against the throttle bore. This will set the fast idle mechanism on the second step. Then, release the choke.
5. Without touching the throttle linkage, start the engine. If the rpm is not 1,400, note the difference.
6. If the speed must be readjusted, stop the engine, open the throttle all the way, and adjust the screw on the choke housing inward to increase the idle or outward to decrease the idle. 1 complete turn equals about 300 rpm.
7. Repeat Steps 4–6 until idle speed is at 1,400 rpm.
8. Open the throttle to open the rear choke. Then repeat Steps 4–6 for the front carburetor.
9. Finally, repeat Step 4 for both front and rear chokes. Both chokes must be set to the proper position while the throttle is held open. Then, both chokes must be held there as the throttle is released. Remove the drill bits, release the chokes, and start the engine. RPM must be 1,800–2,000.

Automatic Choke and Unloader

2002 AND 2002A MODELS

1. Be sure the choke valve shaft will rotate freely in its bore and that the choke cap aligning notch is aligned with the lug on the choke valve housing.
2. Depress the accelerator to allow the choke valve to close under spring tension.

➡**The choke valve should close if the ambient temperature is below 68°F (20°C).**

3. If adjustment is needed, remove the choke cap with the water hoses attached.
4. Depress the choke rod (the vertical shaft inside choke housing) downward to its stop and check the choke valve clearance between the choke valve and the throttle bore. The gap should be 0.2–0.3 inches (6–7mm).
5. An adjusting screw and locknut is located under the choke housing and controls the height of the choke rod. Loosen the locknut and move the screw in or out to change the choke valve gap.
6. Reposition of the choke cover on the carburetor. Be sure the choke arm engages the coil spring loop in the choke cover. Align the notch on the cover with the lug on the choke housing.
7. Connect the heating coil wire terminal to the housing.
8. Adjust the fast idle speed to 2000–2200 rpm with the engine at normal operating temperature.
9. With the choke valve set at a gap of 6mm, adjust the choke connector rod nuts to set the fast idle. Shorten the rod to reduce the rpm.

2500, 2800, BAVARIA, 3000 AND 3.0 MODELS

1. Remove the choke cover, leaving the water hoses attached.
2. Open the throttle and close the choke butterfly.
3. Loosen the lockscrew on the pivot unit at the top of the choke rod. Make sure the adjusting screw inside the choke housing points to the high step of the actuating cam.

4. Raise and lower the rod until the gap between the lower end of the rod and the actuating cam is 0.06 inches (1.5mm). Then, tighten the lockscrew and press the clamping ring on the rod up against the pivot unit.
5. Then, push the rod upward and push the actuating cam against the rod.
6. Check the gap between the lower edge of the choke butterfly and the throttle bore. It should be 0.1 inches (3mm). If not, loosen the locknut and turn the adjusting screw on the choke unloader until the dimension is correct. Tighten the locknut and apply sealer.

Accelerator Pump

A special metering cup is used to measure accelerator pump stroke and performance. If this is not available, the pump stroke (and fuel delivery) can be adjusted as follows:

On the 2002 models adjust the position of the locknuts on the pump lever. On the 2500, 2800, Bavaria, 3000 and 3.0 Series adjust by bending the plunger lever (located under the float bowl cover) at the pivot point.

Make sure, before making adjustment, that idle mixture and ignition timing are correct, that the carburetor is clean, and that the plunger and check valves in the accelerator pump system are in good condition.

Idle Stop Solenoid

◆ **See Figure 3**

The idle stop solenoid prevents any tendency for the engine to run on after the ignition is switched off. The solenoid if non-adjustable, must be replaced if defective. To check operation, pull off the electrical connector when the engine is running. The solenoid is working properly if the engine shuts down. When the connector is replaced, a slight click should be heard. To replace the idle stop solenoid, remove the connector and unscrew the valve assembly from the carburetor. When installing the new solenoid valve, make sure there is a good seal at the taper.

✴✴ WARNING

Tightening torque for the solenoid is only 2 ft. lbs. (3 Nm).

Carburetor Dashpot

A dashpot is used to slow the carburetor throttle return while the vehicle engine is above 1800 rpm on carbureted engines. An electrically controlled set of relays and magnetic switches is used to direct engine speeds under a certain rpm.

Operate the engine at 2500 rpm and slowly decrease the speed to approximately 1800 rpm. The dashpot plunger should contact the throttle linkage at the 1700–1900 rpm mark (for 2002 models, 1500 rpm is the minimum). Adjust the

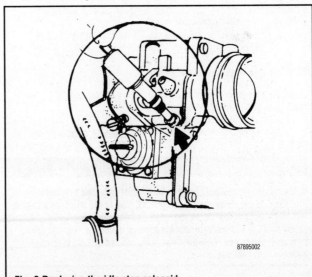

87895002

Fig. 3 Replacing the idle stop solenoid

dashpot plunger as necessary. If adjustment is needed, turn the screw on the dashpot until it contacts the linkage at the desired rpm.

The plunger must be free of the throttle linkage under 1700 rpm (for 2002 models, 1550 is the minimum) when the engine vacuum is directed through the magnetic valve to the dashpot.

If no vacuum is present at the dashpot hose under 1700 rpm, check the engine speed relay connector. Remove the terminal end from the magnetic valve and increase the engine speed to 2000 rpm. If voltage is present at the terminal, the magnetic valve to the dashpot is defective and should be replaced.

If no vacuum is present at the dashpot hose under 1700 rpm, check the engine speed relay connector. Remove the terminal end from the magnetic valve and increase the engine speed to 2000 rpm. If voltage is present at the terminal, the magnetic switch is defective and if no voltage is present, the speed sensitive relay must be replaced.

Compensation Speed Dashpot

1. Pull off vacuum hose.
2. Increase engine speed to approximately 2000 rpm, then slowly decrease.
3. At 1800 rpm, the dashpot plunger must touch the carburetor linkage.
4. Adjust if necessary by turning the dashpot after loosening the locknut.
5. Reconnect vacuum hose.

➡️**If the engine speed is lower than 1700 rpm, but the dashpot plunger does not free the carburetor linkage, check for vacuum to the dashpot. If vacuum is present in the signal line, the dashpot must be replaced.**

REMOVAL & INSTALLATION

1600, 2000 and 2002 Models With Manual Choke

1. Remove the air cleaner assembly, marking the vacuum lines, breather hoses, and air intake hose for reassembly.
2. Disconnect the fuel feed line at the carburetor and plug.
3. Loosen the clamp screw and clamp, and disconnect the choke cable.
4. Lever off the clamp spring connecting the accelerator rod to the carburetor and disconnect the throttle linkage.
5. Label and remove the vacuum line(s) from the carburetor.
6. Remove the carburetor attaching nuts, and lift the carburetor from the manifold. Remove the flange gaskets and carburetor spacer, taking note of their placement.

To install:

7. Install the carburetor to the manifold using new gaskets and installing the spacer.
8. Reconnect all fuel and vacuum lines. Install the air cleaner and breather hose. Connect thc throttle linkage.
9. Adjust the choke cable in the following manner:
   a. Push the choke knob on the dash into the bottom notch.
   b. Press the fast idle cam against its stop so that the outer choke cable projects 0.60 inches (15mm) in front of the cable clamp, and tighten the clamp screw in this position.
   c. Adjust the idle speed as needed. Tighten the attaching nuts to 7–10 ft. lbs. (9–13 Nm).

2002 Models With Automatic Choke

1. Remove the air cleaner assembly, marking the vacuum lines, breather hoses, and air intake hose for reassembly.
2. Disconnect the fuel feed line at the carburetor.
3. Disconnect the electrical cable for the thermostat valve. Drain the radiator of coolant.

✳✳ CAUTION

When draining coolant, keep in mind that cats and dogs are attracted to ethylene glycol antifreeze, and could drink any that is left in an uncovered container or in puddles on the ground. This will prove fatal in sufficient quantity. Always drain the coolant into a sealable container. Coolant should be reused unless it is contaminated or several years old.

4. Remove the retaining screws and lift the choke mechanism cover from the carburetor body.

5. Remove the safety clip from the ball socket at the throttle linkage connection to the carburetor. Press the throttle and down-shift rotary shaft downward and rearward and disconnect the throttle linkage.
6. Label and remove the vacuum line from the carburetor.
7. Remove the 2 carburetor attaching nuts, and lift off the carburetor from the manifold. Remove the flange gaskets and carburetor spacer, taking note of their placement.

To install:

8. Install the carburetor to the manifold using new gaskets and installing the spacer.
9. Reconnect all fuel and vacuum lines. Install the air cleaner and breather hose. Connect the throttle linkage.
10. Insert the automatic choke engaging arm in the eyelet for the bimetallic spring. The choke must be adjusted so that the notch on the choke cover and the projection on the choke housing align. Adjust the idle speed. Tighten the attaching nuts to 7–10 ft. lbs. (9–13 Nm).

2002Ti Models

1. Remove the air cleaner, labeling all hoses.
2. Disconnect the choke cable at the carburetor end and remove the cable at the carburetor end and remove the cable from the bracket.
3. Loosen the dipstick retainer clip.
4. Pull off fuel hoses.
5. Remove the throttle tensioning spring. Remove the 2 carburetor mounting nuts which fasten the mounting bracket for the rotating shaft, and pull the bracket off the manifold studs. Disconnect the rod from the rotating shaft.
6. Remove the remaining mounting nuts and remove the carburetors. Remove all gaskets.

To install:

7. To install, reverse the removal procedure, bearing the following points in mind:
   a. Before installing the carburetor on the right side, position the prong on the choke butterfly lever so it engages with the hole in the linkage of the left hand carburetor by rotating the linkage on the left hand carburetor as necessary.
   b. Make sure the torsion spring on the carburetor synchronizing portion of the throttle mechanism is in the proper position.
   c. Push the choke knob in to the first notch. Open the choke mechanism on the carburetors all the way. Then, clamp the choke cable snugly in place, making sure the cable sheath does not protrude more than 0.6 inches (15mm).

2500, 2800, Bavaria, 3000 and 3.0 Models

1. Drain the radiator of coolant, and remove the air cleaner.

✳✳ CAUTION

When draining coolant, keep in mind that cats and dogs are attracted to ethylene glycol antifreeze, and could drink any that is left in an uncovered container or in puddles on the ground. This will prove fatal in sufficient quantity. Always drain the coolant into a sealable container. Coolant should be reused unless it is contaminated or several years old.

2. Disconnect fuel, vacuum, and water lines.
3. Disconnect and remove the choke cables. Disconnect the fuel return hose at the carburetor, on cars so equipped.
4. Disconnect throttle rod at the carburetor. Remove the carburetor mounting nuts from the studs, and remove the carburetor.

To install:

5. Install in reverse order, noting that the flange gasket must be in position so the smaller opening is situated toward the cylinder head, and the coated side faces down. Synchronize the carburetors and bleed the cooling system when filling it.

OVERHAUL

Carburetor repair kits are recommended for each overhaul. Kits contain a complete set of gaskets and new parts to replace those that generally deteriorate most rapidly. Not substituting all of the new parts supplied in the kits can result in poor performance later.

Zenith/Solex carburetor repair kits are of three basic types-repair: rebuild, and gasket. The following summarizes the parts in each type:

REPAIR KITS:
- All jets and gaskets
- All diaphragms
- Float needle valve
- Volume control screw
- Spring for pump diaphragm
- Spring for pump diaphragm
- Pump ball valve
- Main jet carrier
- Float
- Complete intermediate rod
- Intermediate pump lever
- Complete injector tube
- Some cover hold-down screws and washers

REBUILD KITS:
- All gaskets
- Float needle
- Volume control screw
- All diaphragms
- Spring

GASKET KITS:
- All needed gaskets

Carburetor overhaul should be performed only in a clean, dust-free area. Disassemble the carburetor carefully keeping look-alike parts separated to pre-vent accidental interchange during assembly. Note all jet sizes. When reassembling, make sure all screws and jets are tight in their seats. Tighten all screws gradually, in rotation. Do not tighten needle valves into seats. Uneven jetting will result. Use a new flange gasket.

Wash carburetor parts, except diaphragm and electric choke units, in a carburetor cleaner, rinse in solvent, and blow dry with compressed air.

Carburetors have numerous small passages that can be fouled by carbon and gummy deposits. Soak metal parts in carburetor solvent until thoroughly clean. The solvent will weaken or destroy cork, plastic, and leather components. These parts should be wiped with a clean, lint-free cloth. Clean all fuel channels in float bowl and cover. Clean jets and valves separately to avoid accidental interchange. Never use wire or sharp objects to clean jets and passages as this will seriously alter their calibration.

Check throttle valve shafts for wear or scoring that may allow air leakage affecting starting and idling. Inspect float spindle and other moving parts for wear. Replace if worn. Replace float if fuel has leaked into it.

Accelerator pump check valves should pass air one way but not the other. Test for proper seating by blowing and sucking on valve and replace if necessary. Wash valve again to remove breath moisture. Check bowl cover with with straight edge for warped surfaces. Closely inspect valves and seats valves and seats for wear and damage.

Rebuild kits contain complete, step by step disassembly and assembly instructions, for each specific type of carburetor, so they are not included here.

KUGELFISCHER FUEL INJECTION SYSTEM

The Kugelfischer injection system consists of mechanical type fuel injectors, an engine driven injection pump, cold start valve and electrically controlled switches and sensors. This system was used on 2002Tii models.

Fuel Pressure

TESTING

✳ CAUTION

The following procedure will produce fuel vapors. Make sure there is proper ventilation and take the appropriate fire safety precautions, otherwise personal injury may occur.

Connect a pressure gauge to the union at the front of the injection pump. Idle the engine. The pressure should be 28.5 psi (194 kPa). If pressure is low, check the pump ground. If that is satisfactory and pressure is still low, replace the pump.

Air Container and Throttle Valve Stub Assembly

REMOVAL & INSTALLATION

1. Label and disconnect all hoses from the air cleaner. Remove the air cleaner.
2. Disconnect the fuel hose and cable from the start of the throttle valve stub. Disconnect the vacuum hose from the air container.
3. Loosen all hose clamps and remove the 4 induction pipes.
4. Unhook the return spring from the throttle valve stub linkage. Disconnect the retaining screw for the linkage bracket.
5. Taking care to support the pipe connection while loosening, disconnect the injection pipe at No. 1 cylinder. Remove the injection valve.
6. Remove the 2 retaining bolts for the throttle valve stub support bracket. Disconnect the vacuum hose from the valve stub and the auxiliary air hose from the air container.
7. Taking care to support the pipe connection while loosening, disconnect the injection pipe from No. 4 cylinder.
8. Remove the 6 nuts retaining the air container to the cylinder head and lift off the air container and throttle valve stub assembly.

To install:

9. Install new gaskets at the cylinder head flange and new cord rings at the induction pipes, if necessary.

10. Install the air container to the cylinder head and install the 6 nuts that retain it.
11. Install the valve stub support bracket and retaining bolts.
12. Install the No. 1 injection pipe and connect all 4 induction pipes. Connect the fuel lines and vacuum hose. Reconnect the cable to valve stub.
13. Install the air cleaner and connect all hoses.
14. Check the tightness of the induction pipes by spraying water at the pipe connections. If there is an air leak, the engine will idle unevenly.

Warm-up Sensor

ADJUSTMENT

➡ **The sensor adjustment must be made before the engine is warm.**

1. Remove the air filter housing.
2. Press out the air regulator cone with a screwdriver until special tool 6073 or the equivalent can be inserted into the groove of the air regulator cone.
3. A distance of 0.10–0.11 inches (2.5–3.0mm) should exist between the grub screw and the stop screw. Adjustments can be made at the plate nut.
4. After the engine is at normal operating temperature, the air regulator valve cone must project 0.3–0.4 inches (9–10mm). The plate washer must project above the lever by 0.15 inches (4mm) and the grub screw must be in full contact with the stop screw.
5. If these specifications are not obtained, the warm up sensor must be replaced.

REMOVAL & INSTALLATION

1. Drain the coolant and remove the air filter.

✳ CAUTION

When draining coolant, keep in mind that cats and dogs are attracted to ethylene glycol antifreeze, and could drink any that is left in an uncovered container or in puddles on the ground. This will prove fatal in sufficient quantity. Always drain the coolant into a sealable container. Coolant should be reused unless it is contaminated or several years old.

2. Disconnect the coolant hoses and the auxiliary air hose.

3. Disconnect the return spring and remove the warm-up sensor while disconnecting the accelerator linkage.

4. After installation, adjust the sensor as previously outlined and adjust the idle speed.

Cold Start Valve

TESTING

1. Remove the start valve from the throttle valve section.
2. Turn the ignition switch to **ON** to obtain fuel pressure from the pump, but do not start the engine.
3. Connect a positive current jumper wire to the **SV** connection of the time switch.
4. If fuel is ejected from the start valve, the valve and the feed pipe are considered to be good.

➡**The valve must not drip fuel with the current OFF.**

REMOVAL & INSTALLATION

1. Remove the electrical connector and the fuel line to the valve.
2. Remove the retaining bolts and pull the valve assembly from the air collector.
3. Replace the rubber sealing ring during installation.

Thermo-Time Switch

TESTING

1. Remove the wire terminal from the thermo-time switch.
2. Connect a test lamp to a positive terminal and the **W** terminal of the thermo-time switch.
3. The lamp should light at coolant temperature below 95°F (35°C).
4. Leave the test lamp attached to the **W** terminal and connect a positive jumper wire to terminal **G**.
5. The internal bi-metal control should open after a short time and the light should then go out. If not, replace the thermo-time switch.

Time Switch

TESTING

1. Remove the time switch from the firewall.
2. Connect a test lamp between ground and the **SV** terminal of the time switch.
3. Remove the No. 4 wire from the ignition coil and actuate the starter. The test lamp should go out after a short time.
4. The injection time period of start valve is as follows:
   a. At 4°F (-15°C)—9–15 seconds
   b. At 32°F (0°C)—4–10 seconds
   c. At 95°F (35°C)—1 second
5. Remove the terminal plug from the thermo-time switch. Actuate the starter; the light should go on for one second and then go out.
6. Connect a test lamp between the **TH** terminal and ground. The test lamp must light up as long as the starter is actuated.

Injection Pump

REMOVAL & INSTALLATION

1. Drain the cooling system.

✳✳ CAUTION

When draining coolant, keep in mind that cats and dogs are attracted to ethylene glycol antifreeze, and could drink any that is left in an uncovered container or in puddles on the ground. This will prove fatal in sufficient quantity. Always drain the coolant into a sealable container. Coolant should be reused unless it is contaminated or several years old.

2. Label and disconnect all hoses from the air cleaner. Remove the air cleaner.
3. Disconnect the 4 injection lines and fitting rings at the pump, noting their placement for installation. Plug the pressure valve with dust caps.
4. Disconnect the fuel return hose, oil feed hose, water inflow hose and the oil dipstick support bracket from the pump.
5. Disconnect the coolant return hose, oil return hose and the hose for the auxiliary air from the warm-up runner. Loosen the screw.
6. Disconnect the connecting link from the pump lever.
7. Remove the 4 retaining bolts for the injection pump drive belt dust cover and remove the cover.
8. Rotate the engine until the No. 1 cylinder is at Top Dead Center (TDC). At this point, the notch in the drive belt pulley is aligned with the projection on the lower section of the drive belt dust cover, and the distributor rotor is pointing to the spark plug wire connection for the No. 1 cylinder with the cap removed. Also, the notch in the cogged belt pulley is aligned with the cast-in projection on the pump housing. With the engine at TDC, remove the pump drive pulley retaining nut.
9. Using a puller, remove the pump drive pulley, taking care not to misplace the woodruff key. Remove the cogged belt.
10. Remove the 2 bolts retaining the injection pump to the timing case cover. The, pull out the pump to the rear so that the intermediate shaft may be lifted out at the warm-up sensor housing. Lift out the injection pump.
To install:
11. Install the injection pump to the timing case cover. Using a pulley puller/installer, install the pump drive pulley and install the pump drive pulley retaining nut.
12. Using the procedure outlined below, install the cogged belt. Install the belt cover. Connect the connecting link to the pump lever.
13. Connect the coolant return hose, oil return hose and the hose for the auxiliary air to the warm-up runner.
14. Connect the fuel return hose, oil feed hose, water inflow hose and the oil dipstick support to the pump bracket.
15. Reconnect the injection lines at their fittings at the pump. Install the air cleaner and reconnect all hoses.

Cogged Belt

REMOVAL & INSTALLATION

1. Remove the front air filter hood and the upper dust cover on the pump assembly.
2. Rotate the engine so that No. 1 piston is at TDC on its compression stroke. The crankshaft pulley must point to the mark on the dust cap and the pump pulley must align with the casting mark on the pump body.
3. Loosen the alternator and remove the belt.
4. Mark the V-pulley on the crankshaft and remove the retaining bolts from the pulley.
5. Remove the pulley and do not turn the engine, due to the pulley fitting at 180°.
6. Loosen the upper dust cover bolt, remove all other retaining bolts for the lower dust cover and remove the cogged belt by pulling the dust cover to the front and pulling the cogged belt out between the hub and the front dust cover.
7. Be sure of the pulley alignment for both the crankshaft and the injection pump and reverse the removal procedure to install the cogged belt.

Injection Valve

REMOVAL & INSTALLATION

1. Disconnect the feed line to the injector with fitting wrenches to avoid damage to the threaded areas.
2. Unscrew the injector valve from the induction sleeve.
To install:
3. Insert injector valve into sleeve and screw into place using a new sealing ring.

4. Connect the fuel feed line to the valve using a new sealing ring. Tighten fitting using a flare-end or fitting wrench.

SYNCHRONIZING THE VALVE AND INJECTION PUMP

1. Make sure that the connecting rod (linkage) between the pump and the throttle valve is adjusted to 3.3 inches (85mm). The length of the connecting rod is measured from the centers of the ball sockets of the connecting rod.

2. Remove the 2 screws for the throttle valve cover and lift off the cover. Rotate the idling speed screw until it is no linger in contact with the eccentric. Loosen the 2 clamping screws.

3. Using a 4 inch (100mm) long piece of metal rod (approximately 0.15 inches (4mm) thick in diameter), bent at a 90° angle at the end. Insert the rod

through the upper slotted hole of the regulating lever so that the rod seats in the bore of the injection pump housing.

4. Insert a 0.15 inch (4mm) diameter drift pin into the bore of the throttle valve section Then, with the regulating lever set in position with the metal rod and the throttle valve eccentric pressed against the drift pin, tighten the 2 clamping screws.

5. Remove the drift pin and metal rod and check the synchronization. The synchronization is correct when the eccentric partially overlaps the bore in the throttle valve section.

6. Finally, adjust the idle speed using the screw to approximately 900 rpm.

7. Check the synchronization at full load setting. Disconnect the induction pipe from the No. 1 cylinder. Using the metal rod, insert the rod through the lowest slotted hole of the regulator lever so that the rod seats in the bore of the injection pump housing. Then, adjust the stop screw so that the pump lever is barely contacted.

BOSCH K-JETRONIC (CIS) FUEL INJECTION

♦ **See Figures 4 and 5**

The Bosch K-Jetronic fuel injection system is a continuous fuel injection system which consists of mechanical type fuel injectors, a fuel distributor unit, operated by a sensor plate, and a control valve. Electrical and vacuum operated regulators and switches complete the assembly. An electrical control box is not used.

Relieving Fuel System Pressure

✳✳ CAUTION

Anytime the fuel system is serviced, the generation of spilled fuel and fuel vapor expose the technician to possibility of flash fire or explosion. All work should be performed in a well ventilated area with easy access to a fire extinguisher. All spilled fuel must be removed immediately. Wear protective eyewear. Failure to observe these precautions may result in personal injury.

To relieve the pressure in the system, first find the fuel pump relay plug, located on the cowl, as specified in the applicable Electric Fuel Pump Pressure Checking procedure. Unplug the relay, leaving it in a safe position where the connections cannot ground. If necessary, tape the plug in place or tape over the connector prongs with electrical tape. Then, start the engine and operate it until it stalls. Crank the engine for 10 seconds after it stalls to remove any residual pressure.

Electric Fuel Pump

REMOVAL & INSTALLATION

On all electric pump (fuel injection) equipped cars, the fuel pump is mounted together with the expansion tank for the evaporative emissions control system. The pumps which are mounted together with the expansion tank are located under the rear of the car.

1. To replace the pump, first disconnect the battery and then the electrical connector(s) at the pump.

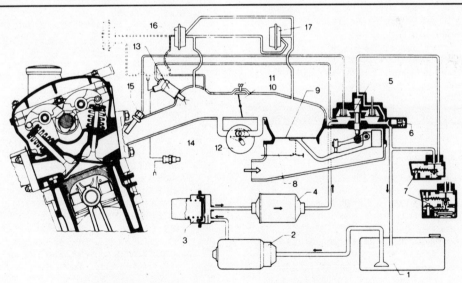

1. Fuel tank with pre-fuel pump
2. Fuel delivery pump
3. Fuel accumulator
4. Fuel filter
5. Fuel distributor
6. System pressure regulator and topping point valve
7. Warming-up regulator
8. Airflow meter
9. Sensor plate
10. Throttle butterfly
11. Idle adjustment screw
12. Aux. air device
13. Electric starting valve
14. Thermo-time switch
15. Injectors
16. Vacuum limiter
17. Start air valve

87895005

Fig. 4 Schematic of Bosch® K-Jetronic system

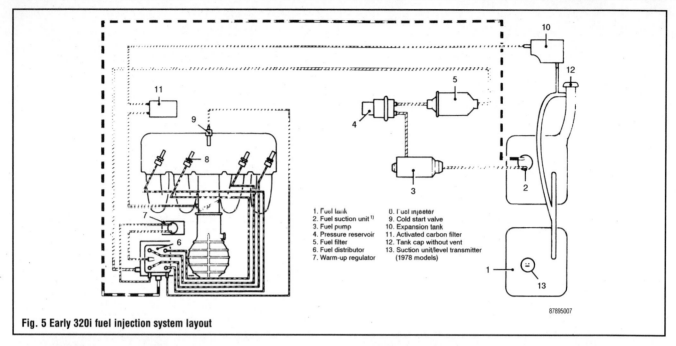

Fig. 5 Early 320i fuel injection system layout

1. Fuel tank
2. Fuel suction unit [1]
3. Fuel pump
4. Pressure reservoir
5. Fuel filter
6. Fuel distributor
7. Warm-up regulator
8. Fuel injector
9. Cold start valve
10. Expansion tank
11. Activated carbon filter
12. Tank cap without vent
13. Suction unit/level transmitter (1978 models)

2. Disconnect both hoses, one at the pump, and one at the expansion tank and plug the openings.

3. Remove the attaching nuts for the mounting bracket. Loosen the clamp bolt, and separate the pump from the pump/expansion tank mounting bracket.

To install:

4. Position the pump the mounting bracket and tighten the clamp bolt.

5. Connect both hoses and the electrical connector at the pump. Connect the negative battery cable and run the engine. Check for fuel leaks.

Basic Throttle Setting

1. Disconnect the accelerator cable and loosen the throttle stop screw.

2. Adjust the distance between the throttle lever and the stop screw to 0.039–0.06 inches (1.0–1.5mm) clearance.

3. Loosen the throttle lever clamping screw and position the throttle valve in the housing to zero play. Tighten the clamping screw.

4. Tighten the throttle stop screw one complete turn and lock it in place.

5. Adjust the accelerator cable to the throttle lever and attach.

Auxiliary Air Regulator

TESTING

1. Disconnect the electrical terminal plug and the 2 air hoses at the auxiliary air regulator.

2. Voltage must be present at the terminal plug with the ignition switch **ON**.

3. Check the air bore of the regulator. With the engine temperature approximately 68°F (20°C), the bore should be half open.

4. Connect the terminal plug and the 2 air hoses tot he auxiliary air regulator.

5. Start the engine and the auxiliary air regulator bore should close within 5 minutes of engine operation by the cut-off valve.

REMOVAL & INSTALLATION

1. Remove the hoses attached to the regulator.

2. Disconnect the electrical harness attached.

3. Remove the 2 Allen bolts securing the regulator assembly to the intake manifold.

To install:

4. Position the regulator on the manifold and secure with the Allen bolts.

5. Connect the electric harness and hoses.

Mixture Control Unit and Sensor Plate

REMOVAL & INSTALLATION

1. Disconnect the large intake pipe (made of rubber) from the unit by loosening the clamp(s) and pulling it off.

2. Loosen the 3 screws in the top of the fuel distributor. Open the clips holding the fuel line to the control unit, and remove the clamp linking the 4 fuel lines together.

3. Lift the distributor off the control unit, using tape to hold the piston up inside the unit, move it aside.

4. Disconnect the electrical plug at the air horn, and the small vacuum hose and large air line connected to the vacuum regulator, mounted near the rear of the mixture control unit.

5. Loosen the 2 mounting nuts located on the wheel well side of the unit and lift it out.

6. Remove the bolts in the flange holding the upper and lower sections of the unit together. Then remove the 6 bolts (3 located inside the lower housing) which retain the air cleaner housing to the mixture control unit.

To install:

7. Replace the mixture control unit lower and upper housings together with an entire new unit. The new unit will have to be split (top and bottom sections separate at the flange). This will permit the air cleaner bolts to be attached from inside. Use a new gasket, and reassemble the upper and lower sections of the new mixture control unit after the air cleaner housing is attached; then, reverse the remaining procedures to install it, using a new seal under the fuel distributor.

ADJUSTMENT

▶ **See Figure 6**

➡**49 state and California control units are not interchangeable.**

1. Remove the air intake cowl at the mixture control unit and throttle housing.

2. Turn the ignition **ON** for approximately 5 seconds, and during this time, slowly raise the sensor plate with a magnet. Turn the ignition switch **OFF**.

➡The amount of resistance should be constant when raising the sensor and no resistance should be felt when pushing the sensor plate down quickly.

3. The sensor plate should be flush to 0.02 inches (0.5mm) below the beginning oft he venturi taper. If adjustment is necessary, remove the mixture control from the intermediate housing and bend the spring accordingly. Center the sensor plate in the bore by loosening the center plate screw. Tighten when aligned.

➡With the sensor plate too high, the engine will run on and with the sensor plate too low, poor cold and warm engine start-up will result.

4. If the sensor plate movement is erratic, the control piston can be sticking. Remove the fuel distributor and inspect the control piston for damage and replace as necessary.

⁂ WARNING

Do not drop the control valve.

SYSTEM PRESSURE TESTING

Install a shut-off valve and an oil pressure gauge between the control pressure line and the fuel distributor, with the pressure gauge next to the fuel distributor.

Cold Engine Pressure Test

1. Disconnect the terminal plug at the mixture control unit to avoid excessive heat.
2. Open the valve for oil flow and turn **ON** the ignition switch to operate the fuel pump, but do not start the engine.
3. Control pressures is dependent upon the engine coolant temperature. At a temperature of 50°F (10°C), oil pressure should be 10–11 psi (68–75 kPa) and at 77°F (25°C), oil pressure should be 22.0 psi (150 kPa). At coolant temperature of 104°F (40°C), the pressure should be over 29.4 psi (200 kPa).

➡If the oil pressure is too low, the warm-up regulator may be defective. If the oil pressure is too high, the fuel return flow may be insufficient or the warm-up regulator may be defective.

4. When complete, turn the ignition **OFF**.

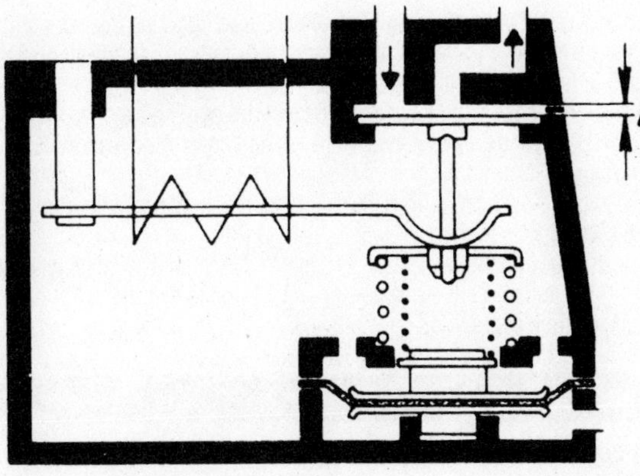

87895016

Fig. 6 Cross-sectional view of valve and opening. Dimension "A" represents the opening

Warm Engine Control Pressure

1. Open the shut-off valve for oil flow. Disconnect the mixture control terminal plug and turn the ignition **ON** to start the fuel pump. Do not start the engine.
2. The control pressure should be 48–54 psi (326–367 kPa) after 3 minutes, with the engine coolant at normal operating temperature. If the control pressure does not rise, check the wire plug terminal for current at the warm-up regulator. If current is present, the heating coil may be defective and would necessitate the replacement of the warm-up regulator.

Testing With Engine Running

1. Connect the wire plugs to the auxiliary air regulator and to the mixture control unit. Install the air intake cowl.
2. With the engine running at idle speed and at normal operating temperature, the control pressure should be 48–54 psi (326–367 kPa).

Cold or Warm Engine System Pressure

1. Close the pressure shut-off valve with the engine stopped and disconnect the mixture control unit terminal plug.
2. Turn the ignition **ON**, but do not start the engine.
3. The speed control pressure should be 64–74 psi (435–503 kPa).
4. Turn the ignition **OFF** and if the pressure is not within specifications, one of the following defects may be the cause:
   a. Leakage at the fuel lines or connections.
   b. Fuel filter clogged.
   c. Engine overruns.
   d. Defective fuel pump.
   e. Pressure adjustment incorrect.
5. If the pressure is too high:
   a. Fuel return flow is restricted.
   b. Incorrect pressure regulator setting.
   c. Control piston stuck.

Shims may be used to change the pressure. Shim thickness changes will vary the pressure as follows:
- 0.01mm–0.85 psi (6 kPa)
- 0.50mm–4.3 psi (29.2 kPa)

6. The transfer valve of pressure regulator must open at 50–57 psi (340–388 kPa).

Cut-off Pressure Testing

➡This is a good test for checking if there is any system leaking.

1. Open the pressure shut-off valve and turn the ignition **ON**.
2. Disconnect the wire plug at the mixture control unit and then reconnect the plug. Turn the ignition **OFF**.
3. Cut-off pressure must not drop below 24 psi (163 kPa) after several minutes.
4. If the pressure drops too early, one of the following may be leaking.
   a. Pressure regulator O-ring.
   b. Warm-up regulator or supply line.
   c. Fuel pump check valve.
   d. Pressure reservoir.
5. Remove the pressure gauge and shut-off valve and reconnect the pressure line.

Vacuum Regulator

TESTING

The coasting vacuum regulator must be open to supply air behind the throttle valve, through the by-pass bore, when the vehicle is coasting.

1. Disconnect the vacuum hose and plug the end.
2. Increase the engine speed to 3000 rpm and release the throttle. The engine speed should drop quickly.

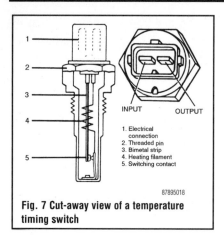

Fig. 7 Cut-away view of a temperature timing switch

1. Electrical connection
2. Threaded pin
3. Bimetal strip
4. Heating filament
5. Switching contact

87895018

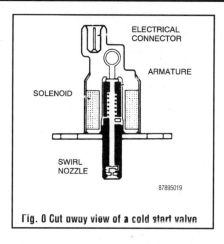

Fig. 0 Cut-away view of a cold start valve

87895019

Fig. 9 When testing a cold start valve, place the valve in a container to test whether fuel is being ejected

87895020

3. Connect the vacuum hose to the regulator valve and again increase the engine speed.

4. Release the throttle. The engine speed should drop slowly if the regulator is functioning properly.

Temperature Timing Switch

▶ See Figure 7

The purpose of the timing switch is to control the cold start valve during the initial start-up of the engine. The function temperature range of this switch is between -4°F (-20°C), where it turns **ON**, and 95°F (35°C), where it turns **OFF**.

TESTING

1. Disconnect the terminal plug from the switch.
2. Connect a test lamp from the positive battery terminal to the **W** post on the temperature timing switch.
3. The test lamp should be on at coolant temperatures below 95°F (35°C) and go out above temperatures of 95°F (35°C).

REMOVAL & INSTALLATION

1. Disconnect the wire harness attached to the switch.
2. Unscrew the switch. Some coolant will spill out, so place a container under the engine to catch any coolant.
To install:
3. Screw the switch in until the crunch washer is squeezed.
4. Connect the harness.

Cold Start Valve

▶ See Figure 8

The purpose of the cold start valve is to inject added fuel into the induction system as dictated by the temperature timing switch.

TESTING

▶ See Figure 9

Remove the colt start valve from the induction header. Connect the relay terminal C87 to a positive battery connector. The cold start valve should eject fuel. If not, it should be replaced.

✳ CAUTION

When testing the cold start valve, eject the fuel into a safe container as fuel is extremely hazardous.

Fig. 10 Cold start valve attached to the intake manifold of a 3 Series BMW

87895P17

REMOVAL & INSTALLATION

▶ See Figure 10

1. Remove the nuts attaching the fuel lines leading to the injectors to the top of the distributor (1 through 4). Unscrew the union nut and disconnect the line leading to the warm-up regulator.

2. Disconnect the large low pressure fuel lines coming from the fuel filter going back to the tank, by removing the attaching bolts. Also disconnect the 2 high pressure lines from the side of the unit in a similar manner.

3. Remove the 3 screws from the unit. Then, lift the unit off the top of the mixture control.

4. Install in reverse order. Clean the control piston in a suitable solvent and replace it, if it is damaged. Use a new gasket where the distributor fits onto the top of the mixture control unit.

Injection Valves

▶ See Figure 11

The injection valves must open at a minimum fuel pressure of 47 psi (320 kPa).

TESTING

1. Connect a pressure valve and shut-off valve in the pressure line to the fuel distributor, with the pressure gauge on the fuel distributor side of the shut-off valve.

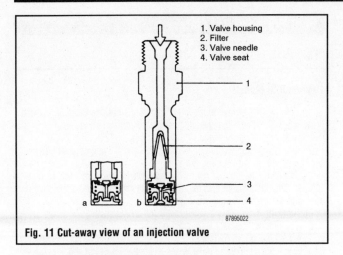

1. Valve housing
2. Filter
3. Valve needle
4. Valve seat

87895022

Fig. 11 Cut-away view of an injection valve

2. Open the shut-off valve, remove the injectors from the intake manifold and turn the ignition switch **ON**.

3. Disconnect the terminal plug from the mixture control unit.

4. Lift the sensor plate for a maximum of 4 seconds.

5. The pressure should not drop more than 4 psi (27 kPa). If the pressure drops more than the specifications, the fuel filter is clogged, fuel pump rate is inadequate or the fuel tank is empty.

REMOVAL & INSTALLATION

1. Remove the rubber intake hose leading from the mixture control unit to the throttle unit. Remove the 4 retaining nuts for each, and then remove No. 2 and No. 3 intake pipes.

2. The injector valves incorporate union nuts and flatted section on each valve to permit the lines to be attached to the valves. However, the injection lines need not be disconnected to remove the valves, which are simply pressed into the intake ports.

3. To remove each valve, simply pass a small prytool downward between the intake header and the cam cover, insert the blade into the groove between the fuel line nut and flatted portion of the injection valve, and pry out. After the valve is out of the port, hold the flatted section of the valve with a wrench, use another wrench to unscrew the union nut, and disconnect the fuel line.

To install:

4. Press the white insulating bushing back into the intake port, if it came out with the valve. Then, press the rubber seal into the grove. Finally, snugly press in the injection valve. Reinstall the intake pipes, using new gaskets.

INJECTION VALVE COMPARISON

If the compression and air induction systems are normal, but the engine is operating erratically, the injector valves should be tested with the use of a special tool (13 5 030) or equivalent.

Testing

1. The tool consists of scaled measuring tubes. Insert each injector valve into one of the tubes and secure. Disconnect the wire terminal plug from the mixture control valve, turn the ignition switch **ON**. Lift the sensor plate so that the injectors will fill the tubes with fuel.

2. Empty the tubes and again fill the tubes with fuel until the 15cc mark is reached on one tube. Compare the difference between the tubes for the fuel levels. The difference should not be over 15%.

3. If the fuel level difference is over 15% between tubes, exchange a good injector valve with a questionable one and repeat the test.

4. If the questionable injector valve flow rate remains the same, the valve is defective and must be replaced. If the injector valve flow rate is normal, the fuel distributor unit is defective and must be replaced.

5. Also check the spray pattern of each injector. Refer to the injector spray pattern chart, and compare to the actual spray pattern of the injector.

BOSCH L-JETRONIC AND MOTRONIC FUEL INJECTION SYSTEMS

♦ **See Figures 12 and 13**

The Bosch L-Jetronic fuel injection system is electronically controlled to regulate the fuel supply in relation to the air flow. An air flow meter, located in the air intake chamber, converts angular movement of an air baffle plate into a voltage signal, which is sent to the control unit.

As the engine begins its revolution, twin contacts, located 180° apart in the base of the distributor, trigger current impulses to the control unit at one impulse per crankshaft rotation.

After computation of the signals, a command signal is sent from the control unit to the electromagnetic injector valve, which are wired in a parallel circuit, causing them to open simultaneously. To obtain smooth combustion, half the total fuel volume necessary for the engine cycle, is injected per half rotation of the camshaft, which corresponds to each rotation of the crankshaft.

Automatic cold start and warm-up devices are incorporated in the system to give better driveability and engine operation during the initial start and warm-up period, when added fuel is needed.

Precautions

The following cautions should be observed to protect the Digital Motor Electronic (DME) equipped system and components:

• Always disconnect the battery, the DME control unit and the ignition coils when using an electric welder on the vehicle or when charging the battery or when the vehicle is placed in a paint drying oven.

• Relieve the fuel system pressure before disconnecting any component of the fuel injection system that contains fuel.

• Remove the main DME relay to disable both the fuel and ignition systems when checking the compression. Never crank the engine after removing the distributor cap or disconnecting the high tension wire on the ignition coil.

• Never disconnect the battery or wires on the alternator, starter or spark plugs when the engine is running.

• Never connect a test lamp on terminal 1 of the ignition coil.

• Never connect terminal 1 of the ignition coil with ground or B+. This means if installing a burglar alarm, terminal 1 should not be used for starter interlocking.

• Whenever performing work on the EML throttle by wire system, a check of the external safety path must be made. This is to check the proper operation of the EML safeguards.

• When working with the EML throttle by wire systems do not place hands or fingers in or near the throttle plates. The throttle motors can close the throttle plates with considerable force.

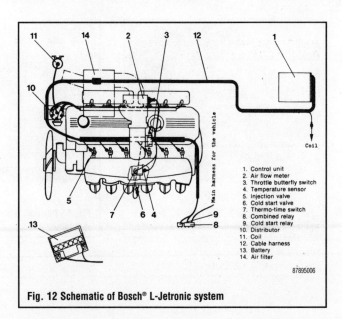

1. Control unit
2. Air flow meter
3. Throttle butterfly switch
4. Temperature sensor
5. Injection valve
6. Cold start valve
7. Thermo-time switch
8. Combined relay
9. Cold start relay
10. Distributor
11. Coil
12. Cable harness
13. Battery
14. Air filter

87895006

Fig. 12 Schematic of Bosch® L-Jetronic system

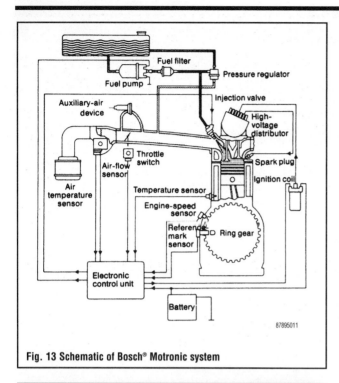

Fig. 13 Schematic of Bosch® Motronic system

Relieving Fuel System Pressure

✸✸ CAUTION

Anytime the fuel system is serviced, the generation of spilled fuel and fuel vapor expose the technician to possibility of flash fire or explosion. All work should be performed in a well ventilated area with easy access to a fire extinguisher. All spilled fuel must be removed immediately. Wear protective eyewear. Failure to observe these precautions may result in personal injury.

To relieve the pressure in the system, first find the fuel pump relay plug, located on the cowl, as specified in the applicable Electric Fuel Pump Pressure Checking procedure. Unplug the relay, leaving it in a safe position where the connections cannot ground. If necessary, tape the plug in place or tape over the connector prongs with electrical tape. Then, start the engine and operate it until it stalls. Crank the engine for 10 seconds after it stalls to remove any residual pressure.

Fuel Pressure Regulator

REMOVAL & INSTALLATION

1982 633CSi Models

1. Remove No. 4 intake tube. Pull off the vacuum hose located on one end of the regulator. Loosen the fuel line hose clamp and pull off the fuel return line that attaches to the opposite end.
2. Using a backup wrench on the flats that are an integral part of the regulator body, loosen the coupling nut and then disconnect the fuel supply line.
3. The fitting that the fuel return line connects to is screwed into the pressure regulator and also mounts the regulator. Unscrew this fitting using an open-end wrench and remove the regulator.
To install:
4. Position the regulator so the return line connection fitting will pass through the hole in the mounting bracket, and then install that fitting. Make the other connections in reverse order. Make all connections tight and then run the engine while checking for leaks.

1982–83 733i Models

Follow the procedure just above for 1982 633CSi models, but note these differences: The regulator connections are identical with those on the unit described above. However, the mounting bracket that fits under the return line connection is bolted together. Once the lines have been disconnected, remove this bolt and remove the unit. Now, remove the return line connection and bracket parts and transfer them to the replacement unit before mounting the unit on the car. Make sure to run the engine and check for leaks.

3 Series; 1983–84 533i, 535i, 633CSi and 635CSi; 1984 733i; All 735i, M5 and M6 Models

⭢ See Figures 14 thru 21

1. Remove the vacuum hose from the unit.
2. Clamp the fuel line into the regulator. Loosen the clamp and pull off the fuel hose.
3. Remove the 2 bolts and pull the unit from the injection tube, or from the body.
To install:
4. Inspect the seal that seals the connection with the injection tube and replace it, if necessary.
5. Install a new seal on the unit and install it into the injection tube. Install the 2 bolts that retain the unit and install the fuel and vacuum hoses.
6. Run the engine and check for leaks.

Fig. 14 Fuel pressure regulator at the side of the intake manifold—3 Series model

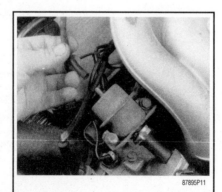

Fig. 15 Remove the vacuum line from the regulator

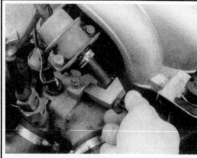

Fig. 16 It is a good idea to clamp off the fuel line hose even though there should be little fuel in the line

Fig. 17 Loosen the clamp, then remove the hose

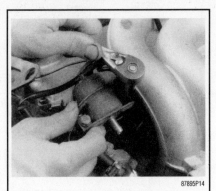

Fig. 18 Remove the bolts securing the regulator

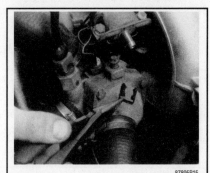

Fig. 19 Depending on the model, some regulators are attached to the fuel rail with a clip, which must be removed

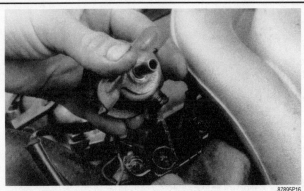

Fig. 20 Remove the regulator from the engine compartment

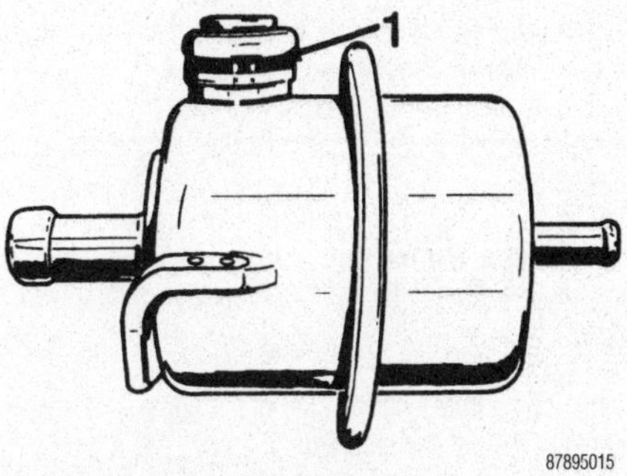

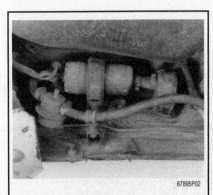

Fig. 21 Check the condition of the seal (1) at the base of the regulator and replace if torn or cracked

Electric Fuel Pump

REMOVAL & INSTALLATION

1982–88 Models

EXCEPT 633CSI, 735I, M5, M6 AND 1987–88 3 SERIES MODELS

▶ **See Figures 22 thru 29**

The fuel pump is an electrical unit, delivering fuel through a pressure regulator, to a fuel distributor or a ring-line for the injection valves. The fuel pump is mounted under the vehicle, near the fuel tank, or in the engine compartment.

1. Relieve fuel system pressure, as described in this section. Disconnect the negative battery connector. Push back any protective caps and disconnect the electrical connector(s).

2. If the fuel lines are flexible, pinch them closed with an appropriate tool. Disconnect the fuel lines and plug the ends.

3. Remove the retaining bolts and remove the pump and expansion tank as an assembly. On the 318i, the pump and mounting bracket come off together. On the 1983–85 733i and 1986 735i, remove the clamp bolt, bend the clamp open, and remove the pump.

4. The pump can be separated from the expansion tank after removal. On the 318i, separate the pump from the mounting bracket and slide the rubber mounting ring from the pump.

To install:

5. Position the pump in its mounting bracket, sliding the rubber ring around it.

6. Install the pump to the expansion tank and mount them both as an assembly, connecting the fuel lines.

7. Connect the electrical leads and the negative battery cable. Run the engine and check for leaks.

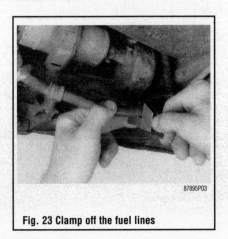

Fig. 22 Fuel pump as seen from under the vehicle—1986 3 Series model

Fig. 23 Clamp off the fuel lines

Fig. 24 In hard to reach areas, a different type clamp tool may be easier to use

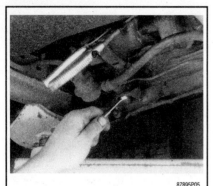

Fig. 25 Remove the nut securing the fuel pump mount(s)

Fig. 26 Tag or paint Identification marks on the wires to the pump

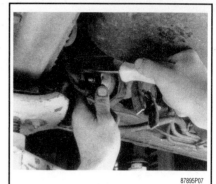

Fig. 27 Loosen the clamp(s) securing the fuel line to the pump

Fig. 28 Slide the hose(s) off the pump assembly

Fig. 29 Remove the pump assembly from the vehicle

1987–88 3 SERIES MODELS

▶ See Figure 30

1. Relieve fuel system pressure. Disconnect the negative battery connector. Going to the pump, which is under the car and near the fuel tank, push back any protective caps, note the routing and disconnect the electrical connector(s).

2. Securely clamp the suction hose (coming from the tank) and plug the discharge hose so no fuel can escape.

3. Open the hose clamp connecting the suction hose to the pump and disconnect it.

4. Remove the 3 attaching nuts which mount the pump and bracket to the floor pan and remove both as an assembly.

5. Remove the bolt passing through the 2 parts of the bracket and also mounting the hose attaching strap to the bracket. Then, pull the pump out of the bracket.

6. Loosen the hose clamp for the discharge hose and disconnect it at the pump. Pull the rubber ring off the pump.

To install:

7. Note the code number on the pump and make sure to replace it with one of the same number. Inspect all the rubber mounts on the pump mounting bracket and replace any that are cracked or crushed.

8. Install the pump in the mounting bracket and install the bolt passing through the bracket.

9. Attach the pump and bracket assembly to the floor pan and secure with the 3 attaching nuts.

10. Attach all hoses to the pump assembly, make sure to correctly route them. Reconnect the electrical leads.

11. Run the engine and check all hose connections for leaks.

633CSI, M5 AND M6 MODELS

1. Relieve fuel system pressure, as described above. Disconnect the battery cables. Working under the fuel tank, pull back the protective caps and then unscrew the attaching nuts and pull off the electrical connections for the fuel pump.

2. Pinch off the inlet line to the fuel pump and the outlet from the filter. Then, loosen the clamps and disconnect these 2 hoses.

3. Remove the nut that clamps the fuel line near the pump. Then, remove the 3 bolts which mount the pump and filter to the bottom of the body and remove the assembly.

4. Remove the bolt fastening the halves of the bracket together and remove the filter from the bracket. Loosen the clamp on the outlet side of the fuel pump and disconnect the line. Then, slide off the rubber bushing in which the pump is mounted.

To install:

5. Check the code number on the side of the pump and make sure the replacement unit carries the same code.

6. Install the pump in the mounting bracket and install the bolt passing through the bracket.

7. Attach the pump and bracket assembly to the floor pan and secure with the 3 attaching nuts.

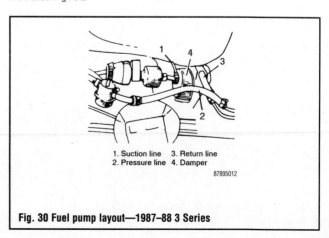

1. Suction line   3. Return line
2. Pressure line 4. Damper

Fig. 30 Fuel pump layout—1987–88 3 Series

8. Attach all hoses to the pump assembly, make sure to correctly route them. Reconnect the electrical leads.

9. Run the engine and check all hose connections for leaks.

735I MODELS

◆ **See Figure 31**

The pump on this car is mounted in the top of the fuel tank along with the fuel level sending unit.

1. If the fuel pump is working well enough to drive the car, run it until the fuel level is as low as possible. If the car cannot be run, devise a safe way to draw fuel out of the tank until the level is low. The best means is some sort of pump and container system designed for this purpose, as siphoning is no longer considered safe because gasoline is a deadly poison.

2. Relieve fuel system pressure, as described above. Remove the trim panels from the trunk. Then, remove the screws from the cover for the pump/sending unit assembly.

3. Label the 3 fuel hoses connecting at the top of the pump/sending unit assembly. Unclamp and disconnect the fuel hoses and then plug them.

4. Slide the collar for the electrical connector to one side and then unplug the connector.

5. Remove the eight attaching screws and remove the pump/sending unit assembly. Replace the gasket.

6. Press the 2 retaining locks for the pump unit inward and slide the pump out of the pump/sending unit assembly.

7. Note the routing of the fuel and electrical lines to the pump from the top of the pump/sending unit assembly. Loosen the 2 hose clamp screws and the screws attaching the electrical connectors to the pump. Disconnect the hose and connector.

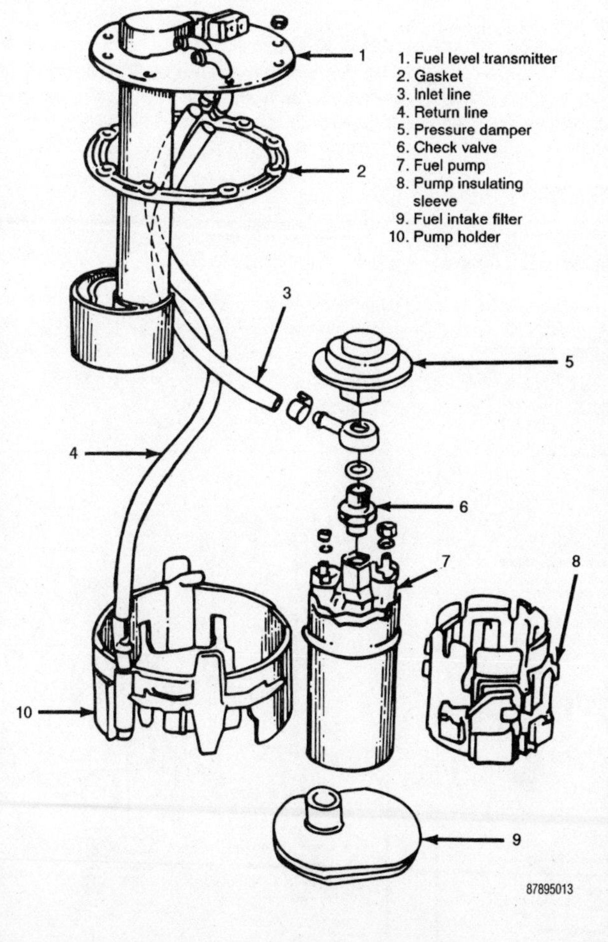

1. Fuel level transmitter
2. Gasket
3. Inlet line
4. Return line
5. Pressure damper
6. Check valve
7. Fuel pump
8. Pump insulating sleeve
9. Fuel intake filter
10. Pump holder

87895013

Fig. 31 Model 735i in-tank fuel pump system layout

8. Unscrew the pressure regulator from the top of the check valve. Then, unscrew the check valve from the top of the pump.

9. Pull the insulating sleeve off the pump. Then, loosen the retaining screw and slide the filter off the pump.

To install:

10. To install the pump, first position the filter on the pump and install the retaining screw.

11. Install the insulating sleeve to the pump. Screw the check valve into the top of the pump and attach the pressure regulator to the pump.

12. Connect the hose and the electrical leads to the pump. slide the pump into the pump/sending unit assembly. Position the sending unit assembly in the tank, using a new gasket, and install the 8 retaining screws.

13. Connect the plug to the top of the sending unit and connect the fuel hoses.

14. Install the trim panels in the trunk and install the pump/sending unit cover. Connect the negative battery cable and run the engine. Check for fuel leaks.

TESTING

✳✳ CAUTION

The following procedure will produce fuel vapors. Make sure there is proper ventilation and take the appropriate fire safety precautions otherwise personal injury may occur.

3.0Si Models

Install a pressure gauge in the line between the fuel filter and the injector feed circuit. The pressure must be 31.2 psi (212 kPa). If not, adjust the pressure. If that will not correct low pressure, replace the pump.

The fuel pressure regulator is located in the circuit which feeds all the injectors between 2 of the injectors. An adjusting bolt and locknut protrude from the top. To adjust it, connect a pressure gauge and idle the engine as described in the pressure check above, loosen the locknut, turn the bolt in or out until the pressure is correct, and then retighten the locknut.

1982–86 325e, 528e, 533i, 633CSi and 1982 733i Models

Relieve fuel system pressure, as described in this section. Connect a pressure gauge in the line leading to the cold start valve from the injector feed circuit. With the engine idling, the pressure must be 33–38 psi (224–258 kPa), or the fuel pump (or filter) is defective.

1987–88 3 Series Models

1. Relieve fuel system pressure, as described in this section. Tee a pressure gauge into the fuel feed line in front of the pressure regulator.

2. Disconnect the fuel pump relay. Connect a remote starter switch between terminals KL30 and KL87 of the relay. Close the switch and check the pressure. It should be 43 psi (292 kPa). If not, the filter is severely clogged or the fuel pump is defective.

M3 Models

1. Relieve fuel system pressure, as described above. Tee a pressure gauge into the fuel return line at the pressure regulator. Then, clamp off the return line so pressure builds up to the maximum level the pump can produce.

2. Remove the trim from the cowl on the right (passenger's side). Then, unplug the fuel pump relay. Connect a remote starter switch between terminals 30 and 87 (left side and top holding the male side of the connector). Energize the switch and check the pressure. It must be 43 psi (292 kPa). Check the filter for excessive clogging. If it is okay, the pump is defective.

1983–88 533i, 535i, 633CSi, 635CSi, 733i, 735i, M5 and M6 Models

1. Relieve fuel system pressure, as in this section. Tee a pressure gauge into the fuel feed line in front of the pressure regulator (on M5 and M6 models, tee in between the cold start valve and the fuel rail). Plug the fuel return hose.

2. Pull off the pump relay. Jumper terminals 87 and 30. Measure the delivery pressure. It should be 43 psi (292 kPa) on these models except the 1987–88 735i. On these models, it should be 48 psi (326 kPa).

Pressure Sensor

REMOVAL & INSTALLATION

Except 3.0Si Models

The pressure sensor is an integral part of the air flow sensor unit and cannot be replaced separately.

3.0Si Models

1. The pressure sensor is located near the firewall on the left side of the engine compartment.
2. Remove the vacuum hose from the pressure sensor.
3. Remove the base plate from the bearing block and if equipped with automatic transmission, remove the starter locking relay.
4. Invert the base plate and remove the pressure sensor retaining bolts.
5. Install the pressure sensor in the reverse order.

➡**Refer to steps 4 and 5 under the 3.0Si control unit removal and installation procedure for proper part replacement.**

Air Flow Sensor

▸ **See Figures 32 and 33**

REMOVAL & INSTALLATION

Except 528e and 530i Models

1. Disconnect the multiple connector. Loosen the air hose clamps at either end of the unit, and detach the hose on the engine side.
2. Remove the air cleaner mounting nuts and remove the air cleaner and air flow sensor. Then, remove the nuts attaching the air flow sensor to the base of the air filter, detach the hose from the air cleaner, and remove the unit. Install in reverse order.

528e and 530i Models

1. Disconnect the multiple connector and then loosen the air hose clamps at either end of the unit.
2. Remove the air cleaner. Lift the volume control out of the bracket.
3. Remove the 3 mounting bolts, and pull the unit out of the bracket.
   To install:
4. Place the unit in the bracket and install the mounting bolts. On the 530i, install the volume control unit. Install the air cleaner and connect the hoses to either end.

Throttle Valve

ADJUSTMENT

Except 3.0Si Models
▸ **See Figure 34**

1. Loosen the throttle lever clamp screw and the throttle stop screw.
2. Press the throttle valve closed and tighten the throttle stop screw until the clearance between the roller and the gate is approximately 0.02–0.4 inches (0.5–1.0mm).
3. Tighten the throttle lever clamp screw. Tighten the throttle stop screw one complete turn and lock with the locknut.
4. Adjust the throttle switch and the idle speed.

3.0Si Models

1. Loosen the locknut and loosen the adjusting screw until there is play between the stop and the screw.
2. Tighten the adjusting screw until the stop just makes contact. Operate the throttle lever several times and allow it to snap back against the stop by spring pressure.
3. Tighten the adjusting screw one full turn and lock the screw with the locknut.

Throttle Valve Switch

▸ **See Figure 35**

The throttle valve switch cuts off the fuel supply to avoid engine overrunning. This is done by switch contacts, which are closed when the throttle valve is in the idling position.

When the throttle valve is moved 2°, the throttle valve switch movement opens the cut-off contacts and closes the acceleration enrichment control. Electrical impulses sent to the control unit determine the fuel quantity required for acceleration. A second switch closes the acceleration enrichment circuit only when the fuel cut-off switch is open.

REMOVAL & INSTALLATION

Except 528e Models

1. Remove the terminal plug from the throttle valve switch.
2. Remove the switch retaining screws and remove the switch from the throttle shaft.
3. To install the switch, engage the throttle shaft into the switch orifice. Install the retaining screws and terminal plug.

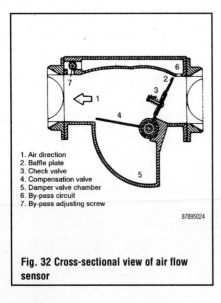

1. Air direction
2. Baffle plate
3. Check valve
4. Compensation valve
5. Damper valve chamber
6. By-pass circuit
7. By-pass adjusting screw

87895024

Fig. 32 Cross-sectional view of air flow sensor

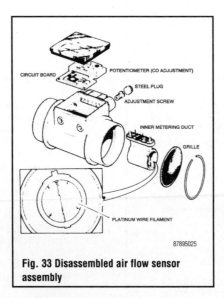

CIRCUIT BOARD
POTENTIOMETER (CO ADJUSTMENT)
STEEL PLUG
ADJUSTMENT SCREW
INNER METERING DUCT
GRILLE
PLATINUM WIRE FILAMENT

87895025

Fig. 33 Disassembled air flow sensor assembly

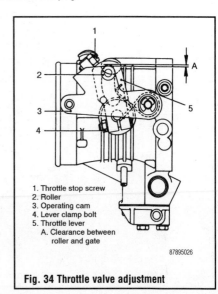

1. Throttle stop screw
2. Roller
3. Operating cam
4. Lever clamp bolt
5. Throttle lever
   A. Clearance between roller and gate

87895026

Fig. 34 Throttle valve adjustment

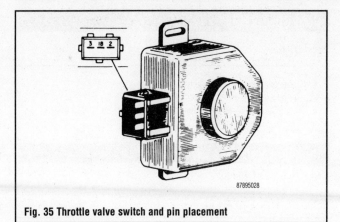

Fig. 35 Throttle valve switch and pin placement

528e Models

1. Unscrew the hose clamp and push back the air hose.
2. Disconnect the accelerator cables.
3. On models with automatic transmissions, disconnect the accelerator cable for the automatic transmission.
4. Disconnect the electrical connector, unscrew the mounting screws and remove the throttle housing.
5. Installation is in the reverse order of removal. Always replace the gasket and adjust the accelerator cable setting.

ADJUSTMENT

Except 3.0Si Models

▶ See Figures 35 and 36

1. Connect an ohmmeter lead to terminals 18 and 2 of the throttle valve switch, after removing the terminal plug.
2. At idle position of the throttle, the meter needle should read 0 resistance.
3. Connect the meter leads to terminals 2 and 3.
4. With the throttle wide open, the meter needle should read 0 resistance.
5. The switch can be moved for small adjustments. If adjustments are unattainable, replace the switch.

3.0Si Models

1. Disconnect the electrical terminal plug from the throttle valve switch and loosen the switch retaining screws.
2. Connect the leads of a calibrated ohmmeter to terminals 17 and 45 of the throttle valve switch.
3. Rotate the switch until the meter needle shows infinity. Rotate the switch in the opposite direction until the meter needle moves to 0 resistance.
4. Mark the housing opposite the center indicator on the switch scale.
5. Rotate the switch clockwise 2° as indicated on the scale.

➡The scale is graduated in ½° increments.

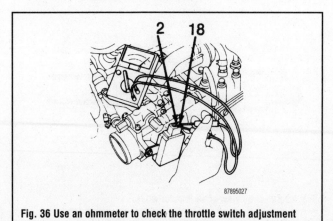

Fig. 36 Use an ohmmeter to check the throttle switch adjustment

6. As the switch is rotated, the meter needle should move to infinity as the switch contacts open.
7. Rotate the switch counterclockwise to the original scale to housing mark. The meter needle should return to 0 resistance.
8. Lock the switch in place with the retaining screws and attach the wire terminal plug.

Air Intake Temperature Sensor

REMOVAL & INSTALLATION

3.0Si Models

The temperature sensor can be unscrewed from the air collector after disconnecting the electrical plug.

TESTING

The desired resistance is listed in the following chart, depending on the temperature reading.

Air Temperature Sensor Adjustment Chart

Degrees F (C)	Resistance (Ohms)
14 (−10)	9.6
32 (0)	6.4
50 (+10)	4.3
68 (20)	3.0
86 (30)	2.1
104 (40)	1.5
122 (50)	1.0
140 (60)	0.79

Coolant Temperature Sensor

REMOVAL & INSTALLATION

All Models

Disconnect the electrical terminal plug and unscrew the coolant temperature sensor.

Coolant Temperature Sensor Adjustment Chart

Degrees F (C)	Resistance (Ohms)
14 (−10)	9.2
32 (0)	5.9
50 (+10)	3.7
68 (20)	2.5
86 (30)	1.7
104 (40)	1.2
122 (50)	0.84
140 (60)	0.60
158 (70)	0.43
176 (80)	0.32
194 (90)	0.25
212 (100)	0.20

TESTING

Except 3.0Si Models

The coolant temperature sensor can be checked with a test lamp. The circuit should open at temperatures above 113°F (45°C) and closed below 113°F (45°C).

3.0Si Models

The desired resistance is noted in the following chart, depending on the temperature reading.

Temperature Timing Switch

REMOVAL & INSTALLATION

Partially drain the coolant and disconnect the electrical connector plug. Pull off the plug (if so equipped) and unscrew the temperature timing switch. After installation, bleed the cooling system.

✳✳ CAUTION

When draining coolant, keep in mind that cats and dogs are attracted to ethylene glycol antifreeze, and could drink any that is left in an uncovered container or in puddles on the ground. This will prove fatal in sufficient quantity. Always drain the coolant into a sealable container. Coolant should be reused unless it is contaminated or several years old.

TESTING

With the use of a test lamp, the switch can be tested at various temperatures for continuity. The operating time is eight seconds at -4°F (-20°C) and declines to 0 seconds at 59°F (15°C).

Cold Start Valve

REMOVAL & INSTALLATION

1. Remove the electrical connector and the fuel line to the valve.
2. Remove the retaining bolts and pull the valve assembly from the air collector.
3. Replace the rubber sealing ring during installation.

TESTING

Except 3.0Si Models

1. Remove the cold start valve from the air collector but do not remove the fuel hose or the electrical connector.
2. Remove the connector plug from the air flow sensor.
3. Install a jumper wire between plug 36 and 39 on the air flow sensor connector.
4. Remove the connector from the cold start relay.
5. Connect a jumper wire from terminal 87 to 30 of the cold start relay connector.
6. Turn the ignition switch **ON**. The cold start valve should eject fuel.

3.0Si Models

The cold start valve should only receive current when the starter or the timer switch is in operation. The use of a test lamp on the terminal end of the starter valve and to ground, will indicate current presence to the switch when starting. The current should stop flowing no longer than eight seconds after the starter is stopped. The temperature timing switch is operable under temperatures of 41°F (5°C).

Cold Start Relay

TESTING

1. Connect a ground wire to terminal 85.
2. Connect a positive lead to terminal 30 and 86 C.
3. The relay is good when the test lamp operates when probed to terminals 87 and 86.

Injection Valves

▶ See Figures 37 and 38

REMOVAL & INSTALLATION

Except 3.0Si, 530i, 630CSi and 633i Models

1. With the injector tube and injector valves removed from the engine, cut the metal hose clamp sleeve and remove the sleeve.
2. Heat the hose with a soldering iron and remove the injector hose from the tube.
3. To install the injector valve assembly on the tube, clean the tube adapter and coat the inside of the hose with fuel.
4. Install the fuel injector hose with the hose sleeve on the injector tube and push against the stop, with the electrical terminal facing up.
5. Complete the installation in the reverse of the removal procedure.

3.0Si Models

1. Remove the electrical plug from the injection valves.
2. Loosen and remove the injection valve from the ring line.

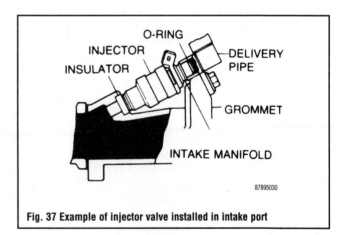

Fig. 37 Example of injector valve installed in intake port

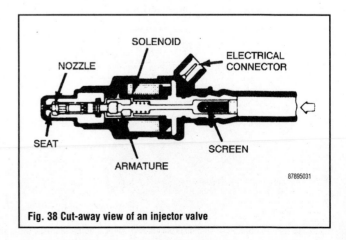

Fig. 38 Cut-away view of an injector valve

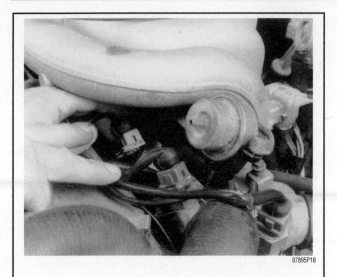

Fig. 39 Unfasten the wire harness(es) attached to the injectors

3. Remove the retaining bolts and pull the injector from the manifold.
4. To install, replace the rubber ring and do not damage the nozzle jet during the installation.

530i, 630CSi and 633i Models

▶ See Figures 39 and 40

1. With the air collector removed, unfasten the electrical connector plugs from the 6 injection valves.

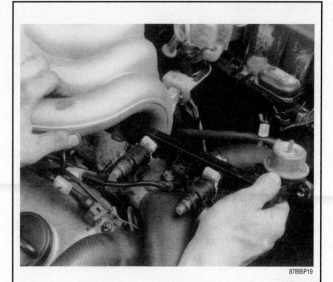

Fig. 40 Sliding the injector fuel supply rail with injectors out from under the intake manifold

2. Remove the valve retaining bolts and remove the injector tube with all the valves attached.
3. Remove the retaining clamps and remove the valves from the injector tube.
4. To install, reverse the removal procedure.

FUEL TANK

Tank Assembly

REMOVAL & INSTALLATION

1600, 2000 and 2002 Models

1. Disconnect the negative battery cable.
2. Drain the fuel from the fuel tank.

✳ CAUTION

Never smoke when working around gasoline! Avoid all sources of sparks or ignition. Gasoline vapors are EXTREMELY volatile!

3. Remove the fiber floor panel from the trunk, if equipped. Disconnect the positive lead and ground wire.
4. Disconnect the fuel feed hose from the immersion tube transmitter.
5. Label and disconnect all evaporative control vapor lines.
6. Disconnect the hose clamp from the bottom of the filler neck and push up on the rubber sleeve.
7. Remove the tank retaining bolts and carefully lift out the tank.
8. Reverse the above procedure to install.

2002Tii Model

1. Disconnect the negative battery cable.
2. Drain the fuel from the tank.

✳ CAUTION

Never smoke when working around gasoline! Avoid all sources of sparks or ignition. Gasoline vapors are EXTREMELY volatile!

3. Remove the fiber floor panels from the trunk, if equipped. Disconnect the leads from the fuel gauge sending unit. Disconnect the fuel feed and return lines from the suction unit.
4. Label and disconnect all evaporative control vapor lines.
5. Disconnect the hose clamp from the filler neck.
6. Remove the tank retaining bolts, separate the filler neck sections and carefully lift out the tank.
7. Reverse the above procedure to install.

2500, 2800, Bavaria, 3000 and 3.0 Models

1. Drain the fuel and disconnect the negative battery terminal.

✳ CAUTION

Never smoke when working around gasoline! Avoid all sources of sparks or ignition. Gasoline vapors are EXTREMELY volatile!

2. Remove the luggage compartment mat and the lining which rests against the right side quarter panel.
3. Remove the fuel hose from the tank sending unit. Pull the electrical connections off, noting that the ground wire (Brown) goes to the rounded connector, the Brown/Yellow wire to the **G** connector, and the Brown Black wire to the **W** connector.
4. Remove the filler cap and slip he rubber ring off the filler neck.
5. Detach the tank from the luggage compartment floor, tilt upwards at the front, and remove it.
To install:
6. Install in reverse order. Before putting the tank into position, check the foam gasket supporting the tank and replace it if necessary. Make sure to install the sealing ring onto the filler neck before the tank goes into final position.

318i and 320i Models

1. Disconnect the battery negative terminal and drain the fuel.

✳✳ CAUTION

Never smoke when working around gasoline! Avoid all sources of sparks or ignition. Gasoline vapors are EXTREMELY volatile!

2. Remove the rear seat. Remove the black guard plate to gain access to fuel lines and the sending unit.

3. Unfasten the electrical connector and the suction and return lines at the sending unit. Disconnect the vent line at the tank.

4. Disconnect the filler neck at the lower end.

5. Remove the mounting screw and remove the guard from behind the connecting hose (which goes to the left side tank).

6. Disconnect the connecting hose. Then, remove the 2 mounting screws on the inboard side of the tank at the bottom, and lower the tank out of the car.

7. For the tank mounted on the left side, perform Steps 5 and 6 in a similar way, but before lifting the tank out of the car, disconnect the small vent line from the top of the tank. If this line should have to be replaced, limit the length of the replacement hose section to 23 inches (600mm).

8. Install the fuel tanks in reverse order.

5 Series Models

1. Disconnect the battery ground cable. Siphon the fuel out of the tank.

2. Fold the floor mat out of the way for access. Remove the 3 screws and remove the round black cover which permit access to the sending unit

3. Disconnect the wires at the sending unit (Brown-ground, Brown/Yellow - G, Brown/Black-W). Detach the unclamped vent line.

4. Detach the feed and return lines at the filter and return pipe (both under the car).

5. Detach the front and rear mounting bushings of the rear-most muffler, and then remove the rear bracket from the body.

6. Loosen the tank mounting bolts at the front and right sides, remove the filler cap, and remove the tank.

7. Install in reverse order.

6 Series Models

1. Disconnect the negative battery cable, and siphon fuel from the tank. Lift the rear compartment rug out of the way. Remove the round access cover.

2. Disconnect the electrical plug and the 2 fuel lines from the top of the sending unit.

3. Remove the fuel tank filler cap and the rubber seal which surrounds the filler neck. Then, disconnect the 4 vent hoses.

4. Remove the bushings from the rear muffler at front and rear, and then remove the mounting bracket at the rear.

5. Bend the tabs down, remove the mounting bolts, and remove the heat shield. Remove the nut and bolt, and remove the stone guard.

6. Remove the 3 mounting bolts from the right side panel, and lower the tank, right side first, and then remove it, being careful to avoid pinching any of the hoses.

7. Install in reverse order, making sure the rubber bumpers against which the tank is held by the mounting straps are in good shape, or replace them, as necessary.

7 Series Models

1. Unscrew the filler cap and siphon out the tank.

2. Disconnect the negative battery cable. Fold the rug in the rear compartment out of the way, and remove the round access panel.

3. Disconnect inlet and outlet hoses at the sending unit.

4. Disconnect the sending unit electrical connector at the plug, located near the wiring harness in the trunk.

5. Remove the mounting bolts from the straps and lower the tank slightly and support it. Pull off the (4) vent hoses. Then, lower the tank out of the car.

6. Install in reverse order, making sure the rubber bumpers against which the tank is held by the mounting straps are in good shape, or replace them, as necessary.

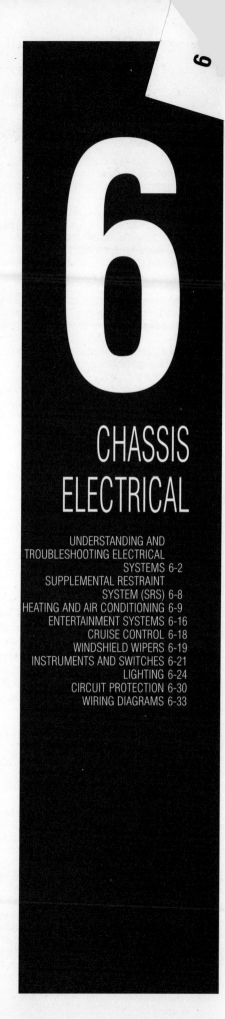

6

CHASSIS ELECTRICAL

UNDERSTANDING AND TROUBLESHOOTING ELECTRICAL SYSTEMS

Basic Electrical Theory

♦ See Figure 1

For any 12 volt, negative ground, electrical system to operate, the electricity must travel in a complete circuit. This simply means that current (power) from the positive (+) terminal of the battery must eventually return to the negative (-) terminal of the battery. Along the way, this current will travel through wires, fuses, switches and components. If, for any reason, the flow of current through the circuit is interrupted, the component fed by that circuit will cease to function properly.

Perhaps the easiest way to visualize a circuit is to think of connecting a light bulb (with two wires attached to it) to the battery—one wire attached to the negative (-) terminal of the battery and the other wire to the positive (+) terminal. With the two wires touching the battery terminals, the circuit would be complete and the light bulb would illuminate. Electricity would follow a path from the battery to the bulb and back to the battery. It's easy to see that with longer wires on our light bulb, it could be mounted anywhere. Further, one wire could be fitted with a switch so that the light could be turned on and off.

The normal automotive circuit differs from this simple example in two ways. First, instead of having a return wire from the bulb to the battery, the current travels through the frame of the vehicle. Since the negative (-) battery cable is attached to the frame (made of electrically conductive metal), the frame of the vehicle can serve as a ground wire to complete the circuit. Secondly, most automotive circuits contain multiple components which receive power from a single circuit. This lessens the amount of wire needed to power components on the vehicle.

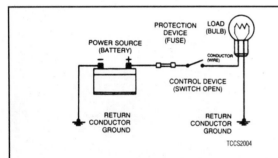

Fig. 1 This example illustrates a simple circuit. When the switch is closed, power from the positive (+) battery terminal flows through the fuse and the switch, and then to the light bulb. The light illuminates and the circuit is completed through the ground wire back to the negative (-) battery terminal. In reality, the two ground points shown in the illustration are attached to the metal frame of the vehicle, which completes the circuit back to the battery

HOW DOES ELECTRICITY WORK: THE WATER ANALOGY

Electricity is the flow of electrons—the subatomic particles that constitute the outer shell of an atom. Electrons spin in an orbit around the center core of an atom. The center core is comprised of protons (positive charge) and neutrons (neutral charge). Electrons have a negative charge and balance out the positive charge of the protons. When an outside force causes the number of electrons to unbalance the charge of the protons, the electrons will split off the atom and look for another atom to balance out. If this imbalance is kept up, electrons will continue to move and an electrical flow will exist.

Many people have been taught electrical theory using an analogy with water. In a comparison with water flowing through a pipe, the electrons would be the water and the wire is the pipe.

The flow of electricity can be measured much like the flow of water through a pipe. The unit of measurement used is amperes, frequently abbreviated as amps (a). You can compare amperage to the volume of water flowing through a pipe. When connected to a circuit, an ammeter will measure the actual amount of current flowing through the circuit. When relatively few electrons flow through a circuit, the amperage is low. When many electrons flow, the amperage is high.

Water pressure is measured in units such as pounds per square inch (psi);

The electrical pressure is measured in units called volts (v). When a voltmeter is connected to a circuit, it is measuring the electrical pressure.

The actual flow of electricity depends not only on voltage and amperage, but also on the resistance of the circuit. The higher the resistance, the higher the force necessary to push the current through the circuit. The standard unit for measuring resistance is an ohm. Resistance in a circuit varies depending on the amount and type of components used in the circuit. The main factors which determine resistance are:

• Material—some materials have more resistance than others. Those with high resistance are said to be insulators. Rubber materials (or rubber-like plastics) are some of the most common insulators used in vehicles as they have a very high resistance to electricity. Very low resistance materials are said to be conductors. Copper wire is among the best conductors. Silver is actually a superior conductor to copper and is used in some relay contacts, but its high cost prohibits its use as common wiring. Most automotive wiring is made of copper.

• Size—the larger the wire size being used, the less resistance the wire will have. This is why components which use large amounts of electricity usually have large wires supplying current to them.

• Length—for a given thickness of wire, the longer the wire, the greater the resistance. The shorter the wire, the less the resistance. When determining the proper wire for a circuit, both size and length must be considered to design a circuit that can handle the current needs of the component.

• Temperature—with many materials, the higher the temperature, the greater the resistance (positive temperature coefficient). Some materials exhibit the opposite trait of lower resistance with higher temperatures (negative temperature coefficient). These principles are used in many of the sensors on the engine.

OHM'S LAW

There is a direct relationship between current, voltage and resistance. The relationship between current, voltage and resistance can be summed up by a statement known as Ohm's law.

Voltage (E) is equal to amperage (I) times resistance (R): $E = I \times R$

Other forms of the formula are $R = E/I$ and $I = E/R$

In each of these formulas, E is the voltage in volts, I is the current in amps and R is the resistance in ohms. The basic point to remember is that as the resistance of a circuit goes up, the amount of current that flows in the circuit will go down, if voltage remains the same.

The amount of work that the electricity can perform is expressed as power. The unit of power is the watt (w). The relationship between power, voltage and current is expressed as:

Power (w) is equal to amperage (I) times voltage (E): $W = I \times E$

This is only true for direct current (DC) circuits; The alternating current formula is a tad different, but since the electrical circuits in most vehicles are DC type, we need not get into AC circuit theory.

Electrical Components

POWER SOURCE

Power is supplied to the vehicle by two devices: The battery and the alternator. The battery supplies electrical power during starting or during periods when the current demand of the vehicle's electrical system exceeds the output capacity of the alternator. The alternator supplies electrical current when the engine is running. Just not does the alternator supply the current needs of the vehicle, but it recharges the battery.

The Battery

In most modern vehicles, the battery is a lead/acid electrochemical device consisting of six 2 volt subsections (cells) connected in series, so that the unit is capable of producing approximately 12 volts of electrical pressure. Each subsection consists of a series of positive and negative plates held a short distance apart in a solution of sulfuric acid and water.

The two types of plates are of dissimilar metals. This sets up a chemical reaction, and it is this reaction which produces current flow from the battery when its positive and negative terminals are connected to an electrical load.

The power removed from the battery is replaced by the alternator, restoring the battery to its original chemical state.

The Alternator

On some vehicles there isn't an alternator, but a generator. The difference is that an alternator supplies alternating current which is then changed to direct current for use on the vehicle, while a generator produces direct current. Alternators tend to be more efficient and that is why they are used.

Alternators and generators are devices that consist of coils of wires wound together making big electromagnets. One group of coils spins within another set and the interaction of the magnetic fields causes a current to flow. This current is then drawn off the coils and fed into the vehicles electrical system.

GROUND

Two types of grounds are used in automotive electric circuits. Direct ground components are grounded to the frame through their mounting points. All other components use some sort of ground wire which is attached to the frame or chassis of the vehicle. The electrical current runs through the chassis of the vehicle and returns to the battery through the ground (-) cable; if you look, you'll see that the battery ground cable connects between the battery and the frame or chassis of the vehicle.

➡ It should be noted that a good percentage of electrical problems can be traced to bad grounds.

PROTECTIVE DEVICES

▶ See Figure 2

It is possible for large surges of current to pass through the electrical system of your vehicle. If this surge of current were to reach the load in the circuit, the

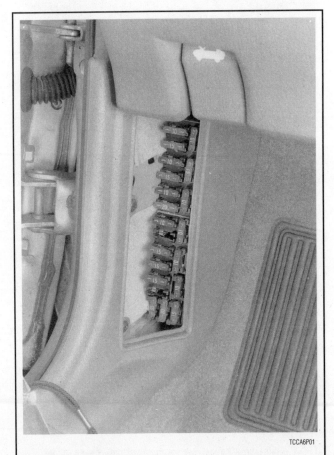

TCCA6P01

Fig. 2 Most vehicles use one or more fuse panels. This one is located on the driver's side kick panel

surge could burn it out or severely damage it. It can also overload the wiring, causing the harness to get hot and melt the insulation. To prevent this, fuses, circuit breakers and/or fusible links are connected into the supply wires of the electrical system. These items are nothing more than a built-in weak spot in the system. When an abnormal amount of current flows through the system, these protective devices work as follows to protect the circuit:

• Fuse—when an excessive electrical current passes through a fuse, the fuse "blows" (the conductor melts) and opens the circuit, preventing the passage of current.

• Circuit Breaker—a circuit breaker is basically a self-repairing fuse. It will open the circuit in the same fashion as a fuse, but when the surge subsides, the circuit breaker can be reset and does not need replacement.

• Fusible Link—a fusible link (fuse link or main link) is a short length of special, high temperature insulated wire that acts as a fuse. When an excessive electrical current passes through a fusible link, the thin gauge wire inside the link melts, creating an intentional open to protect the circuit. To repair the circuit, the link must be replaced. Some newer type fusible links are housed in plug-in modules, which are simply replaced like a fuse, while older type fusible links must be cut and spliced if they melt. Since this link is very early in the electrical path, it's the first place to look if nothing on the vehicle works, yet the battery seems to be charged and is properly connected.

✳✳ CAUTION

Always replace fuses, circuit breakers and fusible links with identically rated components. Under no circumstances should a component of higher or lower amperage rating be substituted.

SWITCHES & RELAYS

▶ See Figures 3 and 4

Switches are used in electrical circuits to control the passage of current. The most common use is to open and close circuits between the battery and the various electric devices in the system. Switches are rated according to the amount of amperage they can handle. If a sufficient amperage rated switch is not used in a circuit, the switch could overload and cause damage.

Some electrical components which require a large amount of current to operate use a special switch called a relay. Since these circuits carry a large amount of current, the thickness of the wire in the circuit is also greater. If this large wire were connected from the load to the control switch, the switch would have to carry the high amperage load and the fairing or dash would be twice as large to accommodate the increased size of the wiring harness. To prevent these problems, a relay is used.

Relays are composed of a coil and a set of contacts. When the coil has a current passed though it, a magnetic field is formed and this field causes the contacts to move together, completing the circuit. Most relays are normally open, prevent-

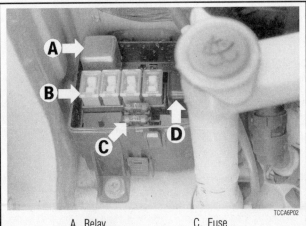

TCCA6P02

| A. Relay | C. Fuse |
| B. Fusible link | D. Flasher |

Fig. 3 The underhood fuse and relay panel usually contains fuses, relays, flashers and fusible links

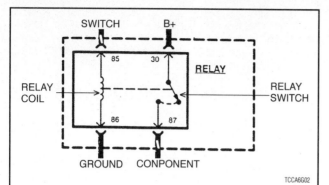

Fig. 4 Relays are composed of a coil and a switch. These two components are linked together so that when one operates, the other operates at the same time. The large wires in the circuit are connected from the battery to one side of the relay switch (B+) and from the opposite side of the relay switch to the load (component). Smaller wires are connected from the relay coil to the control switch for the circuit and from the opposite side of the relay coil to ground

ing current from passing through the circuit, but they can take any electrical form depending on the job they are intended to do. Relays can be considered "remote control switches." They allow a smaller current to operate devices that require higher amperages. When a small current operates the coil, a larger current is allowed to pass by the contacts. Some common circuits which may use relays are the horn, headlights, starter, electric fuel pump and other high draw circuits.

LOAD

Every electrical circuit must include a "load" (something to use the electricity coming from the source). Without this load, the battery would attempt to deliver its entire power supply from one pole to another. This is called a "short circuit." All this electricity would take a short cut to ground and cause a great amount of damage to other components in the circuit by developing a tremendous amount of heat. This condition could develop sufficient heat to melt the insulation on all the surrounding wires and reduce a multiple wire cable to a lump of plastic and copper.

WIRING & HARNESSES

The average vehicle contains meters and meters of wiring, with hundreds of individual connections. To protect the many wires from damage and to keep them from becoming a confusing tangle, they are organized into bundles, enclosed in plastic or taped together and called wiring harnesses. Different harnesses serve different parts of the vehicle. Individual wires are color coded to help trace them through a harness where sections are hidden from view.

Automotive wiring or circuit conductors can be either single strand wire, multi-strand wire or printed circuitry. Single strand wire has a solid metal core and is usually used inside such components as alternators, motors, relays and other devices. Multi-strand wire has a core made of many small strands of wire twisted together into a single conductor. Most of the wiring in an automotive electrical system is made up of multi-strand wire, either as a single conductor or grouped together in a harness. All wiring is color coded on the insulator, either as a solid color or as a colored wire with an identification stripe. A printed circuit is a thin film of copper or other conductor that is printed on an insulator backing. Occasionally, a printed circuit is sandwiched between two sheets of plastic for more protection and flexibility. A complete printed circuit, consisting of conductors, insulating material and connectors for lamps or other components is called a printed circuit board. Printed circuitry is used in place of individual wires or harnesses in places where space is limited, such as behind instrument panels.

Since automotive electrical systems are very sensitive to changes in resistance, the selection of properly sized wires is critical when systems are repaired. A loose or corroded connection or a replacement wire that is too small for the circuit will add extra resistance and an additional voltage drop to the circuit.

The wire gauge number is an expression of the cross-section area of the conductor. Vehicles from countries that use the metric system will typically describe the wire size as its cross-sectional area in square millimeters. In this method, the larger the wire, the greater the number. Another common system for

expressing wire size is the American Wire Gauge (AWG) system. As gauge number increases, area decreases and the wire becomes smaller. An 18 gauge wire is smaller than a 4 gauge wire. A wire with a higher gauge number will carry less current than a wire with a lower gauge number. Gauge wire size refers to the size of the strands of the conductor, not the size of the complete wire with insulator. It is possible, therefore, to have two wires of the same gauge with different diameters because one may have thicker insulation than the other.

It is essential to understand how a circuit works before trying to figure out why it doesn't. An electrical schematic shows the electrical current paths when a circuit is operating properly. Schematics break the entire electrical system down into individual circuits. In a schematic, usually no attempt is made to represent wiring and components as they physically appear on the vehicle; switches and other components are shown as simply as possible. Face views of harness connectors show the cavity or terminal locations in all multi-pin connectors to help locate test points.

CONNECTORS

♦ See Figures 5 and 6

Three types of connectors are commonly used in automotive applications—weatherproof, molded and hard shell.

• Weatherproof—these connectors are most commonly used where the connector is exposed to the elements. Terminals are protected against moisture and dirt by sealing rings which provide a weathertight seal. All repairs require the use of a special terminal and the tool required to service it. Unlike standard blade type terminals, these weatherproof terminals cannot be straightened once they are bent. Make certain that the connectors are properly seated and all of the sealing rings are in place when connecting leads.

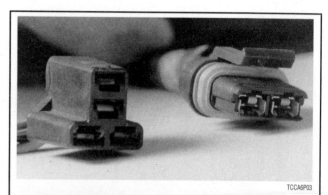

Fig. 5 Hard shell (left) and weatherproof (right) connectors have replaceable terminals

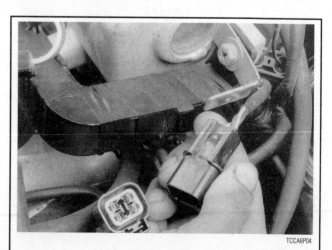

Fig. 6 Weatherproof connectors are most commonly used in the engine compartment or where the connector is exposed to the elements

• Molded—these connectors require complete replacement of the connector if found to be defective. This means splicing a new connector assembly into the harness. All splices should be soldered to insure proper contact. Use care when probing the connections or replacing terminals in them, as it is possible to create a short circuit between opposite terminals. If this happens to the wrong terminal pair, it is possible to damage certain components. Always use jumper wires between connectors for circuit checking and NEVER probe through weatherproof seals.

• Hard Shell—unlike molded connectors, the terminal contacts in hard-shell connectors can be replaced. Replacement usually involves the use of a special terminal removal tool that depresses the locking tangs (barbs) on the connector terminal and allows the connector to be removed from the rear of the shell. The connector shell should be replaced if it shows any evidence of burning, melting, cracks, or breaks. Replace individual terminals that are burnt, corroded, distorted or loose.

Test Equipment

Pinpointing the exact cause of trouble in an electrical circuit is most times accomplished by the use of special test equipment. The following describes different types of commonly used test equipment and briefly explains how to use them in diagnosis. In addition to the information covered below, the tool manufacturer's instructions booklet (provided with the tester) should be read and clearly understood before attempting any test procedures.

JUMPER WIRES

✳✳ CAUTION

Never use jumper wires made from a thinner gauge wire than the circuit being tested. If the jumper wire is of too small a gauge, it may overheat and possibly melt. Never use jumpers to bypass high resistance loads in a circuit. Bypassing resistances, in effect, creates a short circuit. This may, in turn, cause damage and fire. Jumper wires should only be used to bypass lengths of wire or to simulate switches.

Jumper wires are simple, yet extremely valuable, pieces of test equipment. They are basically test wires which are used to bypass sections of a circuit. Although jumper wires can be purchased, they are usually fabricated from lengths of standard automotive wire and whatever type of connector (alligator clip, spade connector or pin connector) that is required for the particular application being tested. In cramped, hard-to-reach areas, it is advisable to have insulated boots over the jumper wire terminals in order to prevent accidental grounding. It is also advisable to include a standard automotive fuse in any jumper wire. This is commonly referred to as a "fused jumper". By inserting an in-line fuse holder between a set of test leads, a fused jumper wire can be used for bypassing open circuits. Use a 5 amp fuse to provide protection against voltage spikes.

Jumper wires are used primarily to locate open electrical circuits, on either the ground (-) side of the circuit or on the power (+) side. If an electrical component fails to operate, connect the jumper wire between the component and a good ground. If the component operates only with the jumper installed, the ground circuit is open. If the ground circuit is good, but the component does not operate, the circuit between the power feed and component may be open. By moving the jumper wire successively back from the component toward the power source, you can isolate the area of the circuit where the open is located. When the component stops functioning, or the power is cut off, the open is in the segment of wire between the jumper and the point previously tested.

You can sometimes connect the jumper wire directly from the battery to the "hot" terminal of the component, but first make sure the component uses 12 volts in operation. Some electrical components, such as fuel injectors or sensors, are designed to operate on about 4 to 5 volts, and running 12 volts directly to these components will cause damage.

TEST LIGHTS

♦ See Figure 7

The test light is used to check circuits and components while electrical current is flowing through them. It is used for voltage and ground tests. To use a 12 volt test light, connect the ground clip to a good ground and probe wherever

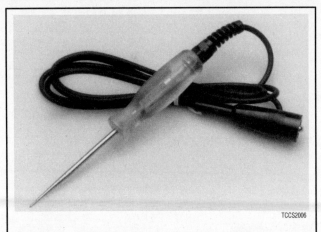

Fig. 7 A 12 volt test light is used to detect the presence of voltage in a circuit

necessary with the pick. The test light will illuminate when voltage is detected. This does not necessarily mean that 12 volts (or any particular amount of voltage) is present; it only means that some voltage is present. It is advisable before using the test light to touch its ground clip and probe across the battery posts or terminals to make sure the light is operating properly.

✳✳ WARNING

Do not use a test light to probe electronic ignition, spark plug or coil wires. Never use a pick-type test light to probe wiring on computer controlled systems unless specifically instructed to do so. Any wire insulation that is pierced by the test light probe should be taped and sealed with silicone after testing.

Like the jumper wire, the 12 volt test light is used to isolate opens in circuits. But, whereas the jumper wire is used to bypass the open to operate the load, the 12 volt test light is used to locate the presence of voltage in a circuit. If the test light illuminates, there is power up to that point in the circuit; if the test light does not illuminate, there is an open circuit (no power). Move the test light in successive steps back toward the power source until the light in the handle illuminates. The open is between the probe and a point which was previously probed.

The self-powered test light is similar in design to the 12 volt test light, but contains a 1.5 volt penlight battery in the handle. It is most often used in place of a multimeter to check for open or short circuits when power is isolated from the circuit (continuity test).

The battery in a self-powered test light does not provide much current. A weak battery may not provide enough power to illuminate the test light even when a complete circuit is made (especially if there is high resistance in the circuit). Always make sure that the test battery is strong. To check the battery, briefly touch the ground clip to the probe; if the light glows brightly, the battery is strong enough for testing.

➡**A self-powered test light should not be used on any computer controlled system or component. The small amount of electricity transmitted by the test light is enough to damage many electronic automotive components.**

MULTIMETERS

Multimeters are an extremely useful tool for troubleshooting electrical problems. They can be purchased in either analog or digital form and have a price range to suit any budget. A multimeter is a voltmeter, ammeter and ohmmeter (along with other features) combined into one instrument. It is often used when testing solid state circuits because of its high input impedance (usually 10 megaohms or more). A brief description of the multimeter main test functions follows:

• Voltmeter—the voltmeter is used to measure voltage at any point in a circuit, or to measure the voltage drop across any part of a circuit. Voltmeters usually have various scales and a selector switch to allow the reading of different voltage ranges. The voltmeter has a positive and a negative lead. To avoid damage to the meter, always connect the negative lead to the negative (-) side of the circuit (to ground or nearest the ground side of the circuit) and connect the positive lead to the positive (+) side of the circuit (to the power source or the nearest power source). Note that the negative voltmeter lead will always be black and that the positive voltmeter will always be some color other than black (usually red).

- Ohmmeter—the ohmmeter is designed to read resistance (measured in ohms) in a circuit or component. Most ohmmeters will have a selector switch which permits the measurement of different ranges of resistance (usually the selector switch allows the multiplication of the meter reading by 10, 100, 1,000 and 10,000). Some ohmmeters are "auto-ranging" which means the meter itself will determine which scale to use. Since the meters are powered by an internal battery, the ohmmeter can be used like a self-powered test light. When the ohmmeter is connected, current from the ohmmeter flows through the circuit or component being tested. Since the ohmmeter's internal resistance and voltage are known values, the amount of current flow through the meter depends on the resistance of the circuit or component being tested. The ohmmeter can also be used to perform a continuity test for suspected open circuits. In using the meter for making continuity checks, do not be concerned with the actual resistance readings. Zero resistance, or any ohm reading, indicates continuity in the circuit. Infinite resistance indicates an opening in the circuit. A high resistance reading where there should be none indicates a problem in the circuit. Checks for short circuits are made in the same manner as checks for open circuits, except that the circuit must be isolated from both power and normal ground. Infinite resistance indicates no continuity, while zero resistance indicates a dead short.

❋❋ WARNING

Never use an ohmmeter to check the resistance of a component or wire while there is voltage applied to the circuit.

- Ammeter—an ammeter measures the amount of current flowing through a circuit in units called amperes or amps. At normal operating voltage, most circuits have a characteristic amount of amperes, called "current draw" which can be measured using an ammeter. By referring to a specified current draw rating, then measuring the amperes and comparing the two values, one can determine what is happening within the circuit to aid in diagnosis. An open circuit, for example, will not allow any current to flow, so the ammeter reading will be zero. A damaged component or circuit will have an increased current draw, so the reading will be high. The ammeter is always connected in series with the circuit being tested. All of the current that normally flows through the circuit must also flow through the ammeter; if there is any other path for the current to follow, the ammeter reading will not be accurate. The ammeter itself has very little resistance to current flow and, therefore, will not affect the circuit, but it will measure current draw only when the circuit is closed and electricity is flowing. Excessive current draw can blow fuses and drain the battery, while a reduced current draw can cause motors to run slowly, lights to dim and other components to not operate properly.

Troubleshooting Electrical Systems

When diagnosing a specific problem, organized troubleshooting is a must. The complexity of a modern automotive vehicle demands that you approach any problem in a logical, organized manner. There are certain troubleshooting techniques, however, which are standard:

- Establish when the problem occurs. Does the problem appear only under certain conditions? Were there any noises, odors or other unusual symptoms? Isolate the problem area. To do this, make some simple tests and observations, then eliminate the systems that are working properly. Check for obvious problems, such as broken wires and loose or dirty connections. Always check the obvious before assuming something complicated is the cause.
- Test for problems systematically to determine the cause once the problem area is isolated. Are all the components functioning properly? Is there power going to electrical switches and motors. Performing careful, systematic checks will often turn up most causes on the first inspection, without wasting time checking components that have little or no relationship to the problem.
- Test all repairs after the work is done to make sure that the problem is fixed. Some causes can be traced to more than one component, so a careful verification of repair work is important in order to pick up additional malfunctions that may cause a problem to reappear or a different problem to arise. A blown fuse, for example, is a simple problem that may require more than another fuse to repair. If you don't look for a problem that caused a fuse to blow, a shorted wire (for example) may go undetected.

Experience has shown that most problems tend to be the result of a fairly simple and obvious cause, such as loose or corroded connectors, bad grounds or damaged wire insulation which causes a short. This makes careful visual inspection of components during testing essential to quick and accurate troubleshooting.

Testing

OPEN CIRCUITS

▶ **See Figure 8**

This test already assumes the existence of an open in the circuit and it is used to help locate the open portion.

1. Isolate the circuit from power and ground.
2. Connect the self-powered test light or ohmmeter ground clip to the ground side of the circuit and probe sections of the circuit sequentially.
3. If the light is out or there is infinite resistance, the open is between the probe and the circuit ground.
4. If the light is on or the meter shows continuity, the open is between the probe and the end of the circuit toward the power source.

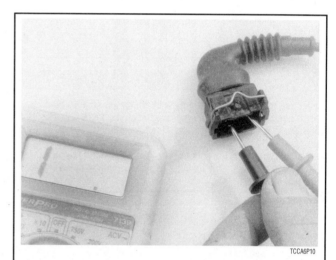

Fig. 8 The infinite reading on this multimeter indicates that the circuit is open

TCCA6P10

SHORT CIRCUITS

➡**Never use a self-powered test light to perform checks for opens or shorts when power is applied to the circuit under test. The test light can be damaged by outside power.**

1. Isolate the circuit from power and ground.
2. Connect the self-powered test light or ohmmeter ground clip to a good ground and probe any easy-to-reach point in the circuit.
3. If the light comes on or there is continuity, there is a short somewhere in the circuit.
4. To isolate the short, probe a test point at either end of the isolated circuit (the light should be on or the meter should indicate continuity).
5. Leave the test light probe engaged and sequentially open connectors or switches, remove parts, etc. until the light goes out or continuity is broken.
6. When the light goes out, the short is between the last two circuit components which were opened.

VOLTAGE

This test determines voltage available from the battery and should be the first step in any electrical troubleshooting procedure after visual inspection. Many electrical problems, especially on computer controlled systems, can be caused by a low state of charge in the battery. Excessive corrosion at the battery cable terminals can cause poor contact that will prevent proper charging and full battery current flow.

1. Set the voltmeter selector switch to the 20V position.
2. Connect the multimeter negative lead to the battery's negative (-) post or terminal and the positive lead to the battery's positive (+) post or terminal.
3. Turn the ignition switch **ON** to provide a load.
4. A well charged battery should register over 12 volts. If the meter reads below 11.5 volts, the battery power may be insufficient to operate the electrical system properly.

VOLTAGE DROP

▶ **See Figure 9**

When current flows through a load, the voltage beyond the load drops. This voltage drop is due to the resistance created by the load and also by small resistances created by corrosion at the connectors and damaged insulation on the wires. The maximum allowable voltage drop under load is critical, especially if there is more than one load in the circuit, since all voltage drops are cumulative.

1. Set the voltmeter selector switch to the 20 volt position.
2. Connect the multimeter negative lead to a good ground.
3. Operate the circuit and check the voltage prior to the first component (load).
4. There should be little or no voltage drop in the circuit prior to the first component. If a voltage drop exists, the wire or connectors in the circuit are suspect.
5. While operating the first component in the circuit, probe the ground side of the component with the positive meter lead and observe the voltage readings. A small voltage drop should be noticed. This voltage drop is caused by the resistance of the component.
6. Repeat the test for each component (load) down the circuit.
7. If a large voltage drop is noticed, the preceding component, wire or connector is suspect.

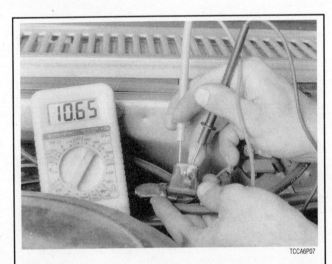

Fig. 9 This voltage drop test revealed high resistance (low voltage) in the circuit

RESISTANCE

▶ **See Figures 10 and 11**

> ❊❊ **WARNING**
>
> **Never use an ohmmeter with power applied to the circuit. The ohmmeter is designed to operate on its own power supply. The normal 12 volt electrical system voltage could damage the meter!**

1. Isolate the circuit from the vehicle's power source.
2. Ensure that the ignition key is **OFF** when disconnecting any components or the battery.

3. Where necessary, also isolate at least one side of the circuit to be checked, in order to avoid reading parallel resistances. Parallel circuit resistances will always give a lower reading than the actual resistance of either of the branches.
4. Connect the meter leads to both sides of the circuit (wire or component) and read the actual measured ohms on the meter scale. Make sure the selector switch is set to the proper ohm scale for the circuit being tested, to avoid misreading the ohmmeter test value.

Fig. 10 Checking the resistance of a coolant temperature sensor with an ohmmeter. Reading is 1.04 kilohms

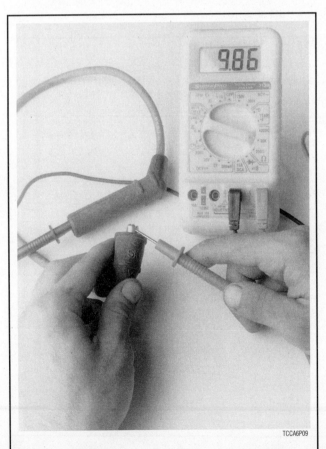

Fig. 11 Spark plug wires can be checked for excessive resistance using an ohmmeter

Wire and Connector Repair

Almost anyone can replace damaged wires, as long as the proper tools and parts are available. Wire and terminals are available to fit almost any need. Even the specialized weatherproof, molded and hard shell connectors are now available from aftermarket suppliers.

Be sure the ends of all the wires are fitted with the proper terminal hardware and connectors. Wrapping a wire around a stud is never a permanent solution and will only cause trouble later. Replace wires one at a time to avoid confusion. Always route wires exactly the same as the factory.

➡**If connector repair is necessary, only attempt it if you have the proper tools. Weatherproof and hard shell connectors require special tools to release the pins inside the connector. Attempting to repair these connectors with conventional hand tools will damage them.**

SUPPLEMENTAL RESTRAINT SYSTEM (SRS)

General Information

BMW provides a Supplemental Restraint System (SRS) for the protection of the driver. An air bag is used in conjunction with the standard seatbelt to lessen the possibility of injury in case of a frontal, or near frontal, collision. Certain 3 and 5 Series models also provide an automatic belt tensioner system to take up slack from the seatbelt at the same time as air bag deployment.

➡**The SRS can only be of use when used in conjunction with the standard seatbelt. This is why it is considered supplemental. Use of the standard seatbelt is mandatory for the best possible protection from all the safety devices built into a BMW vehicle.**

SYSTEM OPERATION

♦ **See Figures 12 and 13**

In the case of a frontal collision, as defined by an area 30 degrees left and right of the centerline of the vehicle and traveling at least 12 mph (20 km/h), the air bag will deploy and if equipped, the seatbelt tensioner will operate. This will provide a cushion for the upper body of the driver and will draw the seatbelts tight providing additional restraint.

The system consists of crash sensors, an air bag in the steering wheel, a control unit, steering wheel contact ring and seatbelt tensioners on vehicles so equipped. All the components and wiring are colored orange to indicate the component being part of the SRS.

When either of the sensors are activated by a collision with a solid object and the sensor is also activated, the control unit sends current to the air bag and the seatbelt retractors. The current sets off the ignitors within the air bag and seatbelt retractors. The solid fuel burns, generating a harmless gas that fills the air bag extremely quickly. The solid fuel in the seatbelt retractor burns and the resulting gas pushes a piston down, taking the slack out of the seatbelt.

The air bag deploys from the center pad of the steering wheel. It fills with gas to full inflation within 30 milliseconds. The deployment sound is that of a loud bang. The inflation rate is so quick, that by the time the occupant strikes the air bag, the air bag is already deflating. This allows a controlled release of energy, preventing injury to the occupant. The occupant will only realize that the air bag deployed after the air bag is fully deflated and has done its job.

Some common misconceptions about air bags have crept into the common knowledge and should be corrected. The air bag will not suffocate the occupant, nor will it block the view of the occupant; the inflation and deflation times are too quick for this to occur. The dust produced after the air bag is deployed is not harmful; it is a combination of the burnt fuel and the talc powder that some air bags are packed in to facilitate smooth deployment. A parking lot tap will not deploy the air bag, unless it is a frontal collision above 12 mph (20 km/h). An air bag is not to be used in lieu of a seatbelt; it must be used in conjunction with a seatbelt. Being rear ended will not deploy the air bag. The air bag can not protect the occupant in a side impact, only the seatbelt can provide any measure of restraint.

➡**Always wear your seatbelt! If it is good enough for use by every race car driver, it should be good enough for you.**

When the ignition switch is activated, the SRS light will illuminate for 6 seconds and extinguish. This indicates normal operation. If the light does not illuminate, illuminates after the 6 second period or flashes for 5 minutes during driving then stays lit, there is a problem with the SRS. Have the system checked by a qualified BMW technician. The SRS does not lend itself to being serviced by a non qualified person. If the SRS is activated, the system must be replaced, as it can only be used once.

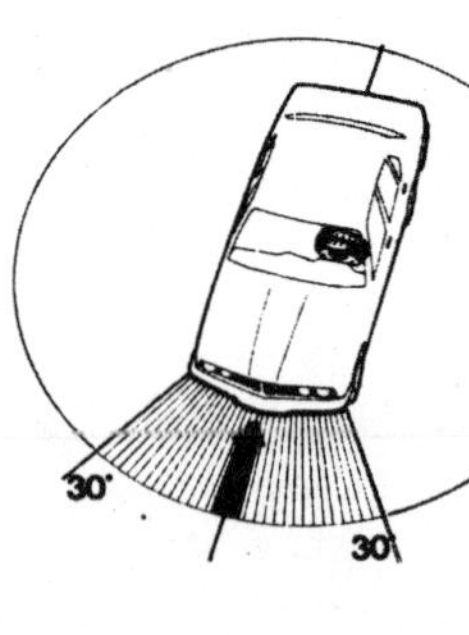

SYSTEM COMPONENTS

87896000

Fig. 12 The air bag will only deploy in a frontal collision within 30 degrees of center

87896001

Fig. 13 The SRS indicator light will appear in the check-control panel. It should remain lit for 6 seconds

Control Module

The control module is located under the left side of the dashboard on 3, 5 and 7 Series models.

The control module monitors the entire SRS and will warn the driver of malfunctions by illuminating the SRS lamp on the dashboard. The control module monitors the operation of the crash sensors and will activate the air bag and seatbelt retractors.

Crash Sensors

The crash sensors are mounted on the left and right inner fenders. The sensors will complete a circuit to the control module if the impact is great enough. The sensors must be mounted with the arrows facing forward; they should not be tampered with or disassembled.

The control unit has a safing sensor built into it. The safing sensor only allows deployment in cases where all criteria for deployment are met. As a result, during an accident, the safing sensor and at least one of the inner fender mounted sensors must be activated.

Air Bag

The air bag is packed in the center pad of the steering wheel assembly. There is an ignitor and solid fuel that produces the gas to fill the air bag. As the fuel starts to burn and the air bag begins to expand, the air bag breaks through the outer skin of the steering wheel center pad. The air bag unfolds and fills to full expansion. Two vents on the back side allow the gases to exit the air bag and release energy.

The air bag is fully deployed within 30 milliseconds and is deflating by the time the occupant strikes the bag. This is to control the levels of forces that the occupant is subjected to and to provide the best possible level of occupant protection.

Seat Belt Tensioners

The are 2 styles of seatbelt tensioners. The 5 and 7 Series models use a pyrotechnic style ignitor and solid fuel, similar to the air bag. The 3 Series uses a mechanical system that operates independently of the air bag. The seatbelt tensioners operate on both the drivers and passenger seatbelts.

On the 5 Series, at the same time the air bag is deployed, the ignitor and solid fuel of the seatbelt tensioner is deployed. The gases produced by the burning fuel in the seatbelt tensioner force a piston down, pulling a steel cable that is attached to the seatbelt reel. The seatbelt is pulled taut, providing a more positive restraint for the occupant

The mechanical system on the 3 Series is similar in operation to the pyrotechnic system of the 5 Series, except the solid fuel and ignitor is replaced by a spring and inertia lock. If the force of the accident is great enough, the inertia lock built into the seatbelt reel assembly, will release the spring, pulling the seatbelt taut.

Steering Wheel Contact Ring

The purpose of the steering wheel contact ring is to provide a continuous electrical path to the ignitor in the air bag. The contact ring allows rotation of the steering wheel while providing the electrical path in an uninterrupted fashion.

SERVICE PRECAUTIONS

✳✳ CAUTION

The service precautions must be adhered to, to prevent personal injury. Unintended deployment of the air bag or seatbelt tensioner can cause injury.

• Before servicing, disarm the air bag system by turning the ignition switch to the **OFF** position, disconnect the negative battery cable and the air bag connector under the steering column.
• Sensors must be installed with their arrows pointing toward the front of the vehicle.
• Always make sure the steering wheel contact ring has been aligned to the center position before installing. Do not turn the steering wheel with the steering gear disconnected.
• Always replace the air bag system fasteners with new ones. Do not reuse the old fasteners.
• Do not disassemble any air bag system components.
• Always carry an air bag with the trim cover pointed away.
• Always place an air bag on the workbench with the pad side facing upward, away from loose objects.

HEATING AND AIR CONDITIONING

➡**All the procedures needing the air conditioner refrigerant lines to be disconnected require that the system be discharged and the refrigerant recovered by a qualified and properly equipped shop using a recovery and recycling machine Do not discharge the refrigerant into the atmosphere. See Section 1 for more information regarding air conditioner refrigerant systems, discharging and charging.**

Core and Blower Assembly

REMOVAL & INSTALLATION

On the following models, the entire heater assembly must be removed from the car to replace either the blower motor or the heater core.

• After deployment, the air bag surface may contain sodium hydroxide dust. Always wear gloves and safety glasses when handling the assembly. Wash hands afterwards.
• Always inspect the air bag sensors and steering wheel pad after the vehicle has been involved in a collision (even in cases of minor collision) where the air bag did not deploy.
• Never disconnect any electrical connection with the ignition switch **ON**.
• Before disconnecting the negative battery cable, make a record of the contents memorized by each memory system like the clock, audio, etc. When service or repairs are completed make certain to reset these memory systems.
• Avoid touching module connector pins.
• Always touch a vehicle ground after sliding across a vehicle seat or walking across vinyl or carpeted floors to avoid static charge damage.
• All sensors are specifically calibrated to a particular vehicle. Do not interchange. The sensors, mounting brackets and wiring harness must never be modified from original design.
• Never strike or jar a sensor, or deployment could happen.
• The air bag must be deployed before it is scrapped. Return the air bag to a dealer for disposal.
• Any visible damage to sensors requires component replacement.
• Never bake dry paint on vehicle or subject the vehicle to temperatures exceeding 200°F (93°C), without disabling the air bag system and removing the air bag, sensors, SRS control module and the steering wheel contact ring.
• Never allow welding cables to lay on, near or across any vehicle electrical wiring.
• Caution labels are important when servicing the air bag system in the field. If they are dirty or damaged, replace them with new ones.
• If the crash sensors or the control unit has been dropped 1.5 ft. (0.5m) or more, they must be replaced.
• Do not subject the air bag to extreme temperatures above 212°F (100°C)

DISARMING THE SYSTEM

1. Place the ignition switch in the **OFF** position.
2. Disconnect the negative battery terminal and cover the battery terminal to prevent accidental contact.
3. Disconnect the crash sensors in the engine compartment.
4. Remove the lower cover of the steering column and disconnect the orange connector. The 3 Series has a small panel on the bottom of the steering column that when pulled down, holds the connector.
5. On the 5 Series, disconnect the seatbelt tensioner connectors.

ENABLING THE SYSTEM

1. Place the ignition switch in the **OFF** position.
2. Connect the sensors, the steering column connector and the seatbelt tensioner connectors.
3. Connect the negative battery terminal.
4. Place the ignition switch in the **ON** position. Check that the SRS light illuminates for 6 seconds and extinguishes. If it illuminates in any other pattern, there is a problem that needs to be rectified by a qualified BMW technician.

1600, 2000 and 2002 Models

▶ **See Figure 14**

1. Disconnect the negative battery cable.
2. Move the heater control lever on the dash all the way to the **WARM** position. Remove the radiator and engine drain cocks and drain the cooling system.

✳✳ CAUTION

When draining coolant, keep in mind that cats and dogs are attracted to ethylene glycol antifreeze, and could drink any that is left in an uncovered container or in puddles on the ground. This will prove fatal in sufficient quantity. Always drain the coolant into a sealable container. Coolant should be reused unless it is contaminated or several years old.

3. Loosen the hose clamp and disconnect the heater return hose from its fitting on the engine side of the firewall. Also, loosen the clamps and disconnect the heater feed hose from the heater control valve at the firewall. Remove the valve and check that it is not blocked with cooling system deposits. Replace it, as necessary.

4. On 1970 models, from the interior of the vehicle, remove the retaining screws and pull the storage tray to the rear. On 1971 and later models, with a full-length console, unscrew the shift knob, pull off the rubber boot, unfasten the screws for the side and center sections, life out the center section, disconnect the electrical connections for the hazard flasher and radio, if equipped, and lift out the remaining sections of the console.

5. Remove the retaining screws and remove the following dashboard finish panels: the lower steering column casing, the lower center trim panel, the outer left-hand trim panel, and the bottom half of the upper steering column casing.

6. Pull off the black knobs for the air control and heater temperature controls. On 1970 models, remove the inner knurled nuts and the Phillips head screw for the air control outer finish panel and lift off the panel. Then remove the 2 Phillips head screws securing the air controls to the dash. Finally, pull out the ashtray, and remove the 2 Phillips head screws retaining the heater temperature control to the dash. On 1971 and later models, lift out the snap-fit clear plastic covers for both the air control and the heater temperature controls. Then, remove the Phillips head screws retaining the controls to the dash, and pull the levers downward and out.

7. Label and disconnect the electrical leads for the heater (3 wires for 2-speed blower; 4 wires for 3-speed blower) underneath the dash. Remove the nut and disconnect the heater ground wire.

8. Pull off the left-hand hot air hose and slightly turn the retaining bracket for the steering column. Loosen the right-hand trim panel and pull off the right-hand hot air hose.

9. Open the glove compartment. Remove the left and right-hand side heater retaining nuts (one on each side). Carefully pull out the heater unit.

10. Drill out the rivets retaining the heater cover. Unsnap the clasps at the rear of the heater housing. Separate the housing valves.

11. Loosen the hose clamp for the heater valve. Loosen the cable clamp screw, and remove the lever pivot screw and the 2 control mounting screws.

12. Remove the rubber sleeves at either side of the blower.

13. Label and disconnect the electrical leads from the blower motor.

14. Disconnect the cable for the heater regulator.

15. Label and disconnect the leads from the heater housing.

16. Unsnap the clips and pull the motor and blower wheel assembly downward.

➡The motor and blower wheel are balanced as an assembly. If the motor is burned out, or if the blower wheel is damaged, the motor and blower wheel should be replaced as a unit., otherwise the blower will vibrate excessively during operation.

To install:

17. Install the blower motor in the assembly and install the retaining clips. Connect the cable for the heater regulator and install the leads on the heater housing.

18. Connect the leads at the blower and install the sleeves at the sides of the blower. Install the heater valve and connect the lever. Attach the halves of the heater case and install retaining screws where the rivets were drilled out.

19. Install the heater unit in the vehicle and install the retaining nuts. Reconnect the hot air hoses and install the trim panels.

20. Reconnect the heater electrical leads under the dash. Install all the air controls to the dash. Install all removed dash panels.

21. Reinstall all console components. Attach all heater hoses and fill the cooling system to the correct level.

22. Connect the negative battery cable.

23. Run the engine to normal operating temperature and check the operation of the heater. Be sure to bleed the cooling system, and check for coolant leaks.

2500, 2800, Bavaria, 3000 and 3.0 Models

1. Disconnect the negative battery cable.

2. Open the hood and remove the cover plate from the top of the cowl.

3. Remove the metal grid from the top of the blower. Unfasten the electrical connectors.

4. Unscrew the motor mount where it attaches to the heater housing. Tilt forward, and remove the unit from the cowl.

5. Release the 4 retaining clips, and pull the motor off the motor mount.

6. Install in reverse order. Make sure the shorter ends of the remaining clips go over the motor mount.

7. Connect the negative battery cable.

528i, 530i and 630CSi Models

▶ **See Figures 15 and 16**

1. Disconnect the negative battery cable.

2. Open the hold and remove the black access cover from the upper portion of the cowl.

3. On the 600 Series, remove the 2 screws on the windshield side, and the 3 screws on the front of the cowl, and remove the blower cover.

4. Open the 3 fasteners on the retaining straps, and then pull off the 2 upper halves of the blower cages.

5. Lift out the motor with wheels attached, and disconnect the wiring; the whole assembly may then be removed.

6. If the motor if faulty, the entire unit must be replaced. Install the unit in reverse order, positioning the flat surfaces on the intake ducts downward. On the

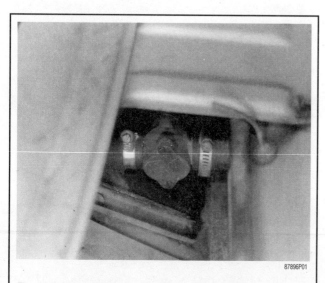

Fig. 14 Heater control valve at firewall—2002 models

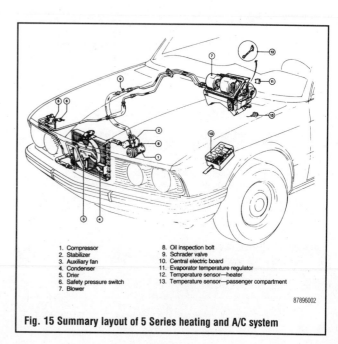

1. Compressor
2. Stabilizer
3. Auxiliary fan
4. Condenser
5. Drier
6. Safety pressure switch
7. Blower
8. Oil inspection bolt
9. Schrader valve
10. Central electric board
11. Evaporator temperature regulator
12. Temperature sensor—heater
13. Temperature sensor—passenger compartment

Fig. 15 Summary layout of 5 Series heating and A/C system

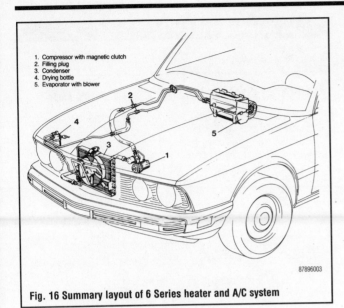

1. Compressor with magnetic clutch
2. Filling plug
3. Condenser
4. Drying bottle
5. Evaporator with blower

87896003

Fig. 16 Summary layout of 6 Series heater and A/C system

530i, make sure the area of the motor between the 2 wiring connectors fits into the notch on the passenger's side of the mounting bracket.

7. Connect the negative battery cable.

320i Models

1. Disconnect the battery ground.
2. Move the selector lever to the **WARM** position.
3. Drain the cooling system into a suitable container.

✳✳ CAUTION

When draining coolant, keep in mind that cats and dogs are attracted to ethylene glycol antifreeze, and could drink any that is left in an uncovered container or in puddles on the ground. This will prove fatal in sufficient quantity. Always drain the coolant into a sealable container. Coolant should be reused unless it is contaminated or several years old.

4. Loosen the hose clamp, and remove the heater core return hose.
5. Disconnect the heater hose between the hot water control valve and the engine.
6. Remove the package tray.
7. Remove outer tube casing.
8. Remove the lower center trim panel.
9. Remove the left side outer trim panel.
10. Remove the upper section of the steering tube casing.
11. Remove the heater control knobs.
12. Remove the heater control trim panel.
13. Remove the right side trim panel.
14. Disconnect the heater electrical lead.
15. Remove the heater housing retaining nuts.
16. Disconnect the left side distribution duct, and move the steering tube outer casing retaining bracket out of the way.
17. Remove the glove box lower trim panel.
18. Disconnect the left side distribution duct, and lift out the heater housing.
19. Remove the housing rivets.
20. Remove the housing clamps, and separate the housing halves.
21. Disconnect the cable from the hot water control valve.
22. Remove the hot water control valve and hose from the water valve bracket on the heater housing.
23. Remove the rubber sleeves from the heater core inlet and outlet tubes.
24. Disconnect the electrical leads at the blower motor.
25. Disconnect the electrical leads at the blower resistor in the heater housing.
26. Open the blower motor support clamps, and remove the blower motor and fan as an assembly.

To install:

27. Install the blower motor in the assembly and install the retaining clips. Connect the cable for the heater regulator and install the leads on the heater housing.
28. Connect the leads at the blower and install the sleeves at the sides of the blower. Install the heater valve and connect the lever. Attach the halves of the heater case and install retaining screws where the rivets were drilled out.
29. Install the heater unit in the vehicle and install the retaining nuts. Reconnect the hot air hoses and install the trim panels.
30. Reconnect the heater electrical leads under the dash. Install all the air controls to the dash. Install all removed dash panels.
31. Reinstall all console components. Attach all heater hoses and fill the cooling system to the correct level.
32. Connect the negative battery cable.
33. Run the engine to normal operating temperature and check the operation of the heater. Be sure to bleed the cooling system, also, check for leaks.

528e, 533i and 1982 633CSi Models

◆ See Figures 15 and 16

1. Disconnect the negative battery cable.
2. Remove the center tray. Remove the instrument panel trim at the bottom right of the tray.
3. Remove the glove box and remove heater controls at the water valve and the air doors. Remove center console if equipped.
4. Push the selector lever to the **WARM** position.
5. Drain the coolant and remove the air conditioning evaporator as follows:

✳✳ CAUTION

When draining coolant, keep in mind that cats and dogs are attracted to ethylene glycol antifreeze, and could drink any that is left in an uncovered container or in puddles on the ground. This will prove fatal in sufficient quantity. Always drain the coolant into a sealable container. Coolant should be reused unless it is contaminated or several years old.

a. Consult a professional mechanic who can remove the refrigerant from the A/C system using an approved recovery/recycling machine. If you are not certified to perform is procedure, and do not have access to the proper equipment, do not take this step on.
b. Remove the no-drip tape type insulation and disconnect both refrigerant lines from the evaporator.

➡**Plug the refrigerant lines immediately to prevent moisture and contaminants from entering the system.**

c. Pull the temperature sensor out of the evaporator housing.
d. Unfasten the evaporator/heater control electrical connector.
e. Remove the right and left screws from the housing inside the vehicle(from area where the housing meets the passenger compartment carpeting).
f. Remove the floor pan-to-evaporator housing bracket. Lift the housing slightly and pull it from under the dash.

✳✳ WARNING

Do not bend the temperature sensor or it will have to be replaced!

g. Disconnect the blower wires and the blower resistor wire. Lift the evaporator slightly and pull the adapter and evaporator from under the dash.
6. Disconnect the heater hoses from the heater core, and remove the rubber seal.
7. Remove the lower instrument panel center trim.
8. Disconnect the heater controls at the instrument panel.
9. Disconnect the control shafts at the joints.
10. Unfasten the multiple electrical connector at the heater.
11. Remove the instrument panel center cover.
12. Working from inside the engine compartment, remove the upper section of the fire shield.
13. Remove the heater assembly retaining nuts, and lift out the heater.

14. Open the heater housing clips, and separate the housing halves and remove the heater core.

15. Disconnect the electrical leads at the blower motor, and remove the motor.

To install:

16. Install the blower motor and connect the electrical leads. install the heater and clip the housing halves together. Install the heater and install the mounting nuts.

17. Install the upper section of fire shield under the hood.

18. Install the instrument panel center cover. Connect the electrical connector at the heater and fasten the control shafts at the joints.

19. Connect the heater controls at the instrument panel. Install the lower instrument panel trim.

20. Reconnect the heater hoses at the heater core. Install the blower wires and install the evaporator. Install the evaporator bracket.

21. Connect both refrigerant lines to the evaporator. Install all heater controls and connect the heater hoses.

22. Install the glove box. Install the center tray and instrument panel lower trim.

23. Have a professional fill the cooling system and recharge the A/C system using an approved recovery/recycling machine.

24. Run the engine and check for leaks. Check the operation of the heating and A/C systems.

1982–86 733i and 735i Models

1. Disconnect the negative battery cable.
2. Drain the coolant from the system.

✳✳ CAUTION

When draining coolant, keep in mind that cats and dogs are attracted to ethylene glycol antifreeze, and could drink any that is left in an uncovered container or in puddles on the ground. This will prove fatal in sufficient quantity. Always drain the coolant into a sealable container. Coolant should be reused unless it is contaminated or several years old.

3. Discharge the refrigerant from the air conditioner using a recovery/recycling machine.

4. Remove the instrument trim panel.

5. Remove the cowl fresh air grille.

6. Remove the heater assembly cover attaching screws, and remove the cover.

7. Disconnect the heater hoses at the heater core.

8. Disconnect the vacuum lines at the heater.

9. Bend open the heater duct mounting clamp.

10. Disconnect the central electrical lead.

11. Pull the duct cover downward, and remove it.

12. Remove the center strut attaching bolts.

13. Remove the insulation from the refrigerant lines.

14. Disconnect the refrigerant lines from the evaporator.

15. Disconnect the evaporator drain tube.

16. Remove the heater assembly retaining bolts, remove the heater and the heater core.

To install:

17. Install the heater and heater core. Install the heater assembly and connect the evaporator drain tube.

18. Connect the refrigerant lines to the evaporator. Install the center strut and install the duct cover.

19. Fasten the electrical lead and connect the vacuum lines at the heater.

20. Connect the heater hoses at the heater core. Install the heater assembly cover. Install the cowl fresh air grille. Install the instrument trim panel.

21. Connect the negative battery cable.

22. Charge the A/C system and fill the cooling system using an approved recovery/recycling machine.

23. Run the engine and check all connections for leaks. Check the operation of the blower.

Heater Assembly and Core

REMOVAL & INSTALLATION

1983–88 528e, 533i, 535i, 633CSi, 635CSi, M5 and M6 Models

1. Disconnect the battery ground. Remove the instrument panel trim at the bottom left. Remove the package tray.

2. Have the air conditioning system discharged by a professional using an approved recovery/recycling machine.

3. Remove the 2 bolts securing the trim panel underneath the evaporator unit.

4. Remove the tape type insulation.

5. Using a backup wrench, disconnect the low and high pressure A/C lines and cap the open ends.

6. Unfasten the electrical connector for the evaporator. Disconnect the temperature sensor plug accessible from the outside of the evaporator housing.

7. Remove the 2 bolts and then remove the bracket that braces the evaporator housing at the firewall. Remove the mounting bolt from either side of the housing.

8. Unclip both fasteners and remove the housing.

9. Now, move into the engine compartment and remove the rubber insulator from the cowl.

10. Remove the mounting bolts for the cover which is located under the windshield.

11. Remove the mounting nuts for the heater housing located on either side of the blower.

12. Drain the cooling system, then disconnect the 2 hoses at the core.

✳✳ CAUTION

When draining coolant, keep in mind that cats and dogs are attracted to ethylene glycol antifreeze, and are could drink any that is left in an uncovered container or in puddles on the ground. This will prove fatal in sufficient quantity. Always drain the coolant into a sealable container. Coolant should be reused unless it is contaminated or several years old.

13. Working from inside the vehicle, remove the 3 electrical connectors for the heater housing. Pull off the 2 air ducts.

14. Remove the 2 mounting nuts and remove the heater unit.

15. Remove the air duct connections from the housing. Push the retaining bar back and then split and remove the 2 blower shells.

16. Remove the retaining clips from the housing halves and split the housing. Then, remove the core.

To install:

17. Reverse the removal procedure, noting the following points:

   a. Cement a new rubber seal on to the core.

   b. Make sure that when reassembling the halves of the housing, all the distributor door flap shafts pass through the holes in the housing.

   c. Before reconnecting the refrigerant lines, coat the threads with clean refrigerant oil.

   d. Refill the cooling system with clean coolant and bleed it.

   e. Have the air conditioning system evacuated and recharged using an approved recovery/recycling machine.

Heater Core

REMOVAL & INSTALLATION

1600, 2000, 2002 and 320i Models

In order to remove the heater core, it is necessary to first remove the entire heater assembly from the car. See the procedure for removing the blower motor, above. Once the heater is out of the car, the core may be removed by drilling out the rivets and unsnapping the clips which hold the housing halves together.

2500, 28000, Bavaria, 3000 and 3.0 Models

1. Drain the coolant from the system.

❄❄ CAUTION

When draining coolant, keep in mind that cats and dogs are attracted to ethylene glycol antifreeze, and could drink any that is left in an uncovered container or in puddles on the ground. This will prove fatal in sufficient quantity. Always drain the coolant into a sealable container. Coolant should be reused unless it is contaminated or several years old.

2. Disconnect the heater hoses from the heater core, and remove the rubber seal.
3. Remove the fresh air outlet grille cover.
4. Remove the heater control cover.
5. Disconnect the air distribution hoses from the discharge nozzles.
6. Remove the intermediate distribution duct.
7. Remove the buttons from the control levers.
8. Remove the threaded knobs for the left instrument panel trim strip.
9. Remove the rear switch plate.
10. Remove the front switch plate.
11. Remove the heater retaining nuts.
12. Tilt the heater and switch plate inwards, and remove the heater.
13. Detach the cable going to the defroster flap.
14. Pull off the retaining clips, remove the seals, and pull apart the halves of the heater housing (the core will stay in the left side of the housing).
15. Slide the core out of the housing, pulling the outer end toward you to permit the hose connections to clear the housing.

To install:

16. 13.Reverse the removal procedure, noting the following points:
    a. Slide the air guide baffle in an angle to properly install.
    b. First insert the switch plate into the dash and then insert the heater. Tighten the attaching nuts firmly. Check the foam rubber seal between the heater and dash panel and replace, if necessary.
    c. When installing the front switch plate, make sure the control levers do not scrape against the trim.
    d. Replace the sealing gasket which goes under the cowl cover.

3 Series Models

1. Disconnect the negative battery terminal. Remove the center console and the drivers side instrument panel trim next to the steering column. Drain the coolant.

❄❄ CAUTION

When draining coolant, keep in mind that cats and dogs are attracted to ethylene glycol antifreeze, and could drink any that is left in an uncovered container or in puddles on the ground. This will prove fatal in sufficient quantity. Always drain the coolant into a sealable container. Coolant should be reused unless it is contaminated or several years old.

2. Loosen the coolant pipe clamp near the heater connection.
3. Remove the duct from the heater to the rear heating duct.
4. Place some rags or a small container under the heater connection to catch any spilled coolant. Remove the bolts from the heater connection and separate the joint.
5. Remove the heater core bolts and remove from the heater housing.

To install:

6. Replace the heater core into the heater housing and replace the bolts. Replace the O-rings on the heater pipe joint. Connect the pipe to the heater core and install the bolts.
7. Install the rear heating duct connection and the pipe holding clamp. Install the instrument panel trim and the center console. Fill the cooling system and bleed. Connect the negative battery terminal.

5 Series Models

EXCEPT 528I AND 530I MODELS

1. Remove the center console and the glove compartment.
2. Disconnect the coolant hoses from the heater. The upper hose is the return line, the middle hose the water feed for the right side and the bottom is the feed for the left side. Blow air into the return connection to remove the remaining coolant from the core.

❄❄ CAUTION

When draining coolant, keep in mind that cats and dogs are attracted to ethylene glycol antifreeze, and could drink any that is left in an uncovered container or in puddles on the ground. This will prove fatal in sufficient quantity. Always drain the coolant into a sealable container. Coolant should be reused unless it is contaminated or several years old.

3. Remove the screws from the holder. Remove the screws from the right holder and remove the holder.
4. Remove the motor for the front vents and disconnect the inside temperature sensor.
5. Disconnect the screws, straps and clips holding the heater cover. Remove the cover to expose the internal coolant pipes.
6. Remove the mounting screws from the coolant pipes and lift out. The heater core remove from the right.

To install:

7. Install the heater core and the coolant pipes with new O-rings. Install the cover and connect the clips, straps and screws.
8. Install the vent motor and connect the inside temperature sensor. Install the holders and screws.
9. Connect the coolant hoses. Install the center console and glove compartment. Fill and bleed the cooling system.

528I AND 530I MODELS

1. Remove the center tray.
2. Remove the glove box.
3. Disconnect the battery ground.
4. Push the selector lever to the **WARM** position.
5. Drain the coolant.

❄❄ CAUTION

When draining coolant, keep in mind that cats and dogs are attracted to ethylene glycol antifreeze, and could drink any that is left in an uncovered container or in puddles on the ground. This will prove fatal in sufficient quantity. Always drain the coolant into a sealable container. Coolant should be reused unless it is contaminated or several years old.

6. Disconnect the heater hoses from the heater core, and remove the rubber seal.
7. Remove the lower instrument panel center trim.
8. Disconnect the heater controls at the instrument panel.
9. Disconnect the control shafts at the joints. To do this, press in locking prongs with needle nose pliers.
10. Unfasten the multiple electrical connector at the heater.
11. Remove the instrument panel center cover.
12. Working from inside the engine compartment, remove the upper section of the fire shield.
13. Disconnect ducts by pulling outward to pull connector pins out of bushings which are in the ducts.
14. Remove clips and remove the outer portion of the lower blower housing. Pull out the motor/blower unit, disconnect the wires, and remove it.
15. Pull the foam rubber seal about halfway off and fold back.
16. Remove the clamp from the pipe leading to the water valve, disconnect the water valve and remove the valve and pipe as an assembly.
17. Remove clips and detach the right side housing. Note this housing covers ears which operate the heater damper.

18. Remove the attaching circlip and remove the smaller gear. Then, pull out the shaft to which the smaller gear is mounted.

19. Remove the housing clips and separate the housing halves.

20. Press out the grommet and pull the wires out from between core pipes and the core. Remove the core from the heater assembly.

To install:

21. Reverse the above, keeping the following points in mind:

a. Glue new rubber seals onto the outside of the core before installing it into the heater.

b. When reassembling the halves of the heater, first position the sleeve on the air flap and position the flap carefully and guide it into the bore on the opposite side of the heater housing.

c. When reinstalling damper gears, mesh the gears so the timing marks line up.

d. Replace the water valve seals.

e. When remounting the lower blower motor, make sure the portion of the motor between the 2 electrical connectors engages with the slot in the heater housing. Then, when reinstalling the blower housing, make sure the flat surface on either side of the intake duct faces down.

f. Secure the cables so that air flaps are closed when the control switch is at **OFF**.

g. Turn the fan switch and water valve and air distribution flaps left to the stop for each when reconnecting the control shafts.

733i and 735i Models

1. Drain coolant from the cooling system.
2. Remove the center console.

✳✳ CAUTION

When draining coolant, keep in mind that cats and dogs are attracted to ethylene glycol antifreeze, and could drink any that is left in an uncovered container or in puddles on the ground. This will prove fatal in sufficient quantity. Always drain the coolant into a sealable container. Coolant should be reused unless it is contaminated or several years old.

3. Remove the 2 bolts and remove the right core mounting bracket. Lift out the front blower motor.

4. Remove the core cover screws. Loosen the wire straps and clips and remove the cover.

5. Unscrew the 6 mounting bolts and lift out the 3 heater pipes. Replace the O-rings. Then, lift out the core from the right side.

To install:

6. Install core by reversing the above procedures. Check all connections for leaks and check the system for correct operation.

Blower Motor

REMOVAL & INSTALLATION

3 Series Models

The blower is accessible by removing the cover at the top of the firewall in the engine compartment.

1. Disconnect the negative battery cable. To remove the motor cover, pull off the rubber weatherstrip, cut off wire ties holding the wire that runs diagonally across the cover, unscrew and remove the bolts, and pull the cover aside.

2. Release the retaining straps, move them to the side, and then remove the blower cover.

3. Pull off both electrical connectors. Disengage the clamp that fastens the assembly in place by pulling the bottom. Lift out the motor/fan assembly, being careful not to damage the flap underneath.

To install:

4. The fan and motor assembly is balanced at the factory. Do not disturb the orientation of the fan and motor during installation. Place the fan and motor into the heater and install the clamp.

5. Connect the wires and install the fan cover. Attach the straps.

6. Install the outside cover and install the 4 bolts. Install new wire ties on the diagonal wire and replace the weather-stripping. Connect the negative battery cable.

5 and 6 Series Models

EXCEPT 528E, 533I, 535I, 633CSI, 635CSI, M5 AND M6 MODELS

1. Disconnect the negative battery cable.

2. Remove the rubber insulator from the cowl. Remove the mounting bolts and the radiator expansion tank located under the windshield on vehicles equipped. Remove the intensive washing fluid reservoir, if necessary.

3. Remove the wire ties holding the cable to the cover. Remove the screws holding the housing cover and remove the cover. Remove the cable and release the clips to remove the blower cover.

4. Disconnect the electrical connector for the motor. Unclip the retaining strap for the motor and remove the motor and blower wheels.

To install:

5. Replace the motor and blower wheels as an assembly (prebalanced). The motor will fit into the housing only one way. The flat surface on the inlet cowls face the body.

6. Install the blower cover and clip into place. Install the housing cover and replace the screws. Replace the cable wire ties.

7. Install the intensive washing fluid reservoir or the expansion tank, as equipped. Install the weather-stripping.

528E, 533I, 535I, 633CSI, 635CSI, M5 AND M6 MODELS

1. Disconnect the battery ground cable.

2. Remove the rubber insulator from the cowl. Remove the mounting bolts for the cover which is located under the windshield.

3. Push back the 3 retaining tabs and remove the 2 shells that cover the blower wheels.

4. Unfasten the electrical connector for the motor. Unclip the retaining strap for the motor and remove the motor and blower wheels.

To install:

5. Replace the motor and blower wheels as an assembly. This is because each assembly is a balance unit. The motor will fit into the housing only one way. Reverse all procedures to install, making sure the flat surface on the inlet cowls face the body.

733i and 735i Models

1. Disconnect the battery ground cable. Pull the rubber cover off the overflow tank for the cooling system. Unfasten the electrical connector and overflow hose from the overflow tank. Then, remove the mounting nuts and put the tank aside without damaging the hose leading to the radiator.

2. Cut the straps for the wiring harness running across the cowl.

3. Remove the attaching screws and remove the blower cover from the cowl.

4. Disconnect the cable and unclip it where it is clipped to the blower cover. Then, open the plastic retainer and take off the cover.

5. Unfasten the electrical connector. Lift off the metal retainer for the blower motor and remove the blower motor.

6. Install a new, prebalanced motor and blower assembly. Install in reverse order.

Heater Water Control Valve

REMOVAL & INSTALLATION

Except 5, 6 and 7 Series Models

1. Disconnect the negative battery terminal. Remove the center console and the drivers side instrument panel trim next to the steering column. Drain the coolant.

✳✳ CAUTION

When draining coolant, keep in mind that cats and dogs are attracted to ethylene glycol antifreeze, and could drink any that is left in an uncovered container or in puddles on the ground. This will prove fatal in sufficient quantity. Always drain the coolant into a sealable container. Coolant should be reused unless it is contaminated or several years old.

2. Disconnect the coolant hoses from the inlet on the firewall. Disconnect the wire or control cable from the control valve.

3. Loosen the coolant pipe clamp. Remove the 2 bolts from the pipe connection at the control valve and the bolts from the heater connection.

To install

4. Replace the O-rings at the connections.

5. Replace the bolts in the connections and attach the pipe clamp. Connect the wire or cable to the control valve.

6. Connect the coolant hose at the firewall. Install the center console and the instrument panel trim. Fill and bleed the cooling system. Connect the negative battery terminal.

5, 6 and 7 Series Models

1. Drain the cooling system. Disconnect the heater hoses from the control valve and the feed hose to the electric water pump, if equipped.

✳✳ CAUTION

When draining coolant, keep in mind that cats and dogs are attracted to ethylene glycol antifreeze, and could drink any that is left in an uncovered container or in puddles on the ground. This will prove fatal in sufficient quantity. Always drain the coolant into a sealable container. Coolant should be reused unless it is contaminated or several years old.

2. Disconnect the electrical plug from the top of the valve. Remove the screws and the clamp.

3. Remove the valve by lifting out.

To install:

4. The valve can be checked by applying battery voltage to the top of the pyramid of terminals and alternately grounding the bottom pins. The valve will actuate.

5. Install the valve, bolts and electrical connector. Connect the coolant hoses. Fill and bleed the cooling system.

Control Panel

REMOVAL & INSTALLATION

Models With Cable Control

1. Disconnect the negative battery cable.

2. Remove the radio as outlined in this section.

3. Remove the control panel retaining screws and pull the panel forward.

4. Disconnect the electrical wires from the rear of the panel.

5. Loosen the tang that holds the cable in position and remove the cable from the control head, by tilting the control head up slightly.

To install:

6. Install the control head in position, first connecting the actuating cable to it.

7. Reconnect the electrical leads and install the panel retaining screws.

8. Install the radio.

9. Reconnect the battery and check the operation of the system and check the levers for freedom of movement.

Models With Vacuum Control

1. Disconnect the negative battery cable.

2. Remove the radio and surrounding trim panel.

3. Remove the screws along the top edge of the control panel and pull the panel out slightly.

4. Disconnect the electrical leads from the back of the panel.

5. Unplug the vacuum line connector, note the position of the connector for installation.

6. Remove the panel from the dash.

To install:

7. Install the control panel in position and reconnect the vacuum connector, note the color coding of the hoses for correct installation, they should match.

8. Reconnect the electrical leads and screw the panel into position.

9. Install the radio and surrounding trim panel.

10. Connect the negative battery cable. Check the operation of the system and check for any vacuum leaks.

Automatic Controls

1. Disconnect the negative battery cable.

2. Remove the radio and surrounding trim panel.

3. Remove the cover from the rear defogger switch.

4. Use a tool to press the clip accessible from the defogger switch opening.

5. Pull the control unit out and disconnect the plugs.

6. Install in reverse order.

Control Cables

REMOVAL & INSTALLATION

Lower Footwell Flap

1. Disconnect the negative battery terminal. Remove the left side lower instrument panel trim and the center console tray. Remove the radio.

2. Remove the switches or covers from the openings above the radio opening. Disconnect the switches from the wiring harness.

3. Remove the screws holding the control panel at the top. The screws are accessible at the openings above the radio opening. Pull the control panel forward.

4. Disconnect the cable clamp and remove the cable end from the lever. Do this at each end of the cable.

To install:

5. Connect the cable at the flap lever and fit the clamp in place. The cable housing must be flush with the clamp.

6. Connect the control lever cable and move the lever fully to the right. Turn the cable sleeve until the cable can be placed in the holder and the clamp secured.

7. Affix the control panel and replace the switches and covers. Install the radio, console tray and the trim panel. Connect the negative battery terminal.

Defogger and Fresh Air Flap

1. Disconnect the negative battery terminal. Remove the left side lower instrument panel trim and the center console tray. Lower the glove compartment door and disconnect the straps. Remove the radio.

2. Remove the switches or covers from the openings above the radio opening. Disconnect the switches from the wiring harness.

3. Remove the screws holding the control panel at the top. The screws are accessible at the openings above the radio opening. Pull the control panel forward.

4. Disconnect the cable clamp and remove the cable end from the lever. Do this at each end of the cable.

To install

5. Connect the cable at the flap lever and fit the clamp in place. The cable housing must be flush with the clamp.

6. Connect the control lever cable and move the lever fully to the right. Turn the cable sleeve until the cable can be placed in the holder and the clamp secured.

7. Affix the control panel and replace the switches and covers. Install the radio, console tray, glove compartment door straps and the trim panel. Connect the negative battery terminal.

Mixing Flap

1. Disconnect the negative battery terminal. Remove the left side lower instrument panel trim and the center console tray. Lower the glove compartment door and disconnect the straps. Remove the radio.

2. Remove the switches or covers from the openings above the radio opening. Disconnect the switches from the wiring harness.

3. Remove the screws holding the control panel at the top. The screws are accessible at the openings above the radio opening. Pull the control panel forward.

4. Disconnect the cable clamp and remove the cable end from the lever. Do this at each end of the cable.

To install:

5. Connect the cable at the flap lever and fit the clamp in place.

6. Connect the temperature selector cable and move the wheel to the **WARM** position. Turn the cable knurl nut so the flap moves to the **WARM** position. Adjust the nut so the cable can be placed in the holder and the clamp secured.

7. Affix the control panel and replace the switches and covers. Install the radio, console tray, glove compartment door straps and the trim panel. Connect the negative battery terminal.

ENTERTAINMENT SYSTEMS

♦ See Figure 17

Radio Receiver

➡Most 1984 and later models are equipped with an electronically tuned stereo system; this system uses push buttons instead of knobs for radio control. Removal and installation procedures for electronically tuned radios appear later in this section.

REMOVAL & INSTALLATION

1600, 2000, 2002, and 320i Models

1. Disconnect the negative battery cable.
2. Unscrew the shift lever and lift off the boot.
3. Remove the screws which retain the console to the dash and transmission tunnel.
4. Remove the screws which retain the left and right-hand side panels of the console to the radio mounting bracket. Remove the side panels, exposing the radio mounting bracket. (The radio mounting bracket houses the mono speaker.)
5. Disconnect the antenna cable from the radio. Unfasten the radio ground cable (if so equipped) from the left-hand heater mounting bolt. Detach the power lead for the radio.
6. Lift the radio mounting bracket forward. The radio may now be disconnected from the speaker by removing the speaker multiple plug from the back of the radio.

➡If the radio is connected to multiple speakers, tag each speaker connection and unfasten.

7. Pry off the radio control knobs exposing the mounting nuts. Unscrew the mounting nuts and remove the radio from its bracket.
To install:
8. Install the radio in its mounting bracket and install the mounting nuts.
9. Install the radio control knobs. Connect the speaker plug to the radio and connect the power and ground leads to the radio.
10. Install the side console panels and install the console retaining screws.
11. Install the shift lever boot, if equipped. Connect the negative battery cable and check the operation of the radio.

2500, 2800, Bavaria, 3000 and 3.0 Models

1. Disconnect the negative battery cable. Remove the screws from the outside of the underdash console while supporting the radio from underneath. Pull the unit out and lay it on the console.

2. Disconnect the antenna cable, ground cable, the speaker plug(s) (from the back of the unit) and the power cable.
To install:
3. Connect the wires to the radio and connect the antenna lead.
4. Slide the unit into position and install the retaining screws.
5. Connect the negative battery cable and check the operation of the radio.

528e, 530i and 630CSi Models

1. Disconnect the negative battery cable. Pull off the radio knobs and ornamental rings.
2. Push up on spring catches and remove them from the control shafts. Remove the radio face plate.
3. Remove the bolts from supports on both sides of the radio.
4. Disconnect the antenna lead, the speaker wires and the power supply.
To install:
5. Connect the power supply, speaker and antenna leads to the radio and install it in the dash.
6. Install the radio mask, ornamental rings, face plate and control knobs to the radio.
7. Connect the negative battery cable and check the radio for proper operation.

Electronically Tuned Radio (ETR)

REMOVAL & INSTALLATION

♦ See Figures 18, 19, 20 and 21

➡Most 1984 and later models are equipped with an electronically tuned stereo system; this system uses push buttons instead of knobs for radio control.

If equipped with a theft deterrent radio, make note of the radio code supplied on a tag with the owners information. As an anti-theft feature, the code must be entered into the radio once power has been removed.
1. Turn the ignition switch to the **OFF** position.
2. Determine the type of removal method needed, and proceed with one of the three options that follow:
• Insert radio removal hooks into the holes at the sides of the radio chassis. Seat the hooks and pull the radio out. Disconnect the plugs.
• If not equipped with holes at the sides of the chassis, pull the knob off and insert the hooks at the holes at the cassette opening and pull out.
• If equipped Allen head with screws at the edges of the chassis, remove the screws and pull the chassis out.
To install:
3. Connect the plugs and place the radio in the opening. Snap into place or install the angled screws.
4. Enter the radio code to activate the radio.

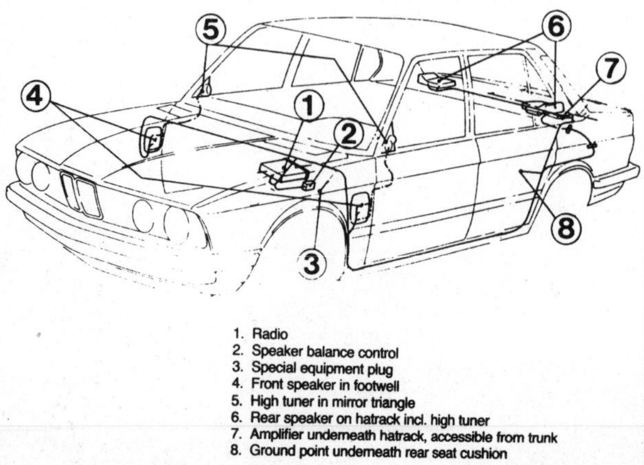

Fig. 17 Example of late model BMW radio component layout— 320i model

1. Radio
2. Speaker balance control
3. Special equipment plug
4. Front speaker in footwell
5. High tuner in mirror triangle
6. Rear speaker on hatrack incl. high tuner
7. Amplifier underneath hatrack, accessible from trunk
8. Ground point underneath rear seat cushion

87896012

Fig. 18 Use a pick tool to open the trim door at the side of the unit—side screw model

87896P02

Fig. 19 Use an Allen key to loosen the retaining screw securing the radio in place

Fig. 20 Unplug the antenna wire from the back of the radio

Fig. 21 Unfasten the power and speaker plugs from the radio

Speakers

REMOVAL & INSTALLATION

Rear Speakers

▶ **See Figures 22, 23, 24 and 25**

1. Remove the speaker grille(s) by removing the screws, if equipped, or pulling up on the grille with a pick tool.
2. Remove the speaker mounting screws and the speakers. Disconnect the wires.

3. Connect the wires and install the speakers in the cutouts. Install the screws and grills.

Door and Dash Mounted Tweeters

1. Remove the grilles by removing the screws, if equipped, or carefully pulling up and prying out the grille.
2. Remove the speaker mounting screws and the speakers. Disconnect the wires.
3. Connect the wires and install the speakers in the cutouts. Install the screws and grills.

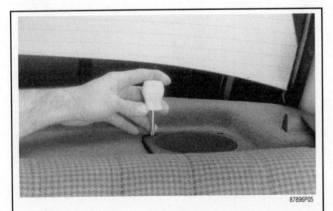

Fig. 22 Remove the screws securing the speaker grille to the rear deck—standard speaker

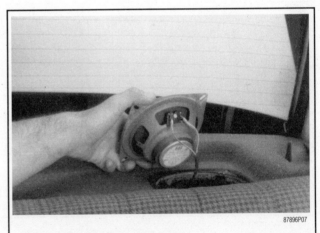

Fig. 24 Lift the speaker out of the hole . . .

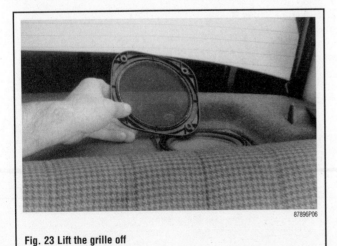

Fig. 23 Lift the grille off

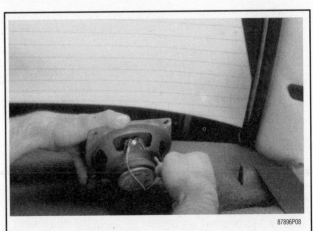

Fig. 25 . . . and unplug the wire connectors at the speaker

Front Speakers

▶ **See Figures 26, 27, 28, 29 and 30**

1. Remove the rubber seal on the side of the kick panel.
2. Remove the hood release lever on the left kick panel side and remove the kick panel trim by unfastening the retaining screws. On 5 and 7 Series models,

remove the door seal and turn the screws 90 degrees. Pull the panel out and to the rear to remove.
3. Remove the screws securing the speaker in place, and unfasten the wires from the speakers and remove.
4. Connect the wires and install the speakers in the cutouts. Install the screws and kick panels.

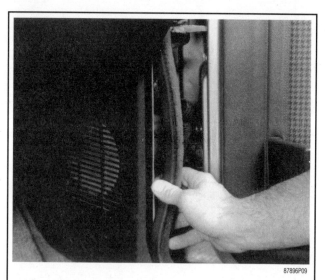

Fig. 26 Lift off the rubber door seal over the kick panel

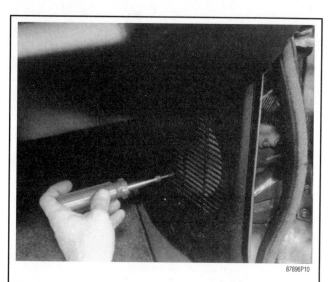

Fig. 27 Remove the retaining screws

Fig. 28 With the panel removed, the speaker is plainly visible

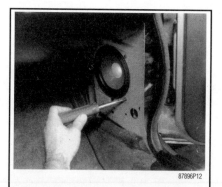

Fig. 29 Remove the retaining screws securing the speaker in place

Fig. 30 Unfasten the wires from the speaker

CRUISE CONTROL

Control Switch

REMOVAL & INSTALLATION

3 Series Models

1. Disconnect the negative battery terminal. Remove the steering wheel.
2. Remove the trim panel at the bottom left of the instrument panel and the lower steering column casing.
3. Remove the screws holding the switch. Remove the switch and disconnect the plug.
   To install:
4. Install the switch and connect the plug. The ground wire must be connected and the retainers must fit into the holes.
5. Install the trim panels and steering wheel. Connect the negative battery terminal.

5, 6 and 7 Series Models

1. Remove the lower dashboard trim panel at the left. Remove the lower section of the steering column casing.
2. Remove the steering wheel and compress the clip to release the switch. Disconnect the plug.
3. Install the switch and connect the plug. Install the steering wheel and trim panels.

Cruise Control Module

REMOVAL & INSTALLATION

3 Series Models

1. Disconnect the negative battery terminal.
2. Open the glove compartment door and remove the upper trim.

3. Remove the Digital Motor Electronics (DME) control unit. The cruise control module is mounted above the DME module. Remove the cruise control module and unfasten the harness.

4. Install the modules and trim. Connect the negative battery terminal.

5, 6 and 7 Series Models

1. Remove the cover from the electronics box at the rear, right side of engine compartment.

2. Turn the ignition switch **OFF**.

3. The control module is between the DME unit at the back of the electronics box and the row of relays. Disconnect the module and remove.

4. Install the module and install the electronics box cover.

WINDSHIELD WIPERS

Wiper Arm

REMOVAL & INSTALLATION

▶ **See Figures 31, 32 and 33**

1. If the wiper arm nut at the base of the arm is covered by a protective cover, carefully pry up on the cover.

2. Paint an alignment mark on the wiper arm and wiper motor or linkage shaft.

3. Remove the nut securing the wiper arm in place.

4. Carefully lift the arm off with a slight back and forth motion.

5. Install the arm by aligning the marks and installing and tightening the nut in place.

6. If the arm is equipped with a cover, push the cover down until secure.

Windshield Wiper Motor

The electric wiper motor assembly is located under the engine hood, at the top of the cowl panel. A few models have covers over the wiper motor assembly, while others have the motors exposed. Link rods operate the left and right wiper pivot assemblies from a drive crank bolted to the wiper motor output shaft.

REMOVAL & INSTALLATION

1600, 2000 and 2002 Models

▶ **See Figure 34**

➡**The motor is accessible from the engine side of the firewall.**

1. Disconnect the negative batter cable.

2. Remove the nut which retains the drive crank linkage to the motor, and disconnect the drive crank.

3. Remove the 3 mounting bolts for the motor.

Actuator

REMOVAL & INSTALLATION

1. Turn the ignition switch to the **OFF** position.

2. Open the engine compartment and access the actuator at the intake manifold.

3. Disconnect the electrical connections from the actuator.

4. Disconnect the actuator cable from the throttle linkage and remove the nuts holding the actuator.

5. Install the actuator and connect the wiring and cable.

4. Label and disconnect the 3 electrical leads from the clear plastic socket connection. Loosen the retaining screw for the ground wire and disconnect the ground wire from the body.

5. Lift out the wiper motor.

To install:

6. Install the wiper motor in position and install the 3 retaining bolts.

7. Connect the electrical leads and attach the ground wire.

8. Connect the drive crank. Reconnect the battery cable and check the operation of the wipers.

2500, 2800, Bavaria, 3000 and 3.0 Models

1. Remove the cover for the heater unit on the cowl panel, if equipped.

2. Remove the crank arm retaining nut and washer.

3. Remove the wiper motor retaining screws, tilt the motor downward and remove.

4. Disconnect the electrical contact plug from the wiper motor.

To install:

5. Connect the electrical contact plug to the wiper motor and install the motor.

6. Install the crank arm retaining nut and washer.

➡**The complete wiper motor, pivot assemblies and linkage can be removed as a unit, if necessary.**

320i, 524td, 528e, 528i, 533i, 535i, 633CSi, 635CSi, M5 and M6 Models

1. Remove the cowl cover to expose the wiper motor. This applies to 320i, 530i and all 5 and 6 Series models after 1983.

2. Disconnect the wiper motor crank arm from the motor output shaft by removing the nut and pulling off the crank arm.

3. Remove the motor retaining screws and disconnect the electrical connector.

4. Remove the wiper motor from the vehicle.

5. Reverse the procedure to install the motor.

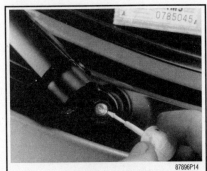

Fig. 31 If equipped with a protective cap, lift up the cap and paint an alignment mark on the wiper arm and shaft

Fig. 32 Loosen and remove the wiper arm retaining nut

Fig. 33 Lift the wiper arm off

Fig. 34 Common 2002 wiper motor. On these models, there is no protective cover over the motor assembly

Fig. 35 With the wiper arm removed, carefully pry up the grille cover

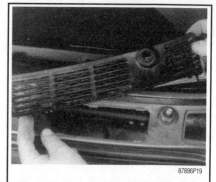

Fig. 36 When you remove the cover, the wiper motor is in the center of the hole

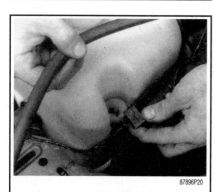

Fig. 37 Remove the wiring harness from the washer motor

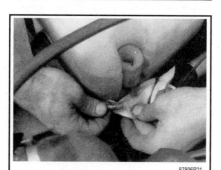

Fig. 38 Twist the hose off the motor. In order to avoid spillage, cap the fitting at the motor

Fig. 39 Remove the washer reservoir retaining hardware

3 Series Models

▶ See Figures 35 and 36

1. Remove the wiper arm assembly.
2. Remove the heater blower motor and the bracket under the wiper motor.
3. Disconnect the motor wiring. If only removing the motor, remove the shaft nut and the 3 mounting nuts. Pull the motor out.
4. Release the clips on the blower plate and disconnect the flaps to remove the blower plate.
5. Remove the wiper arms and the grill. Disconnect the links on the mount for the left pivot.
6. Remove the shaft covers and remove the nut. Remove the washer and pull the linkage out of the opening.

To install:

7. Install the linkage, washer and nuts. Install the shaft covers and connect the left pivot links. Install the grill and the wiper arms.
8. Install the blower plate and clip into place. Install the motor and link on the shaft.
9. Connect the wires, install the mount and the blower motor.
10. Install the wiper arm.

5, 6 and 7 Series Models

1. Cycle the wipers to return to the parked position. Turn the heater blower control to 0 and turn the ignition switch **ON** and **OFF** to close the heater box ventilation flaps. Remove the heater blower and remove the heater linkage cover.
2. Disconnect the negative battery terminal and disconnect the heater linkage. Pull out the temperature sensor. Remove the retainers to pull the inlet cowls out and remove the cover.

3. Disconnect the motor mounting brace. Remove the wiper arms. Remove the cowl cover retainers and the cover.
4. Loosen and remove the wiper arm shaft nuts. Disconnect the wiring plug. Pull the linkage out of the cowl.
5. Mark the relationship of the crank arm to the motor shaft and remove. Remove the 3 mounting bolts to remove the motor.

To install:

6. Install the motor to the linkage. If the position of the motor has been changed or a new motor is being installed, connect the motor to the electrical plug and cycle the motor once to return it to the parked position.
7. Install the crank arm to the original position as marked. If it is a new motor, align the crank arm with the linkage arm so they form a straight line.
8. Install the linkage in the cowl. Connect the motor electrical plug and install the wiper arm shaft nuts. Install the cowl cover and the wiper arms. Install the motor brace.
9. Install the inlet cowls and the cover. Install the temperature sensor and connect the heater linkage. Install the heater blower and connect the negative battery terminal.

Windshield Washer Reservoir and Motor

REMOVAL & INSTALLATION

▶ See Figures 37, 38, 39 and 40

1. Access the washer tank from the engine compartment.
2. Remove the harness attached to the washer motor.

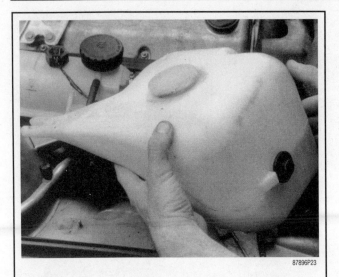

Fig. 40 Lift the washer reservoir out of the engine compartment

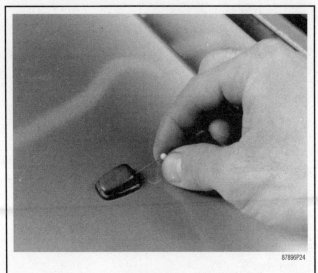

Fig. 41 Use a pin to adjust the washer nozzle spray path

3. Twist off the hose attached to the washer motor.
4. Remove the plastic screws or bolts securing the tank in the engine compartment.
5. Lift the tank out.
To install:
6. Place the tank into position and secure with the hardware.
7. Attach the hose and harness to the washer motor.

INSTRUMENTS AND SWITCHES

Instrument Cluster

REMOVAL & INSTALLATION

Except 3, 5, 6 and 7 Series Models

1. Disconnect the negative battery cable.
2. Remove the lower dash trim from under the steering column by removing the retaining screws. On some models the buzzer module will have to be unclipped to remove the panel from the interior of the vehicle.
3. Remove the steering wheel. Refer to the procedure in Section 8 for details.
4. Remove the 2 screws from the top of the instrument panel hood.
5. Remove the speaker grille and speaker from on top of the instrument panel. After the speaker has been removed, reach in and unfasten the speedometer cable from the back of the speedometer.

WASHER NOZZLE ADJUSTMENT

▶ See Figure 41

To adjust the washer nozzle spray path, or clean out a clogged nozzle, use a straight pin inserted into the nozzle hole. When adjusting the spray path, move the pin slightly, then use the washer to see where the spray pattern is. For optimum performance, the washer fluid should spray the windshield just above the center of the glass.

6. Remove the retaining screws from the lower portion of the dash panel which secure the instrument panel to the dash assembly.
7. Remove the instrument cluster and pull forward.
8. Disconnect the wire harness from the instrument cluster.
9. Install in reverse order or removal. Connect the negative battery cable. Check all cluster components and connections including the gauge lighting and speedometer cable connection.

3 Series Models

▶ See Figures 42 thru 52

1. Disconnect the negative battery cable.
2. Remove the lower dash trim from under the steering column by removing the retaining screws. On some models the buzzer module will have to be unclipped to remove the panel from the interior of the vehicle.
3. Remove the steering wheel. Refer to the procedure in Section 8 for details.

Fig. 42 Before beginning your work, note the location of the major components

Fig. 43 Some lower dash panels have the buzzer attached. To remove, separate the clips

Fig. 44 Remove the retaining screws from the upper portion of the instrument panel hood

Fig. 45 Unfasten the knurled nuts securing the trim panel in front of the steering column

Fig. 46 With the knurled nuts removed, push the trim panel out and remove

Fig. 47 Remove the retaining screws from behind the trim panel

Fig. 48 On most models there is a screw on either side of the steering column

Fig. 49 With all the screws removed, the instrument panel hood can be removed

Fig. 50 Remove the screws securing the instrument panel to the dash panel

Fig. 51 Bring the instrument panel forward and pull out towards you slightly . . .

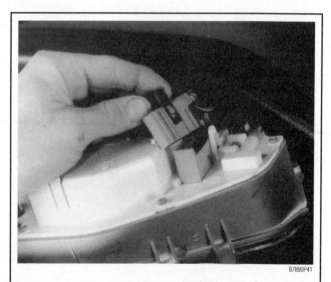

Fig. 52 . . . then unfasten the instrument panel wiring harness

4. Remove the 2 screws from the top of the instrument panel hood.

5. Working from behind the dash panel, remove the 2 knurled nuts which secure the trim panel above the steering column and below the instrument panel. When the nuts are removed, push the trim panel toward you and remove for the dash.

6. Loosen and remove the retaining screws behind the trim panel which secures the lower portion of the instrument panel.

➡**Note the position and length of the screws removed. These screws are not interchangeable as they are different lengths.**

7. Remove the screws from the instrument cluster and pull forward.

8. Pull the clip off the harness plug and disconnect from the instrument cluster.

9. Install in reverse order or removal. Connect the negative battery cable. Check all cluster components and connections including the gauge lighting and speedometer cable connection.

5, 6 and 7 Series Models

1. Disconnect the negative battery cable.
2. Remove the lower dash trim from under the steering column by removing the retaining screws. On some models the buzzer module will have to be unclipped to remove the panel from the interior of the vehicle.
3. Remove the steering wheel. Refer to the procedure in Section 8 for details.
4. Remove the screws from the top of the instrument panel hood.
5. Working from behind the dash panel, remove the 2 knurled nuts which secure the trim panel above the steering column and below the instrument panel. When the nuts are removed, push the trim panel toward you and remove for the dash.

➡ **When pushing out the trim panel pay particular attention not to bend, break or scratch the wood grain panel.**

6. Loosen and remove the retaining screws behind the trim panel which secures the lower portion of the instrument panel.
7. Remove the screws from the instrument cluster and pull forward.
8. Pull the clip off the harness plug and disconnect from the instrument cluster.
9. Install in reverse order or removal. Connect the negative battery cable. Check all cluster components and connections including the gauge lighting and speedometer cable connection.

CLUSTER BULB REPLACEMENT

▶ **See Figures 53, 54 and 55**

The light bulbs in the instrument cluster are installed via a pressure fit or a twist lock assembly.

1. Remove the instrument cluster.
2. Determine which bulb is in need of replacement. If the back of the bulb is round, it is a pressure fit type bulb. If the rear of the bulb is square, the bulb is a twist type bulb.
3. Remove the bulb by either carefully pulling it out, or twisting it ¼ turn to release the connection.
4. Once the bulb is removed, gentle pull the bulb out.
To install:
5. Purchase a bulb of the same watt amount as the removed bulb. If you have any questions on bulb type, consult a BMW dealer.
6. Press the new bulb in place.
7. Install the bulb and socket into the instrument cluster.
8. Install the cluster into the dash panel.
9. Test to make sure the replacement bulb functions correctly.

Service Interval Assembly

The Service Interval (SI) display circuit board, if equipped in your vehicle, is removable only on the 3 Series models. Other vehicles have the Service Interval assembly as an integral part of the instrument panel.

Most problems with the SI stem from bad connections, faulty grounds, relays replaced with nonstandard non diode type relays, or bad batteries. The circuit board can be exchanged or have the batteries replaced by soldering new tab batteries in place. Because of the delicate nature of the repair, it is best if this procedure is performed by a BMW dealer.

REMOVAL & DISASSEMBLY

3 Series Models

1. Remove the instrument cluster.
2. Disassemble the instrument cluster to separate the carrier from the instruments.
3. Remove the screw holding the light guide at the center of the carrier assembly. Slide the Service Interval circuit board out.

Windshield Wiper Switch

REMOVAL & INSTALLATION

➡ **On many models, this switch is a combination unit which also controls the direction signals and headlight dimming. On 3 Series models, this switch is mounted right next to the turn signal switch and its removal is covered specifically under that procedure.**

Except 735i Models

The wiper switch is located on the steering column and in most cases the steering wheel will have to be removed, along with the lower steering column trim panels, to gain access to the switch.

After the retaining screws and electrical connectors are removed, the switch can be lifted from the plate of the steering column.

❊❊ CAUTION

To avoid possible electrical short-circuits, the negative battery cable should be removed before the repairs are attempted.

735i Models

1. Disconnect the negative battery cable. Remove the steering wheel. Remove the lower left instrument panel trim.
2. Remove the screws and remove the lower steering column cover.
3. Push the locking hook for the flasher back and remove the relay, socket facing downward.
4. Take off the upper steering column cover. If the car has airbags, drive out the pins and lift out the expansion rivet first.

❊❊ CAUTION

On vehicles equipped with air bags, DO NOT bang on the steering column very hard or the air bag may be discharged!

Fig. 53 Remove the pressure fit type bulb and socket by gently pulling out

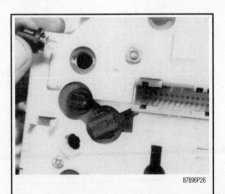

Fig. 54 Remove the twist type bulb by turning and removing

Fig. 55 To remove the bulb, simply pull straight out

5. Press the retaining hooks inward on both sides, pull the switch out, and then disconnect the electrical connector.

6. Reinstall the switch then install the electrical connectors. Install the column cover and lower instrument panel trim.

7. Install the steering wheel and connect the negative battery cable.

Headlight Switch

REMOVAL & INSTALLATION

1600, 2002, 2500, 2800, Bavaria, 3000, 3.0 and 3 Series Models

1. Disconnect the battery ground cable. Remove the lower left trim panel screws and remove the panel.

2. Unscrew the knob from the switch.

3. Pull off the connector plug from behind the dash panel. Pull out the switch from behind and remove it.

4. Install the switch back into position and connect the electrical lead.

5. Screw the knob back onto the switch and install the lower trim panel. Connect the negative battery cable.

528e, 535i, 733i, 735i and M5 Models

1. Disconnect the negative battery cable. The switch is pressed into the left side of the dash. Pry the switch out using a small screwdriver top and bottom.

2. Unplug the switch.

3. Connect the switch to the electrical lead and push it into the dash.

1983–84 633CSi, 635CSi and M6 Models

1. Disconnect the battery ground. Remove the lower left instrument panel trim.

2. Unscrew and remove the light switch knob.

3. Remove the 4 bolts and remove the brace located under the instrument panel.

4. Pull off the switch plug. Then, pull the switch out of the dash from behind.

5. Install the switch into the dash and plug it in.

6. Install the brace under the instrument panel.

7. Screw in the switch control knob. Install the trim panel and connect the negative battery cable.

Speedometer Cable

REMOVAL & INSTALLATION

➡**This applies to vehicles which are not equipped with a speed sensor.**

1600, 2000, and 2002 Models

1. Unscrew the cable fastening bolt on the transmission and pull the cable out.

2. Pull the cable out of the clamp under the car.

3. Remove the cable cover from under the steering column.

4. Reach up behind the instrument cluster and unscrew the cable retaining nut. The cable may now be pulled from the firewall together with the rubber grommet.

To install:

5. Install the cable through the firewall with the grommet and install it into the speedometer.

6. Install the cable cover. Attach the cable to the transmission. Check the operation of the speedometer, if it sticks or makes a clicking noise, check that the cable is correctly routed.

2500, 2800, 3000, Bavaria, 3.0, 3, 5, 6 and 7 Series Models Through 1983

1. Unscrew the retaining bolt, and pull the cable out of the transmission. Pull the cable off the retaining clips under the car.

2. Open the glove compartment on the left side. Reach up behind the instrument cluster and unscrew the cable retaining nut behind the speedometer.

3. Detach the hazard flasher relay, and move it aside. Then, pull the cable and the rubber grommet out of the firewall.

To install:

4. Install the cable through the firewall with the grommet and install it into the speedometer. Reposition the hazard flasher relay.

5. Attach the cable to the transmission. Check the operation of the speedometer, if it sticks or makes a clicking noise, check that the cable is correctly routed.

1984–88 Models

All of the remaining models not previously listed are equipped with an electronic speedometer. This speedometer has no mechanical connection to the transmission. Instead, a sensor in the transmission sends electronic signals to the speedometer which are then translated into the motion of the needle. The only service for any problems with this system is replacement of the speed sensor in the transmission or replacement of the speedometer or circuit board.

1. Raise and safely support the rear of the vehicle.

2. Turn the ignition switch **OFF**.

3. Squeeze the connector of the electrical plug and disconnect the plug on the rear axle cover.

4. Remove the 2 bolts holding the sensor in place. Catch any lubricant that leaks out.

5. Install a new O-ring on the sender and install in the rear axle. Install the electrical connector.

LIGHTING

Headlights

AIMING

Headlights should be precision aimed using special equipment; however, as a temporary measure, you might wish to re-aim your lights to an approximately correct position.

Most of the BMW models covered by this book employ large, knurled knobs, located behind the headlights, for aiming purposes. The horizontal adjustment is located on the right (driver's) side of the light, and the vertical adjustment above the light. Screw the vertical adjustment inward (clockwise) to lower the beam; screw the horizontal adjustment in (clockwise) to turn the beam to left, and vice versa.

The lights may be aimed against a wall. High beams should point just slightly below straight ahead and horizontal. Low beams should point somewhat downward, with the left side beam pointing slightly to the right.

REPLACEMENT

1600, 2000 and 2002 Models

1. Remove the 4 Phillips head screws from the front of the radiator grille.

2. Open the hood. Remove the weather-proof cover, if so equipped. Unscrew the knurled nut which retains the outside edge of the grille to the front panel. Lift off the grille.

3. Disconnect the electrical connector from the back of the sealed beam.

4. Remove the 3 screws which retain the headlight outer ring to the headlight, taking care not to drop the sealed beam.

5. Lift out the headlight.

To install:

6. Reverse the above procedure to install. Have the headlights adjusted at a garage with the proper equipment. If this is not possible, park the car on a level surface about 25 feet (0.6m) from a light colored wall. With the tires properly inflated and a friend sitting in the from seat, adjust the beams to the proper height

using the black knurled knobs located inside the fender well. The upper knob controls the vertical setting and the knob at the side controls the horizontal setting.

2500, 2800, Bavaria, 3000 and 3.0 Models

1. Open the hood and pull the cover off the rear of the headlight. Detach the electrical connector.
2. The bulb is retained by a spring clip-turn the clip back and pull the bulb out to the rear.
3. Installation is the reverse of the removal procedure. Make sure to properly align the reflector.

1975–86 3, 5, 6 and 7 Series Models Except 320i

▶ See Figures 56 thru 61

1. Open the hood and pull the cover off the rear of the headlight. Detach the electrical connector.
2. The bulb is retained by a spring clip. Turn the clip back and pull the bulb out to the rear.
3. Installation is the reverse of the removal procedure. Make sure to properly align the reflector.

320i Models

1. First, remove the top and bottom screws from the parking light. Pull the parking light lens off. Then, open the hood, disconnect the electrical connector for the parking light, and pull the rubber grommet out of the engine compartment wall. Now pull the entire parking light assembly out of the grille.
2. Remove the attaching screws and remove the grille.
3. Loosen the 3 screws on the trim ring (don't let the headlight fall) and then pull the lamp out. Disconnect the connector and remove the lamp.

To install:

4. Install the new lamp in reverse order, making sure the tab on the rear of the lamp is aligned with the notch in the reflector so that the lamp cannot be turned once it is in position.

All 1987–88 Models

▶ See Figure 62

Almost all new models use halogen headlamps, these lamps provide brighter and longer lasting light. The bulbs for the headlight are separate from the reflector, where as conventional bulbs are part of the reflector. Most low beam bulbs are part number 9004, and most high beam bulbs are part number 9006. Use these number when purchasing new bulbs.

➡Halogen bulbs are very sensitive and must be handled carefully. They must not be touched with bare hands. Always use a clean, soft cloth to change the bulbs.

1. Open the hood and disconnect the negative battery cable.
2. Remove the cover from the rear of the headlight assembly.
3. Turn the headlight holder counterclockwise and remove the light assembly.
4. Replace the bulb. Install a new bulb, making sure not to handle it with your bare hands.

Marker Lights and Front Turn Signal Lamps

REMOVAL & INSTALLATION

Except 1987–88 6 and 7 Series Models

▶ See Figures 63 thru 68

The front turn signal and all 4 marker lamp bulbs can easily be replaced. To replace the marker lamp bulbs, just remove the plastic lens and change the bulb. Most of the vehicles are equipped with a 4 watt bulb. On some of the older models the plastic lens will be retained with screws and on the newer models it can be popped out.

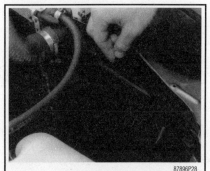

Fig. 56 If equipped with a cover over the headlight in the engine compartment, remove the retaining clips

Fig. 57 Remove the cover from the engine compartment

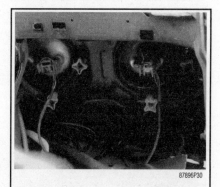

Fig. 58 With the cover removed, the headlights and adjustment knobs are visible

Fig. 59 Unscrew the three retainer screws which secure the collar around the light

Fig. 60 Lift the collar and headlight out . . .

Fig. 61 . . . and unplug the headlight

Fig. 62 Turn the harness and bulb to remove

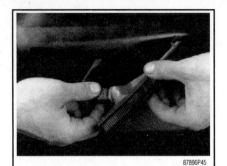

Fig. 63 To remove a side marker light, gently pry the lens and light assembly out of its mount

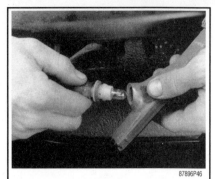

Fig. 64 Twist out the socket and bulb assembly

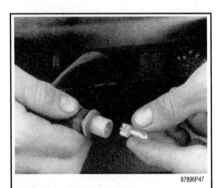

Fig. 65 To remove the bulb, simply pull straight out

Fig. 66 To remove a parking light/turn signal light, remove the retaining screws securing the lens

Fig. 67 With the cover removed, the bulb is visible

Fig. 68 Gently depress, then twist and remove the bulb

The turn signal bulbs in most of the vehicle are in the same housing as the marker lamps.

1987–88 6 and 7 Series Models

The front marker and turn signal lamps on these models are replaced in the same manner as the headlamps. The bulbs are assessable under the hood and are removed by grasping the housing and turning it slightly. The bulbs can then be replaced.

The rear marker lamps are replaced by removing the plastic cover and replacing the bulb.

Fog Lamps

REMOVAL & INSTALLATION

▶ See Figures 69, 70 and 71

To replace the fog lamp bulbs on models so equipped, remove the screws that retain the fog lamp cover. Remove the cover and the rubber seal and replace the bulb. On newer models the bulb is a halogen type bulb and should be handled carefully. Replace the cover, making sure the rubber seal is properly seated.

Fig. 69 Remove the screws from the side of the fog light—late model Bosch® light shown

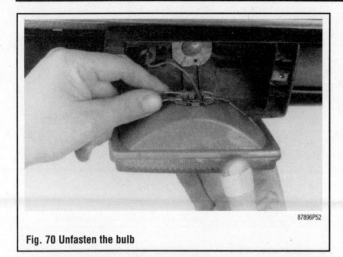

Fig. 70 Unfasten the bulb

Fig. 71 Unplug the bulb

Rear Signal, Brake Lamps and Reverse Lights

REMOVAL & INSTALLATION

Except 1986–88 6 and 7 Series Models

▶ See Figures 72, 73, 74 and 75

1. Open the trunk and remove the rear lining cover.
2. Remove the wing nuts or screws that retain the tail lamp lens and remove the lens.
3. Replace the defective bulb and reinstall the lens assembly.

➡On some of the earlier models, the rear lens assembly was attached by screws on the outside instead of in the trunk.

1986–88 6 Series Models

On these vehicles, remove the defective bulb by first, removing the rear trunk liner and then removing the assembly that the bulbs are housed in. Replace the defective bulb and reinstall.

1986–88 7 Series Models

To replace any of the rear bulbs on these models, open the trunk and pull back the rear liner. The defective bulb can be removed by rotating the socket counterclockwise and removing it. Replace the bulb and turn the socket clockwise to lock into position.

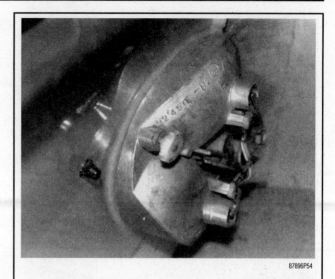

Fig. 72 The early 2002 rear light assembly, secured with round nuts

Fig. 73 Turn the round nuts off and pull the light assembly out to access the bulbs

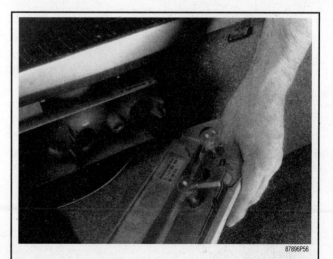

Fig. 74 Depress the tabs and separate the bulb assembly from the lens—3 Series rear lights

Fig. 75 To remove a bulb, gently depress and twist it counterclockwise, then pull straight out

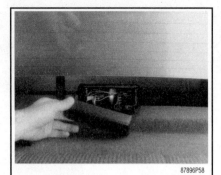

Fig. 76 Remove the screws or press the clips to access the bulb assembly

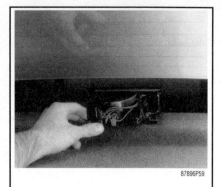

Fig. 77 Unfasten the light assembly

Fig. 78 Twist and pull out the bulb

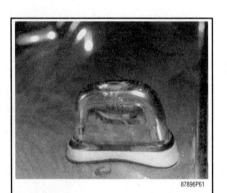

Fig. 79 A 2002 license plate light. The retainer screw is in the center of the lens

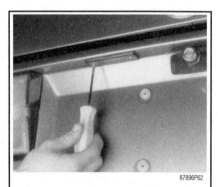

Fig. 80 Remove the retainer screws securing the lens in place—3 Series model

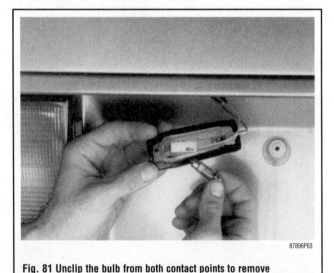

Fig. 81 Unclip the bulb from both contact points to remove

High Mount Brake Light

REMOVAL & INSTALLATION

▶ See Figures 76, 77 and 78

From inside the vehicle, press the clips at the side of the light assembly to separate the light from the lens. Some models are secured by screws attached to the sides. In this case the screws will have to be removed. Remove the lamp cover and then pull the reflector assembly out. Replace the bulb and reinstall the reflector assembly.

License Plate Lights

REMOVAL & INSTALLATION

▶ See Figures 79, 80 and 81

1. Remove the screws from the light and pull out to the side.
2. Remove the bulb from the assembly.
3. Check the contacts for corrosion and secure fit against the bulb when replaced.
4. Install the new bulb and the assembly into the body. Install the screws.

Interior Lights

REMOVAL & INSTALLATION

Dome Light

▶ See Figures 82 and 83

1. Pull the housing down from the headliner.
2. Remove the bulb from the assembly.
3. Check the contacts for corrosion and secure fit against the bulb when replaced.
4. Install the new bulb and the assembly into the body.

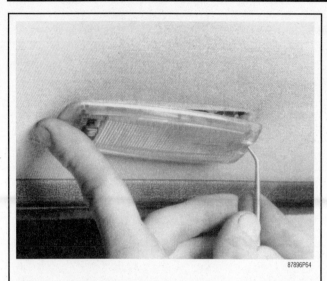

Fig. 82 Carefully pry the interior light assembly from the headliner

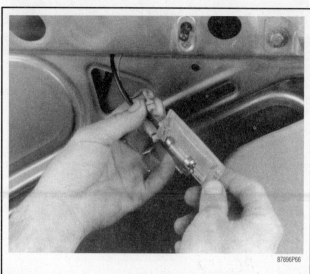

Fig. 84 Carefully pry the light assembly from the trunk lid

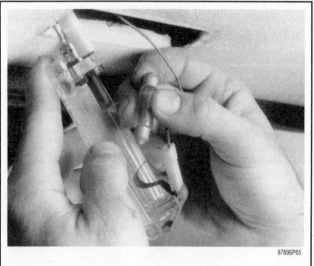

Fig. 83 Unclip the bulb from its contacts

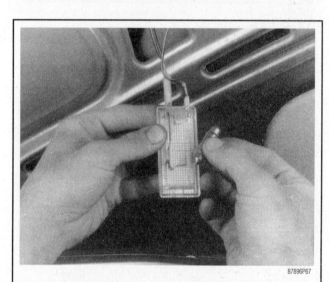

Fig. 85 Unclip the bulb from its contacts

Trunk Light

▶ **See Figures 84 and 85**

1. Pull the housing from the hole in the trunk lid.
2. Remove the bulb from the assembly.
3. Check the contacts for corrosion and secure fit against the bulb when replaced.
4. Install the new bulb and the assembly into the body.

Ashtray Light

▶ **See Figure 86**

1. Lift the ashtray assembly out.
2. Carefully pull the socket and bulb out of its mount.
3. To replace the bulb, pull the bulb out of the socket, and replace with a similar watt bulb.
4. Install socket and new bulb into ashtray and press ashtray into position.

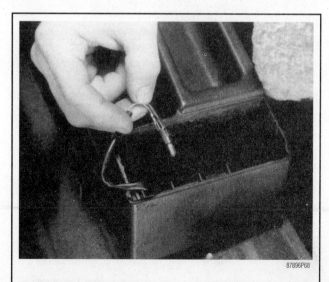

Fig. 86 Ashtray bulb and socket

Fuses

▶ See Figures 87, 88, 89, 90 and 91

The fuse box is located under the hood on the right or left fender well, except on the 3.0 series. On the 3.0 Series it is behind the left glove box door.

The transparent cover lists options served by each circuit, except on the 1600, 2000 and 2002 Series, which are simply coded. Codes are explained in the chart.

Some of the newer model have a solid cover that lists the fuses and their respective circuits on the inside. A removal tool is also inside the cover.

Fuse Specifications— 1600, 2000 and 2002

1970

Fuse Location	Capacity (amps)	Circuits Protected
1	8	Front parking lights (right and left)
2	8	Right taillight and license plate lights
3	8	Left taillight and instrument illumination
4	8	Interior light, clock, cigar lighter and buzzer
5	8	Stop and turn lights, back-up lights
6	16	Heater blower, horn, windshield wiper and washer, fuel and temperature gauges, oil pressure and brake warning lights

1971 and Later

Fuse Location	Capacity (amps)	Circuits Protected
1	5	Taillights and left parking light
2	5	Taillights, right parking light, license plate and instrument illum., side marker lights, fog light relay
3	8	Left low beam
4	8	Right low beam
5	5	Left turn signal
6	5	Right turn signal
7	16	Cigar lighter
8	8	Clock, interior light, ignition buzzer, hazard warning flashers, trailer flashers system
9	16	Heater blower
10	16	Rear window defroster
11	8	Automatic choke, electric fuel pump, oil pressure warning, fuel and temperature indicators, brake fluid warning, and tachometer
12	16	Stoplights, turn signals, horn, windshield wiper/washer, back-up lights

87896C00

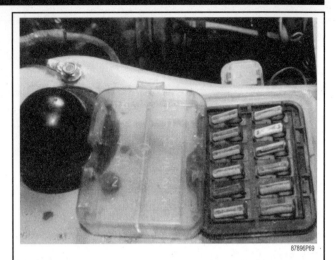

Fig. 87 The 2002 fuse box and cover are in the engine compartment. Notice that the fuses are ceramic

Fig. 88 The 3 Series fuse box and cover

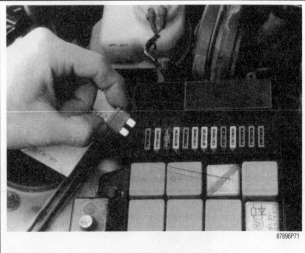

Fig. 89 To remove a fuse, simply pull it out. Always replace a fuse with one of the same amperage rating

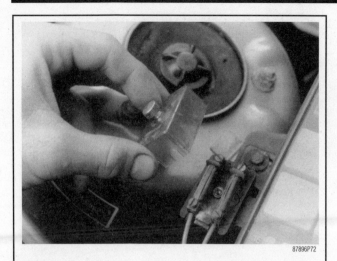

Fig. 90 Some models have additional fuses attached to the side of the main fuse box

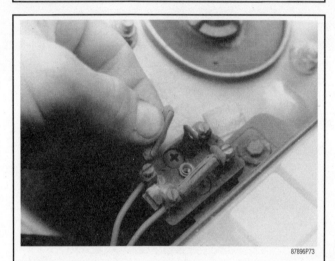

Fig. 91 To remove a ceramic fuse, lift one end up, unclipping the fuse from the contact points

5 SERIES FUSE SPECIFICATIONS

Fuse No.	Current (A)	Description
1	16	Electric fuel pump
2	8	Low beam right
3	8	Low beam left
4	25	Cigar lighter, automatic antenna, seat control, seat heating
5	8	Hazard lights, passenger compartment light, luggage compartment light, reading lamp, clock, central locks, on-board computer, burglar alarm, service indicator, door lock heating, check control
6	8	Indicator lamps, tachometer, mirror, on-board computer, central warning lamp, fuel consumption, service indicator, check control, window regulators, reversing, cruise control, backup lights
7	8	High beam right
8	8	High beam left
9	8	Park/side marker and tail lights right, instrument and license plate lights
10	8	Park/side marker and tail lights left
11	16	Turn signal indicators, windshield wipers and washer, horn relay, headlights
12	8	Stop lights, radio
13	16 (25)	Rear window defogger, electric sun roof
14	25	Heater blower, air conditioner
15	8	Front fog lamp right
16	8	Front fog lamp left
17	25	Supplementary fan

87896C02

7 SERIES FUSE SPECIFICATIONS

Fuse No.	Current (A)	Description
1	15	Left high beam, right low beam
2	15	Right high beam, left low beam
3	15	Auxiliary fan 91°C (196°F)
4	15	Turn signal
5	30	Windshield wipers and washer
6	7.5	Brake light, cruise control
7	15	Horn
8	—	Without connection
9	15	Engine electrical equipment
10	7.5	Instruments
11	15	Main and aux. fuel pump
12	7.5	Radio, check control, instruments, on-board computer
13	7.5	Left low beam
14	7.5	Right low beam
15	—	Without connection
16	30	Heater blower, air conditioner
17	15	Backup light, power outside mirrors, mirror heating, fasten seat belt sign, washer jet heating
18	30	Auxiliary fan 99°C (210°F)
19	30	Power sliding roof, heated seat
20	30	Rear window defogger
21	7.5	Interior lights, radio, glove box, luggage compartment light, rechargeable flashlight, seat belt buzzer, on-board computer, radio memory, clock
22	7.5	Left side lights
23	7.5	Right side lights, engine compartment light, license plate lights, instrument panel lights, make-up mirror light
24	15	Hazard warning lights, open door buzzer
25	—	Without connection
26	30	Seat adjustment, electric window lifts
27	30	Central locking system, door lock heating, burglar alarm, on-board computer
28	30	Cigar lighters, power antenna
29	7.5	Left fog light
30	7.5	Right fog light

87896C04

Flashers

REMOVAL & INSTALLATION

1600, 2000, 2500, 2800, Bavaria, 3000 and 3.0 Models

1. Open the glovebox at the left side. Pull the relay hanger off the panel on which it is hung.
2. Disconnect the electrical connector. Install in the reverse order.

3, 5, 6 and 7 Series Models

1. Remove the screws and remove the bottom center instrument panel trim. Disconnect the negative battery cable.
2. Detach the flasher from the mounting bracket. Unplug the electrical connector and remove the flasher.
3. Install in the reverse order.

Relays

REMOVAL & INSTALLATION

◆ See Figures 92, 93, 94 and 95

1. Access the relay to be removed from under the steering column, behind the glove box or in the main fuse box.
2. To remove, use a relay removal tool or grasp the relay with your fingers and gently move the relay from side to side while pulling upward.
3. Replace with a relay of the same part number as the one removed. If you have any questions, consult a BMW dealer.

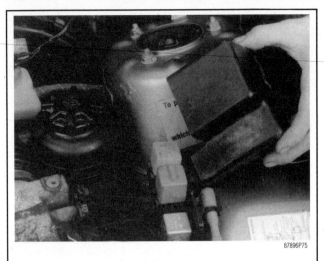

Fig. 92 Some relays have a protective cover over them. To find these relays, consult your owner's manual

Fig. 94 If a relay is difficult to remove, rock it back and forth as you pull upward

Fig. 93 A relay removal tool can be very helpful on tight fitting relays

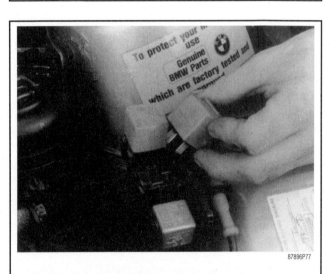

Fig. 95 When removing a relay, be careful not to pull off the cover, or the relay will have to be replaced

5 SERIES RELAY PLACEMENT CHART

Relay	Description
1	High beams
2	Low beams
3	Fog lamps
4	Two-tone horns
5	Power saving relay
6	Wipe/wash intermittent action control unit (intensive cleaning)

87896C01

7 SERIES RELAY PLACEMENT CHART

Relay	Description
K 1	Auxiliary fan—speed 1
K 2	Two-tone horn
K 3	High beams
K 4	Low beams
K 5	Heater blower
K 6	Auxiliary fan—speed 2
K 7	Rear window defogger, power sliding roof, heated seat
K 8	Front fog lamps
K 9	—
K10	Control unit for wipe/wash and intensive cleaning system

87896C03

WIRING DIAGRAMS

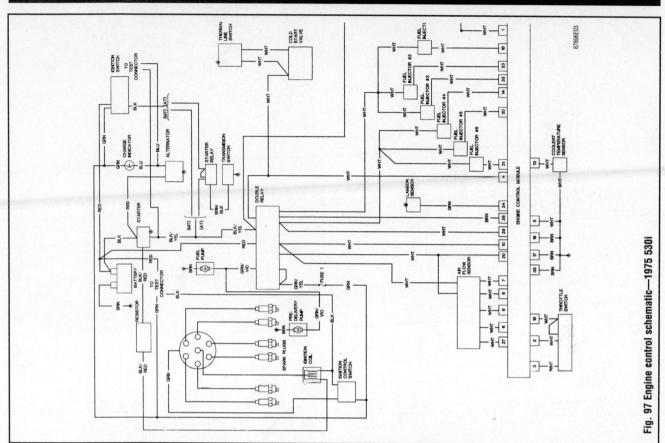

Fig. 97 Engine control schematic—1975 530i

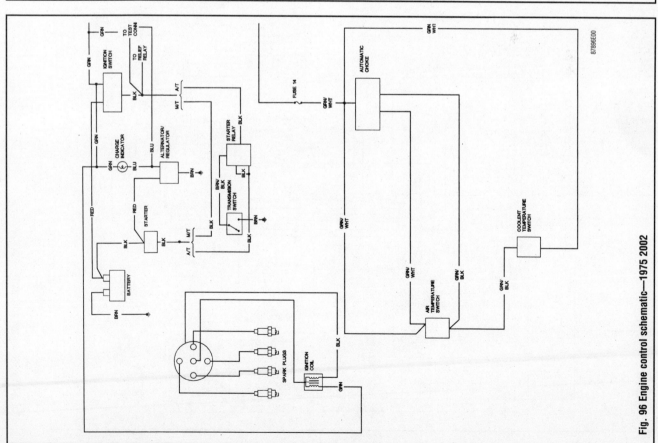

Fig. 96 Engine control schematic—1975 2002

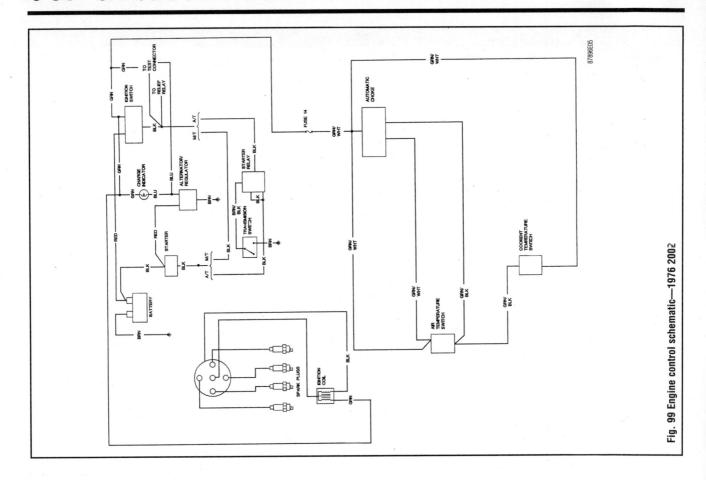

Fig. 99 Engine control schematic—1976 2002

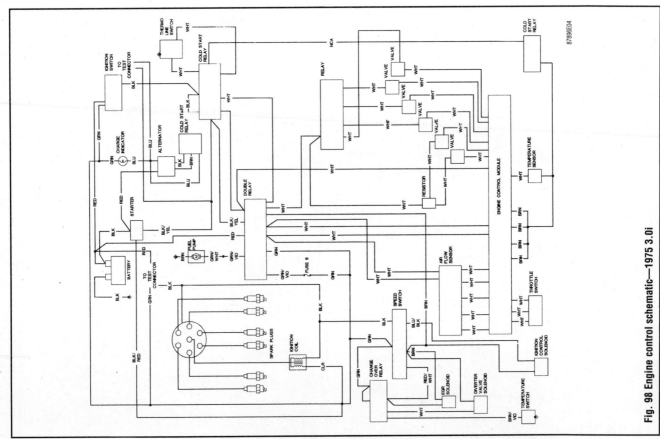

Fig. 98 Engine control schematic—1975 3.0i

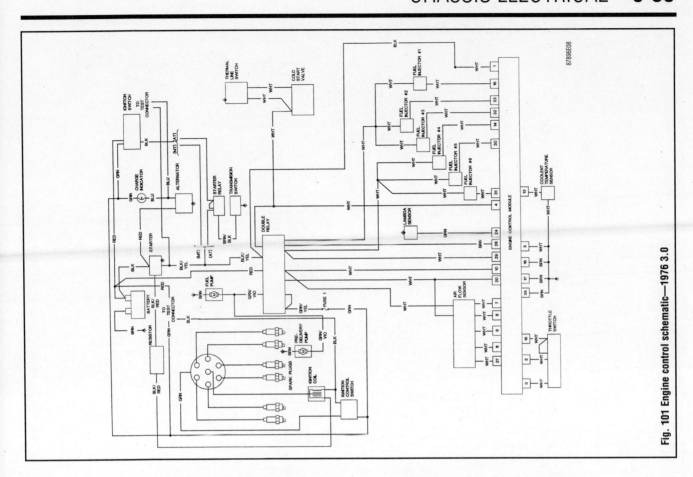

Fig. 101 Engine control schematic—1976 3.0

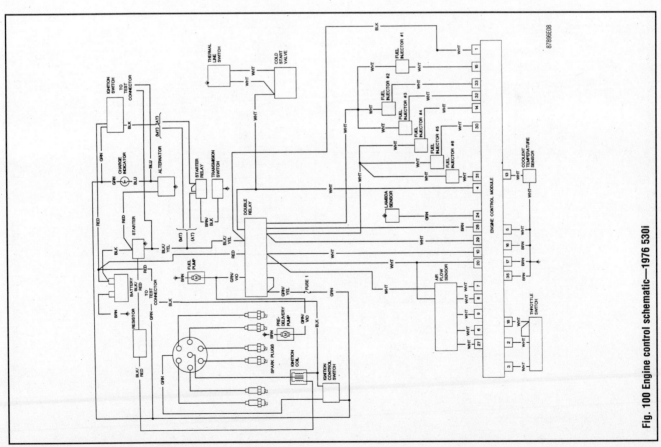

Fig. 100 Engine control schematic—1976 530i

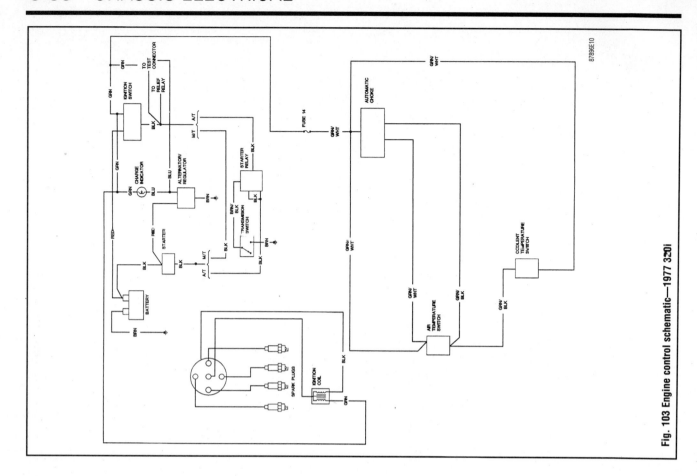

Fig. 103 Engine control schematic—1977 320i

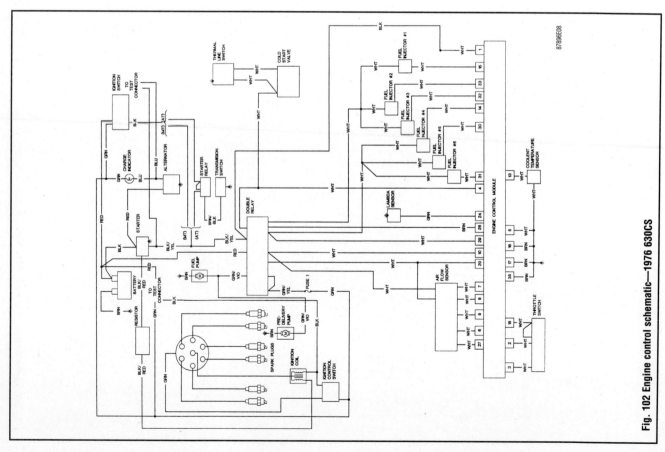

Fig. 102 Engine control schematic—1976 630CS

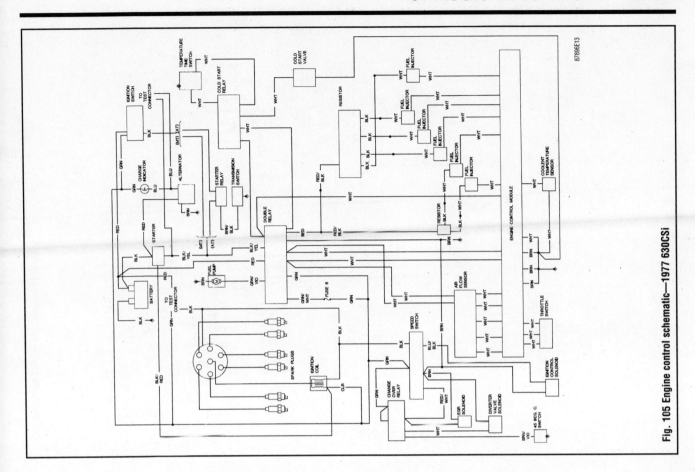

Fig. 105 Engine control schematic—1977 630CSi

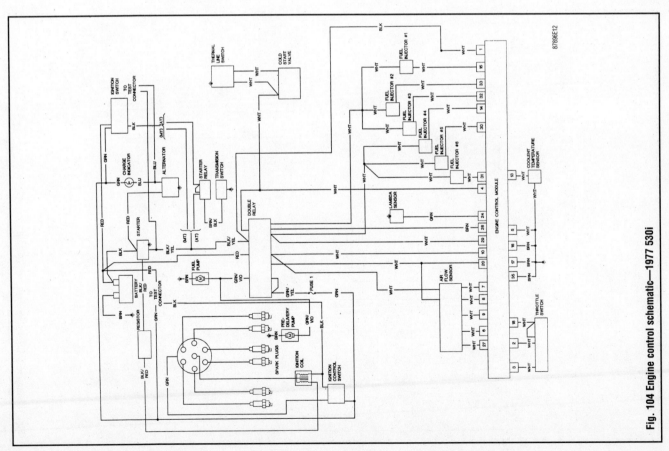

Fig. 104 Engine control schematic—1977 530i

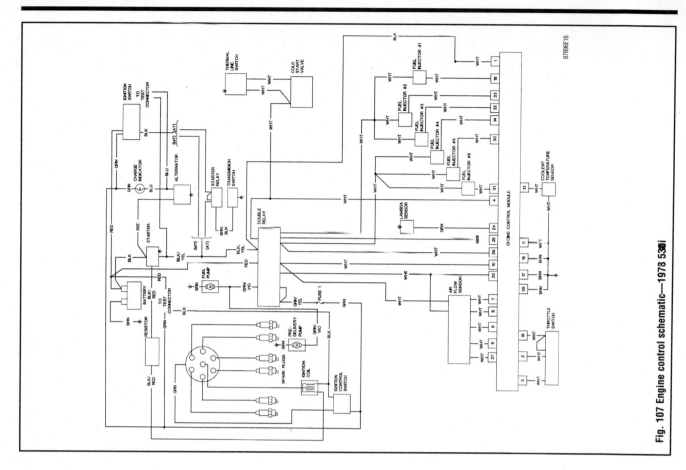

Fig. 107 Engine control schematic—1978 530i

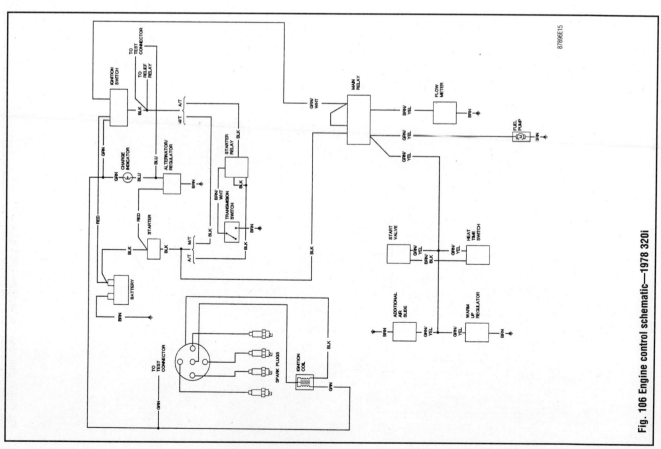

Fig. 106 Engine control schematic—1978 320i

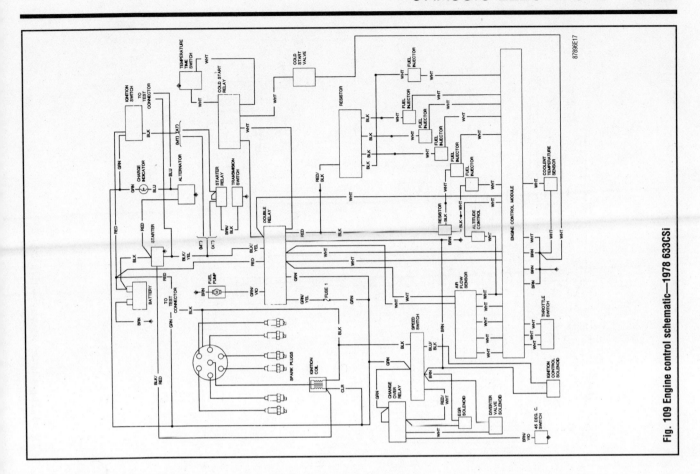

Fig. 109 Engine control schematic—1978 633CSi

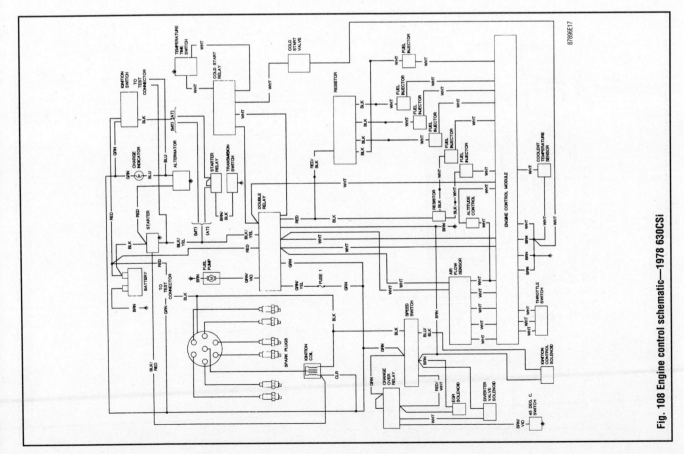

Fig. 108 Engine control schematic—1978 630CSi

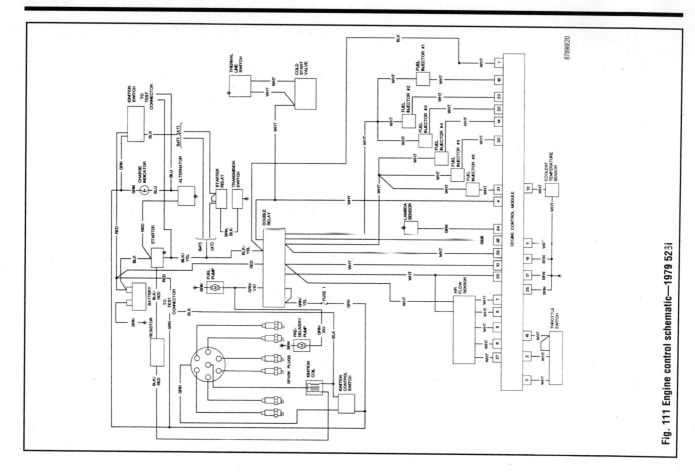

Fig. 111 Engine control schematic—1979 523i

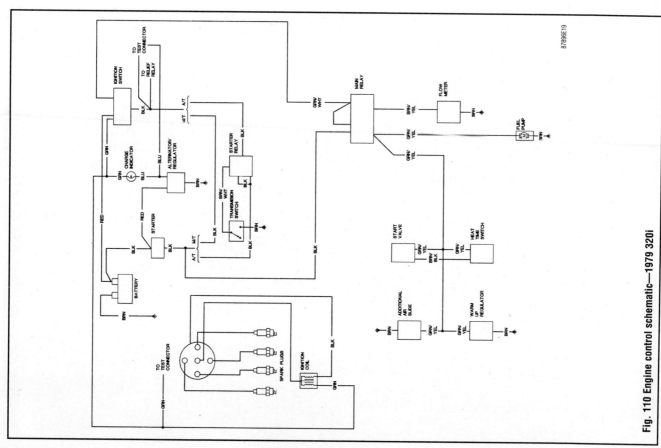

Fig. 110 Engine control schematic—1979 320i

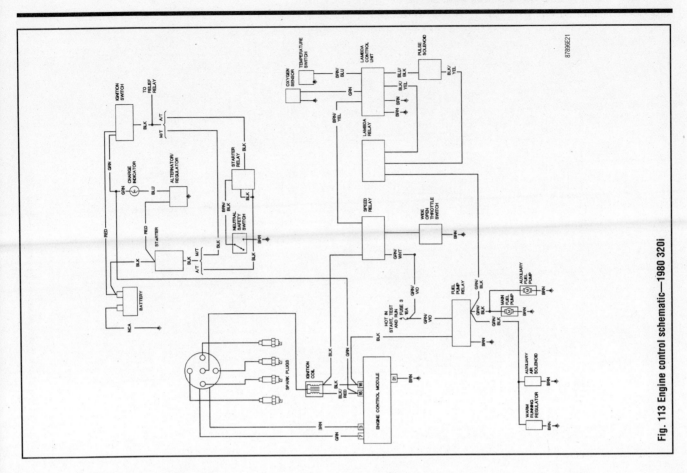

Fig. 113 Engine control schematic—1980 320i

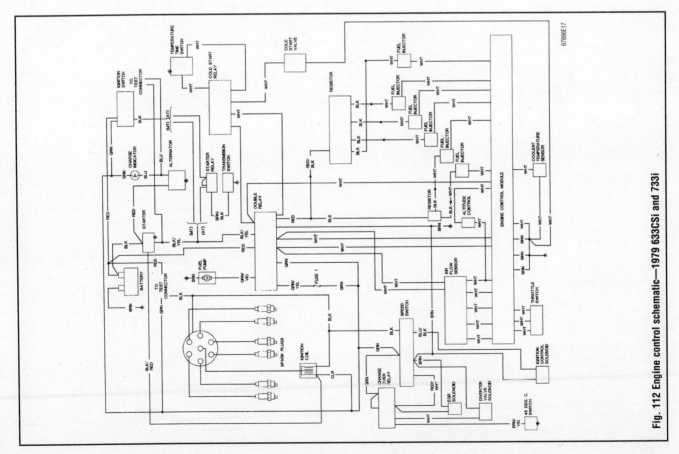

Fig. 112 Engine control schematic—1979 633CSi and 733i

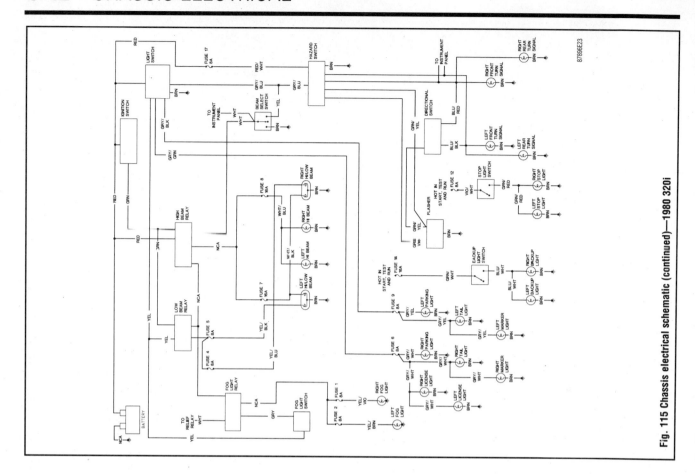

Fig. 115 Chassis electrical schematic (continued)—1980 320i

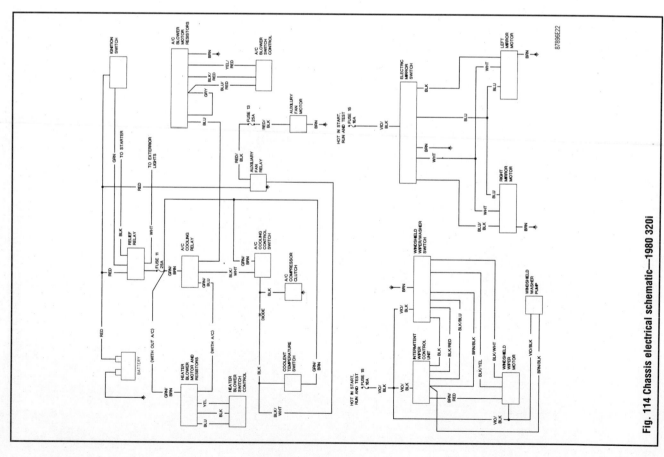

Fig. 114 Chassis electrical schematic—1980 320i

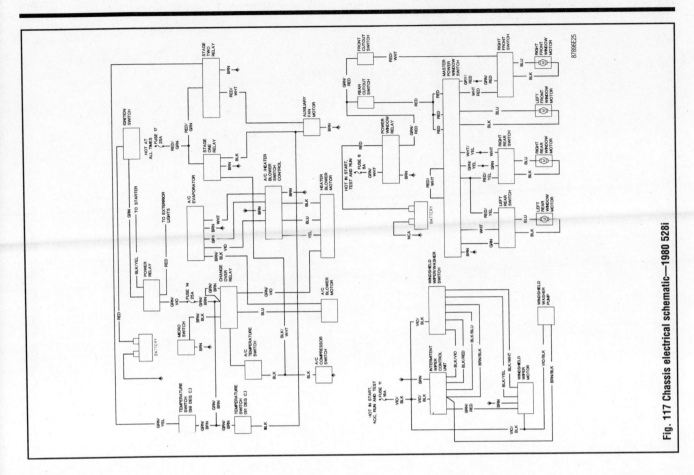

Fig. 117 Chassis electrical schematic—1980 528i

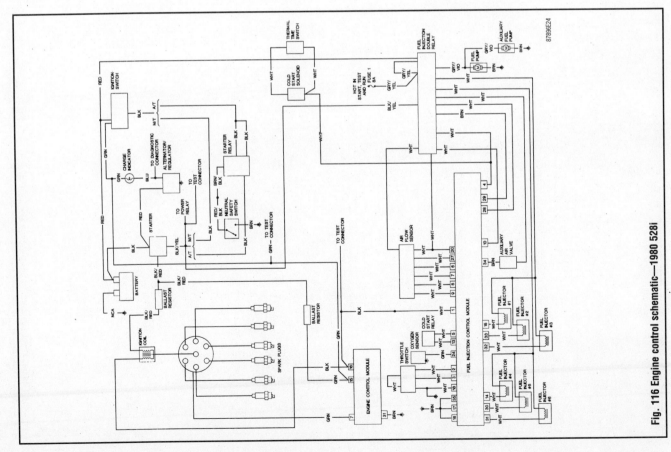

Fig. 116 Engine control schematic—1980 528i

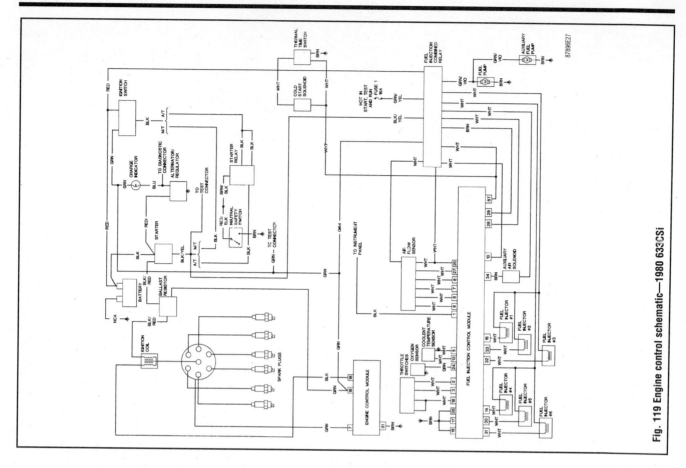

Fig. 119 Engine control schematic—1980 633CSi

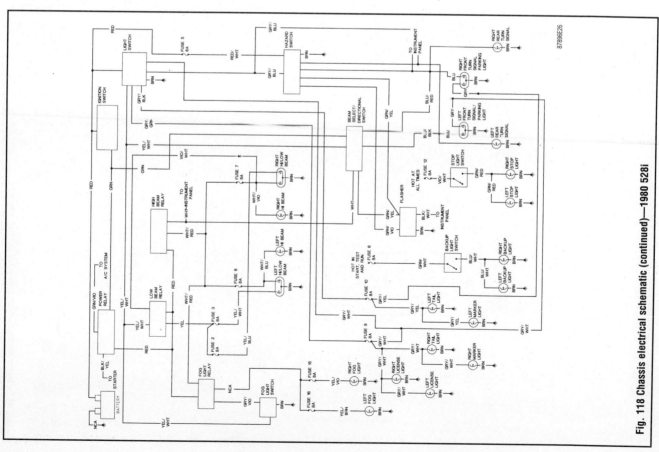

Fig. 118 Chassis electrical schematic (continued)—1980 528i

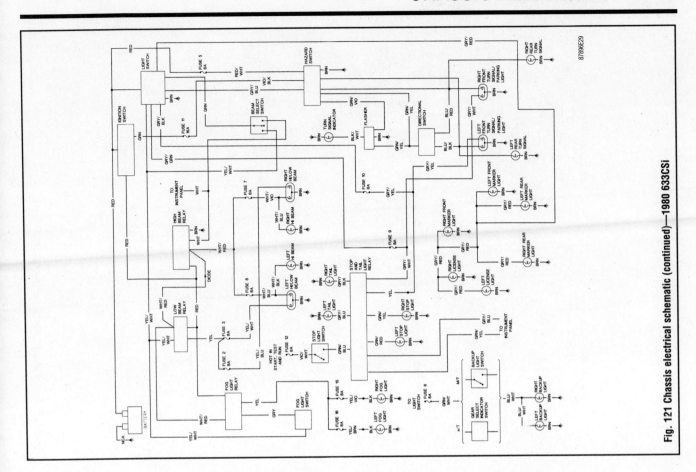

Fig. 121 Chassis electrical schematic (continued)—1980 633CSi

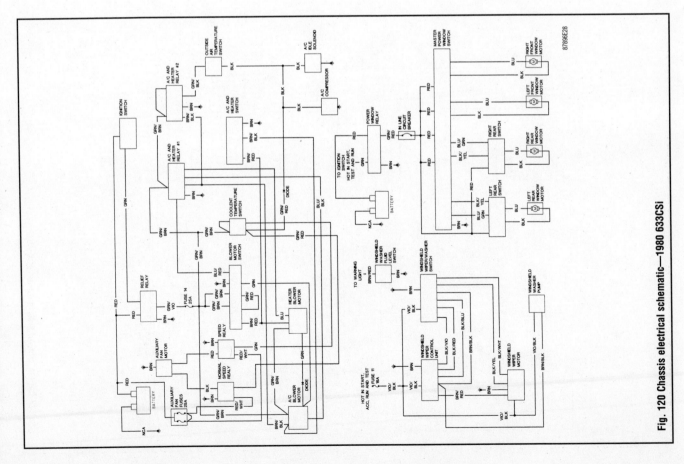

Fig. 120 Chassis electrical schematic—1980 633CSi

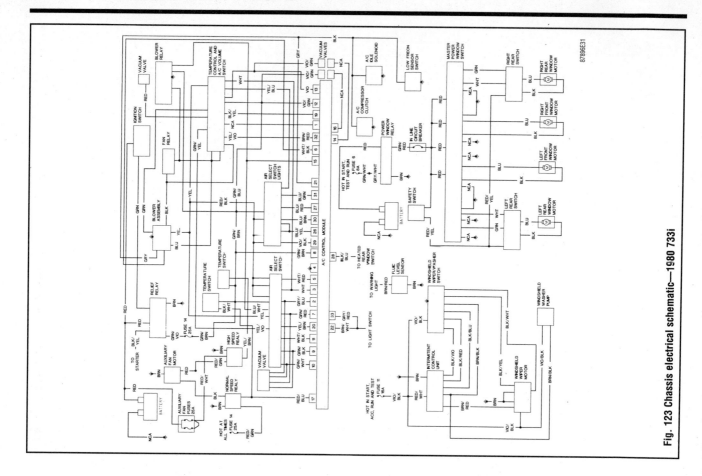

Fig. 123 Chassis electrical schematic—1980 733i

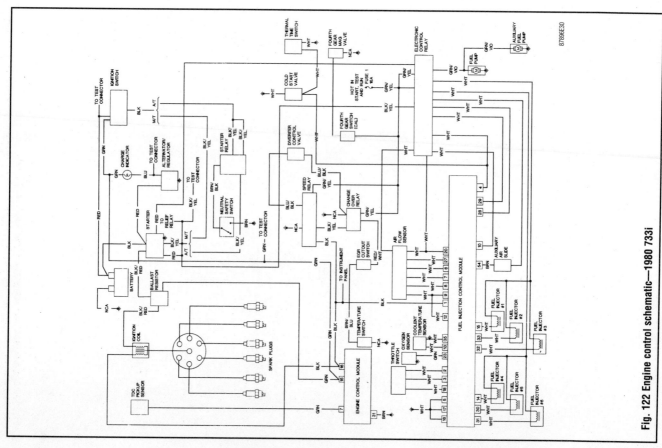

Fig. 122 Engine control schematic—1980 733i

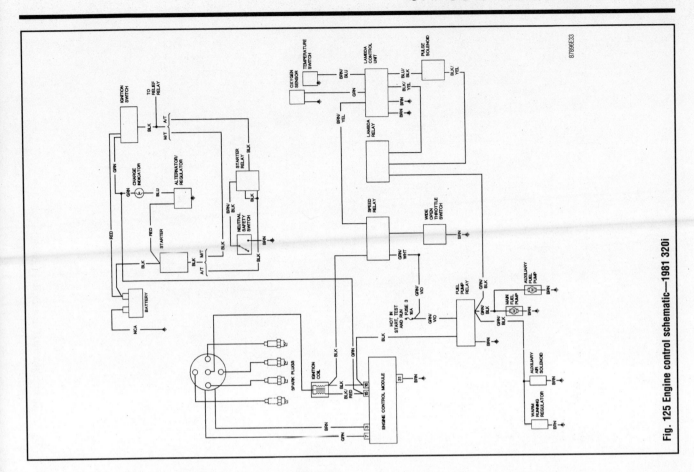

Fig. 125 Engine control schematic—1981 320i

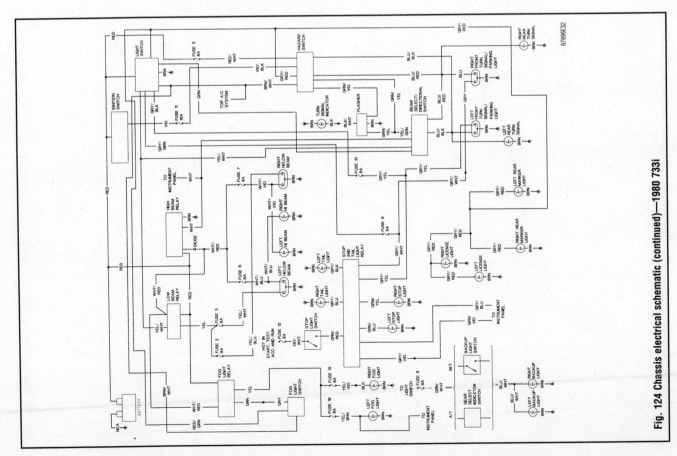

Fig. 124 Chassis electrical schematic (continued)—1980 733i

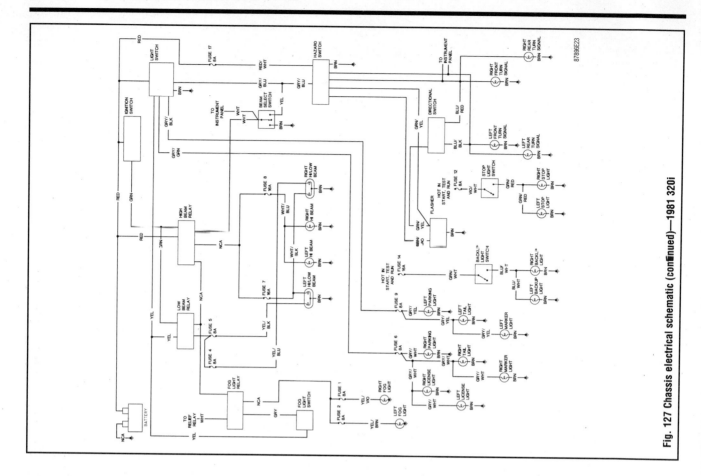

Fig. 127 Chassis electrical schematic (continued)—1981 320i

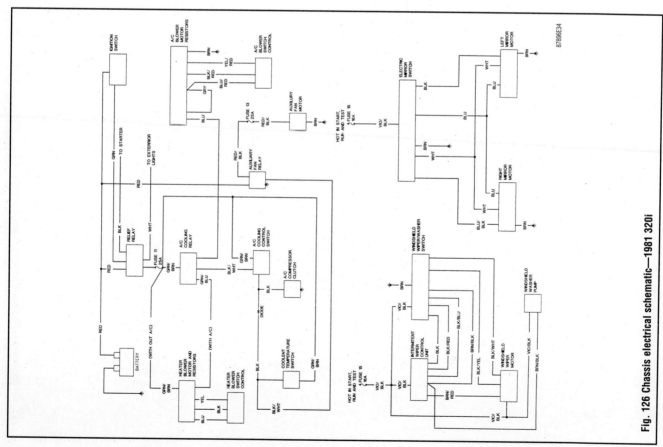

Fig. 126 Chassis electrical schematic—1981 320i

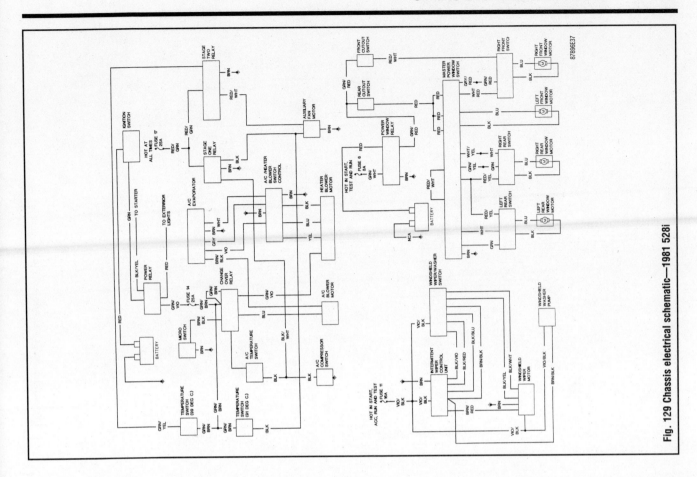

Fig. 129 Chassis electrical schematic—1981 528i

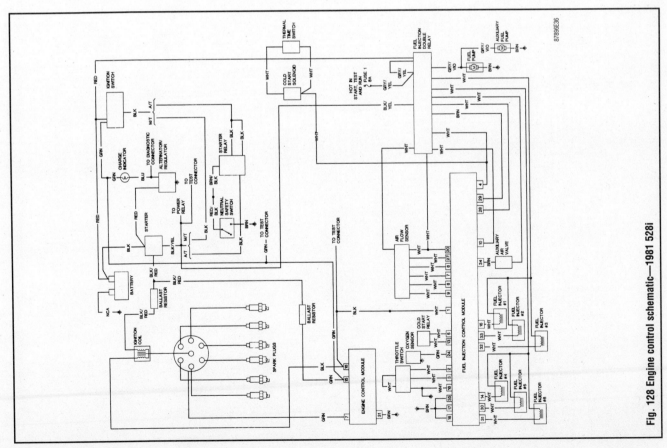

Fig. 128 Engine control schematic—1981 528i

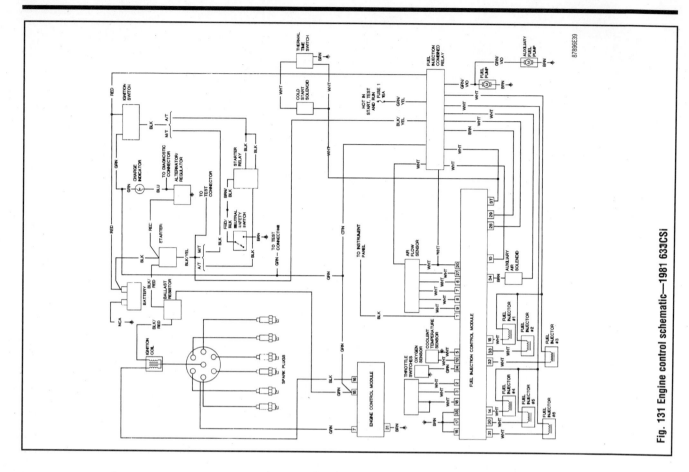

Fig. 131 Engine control schematic—1981 633CSi

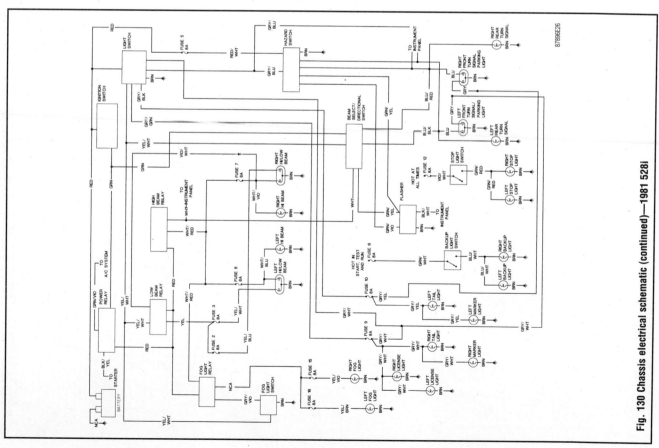

Fig. 130 Chassis electrical schematic (continued)—1981 528i

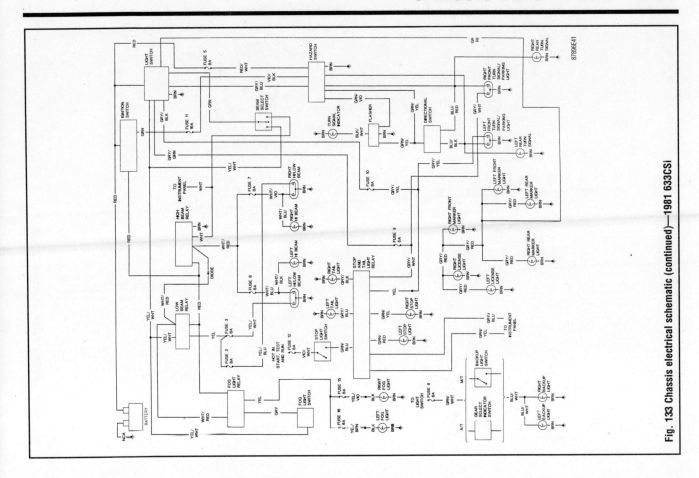

Fig. 133 Chassis electrical schematic (continued)—1981 633CSi

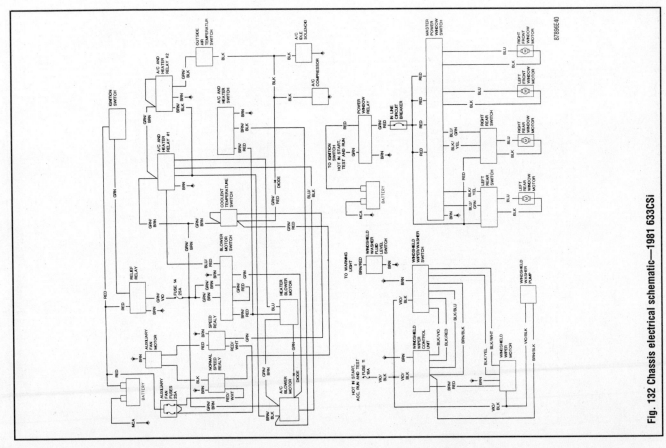

Fig. 132 Chassis electrical schematic—1981 633CSi

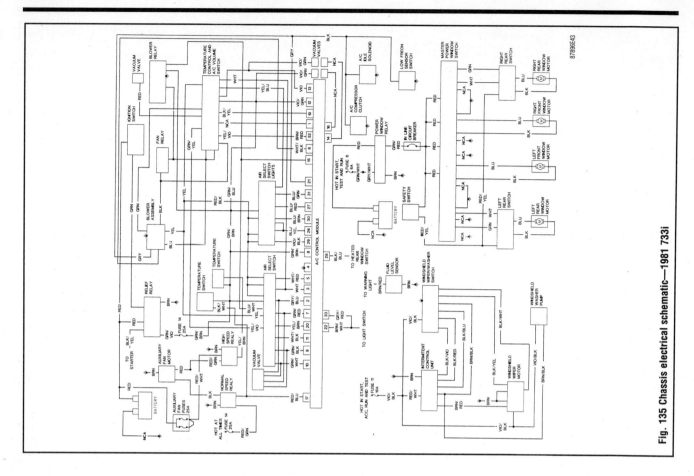

Fig. 135 Chassis electrical schematic—1981 733i

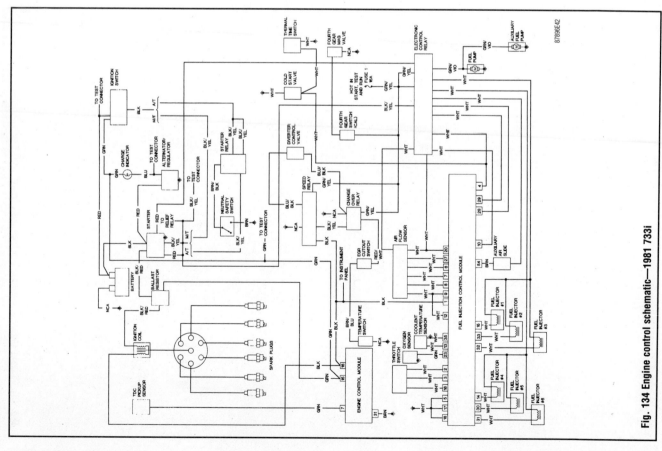

Fig. 134 Engine control schematic—1981 733i

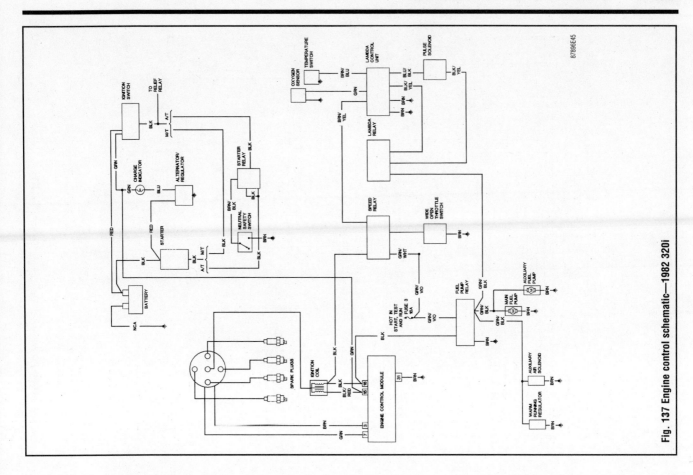

Fig. 137 Engine control schematic—1982 320i

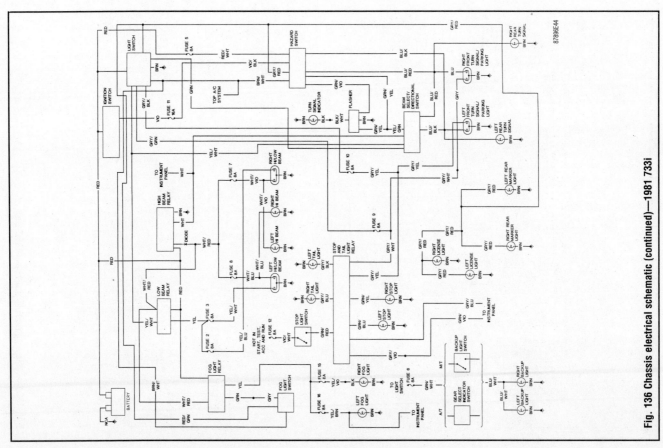

Fig. 136 Chassis electrical schematic (continued)—1981 733i

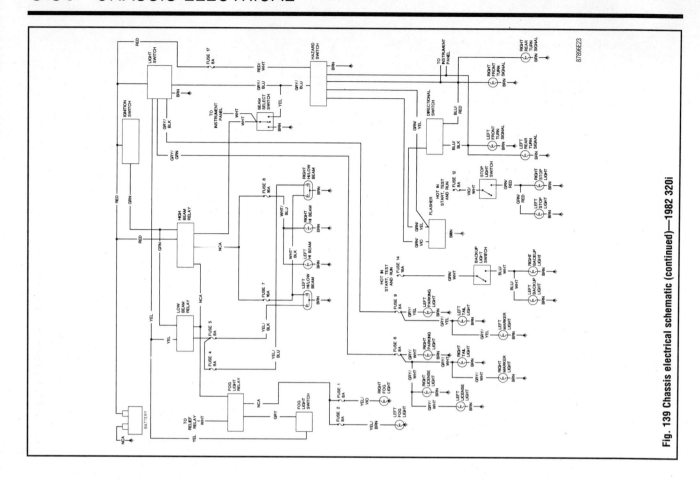

Fig. 139 Chassis electrical schematic (continued)—1982 320i

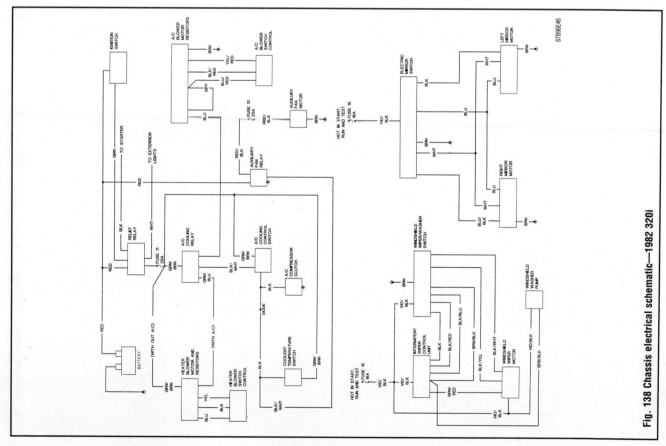

Fig. 138 Chassis electrical schematic—1982 320i

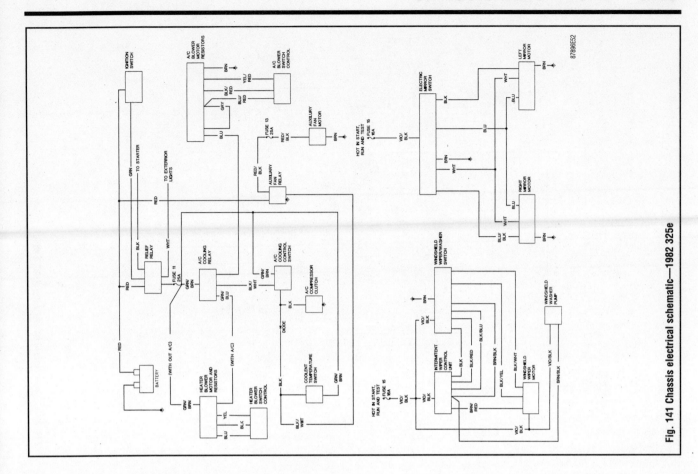

Fig. 141 Chassis electrical schematic—1982 325e

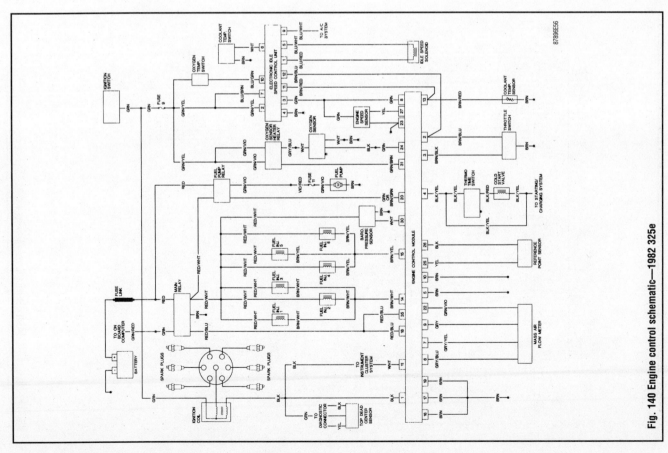

Fig. 140 Engine control schematic—1982 325e

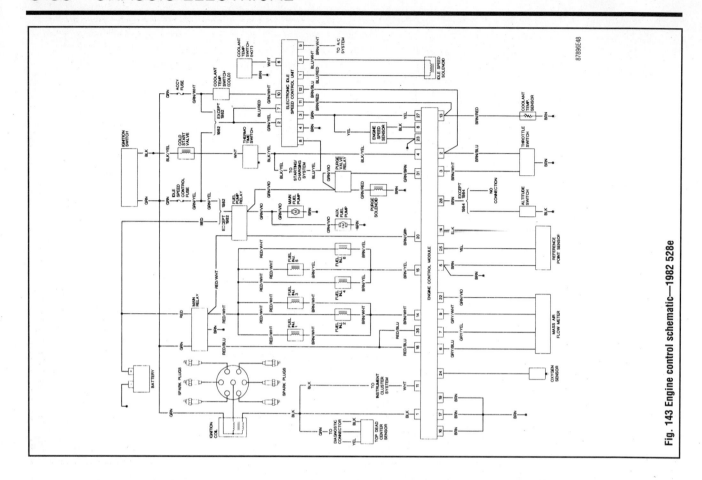

Fig. 143 Engine control schematic—1982 528e

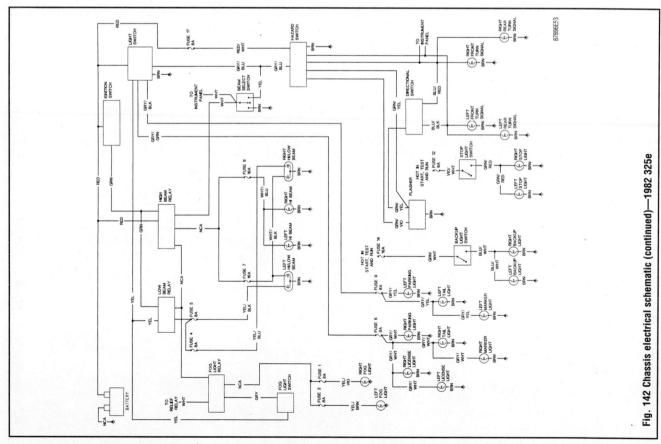

Fig. 142 Chassis electrical schematic (continued)—1982 325e

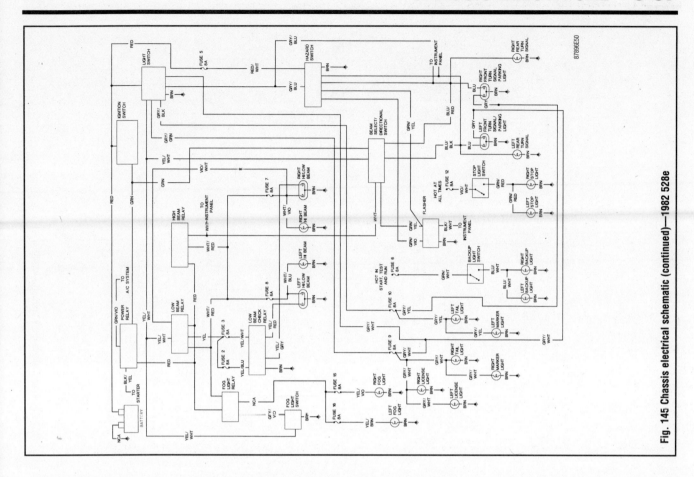

Fig. 145 Chassis electrical schematic (continued)—1982 528e

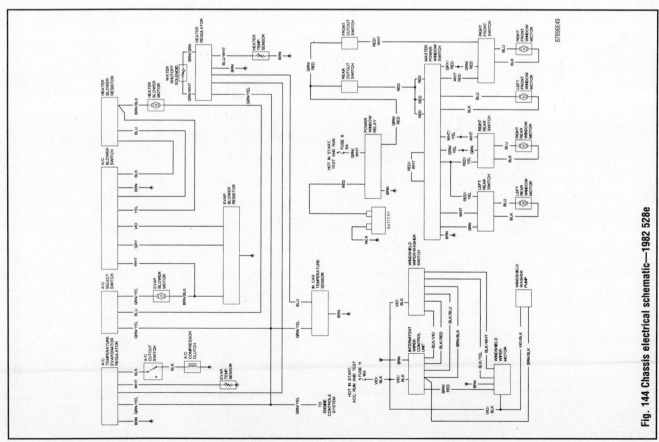

Fig. 144 Chassis electrical schematic—1982 528e

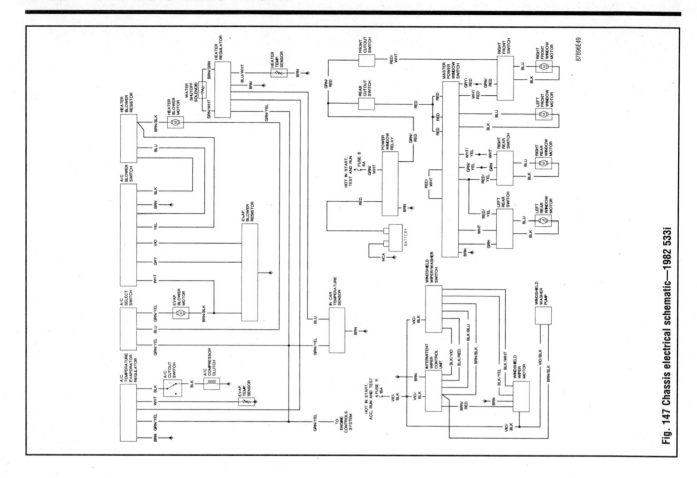

Fig. 147 Chassis electrical schematic—1982 533i

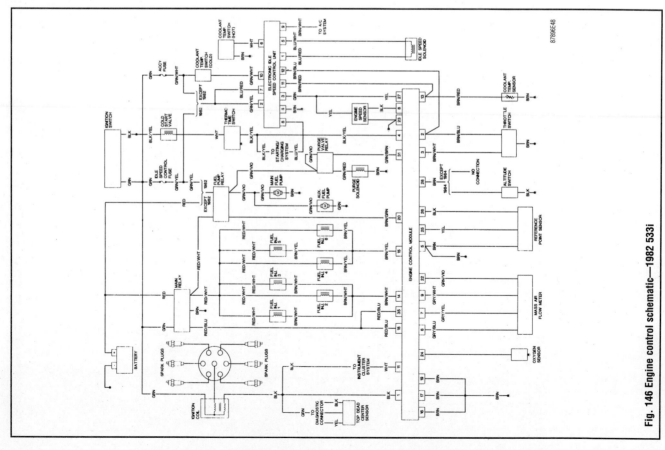

Fig. 146 Engine control schematic—1982 533i

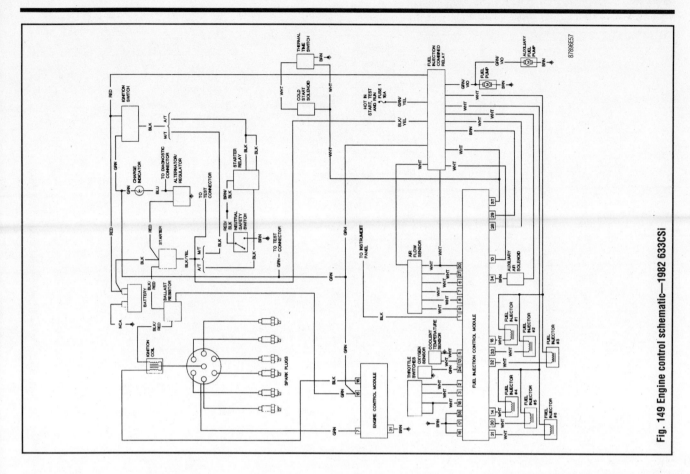

Fig. 149 Engine control schematic—1982 633CSi

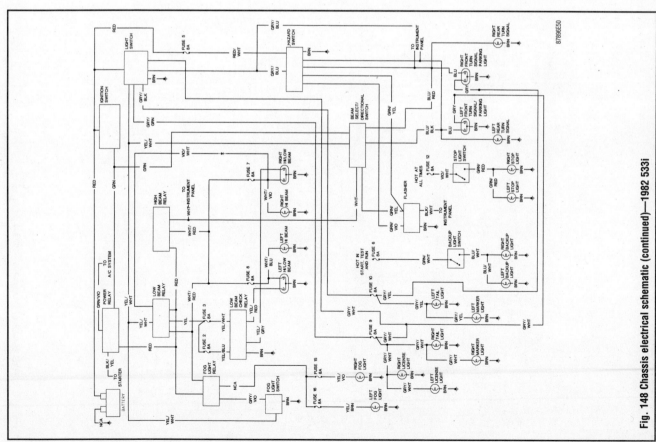

Fig. 148 Chassis electrical schematic (continued)—1982 533i

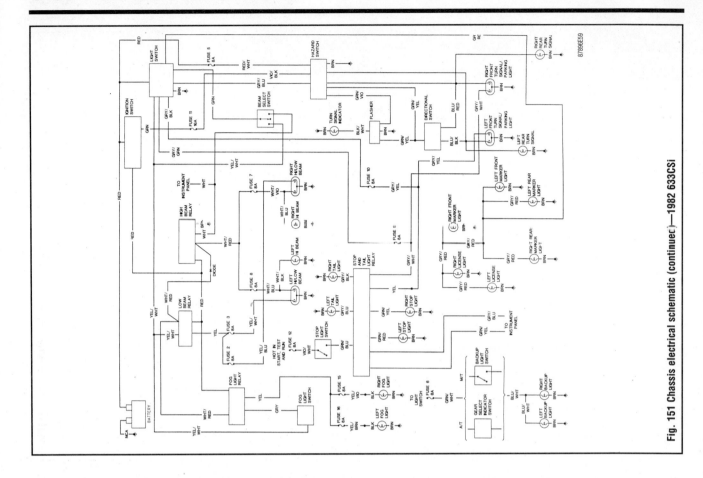

Fig. 151 Chassis electrical schematic (continued)—1982 633CSi

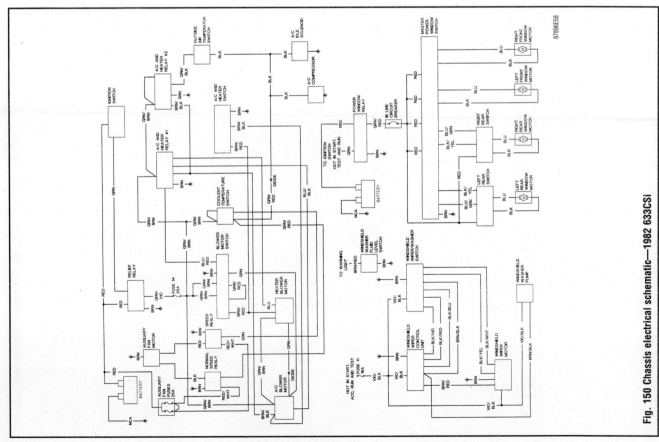

Fig. 150 Chassis electrical schematic—1982 633CSi

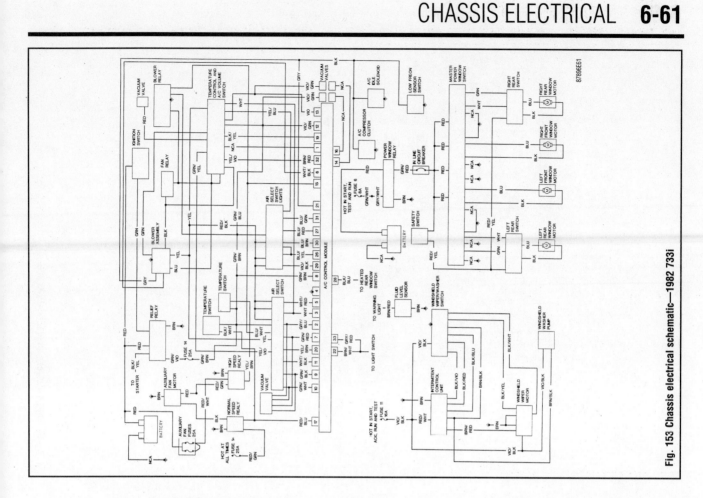

Fig. 153 Chassis electrical schematic—1982 733i

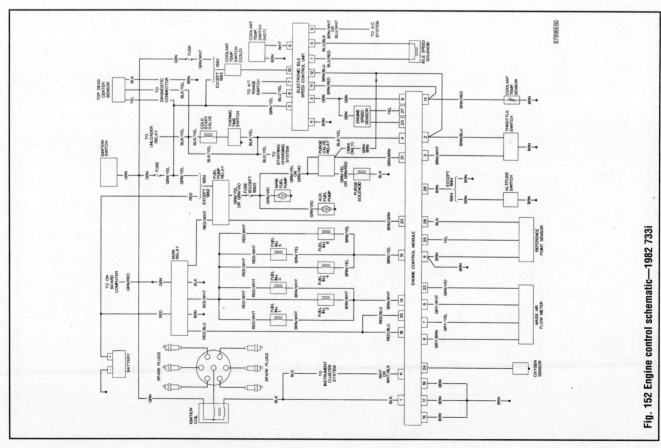

Fig. 152 Engine control schematic—1982 733i

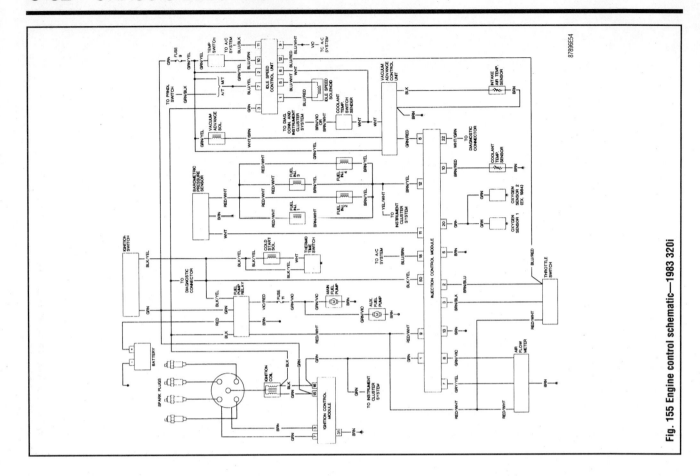

Fig. 155 Engine control schematic—1983 320i

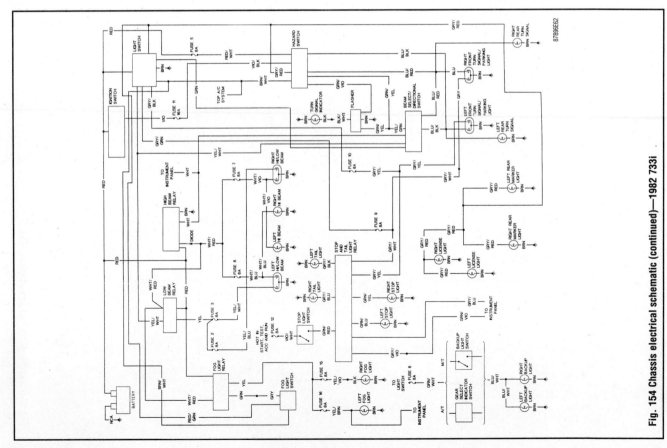

Fig. 154 Chassis electrical schematic (continued)—1982 733i

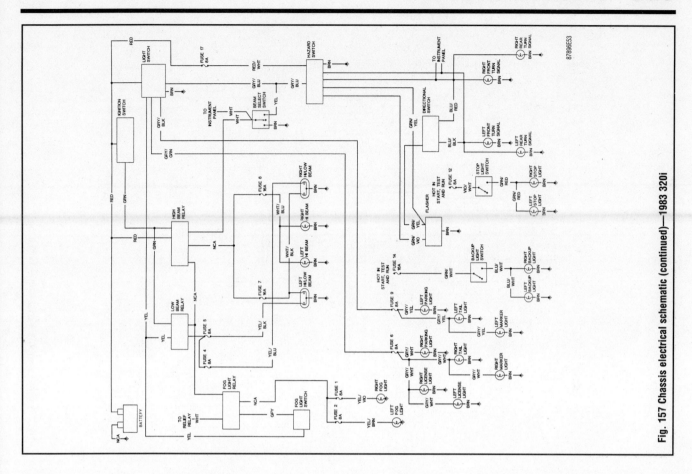

Fig. 157 Chassis electrical schematic (continued)—1983 320i

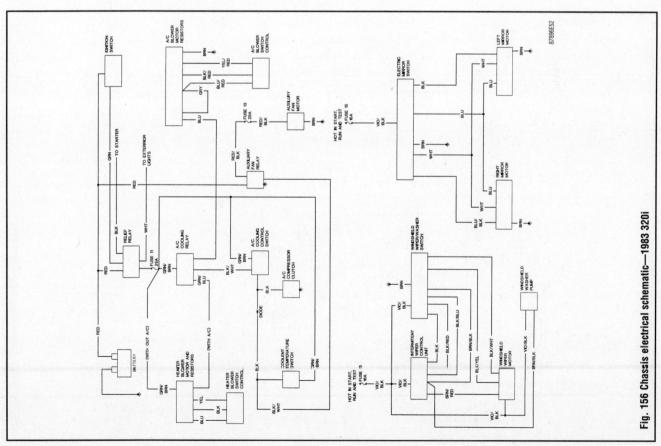

Fig. 156 Chassis electrical schematic—1983 320i

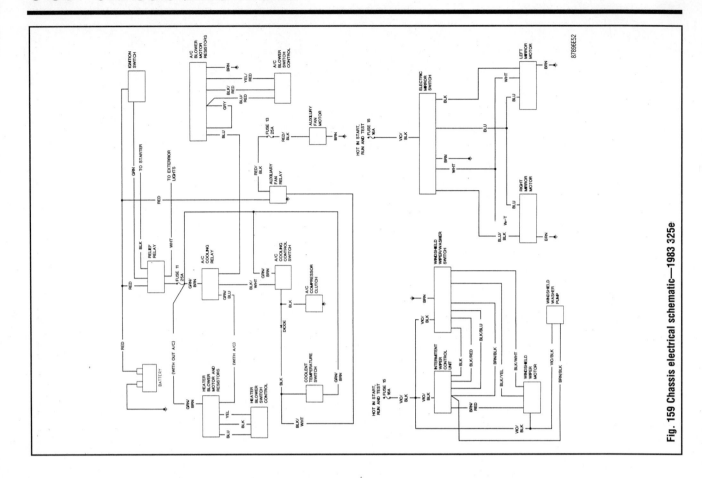

Fig. 159 Chassis electrical schematic—1983 325e

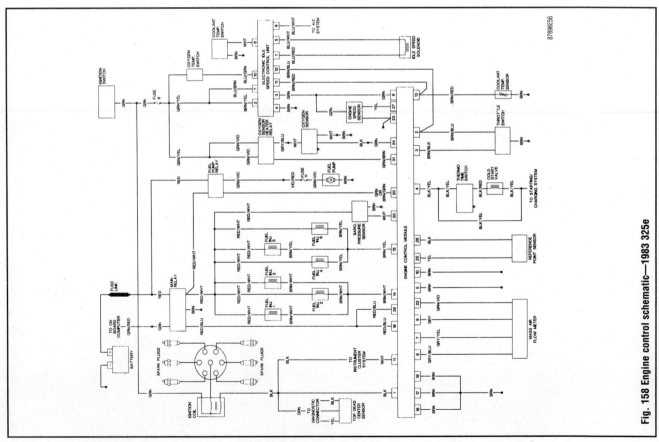

Fig. 158 Engine control schematic—1983 325e

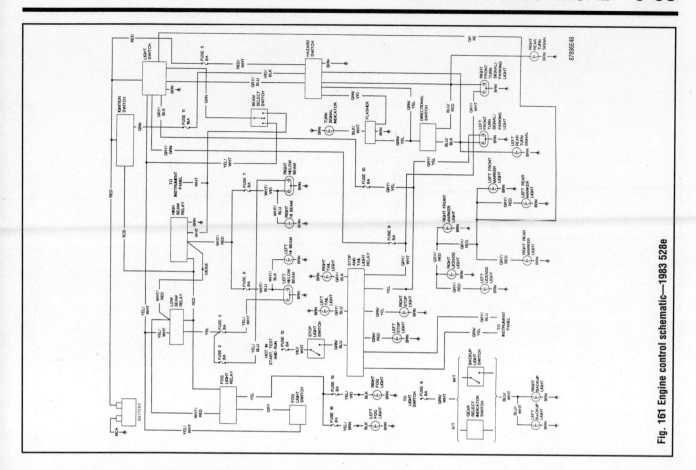

Fig. 161 Engine control schematic—1983 528e

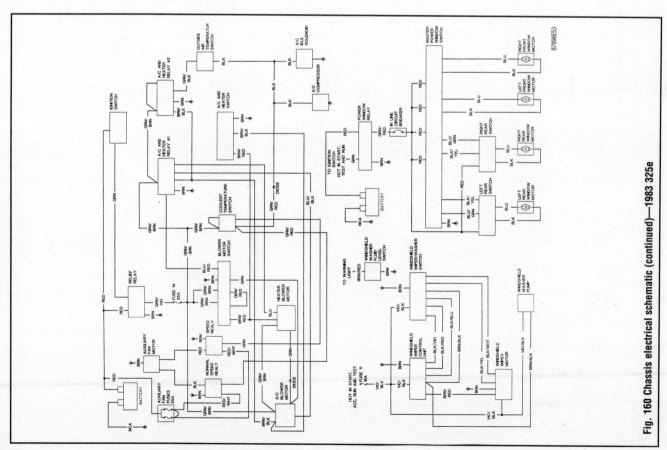

Fig. 160 Chassis electrical schematic (continued)—1983 325e

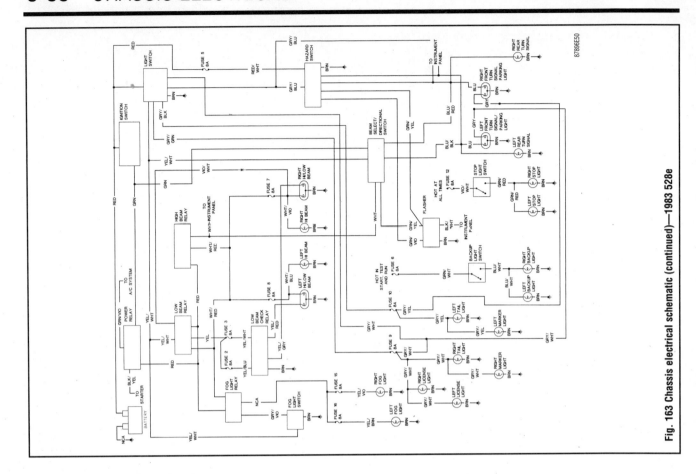

Fig. 163 Chassis electrical schematic (continued)—1983 528e

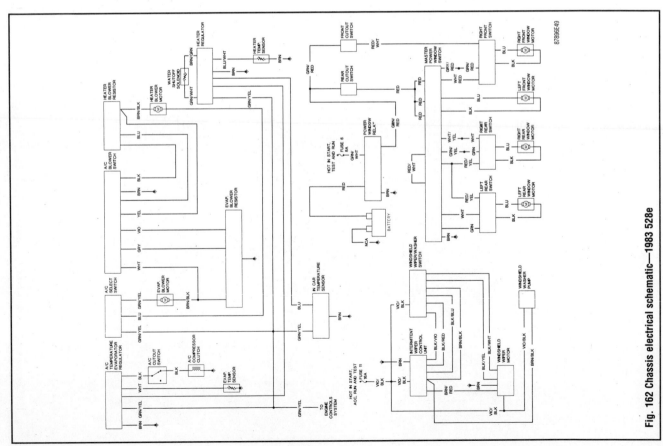

Fig. 162 Chassis electrical schematic—1983 528e

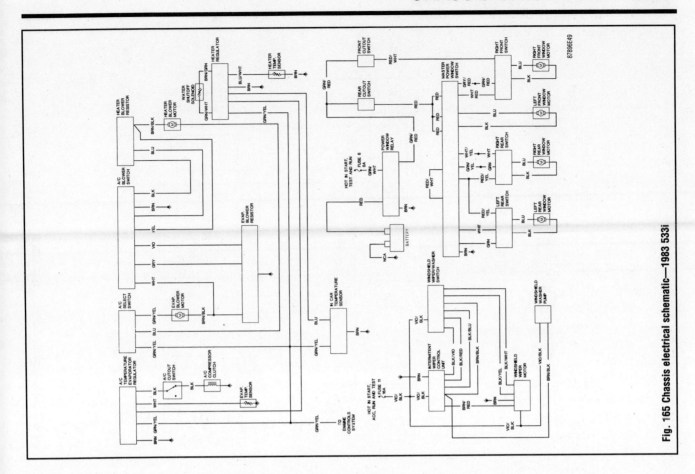

Fig. 165 Chassis electrical schematic—1983 533i

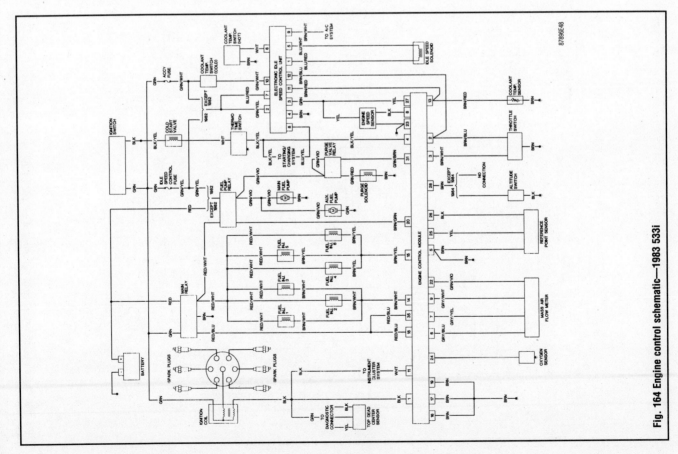

Fig. 164 Engine control schematic—1983 533i

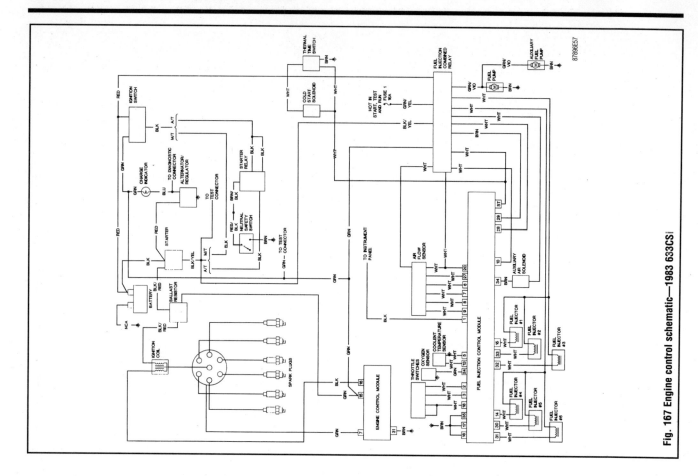

Fig. 167 Engine control schematic—1983 633CSi

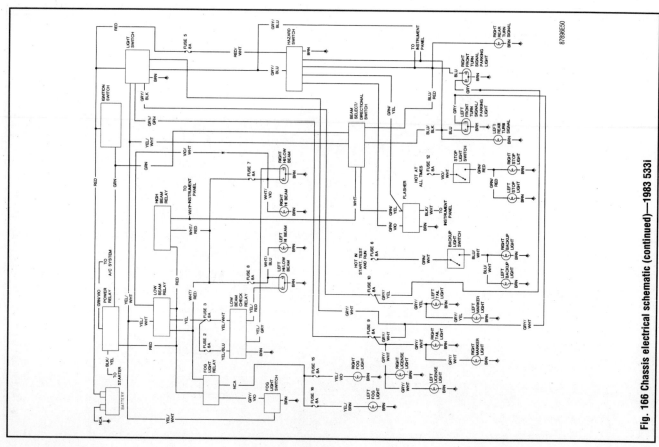

Fig. 166 Chassis electrical schematic (continued)—1983 533i

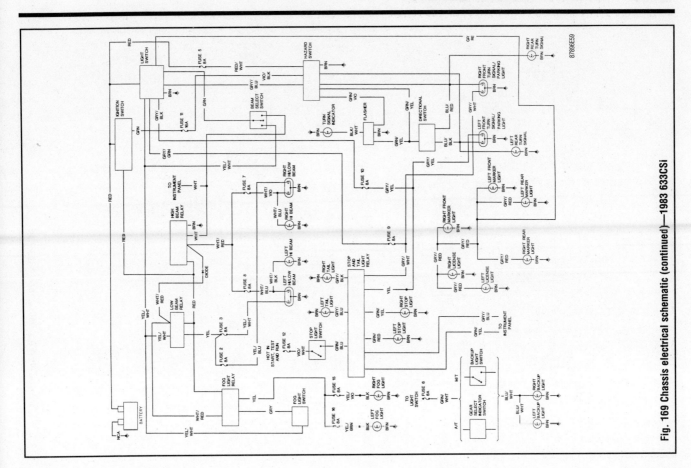

Fig. 169 Chassis electrical schematic (continued)—1983 633CSi

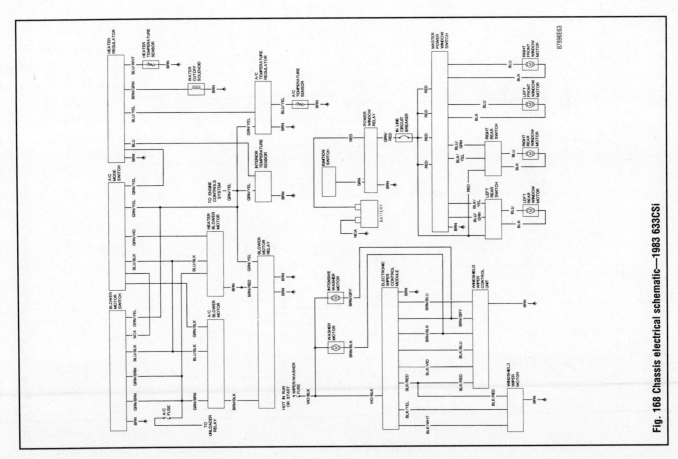

Fig. 168 Chassis electrical schematic—1983 633CSi

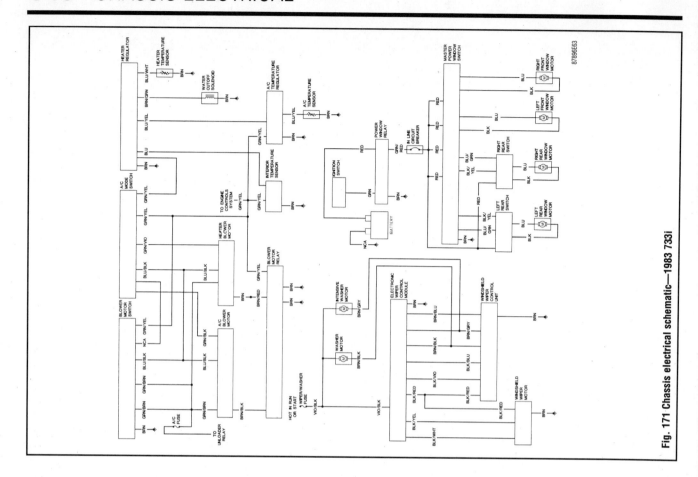

Fig. 171 Chassis electrical schematic—1983 733i

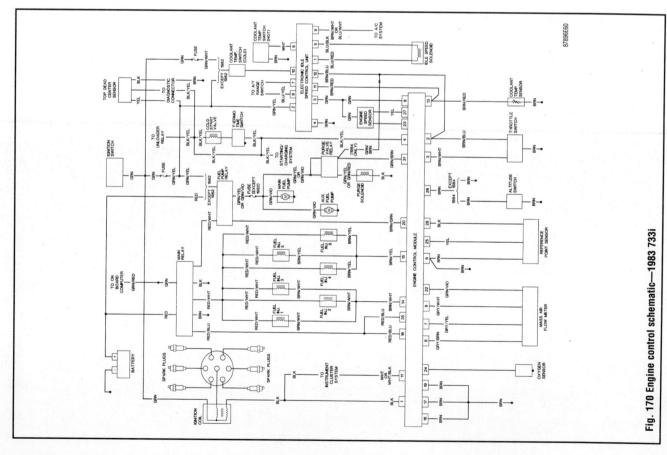

Fig. 170 Engine control schematic—1983 733i

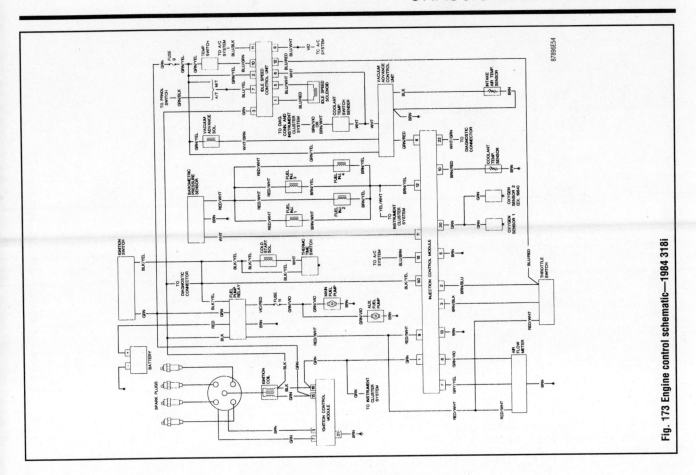

Fig. 173 Engine control schematic—1984 318i

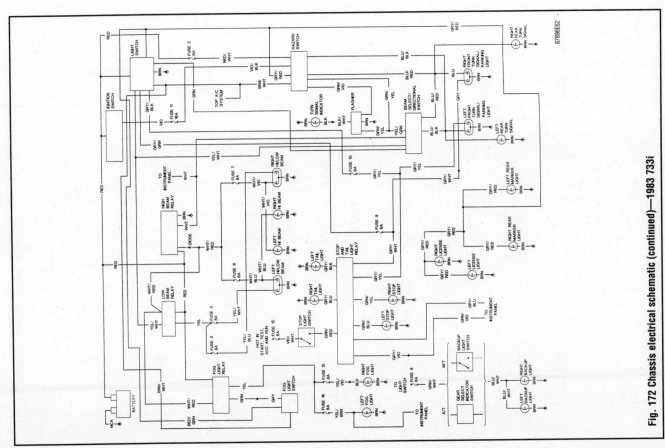

Fig. 172 Chassis electrical schematic (continued)—1983 733i

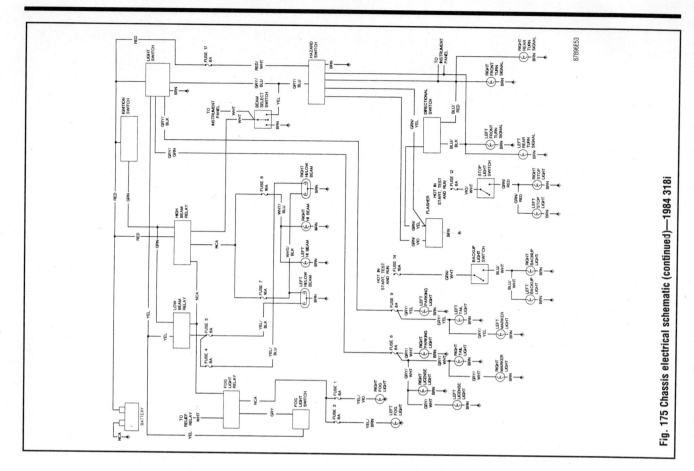

Fig. 175 Chassis electrical schematic (continued)—1984 318i

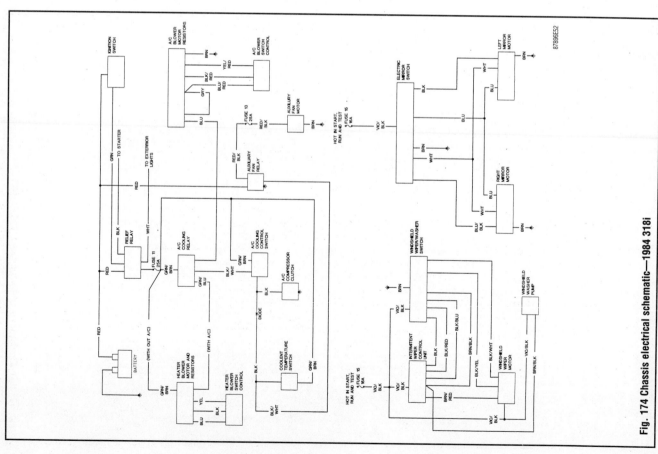

Fig. 174 Chassis electrical schematic—1984 318i

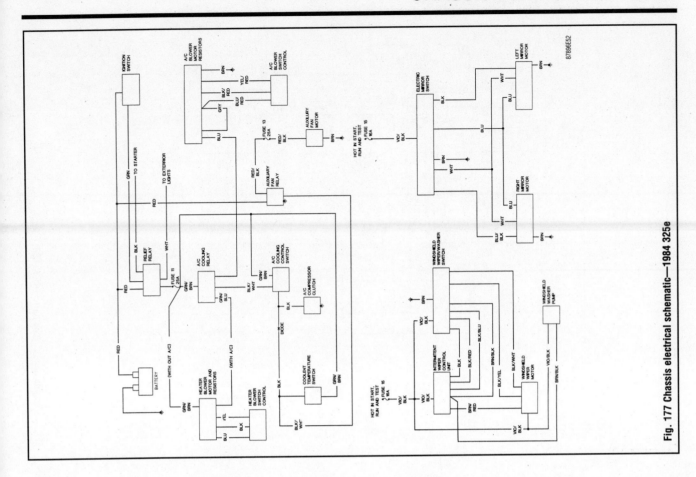

Fig. 177 Chassis electrical schematic—1984 325e

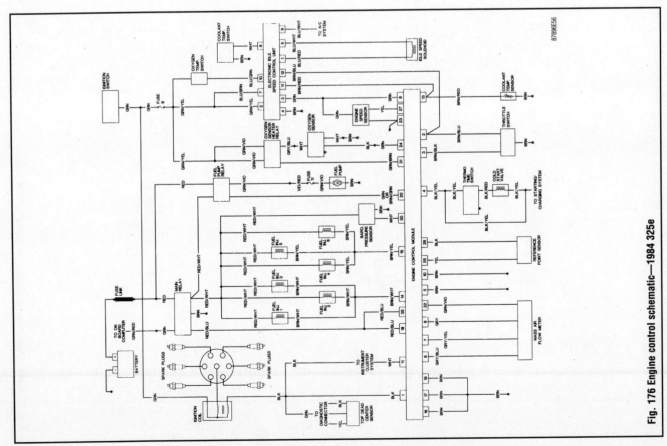

Fig. 176 Engine control schematic—1984 325e

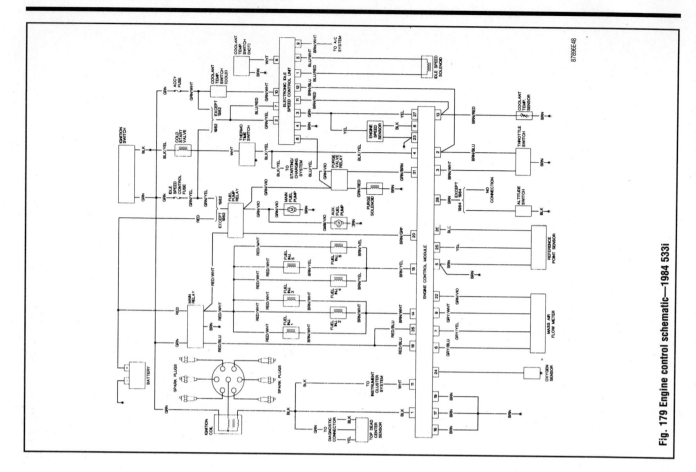

Fig. 179 Engine control schematic—1984 533i

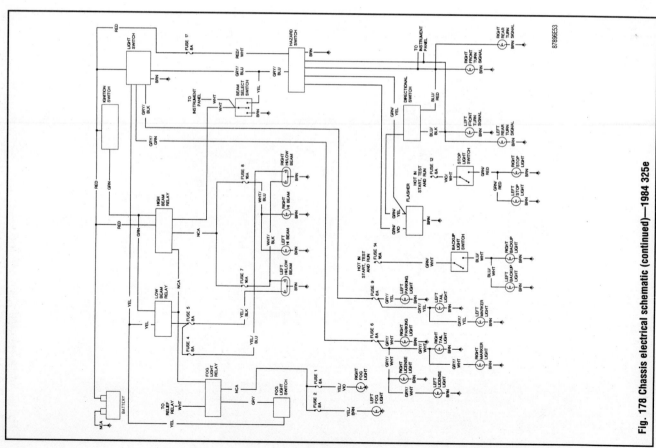

Fig. 178 Chassis electrical schematic (continued)—1984 325e

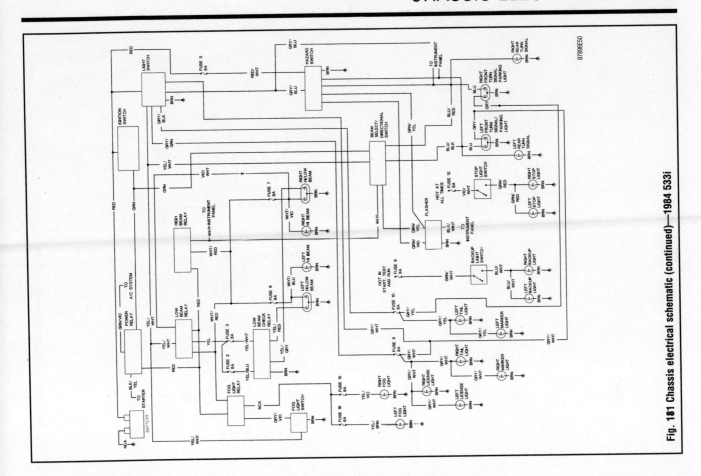

Fig. 181 Chassis electrical schematic (continued)—1984 533i

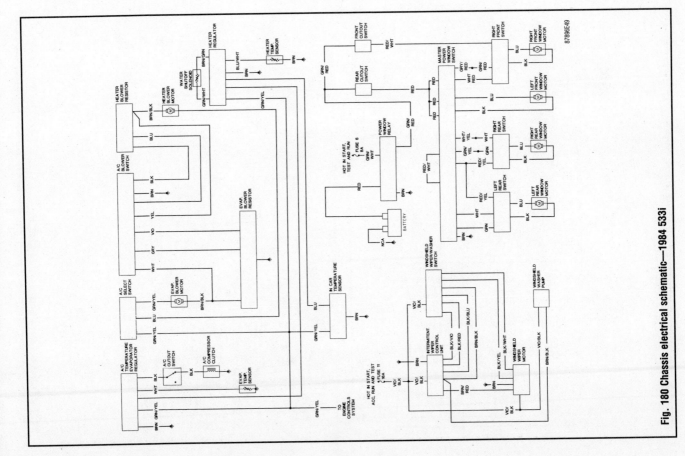

Fig. 180 Chassis electrical schematic—1984 533i

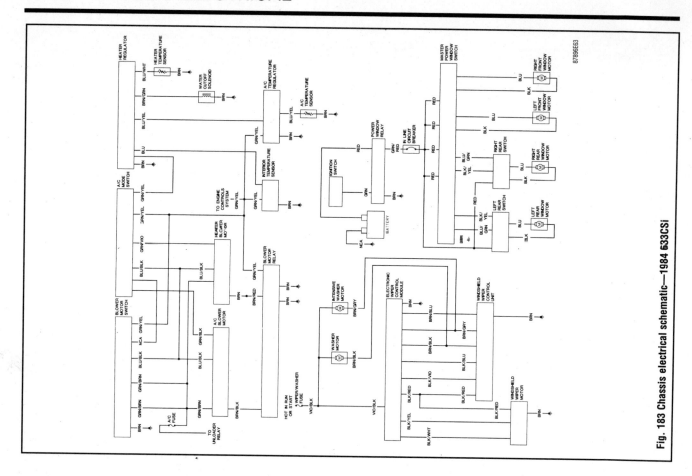

Fig. 183 Chassis electrical schematic—1984 633CSi

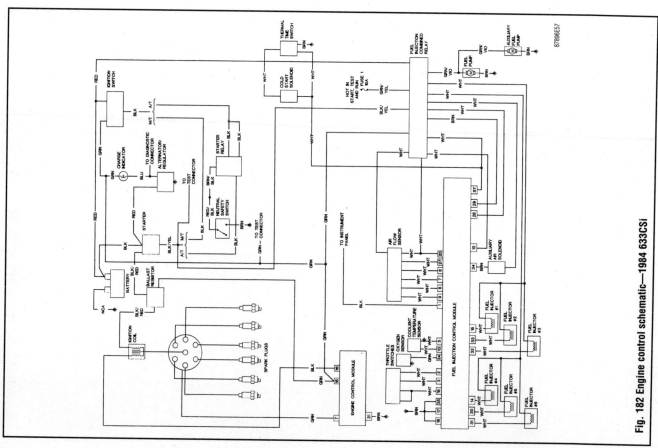

Fig. 182 Engine control schematic—1984 633CSi

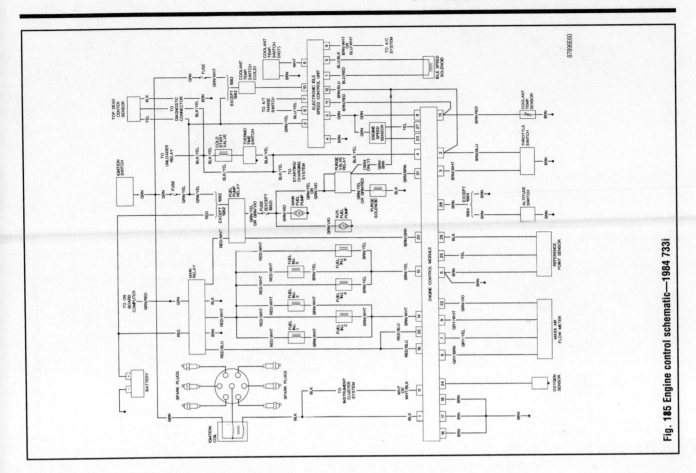

Fig. 185 Engine control schematic—1984 733i

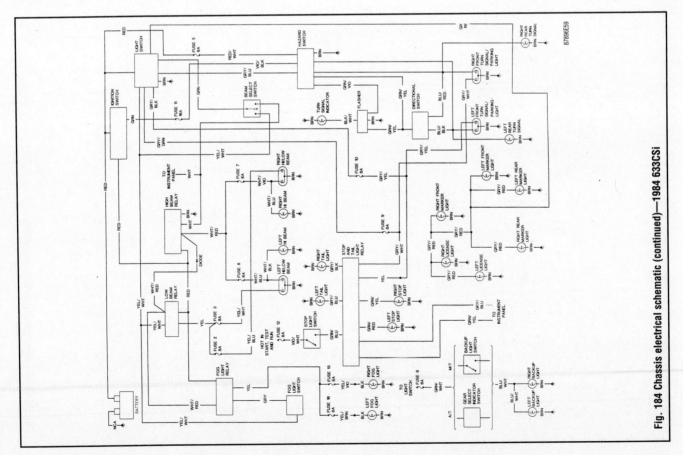

Fig. 184 Chassis electrical schematic (continued)—1984 633CSi

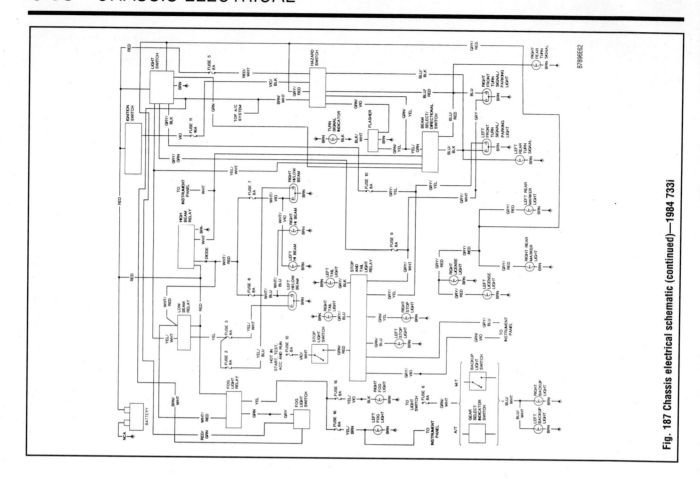

Fig. 187 Chassis electrical schematic (continued)—1984 733i

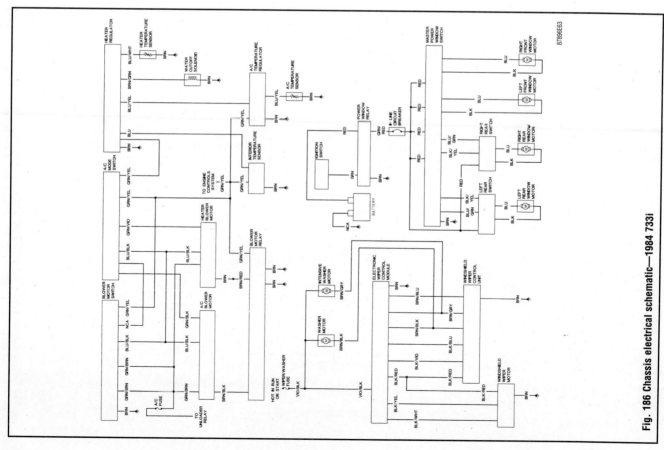

Fig. 186 Chassis electrical schematic—1984 733i

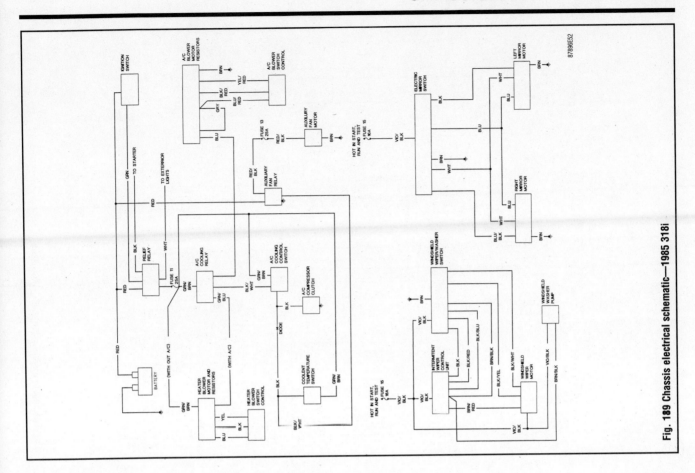

Fig. 189 Chassis electrical schematic—1985 318i

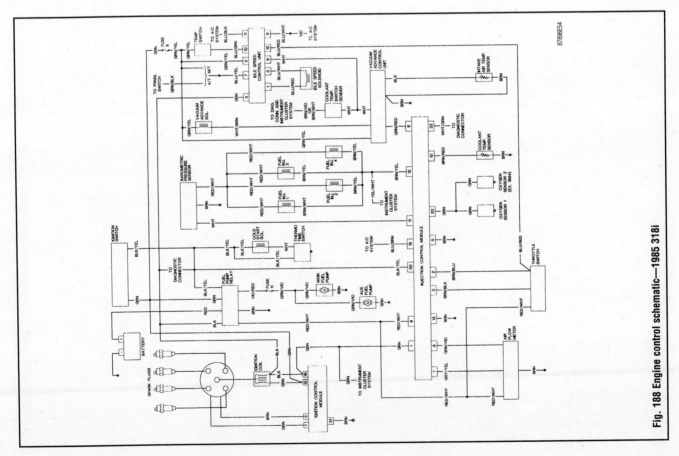

Fig. 188 Engine control schematic—1985 318i

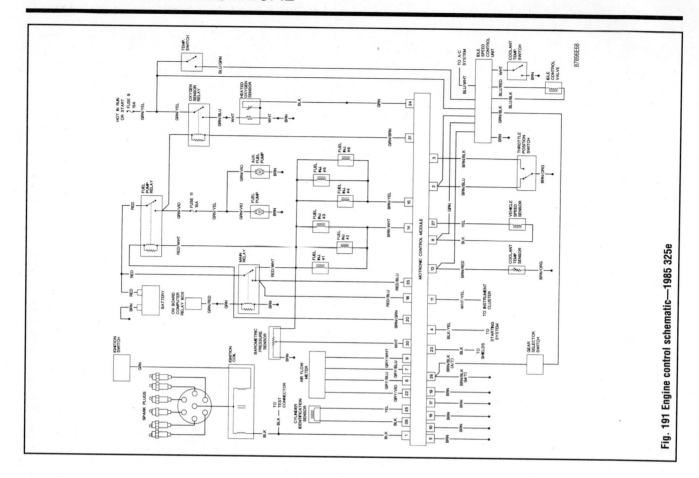

Fig. 191 Engine control schematic—1985 325e

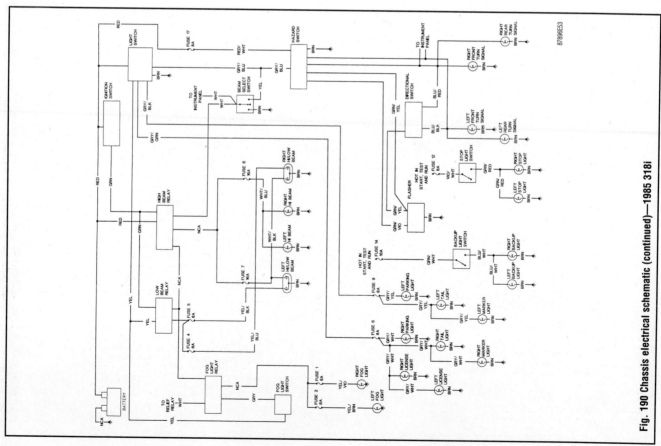

Fig. 190 Chassis electrical schematic (continued)—1985 318i

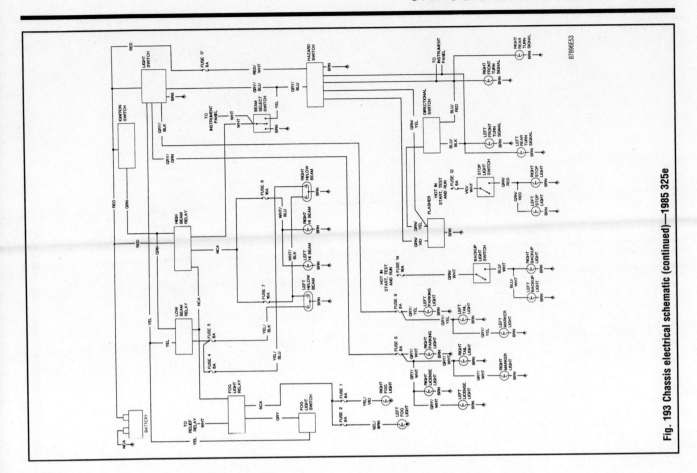

Fig. 193 Chassis electrical schematic (continued)—1985 325e

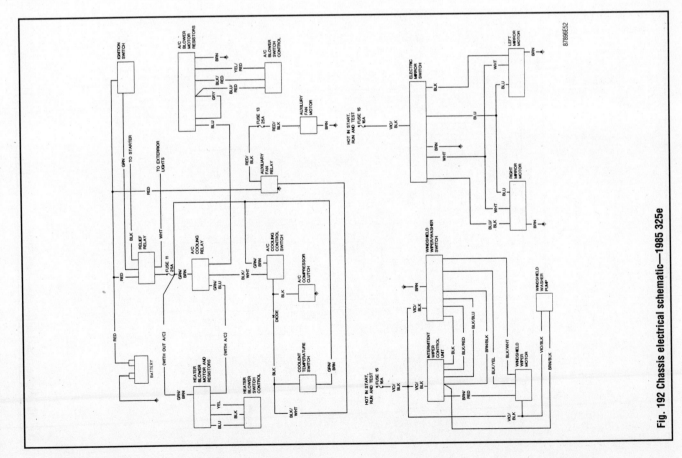

Fig. 192 Chassis electrical schematic—1985 325e

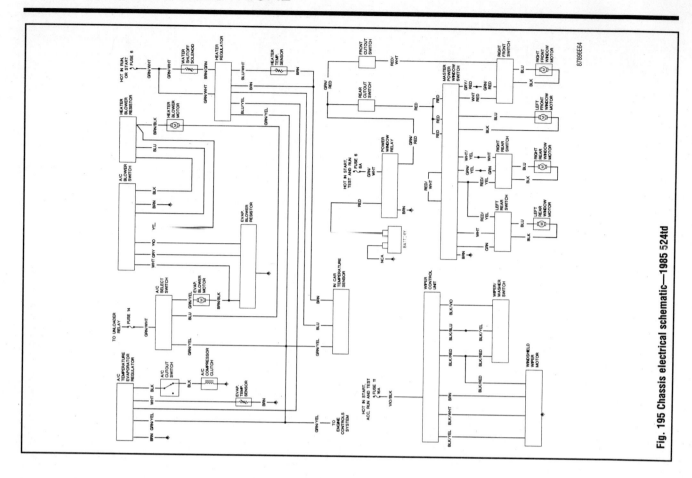

Fig. 195 Chassis electrical schematic—1985 524td

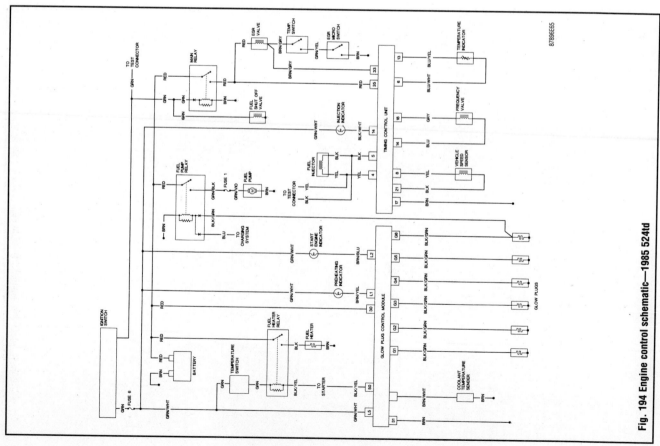

Fig. 194 Engine control schematic—1985 524td

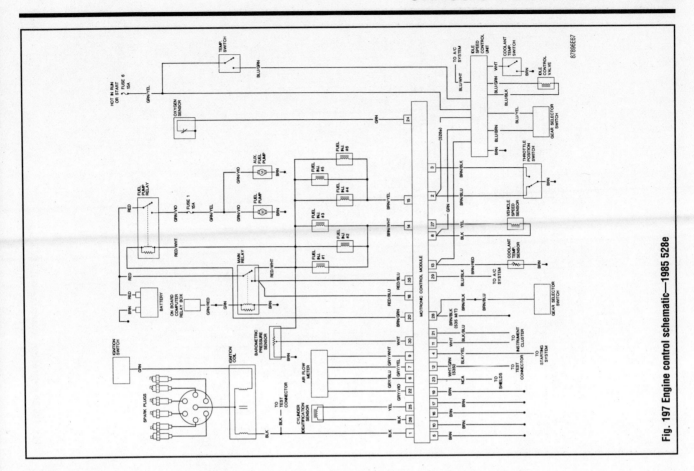

Fig. 197 Engine control schematic—1985 528e

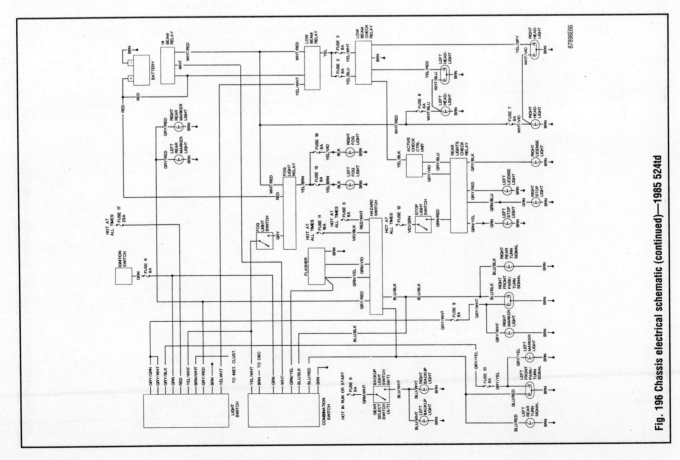

Fig. 196 Chassis electrical schematic (continued)—1985 524td

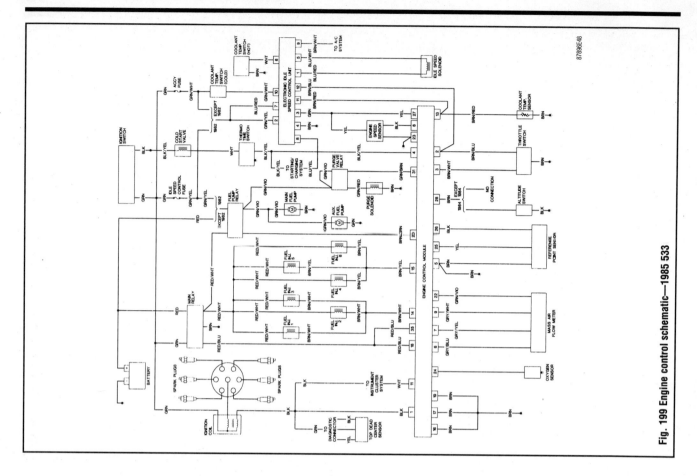

Fig. 199 Engine control schematic—1985 533

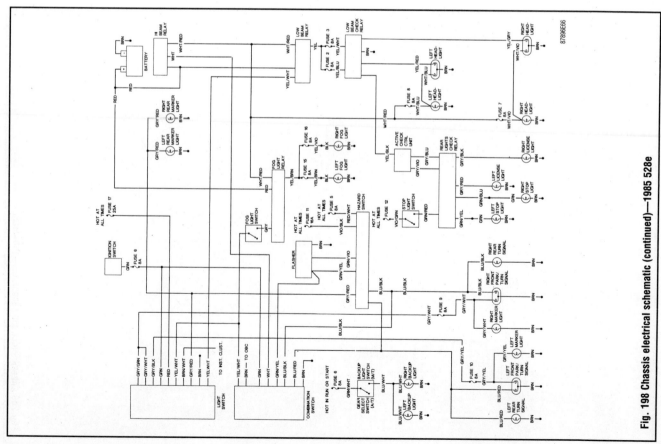

Fig. 198 Chassis electrical schematic (continued)—1985 528e

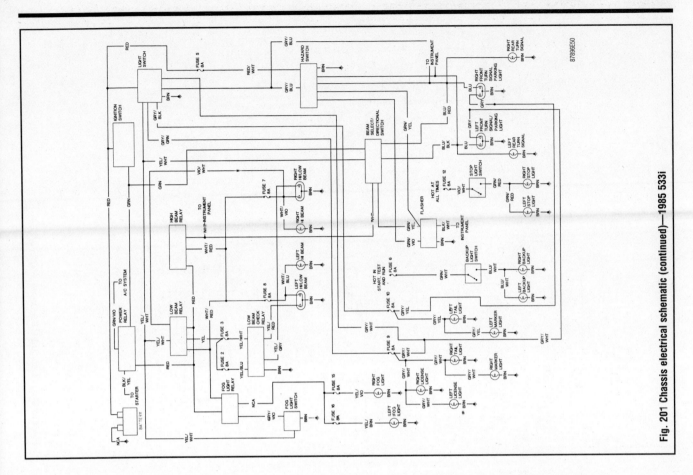

Fig. 201 Chassis electrical schematic (continued)—1985 533i

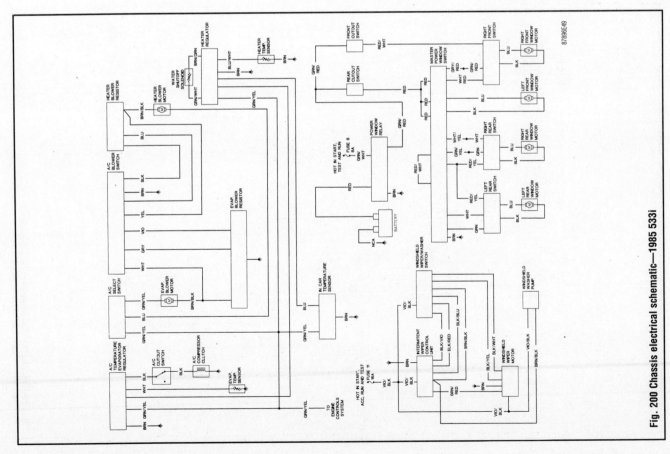

Fig. 200 Chassis electrical schematic—1985 533i

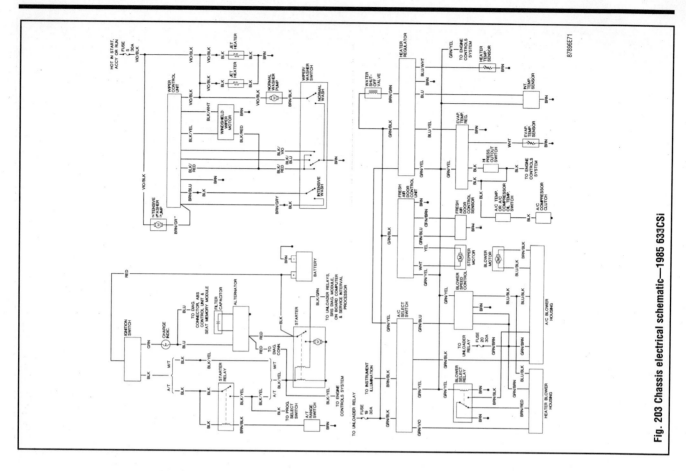

Fig. 203 Chassis electrical schematic—1985 633CSi

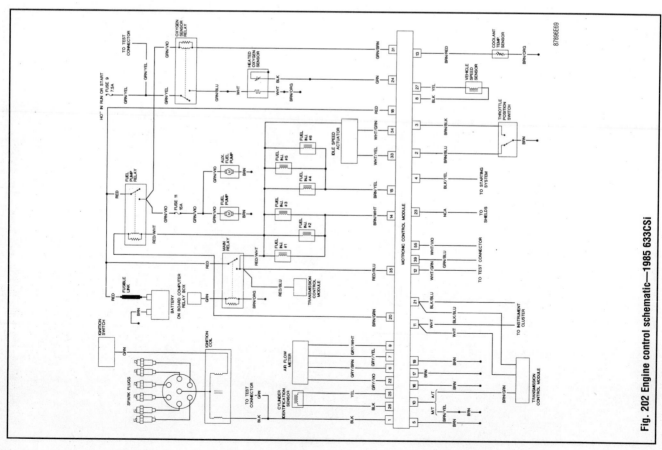

Fig. 202 Engine control schematic—1985 633CSi

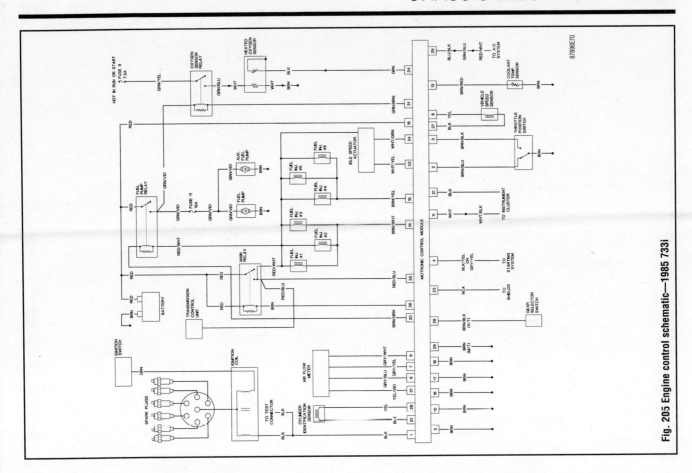

Fig. 205 Engine control schematic—1985 733i

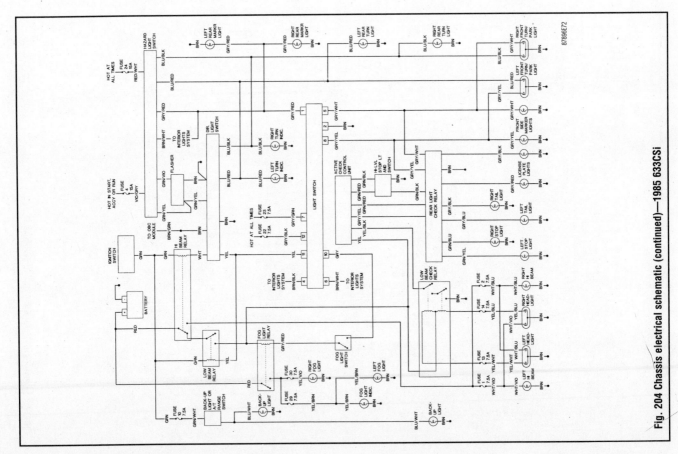

Fig. 204 Chassis electrical schematic (continued)—1985 633CSi

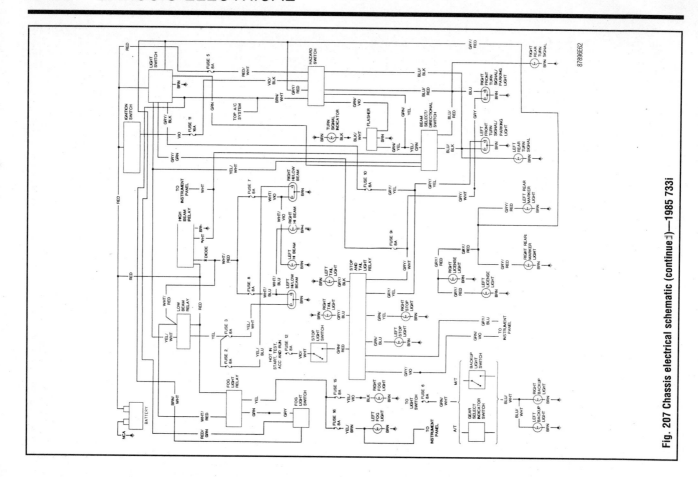

Fig. 207 Chassis electrical schematic (continued)—1985 733i

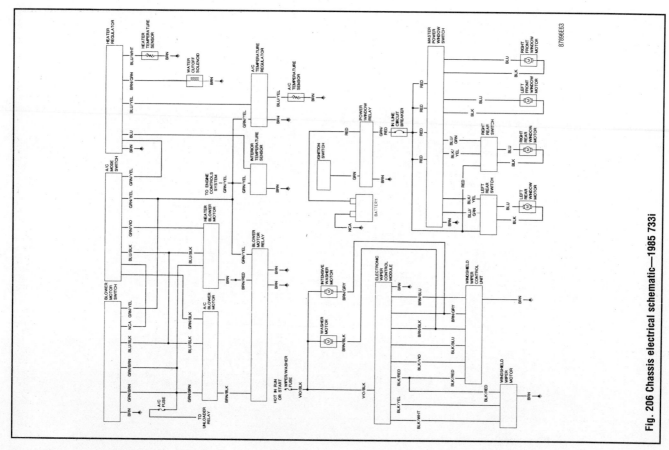

Fig. 206 Chassis electrical schematic—1985 733i

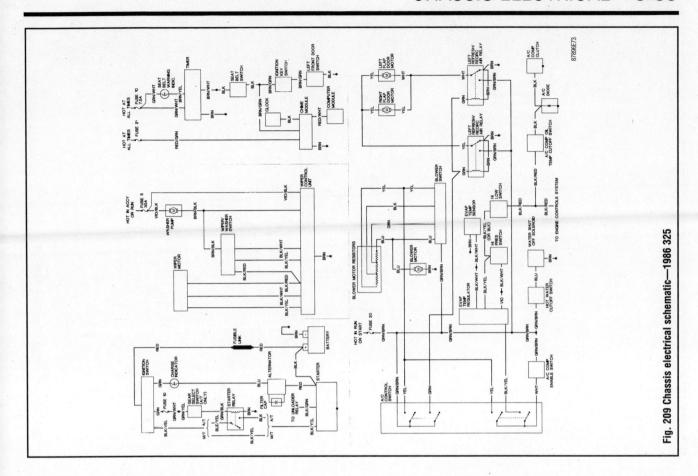

Fig. 209 Chassis electrical schematic—1986 325

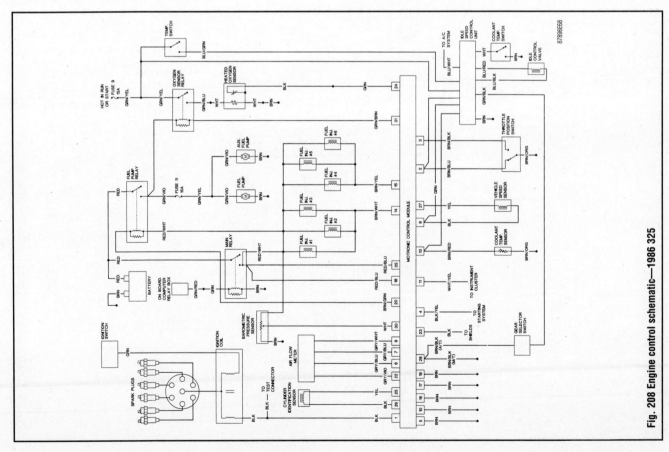

Fig. 208 Engine control schematic—1986 325

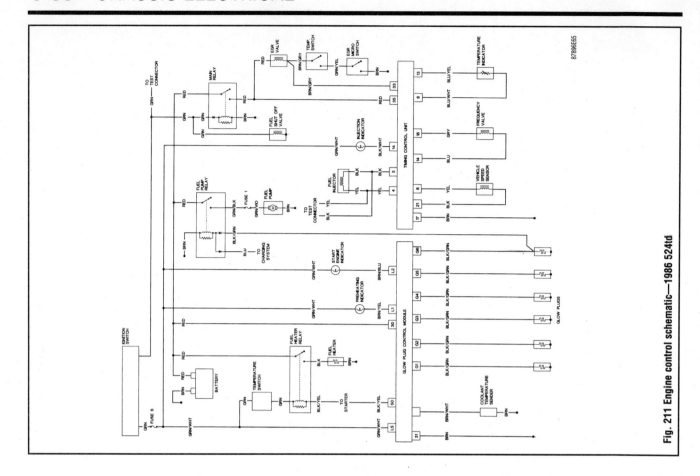

Fig. 211 Engine control schematic—1986 524td

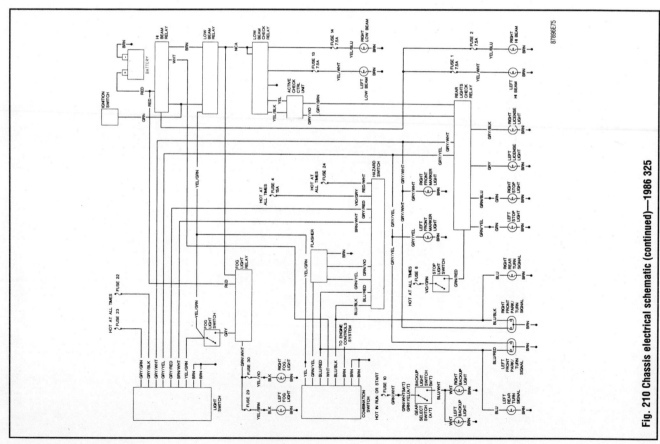

Fig. 210 Chassis electrical schematic (continued)—1986 325

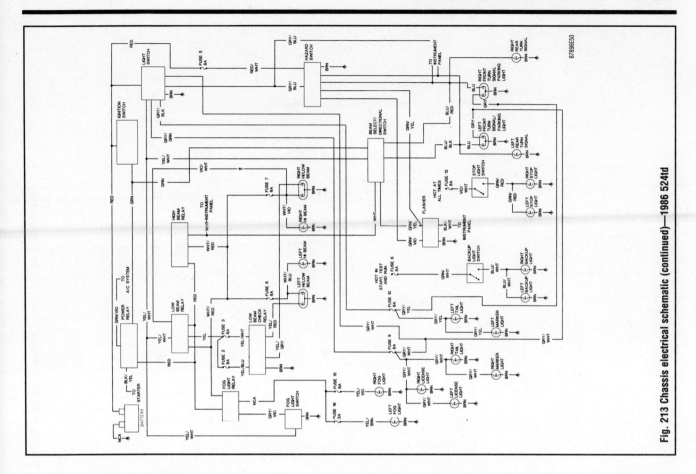

Fig. 213 Chassis electrical schematic (continued)—1986 524td

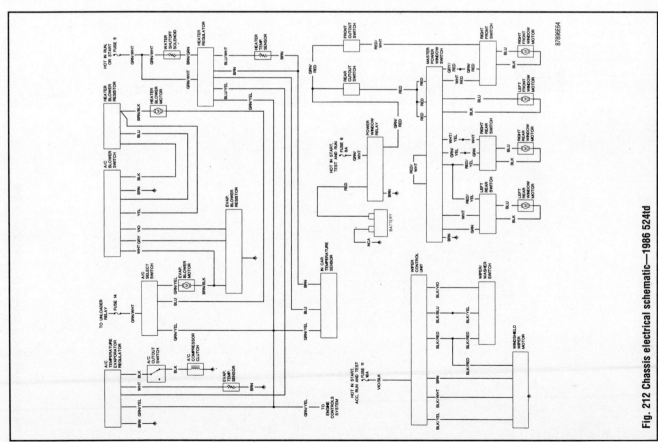

Fig. 212 Chassis electrical schematic—1986 524td

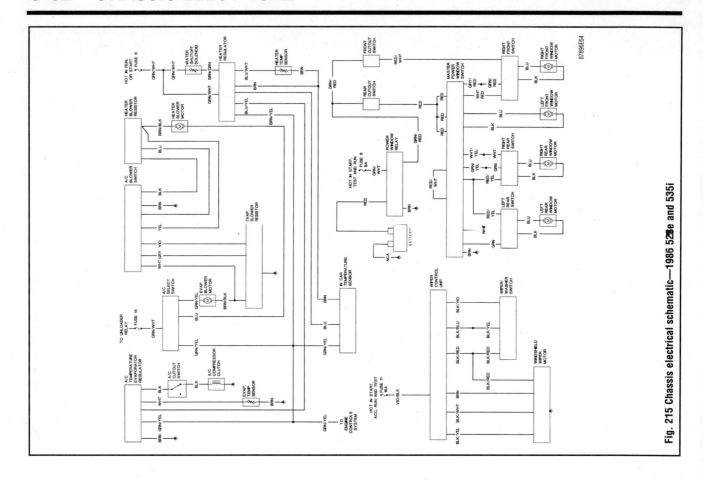

Fig. 215 Chassis electrical schematic—1986 528e and 535i

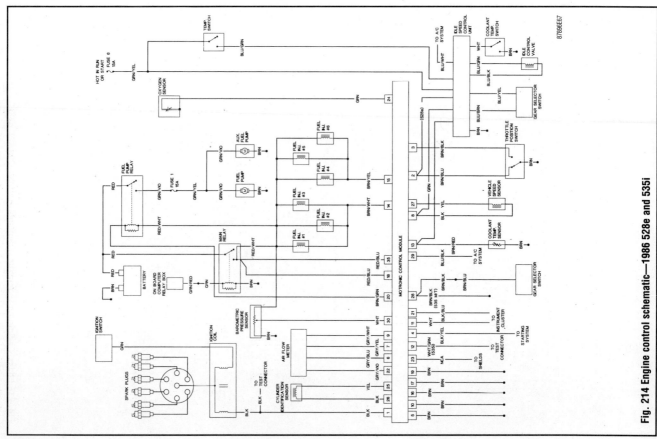

Fig. 214 Engine control schematic—1986 528e and 535i

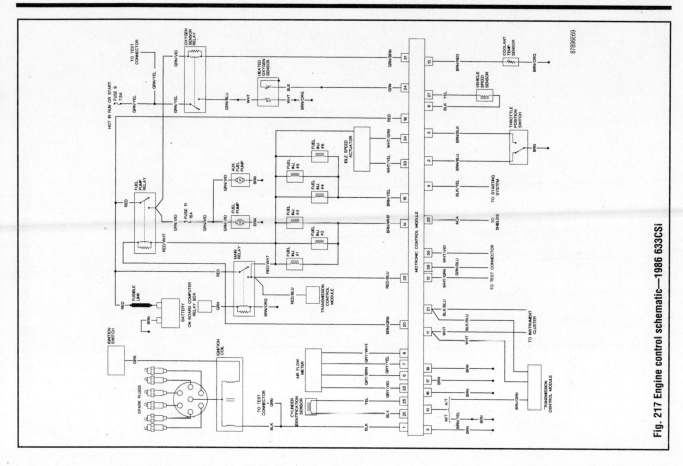

Fig. 217 Engine control schematic—1986 633CSi

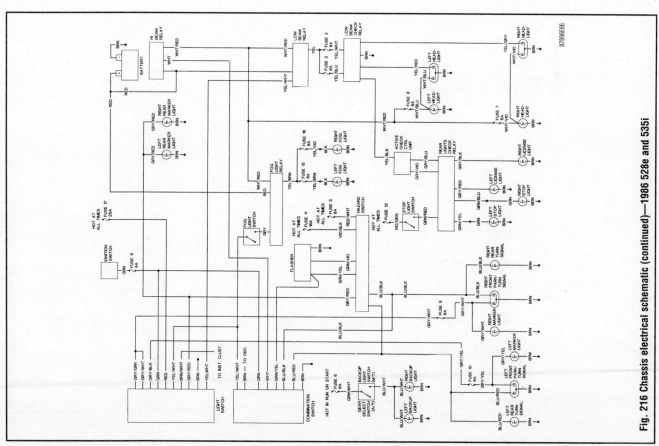

Fig. 216 Chassis electrical schematic (continued)—1986 528e and 535i

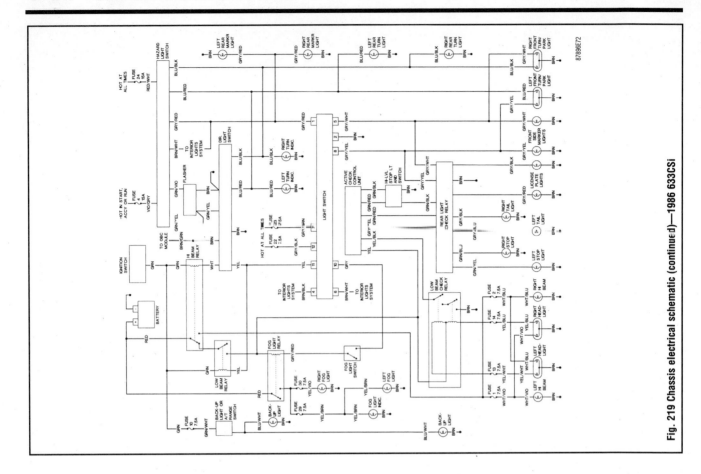

Fig. 219 Chassis electrical schematic (continued)—1986 633CSi

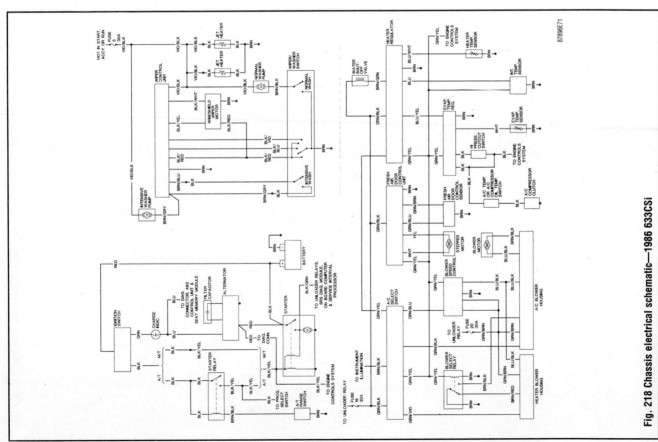

Fig. 218 Chassis electrical schematic—1986 633CSi

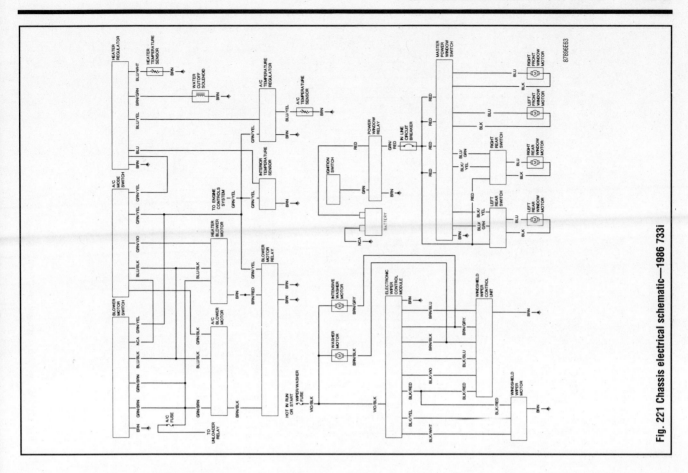

Fig. 221 Chassis electrical schematic—1986 733i

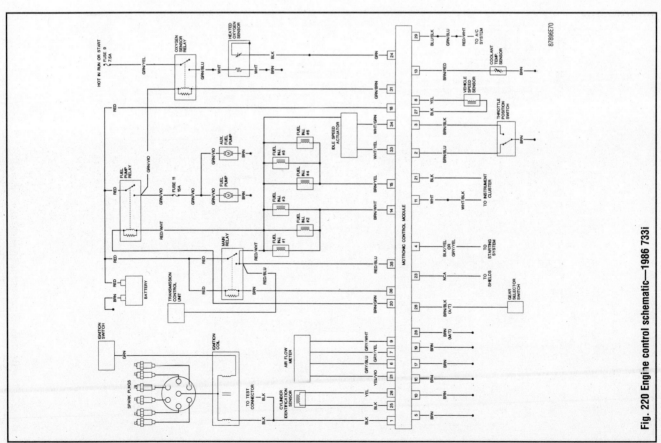

Fig. 220 Engine control schematic—1986 733i

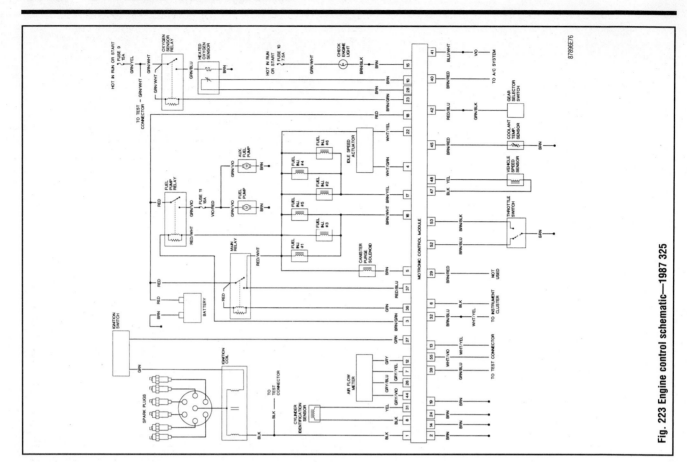

Fig. 223 Engine control schematic—1987 325

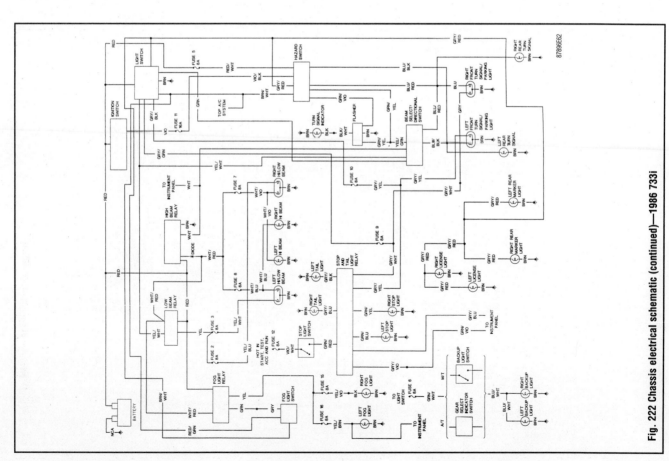

Fig. 222 Chassis electrical schematic (continued)—1986 733i

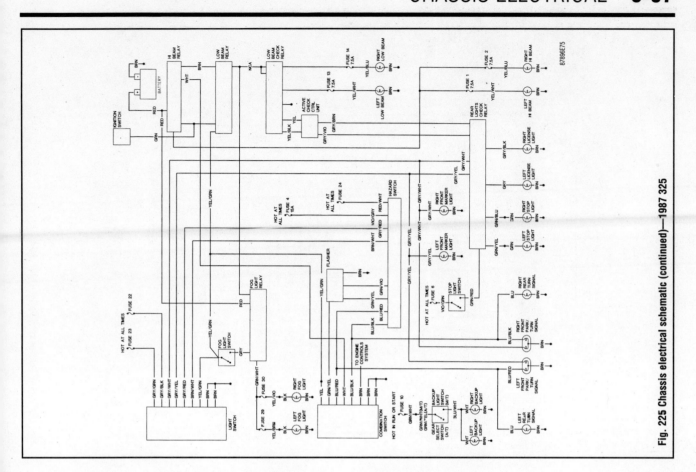

Fig. 225 Chassis electrical schematic (continued)—1987 325

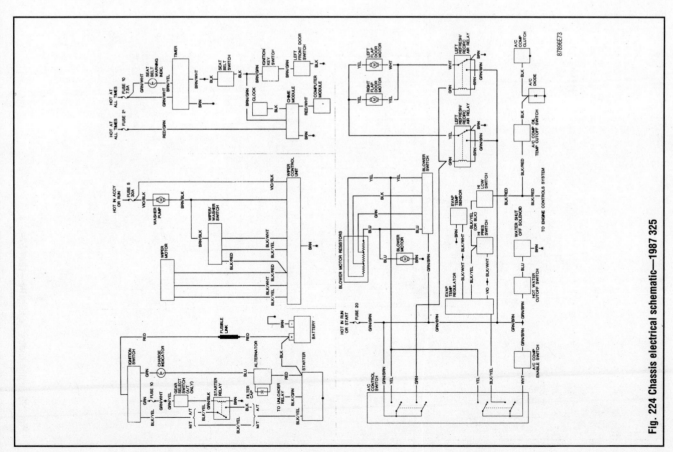

Fig. 224 Chassis electrical schematic—1987 325

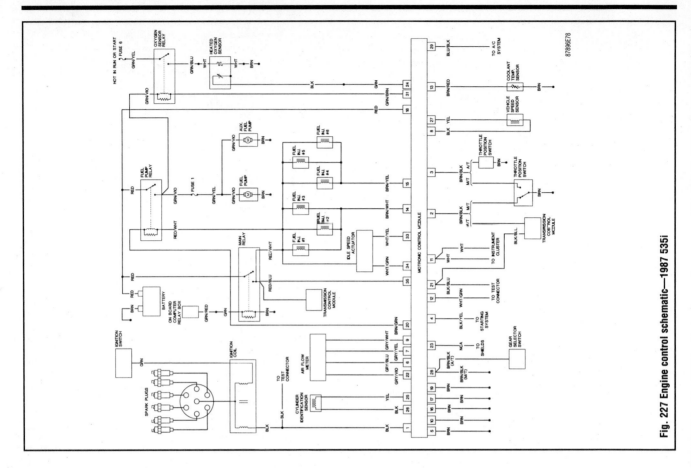

Fig. 227 Engine control schematic—1987 535i

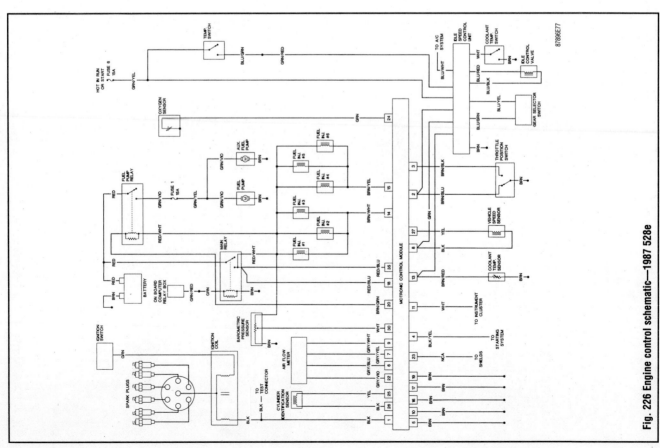

Fig. 226 Engine control schematic—1987 528e

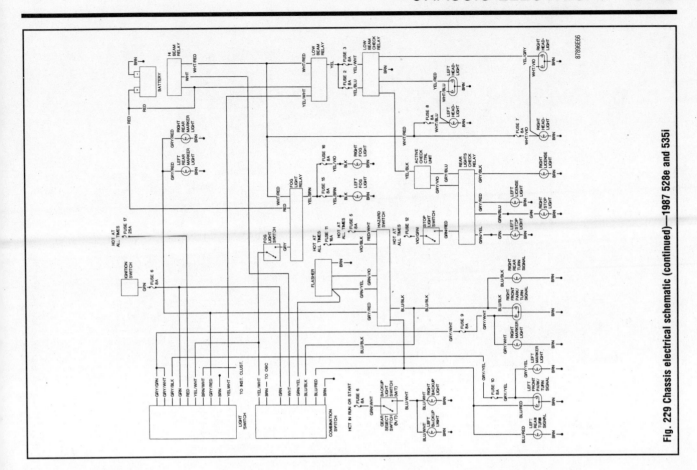

Fig. 229 Chassis electrical schematic (continued)—1987 528e and 535i

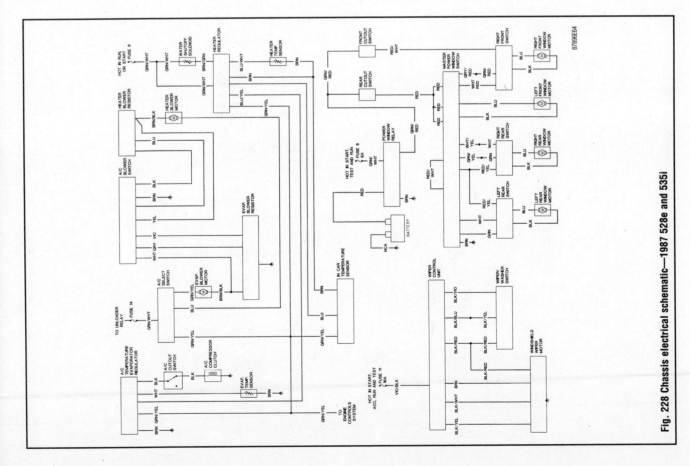

Fig. 228 Chassis electrical schematic—1987 528e and 535i

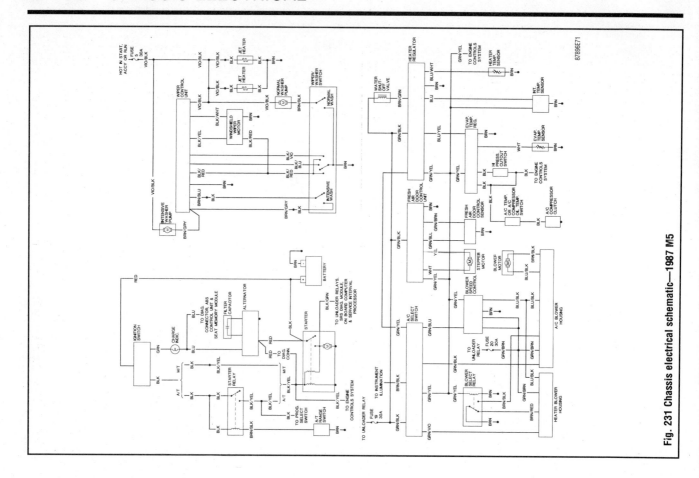

Fig. 231 Chassis electrical schematic—1987 M5

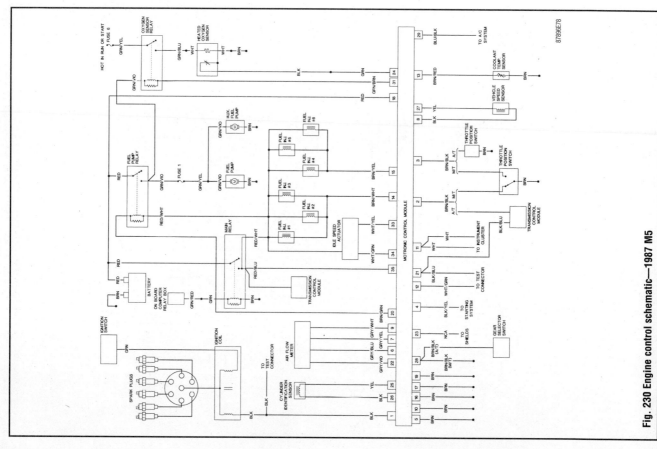

Fig. 230 Engine control schematic—1987 M5

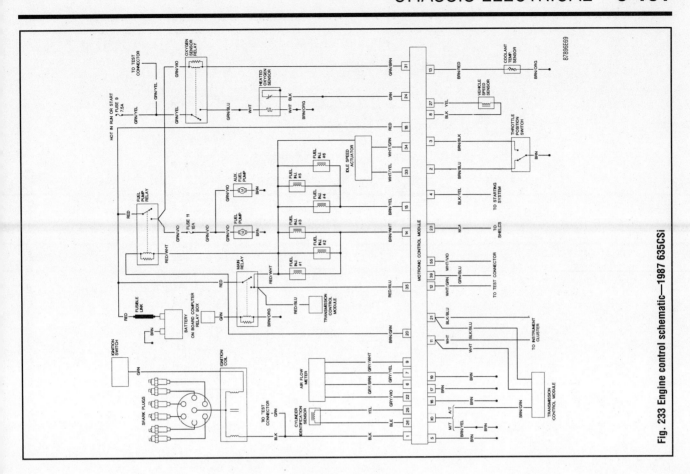

Fig. 233 Engine control schematic—1987 635CSi

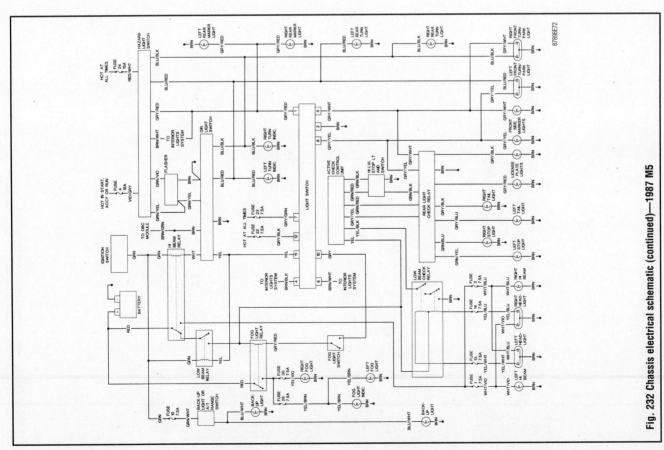

Fig. 232 Chassis electrical schematic (continued)—1987 M5

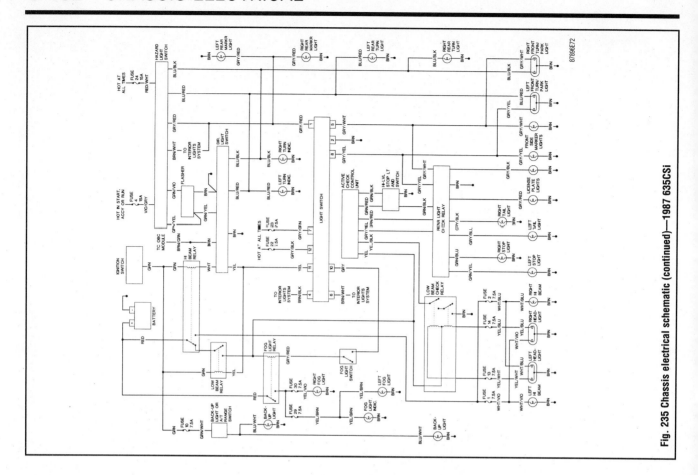

Fig. 235 Chassis electrical schematic (continued)—1987 635CSi

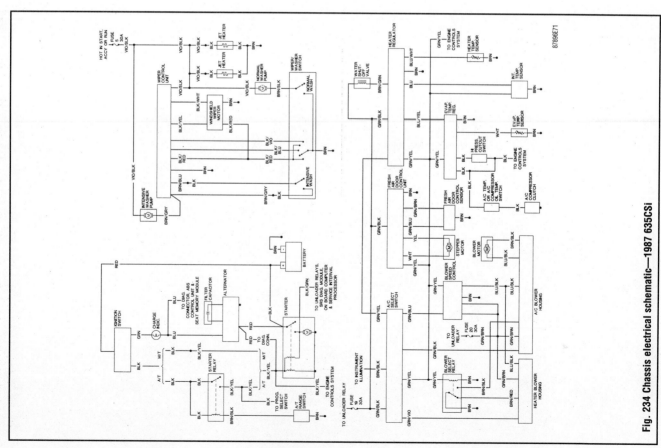

Fig. 234 Chassis electrical schematic—1987 635CSi

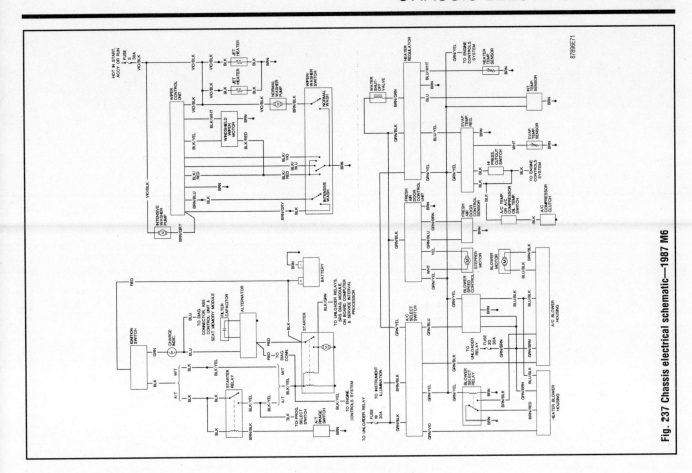

Fig. 237 Chassis electrical schematic—1987 M6

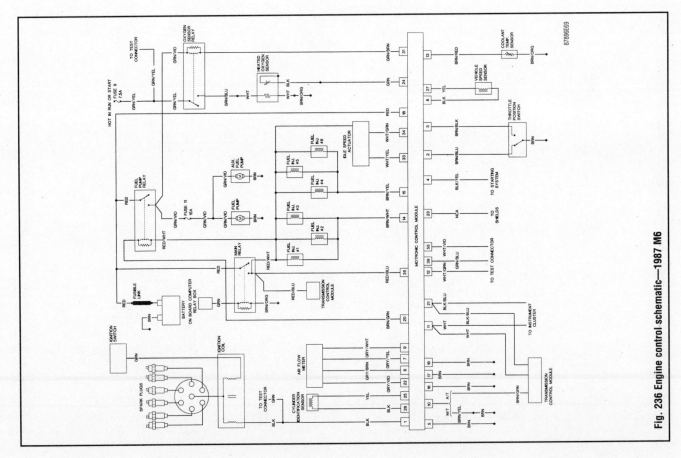

Fig. 236 Engine control schematic—1987 M6

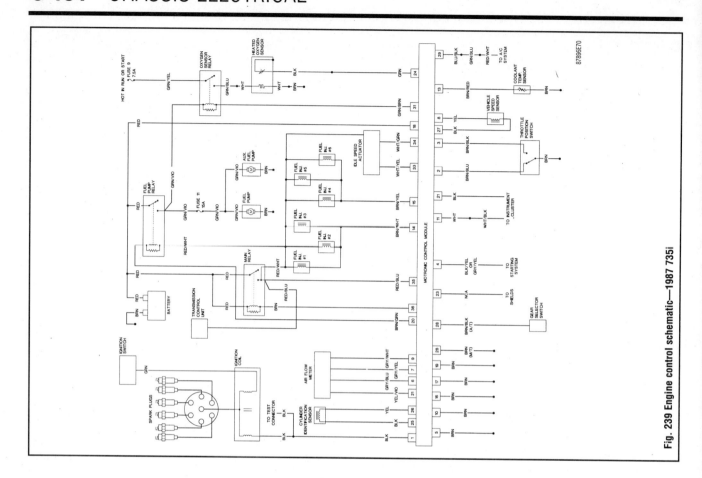

Fig. 239 Engine control schematic—1987 735i

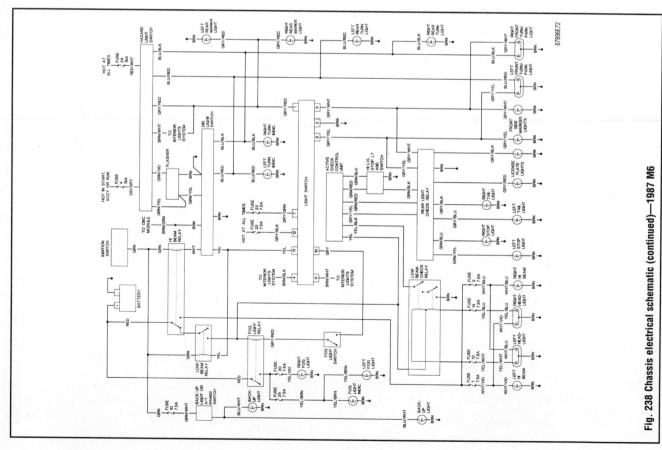

Fig. 238 Chassis electrical schematic (continued)—1987 M6

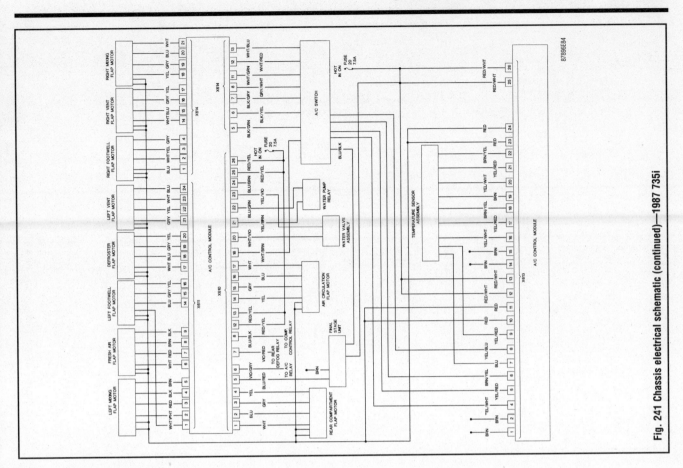

Fig. 241 Chassis electrical schematic (continued)—1987 735i

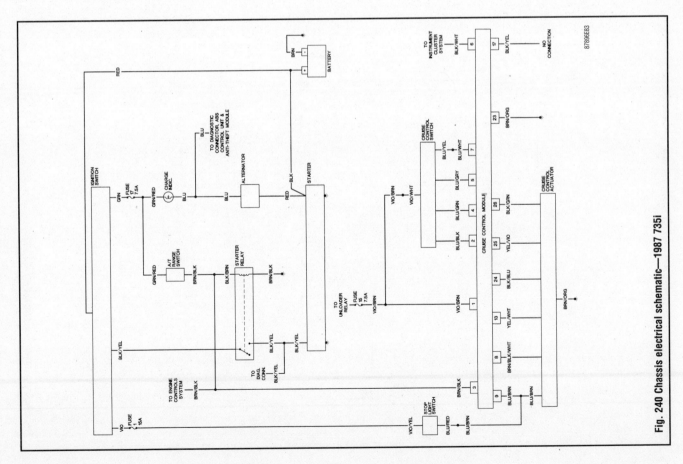

Fig. 240 Chassis electrical schematic—1987 735i

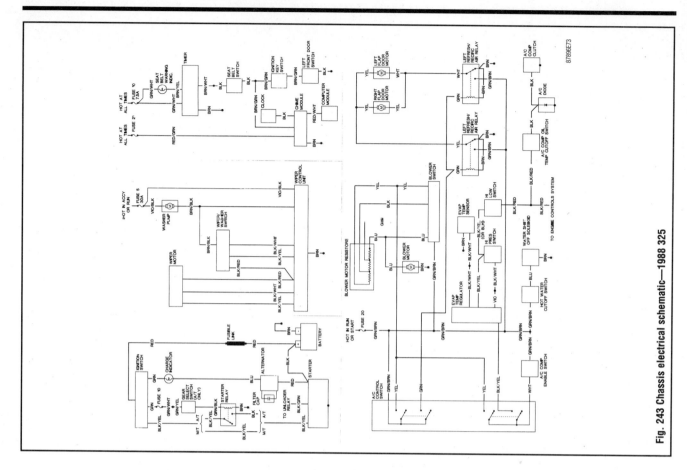

Fig. 243 Chassis electrical schematic—1988 325

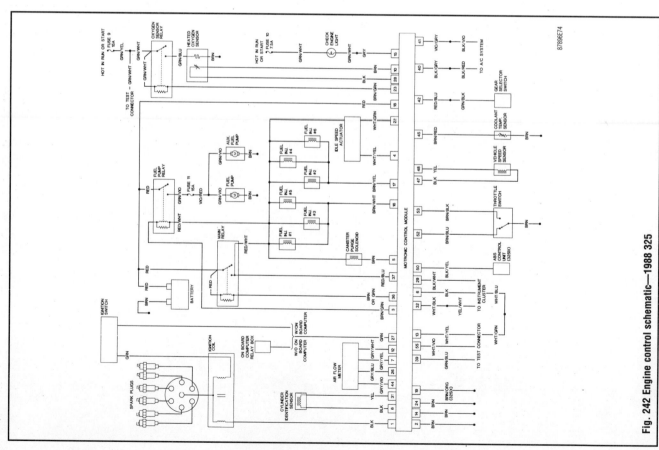

Fig. 242 Engine control schematic—1988 325

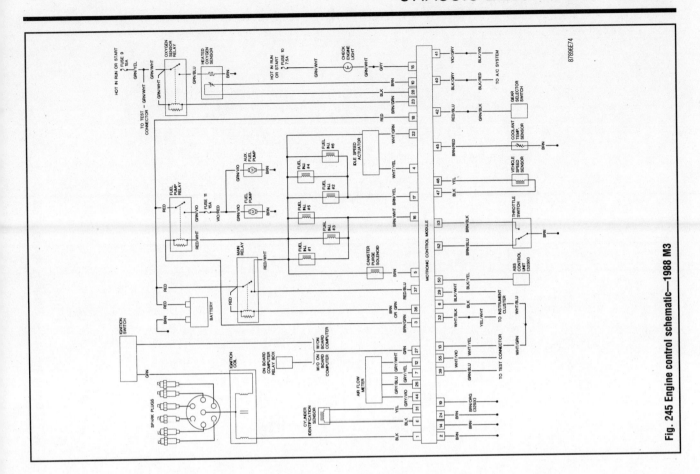

Fig. 245 Engine control schematic—1988 M3

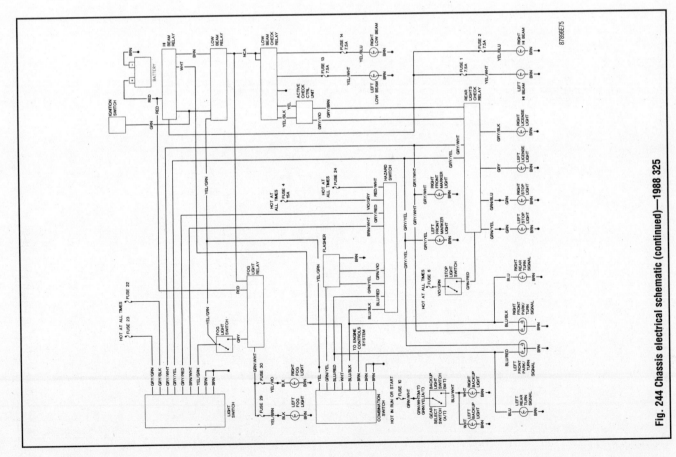

Fig. 244 Chassis electrical schematic (continued)—1988 325

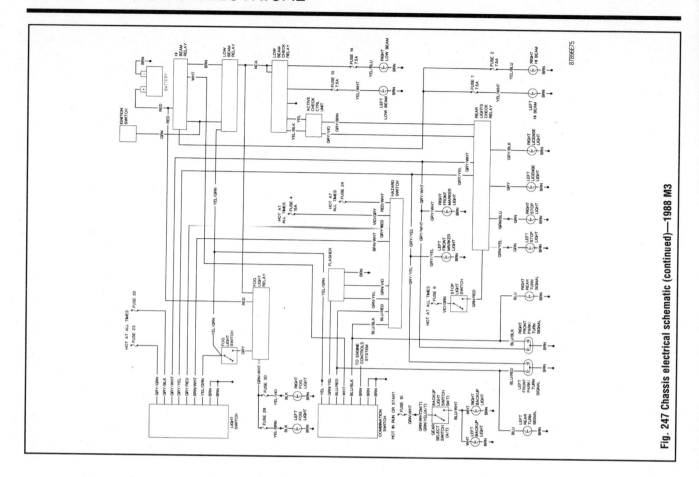

Fig. 247 Chassis electrical schematic (continued)—1988 M3

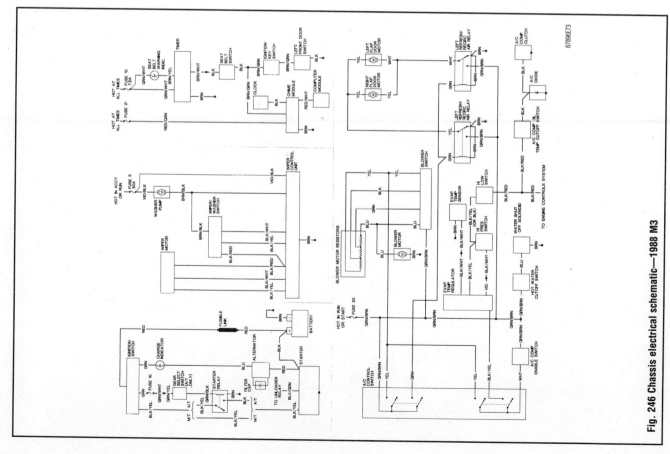

Fig. 246 Chassis electrical schematic—1988 M3

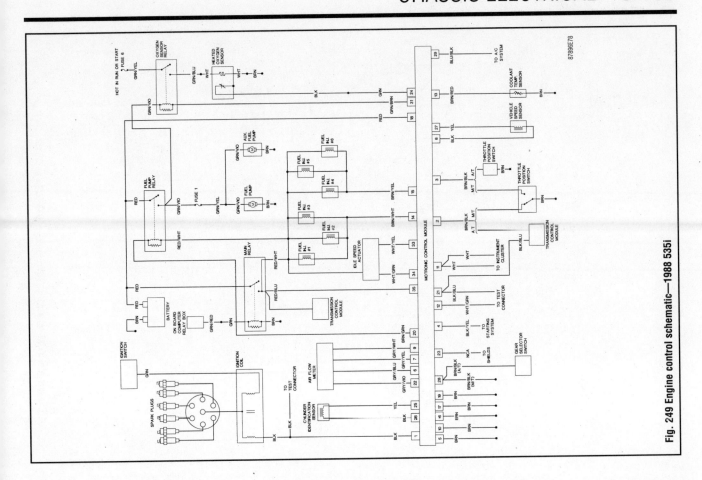

Fig. 249 Engine control schematic—1988 535i

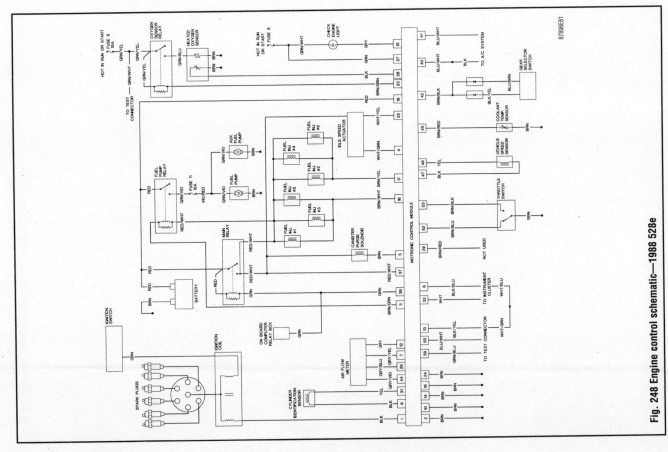

Fig. 248 Engine control schematic—1988 528e

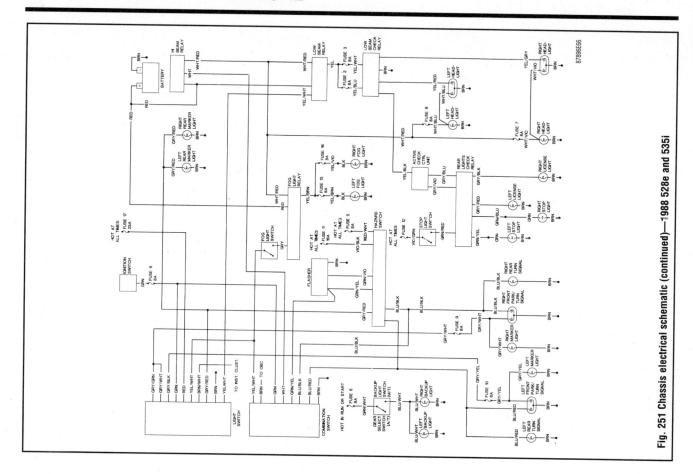

Fig. 251 Chassis electrical schematic (continued)—1988 528e and 535i

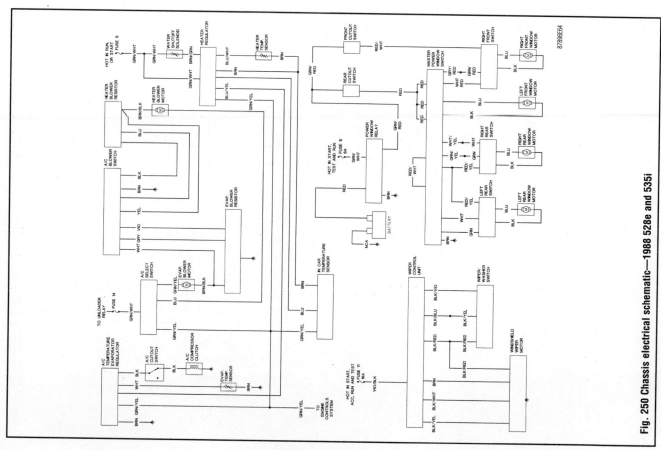

Fig. 250 Chassis electrical schematic—1988 528e and 535i

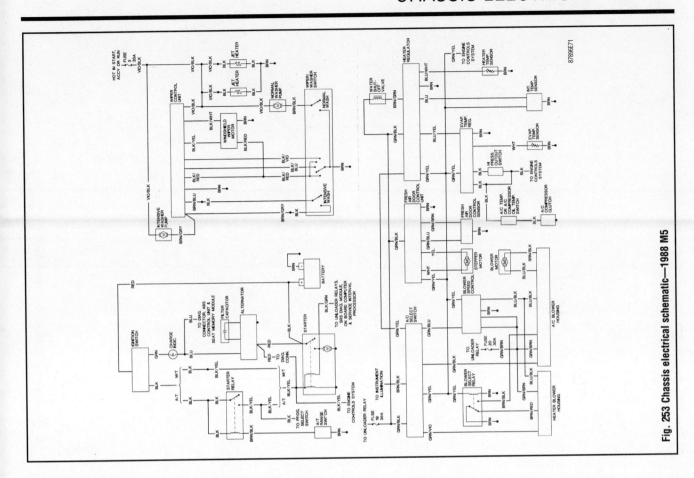

Fig. 253 Chassis electrical schematic—1988 M5

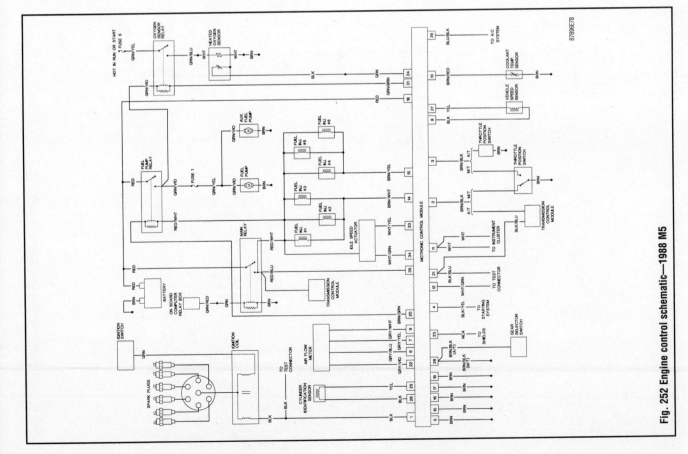

Fig. 252 Engine control schematic—1988 M5

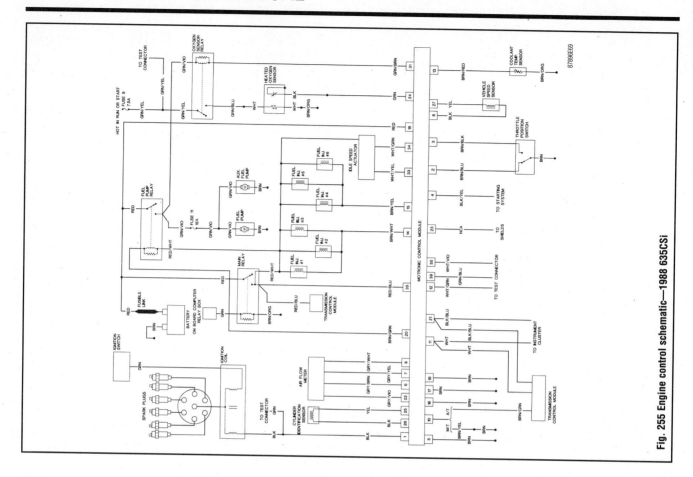

Fig. 255 Engine control schematic—1988 635CSi

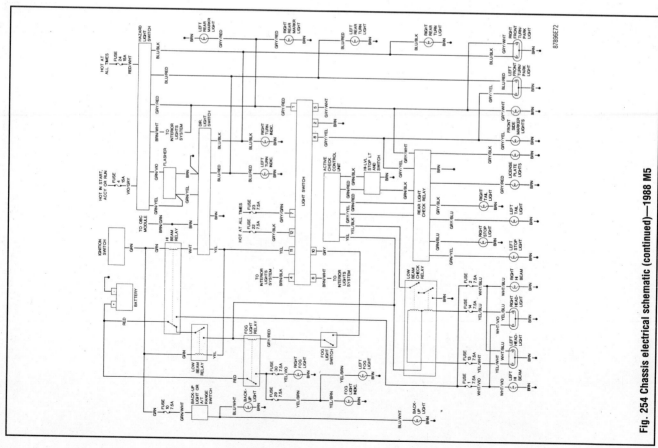

Fig. 254 Chassis electrical schematic (continued)—1988 M5

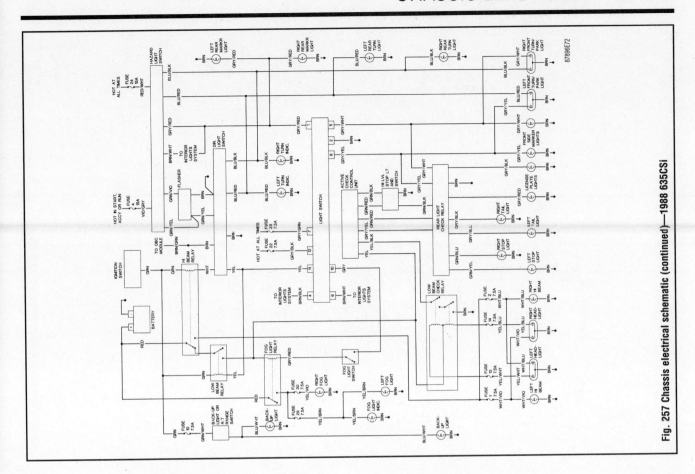

Fig. 257 Chassis electrical schematic (continued)—1988 635CSi

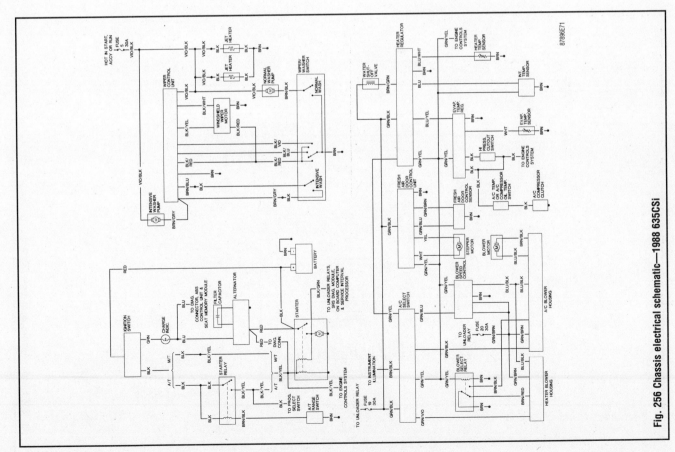

Fig. 256 Chassis electrical schematic—1988 635CSi

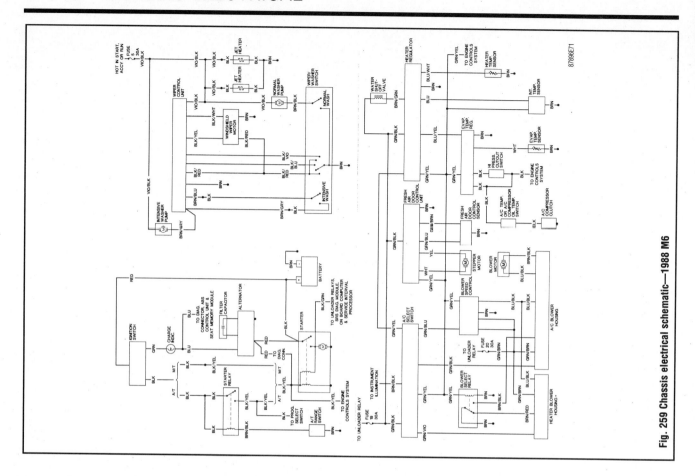

Fig. 259 Chassis electrical schematic—1988 M6

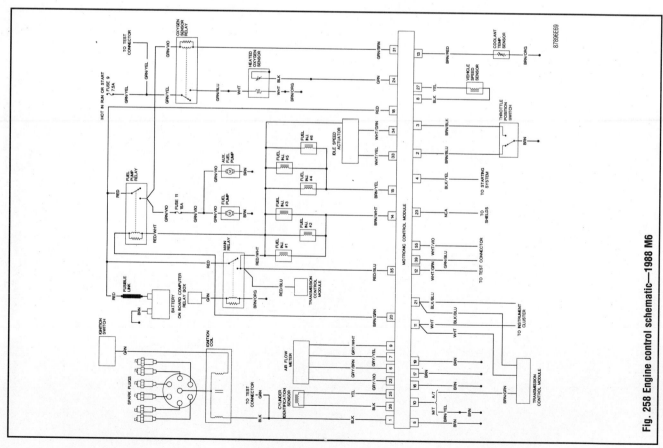

Fig. 258 Engine control schematic—1988 M6

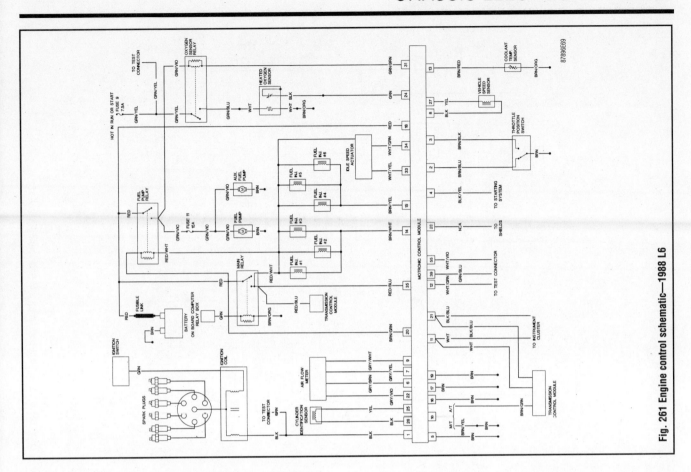

Fig. 261 Engine control schematic—1988 L6

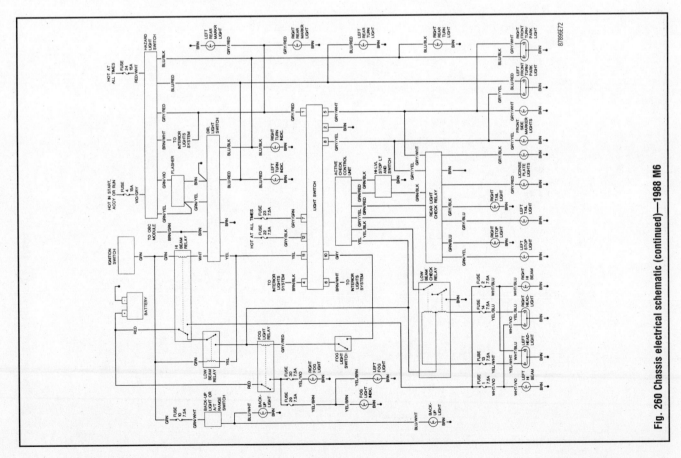

Fig. 260 Chassis electrical schematic (continued)—1988 M6

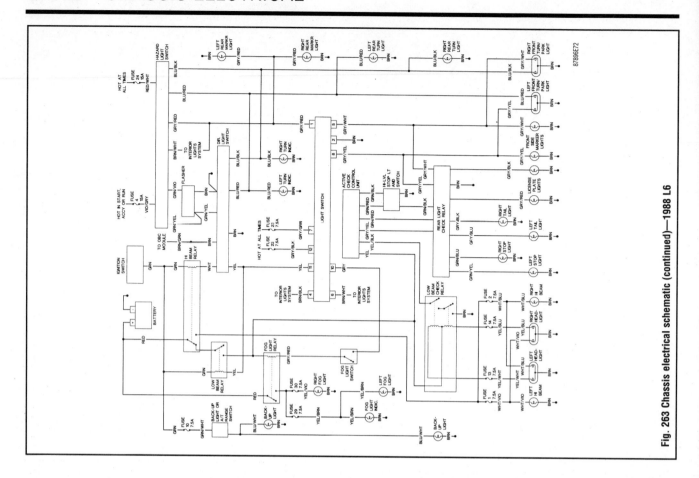

Fig. 263 Chassis electrical schematic (continued)—1988 L6

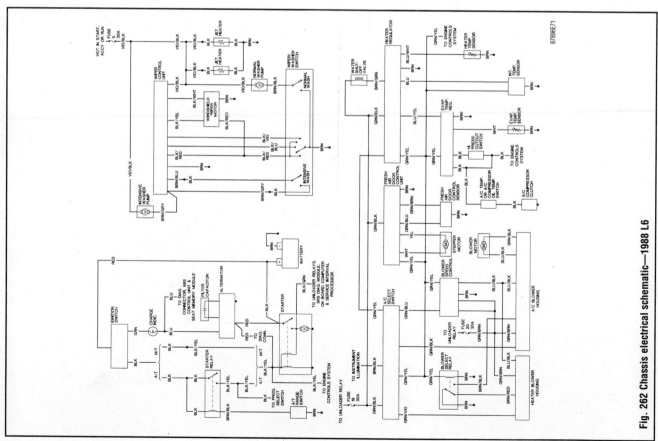

Fig. 262 Chassis electrical schematic—1988 L6

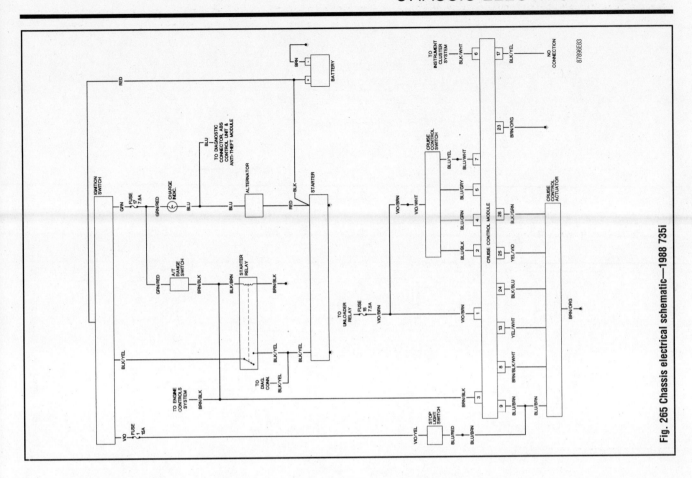

Fig. 265 Chassis electrical schematic—1988 735i

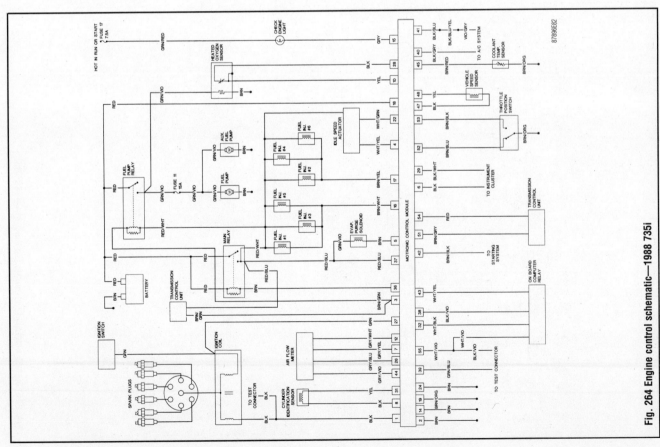

Fig. 264 Engine control schematic—1988 735i

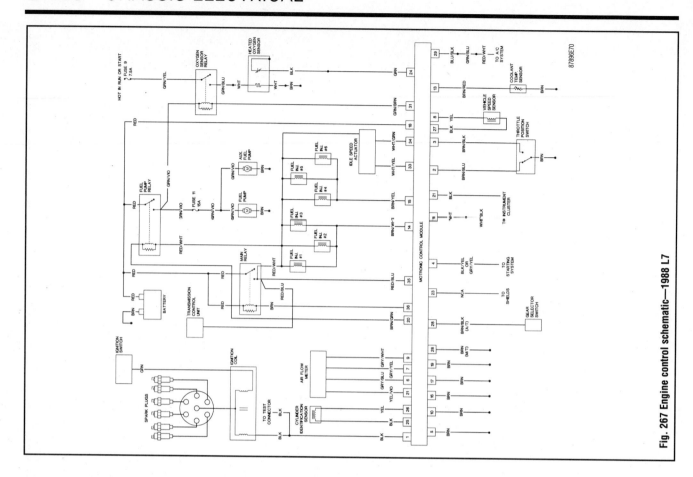

Fig. 267 Engine control schematic—1988 L7

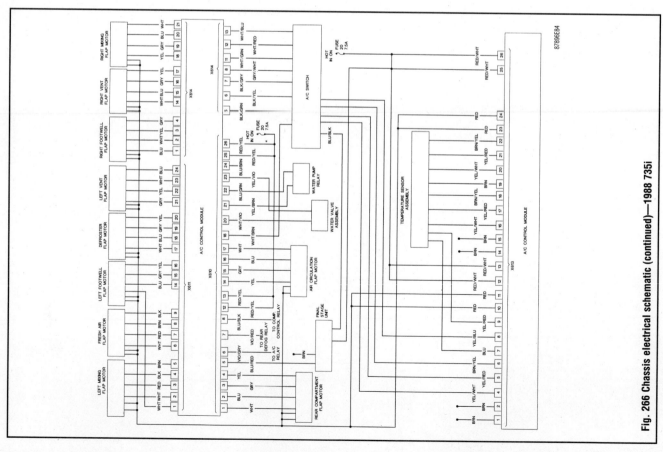

Fig. 266 Chassis electrical schematic (continued)—1988 735i

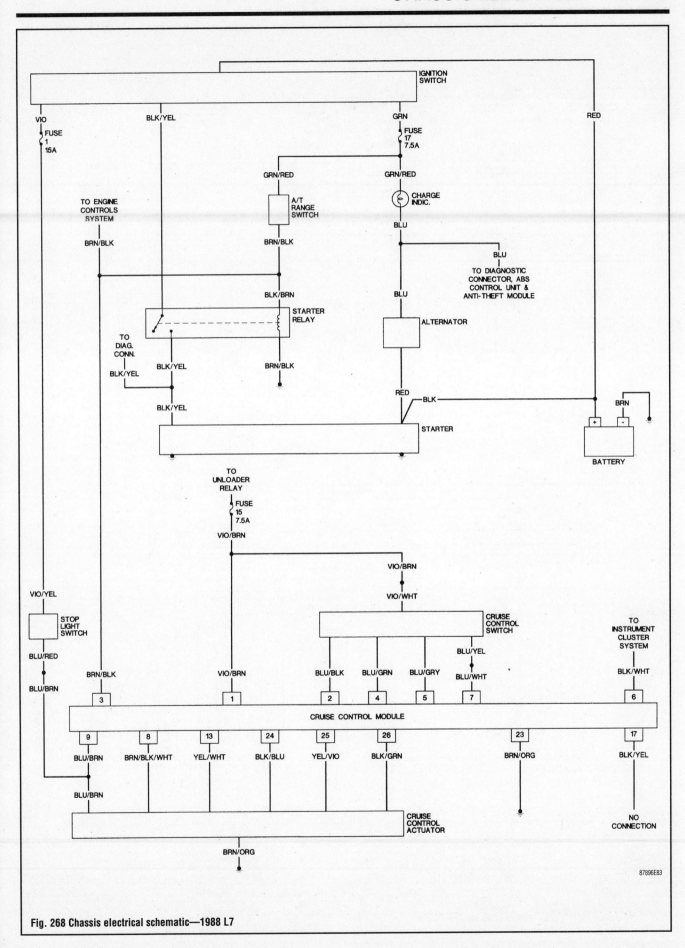

Fig. 268 Chassis electrical schematic—1988 L7

87896E83

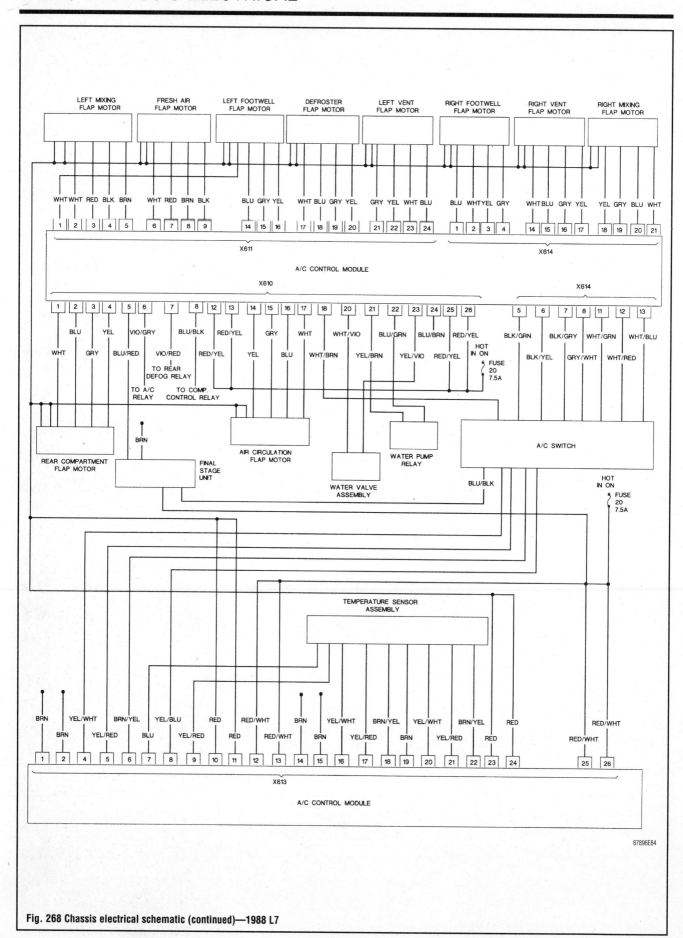

Fig. 268 Chassis electrical schematic (continued)—1988 L7

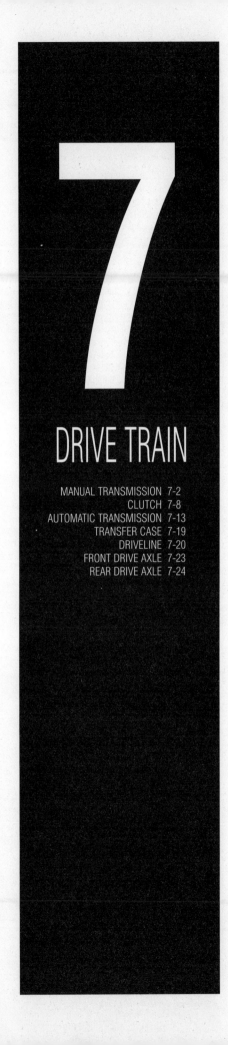

7
DRIVE TRAIN

MANUAL TRANSMISSION

Understanding the Manual Transmission

♦ **See Figure 1**

Because of the way an internal combustion engine breathes, it can produce torque (or twisting force) only within a narrow speed range. Most overhead valve pushrod engines must turn at about 2500 rpm to produce their peak torque. Often by 4500 rpm, they are producing so little torque that continued increases in engine speed produce no power increases.

The torque peak on overhead camshaft engines is, generally, much higher, but much narrower.

The manual transmission and clutch are employed to vary the relationship between engine RPM and the speed of the wheels so that adequate power can be produced under all circumstances. The clutch allows engine torque to be applied to the transmission input shaft gradually, due to mechanical slippage. The vehicle can, consequently, be started smoothly from a full stop.

The transmission changes the ratio between the rotating speeds of the engine and the wheels by the use of gears. 4-speed or 5-speed transmissions are most common. The lower gears allow full engine power to be applied to the rear wheels during acceleration at low speeds.

The clutch driveplate is a thin disc, the center of which is splined to the transmission input shaft. Both sides of the disc are covered with a layer of material which is similar to brake lining and which is capable of allowing slippage without roughness or excessive noise.

The clutch cover is bolted to the engine flywheel and incorporates a diaphragm spring which provides the pressure to engage the clutch. The cover also houses the pressure plate. When the clutch pedal is released, the driven disc is sandwiched between the pressure plate and the smooth surface of the flywheel, thus forcing the disc to turn at the same speed as the engine crankshaft.

The transmission contains a mainshaft which passes all the way through the transmission, from the clutch to the driveshaft. This shaft is separated at one point, so that front and rear portions can turn at different speeds.

Power is transmitted by a countershaft in the lower gears and reverse. The gears of the countershaft mesh with gears on the mainshaft, allowing power to be carried from one to the other. Countershaft gears are often integral with that shaft, while several of the mainshaft gears can either rotate independently of the shaft or be locked to it. Shifting from one gear to the next causes one of the gears to be freed from rotating with the shaft and locks another to it. Gears are locked and unlocked by internal dog clutches which slide between the center of the gear and the shaft. The forward gears usually employ synchronizers; friction members which smoothly bring gear and shaft to the same speed before the toothed dog clutches are engaged.

87897P29

Fig. 1 The manual transmission is mounted to the rear of the engine to transmit flywheel rotation through the driveshaft to the rear axle

Identification

♦ **See Figure 2**

Manual Transmission Application Chart

Vehicle	Transmission	
Model	Model	Speeds
1600	232/6	4
2002	242/6	4
2002Tii	242/4	4
	235/5	5
2500,2800,Bavaria 3000	262/8 ①	4
3.0	ZF-S4-18/3	4
320i	242/9	4
	242/18	4
	242/18.5	4
	265/6	5
528i,6 series,M6,L6	262/9	4
	265/6	5
528e,533i,525i,535i	265/6	5
318i,325e,325is,325ix	265/OD	5
M3,M5	260/5	5
	260/OD	5
	240(ZF-S5-16)	5
733i,735i	262/9.10	4
	262/9.30	4
	265/6	5

① Getrag

87897C02

Fig. 2 Identifying the manual transmission in your vehicle

Transmission

REMOVAL & INSTALLATION

4-Cylinder Engines

1600, 2000 AND 2002 MODELS

1. From inside the car, lift up the rubber boot to the shift lever. Raise the foam rubber ring and unsnap the circlip at the base of the shifter. Then, pull the shifter from the socket. Take care not to lose the shims which take up the clearance in the shifter socket under the circlip.

2. Raise the hood. Drain the cooling system into a suitable container. Disconnect the negative battery cable.

✳✳ CAUTION

When draining coolant, keep in mind that cats and dogs are attracted to ethylene glycol antifreeze, and could drink any that is left in an uncovered container or in puddles on the ground. This will prove fatal in sufficient quantity. Always drain the coolant into a sealable container. Coolant should be reused unless it is contaminated or several years old.

3. Remove the retaining bolts at the top of the transmission which secure the assembly to the engine body.

4. Jack up the front of the vehicle and place jackstands beneath the front jacking points. Place blocks behind the rear wheels and make sure that the parking brake is firmly applied.

✳✳ CAUTION

Test the stability of the supports before climbing under the car.

5. Position a floor jack or transmission stand securely under the transmission. Place the jack under the center of the assembly. Lift the jack enough to touch the transmission, but not enough to lift it.

6. Remove the drain plug from the transmission and drain the contents into a drain pan for inspection. Check the fluid for metal particles. Clean and replace the drain plug.

7. Disconnect the exhaust pipe bracket from the back of the transmission. Disconnect the head pipe from the exhaust manifold.

8. Disconnect the driveshaft from the transmission at the flexible giubo coupling leaving the coupling attached to the driveshaft. Discard the old locknuts. Check the condition of the giubo and replace if excessively cracked or torn.

9. Remove the 2 bolts which retain the driveshaft center support bearing housing to the underbody. Push the driveshaft downward and away from the centering pin on the transmission.

10. Using an Allen wrench, loosen the set screw and drive out the retaining pin from the shift linkage.

11. On 1600 and 2000 models, detach the clutch linkage return spring. Push the retainer downward and remove the pushrod toward the front of the vehicle.

12. On 2002 and 2002Tii models, disconnect the slave cylinder from the throwout lever by lifting out the retaining ring, slipping off the rubber collar, unsnapping the circlip, and withdrawing the slave cylinder forward.

➡**Mark the position of the torsional retainer.**

13. Loosen the bolts for the transmission support bracket. Remove the bolts which retain the flywheel inspection cover to the transmission and remove the cover.

14. Place a wooden block beneath the oil pan between the pan and front crossmember to support the engine.

15. Loosen the speedometer cable set bolt and disconnect the speedometer. Disconnect the reverse light wire leads. Remove the transmission support crossmember.

16. Turn the front wheels to the full right direction. The transmission may now be removed by pulling straight out toward the rear of the vehicle. When the transmission is clear of the pressure plate, carefully lower the jack and transmission to the ground.

To install:

17. Reverse the above procedure to install, using the following installation notes:

a. When hooking up the clutch linkage on 1600 and 2000 models, adjust the linkage as outlined under Clutch Linkage Adjustment.

b. When hooking up the shift linkage, first drive in the retaining pin and then secure it with the Allen head setscrew.

c. When hooking up the driveshaft, check the free-play of the centering bearing and pack it with chassis grease, as necessary. Use new locknuts to install the flexible coupling.

d. When installing the center support for the driveshaft, preload the bearing housing, a distance of 0.08 inches (2mm) to the front. Tightened the bolts after the transmission is installed.

e. When connecting the exhaust pipe support bracket, the bracket must lie tension-free against the head pipe, or severe engine vibration may result.

f. When installing the shift lever, fill the ball socket with chassis grease. Use shims beneath the circlip to obtain a tight fit.

g. Tighten the transmission-to-engine bolts to 18 ft. lbs. (23 Nm) for the small bolts), 34 ft. lbs. (44 Nm) for the large bolts.

h. Remember to fill the transmission to the bottom of the filler plug hole with SAE 80 gearbox oil.

i. Do not forget to fill the cooling system with anti-freeze and connect the negative ground cable.

318I AND 320I MODELS

1. From inside the car, lift up the boot around the shift lever. Raise the foam rubber ring and unsnap the circlip at the base of the shifter. Then, pull out the shifter from its socket. Take care not to lose the shims which take up the clearance in the shifter socket under the circlip.

2. Raise the hood. Drain the cooling system into a suitable container. Disconnect the negative battery cable.

3. On 320i models, remove the retaining bolts at the top of the transmission which secure the assembly to the engine body. Swing up the bracket mounted to the top left bolt.

4. Raise the front of the vehicle and place jackstands beneath the front jacking points. Place blocks behind the rear wheels and make sure that the parking brake is firmly applied.

✳✳ CAUTION

Test the stability of the supports before climbing under the car.

5. Position a floor jack or transmission stand securely under the transmission. Place the jack under the center of the assembly. Lift the jack enough to touch the transmission, but not enough to lift it.

6. Drain the transmission of gear oil.

7. Disconnect the exhaust system support at the rear of the transmission.

8. Detach the exhaust pipe at the manifold.

9. Remove the driveshaft at the transmission by pulling out the bolts from the rear of the giubo coupling (the coupling remains attached to the driveshaft).

10. Remove the heat shield. Remove the bolts for the center bearing bracket, and pull the bracket downward. Bend the driveshaft downward and pull it out of the bearing journal.

11. Remove the bolt and disconnect the speedometer drive cable. Disconnect the reverse light switch wire, and pull the wire out of the transmission.

12. Remove the 2 Allen bolts at the top and pull the console off the transmission.

13. Disconnect the gearshift selector rod by pulling off the circlip, removing the washer and pulling the rod off the pin.

14. Detach the clutch slave cylinder bracket at the front of the transmission, remove the mounting bolts from the slave cylinder mounting, and remove the slave cylinder.

15. Remove the flywheel housing cover.

16. Detach the crossmember by removing the nuts attaching it to the body at either end. On 318i models, remove all front mounting bolts. Remove the 3 remaining front mounting bolts on the 320i, and pull the transmission out toward the rear and lower the jack.

To install:

17. Install the transmission under the vehicle and align it into position. Install the crossmember.

18. Install the flywheel cover. Install 2 of the top transmission-to-engine bolts to retain the transmission.

19. Attach the clutch slave cylinder and mounting bracket. Install the gear selector rod and install the retaining circlip.

20. Connect the speedometer drive cable and then continue the installation in reverse order, noting the following points:

a. Front mounting bolts are tightened to 18–19 ft. lbs. (23–24 Nm) on the 318i model transmissions, 34–37 ft. lbs (44–48 Nm) on the 320i transmissions. Tighten the crossmember rubber mounts to 31–35 ft. lbs. (40–45 Nm).

b. On the 318i, the console has self-locking bolts which must be replaced.

c. When reinstalling the clutch slave cylinder, make sure the bleeder screw faces downward.

d. When installing the driveshaft center support bearing, preload it forward a distance of 0.08 inches (2mm) on 320i, 0.08–0.1 inches (2–4mm) on 318i models.

e. Replace the locknuts on the driveshaft coupling with new locknuts, and tighten the nuts only, not the bolts, to 31–35 ft. lbs. (40–45 Nm).

f. Inspect the gasket at the joint between the exhaust manifold and pipe and replace it if necessary.

g. When reattaching the exhaust system support at the rear, leave the attaching nut/bolt slightly loose. Loosen the 2 nuts/bolts attaching the support via slots to the transmission. Push the support toward the exhaust pipe until all tension is removed and then secure nuts and bolts.

h. Do not forget to fill the transmission with new gear oil, as well as the cooling system.

6-Cylinder Models

EXCEPT 1983–84 533I AND 633CSI; 1982–84 733I; 1985–88 3 SERIES; ALL 535I, 635CSI, 735I, M5 AND M6 MODELS

1. Remove the exhaust system. Drain the transmission gear oil.
2. Remove the circlip and washer at the selector rod and disengage the rod at the transmission.
3. Remove the boot surrounding the gearshift lever. With a pointed object such as a pick tool, release the circlip at the bottom of the gearshift lever and pull the lever upward and out of the transmission. Lubricate the nylon bushings at the bottom of the lever mechanism.
4. Remove the 3 bolts from the giubo coupling at the front of the driveshaft. Leaving the nuts/bolts attached to the driveshaft.
5. Remove the exhaust heat shield. Remove the mounting bolts and remove the center bearing support bracket. Bend the driveshaft downward at the front and slide the spline out of the center bearing.
6. Support the transmission securely with a floorjack and wooden block.
7. Remove the attaching bolt and pull out the speedometer cable. Disconnect the reverse light harness and pull the wire out of the clips on the transmission.
8. Loosen the connection to the rubber bushing at the transmission, remove the mounting nuts at either end, and remove the crossmember.
9. On 633CSi models, lower the transmission to the front axle carrier. Disconnect the mount for the clutch hydraulic line at the front of the transmission.
10. Then, on all models, unscrew the mounting nuts and detach the clutch slave cylinder (with the line connected).
11. Remove the retaining nuts at the clutch housing and separate the transmission and clutch housing.
12. Pull the gearbox toward the rear of the vehicle and lower.

To install:

13. Position the gearbox under the vehicle and move into position. Install the mounting nuts at the clutch housing.
14. Attach the clutch slave cylinder to the transmission.
15. Install the crossmember and rubber mounts. Install the speedometer cable and connect the wire to the reverse light switch.
16. Install the heat shield and the mounting nuts for the center bearing carrier.
17. Complete the installation, keeping the following points in mind:

a. Use the slave cylinder to move the clutch throw-out arm to the correct position. Align the throw-out bearing. Grease the guide sleeve and groove in the throw-out bearing.

b. Put the transmission into gear before installing.

c. Make sure, when installing the clutch slave cylinder, that the hose connection faces downward.

d. Preload the center bearing 0.08 inches (2mm) toward the front.

e. When tightening the flexible giubo coupling, hold the bolt heads and tighten only the nuts to 75 ft. lbs. (97 Nm). Use new locknuts. Tighten the transmission-to-engine bolts to 16–17 ft. lbs. (21–22 Nm) for 5 Series transmissions or 31–35 ft. lbs. (40–45 Nm) for all other transmissions. Tighten the bolt for the rubber bushing on the crossmember to 18 ft. lbs. (23 Nm)

1985–88 3 SERIES MODELS

▶ See Figures 3 thru 25

1. Raise the car and support it securely on jackstands. Remove the entire exhaust system. Remove the crossbrace and heat shield.

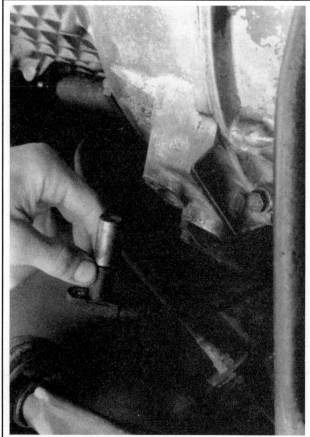

Fig. 6 Slide the flywheel sensor out. If the end is dirty, be sure to clean it before installation

Fig. 3 Support the transmission with a piece of wood and a floor or transmission jack

Fig. 4 Unfasten the reverse light harness

Fig. 5 Use a Torx® socket to remove the retaining bolt for the flywheel sensors. Mark each sensor location

2. On the 325iX, remove the transfer case as outlined in this section.

3. Hold the locknuts on the front of the flexible coupler with one wrench, and remove bolts from the rear. Some models have a vibration damper on the coupler. This damper is mounted on the transmission output flange with bolts that are pressed into the damper. On these models, unscrew and remove the nuts located behind the damper.

4. Loosen the threaded sleeve/collar on the driveshaft. Use a special tool such as BMW 261040 or equivalent to hold the splined portion of the shaft while turning the sleeve.

5. Remove the mounting bolts and remove the center driveshaft mount. Then, bend the driveshaft down at the center and remove from off the transmission output flange. Keep the sections of the driveshaft from pulling apart and suspend it from the car with wire.

6. Remove the retainer and washer, and pull out the shift selector rod.

7. Use a hex head wrench to remove the 2 self-locking bolts that retain the shift rod bracket at the rear of the transmission and remove the bracket. Detach the shift arm, using a prytool to lift the spring clip up off the boss on the case. Then, pull out the shift shaft pin.

8. Unscrew and remove the clutch slave cylinder and support the hydraulic line connected.

9. The transmission incorporates sending units for flywheel rotating speed and position. Remove the heat shield that protects these from exhaust heat. paint identification marks on each sensor and remove the retaining bolt for each sending unit.

➡The speed sending unit, which has no identifying ring goes in the bore on the right, and the reference mark sending unit, which has a marking ring, goes in the bore on the left. If the sending units are installed in reverse order, the engine will not run.

10. Pull these units out of the flywheel housing.

11. Disconnect the wiring connector at the reverse light switch and pull out the harness.

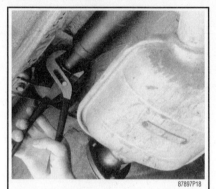
Fig. 7 Loosen the collar at the center of the driveshaft

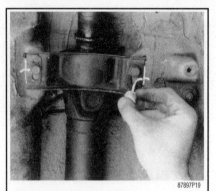
Fig. 8 Paint alignment marks on the center driveshaft bracket

Fig. 9 Remove the bolts securing the center driveshaft bracket

Fig. 10 Lower and separate the driveshaft sections

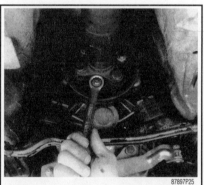
Fig. 11 Loosen the nuts and bolts attaching the rubber giubo to the transmission

Fig. 12 Carefully pry the rubber giubo from the transmission

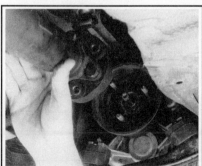
Fig. 13 Notice that once the rubber giubo is separated from the transmission, it remains attached to the driveshaft

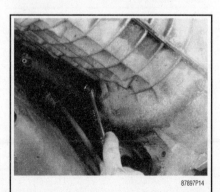
Fig. 14 Remove the retaining bolts securing the slave cylinder to the transmission

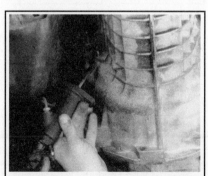
Fig. 15 Slide the slave cylinder out. It is not necessary to remove the slave cylinder fluid line

Fig. 16 Remove the Torx® bolts attaching the transmission to the engine

Fig. 17 Do not forget to remove the small bolts at the side of the transmission, where it mounts to the engine

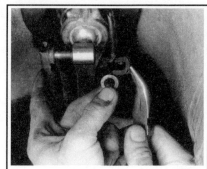

Fig. 18 Remove the circlip securing the shift rod to the shift linkage, then slide it out

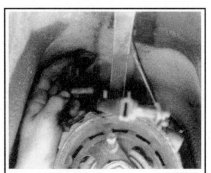

Fig. 19 To completely remove the linkage rod, remove the clip above the transmission and unfasten the rod

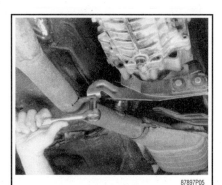

Fig. 20 Remove the exhaust bracket attached to the transmission

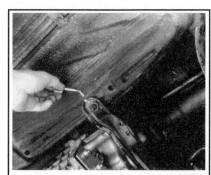

Fig. 21 Paint alignment marks on the rear transmission bracket for ease of reinstallation

Fig. 22 Remove the retainer nuts securing this bracket to the vehicle underside

Fig. 23 Carefully separate the transmission from the engine

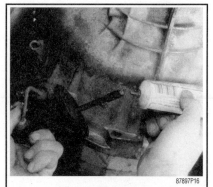

Fig. 24 Before installing the slave cylinder, apply grease to the rod end

12. With the transmission supported underneath in a secure manner, remove the mounting bolts and crossmember holding the rear of the transmission to the body. Then, lower the transmission onto the front axle carrier

13. Using a Torx® socket, remove the Torx® bolts holding the transmission flywheel housing to the engine at the front. Pull the transmission rearward to slide the input shaft out of the clutch disc and lower the transmission and remove it from the vehicle.

To install:

14. Install the transmission in position under the car and install the retaining bolts.

15. Install the crossmember. Connect the wiring to to the reverse light switch.

16. Install the sending units into the transmission.

17. Install the clutch slave cylinder and install the shift shaft and bracket.

18. Install the center driveshaft mount and complete the installation, keeping the following points in mind:

a. Coat the input shaft splines and flywheel housing guide pins with a light coating of a grease such as Microlube GL 261® or equivalent.

b. Make sure the front mounting bolts are installed with their washers. Tighten them to 46–58 ft. lbs. (60–75 Nm).

c. Before installing the 2 sending units for flywheel position and speed, make sure the faces are free of either grease or dirt and coat with a light coating of Molykote Long-term 2® or equivalent grease. Inspect the O-rings and replace if cut, cracked, crushed, or stretched.

d. When installing the shift rod bracket at the rear of the transmission, use new self-locking bolts and make sure the bracket is level before tightening. Tighten the shift rod bracket bolts to 16 ft. lbs. (21 Nm), except on the M3, which uses an aluminum bracket. On the M3, tighten these bolts to 8 ft. lbs. (10 Nm).

e. Install the clutch slave cylinder with the bleed screw downward.

f. When installing the driveshaft center bearing, preload it forward 0.1–0.2 inches (4–6mm). Check the driveshaft alignment with an appropriate

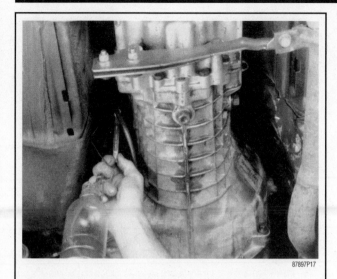

Fig. 25 Bleed the slave cylinder before lowering the vehicle

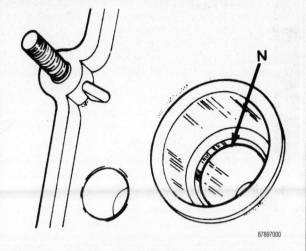

Fig. 26 Pack the groove at the engine block with suitable grease before installing the transmission

tool such as BMW 26 1 030. Replace the nuts and then tighten the center mount bolts to 16–17 ft. lb. (21–22 Nm).

    g. Tighten the flexible giubo coupling bolts to 83–94 ft. lb. (108–122 Nm).

1982 733I MODELS

▶ See Figure 26

➡ This procedure requires a special tool for clamping the flexible drive coupling.

1. Remove the circlip and washer from the front end of the selector rod, and disconnect from the lower end of the shift lever.

2. Push up the dust cover, and with needle nose pliers or equivalent and remove the circlip which holds the gearshift lever in place. Lubricate the nylon bushing surrounding the socket with a permanent lubricant for reassembly.

3. Disconnect the reverse light harness near the gearshift lever. Remove the large circlip which surrounds the gearshift mount.

4. Drain the gear oil into a suitable container. Raise the car and support it on jackstands. Install the special tool (BMW 26 1 011 or equivalent) which clamps around the flexible giubo coupling. Then, unscrew the nuts on the forward side of the coupling Withdraw the bolts out the rear. This requires tightening the clamping tool until the bolts can be pulled out by hand.

5. Remove the web type crossmember located under the driveshaft. Then, loosen the mounting nuts for the center bearing bracket and detach it. Bend the driveshaft downward and pull it off the centering pin.

6. Support the transmission securely with a floor jack or transmission jack.

7. Remove the mounting nut from the crossmember rubber bushing, then the nuts and bolts from either end of the crossmember. Remove the crossmember.

8. Detach the exhaust bracket and remove it.

9. Detach the mounting bracket for the clutch slave cylinder hydraulic line. Remove the 2 mounting bolts and detach the slave cylinder. Detach the 4th gear switch wires, if so equipped.

10. Detach the transmission at the clutch housing and remove by pulling it toward the rear of the vehicle.

To install:

11. Install the transmission in position under the vehicle and slide into the clutch housing. Install the mounting bolts. Attach the mounting bracket for the clutch slave cylinder and attach the slave cylinder.

12. Fasten the crossmember and reattach the exhaust system at the transmission.

13. Install the driveshaft into position.

14. Complete the installation, keeping the following points in mind:

    a. Use the clutch slave cylinder to put the release lever in position. Align the clutch bearing and grease the lubrication groove inside it with Molykote® BR2 750 or equivalent.

    b. Put the transmission into gear prior to installation.

    c. Install the guide sleeve into the bearing, then turn the output flange until the driveshaft slides into the drive plate. Then, remove the slave cylinder while mounting the transmission. Tighten transmission-to-clutch housing bolts to 54–59 ft. lbs. (70–77 Nm).

    d. When installing the clutch slave cylinder, make sure the bleeder screw faces downward.

    e. When remounting the exhaust system bracket, make sure there is no torsional strain on the exhaust system.

    f. Preload the center driveshaft bearing toward the front of the car 0.08 inches (2mm).

    g. When reassembling the flexible drive coupling, use new self-locking nuts. Leave the special tool compressed while installing the bolts. Hold the bolts in position and turn only the nuts.

    h. Tighten the transmission mount-to-crossmember bolt to 36–40 ft. lbs. (47–52 Nm), and the crossmember-to-body nuts to 16–17 ft. lbs. (21–22 Nm).

    i. When installing the shift lever, note that the tab on the damper plate nuts engage in the opening in the shift arm.

1983–84 533I, 633CSI, AND 733I; ALL 535I MODELS

▶ See Figure 26

1. Raise the car and support it securely. Disconnect and lower the exhaust system to provide clearance for transmission removal. Remove the exhaust heat shield brace and transmission heat shield.

2. Support the driveshaft and then unscrew the driveshaft giubo coupling at the rear of the transmission. Use a wrench on both the nut and the bolt.

3. Working at the front of the driveshaft center bearing, unfasten the screw-on type connector which attaches the driveshaft to the center bearing. Then, unbolt the center bearing mount. Bend the driveshaft down and pull it off the centering pin. If the car has a vibration damper, turn it and pull it back over the output flange before pulling the driveshaft off the guide pin. Suspend it from the car with wire.

4. Pull off the wires for the reverse light switch. Unscrew the passenger compartment console and disconnect it from the top of the transmission. Discard the hardware and purchase replacements.

5. Pull out the shifter locking clip, and disconnect the shift rod at the rear of the transmission. Take care to keep all the washers.

6. If the transmission is attached to the shift lever with a link arm, use a small prytool to lift the spring out of the holder on the bracket and raise the arm. Pull out the shift shaft bolt.

7. If the car has a flywheel housing cover, remove the mounting bolts and remove the cover.

8. If the vehicle is equipped with Digital Motor Electronics (DME) speed and reference mark sensors on the flywheel housing, they must be disconnected. Note their locations. Paint identification marks on each before removing.

➡**The speed sensor goes in the upper bore. The reference mark sensor, which has a ring, goes in the lower bore. Check the O-rings for the sensors and install new ones if they are damaged.**

9. Support the transmission securely. Then, unbolt and remove the rear transmission crossmember.

10. Remove the upper and lower attaching nuts and remove the clutch slave cylinder.

11. Disconnect the reverse light harness.

12. Unscrew the Torx® bolts fastening the transmission to the bell housing

13. Pull the transmission rearward until the input shaft has disengaged from the clutch disc and lower and remove.

To install:

14. To install the transmission, first put in gear. Insert the guide sleeve of the input shaft into the clutch pilot bearing carefully. Turn the output shaft to rotate the front of the input shaft until the splines line up and engages the clutch disc.

15. Install the remaining portions of the procedure in reverse order of removal, observing the following points:

a. Make sure the arrows on the rear crossmember point forward.

b. Preload the center bearing mount forward 0.08–0.1 inches (2–4mm). On 7 Series models and 6 Series cars with no integral clutch housing, preload the bearing to 0.1–0.2 inches (4–6mm).

c. In tightening the driveshaft screw on ring, use special Tool No. 26 1 040 or equivalent.

d. Use new locknuts when installing the driveshaft. Turn only the nut, holding the bolts stationary.

e. Make sure DME sensor faces are clean. Coat the sensor outside diameters with Molykote Long-term 2® or equivalent.

f. If the car has a shift arm, lubricate the bolt with a light layer of Molykote Long-term 2® or equivalent.

g. Observe these torque figures:
- Transmission to bell housing: 52–58 ft. lbs. (68–75 Nm)
- Top rear transmission bolts: 46–58 ft. lbs. (60–75 Nm)
- Center mount to body: 16–17 ft. lbs. (21–22 Nm)
- Front joint-to-transmission: 83–94 ft. lbs. (108–122 Nm)

735I MODELS

1. Disconnect the negative battery cable. Remove the exhaust system. Remove the attaching bolts and remove the heat shield mounted just to the rear of the transmission on the floorpan.

2. Support the transmission securely from underneath. Remove the crossmember that supports the transmission it at the rear.

3. Using wrenches on both the bolt heads and nuts, remove the bolts through the giubo coupler at the front of the driveshaft.

4. Remove the center driveshaft mounting bolts. Bend the driveshaft down at the center and pull it off the transmission output flange. Keep the sections of the driveshaft from pulling apart and suspend it from the car with wire.

5. Remove the shifter circlip and washer, then pull the shift selector rod off the transmission shift shaft. Disconnect the reverse light harness, nearby.

6. Lower the transmission slightly for access. Use a prytool to lift the spring out of the shaft holder on the bracket and then raise the arm. Pull out the shift shaft bolt.

7. Remove the upper and lower attaching nuts and remove the clutch slave cylinder and support.

8. Unscrew the bolts securing the transmission to the bell housing using a Torx® wrench. Make sure to retain the washer with each bolt. Pull the transmission rearward until the input shaft has disengaged from the clutch disc and then lower.

To install:

9. Install the transmission in position under the car and install the retaining bolts.

10. Install the crossmember. Connect the wiring to to the reverse light switch.

11. Install the clutch slave cylinder and install the shift shaft and bracket.

12. Install the center driveshaft mount and complete the installation, keeping the following points in mind:

a. Preload the center bearing mount forward 0.1–0.2 inches (4–6mm).

b. When reconnecting the nuts and bolt at the transmission giubo coupling, replace the nuts with new ones and turn only the nut, holding the bolts stationary.

c. When reconnecting the shift arm, lubricate the bolt with a light layer of Molykote Long-term 2® or equivalent and check the O-ring for crushing, cracks or cuts, replacing it if it is damaged.

d. When installing the clutch slave cylinder, make sure the bleeder screw faces downward.

e. Observe these torque figures:
- Center mount to body: 16–17 ft. lbs. (21–22 Nm)
- Front joint-to-transmission: 58 ft. lbs. (75 Nm)

CLUTCH

✳✳ CAUTION

The clutch driven disc may contain asbestos, which has been determined to be a cancer causing agent. Never clean clutch surfaces with compressed air! Avoid inhaling any dust from the clutch surface. When cleaning clutch surfaces use a commercially available brake cleaning solvent.

Understanding the Clutch

The purpose of the clutch is to disconnect and connect engine power at the transmission. A vehicle at rest requires a lot of engine torque to get all that weight moving. An internal combustion engine does not develop a high starting torque (unlike steam engines) so it must be allowed to operate without any load until it builds up enough torque to move the vehicle. To a point, torque increases with engine rpm. The clutch allows the engine to build up torque by physically disconnecting the engine from the transmission, relieving the engine of any load or resistance.

The transfer of engine power to the transmission (the load) must be smooth and gradual; if it weren't, drive line components would wear out or break quickly. This gradual power transfer is made possible by gradually releasing the clutch pedal. The clutch disc and pressure plate are the connecting link between the engine and transmission. When the clutch pedal is released, the disc and plate contact each other (the clutch is engaged) physically joining the engine and transmission. When the pedal is pushed in, the disc and plate separate (the clutch is disengaged) disconnecting the engine from the transmission.

Most clutch assemblies consists of the flywheel, the clutch disc, the clutch pressure plate, the throw out bearing and fork, the actuating linkage and the pedal. The flywheel and clutch pressure plate (driving members) are connected to the engine crankshaft and rotate with it. The clutch disc is located between the flywheel and pressure plate, and is splined to the transmission shaft. A driving member is one that is attached to the engine and transfers engine power to a driven member (clutch disc) on the transmission shaft. A driving member (pressure plate) rotates (drives) a driven member (clutch disc) on contact and, in so doing, turns the transmission shaft.

There is a circular diaphragm spring within the pressure plate cover (transmission side). In a relaxed state (when the clutch pedal is fully released) this spring is convex; that is, it is dished outward toward the transmission. Pushing in the clutch pedal actuates the attached linkage. Connected to the other end of this is the throw out fork, which hold the throw out bearing. When the clutch pedal is depressed, the clutch linkage pushes the fork and bearing forward to contact the diaphragm spring of the pressure plate. The outer edges of the spring are secured to the pressure plate and are pivoted on rings so that when the center of the spring is compressed by the throw out bearing, the outer edges bow outward and, by so doing, pull the pressure plate in the same direction — away from the clutch disc. This action separates the disc from the plate, disengaging the clutch and allowing the transmission to be shifted into another gear. A coil type clutch return spring attached to the clutch pedal arm permits full release of the pedal. Releasing the pedal pulls the throw out bearing away from the diaphragm spring resulting in a reversal of spring position. As bearing pressure is gradually released from the spring center, the outer edges of the spring bow outward, pushing the pressure plate into closer contact with the clutch disc. As the disc and plate move closer together, friction between the two increases and slippage is reduced until, when full spring pressure is applied (by fully releasing the pedal) the speed of the disc and plate are the same. This stops all slipping, creating a direct connection between the plate and disc which results in the transfer of power from the engine to the transmission. The clutch disc is now rotating with the pressure plate at engine speed and, because it is splined to the transmission shaft, the shaft now turns at the same engine speed.

The clutch is operating properly if:

1. It will stall the engine when released with the vehicle held stationary.
2. The shift lever can be moved freely between 1st and reverse gears when the vehicle is stationary and the clutch disengaged.

Adjustments

PEDAL HEIGHT

4-Cylinder Engines

1600, 2000 AND 2002 MODELS

Measure the length of the clutch tension spring (hook-to-hook). Specified length is 3.5 inches (92mm). If the dimension is incorrect, unlock the 2 nuts, rotate them together as necessary to get the correct length, and then relock them.

3 SERIES

▶ See Figure 27

Measure the distance between the bottom edge of the clutch pedal and the firewall (A). It should be roughly 10 inches (255mm).

➡1987–88 325 models and M3 do not require clutch pedal adjustment. If out of specification, loosen the locknut and rotate the piston rod on the pedal to correct.

6-Cylinder Engines

EXCEPT 3 SERIES

▶ See Figures 28, 29 and 30

Measure the length of the over-center spring (Dimension A) and, if necessary, loosen the locknut and rotate the shafts as necessary to get the proper

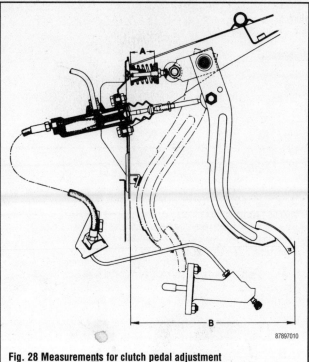

Fig. 28 Measurements for clutch pedal adjustment

	Dimension "A"	Dimension "B"
733i	1.338 in.	10.472–10.787 in.
630CSi, 633CSi, 528i,	1.138–1.358 in.	9.644–9.960 in.
530i, 2800,	1.283–1.302 in.	10.078–9.764 in.
3.0	1.34–1.36	10.35–10.63 in.

Fig. 29 Clutch Pedal Adjustment Chart—1970–82 6-cylinder engine equipped models

1983–88 Models	Dimension "A" (in.)	Dimension "B" (in.)
733i,	1.358	10.472–10.787
735i,	–	10.433–10.827
633CSi, 635CSi, M6	1.358	10.669–11.102
528e, 524td, 533i, 535i	1.358	9.843–10.276

Fig. 30 Clutch Pedal Adjustment Chart—1983–88 6-cylinder engine equipped models

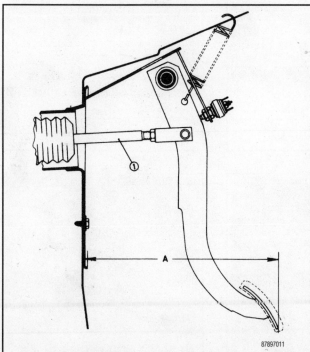

Fig. 27 Adjusting clutch pedal height—4-cylinder and 3 Series models

clearance. Measure the distance (Dimension B) from the firewall to the tip of the clutch pedal and move the pedal in or out, if necessary, by loosening the locknut and rotating the shaft.

3 SERIES

▶ See Figure 27

Measure the distance between the bottom edge of the clutch pedal and the firewall (A). It should be roughly 10 inches (25cm).

FREE-PLAY

1600 and 2000 Models

On 1600 and 2000 models, the free-play of the thrust rod at the release lever is adjusted at 8,000 mile (13,000 km) intervals. Loosen the locknut and turn the nut until 0.1–0.13 inches (3.0–3.5mm) clearance exist between the release lever and the adjustment nut on the thrust rod. Tighten the locknut.

Except 1600 and 2002 Models

The 1600 and 2002 vehicles are the only models covered by this manual to utilize a cable clutch actuating system. All other models use a hydraulic system for which no free-play adjustments are necessary or possible.

Driven Disc and Pressure Plate

REMOVAL & INSTALLATION

▶ See Figures 31 thru 37

1. On 1984–88 models equipped with Digital Motor Electronics (DME), remove the protective heat shield attaching bolts from the right side of the transmission.

2. Tag then disconnect the speed and reference mark sensors at the flywheel housing.

3. Remove the transmission and clutch housing as described in this section. On some models, a Torx® socket is required to remove the lower transmission retaining bolts.

4. Prevent the flywheel from turning, using a suitable locking tool.

5. Loosen the mounting bolts one after another gradually (1 1½ turns at a time) to relieve tension from the clutch.

6. Remove the mounting bolts, clutch, and drive plate. Coat the splines of the transmission input shaft with Molykote® Long-term 2, Microlube® GL 2611,

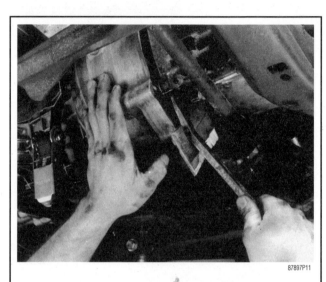
Fig. 31 Carefully remove the transmission from the engine

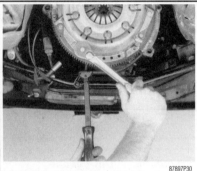
Fig. 32 Lock the flywheel/clutch assembly, then loosen and remove the clutch retaining bolts

Fig. 33 Remove the pressure plate from the flywheel . . .

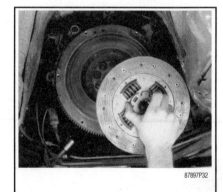
Fig. 34 . . . then remove the driven disc

Fig. 35 Clean the flywheel and inspect carefully

Fig. 36 If the flywheel needs to be removed, lock in place and remove the bolts

Fig. 37 Apply suitable grease to the pilot hole before installing the clutch and transmission

or equivalent grease. Make sure the clutch pilot bearing, located in the center of the crankshaft, turns easily.

7. Check the clutch disc for excessive wear or cracks. Check the integral torsional dampening springs used with lighter flywheels, for a tight fit so they cannot rattle or become dislocated. Inspect all rivets to make sure they are tight. Check the flywheel to make sure it is not scored or cracked. Use a straight edge to make sure the contact surface is true. Replace any defective parts.

To install:

8. Fit the new clutch plate and disc in place and install the mounting bolts.

9. When installing the clutch retaining bolts turn them gradually in a criss-cross pattern to evenly tighten the clutch disc and prevent warpage.

10. Install the transmission and the clutch housing.

11. On vehicles equipped, install the speed and reference mark sensors. Install the protective heat shield.

12. Note that on late model 6-cylinder engines, the clutch pressure plate must fit over dowel pins. Tighten the clutch mounting bolts to 16–17 ft. lbs. (21–22 Nm) for 1970–82 vehicles, and 17–19 ft. lbs. (22–23 Nm) for 1983–88 models.

Pilot Bearing

The pilot bearing is located in the end of the crankshaft and holds the end of the transmission input shaft in alignment. If the pilot shaft seizes, the transmission will grind into gear or not shift properly. Sometimes what are thought to be transmission problems can be cured with a new pilot bearing. It is always a good idea to replace the pilot bearing when replacing the clutch.

REMOVAL & INSTALLATION

▶ **See Figures 38, 39, 40, 41 and 42**

1. Remove the transmission and clutch.

2. Use a small bore bearing puller to remove the bearing from the end of the crankshaft. Note the order of washers and spacers when removing.

3. Clean the bore in the crankshaft of the old grease.

4. Lubricate the new bearing with 1 gram of grease and drive into the crankshaft bore.

5. Install the washers and spacers onto the crankshaft. Clean any excess grease from the surrounding area.

6. Install the clutch and transmission.

Clutch Master Cylinder

▶ **See Figure 43**

REMOVAL & INSTALLATION

▶ **See Figure 44**

1. Remove the necessary trim panel or carpet from below the steering column.

2. On 320i models, disconnect the accelerator cable and pull it forward out of the engine firewall.

3. Disconnect the pushrod at the clutch pedal.

4. Remove the cap on the reservoir tank.

➡On some models, there is a clutch master cylinder reservoir, while on other models there is a common reservoir shared with the brake master cylinder.

5. Remove the float container and screen, if equipped. Remove enough brake fluid from the tank until the level drops below the refill line or the hose connection.

Fig. 38 The pilot bearing is visible at the center of the flywheel

Fig. 39 Remove all the washers from the bore

Fig. 40 Some washers may have to be removed using a pick tool

Fig. 41 Apply grease before installing the bearing

Fig. 42 Use a socket and hammer to tap the bearing into place

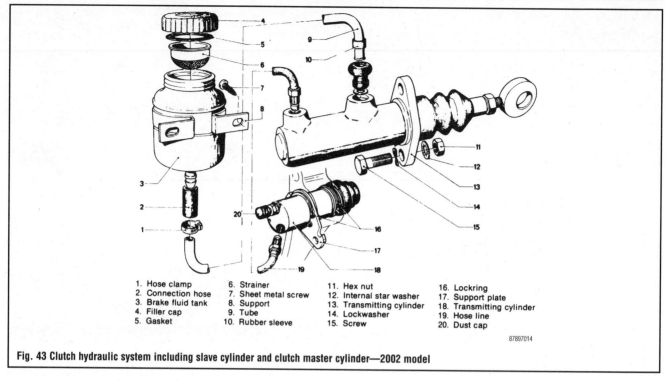

1. Hose clamp	6. Strainer	11. Hex nut	16. Lockring
2. Connection hose	7. Sheet metal screw	12. Internal star washer	17. Support plate
3. Brake fluid tank	8. Support	13. Transmitting cylinder	18. Transmitting cylinder
4. Filler cap	9. Tube	14. Lockwasher	19. Hose line
5. Gasket	10. Rubber sleeve	15. Screw	20. Dust cap

87897014

Fig. 43 Clutch hydraulic system including slave cylinder and clutch master cylinder—2002 model

6. On 733i and 735i models, disconnect the coolant expansion tank without removing the hoses and place aside.

7. Remove the retaining nut from the end of the master cylinder actuating rod where it attaches to the pedal mechanism.

8. Disconnect the hydraulic line attached to the master cylinder. Remove the retaining bolts and remove the master cylinder from the firewall.

To install:

9. Installation is the reverse of removal.

10. On all 1983–88 models the piston rod bolt should be coated with Molykote® Long-term 2 or equivalent. Make sure all bushings remain in position. Bleed the system and adjust the pedal pushrod travel to 6 inches (15cm).

Clutch Slave Cylinder

▶ See Figure 43

REMOVAL & INSTALLATION

▶ See Figures 45, 46, 47 and 48

1. Remove enough brake fluid from the reservoir to drop the fluid level below the refill line or hose connection.

2. From underneath the vehicle, remove the circlip or retaining bolts, depending on the model, which secure the slave cylinder to the transmission case.

3. Disconnect the brake line and remove the slave cylinder. Place a container below the hydraulic line to catch any dripping brake fluid.

To install:

4. Installation is the reverse or removal. Make sure to install the cylinder with the bleed screw facing downward. When installing the front pushrod, coat it with Molykote® Long-term 2 or equivalent anti-seize compound. Bleed the system.

➡On the 325 Series and M3, if the engine uses a 2-section flywheel, make sure you use a larger slave cylinder with a diameter of 22mm, instead of the usual cylinder diameter of 20.5mm.

BLEEDING THE CLUTCH SYSTEM

▶ See Figure 48

1. Fill the reservoir.

2. Connect a bleeder hose from the bleeder screw on the slave cylinder to a container filled with brake fluid.

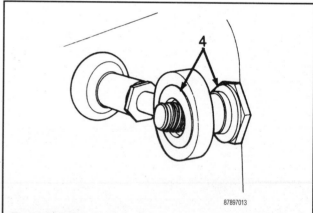

87897013

Fig. 44 On 7 Series models, make sure the bushing on the linkage (4) is properly positioned

87897P14

Fig. 45 Loosen the retaining bolts securing the slave cylinder to the transmission body

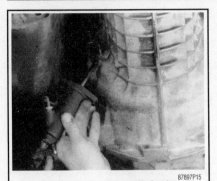

Fig. 46 Remove the slave cylinder from the vehicle. Notice the direction of the bleed screw

Fig. 47 Before installing the slave cylinder, apply grease to the end of the pushrod

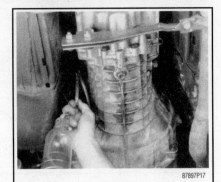

Fig. 48 After the installation is complete, bleed the clutch hydraulic system

3. Pump the clutch pedal about 10 times and hold down.

4. Open the bleeder screw and watch the stream of escaping fluid. When no air bubbles escape, close the bleeder screw and tighten.

5. If this procedure fails to produce a bubble-free stream:

a. Pull the slave cylinder off the transmission without disconnecting the fluid line.

➡**Do not depress the clutch pedal while the slave cylinder is removed.**

b. Depress the pushrod in the cylinder until it hits the internal stop. Then, reinstall the cylinder.

c. Repeat the bleeding procedure.

AUTOMATIC TRANSMISSION

Understanding the Automatic Transmission

The automatic transmission allows engine torque and power to be transmitted to the rear wheels within a narrow range of engine operating speeds. It will allow the engine to turn fast enough to produce plenty of power and torque at very low speeds, while keeping it at a sensible rpm at high vehicle speeds (and it does this job without driver assistance). The transmission uses a light fluid as the medium for the transmission of power. This fluid also works in the operation of various hydraulic control circuits and as a lubricant. Because the transmission fluid performs all of these functions, trouble within the unit can easily travel from one part to another.

Identification

◆ See Figure 49

Refer to the transmission designation chart for 1970–82 models. For 1983–88 vehicles, BMW offered two

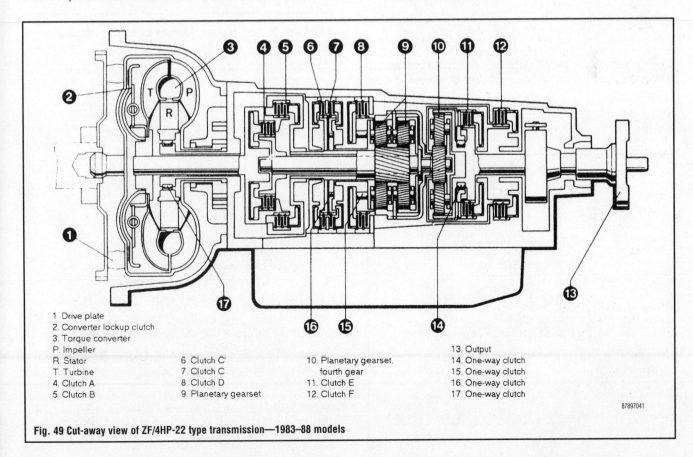

1. Drive plate
2. Converter lockup clutch
3. Torque converter
P. Impeller
R. Stator
T. Turbine
4. Clutch A
5. Clutch B
6. Clutch C'
7. Clutch C
8. Clutch D
9. Planetary gearset
10. Planetary gearset, fourth gear
11. Clutch E
12. Clutch F
13. Output
14. One-way clutch
15. One-way clutch
16. One-way clutch
17. One-way clutch

Fig. 49 Cut-away view of ZF/4HP-22 type transmission—1983–88 models

ZF transmission types. The two units are almost identical, except that the new one is a 4-speed unit instead of a 3-speed.

1970 - 82 AUTOMATIC TRANSMISSION CHART

Vehicle	Transmission	Cover Designation
2002A	ZF/3HP–12	028
2500, 2800	ZF/3HP–20	1019
3000, Bavaria, 3.0	ZF/BW–65	——
320i ('77–'79)	ZF/3HP–22	A ①, Red ②
('80–'82)	ZF/3HP–22	T ①
538e	ZF/3HP–22	RB
528i	ZF/3HP–22	N ①
530i ('75–'76)	ZF/BW–65	
('77–'78)	ZF/3HP–22	Silver/Black ②, N ①
630CSi	ZF/3HP–22	Silver/Black ②, N ①
633CSi	ZF/3HP–22	Q ①
733i ('78–'80)	ZF/3HP–22	J
('81–'82)	ZF/3HP–22	AG

ZF: Zahnradfabrik Friedrichshafen AG
BW: Borg Warner
① With deep oil pan
② With flat oil pan

87897C08

Adjustments

NEUTRAL SAFETY SWITCH

♦ See Figure 50

The neutral safety switch (starter lock switch) used in the ZF type automatic transmission is combined with the reverse light switch. Therefore, if you are having problems with the reverse lights, chances are that you might have difficulty starting the car with the selector lever in PARK or NEUTRAL.

1. Check the operation of the switch by disconnecting the 2 leads at terminals 50. Ground the brown terminal. Connect a 12 volt test lamp to the positive terminal and probe the second terminal tag. The test lamp should light when the selector lever is placed in **P** or **N**.

2. If the switch is in need of adjustment, unscrew the switch and place correspondingly thicker seals (shims) behind the switch and the transmission housing.

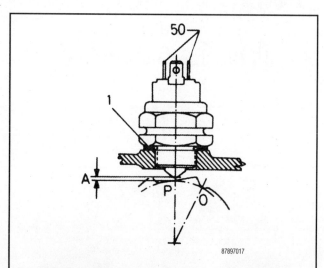

87897017

Fig. 50 Cross-section of neutral safety switch. Note that distance A is 0.02 inches (0.5mm)

BRAKE BANDS

♦ See Figure 51

These adjustments are made externally. Each is made in a square headed bolt retained by a hex type locknut. Adjustment is required after the first 600 miles (966 km) and every 15,000 miles (24,000 km) thereafter.

1. Loosen the locknut (1) about 1 turn (an offset hex wrench will be helpful). Tighten the adjusting bolt (2) to 50–51 ft. lbs. (65–66 Nm).

2. Note the exact position of the adjusting bolts, and loosen it exactly ¾ of a turn. Then, tighten the locknut.

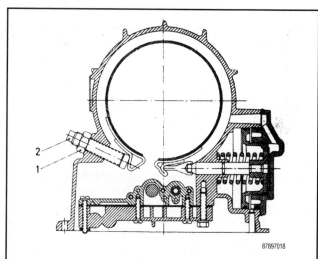

87897018

Fig. 51 Transmission adjusting band. (1) is a locknut and (2) is an adjusting bolt

SELECTOR LEVER

Except 635CSi, 735i, M5, M6, 1983–84 633CSi and 733i Models

1. Detach the selector rod at the selector lever lower section.
2. Move the selector lever on the transmission to position **0** or **N**.
3. Press the selector lever against the stop on the shift gate.
4. Adjust the length of the selector rod until the pin aligns with the bore in the selector lever lower section. Shorten the selector rod length by:
   - 1 turn for 320i models
   - 1–2 turns for 318i, 325e, 325i, 325iX, 524td, 528e, 535, 633CSi and 733i models
   - 2–2½ turns for 530i models

1983–84 633CSi and 733i; All 635CSi, 735i, M5 and M6 Models

1. Move the selector lever to PARK position. Loosen the nut.
2. Push the transmission lever to the DRIVE or PARK position. Then push the cable rod in the opposite direction.
3. Tighten the nut to 7–8 ft. lbs. (9–10 Nm).

ACCELERATOR LINKAGE

Except 2002, 3.0, 528i, and 530i Models

1. On the injection system throttle body, loosen the 2 locknuts at the end of the throttle cable and adjust the cable until there is a play of between 0.010–0.030 inches (0.2–0.8mm).

2. Loosen the locknut and lower the kickdown stop under the accelerator pedal. Have someone depress the accelerator pedal until the transmission detent can be felt. Then, back the kickdown stop out until it just touches the pedal.

3. Check that the distance from the seal at the throttle body end of the cable housing is at least 1.7 inches (4.3cm) from the rear end of the threaded sleeve. If this dimension is correct, tighten all the locknuts.

2002 Models

1. Remove the air cleaner.
2. Remove the accelerator cable.
3. Press the accelerator pedal down to the kick down stop into the full acceleration position. In this position the throttle valve must be fully open and not extend beyond the vertical position. When adjusting, bend the stop.
4. Adjust the length of the accelerator linkage using the eye bolt.

3.0, 528i, and 530i Models

▶ **See Figure 52**

1. Synchronize the idle speed with the engine at operating temperature.
2. Detach the linkage (1).
3. Detach the accelerator cable at the operating lever (2).
4. Adjust linkage so that the operating lever (2) rests on stop (3).

➡**Make sure that linkage(1) is not pulled down into the kickdown position.**

5. The swivel joint (5) must align with the hole in the operating lever (2) leaving a play of 0.009–0.02 inches (0.23–0.48mm) between nipple (4) and the end of the cable sleeve.
6. The accelerator must not sag. Press lever (6) against the acceleration stop (7) and adjust the linkage (8) until the distance between nipple (4) and the end of the cable sleeve is 1.4 inches (37mm). When in the kickdown position, the nipple (4) should be at least 1.7 inches (43mm) from the end of the cable sleeve.

➡**If the idle speed is altered, repeat the above procedure.**

ACCELERATOR CABLE

1600, 2000 and 2002 Models

1. Remove the accelerator cable from the rotary shaft.
2. Press down the accelerator to the full acceleration position.
3. Pull the accelerator cable to determine the full acceleration position. The holes in the fork head must coincide with the hole in the rotary selector so that the bearing pin can be inserted with correct alignment.
4. Turn the fork head to adjust the cable length.

1982 533i, 633CSi and 733i Models

▶ **See Figure 53**

1. Adjust the play in (S) to 0.010–0.30 inches (0.25–0.75mm) via the adjustment nut (2) when the vehicle is in NEUTRAL.
2. Press the accelerator pedal against the stop.
3. Adjust the pressure rod (7) until the distance from the seal (3) to the end of the cable (4) is 1.7–2.0 inches (44–51mm).

1983–84 533i, 633CSi; 635CSi, 733i, 735i, M5 and M6 Models

1. On the injection system throttle body, loosen the 2 locknuts at the end of the throttle cable and adjust the cable until there is a play of 0.010–0.030 inches (0.25–0.75mm).
2. Loosen the locknut and lower the kickdown stop under the accelerator pedal. Have someone depress the accelerator pedal until the transmission detent is felt. Then, back the kickdown stop out until it just touches the pedal.
3. Check that the distance from the seal at the throttle body end of the cable housing is at least 1.7 inches (44mm) from the rear end of the threaded sleeve. If this dimension is correct, tighten the locknuts.

3 Series

320I MODELS

▶ **See Figure 54**

1. Adjust the accelerator cable at nuts (1) until the accelerator cable eye (2) has a play of 0.008–0.01 inches (0.2–0.3mm).
2. Depress the accelerator pedal (3) to the full throttle stop screw (4).
3. There must be 0.010 inches (0.5mm) play between the operating lever (5) and stop nut (6).
4. Adjust by the full throttle stop screw (4).

EXCEPT 320I MODELS

1. Adjust the cable for zero tension with the throttle closed and accelerator pedal released.
2. Loosen the locknut on the throttle stop bolt. Now adjust the bolt inward just until it suspends the accelerator pedal at the point where the throttle just reaches the wide open position. Make sure the throttle is in full detent position.

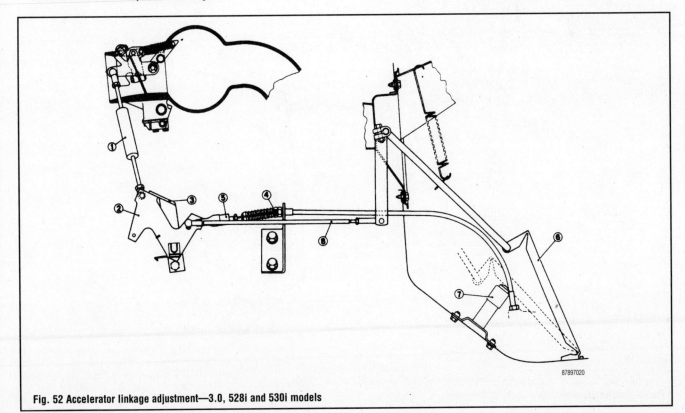

87897020

Fig. 52 Accelerator linkage adjustment—3.0, 528i and 530i models

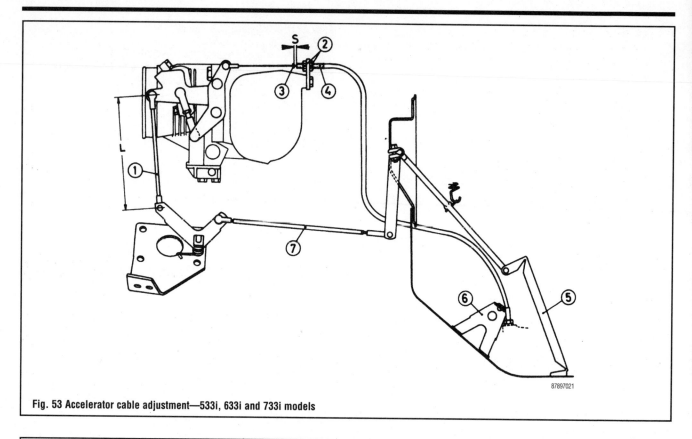

Fig. 53 Accelerator cable adjustment—533i, 633i and 733i models

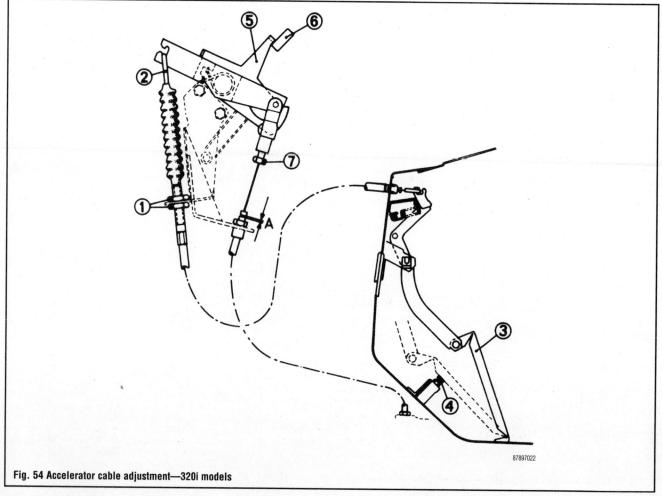

Fig. 54 Accelerator cable adjustment—320i models

Now, turn the stop screw 1½ turns lower to get a clearance of 0.010 inches (0.5mm) between the accelerator pedal and stop bolt at full throttle. Tighten the locknut.

528e and 530i Models

▶ See Figure 55

1. Adjust the free-play (S) of the cable with the transmission in the **N** position to 0.010–0.030 inches (0.25–0.75mm). Use cable adjuster nuts (1) to adjust the free-play.
2. From inside the vehicle, loosen the kickdown switch. Screw in the kickdown stop (2) all the way in the direction of the floor pan.
3. Press down on the accelerator pedal (4) to the transmission pressure point. Unscrew the kickdown stop (2) until it contacts the accelerator pedal.
4. Press the accelerator to the kickdown (wide open throttle position).
5. In the kickdown position, the distance should be 1.7 inches (44mm). The distance (s) equals the distance from the cable seal (5) to the end of the cable sleeve (6).

TRANSMISSION CABLE ADJUSTMENT

320i Models

▶ See Figure 54

➡ **The accelerator cable must be correctly adjusted.**

1. With the transmission in the NEUTRAL position, adjust the play to 0.10–0.30 inches (0.25–0.75mm) with the adjustment screw.
2. Depress the accelerator pedal to kickdown stop. The play should be between 1.7–2.0 inches (43–51mm). If adjustment is needed, adjust using the screw (4).

3 Series Models Except 320i

▶ See Figure 56

1. Adjust the play in **S** to 0.10–0.30 inches (0.25–0.75mm). Make sure both cable locknuts are loose.
2. Back off the accelerator pedal kickdown stop and depress the accelerator pedal until the transmission just reaches the detent and some resistance is felt.
3. Run the kickdown stop out until it just touches the bottom of the pedal.
4. Depress the accelerator through the detent and hold while measuring distance **S** from the lead seal to the end of the sleeve. It must be at least 1.7 inches (44mm). Adjust further, if needed.
5. Tighten all locknuts.

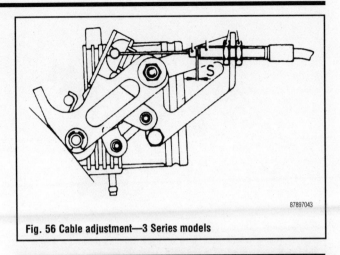

Fig. 56 Cable adjustment—3 Series models

Transmission

REMOVAL & INSTALLATION

3-Speed Models

▶ See Figure 57

1. Disconnect the negative battery cable.
2. Disconnect the accelerator cable.
3. On 4–cylinder engines remove all of the transmission mounting bolts which are accessible from the engine compartment.
4. Raise and support the vehicle safely on jackstands.
5. Detach the transmission fluid filler neck and drain the fluid into a suitable container.
6. On 4–cylinder engines, remove the exhaust pipe support bracket and separate the pipe from the exhaust manifold. On 318i and 325 models, remove the entire exhaust system and detach the heat shield.
7. On 6–cylinder engines except 733i models, remove the entire exhaust system.
8. Detach the oil cooler lines from the transmission, if equipped, and drain fluid into a container.
9. Disconnect the driveshaft at the transmission, On 733i models, use a clamping tool around the coupler. On 318i and 325 models, disconnect the selector rod from the transmission.
10. Disconnect the speedometer cable.
11. Remove the center bearing and bend down the driveshaft and pull off.

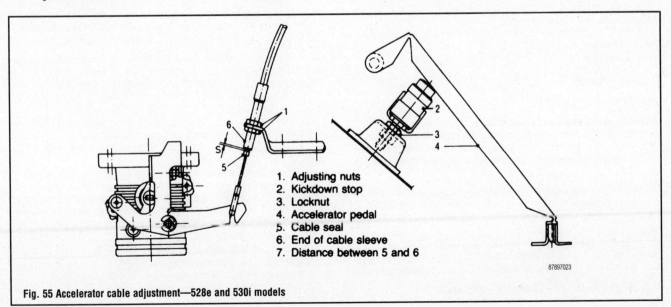

1. Adjusting nuts
2. Kickdown stop
3. Locknut
4. Accelerator pedal
5. Cable seal
6. End of cable sleeve
7. Distance between 5 and 6

Fig. 55 Accelerator cable adjustment—528e and 530i models

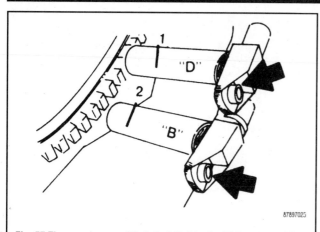

Fig. 57 The speed sensor (1), is installed in the (D) location, while the reference sensor (2) is installed in the (B) location

12. Remove the torque converter cover and remove the 4 bolts that attach the torque converter to the drive plate. Turn the engine for this procedure, using the vibration damper.

13. Use paint to mark identification points on the speed and reference sensors, then remove. If the tips are dirty, clean with a rag

14. Support the transmission and disconnect the crossmember at the body.

15. Remove the remaining transmission mounting bolts.

16. Separate the transmission from the engine and take off the torque converter at the same time. On 1983–88 733i and 735i models, this is done by removing the protective grill on the side of the converter housing and gently prying it toward the transmission as it is pulled rearward. On 318i models, lower the transmission onto the front axle carrier. Remove the grill from the torque converter housing and gently pry the torque converter backwards as the transmission is pulled off.

To install:

17. Install the transmission into the vehicle and push the torque converter back against the stop on the transmission and rotate it to align the bolt holes with the drive plate holes before installing.

➡**On 1983–88 733i and 735i models, the drive connections on the front of the converter must be indented inside the converter housing at least 0.3 inches (9mm).**

18. Install the speed transmitter and reference sensors. The speed sensor faces the gear ring. The reference transmitter faces the flywheel. The engine will not start if the plugs are installed wrong.

19. Install the driveshaft, using new locknuts on the driveshaft flexible giubo coupling. Tighten the driveplate bolts to 16–17 ft. lb. (21–22 Nm).

20. Install the exhaust suspension without twisting. When installing the driveshaft center bearing, preload the center bearing 0.8 inches (2mm).

21. Make sure the torque converter is positioned correctly before installing. Fill the transmission with new fluid.

22. Lower the vehicle and connect the negative battery cable.

4–Speed Automatic

EXCEPT 3 SERIES MODELS

➡**To perform this operation, a support for the transmission, BMW tool 24 0 120 and 00 2 020 or equivalent and a tool for tightening the drive-shaft locking ring, BMW tool 26 1 040 or equivalent are required. If the vehicle has a 6–cylinder engine, a special socket (which retains the bolts) 24 1 110 or equivalent will be needed.**

1. Disconnect the battery ground cable.

2. Loosen the throttle cable adjusting nuts and release the cable tension. Disconnect the cable at the throttle lever. Then, remove the nuts, and pull the cable housing out of the bracket.

3. Raise and safely support the vehicle on jackstands.

4. Disconnect the exhaust system at the manifold and hangers, then lower it out of the way. Remove the hanger that runs across and under the driveshaft. Remove the exhaust heat shield.

5. Support the transmission via a floorjack and BMW tool 24 0 120 which goes under the transmission oil pan. When installed, remove the crossmember which supports the transmission at the rear.

6. Remove the driveshaft giubo coupling through bolts and nuts. Discard the used self–locking coupling nuts.

7. Unscrew the transmission locking ring at the center mount (if equipped). Then, remove the bolts and center mount. Bend the driveshaft downward and pull it off the centering pin. Suspend it with wire from the underside of the car.

8. Drain the transmission fluid and discard it. Remove the fluid filler neck. Disconnect the oil cooler lines at the transmission, if equipped, by unscrewing the flare nuts and plug the open connections.

9. Remove the converter cover by removing the Torx® bolts from behind as well as the bolts from underneath. On 6–cylinder equipped models pull the cover out of the bottom of the transmission housing, just behind the oil pan.

10. Remove the bolts fastening the torque converter to the drive plate, turning the flywheel as necessary to gain access from below. Use a special socket (that retains the bolts) 24 1 110 or equivalent on cars with the 6-cylinder engine.

11. If equipped, remove the guard for the speed and reference mark sensors. Paint location marks on each sensor, then remove the attaching bolt for each and lift out each sensor.

➡**Vehicles equipped with a diesel engine are equipped only with a reference mark sensor.**

12. Check the condition of each sensor and clean if needed.

13. Disconnect the shift cable by loosening the locknut fastening it to the shift lever and disconnecting the cable at the cable housing bracket.

14. If the transmission has an electrical connection, turn the bayonet fastener to the left to release the harness.

15. Lower the transmission as far as possible. Then, remove all the Torx® or standard type bolts attaching the transmission to the engine.

16. Remove the small grill from the bottom of the transmission. Then press the converter off with a large screwdriver passing through this opening while sliding the transmission out.

To install:

17. Install the transmission and observe the following points:

a. Make sure the converter is fully installed onto the transmission, such that the ring on the front is inside the edge of the case.

b. When reinstalling the driveshaft, tighten the lockring with special tool 26 1 040 or equivalent.

c. If the driveshaft has a simple coupling (524td), make sure to replace the self-locking nuts and to hold the bolts still while tightening the nuts to keep from distorting the coupling.

d. When installing the center mount, preload it forward 0.1–0.2 inches (4–6mm).

e. Adjust the throttle cables.

3 SERIES MODELS

➡**To perform this operation, a support for the transmission, BMW tool 24 0 120 and 00 2 020 or equivalent and a tool for tightening the drive-shaft locking ring, BMW tool 26 1 040 or equivalent, are required.**

1. Disconnect the battery ground cable. Loosen the throttle cable adjusting nuts, release the cable tension, and disconnect the cable at the throttle lever. Then, remove the nuts, and pull the cable housing out of the bracket.

2. Raise and safely support the vehicle on jackstands.

3. Disconnect the exhaust system at the manifold and hangers and lower. Remove the hanger bracket that runs across and above the driveshaft. Remove the exhaust heat shield from under the center of the vehicle.

4. On the 325iX, remove the transfer case from the rear of the transmission.

5. Drain the transmission fluid into a suitable container and discard it. Remove the fluid filler neck. Disconnect the oil cooler lines at the transmission, if equipped, by unscrewing the flare nuts and plug the open connections.

6. Support the transmission with a floorjack, transmission jack or other suitable tool. Separate the torque converter housing from the transmission by removing the Torx® bolts and the regular bolts from the bottom and sides of the transmission. Retain the washers used with the Torx® bolts.

7. On the 325iX, disconnect the front driveshaft.

8. Remove the bolts attaching the torque converter housing to the engine, making sure to retain the spacer used behind one of the bolts. Then, loosen the

mounting bolts for the oil level switch just enough so the plate can be removed while pushing the switch mounting bracket to one side.

9. Remove the bolts attaching the torque converter to the drive plate. Turn the flywheel as necessary to gain access to each of the bolts. Make sure to re-use the same bolts and retain the washers.

10. To remove the speed and reference mark sensors, paint identification marks on each sensor, then remove the attaching bolt for each and slide out. Keep the sensors clean.

11. Turn the bayonet type electrical connector counterclockwise and unfasten the plug out of the socket. Lift the wiring harness out of the harness bails.

12. While supporting the transmission securely, remove the crossmember that supports the transmission at the rear.

13. Disconnect the transmission shift rod.

14. Remove the nuts and through bolts from the damper-type U-joint at the front of the transmission.

15. Unscrew the driveshaft spline locking ring at the center mount, if equipped, using the BMW special tool or equivalent. Remove the nuts from the center mount and lower the center mount. Bend the driveshaft downward and pull it off the centering pin. Suspend it with wire from the underside of the vehicle.

16. Lower the transmission as far as possible. Then, remove all the Torx® or standard type bolts attaching the transmission to the engine.

17. Remove the small grill from the bottom of the transmission. Then press the converter off with a large prytool passing through this opening while sliding the transmission out.

To install:

18. Install the transmission in position under the vehicle and raise it up into place. Observe the following points:

    a. Make sure the converter is fully installed onto the transmission, such that the ring on the front is inside the edge of the case. Only use M10x16mm bolts as originally equipped or damage may occur.

    b. When reinstalling the driveshaft, tighten the lockring with the proper tool.

    c. Make sure to replace the self-locking nuts on the driveshaft flexible U-joint and to hold the bolt while tightening the nuts to keep from distorting it.

    d. When installing the center mount, preload it forward 0.1–0.2 inches 4–6mm).

    e. When reconnecting the bayonet type electrical connector, make sure the alignment marks are correct after the plug it twisted into its final position.

    f. When reinstalling the speed and reference mark sensors, inspect the O-rings used on the sensors and install new ones, if needed. Make sure to install the speed sensor into the bore marked D and the reference mark sensor, which is marked with a ring, into the bore marked B.

    g. Tighten the crossmember mounting bolts to 16–17 ft. lbs. (21–23 Nm).

    h. If O-rings are used with the transmission oil cooler connections, replace them.

    i. Adjust the throttle cables.

19. Connect the negative battery cable.

Rear Output Seal

REMOVAL & INSTALLATION

1. Disconnect the driveshaft from the output flange and support with wire.
2. Counterhold the output flange and remove the nut. Pull off the output flange.
3. Use a seal puller to remove the seal.
4. Install the new seal with the lip facing in. Use a seal driver to install.
5. Install the output flange and tighten the nut to 72 ft. lbs. (100 Nm). Install the driveshaft.

TRANSFER CASE

Case Assembly

REMOVAL & INSTALLATION

Manual Transmission Equipped Models

➡ **To perform this procedure, a special, large wrench that locks onto the flats on alternate sides of the rear driveshaft is required. Use tool 26 1 060 or an equivalent.**

1. Disconnect the negative battery cable. Raise and safely support the vehicle. Remove the exhaust system. Unbolt and remove the exhaust system heat shield located behind and below the transfer case.

2. Unscrew the rear section of the driveshaft at the sliding joint located behind the output flange of the transfer case.

3. Hold the through-bolts stationary and remove the self-locking nuts from in front of the flexible coupling at the transfer case output flange. Discard the self-locking nuts and replace them.

➡ **During the next step, be careful not to let the driveshaft rest on the metal fuel line that crosses under it.**

4. Slide the sections of the driveshaft together at the joint and then pull the front of the driveshaft off the centering pin at the transmission output shaft.

5. Remove the nuts and through-bolts from the flexible giubo coupling linking the transmission with the short driveshaft between the transmission and the transfer case.

6. Support the transmission from underneath in a secure manner. Mark each of the 4 bolts fastening the crossmember that supports the transmission at the rear to the body.

➡ **These bolts are of different lengths.**

7. Remove the crossmember.

8. Lower the transmission/transfer case unit just enough to gain access to the bolts linking the 2 boxes together. Remove the lower and upper bolts. It is possible to gain access to the upper bolts using a socket wrench with a U-joint and extension.

9. There is a protective cap on the forward driveshaft where it links up with the transfer case. The cap is made of a brittle material, so it must be handled carefully. Gently slide the cap forward until is free of the transfer case.

10. Slide the transfer case to the rear so it can be separated from both the transmission and the forward driveshaft. When free, remove it.

To install:

11. Install the transfer case under the vehicle and raise it into position, bearing the following points in mind:

    a. Inspect the dowel holes locating the transfer case with the transmission and the guide hole for the output shaft where it slides into the transfer case to make sure these parts are properly aligned. Lubricate the guide pin and the splines of the front driveshaft section with grease.

    b. When fitting the transfer case onto the transmission, check to make sure the output flange of the transmission is properly aligned with the flexible coupling. Install the bolts through the flexible coupling and position and tighten the nuts to 65 ft. lbs. (88 Nm) while holding the bolts stationary.

    c. When reconnecting the transfer case to the gearbox, tighten the bolts to 30 ft. lbs. (41 Nm).

    d. Before fitting the driveshaft back onto the rear of the transmission, retain the seal in the protective cap by applying grease to it.

    e. Tighten the transmission crossmember bolts to 17 ft. lbs. (23 Nm).

    f. Check the fluid level and fill with the recommended lubricant.

Automatic Transmission Equipped Models

➡ **To perform this procedure, a special, large wrench that locks onto the flats on alternate sides of the rear driveshaft is required. Use tool 26 1 060 or an equivalent.**

1. Disconnect the negative battery cable. Raise and safely support the vehicle. Remove the exhaust system. Unbolt and remove the exhaust system heat shields located behind and below the transfer case.

2. Unscrew the rear section of the driveshaft at the sliding joint located behind the output flange of the transfer case.

3. Hold the through-bolts stationary and remove the self-locking nuts from in front of the flexible coupling at the transfer case output flange. Discard the self-locking nuts and replace them.

➡️**During the next step, be careful not to let the driveshaft rest on the metal fuel line that crosses under it.**

4. Slide the sections of the driveshaft together and pull the front of the driveshaft off the centering pin at the transmission output shaft.

5. Remove the nuts and through bolts from the flexible giubo coupling linking the transmission flange with the short driveshaft linking the transmission and the transfer case.

6. Note the locations of all the washers and then loosen the retaining nut and disconnect the range selector cable at the transmission by pulling out the pin. Be careful not to bend the cable. Loosen the nuts that position the cable housing onto the transmission and slide the housing backward so it can be separated from the bracket on the transmission housing.

7. There is a protective cap on the forward driveshaft where it links with the transfer case. The cap is made of a brittle material, so it must be handled carefully. Gently slide the cap forward until is free of the transfer case.

8. Remove the drain plug in the bottom of the pan and drain the fluid.

9. Support the transmission from underneath in a secure manner. Then, mark each of the 4 bolts fastening the crossmember that supports the transmission at the rear to the body, bolts are of different lengths. Remove the crossmember.

10. Remove the nuts fastening the transfer case to the transmission housing. Note the location of the wiring holder so it will be possible to reinstall it on the same bolt.

11. Slide the transfer case to the rear and off the transmission.

To install:

12. Install the transfer case under the vehicle and raise it into position, bearing the following points in mind:

a. Inspect the sealing surfaces as well as the dowel holes in the transfer case to make sure they will seal and locate properly. Clean the sealing surfaces and replace the gasket.

b. When sliding the transfer case back onto the transmission, turn the front driveshaft slightly to help make the splines mesh.

c. When reconnecting the shift cable, inspect the rubber mounts and replace any that are cut, crushed or cracked. Adjust the shift cable.

d. Before fitting the driveshaft back onto the rear of the transmission, retain the seal in the protective cap by applying grease.

e. When fitting the transfer case onto the transmission, check to make sure the output flange of the transmission is properly aligned with the flexible coupling. Put the bolts through the flexible coupling and then position and tighten the nuts to 65 ft. lbs. (88 Nm) while holding the bolts stationary.

f. Tighten the bolts holding the transfer case to the transmission to 65 ft. lbs. (88 Nm).

g. Tighten the transmission crossmember bolts to 17 ft. lbs. (23 Nm).

h. Check the fluid level and fill with the recommended lubricant.

DRIVELINE

Front Driveshaft

REMOVAL & INSTALLATION

1. Disconnect the negative battery cable.
2. Raise and support the vehicle on jackstands.
3. Remove the 6 bolts from the flexible giubo coupling at the front differential.
4. Push the driveshaft back, then down and out of the transfer case.
5. Plug the opening in the transfer case.
6. Check the condition of the transfer case seal and the dust cap. Replace if needed.

To install:

7. Install the driveshaft into the transfer case. Install a new flex giubo coupling at the front differential.

➡️**The arrows on the giubo coupler must face the arms of the flanges.**

8. Install the bolts and tighten the M10-8.8 bolts to 35 ft. lbs. (48 Nm) and the M10-10.9 bolts to 52 ft. lbs. (72 Nm). Hold the nut or bolt at the flex giubo coupling side and turn of the flange side. This prevents stressing the flex coupling.

9. Slide the dust cap into position.

Rear Driveshaft

REMOVAL & INSTALLATION

1600, 2000 and 2002 Models

1. Support the transmission from underneath with a transmission jack or other secure jacking device. Loosen but do not remove the nuts located underneath which fasten the crossmember to the body. Then, slide this crossmember as far to the rear as it will go.

2. Unscrew the fastening nuts on the forward end of the flexible giubo coupler and discard them.

3. Using a prybar to keep the driveshaft from turning, remove the self locking nuts and bolts fastening the rear of the driveshaft to the final drive.

4. Remove the bolts fastening the center mount to the body. Bend the driveshaft down and pull the coupler off the transmission flange.

To install:

5. Install in the reverse order keeping in mind the following points;

a. Replace the self-locking nuts used at either end of the shaft.

b. Preload the center mount forward by 0.0–0.2 inches (4–5mm).

3 Series Models

2-WHEEL DRIVE

▸ **See Figures 58 thru 66**

1. Remove the entire exhaust system. Remove the crossbrace under the driveshaft. Remove the heatshield.

2. Mark the position of the center bearing bracket with paint. Remove the retaining bolts securing the center bearing bracket.

3. Paint alignment marks on either side of the center bearing bracket.

4. Use tool 26 1 040 or equivalent to loosen the spline locking ring behind the center bearing.

5. Support the transmission and remove the crossmember. Remove the bolts holding the flexible giubo coupling to the transmission output flange. If equipped with a vibration damper, rotate the damper and pull off with the flex coupling.

6. Remove the bolts between the driveshaft and differential flange.

7. Pull the driveshaft down and out. Avoid catching the fuel tank connector pipe at the rear. Avoid severe angles at the joints.

To install:

8. Install the driveshaft and loosely install the center bearing to the body. Connect the rear joint to the differential. If equipped with U-joints, tighten to 52 ft. lbs. (72 Nm). If equipped with a constant velocity joint, tighten the M8 bolts to 23 ft. lbs. (32 Nm) and the M10 bolts to 46 ft. lbs. (64 Nm).

9. Install the front flex coupling and vibration damper. Tighten the M10-8.8 bolts to 35 ft. lbs. (48 Nm) and the M10-10.9 bolts to 52 ft. lbs. (72 Nm).

10. Install the transmission crossmember. Preload the center bearing forward 0.1–0.2 inches (4–6 mm) and tighten. Tighten the spline locking ring to 12 ft. lbs. (17 Nm).

11. Install the heatshields and crossmember. Install the exhaust system.

4-WHEEL DRIVE

1. Remove the entire exhaust system. Remove the crossbrace under the driveshaft. Remove the heatshield.

2. Use tool 26 1 040 or equivalent to loosen the spline locking ring at the rear of the shaft.

Fig. 58 Paint alignment marks on and next to the center bearing bracket

Fig. 59 Remove the center bearing bracket bolts

Fig. 60 Paint alignment marks on the driveshaft to either side of the bearing

Fig. 61 After loosening the collar, carefully pull apart the sections

Fig. 62 Separated driveshaft sections

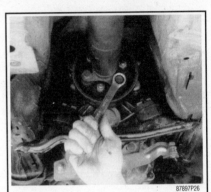
Fig. 63 Loosen the bolts securing the flexible giubo coupler

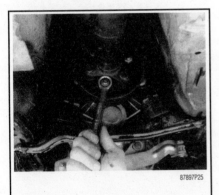
Fig. 64 Loosening the giubo retaining nuts

Fig. 65 Carefully pry the driveshaft section away from the transmission

Fig. 66 Note that the giubo remains attached to the driveshaft after separation from the transmission

3. Remove the bolts holding the flexible giubo coupler to the transmission output flange. If equipped with a vibration damper, rotate the damper and pull off with the flex coupling.

4. Remove the bolts between the driveshaft and differential flange.

5. Remove the center bearing bolts and pull the driveshaft down. Avoid catching the fuel tank connector pipe at the rear. Avoid severe angles at the joints.

To install:

6. Install the driveshaft and loosely install the center bearing to the body. Connect the rear joint to the differential. If equipped with U-joints, tighten to 52 ft. lbs. (72 Nm). If equipped with a constant velocity joint, tighten the M8 bolts to 23 ft. lbs. (32 Nm) and the M10 bolts to 46 ft. lbs. (64 Nm).

7. Install the front flex coupling and vibration damper. Tighten the M10-8.8 bolts to 35 ft. lbs. (48 Nm) and the M10-10.9 bolts to 52 ft. lbs. (72 Nm).

8. Preload the center bearing forward 0.1–0.2 inches (4–6 mm) and tighten. Tighten the spline locking ring to 16 ft. lbs. (22 Nm).

9. Install the heatshields and crossmember. Install the exhaust system.

5, 6 and 7 Series

EXCEPT MODELS EQUIPPED WITH CV-JOINT TYPE DRIVESHAFTS AND 1987–88 735I MODELS

1. Remove the entire exhaust system. Remove the crossbrace under the driveshaft. Remove the heatshield. Mark the relationship of the driveshaft flanges to the differential flange and the transmission output flange.

2. Use tool 26 1 040 or equivalent to loosen the spline locking ring behind the center bearing.

3. Support the transmission and remove the transmission crossmember. Remove the bolts holding the flexible giubo coupling to the transmission output flange. If equipped with a vibration damper, rotate the damper and pull off with the flex coupling.

4. Remove the bolts between the driveshaft and differential flange.

5. Remove the center bearing bolts and pull the driveshaft down. Avoid catching the fuel tank connector pipe at the rear. Avoid severe angles at the joints.

To install:

6. Install the driveshaft and loosely install the center bearing to the body. Connect the rear joint to the differential. If equipped with U-joints, tighten to 52 ft. lbs. (72 Nm). If equipped with a constant velocity joint, tighten the M8 bolts to 23 ft. lbs. (32 Nm) and the M10 bolts to 46 ft. lbs. (64 Nm).

7. Install the front flex coupling and vibration damper. Tighten the M10-8.8 bolts to 35 ft. lbs. (48 Nm) and the M10-10.9 bolts to 52 ft. lbs. (72 Nm).

8. Install the transmission crossmember. Preload the center bearing forward 0.1–0.2 inches (4–6 mm) and tighten. Tighten the spline locking ring to 12 ft. lbs. (17 Nm).

9. Install the heatshields and crossmember. Install the exhaust system.

1987–88 735I MODELS

➡️**If the car has a front universal joint, use special tools 24 0 120 and 00 2 020 to support the transmission during this operation.**

1. Remove the entire exhaust system. Remove the heat shield from the floorpan. Remove the nuts and bolts fastening the driveshaft to the transmission at the flexible coupling. Replace the self-locking nuts.

2. If the car has a front U-joint, support the transmission from underneath with tools 24 0 120 or the equivalent. When the transmission is securely supported, remove the bolts and remove the rear transmission mounting crossmember.

3. Remove the self-locking nuts and then the bolts fastening the driveshaft to the final drive. Replace the self-locking nuts. Remove the driveshaft, taking care to keep it protected from dirt.

4. Remove the bolts from the crossbrace underneath and remove the center driveshaft mount. Then, bend the shaft at the middle and remove it from the car by pulling it off the centering pin on the forward end.

To install:

5. Install in reverse order, keeping the following points in mind:

a. Repack the CV joining with Moly-type grease and replace the gasket, if necessary.

b. Check the center bearing for lubrication and if it's dry, lubricate with Molykote® Long-term 2 or equivalent grease.

c. When remounting the center mount, preload it forward from its most natural position 0.1–0.2 inches (4–6mm).

d. Tighten the U-joint bolts to 52 ft. lbs. (68 Nm) and CV-joint bolts to 51 ft. lbs. (66 Nm)

528E, 535I AND 633CSI WITH CV-JOINT

➡️**To perform this procedure, procure a set of tools designed to support the transmission via the pan BMW tools 24 0 120 and 00 2 020 or equivalent.**

1. Support the transmission from underneath. Remove the nuts and washers from the transmission mounts on top of the transmission crossmember. Loosen but do not remove the nuts located underneath which fasten the crossmember to the body. Then, slide the crossmember as far to the rear as it will go.

2. Unscrew the fastening nuts on the forward end of the CV-joint and then discard.

3. Using a prybar to keep the driveshaft from turning, remove the self-locking nuts and bolts fastening the rear of the driveshaft to the final drive.

4. Remove the bolts fastening the center mount to the body. Bend the driveshaft down and pull the CV-joint off the transmission flange. Cover the joint to keep it clean.

To install:

5. Replace the gasket that fits between the joint bolts. Install in reverse order, keeping these points in mind:

a. Replace the self-locking nuts used at either end of the shaft.

b. Preload the center mount forward by forcing the bracket 0.1–0.2 inches (4–5mm) forward from the neutral position on 5 Series cars and 0.1–0.2 inches (4–6mm) forward on 6 Series cars.

Center Bearing

REMOVAL & INSTALLATION

With Splines

➡️**Models equipped with splined driveshafts have no visible bolts securing the driveshaft sections to the center bearing. If your model has bolts visible, please refer to the procedure for non-splined driveshafts.**

1600, 2000 AND 2002 MODELS

1. With the driveshaft removed, remove the coupling nut.

2. Using a standard puller, pull off the center bearing without the dust guard plate.

3. Remove the grooved ball bearing with a suitable puller.

To install:

4. Using a standard puller, install the ball bearing and install the driveshaft.

3, 5 AND 7 SERIES MODELS (EXCEPT 320I)

1. Paint alignment marks on the driveshaft at the center bearing for installation back into its original orientation. It is critical for balance that the 2 halves of the driveshaft be replaced into their original relationship.

2. Remove the driveshaft.

3. Loosen the spline locking sleeve at the center bearing and separate the front section from the rear section.

4. Remove the snapring at the splines.

5. Use a puller or press to remove the center bearing from the shaft. Note the location of the dust shields.

To install:

6. Press the new center bearing onto the driveshaft. The dust shield should be flush with the center mount.

7. Clean the splines and coat with moly type lubricant. Install the front half to the rear in the same position as it was removed.

8. Install the driveshaft and tighten the spline locking sleeve to 12 ft. lbs. (17 Nm), except for 4-wheel drive which is 16 ft. lbs. (22 Nm). If not equipped with splines, use a threadlocking compound and tighten to 70 ft. lbs. (97 Nm).

320I MODELS

1. With the driveshaft removed, mark the shaft's location to the coupling.

2. Remove the circlip and pull out the driveshaft.

3. Using a standard puller remove the center bearing without its dust cover.

4. Drive the grooved ball bearing out of the center bearing.

5. Installation is the reverse of removal.

Without Splines

Certain models of the 528e, 530i, 535i, 633CSi, 635i, M5 and M6 may be equipped with non-splined driveshafts. These models are easily identified by the bolts securing the two driveshaft sections together.

➡️**This type of driveshaft has the 2 sections bolted together just behind the center bearing. Use a press and a puller to complete this operation.**

1. Remove the driveshaft as described in this section. Matchmark the relationship between the forward and rear sections of the shaft at the center bearing.

2. Remove the bolt that fastens the forward U-joint section to the center mount.

3. Using a standard puller remove the center mount and bearing without the dust guard.

4. Press the old bearing out of the mount and press a new one in. Then, use a mandrel 24 1 040 or equivalent to drive the bearing center race onto the driveshaft.

5. Assemble the driveshaft in reverse order, lining up its halves with the matchmarks. Install the bolt fastening the shaft sections together with a locking type of sealer, tightening to 72 ft. lbs. (98 Nm).

Flexible Coupling Centering Ring

REMOVAL & INSTALLATION

1600, 2000, 2002, 2500, 2800, Bavaria, 3000 and 3.0 Models

1. Press off the sealing cap.
2. Lift out the circlip.
3. Take out the ball cup, centering ring, disc and spring.
4. Fill the centering assembly with approximately 6g (0.2 oz.) of grease and install the ball cup, centering ring, disc and spring. Install the circlip. Install the sealing cap.

Flex Coupling (Giubo Disk)

REMOVAL & INSTALLATION

1. Remove the entire exhaust system. Remove the crossbrace under the driveshaft. Remove the heatshields. Mark the relationship of the driveshaft flange to the transmission output flange for installation.

2. Use tool 26 1 040 or equivalent to loosen the spline locking ring behind the center bearing.

3. Support the transmission and remove the transmission crossmember, if blocking the access to the coupling. Remove the bolts holding the flex coupling to the transmission output flange and the driveshaft. If equipped with a vibration damper, rotate the damper and pull off with the flex coupling.

FRONT DRIVE AXLE

Halfshafts

REMOVAL & INSTALLATION

➡ **A number of special tools are required to perform this operation. Use the BMW factory numbers given to shop for these from factory sources, or to cross-reference similar tools that may be available in the aftermarket. Use 33 4 050 and 00 5 500 to drive in a new lockplate for the brake disc. The tie rod must be pressed off with 342 2 070. Control arms are pressed off with 31 2 160. Use 33 2 112 and 33 2 113 to press the output shafts out of the brake discs and 33 2 112, 33 2 124 and 33 4 042 to press them back in. On the left side, the output shaft is pulled out of the drive axle with 31 5 011 and 30 31 581. On the right side, 31 5 011 and 31 5 012 are used to pull the output shaft out of the axle.**

1. Raise the car and support it securely. Remove the front wheels. Remove the drain plug and drain the oil from the front axle.

2. Lift out the lockplate in the center of the brake disc with a suitable prytool. Then, unscrew the collar nut.

3. Remove the attaching nut from each tie rod and then press the rod off the steering knuckle with 33 2 070.

4. Remove the retaining nut and press the control arm off the steering knuckle on either side.

5. Mount 33 2 112 and 33 2 113 to the brake disc with 2 wheel bolts. Press the output shaft out of the center of the steering knuckle on that side. Repeat on the other side.

To install:

4. Install the front flex coupling and vibration damper. The arrows must face the flange arms. Tighten the M10-8.8 bolts to 35 ft. lbs. (48 Nm) and the M10-10.9 bolts to 52 ft. lbs. (72 Nm).

5. Install the transmission crossmember. Tighten the spline locking ring to 12 ft. lbs. (17 Nm) for 2 wheel drive and 16 ft. lbs. (22 Nm) for 4-wheel drive.

6. Install the heatshields and crossmember. Install the exhaust system.

Driveshaft End Bearing

REMOVAL & INSTALLATION

1. Remove the entire exhaust system. Remove the crossbrace under the driveshaft. Remove the heatshields. Mark the relationship of the driveshaft flange to the transmission output flange for installation.

2. Use tool 26 1 040 or equivalent to loosen the spline locking ring behind the center bearing.

3. Support the transmission and remove the transmission crossmember, if blocking the access to the coupling. Remove the bolts holding the flex coupling to the transmission output flange. If equipped with a vibration damper, rotate the damper and pull off with the flex coupling.

4. Fill the opening of the bearing with grease. Use a tool the same diameter as the bore in the bearing and drive in. The hydraulic force developed will drive the bearing out from the back side.

To install:

5. Clean the grease from the bore and fill with 2 grams of moly-type lubricant grease. Drive the new bearing in until so it protrudes 0.2 inch (4mm).

6. Install the front flex coupling and vibration damper, if equipped. The arrows must face the flange arms. Tighten the M10-8.8 bolts to 35 ft. lbs. (48 Nm) and the M10-10.9 bolts to 52 ft. lbs. (72 Nm).

7. Install the transmission crossmember. Tighten the spline locking ring to 12 ft. lbs. (17 Nm) for 2 wheel drive and 16 ft. lbs. (22 Nm) for 4 wheel drive.

8. Install the heatshields and crossmember. Install the exhaust system.

6. To remove the drive axle from the differential on the left side: Install special tool 31 5 011 by bolting it together around the axle so that the ring on its inner diameter fits into the groove on the shaft. Install 30 31 581 onto the shaft so it will rest against the housing and the bolt heads of 31 5 011 will rest against it. Screw the 2 bolts in, alternately in small increments, to get even pressure on the shaft, pulling it out of the differential.

7. To remove the drive axle on the right side: Install 31 5 012 on the diameter of the shaft directly against the housing. Install 31 5 011, by bolting it together around the axle so that the ring on its inner diameter fits into the groove on the shaft. Screw the 2 bolts in, alternately in small increments, to get even pressure on the shaft, pulling it out of the differential.

To install:

8. Install the halfshafts, bearing the following points in mind:

a. Install the shafts into the housing until the snapring inside engages in the groove of the shaft. It may be necessary to install the removal tool and tap against it with a plastic-tipped hammer to drive the shaft far enough into the housing.

b. Before installing the shafts in the steering knuckle, coat the spline with light oil.

c. When installing the control arms onto the steering knuckle, tighten the nut to 61.5 ft. lbs. (84 Nm) and use a new cotter pin. When installing the tie rod onto the steering knuckle, tighten to 61.5 ft. lbs. (84 Nm) and use a new self-locking nut.

d. Drive a new lockplate into the brake disc with 33 4 050 and 00 5 500. Tighten the nut to 181 ft. lbs. (245 Nm).

e. Replace the drain plug and refill the final drive unit with the required lubricant.

Hub and Bearings

REMOVAL & INSTALLATION

➡A number of special tools are required to perform this operation. Read through the procedure and procure these before attempting to start work. Factory part numbers for tools are given, but it is possible to shop for equivalent tools, using these part numbers, in the aftermarket.

1. Raise the car and support it securely. Remove the output halfshaft as described in this section. Then, remount the control arm with the nuts finger-tight, to keep the spring strut in position.

2. Remove the upper and lower attaching bolts and remove the brake caliper, suspending it nearby with wire.

3. Remove the Allen bolt and remove the brake disc.

4. Bolt special tool 31 2 090 or equivalent to the knuckle with its 3 bolts. Then, mount 33 1 307 hooked around the tie rod arm and press the drive flange off. If it is scored, pull the bearing's inner race out of the drive flange with 33 1 307 and 00 7 500 or equivalent.

5. Compress the snapring and remove it.

6. Remove 31 2 090 or the equivalent and replace 33 1 307 or its equivalent with a tool such as 31 2 070. Again install and use the combination, this time to press out the bearing.

7. Screw out the spindle of 31 2 090 and install 33 4 032 or equivalent so it is flush with the surface of 31 2 090. Use 33 4 034 and 33 4 038 to pull in the new bearing. Then, remove 31 2 090.

8. Install the snapring.

9. Pull the drive flange into place with 33 4 032 or equivalent, 33 4 038 or equivalent, 33 4 045 or equivalent, and 33 4 048 or equivalent.

10. Install the brake disc and caliper and the wheel in reverse order.

REAR DRIVE AXLE

Halfshaft

REMOVAL & INSTALLATION

▶ **See Figures 67, 68, 69 and 70**

1. Remove the rear wheel. Pull out the lockplate and remove the axle nut.
2. Remove the constant velocity joint bolts at the final drive output flange.
3. Use tool 33 2 110 or equivalent to press the axle through the bearing and out of the vehicle. Do not allow the halfshaft to drop.

To install:

4. Place the halfshaft through the bearing and into place using tool 33 2 110 or equivalent.
5. Secure the constant velocity joint bolts at the final drive output flange and tighten to 42 ft. lbs. (58 Nm).
6. Lubricate the axle nut with oil. Tighten the axle nut to 145 ft. lbs. (200 Nm) and install the lockplate with tools 33 4 050 and 00 5 500 or equivalent. Install the rear wheel.

Rear Axle Shaft, Wheel Bearings, and Seals

REMOVAL & INSTALLATION

6-Cylinder Models

EXCEPT 320I, 528E, 530I, 633I, 735I AND 1983–84 733I

▶ **See Figures 71 and 72**

1. Remove the wheel.
2. Loosen the brake caliper and leave the brake line connected.
3. Remove the brake disc.
4. Remove the driving flange as follows:
    a. Disconnect the output shaft.
    b. Remove the lockplate.
    c. Loosen the collared nut and pull off the drive flange.
5. Tighten the collared nut and drive off the rear axle shaft.
6. Drive off the wheel bearings and seals toward the outside.
7. Install the wheel bearings and seals. Install the drive flange and lockplate. Install the brake disc and caliper. Install the wheel.

320I MODELS

1. Remove the wheel.
2. Remove the cotter pin from the castellated nut.
3. Apply the handbrake.

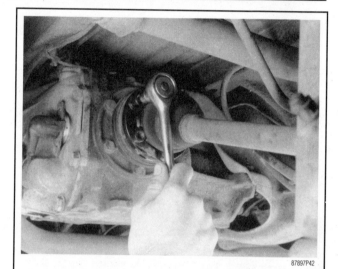

Fig. 67 Remove the inner retaining bolts from the halfshaft

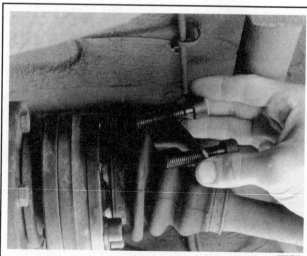

Fig. 68 Each bolt slides through a bracket

Fig. 69 With the bolts removed, the inner portion of the shaft is free to drop. Support it with one hand . . .

Fig. 71 Halfshaft nut and lockplate removed

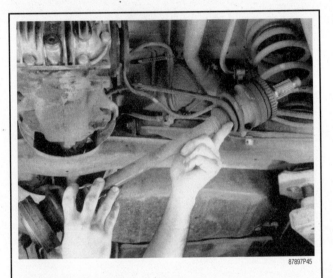

Fig. 70 . . . as you slide the halfshaft out

Fig. 72 Installing the wheel bearing

4. Loosen the castellated nut.
5. Release the handbrake.
6. Remove the brake drum.
7. Pull off the drive flange with a puller.
8. Disconnect the output shaft and tie it up.
9. Drive out the halfshaft with a plastic hammer using the castellated nut to protect the end of the shaft.
10. Drive out the bearing and sealing ring.
11. Take out the spacer sleeve and shim.
To install;
12. Install bearing and seal ring, install the drive flange and connect the output shaft.
13. Install the brake drum and tighten the castellated nut, use a new cotter pin.
14. Install the wheel.

528E, 530I, 535I, 633CSI, 735I, M5, M6 AND 1983–84 733I

1. Remove the rear wheel. Disconnect the output shaft at the outer flange and suspend it with wire.

2. Unbolt the caliper and suspend it with the brake line connected. Unbolt and remove the rear disc.
3. Remove the large nut and remove the lockplate. If the car has ABS, disconnect and then remove the ABS speed sensor.
4. Use a special tool BMW 33 4 000 or equivalent and 2 M10 x 30 bolts to unscrew the collar nut. Then, pull off the drive flange with tools 00 7 501 and 00 7 502.
5. Screw on the collar nut until it is just flush with the end of the shaft and use a soft-tipped hammer to knock out the shaft.
6. Remove the circlip. Then, use special tools 33 4 031, 33 4 032 and 33 4 038 or equivalent to pull off the wheel bearings.
7. Pull the inner bearing race off the axle shaft with special tool 00 7 500 or equivalent.
To install:
8. Pull the new bearing assembly in with special tools 33 4 036, 33 4 032, and 33 4 038 or equivalent.
9. Install special tool 33 4 037 or equivalent. Then, reinstall the circlip.
10. Pull the rear axle shaft through with special tools 23 1 300, 33 4 080 and 33 4 020 or equivalent.

11. Use special tool 33 4 000 or equivalent to tighten the collar nut.

12. Fit special tool 33 4 060 or equivalent into the lockplate and top it in with a slide hammer 00 5 000 or equivalent.

13. Reconnect the output shaft. Remount the brake disc and caliper.

Front Wheel Drive Hub and Bearings

REMOVAL & INSTALLATION

→A number of special tools are required to perform this operation. Read through the procedure and procure these before attempting to start work. Factory part numbers for tools are given, but it is possible to shop for equivalent tools, using these part numbers, in the after-market.

1. Raise the car and support it securely. Remove the output halfshaft as described in this section. Then, remount the control arm with nuts just finger-tight, to keep the spring strut in position.

2. Remove the upper and lower attaching bolts and the brake caliper, suspending it nearby with wire.

3. Remove the Allen bolt and remove the brake disc.

4. Bolt special tool 31 2 090 or equivalent to the knuckle with its 3 bolts. Then, mount 33 1 307 hooked around the tie rod arm and press the drive flange off. If it is scored, pull the bearing's inner race out of the drive flange with 33 1 307 and 00 7 500 or equivalent.

5. Compress the snapring with snapring pliers and remove it.

6. Remove 31 2 090 or the equivalent and replace 33 1 307 or its equivalent with a tool such as 31 2 070. Again install and use the combination, this time to press out the bearing.

7. Screw out the spindle of 31 2 090 and install 33 4 032 or equivalent so it is flush with the surface of 31 2 090. Use 33 4 034 and 33 4 038 to pull in the new bearing. Then, remove 31 2 090.

8. Install the circlip again, with snapring pliers, making sure the open end faces downward.

9. Pull the drive flange into place with 33 4 032 or equivalent, 33 4 038 or equivalent, 33 4 045 or equivalent, and 33 4 048 or equivalent.

10. Install the brake disc and caliper and the wheel in reverse order.

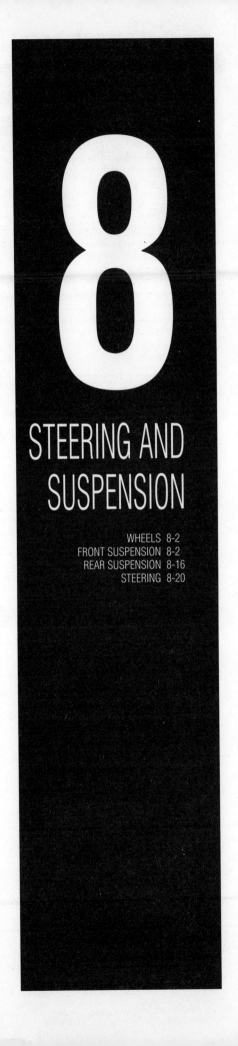

8

STEERING AND SUSPENSION

WHEELS

Wheel and Tire Assembly

REMOVAL & INSTALLATION

▶ See Figures 1 and 2

1. With the vehicle resting on the ground and the parking brake set, loosen the lug nuts or bolts depending on year, but do not remove.
2. Block the wheel at the opposite corner of the vehicle with a chock. Raise the vehicle at the jacking point.
3. Place a jackstand under the vehicle at the jacking point before continuing work.
4. Mark the relationship of the wheel to the hub to maintain the finish balance. Remove the lug nuts or bolts and remove the wheel.

To install:

5. Clean the surfaces of the wheel and the hub where they meet. Coat the hub with a thin layer of anti-seize.
6. If your vehicle wheels are attached via lug bolts, place the alignment tool provided in the vehicles tool kit into one of the bolt holes. This tool is the metal

Fig. 2 Placing an anti-seize compound around the hub before installing the wheel

rod with the plastic fitting on the end. Slide the wheel over the alignment tool and onto the hub. The alignment tool matches the lug holes in the wheel with the threaded holes in the hub.

7. Install the lug bolts and remove the alignment tool. Snug the lug bolts.
8. If your vehicle wheels are attached via lug nuts, position the wheel over the studs and install the nuts.
9. Lower the vehicle and tighten the lug bolts to 65–79 ft. lbs. (90–110 Nm) or lug nuts to 59–62 (77–81 Nm) in a crisscross pattern.

INSPECTION

With the wheel removed, check for obvious bends, dents or chip missing from the rim. Check for cracks at the spokes, inside and outside. With the wheel installed, spin the wheel on the hub to check for bends and wobbles not noticeable with the wheel removed.

Do not try to repair a damaged wheel by hammering it straight. Have an alloy wheel professionally repaired or replace it. Replace damaged steel wheels. Use only OEM approved replacement wheels and check with BMW or your dealer for approved makes of wheels. Do not change the size, width or offset without first checking with BMW if the change is acceptable.

Fig. 1 An example of a BMW alloy wheel and tire assembly. The center cap is removable on both steel and alloy wheels

FRONT SUSPENSION

▶ See Figures 3, 4, 5, 6 and 7

The front suspension on all BMWs is fully independent, utilizing MacPherson type struts with integral coil springs (the springs surround the structure of the strut, which contains the shock absorber). Transverse mounted wishbones are used on many models at the bottom to locate the lower end of the strut laterally as it moves up and down in relation to the body. A stabilizer bar is available which is mounted between the front

crossmember and the lower wish- bones. All suspension mounts are rubber cushioned.

✳✳ CAUTION

When removing front suspension components, be sure to support the car securely via the reinforced boxmember area adjacent to the front jacking points.

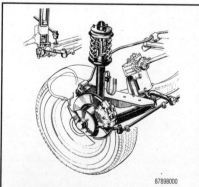

Fig. 3 An example of a BMW 2002 front steering and suspension assembly

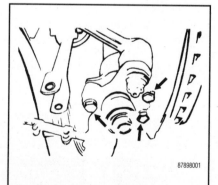

Fig. 4 An example of a BMW 320i front steering and suspension assembly

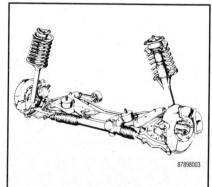

Fig. 5 An example of a BMW 3 Series front steering and suspension assembly

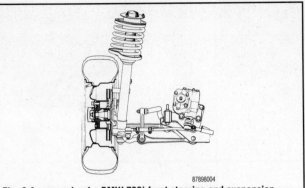

Fig. 6 An example of a BMW 733i front steering and suspension assembly

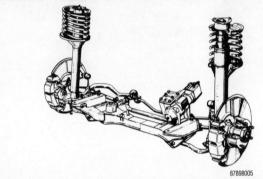

Fig. 7 An example of a BMW 528e front steering and suspension assembly

MacPherson Strut Assembly

REMOVAL & INSTALLATION

➡Not too much in the way of special tools and equipment is required to remove the struts from the front of your BMW, although care should be taken in ensuring proper torquing of the fasteners during reassembly. However, once the strut is off the car, special equipment is required to disassemble it safely. You will either have to purchase a special spring compressor or take the strut to a qualified repair shop. Rebuilding the shock absorbers contained within the body of the strut requires a good deal of specialized equipment and knowledge. By removing the strut and, if you're equipped to handle it, removing the spring, you could, however, substantially reduce the cost of doing the work.

1600, 2000 and 2002 Models

▶ See Figure 8

1. Raise the vehicle and support it safely on jackstands. Remove the wheel.
2. Disconnect the angle bracket from the strut assembly.
3. Disconnect the caliper, leaving the brake line attached. Tie the caliper to the vehicle body with a piece of wire so that the weight is not supported by the brake hose.
4. Disconnect the lower arm from the axle beam.
5. Remove the lockwire and disconnect the track rod arm from the strut assembly.
6. Remove the 3 retaining nuts and detach the strut assembly at the wheelhouse.
To install:
7. Install the strut assembly at the wheelhouse.
8. When reattaching the wishbone at the front axle beam, use a new self-locking nut and make sure the spacer touches the axle beam.
9. Tighten the components as follows:
  • Strut thrust bearing at wheelhouse: 16–17 ft. lbs. (21–22 Nm)

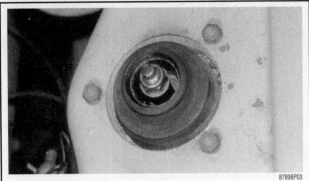

Fig. 8 Front strut upper mount on a 1600, 2000 and 2002—as seen from the engine compartment

  • Lower arm-to-axle: 123–137 ft. lbs. (160–178 Nm). This should be finalized after the vehicle has been lowered to the ground.
  • Track rod arm from strut: 18–24 ft. lbs. (23–31 Nm)
  • Caliper-to-strut: 58–69 ft. lbs. (75–90 Nm)

2500, 2800, Bavaria, 3000 and 3.0 Models

1. Raise the vehicle and support it safely. Remove the wheel.
2. Disconnect the brake caliper and suspend it from the vehicle body with a wire. Do not remove the brake hose.
3. Disconnect the angle bracket from the strut assembly.
4. Remove the lock wire and disconnect the track rod arm from the strut assembly.
5. Remove the 3 retaining nuts and detach the strut assembly at the wheel house.
To install:
6. Install the strut assembly at the wheel house and connect the track rod.
7. Complete the installation and use the following torque figures:
  • Brake caliper-to-strut: 59–70 ft. lbs. (77–91 Nm)
  • Track rod-to-strut: 33–44 ft. lbs. (43–57 Nm)
  • Bearing-to-wheelhouse: 16–18 ft. lbs. (21–23 Nm)

3 Series Models

320I MODELS

1. Raise the vehicle and support safely. Remove the wheel.
2. Detach the bracket at the strut assembly.
3. Disconnect and suspend the bake caliper with a wire from the vehicle body. Do not disconnect the brake line.
4. Remove the cotter pin and castle nut. Press the tie rod off the steering knuckle.
5. Remove the 3 retaining nuts and detach the strut assembly at the wheel house.
6. Install the strut assembly into the vehicle and attach it at the wheel house.
7. Install the cotter pin and castle nut and install the tie rod.
8. Connect the brake caliper and install the wheel.

2-WHEEL DRIVE MODELS (EXCEPT 320I)

▶ See Figures 9 thru 16

1. Disconnect the negative battery cable.
2. Raise and safely support the vehicle on jackstands. Remove the tire and wheel assembly.
3. Disconnect the brake pad wear indicator plug and ground wire. Pull the wires out of the holder on the strut. Remove the ABS pulse sender, if equipped.
4. Unbolt the caliper and pull it away from the strut, suspending it with a piece of wire from the body. Do not disconnect the brake line.
5. Remove the attaching nut and then detach the push rod on the stabilizer bar at the strut.
6. Unscrew the attaching nut and press off the ball joint stud with the proper tool.
7. Unscrew the nut and press off the tie rod joint.

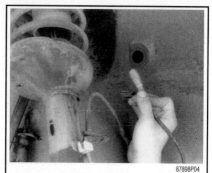

Fig. 9 If equipped with ABS or brake wear sensors, the harnesses should be unplugged

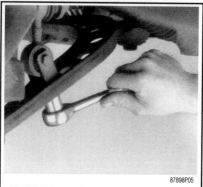

Fig. 10 Remove the outer stabilizer mount attached to the control arm

Fig. 11 Remove the ball joint nut . . .

Fig. 12 . . . and remove the ball joint from the strut assembly

Fig. 13 Remove the tie rod nut . . .

Fig. 14 . . . and remove the tie rod from the strut /steering knuckle assembly

Fig. 15 Remove the upper mounting nuts (in the engine compartment), but be sure the strut is supported from underneath

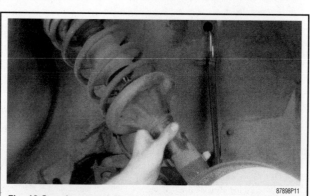

Fig. 16 Once free, carefully remove the strut assembly (note the strap used to support the brake caliper)

➡ Do not turn the steering rack to full lock or damage to the seals can occur.

8. Press the bottom of the strut outward and push it over the ball joint stud. Support the bottom of the strut.

9. Unscrew the nuts at the top of the strut, from inside the engine compartment, then remove the strut.

To install:

10. Install the strut into the wheel housing and install the nuts. Press down on the control arm and install the ball joint stud into the strut bore. Using new nuts, tighten the ball joint to 61 ft. lbs. (85 Nm) and the top strut mounting nuts to 16–17 ft. lbs. (21–23 Nm).

11. Install the tie rod into the steering arm and tighten the new nut to 26 ft. lbs. (37 Nm).

12. Install the stabilizer bar link and tighten to 43 ft. lbs. (59 Nm).

13. Install the brake caliper and tighten to 80 ft. lbs. (110 Nm).

14. Install the ABS sensor, the brake pad wear sensor and the brake hose. Connect the negative battery terminal.

15. Lower the vehicle. Have the alignment checked.

4-WHEEL DRIVE MODELS

1. Disconnect the negative battery cable.

2. Raise and safely support the vehicle. Remove the front tire and wheel assembly. Unplug the ABS pulse transmitter.

3. Lift out the lock plate at the center of the brake disc with a small prybar. Unscrew the collar nut.

4. Disconnect the brake pad wear indicator plug and the ground wire. Pull the wires and brake hose out of the clip on the spring strut. Then, disconnect the small rod at the strut.

5. Remove the brake caliper mounting bolts and support the assembly with a piece of wire, keeping stress off the brake hose.

6. Remove the attaching nut from the tie rod end. Then press the stud off the knuckle with the proper tool.

➡ Do not turn the steering rack to full lock or damage to the seals can occur.

7. Remove the attaching nut for ball joint and then press the stud off the knuckle with an appropriate tool.

8. Press the output shaft out of the center of the knuckle.

9. Support the spring strut from underneath. Remove the 3 bolts from the upper mount at the wheel housing. Remove the strut.

To install:

10. Install the strut into the wheel housing and install the nuts. Press down on the control arm and install the ball joint stud into the strut bore. Using new nuts, tighten the ball joint to 61 ft. lbs. (85 Nm) and the top strut mounting nuts to 16–17 ft. lbs. (21–23 Nm).

11. Pull the axle through the bearing. Install a new nut and tighten to 180 ft. lbs. (250 Nm). Install a new lockplate.

12. Install the tie rod into the steering arm and tighten the new nut to 26 ft. lbs. (37 Nm).

13. Install the stabilizer bar link and tighten to 43 ft. lbs. (59 Nm).

14. Install the brake caliper and tighten to 80 ft. lbs. (110 Nm).

15. Install the ABS sensor, the brake pad wear sensor and the brake hose. Connect the negative battery terminal. Have the alignment checked.

533i, 630CSi and 633CSi Models

1. Raise the vehicle and support safely on jackstands. Remove the wheel.

2. Disconnect the bracket at the strut assembly.

3. Disconnect the brake caliper and suspend from the vehicle body with wire. Do not remove the brake hose.

4. Remove the lock wire and disconnect the tie rod arm at the strut assembly.

5. Remove the 3 retaining nuts and detach the strut assembly at the wheelhouse.

To install:

6. Install the strut assembly into the vehicle and attach it at the wheel house.

7. Install the cotter pin and castle nut and install the tie rod.

8. Connect the brake caliper and install the wheel.

528e, 530i, 535i, 635CSi, M5, M6 and 735i Models

▶ **See Figure 17**

1. Raise the vehicle and support it securely on jackstands. Remove the front wheel.

2. Disconnect the brake caliper and suspend it with a piece of wire so there is no tension on the brake hose (do not disconnect the hose).

3. If removing the left side strut, lift the electrical plug out of the clip on the strut, disconnect the ground wire, and disconnect the plug.

4. On cars with ABS, disconnect the ABS pulse transmitter at the strut.

5. Disconnect the stabilizer push rod at the bracket on the side of the strut; To do this, use a wrench to hold the rod end on the flats just outside the bracket and unscrew the nut from the inside of the bracket.

6. Remove the bolts from the underside of the tie rod arm that attach the bottom of the strut to the arm. Then, move the strut outward.

7. On the 735i, remove the cap. Support the bottom of the strut and then remove the 3 nuts attaching the strut to the top of the fender well.

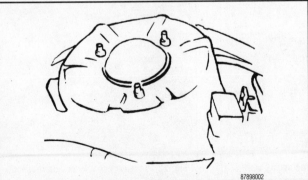

87898002

Fig. 17 Upper strut mount assembly accessed from the engine compartment—5 and 7 Series models

To install:

8. Install the strut in position on the vehicle.

9. Use new self-locking nuts on the studs that pass through the fender well. Align the bottom of the strut with the tie rod arm so the tab on the arm fits into the notch on the bottom of the strut.

733i Models

1. Raise the vehicle and support safely on jackstands. Remove the wheel.

2. Disconnect the vibration strut from the control arm.

3. Disconnect the bracket and clamps from the strut assembly.

4. Disconnect the wire connection and press out the wire from the clamp on the spring strut tube.

5. Remove the brake caliper and suspend it from the vehicle body with a wire. Do not remove the brake hose.

6. Disconnect the tie rod from the shock absorber.

7. Remove the 3 retaining nuts and disconnect the strut assembly from the wheelhouse.

To install:

8. Install the strut assembly into the vehicle and attach it at the wheel house.

9. Install the cotter pin and castle nut and install the tie rod.

10. Connect the brake caliper and install the wheel.

Strut Spring

REMOVAL & INSTALLATION

▶ **See Figure 18**

➡ **These procedures are for struts assemblies that have been removed from the vehicle.**

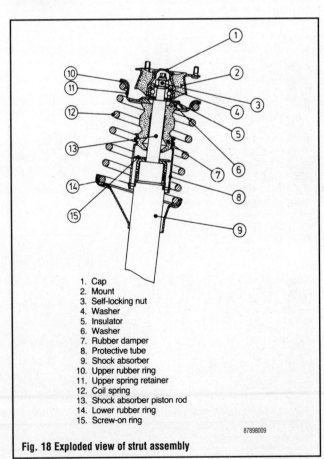

1. Cap
2. Mount
3. Self-locking nut
4. Washer
5. Insulator
6. Washer
7. Rubber damper
8. Protective tube
9. Shock absorber
10. Upper rubber ring
11. Upper spring retainer
12. Coil spring
13. Shock absorber piston rod
14. Lower rubber ring
15. Screw-on ring

87898009

Fig. 18 Exploded view of strut assembly

1600, 2000 and 2002 Models

♦ **See Figures 19 and 20**

✳✳ **CAUTION**

In order to disassemble the spring and shock absorber strut assembly, it is necessary to use a special spring compressor. It is extremely dangerous to use any other method of compressing the spring, as the spring could slip while compressed, possibly striking you and causing serious injury. For this reason, if a spring compressor of the proper type is not available, this procedure is best left to your dealer or a qualified repair shop.

➡ **If a spring is determined to be worn out or broken, it is necessary also to replace the other spring on the same axle.**

1. Install the special spring compressor on the strut assembly and compress the spring.
2. Lift off the plastic sealing cap from the top of the strut. Unscrew the elastic locknut, while holding the shock absorber piston rod steady. Lift out the telescopic leg support bearing assembly from the top of the strut.
3. Remove the upper spring cup and support.
4. Slowly release the compressor tool until the spring is completely tension-free. Remove the coil spring, and lower spring cup.
5. Check the condition of the upper and lower spring cups (collars), and the inner rubber bump stop buffer. Replace them if they are cracked, dry-rotted or otherwise damaged.
6. Inspect the coil spring and shock absorber. Coil spring free length is 13 inches (33cm). If the spring is sagged much beyond this, it should be replaced, of course along with the other front spring as they are a matched pair.
7. If the shock absorber is leaking excessively or it displays weak damping action, it and the one on the other side should be replaced.

8. Install the spring onto the strut using the following assembly notes:
   a. The conical end of the inner rubber auxiliary spring must face the lower spring cup.
   b. The coil spring must be compressed and the ends must locate on the stops in the upper and lower spring cups.
   c. When installing the telescopic leg support bearing, make sure that the inner curvature of the sealing washer faces the support bearing.
   d. Tighten the locknut for the strut assembly to 52 ft. lbs (68 Nm). Only after the locknut is tightened to its final figure should you release the spring compressor, and then, very slowly.

2500, 2800, Bavaria, 3000 and 3.0 Models

1. Compress the coil spring with a spring compressor.
2. Remove the rubber cap, lock the piston rod with one wrench, and use another wrench to remove the locknut.
3. Remove the strut thrust bearing from the top of the strut.
4. Gradually loosen the spring compressors and remove the spring plate and spring.
5. Check the rubber bushings above and below the spring and replace if necessary.
6. Wind the spring into the spring plates to spring ends rest against stops, and then reverse the remaining procedures to install, keeping the following points in mind:
   a. The internal dish of the sealing washer that goes right above the thrust bearing should face the spring. Another washer goes on top of that.
   b. Tighten the retaining nut to 53–59 ft. lbs. (69–77 Nm).

3, 5, 6 and 7 Series Models

EXCEPT 318I AND 320I

♦ **See Figures 21 thru 28**

✳✳ **CAUTION**

This procedure calls for the spring to be compressed. A compressed spring has high potential energy and if released suddenly can cause severe damage and personal injury. If not comfortable with dealing with a compressed spring, have a professional technician remove the spring from the strut for you.

1. Remove the strut from the vehicle.
2. Using a proper spring compressor, compress the spring.
3. Remove the top nut of the strut mount. Counterhold the strut rod during removal.
4. Pull the strut mount off the strut rod. Note the positioning of the spacers and washer for replacement.
5. Pull the spring off the strut.
6. Remove the rubber bump stop and inspect. If torn, replace with new piece.

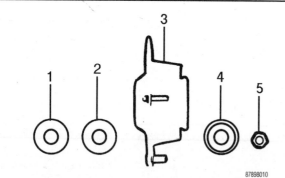

87898010

Fig. 19 Disassembled upper strut mount assembly. Numbers indicate order of installation from the spring to the locknut

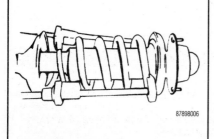

87898006

Fig. 20 Strut assembly mounted in spring compressor. Other models of spring compressors are available

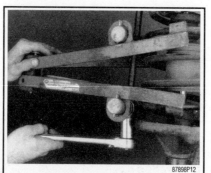

87898P12

Fig. 21 Using a scissor type spring compressor tool to safely compress the strut spring

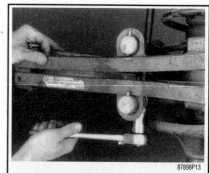

87898P13

Fig. 22 The spring should be compressed until there is space between the upper portion of the spring and the metal cap

Fig. 23 Remove the locknut and washer at the top of the strut

Fig. 24 Remove the upper strut mount

Fig. 25 Remove the washer between the upper strut mount and the spring cap

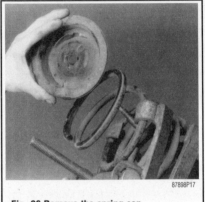

Fig. 26 Remove the spring cap

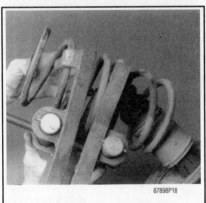

Fig. 27 Lift the compressed spring off

Fig. 28 Inspect the rubber bump stop (replace if worn)

To install:

7. Install the spring and strut mount with all the spacers and washers in their original positions. Tighten the new strut rod nut to 47 ft. lbs. (65 Nm).

8. Release the spring slowly and check that it seats in the spring holders. Install the strut in the vehicle.

318I AND 320I MODELS

♦ See Figure 19

1. Compress the spring coil with a special tool such as BMW 313 110. Lift off the rubber cap.

2. Hold the piston rod with one wrench while removing the self-locking nut with another.

3. Release the spring and remove the strut support bearing.

4. Install the spring on the strut assembly, keeping the following points in mind:

   a. A tapered special tool is available to facilitate installation of the support bearing over the shock absorber piston rod.

   b. Check mounting rings for the spring, auxiliary spring (which fits over the piston rod) and outer tube, and replace any which are faulty.

   c. Make sure the spring ends rest on the locating shoulders in both upper and lower spring retainers before compressing the spring and support bearing. Replace the self locking nut which goes on the piston rod, and tighten to 57–62 ft. lbs. (74–81 Nm).

   d. Sequence of installing the spring is: large washer, sealing washer, support bearing, concave washer and self locking nut.

Strut Inserts

TESTING

The basic test for strut insert performance is the vehicle"s behavior on the road. Strut insert have the job of eliminating spring bounce shortly after the car hits a bump. If the car tends to lose control over washboard surfaces or if there is any sign of fluid leakage, strut insert work is required.

If you're uncertain about strut insert performance, you can jounce test the car. To do this, rest your weight on the front bumper and bounce it repeatedly, in sympathy with the natural rhythm of the springs until the car is bouncing up and down as fast as you can make it. Then release it, and carefully observe its behavior. The car should move upward, then return to its normal riding height and virtually stop. Several bounces after release indicates worn strut inserts.

REMOVAL & INSTALLATION

With the MacPherson strut type front suspension used on BMWs, the strut inserts are an integral part of the strut. Since the strut and associated parts are a very expensive assembly, the strut inserts in front are replaceable. This is an extremely difficult job requiring a good deal of specialized mechanical skill and a number of special tools.

All Models

♦ See Figures 29, 30 and 31

✶✶✶ CAUTION

This procedure calls for the spring to be compressed. A compressed spring has high potential energy and if released suddenly can cause severe damage and personal injury. If not comfortable with dealing with a compressed spring, have a professional technician remove the spring from the strut for you.

1. Remove the strut from the vehicle and mount in a vise using a strut holder. This will prevent damage to the strut tube.

2. Using a proper spring compressor, compress the spring and lock into place. Use all the safety hooks provided and never point the compressed spring at a person.

3. Remove the top nut of the strut mount. Counterhold the strut rod during removal.

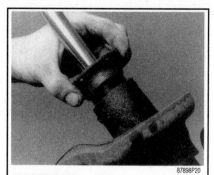

Fig. 29 With the spring and rubber bump stop removed, loosen and remove the strut insert gland nut

Fig. 30 Slide the strut insert out of the housing. Some inserts will come out in pieces

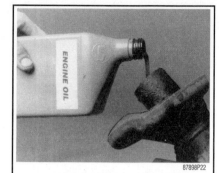

Fig. 31 Before installing the new insert, pour oil or full strength engine coolant into the strut housing

4. Pull the strut mount off the strut rod. Note the positioning of the spacers and washer for replacement.

5. Pull the spring off the strut and place somewhere safe. Do not release the compression of the spring.

6. Remove the rubber bump stop, and replace if worn.

7. Remove the gland nut at the top of the strut housing. Turn the nut and allow the pressure to bleed off. A special tool is sometimes needed to remove the nut. Some aftermarket strut manufacturers provide a tool with the replacement cartridges.

8. Pull the old cartridge out of the strut and pour out the oil or fluid in the strut housing.

To install:

9. Fill the strut tube with enough engine oil or full strength anti-freeze so when the new cartridge is installed, oil fills the tube but doesn't overflow. If the strut rod diameter is greater than 1.3 inches (33mm) do not use oil.

10. Install the new cartridge and any spacers that where provided by the strut insert manufacturer. Install the gland nut and tighten to 94 ft. lbs. (130 Nm).

11. Install the spring and strut mount with all the spacers and washers in their original positions. Tighten the new strut rod nut to 47 ft. lbs. (65 Nm).

12. Release the spring slowly and check that it seats in the spring holders. Install the strut in the vehicle.

Wishbone Arm

REMOVAL & INSTALLATION

1600, 2000 and 2002 Models

1. Raise the vehicle and support it safely on jackstands. Remove the wheel.

2. Disconnect the trailing link at the lower arm.

3. Disconnect the lower arm from the front axle beam and push off at the trailing link.

4. Remove the cotter pin and castle nut. Press off the track rod at the track rod arm with special tool such as BMW 00 7 500 or equivalent.

5. Remove the lockwire and nuts. Remove the track rod arm with the lower arm.

6. Remove the cotter pin and nut. Press off the track rod arm from the guide joint with a special tool such as BMW 00 7 500 or equivalent.

To install:

7. Install the track rod arm and lower arm into position. Note the following points:

   a. Use a new self-locking nut where the trailing link connects to the wishbone, and tighten to 51–65 ft. lbs. (66–84 Nm). (Also, make sure the convex faces of both washers face the wishbone.

   b. Use a new self-locking nut where the wishbone attaches to the front axle beam. Also make sure the spacer is on the axle beam side and that you install washers on either side of the wishbone.

   c. Tighten the track rod-to-track arm castellated nut to 25–29 ft. lbs. (32–38 Nm).

   d. Tighten the nuts attaching the track rod arm and wishbone to the bottom of the strut to 18–24 ft. lbs. (23–31 Nm). Replace the lockwire.

   e. Tighten the castellated nut attaching the track rod arm to the wishbone to 43–50 ft. lbs. (56–65 Nm).

   f. Check the guide (ball) joint end play and if it exceeds 0.08 inches (2mm) replace the guide joint.

2500, 2800, Bavaria, 3000 and 3.0 Models

1. Raise the vehicle and support it safely on jackstands. Remove the wheel.

2. Remove the locknut and disconnect the track rod arm from the strut assembly.

3. Press the guide (ball) joint out of the track rod arm with an extractor.

4. Disconnect the lower arm from the axle carrier.

5. Disconnect the trailing link from the lower arm.

6. Connect the trailing link to the lower arm and connect the lower arm to the axle carrier. Note the following points during installation:

   a. Tighten the bolts fastening the track rod arm to the strut to 33–44 ft. lbs. (56–57 Nm). Use new locknut(s).

   b. When attaching the wishbone to the front axle carrier, tighten it snugly, complete assembly of the front suspension, and then lower the vehicle and allow it to sit at its normal ride height. Tighten the stop nut to 60–66 ft. lbs. (78–86 Nm).

   c. Make sure, when reattaching the trailing link to the wishbone that the convex faces of the washers are outward. Check the play of the guide (ball) joint and replace it if the play is greater than 0.08 inches (2mm).

   d. Some wishbones and some track rods have metal stops cast integrally into the structure. A wishbone with a stop may be used in conjunction with a track rod arm without a stop, but if the track rod arm has a stop, the wishbone must also have a stop.

   e. Tighten the nut attaching the trailing link to the wishbone to 52–66 ft. lbs. (66–86 Nm).

Control Arm

REMOVAL & INSTALLATION

3 Series Models

♦ See Figures 32, 33, 34, 35 and 36

1. Raise and safely support the vehicle on jackstands. Remove the front wheel assembly.

2. Disconnect the rear control arm bushing bracket where it connects to the body by removing the bolts.

3. Remove the nut and disconnect the link on the front stabilizer bar where it connects to the stabilizer bar.

4. Unscrew the nut which attaches the control arm to the crossmember and remove the nut from above the crossmember. Then, use a plastic hammer to knock the stud out of the crossmember.

5. Unscrew the nut and press off the ball joint where the control arm attaches to the lower end of the strut, using the proper tool.

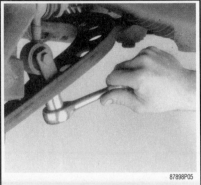

Fig. 32 Remove the stabilizer bar retaining nut attached to the control arm

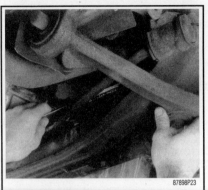

Fig. 33 Remove the nut securing the center portion of the control arm

Fig. 34 Remove the nut securing the ball joint

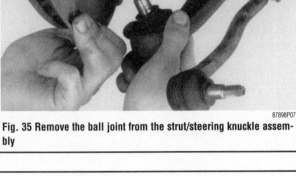

Fig. 35 Remove the ball joint from the strut/steering knuckle assembly

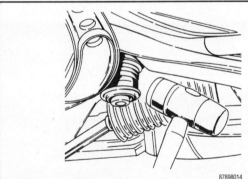

Fig. 36 Use a soft-faced hammer to loosen any control arm mounts which will not come free

To install:

6. Make sure the ball joints studs and the bores in the crossmember and strut are clean before inserting the studs. Replace the original nuts with replacement nuts and washers. Tighten the ball joint nut to 47 ft. lbs. (65 Nm) for 2-wheel drive and 61.5 ft. lbs. (93 Nm) for 4-wheel drive. Tighten the control arm to subframe nut to 61 ft. lbs. (85 Nm) for 2-wheel drive and 72 ft. lbs. (100 Nm) for 4-wheel drive.

7. Install the control arm bushing bracket and tighten the bolts to 30 ft. lbs. (42 Nm).

8. Install the stabilizer bar link and tighten to 43 ft. lbs. (59 Nm).

320i Models

1. Raise the vehicle and support it safely, remove the wheel. Disconnect the stabilizer at the control arm.

2. Disconnect the control arm at the front axle support.

3. Remove the cotter pin and castellated nut.

4. Press the control arm off the steering knuckle with special tool BMW 31 1 100 or equivalent.

5. Install the control arm to the steering knuckle using the special tool.

6. Install the castle nut and cotter pin. Connect the control arm at the front axle and connect the stabilizer bar.

528e, 530i, 533i and 633CSi Models

▶ **See Figure 37**

1. Raise the vehicle and support safely on jackstands. Remove the wheel.

2. Disconnect the stabilizer bar at the control arm.

3. Remove the tension strut nut on the control arm.

4. Disconnect the control arm at the front axle support and remove it from the tension strut.

5. Remove the lock wire, remove the bolts and take the control arm off the spring strut.

6. Remove the cotter pin and nut.

7. Using special tool BMW 00 7 500 or equivalent, pull the guide joint from the tie rod arm.

To install:

8. Install the guide joint to the tie rod with the special tool.

9. Install the control arm to the spring strut and connect it to front axle support. Install the stabilizer to the control arm.

535i, 635i, M5, M6, 635CSi and 735i Models

1. Raise and support the vehicle securely on jackstands. Remove the wheel.

2. Remove the 3 bolts that fasten the bottom of the strut to the steering knuckle.

3. Remove the cotter pin and castellated nut. Use a ball joint remover (BMW 31 1 110 or equivalent) to press the ball joint end of the control arm off the steering knuckle.

4. Remove the self locking nut. Then, remove the through bolt and the 2 washers, slide the inner end of the strut and bushing out of the front suspension crossmember.

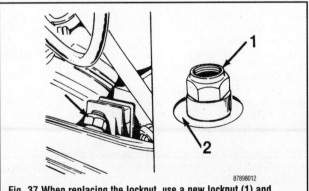

Fig. 37 When replacing the locknut, use a new locknut (1) and washer(2)

5. Install the control arm to the vehicle, noting the following points:

    a. Make sure both washers are replaced to cushion the bushing where it contacts the suspension crossmember.

    b. Replace the bushing if it is worn or cracked.

    c. Use a new self-locking nut on the bolt fastening the inner end of the strut.

    d. Align the bottom of the strut with the steering knuckle so the tab on the arm fits into the notch on the bottom of the strut. Install the bolts with a locking type sealer.

    e. When installing the arm ball joint onto the steering knuckle, tighten the nut until a castellation lines up with the cotter pin hole and then use a new cotter pin in the nut.

    f. Final tighten the through bolt for the inner end of the arm after the car is on the ground and at normal ride height.

733i Models

1. Raise the vehicle and support safely. Remove the wheel.
2. Disconnect the vibration strut from the control arm.
3. Disconnect the control arm from the axle carrier.
4. Disconnect the tie rod arm from the front strut.
5. Remove the cotter pin and castellated nut. Press off the control arm with special tool BMW 31 1 110 or equivalent.
6. Install the control arm onto the vehicle. Connect the tie rod to the front strut and connect the control arm to the axle carrier.
7. Use new self-locking nuts on the connections at the vibration strut and axle carrier. On 1983–88 models, when reconnecting the arm to the tie rod arm, use a bolt tightener BMW No. 81 22 9 400 086 and make sure the threads and bolt holes are clean.

BUSHING REPLACEMENT

The bushings must be pressed out of the housing bores. BMW bushings are notoriously hard to press out of the housings. Use a high capacity hydraulic press, penetrating lubricant and the proper sized mandrels for the press. Do not use sockets to try to replace the bushings. Mark the relationship of the bushing to the bore for correct replacement positioning. Because of the difficult nature of this job, it is recommended that a BMW or professional mechanic perform this job.

Thrust Rod

REMOVAL & INSTALLATION

1986–88 5 and 7 Series Models

♦ See Figure 38

The 5 Series BMW uses a multi-link type suspension. There is a lower control arm to support the strut housing and a thrust rod to control fore and aft motion. The thrust rod is not used on 3 Series vehicles.

Always replace the strut rods in pairs. If the strut rods are not replaced in pairs, uneven driving response may result.

1. Raise and safely support the front end on jackstands. Do not place the jackstands under any suspension parts. Remove the wheel.
2. Remove the thrust rod ball joint nut and press the stud out of the steering knuckle with a ball joint remover tool.
3. Remove the nut and bolt at the subframe end of the strut rod. Remove the strut rod.

To install:

4. Install the strut to the subframe using a new nut and washer on both sides. Do not tighten at this point.
5. Clean the grease and dirt off of the ball joint stud and bore. Install the ball joint stud into the steering knuckle and tighten the new nut to 67 ft. lbs. (93 Nm).
6. Install the wheel and lower the vehicle to the ground. Load 150 lbs. into each of the front seats and in the center of the rear seat. Tighten the control arm to subframe bolt to 92 ft. lbs. (127 Nm).

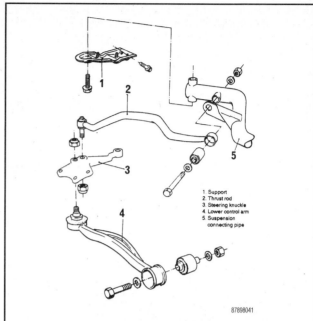

Fig. 38 Exploded view of 5 and 7 series control arm and thrust rod assembly

BUSHING REPLACEMENT

The bushings must be pressed out of the housing bores. BMW bushings are notoriously hard to press out of the housings. Use a high capacity hydraulic press, penetrating lubricant and the proper sized mandrels for the press. Do not use sockets to try to replace the bushings. Mark the relationship of the bushing to the bore for correct replacement positioning. Because of the difficult nature of this job, it is recommended that a BMW or professional mechanic perform this job.

Stabilizer Bar

REMOVAL & INSTALLATION

1600, 2000, 2002, 2500, 2800, 3000, Bavaria and 3.0 Models

1. Raise and support the front end securely on jackstands.
2. Disconnect the stabilizer bar at the control arms.
3. Remove the attaching nut and then detach the push rod on the stabilizer bar at the strut assembly.
4. Unscrew the nut which attaches the front of the stabilizer bar to the crossmember and remove the nut from above the crossmember.
5. Lower the stabilizer bar down and away from the engine.
6. Installation is the reverse of removal. Tighten the pushrod nuts to 24–34 ft. lbs. (31–44 Nm).

1975–83 3, 5, 6 and 7 Series Models

1. Raise and support the front end on jackstands.

    a. On the 320, 528e, 533i and 633CSi models, disconnect the stabilizer bar at the control arms.

    b. On the 318i models remove the attaching nut and then detach the push rod on the stabilizer bar at the strut.

    c. On the 524td, 528e, 633CSi models, disconnect the stabilizer push rod at the bracket on the side of the strut. To do this, use a wrench to hold the rod end on the flats just outside the bracket and unscrew the nut from the inside of the bracket.

    d. On the 318i models, remove the nut and disconnect the thrust rod on the front stabilizer bar where it connects to the center of the control arm.

e. On the 318i models. unscrew the nut which attaches the front of the stabilizer bar to the crossmember and remove the nut from above the crossmember. Then, use a plastic hammer to knock this support pin out of the crossmember.

2. Installation is the reverse of removal. Tighten the pushrod nuts to 24–34 ft. lbs. (31–44 Nm).

1984–88 3 Series Models

▶ See Figures 39 and 40

1. Raise and support the front end on jackstands.
2. Remove the stabilizer bar link nuts at the stabilizer bar. Disconnect the links from the bar on both sides.
3. Remove the bolts holding the left control arm bracket.
4. Remove the bolts holding the stabilizer bar and bushings to the body. Remove the stabilizer bar out from the left side.

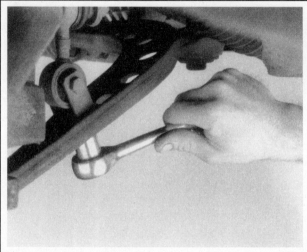

87898P05

Fig. 39 Remove the stabilizer mount attached to the control arm

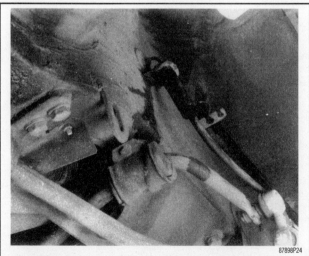

87898P24

Fig. 40 Stabilizer bar mount behind the front of the control arm on the vehicle frame

To install:

5. Install the stabilizer bar and bushings. Tighten the bushing mounts to 16 ft. lbs. (22 Nm) with the wrench flats parallel to the edges of the bar. Install the left control arm bracket and tighten the bolts to 30 ft. lbs. (42 Nm).
6. Install the stabilizer bar links and tighten the nuts to 43 ft. lbs. (59 Nm). Tighten the control arm mounting nut to 30 ft. lbs. (42 Nm).

1984–88 5, 6 and 7 Series Models

1. Raise and support the front end.
2. Remove the stabilizer bar link nuts at the stabilizer bar. Disconnect the links from the bar on both sides.
3. Remove the bolts holding the stabilizer bar and bushings to the body. Remove the stabilizer bar.

To install:

4. Install the stabilizer bar and bushings. The bushing slit will face down. Tighten the bushing mounts to 16 ft. lbs. (22 Nm).
5. Install the stabilizer bar links and tighten the nuts to 43 ft. lbs. (59 Nm) with the wrench flats parallel to the edges of the bar. Tighten the link to control arm mounting nut to 30 ft. lbs. (42 Nm).

Ball Joint

REMOVAL & INSTALLATION

➡These joints are replaceable only on the 1600 and 2002 Series. On other models, the entire control arm must be replaced if the joint is defective.

1. Remove the lower wishbone from the car as outlined in this section.
2. Clamp the wishbone in a vise.
3. Drill out the rivets which retain the ball joint to the wishbone.
4. Install a new guide joint using new hex bolts and nuts.
5. Install the lower wishbone as outlined in this section.

Front Wheel Bearings

ADJUSTMENT

➡Refer to the procedure in Section 9 of this manual for a detailed explanation.

REMOVAL & INSTALLATION

➡Wheel bearings on 1983–88 318i, 325, 5 and 6 Series models, and 1987–88 7 Series are permanently sealed bearings and do not require periodic disassembly and packing.

1600, 2000 and 2002 Models

1. Remove the wheel. Unbolt and remove the caliper. Hang it from the body. Do not disconnect or stress the hose. On models with a separate disc, remove the locking cap by gripping carefully on both sides with a pair of pliers, remove the cotter pin from the castellated nut, and remove the nut and, where equipped, the slotted washer. Then, remove the entire hub and bearing.
2. Remove the shaft sealing ring and take out the roller bearing.
3. The outer bearing race may be forced out through the recesses in the wheel hub. A BMW puller 00 8 550 or the equivalent may also be used.
4. Clean all bearings and races and the interior of the hub with alcohol, and allow to air dry.

➡Do not dry with compressed air as this can damage the bearings by rolling them over one another unlubricated or force one loose from the cage causing injury. Replace all bearings and races if there is any sign of scoring or galling.

5. Press in the outer races with a suitable sleeve. Pack a new shaft seal with grease and refill the hub with fresh grease.

6. Assemble in this order: outer race; inner race; outer race; inner race; shaft seal.

7. If necessary, adjust the wheel bearing play.

3 Series Models

▶ **See Figure 41**

➡**The bearings on the 318i and 325 models are only removed if they are worn. They cannot be removed without destroying them (due to side thrust created by the bearing puller). They should not be disassembled or repacked.**

1. Remove the front wheel and support the car. Remove the attaching bolts and remove and suspend the brake caliper, hanging it from the body so as to avoid putting stress on the brake line.

2. Remove the setscrew with an Allen wrench. Pull off the brake disc and pry off the dust cover with a small prybar.

3. Using a chisel, knock the tab on the collar nut away from the shaft. Unscrew and discard the nut.

4. Pull off the bearing with a puller set such as 31 2 101/102/104 or equivalent and discard it. On the M3, use a puller set such as 31 2 102/105/106. On the M3, install the main bracket of the puller with 3 wheel bolts.

5. If the inside bearing inner race remains on the stub axle, unbolt and remove the dust guard. Bend back the inner dust guard and pull the inner race off with a special tool capable of getting under the race (BMW 00 7 500 and 33 1 309 or equivalent). Reinstall the dust guard.

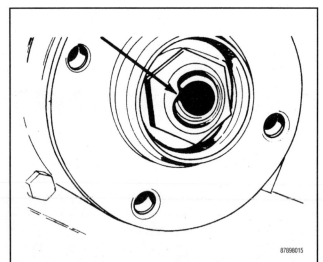

Fig. 41 An example of a collar nut which is locked by tapping with a chisel or other suitable tool

To install:

6. If the dust guard has been removed, install a new one. Install a special tool (BMW 31 2 120 or equivalent. On M3 models, use 31 2 110 or equivalent) over the stub axle and screw it in for the entire length of the guide sleeve's threads. Press the bearing on.

7. Reverse the remaining removal procedures to install the disc and caliper. Tighten the wheel hub collar nut to 188 ft. lbs. (244 Nm) Lock the collar nut by bending over the tab.

4-Wheel Drive Models

Please refer to Section 7 of this manual for details of front wheel bearing removal on 4-wheel drive vehicles.

528e, 530i, 535i, 633CSi, 635CSi, M5 and M6 Models

1. Raise the vehicle and support it securely on jackstands. Unbolt and remove the caliper, suspending it so the brake line will not be stressed.

2. Remove the Allen bolt and remove the brake disc.

3. Remove the grease cap. Use a flat punch and hammer to push the punched-in area of the retaining nut away from the groove in the axle. If necessary, chisel the nut off. Then unscrew the bearing retaining nut.

4. Install a puller 31 2 100 or equivalent. Screw the tool's bolt inward to pull the bearing housing out of the axle.

To install:

5. Install a new bearing assembly cover on the stub axle. Use special tool set 31 2 110 to pull the new bearing assembly into the axle.

6. Install a washer and a new retaining nut. Tighten the nut to 210 ft. lbs. (273 Nm). Use a center punch and hammer to punch the inner edge of the nut into the indentation on the axle shaft. Install a new grease cap coated with a sealer such as BMW 88 228 407 420.

733i Models

1. Remove the front wheel. Detach the brake line clamp and bracket on the strut. On cars with ABS, remove the rubber boot, then unbolt and remove the anti-lock sensor.

2. Detach the caliper without disconnecting the brake line and suspend it with a piece of wire.

3. Use a tool such as 21 2 000 to remove the end cap. Remove the cotter pin and unscrew the castellated nut. Then, remove the stepped washer, brake disc, and wheel hub.

4. Use an Allen type wrench to unscrew the bolt and separate the disc from the wheel hub.

5. Lift out the shaft seal. Remove the tapered roller bearings. Knock out the outer races if they show scoring with a punch by tapping all around.

6. Press in new outer races with special tools such as 31 2 061 for the inside bearings and 31 2 062 for the outside bearings.

To install:

7. Pack the inner races with wheel bearing grease. The order of installation is: outer race, inner race, outer race, inner race, shaft seal. To install the seal, lubricate the sealing lip of the shaft seal with grease and install the seal with a tool such as 31 2 040. Repack all bearings thoroughly with wheel bearing grease before installation.

8. Adjust the wheel bearings as described in this section.

735i Models

▶ **See Figure 41**

1. Remove the front wheel and support the car. Remove the attaching bolts and remove and suspend the brake caliper, hanging it from the body so as to avoid putting stress on the brake line.

2. Remove the setscrew with an Allen wrench. Pull off the brake disc and pry off the dust cover with a small prybar.

3. Using a chisel, knock the tab on the collar nut away from the shaft. Unscrew and discard the nut.

4. Install a puller collar such as 31 2 105 to the bearing housing with 3 bolts. Install a puller such as 31 2 102 and 312 2 106 and pull off the bearing and discard it.

5. If the inside bearing inner race remains on the stub axle, unscrew and remove the dust guard, using a socket extension. Bend back the inner dust guard and pull the inner race off with a special tool capable of getting under the race (BMW 31 2 100 and 31 2 102 or equivalent). Reinstall the dust guard and install a new dust cover.

To install:

6. Install a special tool (BMW 31 2 110 or equivalent) over the stub axle and screw it in for the entire length of the guide sleeve's threads. Slide the bearing on and follow it with 31 2 100 or equivalent, and use this tool to press the bearing on.

7. Reverse the remaining removal procedures to install the disc and caliper. Tighten the wheel hub collar nut to 210 ft. lbs. (273 Nm). Lock the collar nut by bending over the tab.

8. Install a new grease cap coated with a sealer such as BMW 88 228 407 420.

Wheel Alignment

If the tires are worn unevenly, if the vehicle is not stable on the highway or if the handling seems uneven in spirited driving, the wheel alignment should be checked. If an alignment problem is suspected, first check for improper tire inflation and other possible causes. These can be worn suspension or steering components, accident damage or even unmatched tires. If any worn or damaged components are found, they must be replaced before the wheels can be properly aligned. Wheel alignment requires very expensive equipment and involves minute adjustments which must be accurate; it should only be performed by a trained technician. Take your vehicle to a properly equipped shop.

Following is a description of the alignment angles which are adjustable on most vehicles and how they affect vehicle handling. Although these angles can apply to both the front and rear wheels, usually only the front suspension is adjustable.

CASTER

▶ **See Figure 42**

Looking at a vehicle from the side, caster angle describes the steering axis rather than a wheel angle. The steering knuckle is attached to a control arm or strut at the top and a control arm at the bottom. The wheel pivots around the line between these points to steer the vehicle. When the upper point is tilted back, this is described as positive caster. Having a positive caster tends to make the wheels self-centering, increasing directional stability. Excessive positive caster makes the wheels hard to steer, while an uneven caster will cause a pull to one side. Overloading the vehicle or sagging rear springs will affect caster, as will raising the rear of the vehicle. If the rear of the vehicle is lower than normal, the caster becomes more positive.

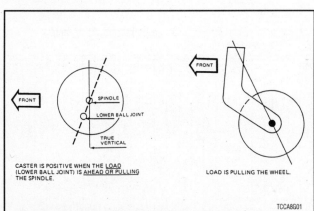

Fig. 42 Caster affects straight-line stability. Caster wheels used on shopping carts, for example, employ positive caster

CAMBER

▶ **See Figure 43**

Looking from the front of the vehicle, camber is the inward or outward tilt of the top of wheels. When the tops of the wheels are tilted in, this is negative camber; if they are tilted out, it is positive. In a turn, a slight amount of negative camber helps maximize contact of the tire with the road. However, too much negative camber compromises straight-line stability, increases bump steer and torque steer.

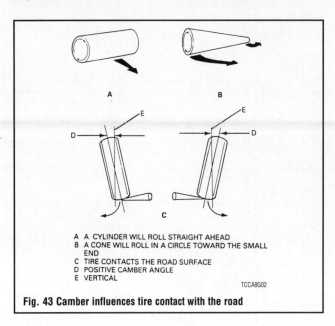

A A CYLINDER WILL ROLL STRAIGHT AHEAD
B A CONE WILL ROLL IN A CIRCLE TOWARD THE SMALL END
C TIRE CONTACTS THE ROAD SURFACE
D POSITIVE CAMBER ANGLE
E VERTICAL

Fig. 43 Camber influences tire contact with the road

TOE

▶ **See Figure 44**

Looking down at the wheels from above the vehicle, toe angle is the distance between the front of the wheels, relative to the distance between the back of the wheels. If the wheels are closer at the front, they are said to be toed-in or to have negative toe. A small amount of negative toe enhances directional stability and provides a smoother ride on the highway.

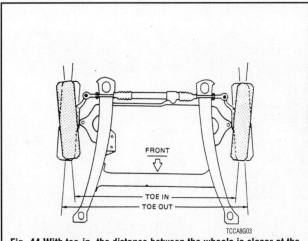

Fig. 44 With toe-in, the distance between the wheels is closer at the front than at the rear

Wheel Alignment

Year	Model		Caster Range (deg.)	Caster Preferred Setting (deg.)	Camber Range (deg.)	Camber Preferred Setting (deg.)	Toe-in (in.)	Steering Axis Inclination (deg.)
1970–76	1600,2000,2002	Front	—	4P	—	½P	.07	8½P
		Rear	—	2N	—	—	—	—
1970–76	2500,Bavaria	Front	—	9⅔P	—	½P	.07	8½P
	2800,3.0	Rear	—	2N	—	—	—	—
1977–81	320i	Front	—	8⅓P	—	0	.07	10½P
		Rear	—	2N	—	—	—	—
1977–78	530i	Front	—	7⅔P	—	½P	.07	8½P
		Rear	—	2N	—	—	—	—
1979–81	528i	Front	—	7⅔P	—	0	.06	8½P
		Rear	—	2N	—	—	—	—
1978–81	633CSi	Front	—	7⅔P	—	0	.06	8P
		Rear	—	2N	—	—	—	—
1978–79	733i	Front	—	9P	—	0	.03	11½P
		Rear	—	1½N	—	—	—	—
1982	320i	Front	—	8⁵⁄₁₆P	—	0	¹⁄₆	10⁵⁄₁₆P
		Rear	—	8⁵⁄₁₆P	—	0	¹⁄₆	10⁵⁄₁₆P
	633CSi	Front	—	7⅔P	—	0	.060	8P
		Rear	—	—	—	2N	.080	—
	733i	Front	—	9P	—	0	³⁄₆₄P	11⁹⁄₁₆
		Rear	—	—	—	1½N	³⁄₁₆P	—
1983	320i	Front	—	8⁵⁄₁₆P	—	0	¹⁄₆	10⁵⁄₁₆P
		Rear	—	—	—	2N	¹⁄₃₂P	—
	63CSi	Front	—	8¼P	—	⁵⁄₁₆N	⁵⁄₆₄P	12³⁄₁₆P
		Rear	—	—	—	2⁵⁄₁₆N	⁵⁄₆₄P	—
	733i	Front	—	8¼P	—	⅓N	.078	12³⁄₁₆P
		Rear	—	—	—	2N	.08	—
1984	318i	Front	8¼P–9¼P	8¾P	1¹⁄₁₀N–¹⁄₁₀N	⅔N	0.079 ①	13⅔P
		Rear	—	—	—	1¹³⁄₁₆N	0.079 ①	—
	528e	Front	7¾P–8¾P	8¼P	½N–¹⁄₁₀P	¹⁄₁₃N	³⁄₃₂P	12³⁄₁₆P
		Rear	—	—	—	2N	³⁄₃₂P	—
	533i	Front	7¾P–8¾P	8¼P	½N–¹⁄₁₀P	¹⁄₁₃N	³⁄₃₂P	12³⁄₁₆P
		Rear	—	—	—	2N	³⁄₃₂P	—
	633CSi	Front	—	8¼P	—	⁵⁄₁₆N	⁵⁄₆₄P	12³⁄₁₆P
		Rear	—	—	—	2⁵⁄₁₆N	⁵⁄₆₄P	—
	733i	Front	9P–10P	9½P	½N–¹⁄₁₂P	0	½	11⅓P
		Rear	—	—	—	2N	³⁄₃₂P	—
1985	318i	Front	8¼P–9¼P	8¾P	1¹⁄₁₀N–¹⁄₁₀N	⅔N	0.079 ①	13⅔P
		Rear	—	—	—	1¹³⁄₁₆N	0.079 ①	—
	325e	Front	8¼P–9¼P	8¾P	1¹⁄₁₀N–¹⁄₁₀N	⅔N	0.079 ①	13⅔P
		Rear	—	—	—	1¹³⁄₁₆N	0.079 ①	—
	528e	Front	7¾P–8¾P	8¼P	½N–¹⁄₁₀P	⅓N	³⁄₃₂P	12¹³⁄₁₆P
		Rear	—	—	—	2N	³⁄₃₂P	—
	533i	Front	7¾P–8¾P	8¼P	½N–¹⁄₁₀P	⅓N	³⁄₃₂P	12¹³⁄₁₆P
		Rear	—	—	—	2N	³⁄₃₂P	—
	635CSi	Front	7¾P–8¾P	8¼P	½N–¹⁄₁₀P	⅓N	0.079 ①	12³⁄₁₆P
		Rear	—	—	—	2⅓N	0.079 ①	—
	735i	Front	9P–10P	9½P	½N–½P	0	0.020 ②	11⅓P
		Rear	—	—	—	2⅓N	0.079 ①	—

87898C02

Wheel Alignment (cont.)

Year	Model		Caster Range (deg.)	Caster Preferred Setting (deg.)	Camber Range (deg.)	Camber Preferred Setting (deg.)	Toe-in (in.)	Steering Axis Inclination (deg.)
1986	325e	Front	8¼P–9½P	8¾P	1¹⁄₁₀N–¹⁄₁₀N	⅔N	0.079 ①	13⅔P
		Rear	—	—	—	1¹³⁄₁₆N	0.079 ①	—
	528e	Front	7¾P–8¾P	8¼P	½N–¹⁄₁₀P	⅓N	0.079 ①	12¹³⁄₁₆P
		Rear	—	—	—	2⅓N	0.079 ①	—
1986	535i	Front	7¾P–8¾P	8¼P	½N–¹⁄₁₀P	⅓N	0.079 ①	12¹³⁄₁₆P
		Rear	—	—	—	2⅓N	0.079 ①	—
	635CSi	Front	7¾P–8¾P	8¼P	½N–¹⁄₁₀P	⅓N	0.079 ①	12¹³⁄₁₆P
		Rear	—	—	—	2⅓N	0.079 ①	—
	735i	Front	9P–10P	9½P	½N–½P	0	0.020 ②	11⅓P
		Rear	—	—	—	2⅓N	0.079 ①	—
1987	325e	Front	8¼P–9¼P	8¾P	1¹⁄₁₀N–¹⁄₁₀N	⅔N	0.079 ①	13⅔P
		Rear	—	—	1½N–2⅓N	1⅚N	0.079 ①	—
	528e	Front	7¾P–8¾P	8¼P	½N–¹⁄₁₀P	⅓N	0.079 ①	12¹³⁄₁₆P
		Rear	—	—	—	2⅓N	0.079 ①	—
	535i	Front	7¾P–8¾P	8¼P	½N–¹⁄₁₀P	⅓N	0.079 ①	12¹³⁄₁₆P
		Rear	—	—	—	2⅓N	0.079 ①	—
	325	Front	8P–9P	8½P	1¹⁄₁₀N–⅙P	⅔N	0.079	13⁵⁄₁₆P
		Rear	—	—	1⅓N–2⅓P	1⁵⁄₁₆N	0.079	—
	325 ③	Front	8¼P–8¾P	8¾P	1⅔N–⅔N	1⅙N	0.079	14⅓P
		Rear	—	—	1⅓N–2⅓P	1⁵⁄₁₆N	0.079	—
	325iX	Front	1P–1⅓P	1⅓	1½P–½N	1N	0.024	12⅔P
		Rear	—	—	1¾N–2¾N	2¼N	0.102	—
	635CSi	Front	7½P–8½P	8P	⅚N–⅙P	⅓N	0.079	12P
		Rear	—	—	2⅚N–1⅚N	2⅓N	0.079 ⑤	—
	M6	Front	7½P–8½P	8¼P	⅚N–⅙P	⅓N	0.079	12P
		Rear	—	—	2⅚N–1⅚N	2⅓N	0.079 ①	—
	528e	Front	7½P–8½P	8P	⅚N–⅙P	⅓N	0.079 ⑤	12P
		Rear	—	—	1⅚N–2⅚N	2⅓N	0.079 ⑤	—
	535i	Front	7½P–8½P	8P	⅚N–⅙P	⅓N	0.079 ⑤	12P
		Rear	—	—	1⅚N–2⅚N	2⅓N	0.079 ⑤	—
	M5	Front	7½P–8½P	8P	⅚N–⅙P	⅓N	0.098 ①	12P
		Rear	—	—	1⅚N–2⅚N	2⅓N	0.098 ①	—
	735i	Front	7½P–8½P	8P	¾N–¼P	¼N	0.087 ⑥	12P
		Rear	—	—	—	2⅓N	0.079 ①	—

87898C03

Wheel Alignment (cont.)

Year	Model		Caster Range (deg.)	Caster Preferred Setting (deg.)	Camber Range (deg.)	Camber Preferred Setting (deg.)	Toe-in (in.)	Steering Axis Inclination (deg.)
1988–89	325e	Front	8P–9P	$8\frac{1}{2}$P	$1\frac{1}{10}$N–$\frac{1}{10}$N	$\frac{2}{3}$N	0.079	$13\frac{5}{8}$P
		Rear	—	—	$1\frac{1}{3}$N–$2\frac{1}{3}$N	$1\frac{5}{16}$N	0.079	—
	325	Front	8P–9P	$8\frac{1}{2}$P	$1\frac{1}{10}$N–$\frac{1}{6}$N	$\frac{2}{3}$N	0.079	$13\frac{5}{16}$P
		Rear	—	—	$1\frac{1}{3}$N–$2\frac{1}{3}$P	$1\frac{5}{16}$N	0.079	—
	325 ③	Front	$8\frac{1}{4}$P–$8\frac{3}{4}$P	$8\frac{3}{4}$P	$1\frac{2}{3}$N–$\frac{2}{3}$N	$1\frac{1}{6}$N	0.079	$14\frac{1}{3}$P
		Rear	—	—	$1\frac{1}{3}$N–$2\frac{1}{3}$P	$1\frac{5}{16}$N	0.079	—
	326iX	Front	1P–$1\frac{2}{3}$P	$1\frac{1}{3}$P	$1\frac{1}{2}$N–$\frac{1}{2}$N	1N	0.024	$12\frac{2}{3}$P
		Rear	—	—	$1\frac{3}{4}$N–$2\frac{1}{3}$P	$1\frac{5}{16}$N	0.079	—
1988–89	325iX ③	Front	1P–$1\frac{2}{3}$P	$1\frac{1}{3}$P	$1\frac{15}{16}$N–$\frac{5}{16}$N	$1\frac{1}{3}$N	0.024	$12\frac{2}{3}$P
		Rear	—	—	$1\frac{3}{4}$N–$2\frac{1}{3}$P	$1\frac{5}{16}$N	0.079	—
1988	325 Convertible	Front	8P–9P	$8\frac{1}{2}$P	$1\frac{1}{10}$N–$\frac{1}{6}$N	$\frac{2}{3}$N	0.079	$13\frac{5}{16}$P
		Rear	—	—	$1\frac{1}{3}$N–$2\frac{1}{3}$N	$1\frac{5}{8}$N	0.079	—
	528e	Front	$7\frac{3}{4}$P–$8\frac{3}{4}$P	$8\frac{1}{4}$P	$\frac{1}{2}$N–$\frac{1}{10}$P	$\frac{1}{3}$N	0.079 ①	$12\frac{13}{16}$P
		Rear	—	—	—	$2\frac{1}{3}$N	0.079 ①	—
	535i	Front	$7\frac{3}{4}$P–$8\frac{3}{4}$P	$8\frac{1}{4}$P	$\frac{1}{2}$N–$\frac{1}{10}$P	$\frac{1}{3}$N	0.079 ①	$12\frac{13}{16}$P
		Rear	—	—	—	$2\frac{1}{3}$N	0.079 ①	—
	635CSi	Front	$7\frac{1}{2}$P–$8\frac{1}{2}$P	8P	$\frac{5}{6}$N–$\frac{1}{6}$P	$\frac{1}{3}$N	0.079 ⑤	12P
		Rear	—	—	$2\frac{5}{6}$N–$1\frac{5}{6}$N	$2\frac{1}{3}$N	0.079 ⑤	—
	M6	Front	$7\frac{3}{4}$P–$8\frac{3}{4}$P	8P	$\frac{5}{6}$N–$\frac{1}{6}$P	$\frac{1}{3}$N	0.079 ⑤	12P
		Rear	—	—	$2\frac{5}{6}$N–$1\frac{5}{6}$N	$2\frac{1}{3}$N	0.079 ⑤	—
	528e	Front	$7\frac{1}{2}$P–$8\frac{1}{2}$P	8P	$\frac{5}{6}$N–$\frac{1}{6}$P	$\frac{1}{3}$N	0.079 ⑤	12P
		Rear	—	—	$1\frac{5}{6}$N–$2\frac{5}{6}$N	$2\frac{1}{3}$N	0.079 ⑤	—
	535i	Front	$7\frac{1}{2}$P–$8\frac{1}{2}$P	8P	$\frac{5}{6}$N–$\frac{1}{6}$P	$\frac{1}{3}$N	0.079 ⑤	12P
		Rear	—	—	$1\frac{5}{6}$N–$2\frac{5}{6}$N	$2\frac{1}{3}$N	0.079 ⑤	—
	M5	Front	$7\frac{1}{2}$P–$8\frac{1}{2}$P	8P	$\frac{5}{6}$N–$\frac{1}{6}$P	$\frac{1}{3}$N	0.098	12P
		Rear	—	—	$1\frac{5}{6}$N–$2\frac{5}{6}$N	$2\frac{1}{3}$N	0.098	—
	735i	Front	$7\frac{1}{2}$P–$8\frac{1}{2}$P	8P	$\frac{3}{4}$N–$\frac{1}{4}$P	$\frac{1}{4}$N	0.087 ⑥	12P
		Rear	—	—	$2\frac{5}{6}$N–$1\frac{5}{6}$N	$2\frac{1}{3}$N	0.087	—
	750iL	Front	$7\frac{1}{2}$P–$8\frac{1}{2}$P	8P	$\frac{3}{4}$N–$\frac{1}{4}$P	$\frac{1}{4}$N	0.087 ⑥	12P
		Rear	—	—	$2\frac{5}{6}$N–$1\frac{5}{6}$N	$2\frac{1}{3}$N	0.087	—

All 300, 500 and 700 series models aligned with 150 lbs. in each front seat, 150 lbs. in rear seat and 46 lbs. in trunk.
All 600 series models aligned with 150 lbs. in each front seat and 30 lbs. in trunk on left side
① 14P—1986 and later models
F Front
R Rear
N Negative
P Positive

① .083 with TRX tires
② .024 with TRX tires
③ With "M" suspension
④ .122 with 16 in. rims
⑤ .083 with TRX 390 rims
⑥ .094 with TRX 415 rims

87898C04

REAR SUSPENSION

♦ **See Figures 45, 46, 47, 48 and 49**

The BMW rear suspension incorporates semi-trailing arms pivoting on maintenance-free rubber bushings. Springs are coil type, and the spring strut incorporates the double acting shock absorber on later models. Some models include a rear stabilizer bar. All are fully independent for maximum ride comfort and control.

Rear Shock/Strut Assembly

♦ **See Figure 50**

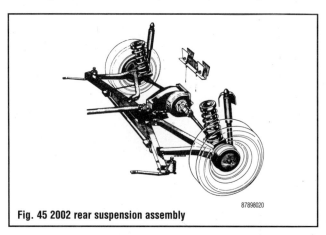

Fig. 45 2002 rear suspension assembly

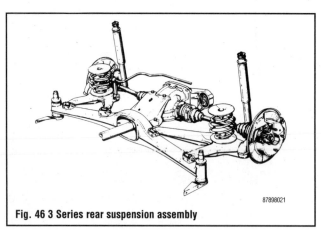

Fig. 46 3 Series rear suspension assembly

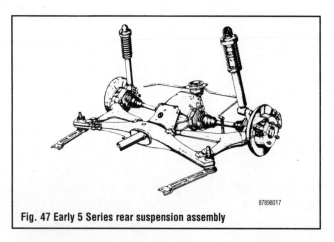

Fig. 47 Early 5 Series rear suspension assembly

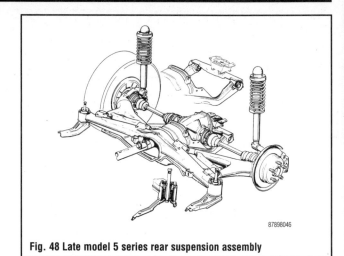

Fig. 48 Late model 5 series rear suspension assembly

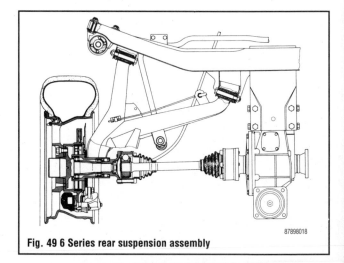

Fig. 49 6 Series rear suspension assembly

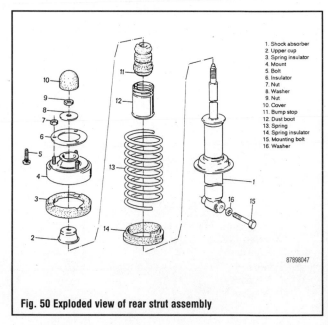

1. Shock absorber
2. Upper cup
3. Spring insulator
4. Mount
5. Bolt
6. Insulator
7. Nut
8. Washer
9. Nut
10. Cover
11. Bump stop
12. Dust boot
13. Spring
14. Spring insulator
15. Mounting bolt
16. Washer

Fig. 50 Exploded view of rear strut assembly

REMOVAL & INSTALLATION

> ❊❊ **CAUTION**

MacPherson strut springs are under tremendous pressure and any attempt to remove them without proper tools could result in serious personal injury!

1600, 2000 and 2002 Models

◗ **See Figures 51 and 52**

➡The shocks on these models are separate of the coil spring.

1. Raise the car and support the control arms with jackstands.
2. Remove the lower shock retaining bolt.
3. Remove the trim over the wheel arch, if equipped, in the trunk compartment and disconnect the upper strut retaining nuts at the wheel arch and remove the assembly.

To install:

4. Install the assembly back into position, using new gaskets between the shock and the wheel arch, and new self-locking nuts on top of the strut.
5. Tighten the shock-to-body nuts to 16–17 ft. lbs. (21–22 Nm), and lower bolt to 52–63 ft. lbs. (16–82 Nm).
6. Install ant trim panels in the trunk compartment, if removed earlier. Lower the vehicle.

1970–80 6-Cylinder Models

1. On the 2500, 2800, Bavaria and 3.0, remove the sleeve which surrounds the shock absorber and the auxiliary spring as well as: the rubber washer; large metal washer; spacer tube; and the fastening plate.
2. On other models, remove the support disc, auxiliary spring (which fits

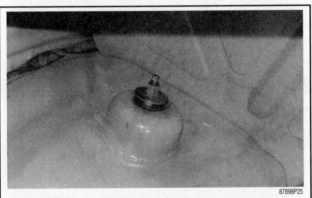

Fig. 51 2002 rear shock mount accessed from the trunk compartment

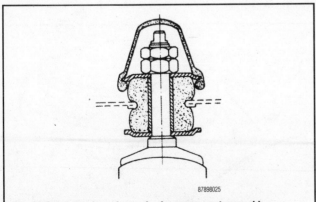

Fig. 52 Cut-away view of rear shock upper mount assembly

around the shock absorber piston rod), and the outer tube. Remove both upper and lower lines, and inspect them, replacing if necessary.

3. Install in reverse order. In case you are replacing a shock absorber which has failed prematurely (especially due to leakage), it may be possible to avoid the cost of replacing the unit located on the opposite side. BMW dealers and some other shops are equipped with equipment designed for testing the shocks. You might be able to remove both shocks and have the performance of a new shock compared with that of the apparently effective old shock. If testing proves the performance of a new shock and slightly used shock to be sufficiently similar, re-use is possible. However, it is dangerous to risk replacing the only one rear shock without machine testing!

1981–83 6-Cylinder Models

1. On 1981–82 733i, remove the rear seat and back rest..
2. Raise the car and support the control arms with jackstands.

> ❊❊ **CAUTION**

The coil spring, shock absorber assembly acts as a strap so the control arm should always be supported!

3. Remove the lower shock retaining bolt.
4. Remove any trim needed to access the assembly and disconnect the upper strut retaining nuts at the wheel arch and remove the assembly. On 733i models , the retaining nut is accessed from the rear seat compartment.
5. Remove the shock assembly from the vehicle.

To install:

6. Install the shock assembly back into position, using new gaskets between the shock and the wheel arch, and new self-locking nuts on top of the strut.
7. Tighten the shock-to-body nuts to 16–17 ft. lbs. (21–22 Nm), spring retainer-to-wheel house nuts to 16–17 ft. lbs. (21–22 Nm), lower bolt to 90–103 ft. lbs. (117–134 Nm).
8. On 733i models, replace the gasket that goes between the top of the strut and the lower surface of the wheel well. Final torquing of the lower strut bolt should be done with the car in the normal riding position.

3 Series Models

➡The shock in these vehicles is separate from the coil spring.

◗ **See Figures 53, 54 and 55**

1. Remove the trunk trim panel, if needed to expose the upper shock mounts.
2. Raise the rear of the vehicle and support safely.
3. Support the lower control arm and remove the lower mounting bolt.
4. If equipped with a rubber cap over the mount in the trunk compartment, remove it and place aside.
5. Remove the upper mounting nuts and remove the shock from the vehicle.

To install:

6. Exchange or replace the upper shock mount and tighten the upper shock nut to 11 ft. lbs. (15 Nm).
7. Install the shock and tighten the retainer nuts to 11 ft. lbs. (15 Nm). Install the trunk panel.
8. Install the lower shock mounting bolt and lower the vehicle. With the vehicle resting at standard ride height, tighten the mounting bolt to 63 ft. lbs. (87 Nm) or if marked grade 10.9 on the bolt head, tighten to 94 ft. lbs. (130 Nm).

5, 6 and 7 Series Models

EXCEPT RIDE CONTROL

➡The shock and spring are combined into a strut assembly.

1. Raise and support the rear of the vehicle.
2. Remove the rear seat cushion and backrest. Remove the trim panel over the strut mount.
3. Support the control arm and remove the nuts at the top of the strut mount.
4. Remove the lower mounting bolt and lower the spring strut assembly. Remove the assembly from the vehicle.

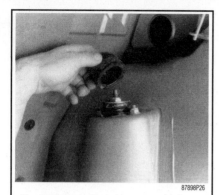

Fig. 53 Remove the rubber cap over the shock mount in the trunk compartment

Fig. 54 Remove the retaining nuts from the sides of the shock

Fig. 55 Remove the retaining bolt from the bottom of the shock

5. Use a spring compressor and compress the spring. Remove the top nut, then pull the top mount off. Remove the spring.

To install:

6. Compress the spring and position on the strut assembly. Install the mount and washers. Use a new locknut and tighten to 18 ft. lbs. (25 Nm). Release the spring.

7. Install the spring strut and tighten the upper mount nuts to 16 ft. lbs. (21.5 Nm). Loosely install the lower mounting bolt.

8. With the vehicle lowered to the ground and at standard riding height, tighten the lower mount to 94 ft. lbs. (130 Nm).

9. Install the trim and seat cushions.

1987–88 7 SERIES WITH RIDE CONTROL

➡ The shock and coil spring are combined into a strut assembly.

1. Raise the car and support the control arms with jackstands.

2. For models with ride control, proceed with the following;

a. Pull off and bridge (electrically) the low pressure switch electrical connection and turn **ON** the ignition.

b. Disconnect the control rod nut, holding the collar with a wrench. Do not disconnect the rod at the ball joint.

c. Operate the lever on the control switch in the **DISCHARGE** direction for about 20 seconds to discharge fluid from the lines.

d. Disconnect the hydraulic line on the shock absorber.

3. Remove the lower shock retaining bolt.

4. Remove the assembly from the vehicle.

5. Use a spring compressor and compress the spring. Remove the top nut and pull the top mount off. Remove the spring.

To install:

6. Compress the spring and position on the strut assembly. Install the mount and washers. Use a new locknut and tighten to 18 ft. lbs. (25 Nm). Release the spring.

7. Install the assembly back into position on the vehicle, using new gaskets between the unit and the wheel arch, and new self-locking nuts on top of the strut.

8. Tighten the shock-to-body nuts to 16–17 ft. lbs. (21–22 Nm), lower bolt to 90–103 ft. lbs. (117–134 Nm).

9. Replace the gasket that goes between the top of the strut and the lower surface of the wheel well.

10. Final torquing of the lower strut bolt should be done with the car in the normal riding position.

TESTING

The shock absorbers should be checked on a regular basis. Visual inspection for leaking oil and damage is a primary indicator of worn or broken shocks. A quick glance at the shocks will provide advance warning of shocks in need of replacement. If oil is visible in any amount more than a very slight coating, the shock need to be replaced. If any visible physical damage is noted, the shock should also be replaced.

The old time method of checking shocks by bouncing the corner of the vehicle is being outmoded by the use of gas pressure and deflecting disk technology shock absorbers. By the time the vehicle does bounce more than once

during this type of test, the shocks have been in need of replacement for a long time. A gradual reduction in the handling capacity may not be noticed as it occurs over a long period of time. Some manufactures of shock absorbers use a design called deflecting disk. This design is inherently self-adjusting for wear and use. An indicator of worn shocks is uneven tire wear and a lack of suspension dampening while traveling over rough roads.

The shocks should always be replaced in pairs. It is also recommended to replace the springs on high mileage vehicles to restore original handling characteristics. Replace the shock mounts and rubber bushings. Check the condition of the stabilizer bar and the mounts

Rear Coil Springs

REMOVAL & INSTALLATION

1600, 2000 and 2002 Models

▶ **See Figure 56**

➡ The coil spring is separate from the shock on these vehicles

✳ CAUTION

Make sure that the car is firmly supported with jackstands.

1. Remove the shock absorber as outlined in this section. Make sure that the trailing arm is securely supported with a jack.

2. Remove the rear wheel and tire assembly.

3. If equipped, disconnect the stabilizer bar from the mount on the trailing arm.

4. Disconnect the output shaft at the halfshaft flange and tie the output shaft up to an underbody component so that it does not hang down.

5. Safety wire or chain the bottom coil of the spring to an underbody component to protect yourself from injury should the spring slip off its lower mount during removal.

Fig. 56 Rubber lower coil spring damper. When installing, make sure the indent aligns properly

6. Slowly lower the jack supporting the trailing arm and carefully release the spring and wire.

7. Inspect the condition of the rubber damping rings. Replace if damaged or dry-rotted. Make sure that the lower ring's locating recess fits into the projection on the lower mounting plate. If the spring is broken, it is recommended that both springs be removed and replaced with new ones of the same size, diameter, free length, and color coding (spring rate).

To install:

8. Install the spring into position,
9. Reconnect the output shaft at the half shaft. Reconnect the stabilizer bar.
10. Install the wheel and tire and install the shock absorber.

➡Take care to rotate the coil spring so that the spring ends locate on the stop (projection) of the upper and lower damping rings.

3 Series Models

▶ See Figure 57

➡The coil spring is separate from the shock on these vehicles.

1. Disconnect the rear portion of the exhaust system and hang it from the body.
2. Disconnect the final drive rubber mount, push it down, and hold it down with a wedge.
3. Remove the bolt that connects the rear stabilizer bar to the strut on the side being worked on. Be careful not to damage the brake line.

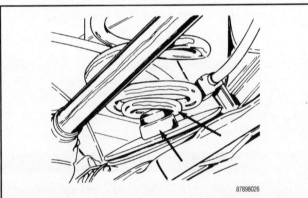

87898026

Fig. 57 Lower the control arm only enough to remove the coil spring

➡Support the lower control arm securely with a jack or other device that will permit it to be lowered gradually, while maintaining secure vehicle support.

4. Then, to prevent damage to the output shaft joints, lower the control arm only enough to slip the coil spring off the retainer.

To install:

5. In replacing the spring, make sure the parts are the same in terms of part number and/or color code.
6. Install the spring, making sure that the spring is in proper position.
7. Keep the control arm securely supported while raising, then replace the shock bolt. Install the bolts in the final drive rubber mount and tighten to 69 ft. lbs. (95 Nm).
8. Tighten the stabilizer bolt to 16 ft. lbs. (21 Nm), and the shock bolt to 63 ft. lbs. (87 Nm) with the control arm in the normal ride position. Install the exhaust system.

5, 6 and 7 Series Models

1. Raise and support the rear of the vehicle.
2. Remove the rear seat cushion and backrest if the assembly must be accessed from the rear seat compartment. Remove the trim panel over the strut mount.
3. Support the control arm and remove the nuts at the top of the strut mount.
4. Remove the lower mounting bolt and lower the spring strut assembly. Remove the assembly from the vehicle.

5. Use a spring compressor to compress the spring. Remove the top nut and pull the top mount off. Remove the spring.

To install:

6. Compress new spring and position on the strut assembly. Install the mount and washers. Use a new locknut and tighten to 18 ft. lbs. (25 Nm). Release the spring.
7. Install the spring/strut and tighten the upper mount nuts to 16 ft. lbs. (21.5 Nm). Loosely install the lower mounting bolt.
8. With the vehicle lowered to the ground and at standard riding height, tighten the lower mount to 94 ft. lbs. (130 Nm).
9. Install the trim and seat cushions.

Rear Stabilizer Bar

REMOVAL & INSTALLATION

1. Disconnect the stabilizer from the trailing arm on either side by removing the connecting bolt from the lower end of the link.
2. Disconnect the stabilizer on the crossmember.
3. Check the rubber bushings for wear and replace as necessary.
4. Installation is the reverse of removal.

Rear Control Arm

REMOVAL & INSTALLATION

5 Series Models

➡If equipped with anti-lock brakes, expensive and specialized equipment is needed to bleed the ABS brake system. If you do not own or have access to this equipment, consult a suitably equipped professional who can perform this procedure.

1. Apply the parking brake and then remove the rear wheel. Disconnect the driveshaft at the outer flange by removing the bolts.
2. Remove the parking brake lever.
3. Plug the front hose to prevent loss of brake fluid in the reservoir.
4. Support the body.
5. Disconnect the brake line at the brake hose.
6. Disconnect the stabilizer and coil spring at the control arm.
7. Disconnect the control arm at the axle carrier.
8. Reconnect the control arm, stabilizer bar and coil spring. Reconnect the brake line.
9. Install the parking brake lever and install the rear wheel.
10. Bleed the brake system.

7 Series Models

➡If equipped with anti-lock brakes, expensive and specialized equipment is needed to bleed the ABS brake system. If you do not own or have access to this equipment, consult a suitably equipped professional who can perform this procedure.

1. Remove the rear wheel.
2. Apply the parking brake to hold the driveshaft stationary. Disconnect the output shaft at the drive flange. Hang the shaft from the body by a piece of wire.
3. Disconnect the parking brake cable at the lever.
4. Remove the float housing from the brake fluid reservoir and then remove as much fluid as possible from the reservoir, using a syringe used only for brake fluid (or a new one).
5. Pull the brake cable housing out of the mounting bracket near the control arm. Disconnect the brake line.
6. On 735i models with ABS, carefully, pull the wiring for the pulse transmitter out of its mount so it will be possible to unplug it.
7. Support the trailing arm from underneath in a secure manner.
8. Remove the nuts and then remove the 2 through bolts to disconnect the control arm from the rear axle carrier.
9. If the car has a stabilizer bar, remove the bolts and remove the attaching bracket for the stabilizer bar.
10. Disconnect the shock absorber and remove the control arm.

To install:

11. Install the shock absorber in position under the vehicle. When reattaching the control arm, insert the bolt on the inner bracket first. Finally, tighten all mounting bolts with the car resting on its wheels. Tighten the bolts attaching the control arm to the axle carrier to 49–54 ft. lbs. (64–70 Nm). Refill and bleed the brake system.

Rear Trailing Arm

REMOVAL & INSTALLATION

528e, 530i, 533i and 633CSi Models

➡If equipped with anti-lock brakes, expensive and specialized equipment is needed to bleed the ABS brake system. If you do not own or have access to this equipment, consult a suitably equipped professional who can perform this procedure.

1. Raise the vehicle and remove the rear wheel. Apply the parking brake and disconnect the output shaft at the rear axle shaft. Then, disconnect the parking brake cable at the handbrake. Remove the parking brake lever.
2. Remove the rear wheel.
3. Support the body.
4. Pull the parking brake cable out of the pipe.
5. Disconnect the stabilizer and spring strut at the trailing arm.
6. Disconnect the brake line at the brake hose.
7. Disconnect the driveshaft at the outboard flange.
8. Disconnect the brake pad wear indicator wire at the right trailing arm and take the wire out of the clamps.
9. Disconnect the trailing arm at the rear axle support.

To install:

10. Install the trailing arm at the rear axle support.
11. Reconnect the brake pad wear indicator. Connect the stabilizer and spring to the trailing arm.

12. Reconnect the driveshaft at the outboard flange. Reattach the parking brake cable and lever.
13. Refill and bleed the brake system.

3 Series Models

➡If equipped with anti-lock brakes, expensive and specialized equipment is needed to bleed the ABS brake system. If you do not own or have access to this equipment, consult a suitably equipped professional who can perform this procedure.

1. Raise the vehicle and remove the rear wheel. Apply the parking brake and disconnect the output shaft at the rear axle shaft. On 320i models, disconnect the parking brake cable at the handbrake. On the 318i and 325, remove the parking brake lever.
2. Remove the brake fluid from the master cylinder reservoir on 318i and 325 models. To do this, it will be necessary to remove the strainer at the top of the reservoir.
3. Disconnect the brake line connection on the rear control arm. Plug the openings.
4. Support the control arm securely. Disconnect the shock absorber at the control arm. On 318i and 325 models, lower the control arm slowly and remove the spring. On 320i models, the control arm need not be lowered slowly because the spring is integral with the strut.
5. Remove the nuts and then slide the bolts out of the mounts where the control arm is mounted to the axle carrier.

To install:

6. Install the trailing arm into position. Install the bolt that goes into the inner bracket first.
7. Tighten the bolts holding the trailing arm to the axle carrier to 48–54 ft. lbs. (62–70 Nm).
8. On 318i and 325 models, make sure the spring is positioned properly top and bottom. Tighten the strut bolt to 52–63 ft. lbs. (68–82 Nm).
9. Reinstall the handbrake or reconnect the cable and adjust. Then apply the brake and reconnect the output shaft.
10. Reconnect the brake line, replenish with the proper brake fluid, and bleed the system.

STEERING

※※ CAUTION

On models equipped with air bags, extreme caution must be used so as not to accidentally discharge the air bag. DO NOT hammer on the steering wheel.

Steering Wheel

REMOVAL & INSTALLATION

1600, 2000, 2002, 2500, 2800, 3000, 3.0 and Bavaria Models

➡Remove and install steering wheel in a straight ahead position. Mark the relationship between the wheel and spindle.

1. Disconnect the negative battery cable.
2. Remove steering wheel pad or BMW emblem. If the horn button is the pad, disconnect the wire attached to the pad.
3. Mark the relationship between the steering wheel and shaft for installation in the same position.
4. Unscrew retaining nut and remove the wheel.

※※ CAUTION

Be careful not to damage the direction signal cancelling cam, which is right under the steering wheel, in performing this operation.

To install:

5. Position the wheel on the column with the marks mark earlier aligned correctly.

6. On the 1600, 2000 and 2002, tighten the nut to 40 ft. lbs. (52 Nm), on 2500 to 61 ft. lbs. (79 Nm) and on the 2800, Bavaria and 3.0, tighten the nut to 69 ft. lbs. (90 Nm).
7. Connect the negative battery cable.

Without SRS (Air Bag)

▶ See Figures 58, 59, 60, 61 and 62

1. Disconnect the negative battery cable.
2. Unlock the steering column with the ignition key.
3. Carefully pry the center emblem out of the steering wheel.
4. Hold the steering wheel and remove the nut from the steering shaft.

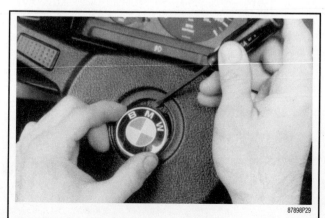

Fig. 58 Pry the emblem from the center of the steering wheel . . .

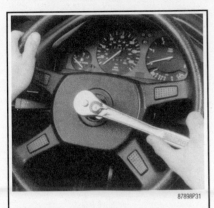

Fig. 59 . . . then remove the retaining nut

Fig. 60 Remove the washer around the steering column

Fig. 61 Scribe an alignment mark between the wheel and column with a pen

Fig. 62 On late model vehicles the key must be in the ignition to depress the lock tab and free the wheel

5. Mark the relationship of the steering wheel to the shaft and pull the steering wheel off the shaft.

6. Remove the steering wheel from the column. If the wheel will not come off, DO NOT FORCE it. Put in key in the ignition and try again. Many vehicles have a wheel lock that is activated when the key is in the ignition.

To install:

7. Install the steering wheel in its original position. Install the washer and a new locknut. Tighten the nut to 58 ft. lbs. (80 Nm). Do not use the steering column lock to hold the steering wheel. Hold the wheel during tightening.

8. Connect the negative battery cable.

9. Install the center emblem by pressing down into the opening. Check for smooth rotation of the wheel and operation of the horn.

With SRS (Air Bag)

✳✳ CAUTION

All precautions must be adhered to or premature deployment of the air bag may occur causing personal injury. If the air bag system is damaged or rendered inoperative, the additional protection an air bag provides in a frontal collision will not be available and may lead to greater injury in an accident. Refer to Section 6 for SRS precautions and procedures.

1. Disarm the SRS system, then disconnect the negative battery terminal. Remove the lower steering column trim and disconnect the orange connector.

2. Use tool 00 2 110 or equivalent, to remove the air bag module bolts from behind the steering wheel. Remove the air bag module and disconnect the wire on the back. Place the air bag module in the trunk with the pad facing up.

3. Unlock the steering column with the ignition key. Turn the steering wheel to the straight ahead position.

4. Hold the steering wheel and remove the nut from the steering shaft.

5. Mark the relationship of the steering wheel to the shaft and pull the steering wheel off the shaft.

To install:

6. Install the steering wheel in its original position with the lock pin in the bore. Install the washer and a new locknut. Tighten the nut to 58 ft. lbs. (80 Nm). Do not use the steering column lock to hold the steering. Hold the wheel during tightening.

7. If the contact ring has moved out of position and needs to be return to the center, press the spring and rotate the ring completely left or right to the stop. Turn the ring in the opposite direction 3 turns to align the marks.

8. Install the air bag module and connect the wires. Tighten the mounting bolts to 6 ft. lbs. (8 Nm), right side first.

9. Connect the negative battery cable.

10. Check for smooth rotation of the wheel and operation of the horn.

Turn Signal Switch (Combination Switch)

REMOVAL & INSTALLATION

1600, 2000, and 2002 Models

1. Disconnect the negative battery cable.

2. Remove the steering wheel. Unscrew and remove the padded trim surrounding the column.

3. Unscrew the choke knob, if equipped and the retaining nut behind it. Unscrew the mounting screws and remove the steering column lower surround panel.

4. Mark the position of the turn signal switch, then remove the attaching screws and remove the switch.

To install:

5. During installation, note that the switch is mounted via slots. Before tightening the mounting screws, slide the switch back and forth until the gap between the canceling cam and the actuating dog on the switch is 0.01 inches (0.3mm).

6. Connect wiring to the switch as follows:
   a. Gray—P
   b. Green/Yellow—54
   c. Blue/Black—R
   d. Blue/Red—L
   e. Brown/Black—H
   f. Gray/Green—PR
   g. Gray/Black—PI

7. Mount the steering wheel and connect the negative battery cable.

2500, 2800, Bavaria, 3000 and 3.0 Models

1. Disconnect the negative battery cable.

2. Put the steering wheel in the straight ahead position. Remove the lower steering column housing and the lower center instrument panel trim on the left side.

3. Remove the steering wheel.

4. Remove the attaching screws and remove the turn signal switch.

5. Extract the cable harness from the retaining clips. Pull out the control lever light, detach the plug, and separate the cable connector.

6. Pull off the black multiple connector and the gray/blue cable.

To install:

7. Install the switch, with the switch in the center position and the actuating peg pointing toward the center of the canceling cam.

8. Check that the clearance between the canceling cam and switch cam follower is 0.01 inches (0.3mm). The switch is slotted at the mounting points to allow for adjustment before the mounting screws receive final tightening.

9. Install the steering wheel and connect the negative battery cable.

318i and 320i Models

> ✸✷✸ **CAUTION**
>
> **With air bag equipped models, all precautions must be adhered to or premature deployment of the air bag may occur causing personal injury. If the air bag system is damaged or rendered inoperative, the additional protection an air bag provides in a frontal collision will not be available and may lead to greater injury in an accident. Refer to Section 6 for SRS precautions and procedures.**

1. Disarm the SRS system if equipped.
2. Disconnect the negative battery cable.
3. Turn the steering wheel to the straight ahead position. Remove the steering wheel and the lower steering column cover.
4. Disconnect the direction signal switch multiple connector from under the dash by squeezing in the locks on either side and pulling it off.
5. Remove the cable straps from the column.
6. Loosen the mounting screws and remove the switch and harness.

To install:

7. Install the switch in position, noting the following points:

a. Make sure to mount the ground wire.

b. Make sure the switch is in the middle position and that the follower faces the center of the cancelling cam on the steering column shaft. Then, before finally tightening the switch mounting screws, adjust the switch on the slotted mounting holes so the gap between the cam and follower is 0.1 inches (3mm).

8. Mount the steering wheel and connect the negative battery cable.

3 Series Models

> ✸✷✸ **CAUTION**
>
> **With air bag equipped models, all precautions must be adhered to or premature deployment of the air bag may occur causing personal injury. If the air bag system is damaged or rendered inoperative, the additional protection an air bag provides in a frontal collision will not be available and may lead to greater injury in an accident. Refer to Section 6 for SRS precautions and procedures.**

1. Disarm the SRS system, if equipped.
2. Disconnect the negative battery terminal. Remove the steering wheel.
3. Remove the trim panel at the bottom left of the instrument panel and the lower steering column casing.
4. Remove the screws holding the switch. Remove the switch and disconnect the plug.

To install:

5. Install the switch and connect the plug. The ground wire must be connected and the retainers must fit into the holes.
6. Install the trim panels and steering wheel. Connect the negative battery terminal.

528e, 530i, 535i, 635CSi, M5 and M6 Models

> ✸✷✸ **CAUTION**
>
> **With air bag equipped models, all precautions must be adhered to or premature deployment of the air bag may occur causing personal injury. If the air bag system is damaged or rendered inoperative, the additional protection an air bag provides in a frontal collision will not be available and may lead to greater injury in an accident. Refer to Section 6 for SRS precautions and procedures.**

1. Disarm the SRS system, if equipped.
2. Disconnect the battery ground cable. Remove the steering wheel as described in this section.
3. Remove the instrument panel trim which is near the bottom of the steering wheel on the left side.
4. Remove the 2 screws from underneath and remove the steering column lower cover.
5. Unfasten the electrical connectors near the bottom of the column and at the area just under the front of the dash.
6. Unscrew the 2 screws fastening the switch and one ground wire to the column just to the left of the steering shaft. Pull off the plug connecting the switch to the relay on the right side of the column. Remove the switch.

To install:

7. Install the switch in position and connect the wiring. Install the steering column covers and the lower instrument panel trim.
8. Install the steering wheel and connect the negative battery cable.

533i and 633CSi

Follow the procedure for 318i and 320i above exactly; when adjusting the gap between the cancelling cam and the switch follower, use the dimension of 0.1 inch (3mm).

1982 733i Models

1. Remove the steering wheel and disconnect the battery ground cable.
2. Remove the trim from below the steering column. Remove the mounting screws and detach the switch from the switch plate.
3. Loosen the straps holding the switch cable to the steering column. Pull the center plug out of the panel on the cowl and remove the switch.

To install:

4. Install the switch in position and connect the wiring. Install the steering column covers and the lower instrument panel trim.
5. Install the steering wheel and connect the negative battery cable. .

1983–85 733i and 1985–86 735i Models

> ✸✷✸ **CAUTION**
>
> **With air bag equipped models, all precautions must be adhered to or premature deployment of the air bag may occur causing personal injury. If the air bag system is damaged or rendered inoperative, the additional protection an air bag provides in a frontal collision will not be available and may lead to greater injury in an accident. Refer to Section 6 for SRS precautions and procedures.**

1. Disarm the SRS system, if equipped.
2. Disconnect the negative battery cable. Remove the steering wheel in this section.
3. Remove the lower steering column cover.
4. Remove the 2 screws located to the left of the steering shaft (the lower screw mounts a ground wire).
5. Disconnect the electrical connector for the switch and the flasher relay, located along the front of the column. Pull the flasher relay out of the holder.
6. Follow the wiring to the area under the dash. Open the ties and unplug the electrical connector. Remove the switch.
7. Install the switch into position, making sure to secure (using wire tie-straps) the electrical wiring going under the dash and to reconnect the ground wire to the lower switch mounting screw.

1987–88 735i

> ✸✷✸ **CAUTION**
>
> **With air bag equipped models, all precautions must be adhered to or premature deployment of the air bag may occur causing personal injury. If the air bag system is damaged or rendered inoperative, the additional protection an air bag provides in a frontal collision will not be available and may lead to greater injury in an accident. Refer to Section 6 for SRS precautions and procedures.**

1. Disarm the SRS system, if equipped.
2. Disconnect the battery ground. Remove the steering wheel as described above.
3. Remove the instrument panel trim below and to the left of the steering wheel.
4. Remove the lower steering column cover.
5. Compress the retaining hook and pull off the flasher relay socket facing downward.
6. On cars with airbags, drive out the pin and pry out the expansion rivet. Then, on all cars, remove the upper steering column cover.
7. Pull off the connector plug. This is located between the column and the dash in front of and above where the steering wheel is normally located.
8. Compress the retaining hooks and remove the switch (located to the left of the steering shaft). Disconnect all electrical plugs and remove the switch.

To install:
9. Install the switch in position and connect the wiring. Reinstall all other components that were removed. Install the steering column covers and the lower instrument panel trim.
10. Install the steering wheel and connect the negative battery cable.

Ignition Switch

REMOVAL & INSTALLATION

3 Series Models

EXCEPT 318I AND 320I MODELS

> ✳✳ **CAUTION**
>
> With air bag equipped models, all precautions must be adhered to or premature deployment of the air bag may occur causing personal injury. If the air bag system is damaged or rendered inoperative, the additional protection an air bag provides in a frontal collision will not be available and may lead to greater injury in an accident. Refer to Section 6 for SRS precautions and procedures.

1. Disarm the SRS system, if equipped.
2. Disconnect negative battery terminal.
3. Remove lower steering column casing.
4. Shear off the 4 tamper-proof screws with a chisel or other suitable tool.
5. Unscrew the set screw and remove the switch.
6. Disconnect the central fuse/relay plate plug.
7. Installation is the reverse of removal.

➡Turn ignition key all the way back and set the switch at the "0" position before installing. Marks on the switch must be opposite each other.

318I AND 320I MODELS

▸ **See Figures 63 and 64**

1. Disconnect the battery ground cable. Remove the steering wheel.
2. Remove the 4 tamper-proof screws, and remove the lower steering column cover.
3. Disconnect the turn signal/wiper switch by removing the 4 screws and disconnecting the wires.
4. Remove the collar from the steering column shaft. Then, remove the snapring (1), washer (2), spring (3) and seating ring (4).

> ✳✳ **CAUTION**
>
> In the next step, pry carefully. Don't use too much force, because a screwdriver can slip and cause injury!

5. Pry off the steering spindle bearings with 2 screwdrivers. Pry by the inner race only.
6. Disconnect the main electrical plug at the bottom of the steering column.
7. Use a chisel to remove the tamper proof screw. Pull the lock assembly with the upper section of the casting off the outer column.

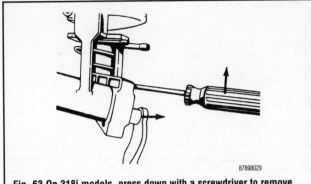

Fig. 63 On 318i models, press down with a screwdriver to remove the ignition lock

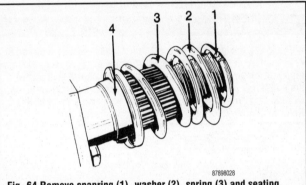

Fig. 64 Remove snapring (1), washer (2), spring (3) and seating ring (4)

8. With a suitable tool, press downward on the lock and then slide the switch off, noting the switch position and that of the lock assembly.

To install:
9. To install, locate the switch in the correct position and install it, noting these points:
   a. When installing the switch, make sure its position is the same in relationship with the lock, so the actions of the 2 will be synchronized.
   b. Use a Torx® screwdriver for the tamper proof screw.
   c. Drive the steering spindle bearings back on by the inner races only.
   d. When installing the seating ring that goes on the shaft, make sure the spring seat faces outward. Use a piece of pipe slightly larger than the shaft and tap it with a hammer to install the snapring. Then, make sure the collar that goes on next locks the snapring in place.

1985–86 528e, 530i, 533i and 633i

> ✳✳ **CAUTION**
>
> With air bag equipped models, all precautions must be adhered to or premature deployment of the air bag may occur causing personal injury. If the air bag system is damaged or rendered inoperative, the additional protection an air bag provides in a frontal collision will not be available and may lead to greater injury in an accident. Refer to Section 6 for SRS precautions and procedures.

1. Disarm the SRS system, if equipped.
2. Disconnect the battery ground cable. Remove the steering wheel as described in this section.
3. Remove the instrument panel lower trim and the steering column lower cover.
4. Unplug the flasher relay and then pull the relay and holder off the front of the column. Then, remove the 4 screws retaining the headlight dimmer and wiper combination switch.
5. Use a hammer and chisel to shear off the 5 screws mounting the switch.
6. Remove the setscrew. Then, press downward on the steering column and pull the steering lock out.

To install:

7. Install the position in the correct position, using new shear-off type screws to mount the switch. Make sure to install the switch so it is properly positioned in relation to the steering lock.

8. Apply paint to the setscrew to lock it in position after it has been installed and tightened.

9. Connect the negative battery cable.

1987–88 528e, 535i, M5, 635i and M6

▶ **See Figure 64**

➡ **To perform this operation, use special tools 32 3 052 and 32 3 050 or equivalent. These are a sleeve, tapered at the outer end, which permits mounting a snapring over the threaded end of the steering shaft without damaging those threads. There is also a pipe which fits over the sleeve and permits the snapring to be forced down the sleeve while being kept square.**

1. Remove the steering wheel as described in this section.

※※ CAUTION

With air bag equipped models, all precautions must be adhered to or premature deployment of the air bag may occur causing personal injury. If the air bag system is damaged or rendered inoperative, the additional protection an air bag provides in a frontal collision will not be available and may lead to greater injury in an accident. Refer to Section 6 for SRS precautions and procedures.

2. Disarm the SRS system, if equipped.
3. Disconnect the negative battery cable.
4. Remove the steering column lower cover.
5. Unplug the flasher relay and then pull the relay and holder off the front of the column. Pull the plug off the horn contact.
6. Note the location of the 2 ground wires. Then, remove the 4 screws and remove the headlight/wiper switch.
7. Pull the collar off the steering shaft. Then, remove, in order, the snapring, washer, spring, and seating ring.
8. Press downward on the locking hook and pull the ignition switch off the column.

To install:

9. Install the switch in position. Install the seating ring with the flat side outward. Use the special tools to fit the snapring on as described in the note above.

10. Mount the collar with the recess downward. Make sure to reconnect the ground wires to the bottom left screw.

11. Connect the negative battery cable.

1983–84 733i

1. Disconnect the negative battery cable.
2. Remove the outer steering column cover.
3. Lift the flasher relay out of its holding clamp. Unscrew the attaching screw and pull out the switch.
4. Open the wire strap and pull off the plug.
5. Install the switch into position, noting these points:
   a. With the ignition key in the new switch, turn the key slowly back and forth while sliding in the switch until it engages. Apply a new coating of locking sealer.
   b. Connect the black wire from the ignition switch to the black wire coming from the power saving relay. Use new straps to tie the wiring harness back in place.
6. Install the steering wheel and connect the negative battery cable.

1985–86 735i

※※ CAUTION

With air bag equipped models, all precautions must be adhered to or premature deployment of the air bag may occur causing personal injury. If the air bag system is damaged or rendered inoperative, the additional protection an air bag provides in a frontal collision

will not be available and may lead to greater injury in an accident. Refer to Section 6 for SRS precautions and procedures.

1. Disarm the SRS system, if equipped.
2. Disconnect the battery ground cable. Remove the steering wheel as described above.
3. Remove the steering column lower cover.
4. Then, remove the 4 screws retaining the headlight dimmer and wiper switches.
5. Use a hammer and chisel to shear off the 4 screws mounting the switch to the switch plate.
6. Remove the setscrew. Then, pull the ignition switch out.

To install:

7. To synchronize the positions of the ignition lock and switch, use the key to turn the ignition lock as far back from the on position as it will go, and set the ignition switch to the **0** position. Complete the installation in reverse order, using new shear-off type screws to mount the switch. Make sure to install the switch so it is properly positioned in relation to the steering lock.

8. Apply clear lacquer to the setscrew to lock it in position after it has been installed and tightened.

1987–88 735i

※※ CAUTION

With air bag equipped models, all precautions must be adhered to or premature deployment of the air bag may occur causing personal injury. If the air bag system is damaged or rendered inoperative, the additional protection an air bag provides in a frontal collision will not be available and may lead to greater injury in an accident. Refer to Section 6 for SRS precautions and procedures.

1. Disarm the SRS system, if equipped.
2. Disconnect the battery ground cable. Remove the steering wheel as described above. Remove the instrument panel trim located just below the steering column.
3. Remove the steering column cover casing by removing the 2 screws from underneath and the 2 from the front of the column.
4. Remove the bolt and nut fastening the lower end of the steering spindle (the bolt passes through a groove in the spindle). Mark alignment of the steering shaft splines with a spot of paint on each side.
5. Remove the bolts and nuts at the forked lower end of the steering column. Replace the nuts, which are self-locking.
6. Remove the 2 bolts fastening the upper column to the dash. Remove the column by pressing it downward.
7. Pull off the ignition switch connector. Then, compress the locking hooks and pull off the combination switch.
8. Turn the ignition switch to **R** position. Use a center punch to press the retainer into the locking bore in the case and then pull the ignition switch out of the case.

To install:

9. Install the switch into position, noting the following points:
   a. Make sure to remount the spacer sleeve that goes in the column mounting bracket.
   b. After realigning the splines of the steering shaft and lower column, tighten the adjusting nut so the sliding force of the column is about 10 lbs.
   c. Make sure the bolt which fastens the steering spindle in place passes through the groove in the spindle.
   d. Check the position of the concave collar located just under the steering wheel. It must fit over the snapring.
   e. Double check to make sure to replace all self-locking nuts.

Ignition Lock Cylinder

REMOVAL & INSTALLATION

1984–88 3, 5, 6 and 7 Series Models

1. Disconnect the negative battery cable.
2. Remove the steering wheel and combination switch assembly.

3. Insert the ignition key and turn 60 degrees.

4. Use a 3/64 inch (1.2mm) wire to press down into the small bore on the face of the lock.

5. Pull the lock cylinder out.

6. If there is no bore, remove the steering column trim and press the bore on the side of the cylinder with punch to remove the cylinder.

7. Installation is the reverse of removal.

Steering Linkage

REMOVAL & INSTALLATION

Outer Tie Rod

▶ See Figures 65, 66, 67, 68 and 69

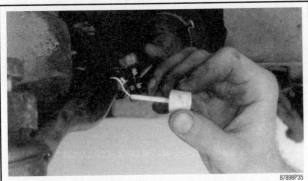

Fig. 65 Use paint to mark the thread location of the tie rod in the steering rack arm

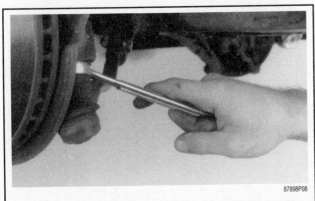

Fig. 66 Remove the nut securing the tie rod to the steering knuckle

1. Raise and safely support the front of the vehicle on jackstands. Remove the front wheel.

2. Use paint to mark the relative position of the tie rod screw threads. This is most effective if the tie rod is to be reinstalled.

3. Remove the cotter pin, if equipped and castle nut at the steering knuckle.

4. Press the outer tie rod off the steering knuckle.

5. If equipped with a locking nut at the tie rod on the steering rack arm loosen this nut.

6. Loosen the nut and bolt which secure the clamp, if equipped, around the steering rack arm over the end of the tie rod.

7. Unscrew the tie rod from the steering rack arm.

To install:

8. If installing a new tie rod, measure the length from the original tie rod in which the new tie rod will need to be screwed into the steering rack arm.

9. Install the tie rod into the arm.

10. Tight the clamp or locking nut at the steering arm.

11. Attach the tie rod at the steering knuckle.

12. Tighten the nut and bolt at the steering rack arm.

13. Install the castle nut and cotter pin, if equipped. Install the front wheel.

14. Have the alignment checked.

Inner Tie Rod

➡The inner tie rod and steering rack arm on models produced after 1981 are installed together. In the event the inner tie rod fails, the entire assembly will have to be replaced.

REPLACEABLE TIE ROD

1. Remove the cotter pin, castle nut and press the outer tie rod off the steering knuckle.

2. Remove the cotter pin and nut from the inner tie rod and press the inner tie rod off the steering rack.

3. Unscrew the clamp, or locking nut securing the tie rod to the arm.

4. Place the arm assembly on a clean surface and use paint to mark the thread position of the inner tie rod in relation to the steering rack control arm.

5. Unscrew the tie rod.

To install:

6. If installing a new tie rod, measure the length from the original tie rod in which the new tie rod will need to be screwed into the steering rack arm.

7. Install the tie rod into the arm.

8. Tight the clamp or locking nut at the steering arm.

9. Attach the reassembled arm to the steering knuckle and steering rack.

10. Tighten the nut and bolt at the steering rack arm.

11. Install the castle nut and cotter pin, if equipped. Install the front wheel.

12. Have the alignment checked.

NON-REPLACEABLE TIE ROD

➡The inner tie rod and steering rack arm on models produced after 1981 are installed together. In the event the inner tie rod fails, the entire assembly will have to be replaced.

Fig. 67 Separate the tie rod from the steering knuckle

Fig. 68 Loosen the nut and bolt securing the retainer clamp around the steering rack arm

Fig. 69 Unscrew the tie rod from the steering rack arm

1. Remove the cotter pin, castle nut and press the outer tie rod off the steering knuckle.

2. Remove the robber boot covering the inner tie rod assembly. Depending on the model one or more clamps will have to be removed or cut off. Peel back the rubber boot. Check the condition of the boot and replace if torn or cracked

3. Lift up the locking tab attaching the tie rod assembly to the rest of the steering rack.

4. Unscrew the tie rod and arm assembly off the steering rack.

To install:

5. If the new assembly did not come with a new boot, remove the boot from the original unit and slide over the replacement assembly.

6. Screw the new tie rod on to the steering rack and lock in place by pushing the locking tab down in to to groove in the tie rod.

7. Install the cover boot over the steering rack and steering rack arm grooves and secure with one or more clamps, depending on model and year.

8. Attach the reassembled arm to the steering knuckle.

9. Install the castle nut and cotter pin, if equipped. Install the front wheel.

10. Have the alignment checked.

Center Tie Rod

1. If equipped, remove the heat guard.

2. Remove the cotter pins, loosen the castle nuts and press the left and right tie rods off the center tie rod.

3. If reinstalling the tie rods, use paint to mark the position of the tie rod in relation to the control arm.

4. Press the center tie rod off of the steering control arm.

To install:

5. Attach the center tie rod to the steering control arm and install the left and right tie rods.

6. Align the front axle.

Center Link

1. Raise and support the front end of the vehicle.

2. Remove the joint nuts and press the studs out of the center link with a tie rod removal tool.

3. Check the length between the studs. It should be 21.023 in. (534mm).

4. Install the center link. Clean the bores and studs. Use new nuts and tighten to 23–29 ft. lbs. (33–40 Nm). Do not use a locknut on a tie rod that has a hole for a cotter pin. If originally equipped with a locknut, use a new locknut for installation.

5. Have the alignment checked and adjusted.

Idler Arm

1. Raise and support the front end of the vehicle.

2. Remove the center link ball joint nut and press the stud out of the center link with a tie rod removal tool.

3. Remove the nut and bolt holding the idler arm. Remove the idler arm taking note of the positioning of the washer between the arm and the subframe. The bushing can be pressed out and replaced.

To install:

4. Install the idler arm and tighten the nut to 30 ft. lbs. (42 Nm) if it is M10 or 61 ft. lbs. (85 Nm) if it is M12.

5. Clean the bores and studs. Use new nuts and tighten the center link ball joint to 23–29 ft. lbs. (33–40 Nm). Do not use a locknut on a joint that has a hole for a cotter pin. If originally equipped with a locknut, use a new locknut for installation.

6. Have the alignment checked and adjusted.

Manual Steering Rack

♦ See Figure 70

REMOVAL & INSTALLATION

1600, 2000, 2002, 2500, 2800, Bavaria, 3000 and 3.0 Models

1. Loosen the bolt and locking nut connecting the coupling flange to the steering column and remove to separate the column from the rack.

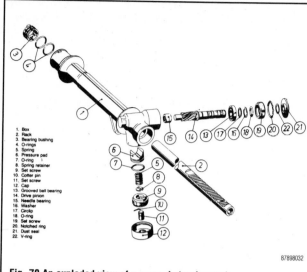

1. Box
2. Rack
3. Bearing bushing
4. O-rings
5. Spring
6. Pressure pad
7. O-ring
8. Spring retainer
9. Set screw
10. Cotter pin
11. Set screw
12. Cap
13. Grooved ball bearing
14. Drive pinion
15. Needle bearing
16. Washer
17. Circlip
18. O-ring
19. Set screw
20. Notched ring
21. Dust seal
22. V-ring

87898032

Fig. 70 An exploded view of a manual steering rack

➡ **On the 2002, do not reuse self-locking nuts.**

2. Remove the castle nut and press off the left track rod from the center track rod.

3. Press the center track rod from the steering drop arm.

4. Detach and remove the steering box from the front axle beam.

To install:

5. Install the steering box to the front axle beam and attach the drop arm to the track rod. Connect the left track rod to the center track rod.

6. Connect the steering column coupling to the steering box flange.

➡ **The steering wheel must be in the straight ahead position and the markings on the steering box and the pitman shaft must align.**

320i Models

1. Loosen the front wheels.

2. Raise and safely support the front of the vehicle on jackstands.

3. Remove the cotter pins, if equipped, and castle nut from the steering knuckles.

4. Press the tie rods off of the steering knuckles.

5. Loosen and remove the nut and bolt securing the universal joint at the steering column to the steering rack. Separate the steering column from the steering rack.

6. Remove the retainer bolts attaching the steering rack to the vehicle body.

7. Lift the rack away from the car. Inspect the steering boots, and replace any that are torn or excessively cracked.

To install:

8. Install the steering rack to the vehicle and secure with the retaining bolts. Tighten the retainer bolts securely.

9. Attach the steering column universal joint to the steering rack, making sure the splines on each align correctly, and the nut and bolt slide through the mounting holes easily. Do not force any part. If necessary separate the parts and try again.

10. Attach the tie rods to the steering knuckles. Install the castle nuts and cotter pins to the tie rods. Install the front wheel.

11. Have the vehicle front end alignment checked.

ADJUSTMENT

1600, 2000, 2002, 2500, 2800, Bavaria, 3000 and 3.0 Models

1. Remove the air intake filter on 2002 models.

2. Position the front wheels straight ahead.

3. The marking on the worm shaft must be in alignment with the marking on the steering box.

4. Remove the castle nut and press the left hand tie rod from the center tie rod.

5. Remove the castle nut and press the center tie rod from the drop arm with special tool 7009, or the equivalent.

6. Remove the steering wheel center and install a friction gauge.

7. Turn the steering wheel one turn to the left from the straight ahead position. In this position the worm cannot be pressed one-sided into its bearing by the steering roller shaft, which might indicate absence of play.

8. Turn the adjustment screw until the specified friction coefficient is reached when passing through the straight ahead position.

320i Models

1. Remove the steering gear from the car.

2. Clamp the special tool 32 1 100, or equivalent, in a vise and place the steering gear assembly into the tool.

3. Unscrew the nut on the steering damper and slide it back.

4. Remove the cap and unscrew the socket head cap about 12mm.

5. Pressure pad adjustment:

   a. Remove the cotter pin. Tighten the set screw with special 32 1 100, or equivalent, and a tighten wrench, to 4 ft. lbs. (52 Nm). Loosen the set screw by one full castle slot to align the cotter pin bore.

   b. Use special tools 32 1 00 and 00 2 000 or equivalent to move rack to the left and right over the entire stroke and check for sticking and hooking. If this is the case, loosen the set screw by one more castle slot and insert the cotter pin.

   c. Repeat the test. If there is still sticking or hooking, replace rack, drive pinion or the entire steering gear. Never loosen the screw by 2 castle slots regardless of circumstances.

6. Turning torque adjustment:

   a. Move rack to the center position. Place special tools 00 2 000 and 32 1 000 or equivalent on the drive pinion, check the turning torque. If it is not between 8–11 ft. lbs. (9–14 Nm), adjust the set screw.

   b. Turn to the right to increase friction, and turn to the left to decrease friction.

   c. Install the cap.

Power Steering Rack

▶ See Figure 71

REMOVAL & INSTALLATION

Except 3, 5, 6 and 7 Series Models

1. Turn the steering to left lock.

2. On models, which share the hydraulic system with the power brakes, discharge pressure from the system by operating the brake pedal hard about 20 times. Then, drain brake fluid out of the reservoir. Remove the 2 mounting nuts/bolts and remove the pipe connecting the steering unit and the rest of the system.

3. On all other systems, drain the steering fluid at this point.

4. Remove the cotter pin and loosen the castellated nut. Then, press the center tie rod off the steering drop arm.

5. Remove the screw or nut(s) and bolt(s) and slide the U-joint off the steering box or slide the flange coupling the steering column and steering gear upward. Replace all self-locking nuts.

6. Disconnect the hoses at the steering gear and plug the openings.

7. Detach and remove the steering gear mounting bolts at the front axle carrier, working below it. Be careful to retain all washers. They are used on both side of the front axle carrier members.

   To install:

8. Install the steering gear into position. Use new seals on the hydraulic lines.

9. The U-joint bolts must pass through the locking grooves on the steering shaft and steering unit shaft.

10. If equipped with alignment marks on the steering shaft and gearbox, align the marks so the steering wheel will be in the straight ahead position.

11. Use a new cotter pin on the castellated nut. Replace all self-locking nuts. A new, self locking nut is available to replace the castellated nut on the steering drop arm. Use new hydraulic fluid.

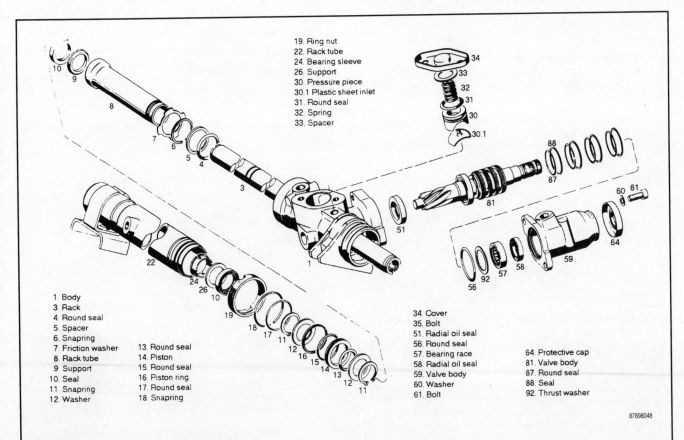

19. Ring nut
22. Rack tube
24. Bearing sleeve
26. Support
30. Pressure piece
30.1 Plastic sheet inlet
31. Round seal
32. Spring
33. Spacer

1. Body
3. Rack
4. Round seal
5. Spacer
6. Snapring
7. Friction washer
8. Rack tube
9. Support
10. Seal
11. Snapring
12. Washer
13. Round seal
14. Piston
15. Round seal
16. Piston ring
17. Round seal
18. Snapring

34. Cover
35. Bolt
51. Radial oil seal
56. Round seal
57. Bearing race
58. Radial oil seal
59. Valve body
60. Washer
61. Bolt
64. Protective cap
81. Valve body
87. Round seal
88. Seal
92. Thrust washer

87898048

Fig. 71 An exploded view of a power steering rack

➡The power steering system must be bled with the front wheels in the straight ahead position. Marks on the housing and propeller shaft must align. Use new self locking nuts on all models.

3 Series Models

2-WHEEL DRIVE MODELS

▶ See Figures 72, 73, 74, 75 and 76

➡On models with SRS, observe all safety precautions. Special care should be taken when handling the column, so as not to damage the shear pins. Damage to the shear pins could cause the column not to collapse in the event of an accident.

1. Disarm the SRS system, if equipped.
2. Raise and support the front end of the vehicle. Remove the front wheels.
3. Remove the steering wheel. Remove the steering rack coupling bolt. Loosen the upper bolt so the coupling can be disconnected from the steering rack.
4. Remove the power steering fluid from the reservoir and discard. Disconnect and plug the fluid return line from the rack. Remove the pressure line hollow bolt from the rack and plug.
5. Disconnect the tie rods from the steering knuckles. Remove the steer-

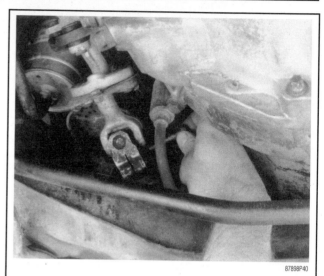

Fig. 74 After removing the bolt, separate the coupler from the rack

Fig. 72 Loosen and remove the nut and bolt securing the universal joint to the steering rack

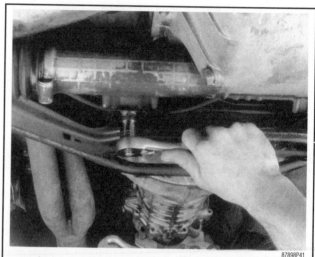

Fig. 75 Remove the bolts securing the steering rack to the vehicle subframe

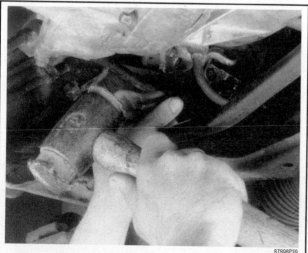

Fig. 73 In some cases the bolt may have to be tapped out with a punch

Fig. 76 With the engine lifted slightly, the steering rack can be removed

ing rack mounting bolts. Note which holes the steering rack was mounted to. If equipped, disconnect the engine mounts located above the steering rack.

6. Raise the engine about 2 in. (50mm) and remove the steering rack.

To install:

7. Install the steering gear. Use the rear holes in the crossmember or the ones originally used if not the rear holes. Lower the engine.

8. Tighten the steering gear bolts to 30 ft. lbs. (42 Nm). Tighten the engine mount nuts to 16 ft. lbs. (22 Nm) for grade M8 bolts and 30 ft. lbs. (42 Nm) for grade M10 bolts.

9. Connect the tie rods to the steering knuckles and tighten the nuts to 23–29 ft. lbs. (33–40 Nm). Do not use a locknut on a joint that has a hole for a cotter pin. If originally equipped with a locknut, use a new locknut for installation.

10. Connect the return line to the steering rack. Connect the pressure line to the steering rack using new crush washers. Tighten the hollow bolt to 7 ft. lbs. (10 Nm) for grade M10 bolts and 14.5 ft. lbs. (20 Nm) for grade M12 bolts.

11. Align the mark on the steering rack shaft with the mark on the rack housing. Align the slot of the universal joint with the shaft and housing marks. This is the centered position. Install the bolts and tighten to 16 ft. lbs. (22 Nm).

12. Install the steering wheel in the centered position.

13. Fill and bleed the power steering reservoir. Have the alignment checked.

4-WHEEL DRIVE MODELS

➡ **To remove the steering gear on 4WD vehicles, use a special tool to support the engine via the body. It is also advisable to use a special tool to support the front axle carrier without damaging it. It is necessary to remove the entire front axle carrier to gain access to the mounting bolts for the steering gear on this vehicle.**

1. Raise the vehicle and support it securely on jackstands. Remove the lower splash guard. Remove the front wheels.

2. Remove the air cleaner. Use a clean turkey baster to remove the power steering fluid from the pump reservoir.

3. Attach the engine support tool and connect it to the engine hooks to be sure the engine is securely supported.

4. Remove the through bolts from the right and left engine mounts.

5. Disconnect both the hydraulic lines running from the power steering pump to the steering gear, and then plug the openings.

6. Loosen both the retaining bolts and then disconnect the steering column spindle off the steering rack.

7. Remove the retaining nuts on both sides and then press the tie rod ends off the steering knuckles with the proper tools. Be careful to keep grease out of the bores and off the tie rod ball studs.

8. Remove the cotter pins, and retaining nuts on both sides and press the control arm ball joint studs out of the steering knuckles. Be careful to keep grease out of the bores and off the control arm ball studs.

9. Remove the bolts on either side attaching the control arm brackets to the body.

10. Remove the bolts and remove the stabilizer bar mounting brackets from the front axle carrier on both sides.

11. Support the front axle carrier with a suitable jacking device. Then, remove the mounting bolts on either side and remove the axle carrier. Remove the mounting bolts and remove the steering gear from the axle carrier.

To install:

12. Install in reverse order, noting these points:

   a. Clean the bores into which the axle carrier bolts are mounted. Use some sort of locking sealer and tighten the bolts to 30 ft. lbs. (41 Nm).

   b. Tighten the mounting bolts holding the steering gear to front axle carrier to 30 ft. lbs. (41 Nm).

   c. Install new cotter pins on the retaining nuts for the control arm ball studs. Tighten to 61.5 ft. lbs. (84 Nm).

   d. Replace the self-locking nuts on the tie rod end ball studs and connecting the steering column spindle to the steering box. Tighten tie rod ball stud nuts to 24–29 ft. lbs. (33–40 Nm).

   e. Replace the gaskets on power steering hydraulic lines.

13. Refill the fluid reservoir with specified fluid. Idle the engine and turn the steering wheel back and forth until it has reached right and left lock 2 times each. Then, turn off the engine and refill the reservoir.

5, 6 and 7 Series Models

➡ **On models with SRS, observe all safety precautions. Special care should be taken when handling the column, so as not to damage the shear pins. Damage to the shear pins could cause the column not to collapse in the event of an accident.**

1. Disarm the SRS system, if equipped.

2. Disconnect the negative battery cable.

3. Remove the steering wheel, if equipped with an air bag (SRS).

4. Discharge the pressure reservoir by pushing in on the brake pedal until the pedal feels hard. Draw off hydraulic fluid in the supply tank.

5. Unscrew the bolt and press the tie rod off the steering drop arm.

6. Remove the heat shield on the steering gear and disconnect the ride level height control pipes, if equipped.

7. Remove the bolt and push the U-joint from the steering gear. Disconnect and plug the hydraulic lines.

8. Unscrew the steering gear mounting bolts and remove the steering gear.

➡ **If necessary, move the steering drop arm by turning the steering stub to enable the removal of the gear assembly.**

To install:

9. Install the steering gear and tighten the mounting bolts. Tighten the grade M10 bolts to 30 ft. lbs. (42 Nm) and the grade M12 bolts to 52–64 ft. lbs. (72–88 Nm).

10. Connect the hydraulic lines, using new seals. Tighten the grade M14 bolts to 25 ft. lbs. (35 Nm) and the grade M16 bolts to 29 ft. lbs. (40 Nm).

11. Turn the steering wheel counterclockwise or clockwise against the stop and then it back about 1.7 turns until the marks are aligned.

12. Connect the U-joint to the steering gear making sure the bolt is in the locking groove of the steering stub.

13. Install the tie rod to the steering drop arm and replace the self locking nut.

14. Replace the heat shield on the steering gear and connect the ride level height control pipes if equipped.

15. Refill the hydraulic fluid and replace the steering wheel, if equipped with an air bag (SRS).

16. Connect the negative battery cable.

ADJUSTMENT

1. Remove the steering wheel center or the air bag.

2. With the front wheels in the straight ahead position, remove the cotter pin and loosen the castle nut.

3. Press the center tie rod off the steering drop arm.

4. Turn the steering wheel to the left about 1 turn. Install a friction gauge and turn the wheel to the right, past the point of pressure and the gauge should read 0.72–0.87 ft. lbs. (0.93–1.1 Nm).

5. To adjust, turn the steering wheel about 1 turn to the left. Loosen the counter nut and turn the adjusting screw until the specified friction is reached when passing over the point of pressure.

Power Steering Pump

REMOVAL & INSTALLATION

Except 7 Series

1. Disconnect the negative battery cable. Release the pressure from the reservoir.

2. Draw the hydraulic fluid from the pump reservoir. Disconnect and plug the hydraulic lines.

3. Disconnect and plug the hydraulic lines. Remove the bolts and loosen the nuts to turn the adjusting pinion.

4. Remove the drive belt.

5. Remove the bolts from the brackets holding the pump and remove the pump assembly.

6. Reverse the removal procedure for installation. Tighten the adjusting pinion to 6 ft. lbs. (8 Nm).

7. If equipped with a tandem pump the removal and installation procedure is the same.

733I AND 735I MODELS

➡ If the pump is damaged, the pressure control regulator must also be replaced.

1. Discharge the hydraulic accumulator, by depressing the brake pedal with the force required for full stop breaking (about 20 times).

2. Use a syringe to draw the fluid out of the pump reservoir and discard it. Detach all hoses at the pump and plug the openings.

3. Loosen the 2 locknuts and turn the adjusting pinion nut to release the belt tension. Remove the drive belt.

4. Remove the bolts from the brackets holding the pump in place at both top and bottom.

5. Install the pump and its mounting bolts. Reconnect the hoses to the pump in such a way that they will not rub against body parts. Note that on 1983–88 models, the belt tension is released or tightened by unscrewing the splash guard, loosening the locknut and bolts at top and bottom of the pump, and then turning the geared locking element.

6. In adjusting the belt, tighten this locking element in the tightening direction to 69–73 in. lbs. and then tighten the locknut. Use new seals on the hydraulic lines.

➡ Run the engine 10 minutes and turn the steering wheel several times from stop to stop. Operate the brake booster quickly, to obtain hard resistance, about 10 times to discard the oil leaving the return hose.

7. Stop the engine, drain the oil from the tank and connect the booster return hose on the tank.

BELT ADJUSTMENT

Tighten the belt so that when pressure is applied to the belt, the distance between both belt pulleys is 0.2–0.4 inches (5–10mm).

On 1983–88 733i and 735i models tighten the geared locking element in the tightening direction to 69–73 in. lbs. (8–9 Nm) and then tighten the locknut.

SYSTEM BLEEDING

Without Ride Height Control

1. Fill the reservoir to the edge with the proper fluid.
2. Start the engine and all oil until the oil level remains constant.
3. Turn the steering wheel from lock to lock quickly until air bubbles are no longer present in the reservoir.
4. On models incorporating a combination power steering and power brake system, operate the brake pedal to discharge the hydraulic accumulator until the oil level stops rising or noticeable resistance on the brake pedal is felt.

With Ride Height Control

1. Fill the reservoir to the level of the strainer.
2. Rotate the steering in both directions fully at least 2 times.
3. Raise the vehicle so the rear wheels are off the ground.
4. Check the oil level. The level should be about ¼ in. (5 mm) above the strainer after 2 minutes. Fill to the specified mark, if necessary.

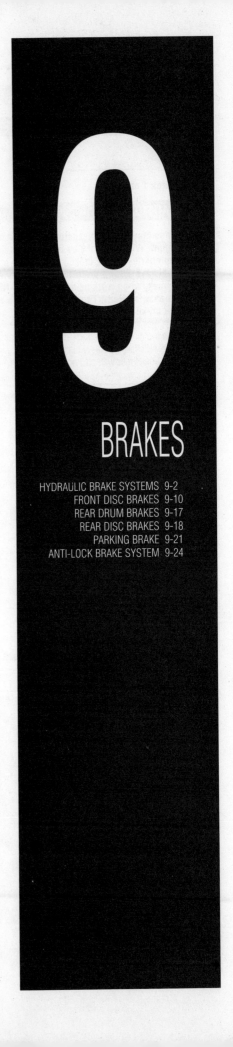

9

BRAKES

HYDRAULIC BRAKE SYSTEMS

Types of Brakes

DISC BRAKES

♦ **See Figures 1 and 2**

> ※※ **CAUTION**
>
> **Brake linings may contain asbestos. Asbestos is a known cancer-causing agent. When working on brakes, remember that the dust which accumulates on the brake parts and/or in the drum contains asbestos. Always wear a protective face covering, such as a painter's mask, when working on the brakes. NEVER blow the dust from the brakes or drum! There are solvents made for the purpose of cleaning brake parts. Use them!**

Disc brake systems utilize a disc (rotor) with brake pads positioned on either side of it. Braking effect is achieved in a squeezing manner. The disc (rotor) is a metal casting, sometimes with cooling fins between the braking surfaces to enable air to circulate between the braking surfaces making them less sensitive to heat buildup and more resistant to fade.

Dirt and water do not affect braking action since contaminants are thrown off by the centrifugal action of the rotor or scraped off the by the pads. Also, the equal clamping action of the two brake pads tends to ensure uniform, straight-line stops. Most disc brakes are inherently self-adjusting.

There are three general types of disc brake:
1. A fixed caliper.
2. A floating caliper.
3. A sliding caliper.

The fixed caliper design uses two pistons mounted on either side of the rotor (in each side of the caliper). The caliper is mounted rigidly and does not move.

Sliding and floating designs are quite similar. In fact, these two types are often lumped together. In these designs, the pad on the inside of the rotor is moved into contact with the rotor by hydraulic force. The caliper, which is not held in a fixed position, moves slightly, bringing the outside pad into contact with the rotor. There are various methods of attaching floating calipers. Some pivot at the bottom or top, whereas others slide on mounting bolts. In any event, the end result is the same.

DRUM BRAKES

> ※※ **CAUTION**
>
> **Brake linings may contain asbestos. Asbestos is a known cancer-causing agent. When working on brakes, remember that the dust which accumulates on the brake parts and/or in the drum contains asbestos. Always wear a protective face covering, such as a painter's mask, when working on the brakes. NEVER blow the dust from the brakes or drum! There are solvents made for the purpose of cleaning brake parts. Use them!**

Drum brakes employ two brake shoes mounted on a stationary backing plate. These shoes are positioned inside a circular drum which rotates with the wheel assembly. The shoes are held in place by springs which allow them to slide toward the drums (when they are applied) while keeping the linings and drums in alignment. The shoes are actuated by a wheel cylinder which is mounted at the top of the backing plate. When the brakes are applied, hydraulic pressure forces the wheel cylinder's actuating links outward. Since these links bear directly against the top of the brake shoes, the tops of the shoes are then forced against the inner side of the drum. This action forces the shoes to contact the brake drum by rotating the entire assembly slightly (known as servo action). When pressure within the wheel cylinder is relaxed, return springs pull the shoes back away from the drum.

Most modern drum brakes are designed to self-adjust themselves during application when the vehicle is moving in reverse. This motion causes both shoes to rotate very slightly with the drum, rocking an adjusting lever, thereby causing rotation of the adjusting screw.

Adjustments

HANDBRAKE & DRUM

1600, 2000 2002 and 320i Models

Adjustment of the drum and handbrake is recommended at 8,000 miles (13,000 km) intervals for 1970–74 models, and 12,500 miles (20,000 km) intervals for 1975–88 models. In addition, if the handbrake can be pulled up more than four notches on 1970–74 vehicles, or five notches on 1975–88 models, adjustment should be performed.

To adjust the rear brakes, proceed as follows:
1. Support the rear of the car securely on jackstands.
2. Release the handbrake lever fully.
3. The brake adjusting bolt is located at the rear of the backing plate, behind the drive axle. Turn counterclockwise on the left side and clockwise on the right

Fig. 1 An example of a disc front brake assembly

Fig. 2 Although this looks like a disc brake assembly, it also includes a hand drum brake inside the rotor cap

side to tighten the brakes Spin the wheel and gradually adjust until the wheel stops and cannot be easily turned. Then, loosen exactly ⅛ turn; just to the point where there is no drag felt. Repeat on the other side.

To adjust the parking brake cable, proceed as follows:

4. Pull the handbrake lever up five notches on 1975–88 vehicles, or four notches on 1970–74 vehicles. Measure the distance between the middle of the handbrake lever and the driveshaft tunnel. It should be 4–5 inches (109–119mm). If it is not within specification, reset the handbrake into another notch until the dimension is correct.

5. Pull up the rubber boot, loosen locknut on the top, then tighten the adjusting nut until the wheel on that side is locked. Repeat for the other side. Tighten both locknuts and install the rubber boot.

6. Check to make sure the adjustment is correct by checking that the wheels are released completely when the brake is released, as well as that both wheels are slowed at the same time as the lever Is raised. Repeat the adjustments if necessary.

All Other Models

If the handbrake can be pulled up mode than five notches, cable adjustment is needed.

1. Raise the rear of the vehicle and support securely on jackstands

2. If the handbrake has a leather or rubber cover over it, remove the cover by lifting up on the rear of the cover and sliding it forward down the length of the handbrake. If there is no rubber or leather cover, remove the center console to access the handbrake adjustment nut.

3. Lift the handbrake up four notches. Use a hand and try and rotate the rear wheels. They should move, but with some resistance from the brakes.

➡**If the wheels move freely, the brake shoes also need adjusting. Refer to the appropriate procedure in this section.**

4. At the base of the handbrake is the adjustment nut. Using a ratchet and socket or other suitable tool to tighten the adjusting nut. After a couple of turns, try and move the rear wheels again. Tighten the nuts until the wheels no longer move.

5. Before lowering the car, with the handbrake off, rotate the wheels until they rotate freely, As the wheel is rotating, slowly raise the hand brake one successive notch. At the first notch the rotation should be unaffected. With each additional notch, the wheel should slow down as the brake shoes grasp. By the third notch the wheel should stop. If the wheel stops any sooner, the brake cable is too tight and should be loosened.

6. Install the handbrake cover or console. Lower the vehicle.

Brake Light Switch

▶ **See Figure 3**

The brake light switch is located at brake pedal. There are different styles of switches. If there is a single threaded body switch, the switch will need to be manually adjusted. If the body is not threaded, it only has to be adjusted once during installation. If there are 2 switches at the brake pedal, one threaded and one that is not, the non-threaded unit operates the brake lights and the threaded body switch is the test switch.

REMOVAL & INSTALLATION

Threaded Body

1. Remove the lower dashboard trim to access the brake light switch.
2. Pull the wire connectors off the switch.
3. Loosen the switch locknuts and thread the switch out of the holder.
4. Install in reverse order. Adjust the switch there is 0.236 inches (6mm) from the pedal to the edge of the switch threads.
5. Connect the wires and install the trim.

Non-Threaded Body

1. Disconnect the wiring harness from the brake light switch.
2. Press the brake pedal and hold down. Pull the plunger and sleeve of the brake switch forward and pull the switch out of the holder.

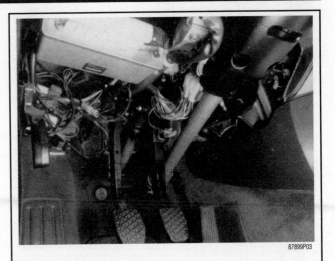

87899P03

Fig. 3 The brake light switch is located near the top of the brake pedal—3 Series shown

3. Depress and hold the brake pedal down. Pull the sleeve and plunger to the full out position. Install in the holder and slowly release the brake pedal. This will automatically adjust the switch position.
4. Connect the harness plug.

ADJUSTMENT

Threaded Body

1. Remove the lower dashboard trim to access the brake light switch.
2. Pull the wire connectors off the switch.
3. Loosen the switch locknuts.
4. Adjust the switch there is 0.236 inches (6mm) from the pedal to the edge of the switch threads.

Non-Threaded Body

1. Disconnect the wiring harness from the brake light switch.
2. Press the brake pedal and hold down. Pull the plunger and sleeve of the brake switch forward and pull the switch out of the holder.
3. Depress and hold the brake pedal down. Pull the sleeve and plunger to the full out position. Install in the holder and slowly release the brake pedal. This will automatically adjust the switch position.
4. Connect the harness plug.

Master Cylinder

➡**Models equipped with anti-lock brakes require expensive and specialized equipment to bleed the brake system. If you do not own or have access to this equipment, it is best to have a properly equipped professional perform this procedure.**

REMOVAL & INSTALLATION

➡**When removing or installing brake line or hoses, always use a backup wrench on the fitting to prevent twisting. Avoid bending the lines or damaging the coating.**

Except 3, 5, 6 and 7 Series Models

▶ **See Figure 4**

➡**When removing brake fluid, always replace with new DOT 3 or 4 grade brake fluid**

1. Remove the air cleaner assembly if necessary.
2. Drain as much brake fluid from the master cylinder.

Fig. 4 From left-to-right, the master cylinder is bolted to the brake booster and pedal assembly—2002 model

✴✴ CAUTION

Exercise extreme care in handling brake fluid near the painted surface of vehicle as fluid will destroy the paint finish if allowed to come into contact with it.

3. Disconnect the brake fluid reservoir. The brake fluid reservoir will be mounted in one of two ways: (1) installed directly on top of the master cylinder. In this case, tilt the reservoir to one side and prying carefully from underneath, lift the reservoir off of the master cylinder, or (2) the reservoir is mounted to the inner fender sheet metal by means of retaining bolts. To remove, carefully disconnect the hoses leading to the master cylinder and allow any remaining brake fluid to drain into a container.

4. Mark, then disconnect all brake lines from the master cylinder.

5. Remove the master cylinder-to-power booster attaching nuts, and remove the master cylinder from the booster and vehicle. Observe the correct seating of the master cylinder-to-power booster seal.

➡Check for proper seating of the master cylinder-to-power booster O-ring. Check the clearance between the master cylinder piston and pushrod with a plastic gauge, and, if necessary, adjust to 0.0020 inches (0.05mm) by placing shims behind the head of the pushrod.

To install:

6. Position the master cylinder onto the studs protruding from the power booster. Install and tighten the attaching nuts to 14 ft. lbs. (20 Nm).

7. Connect the brake lines in their correct order to the master cylinder. Begin Installing each line by finger-tightening the connection to prevent any crossthreading. Tighten the fittings to 10 ft. lbs. (14 Nm)

8. Install the brake fluid reservoir and fill with brake fluid.

9. Bleed the brake and clutch (if equipped) system.

3 Series Models

▶ See Figures 5 thru 10

➡Models equipped with anti-lock brakes require expensive and specialized equipment to bleed the brake system. If you do not own or have access to this equipment, it is best to have a properly equipped professional perform this procedure.

1. If working on a 320i, remove the fuel mixture control unit.

➡When removing brake fluid, always replace with new DOT 3 or 4 grade brake fluid

2. Disconnect the brake fluid level indicator plug, and place aside.

Fig. 5 Use a turkey baster to remove as much brake fluid from the reservoir as possible

Fig. 6 Disconnect the wires attached to the fluid cap and the clutch master cylinder hydraulic hose

Fig. 7 Mark each brake line attached to the master cylinder for correct placement identification

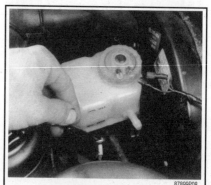

Fig. 8 Use a flare-end wrench to remove the brake line from the master cylinder

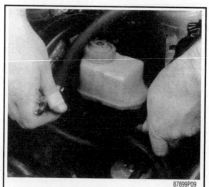

Fig. 9 Remove the nuts securing the master cylinder to the brake booster

Fig. 10 Lift the master cylinder off the studs and out of the vehicle

➡When removing or installing brake line or hoses, always use a backup wrench on the fitting to prevent twisting. Avoid bending the lines or damaging the coating.

3. Unfasten the clutch master cylinder hose at the fluid reservoir. Cap the hose end, or allow it to dip into a suitable container.

✳✳ CAUTION

Exercise extreme care in handling brake fluid near the painted surface of vehicle as fluid will destroy the paint finish if allowed to come into contact with it.

4. Remove the brake fluid from the reservoir, then disconnect the brake fluid reservoir from the master cylinder by unfastening the hoses. Check the condition of each hose and replace if needed.
5. Tag for identification each brake line. Disconnect the brake lines from the master cylinder.
6. On the 320i, work from the underside of the left side inner fender panel (wheel opening area) and remove the two master cylinder support bracket attaching nuts.
7. Remove the master cylinder-to-power booster attaching nuts. Slide the master cylinder out and remove the master cylinder. Inspect the rubber vacuum seal in the end of the unit and replace, if necessary.

To install:
8. Install the master cylinder to the power booster.studs and secure with the retaining nuts tightened to 14 ft. lbs. (20 Nm).
9. Reconnect the brake lines in their correct order. Tighten each fitting to 10 ft. lbs. (14 Nm). Install the fluid reservoir filling with clean brake fluid. Connect the fluid level indicator.
10. Bleed the brake and clutch (if equipped) system.

5 and 6 Series Models

WITH VACUUM POWER BRAKES

➡Models equipped with anti-lock brakes require expensive and specialized equipment to bleed the brake system. If you do not own or have access to this equipment, it is best to have a properly equipped professional perform this procedure.

1. Remove as much brake fluid from the brake reservoir as possible. Disconnect the brake fluid line going to the clutch master cylinder and plug it or allow it to drip into a suitable container.

➡When removing or installing brake line or hoses, always use a backup wrench on the fitting to prevent twisting. Avoid bending the lines or damaging the coating.

✳✳ CAUTION

Exercise extreme care in handling brake fluid near the painted surface of vehicle as fluid will destroy the paint finish if allowed to come into contact with it.

2. Tag for identification, then disconnect the two brake lines connected to the side of the master cylinder.
3. Remove the mounting hardware which secures the master cylinder to the booster. Slide out and remove the master cylinder from the power booster.
4. Inspect the rubber O-ring located in the groove of the rear of the master cylinder. Replace it if damaged.

To install:
5. Install the master cylinder in position, securing the hardware to 18–21 ft. lbs. (25–29 Nm) on the booster. Reconnect the fluid lines tightening to 10 ft.lbs. (10 Nm). Connect all hoses removed earlier.
6. Bleed the the brake and clutch (if equipped) system.

WITH HYDRAULIC POWER BRAKES

➡Models equipped with anti-lock brakes require expensive and specialized equipment to bleed the brake system. If you do not own or have access to this equipment, it is best to have a properly equipped professional perform this procedure.

1. Depress the brake pedal with maximum force about 20 times to remove all residual hydraulic pressure. Remove as much brake fluid from the brake

fluid reservoir as possible using a turkey baster or other suitable clean instrument.

➡When removing or installing brake line or hoses, always use a backup wrench on the fitting to prevent twisting. Avoid bending the lines or damaging the coating.

✳✳ CAUTION

Exercise extreme care in handling brake fluid near the painted surface of vehicle as fluid will destroy the paint finish if allowed to come into contact with it.

2. Disconnect and cap the hydraulic hoses and remove the fluid storage tank from the top of the master cylinder.
3. Remove the mounting hardware fastening the master cylinder to the booster. Slide the unit off and remove it from the vehicle.
4. Check the master cylinder sealing O-ring and replace if needed.
To install:
5. Install the master cylinder on the booster tightening the retaining hardware to 18–21 ft. lbs. (25–29 Nm). Reconnect the brake lines, tightening the fitting to 10 ft. lbs. (14 Nm). Fill the master cylinder and bleed the system.

7 Series Models

➡Models equipped with anti-lock brakes require expensive and specialized equipment to bleed the brake system. If you do not own or have access to this equipment, it is best to have a properly equipped professional perform this procedure.

1. Remove or drain any brake fluid from the brake reservoir.

✳✳ CAUTION

Exercise extreme care in handling brake fluid near the painted surface of vehicle as fluid will destroy the paint finish if allowed to come into contact with it.

➡When removing or installing brake line or hoses, always use a backup wrench on the fitting to prevent twisting. Avoid bending the lines or damaging the coating.

2. Tag for identification, then disconnect the brake lines from the master cylinder.
3. Remove the master cylinder-to-hydraulic booster attaching bolts, and remove the master cylinder from the vehicle.
4. Check the condition of the master cylinder sealing O-ring and replace if needed.
5. Install the master cylinder on the booster securing the retaining bolts to 18–21 ft. lbs. (25–29 Nm).
6. Reconnect the brake lines tightening the fittings to 10 ft. lbs. (14 Nm).
7. Install the fluid reservoir, and fill with clean brake fluid. Complete the job by bleeding the brake system

Vacuum Operated Power Brake Booster

REMOVAL & INSTALLATION

3 Series

EXCEPT 320I

➡Models equipped with anti-lock brakes require expensive and specialized equipment to bleed the brake system. If you do not own or have access to this equipment, it is best to have a properly equipped professional perform this procedure.

✳✳ CAUTION

Exercise extreme care in handling brake fluid near the painted surface of vehicle as fluid will destroy the paint finish if allowed to come into contact with it.

1. Disconnect the negative battery cable.

➡️**When removing or installing brake line or hoses, always use a backup wrench on the fitting to prevent twisting. Avoid bending the lines or damaging the coating.**

2. Draw off brake fluid in the reservoir and discard.

➡️**When removing brake fluid, always replace with new DOT 3 or 4 grade brake fluid**

3. Remove the reservoir, then disconnect and cap the clutch hydraulic hose.
4. Tag for identification, then disconnect all brake lines from the master cylinder.
5. Unfasten the retaining hardware securing the master cylinder to the booster, and remove the master cylinder from the vehicle.
6. Remove the lower instrument panel trim from the driver's side of the passenger compartment.
7. Remove the return spring from the brake pedal. Press off the clip and remove the pin which connects the booster rod to the brake pedal.
8. Remove the four nuts securing the booster, and pull the booster and master cylinder out of the engine compartment.
9. If the filter in the brake booster is clogged, it will have to be cleaned. To do this, remove the dust boot, retainer, damper, and filter, then clean the damper and filter. Make sure when reinstalling that the slots in the damper and filter are offset 180°.

To install:
10. Install the booster and master cylinder back into position. Tighten the retaining nuts to 16 ft. lbs. (22 Nm).
11. Connect the booster rod to the brake pedal using the clip removed earlier. Do not forget to install the spring. Adjust the stoplight switch for a clearance of 0.19–0.23 inches (5–6mm). When complete, position and secure the lower trim panel.
12. Inspect the rubber seal between the master cylinder and booster and replace it if necessary.
13. Install the master cylinder to the booster, followed by the reservoir and hoses.
14. Fill the reservoir with brake fluid and bleed the brake/clutch system.

320I MODELS

➡️**When removing or installing brake line or hoses, always use a backup wrench on the fitting to prevent twisting. Avoid bending the lines or damaging the coating.**

⁂ CAUTION

Exercise extreme care in handling brake fluid near the painted surface of vehicle as fluid will destroy the paint finish if allowed to come into contact with it.

1. Remove the master cylinder.

➡️**When removing brake fluid, always replace with new DOT 3 or 4 grade brake fluid**

2. Disconnect the vacuum line at the power booster.
3. Remove the brake pedal apply-rod to power booster pushrod pin from the pedal assembly inside the passenger compartment.
4. Remove the power booster attaching nuts, and remove the power booster from the vehicle.

To install:
5. Position the booster and secure with the attaching nuts tightened to 16 ft. lbs. (22 Nm).
6. Connect the brake pedal rod using the pin removed earlier.
7. Install the master cylinder and brake lines. Reconnect all hoses and vacuum lines.
8. Adjust the extended visible length of the brake light switch head to 0.19–0.23 inches (5–6mm).
9. Bleed the brake system as needed.

5 and 6 Series

1975–85 MODELS

▶ **See Figure 11**

➡️**Models equipped with anti-lock brakes require expensive and specialized equipment to bleed the brake system. If you do not own or have**

access to this equipment, it is best to have a properly equipped professional perform this procedure.

⁂ CAUTION

Exercise extreme care in handling brake fluid near the painted surface of vehicle as fluid will destroy the paint finish if allowed to come into contact with it.

1. Remove the coolant reservoir from the engine compartment.
2. Remove the brake hoses, steel lines and master cylinder. If needed, mark any lines or hose to ease reinstallation.

➡️**When removing or installing brake line or hoses, always use a backup wrench on the fitting to prevent twisting. Avoid bending the lines or damaging the coating.**

➡️**When removing brake fluid, always replace with new DOT 3 or 4 grade brake fluid**

3. Disconnect the vacuum hose at the power booster.
4. Remove the driver's side lower trim panel and disconnect the power booster apply rod at the brake pedal.
5. Remove the power booster attaching bolts.
6. Remove the power booster from the vehicle.

To install:
7. Install the booster to the vehicle, tightening the attaching nuts to 16 ft. lbs (22 Nm), and connect the brake pedal rod. Install the master cylinder steel lines and hoses. Reconnect the vacuum line.
8. Adjust the brake pedal distance to 9.0–9.3 inches (230–240mm). Check and adjust the stop light switch distance as described below:
   a. Unfasten the electrical connector and loosen the locknut.
   b. Measure the distance between the button on the end of the switch and the brake pedal. It must be 0.19–0.23 inches (5–6mm). If necessary, turn the stoplight switch to adjust the distance.
   c. Tighten the locknut and reconnect the electrical connector.

1986–88 MODELS

▶ **See Figure 11**

➡️**Models equipped with anti-lock brakes require expensive and specialized equipment to bleed the brake system. If you do not own or have access to this equipment, it is best to have a properly equipped professional perform this procedure.**

⁂ CAUTION

Exercise extreme care in handling brake fluid near the painted surface of vehicle as fluid will destroy the paint finish if allowed to come into contact with it.

1. Remove all brake fluid from the master cylinder.

➡️**When removing brake fluid, always replace with new DOT 3 or 4 grade brake fluid**

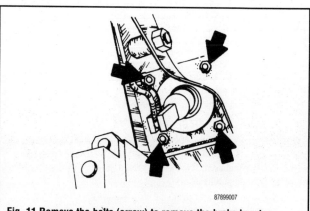

87899007

Fig. 11 Remove the bolts (arrow) to remove the brake booster

2. Disconnect the negative battery cable.

3. Disconnect the electrical plugs from the cap on the fluid reservoir. Disconnect and cap the hose going to the hydraulic clutch.

4. Tag for identification, then disconnect the two brake lines on the outboard side of the master cylinder.

➡**When removing or installing brake line or hoses, always use a backup wrench on the fitting to prevent twisting. Avoid bending the lines or damaging the coating.**

5. Remove the lower instrument panel trim and remove the brake pedal return spring. Then, remove the retaining clip and pull out the clevis pin connecting the pedal linkage to the booster.

6. Remove the four nuts securing the booster to the firewall. Then, remove the booster and master cylinder from the engine compartment.

7. Remove the two mounting bolts and disconnect the master cylinder from the booster.

➡**If the original power booster unit is to be reused, remove the dust boot and clean the silencer and filter. Position the slots in the silencer 180° away from the slots in the filter.**

8. Check the O-ring located in the end of the master cylinder and replace if worn or cracked.

To Install:

9. Install the booster/master cylinder using the attaching nuts tightened to 16 ft. lbs. (22 Nm).

10. Install the pedal linkage, clevis pin and return spring.

11. Adjust the stoplight switch as follows:

  a. Disconnect the electrical connector and loosen the locknut.

  b. Measure the distance between the button on the end of the switch and the brake pedal. It must be 0.19–0.23 inches (5–6mm). If necessary, turn the stoplight switch to adjust the distance.

  c. Tighten the locknut and reconnect the electrical connector.

12. If not already done, fill the reservoir with clean DOT 3 or 4 brake fluid and bleed the brake system completely.

Hydraulically Operated Power Brake Booster

REMOVAL & INSTALLATION

5, 6 and 7 Series Models

▶ See Figure 12

➡**Models equipped with anti-lock brakes require expensive and specialized equipment to bleed the brake system. If you do not own or have access to this equipment, it is best to have a properly equipped professional perform this procedure.**

❊❊ CAUTION

Exercise extreme care in handling brake fluid near the painted surface of vehicle as fluid will destroy the pain finish if allowed to come into contact with it.

1. Release the pressure in the hydraulic accumulator by operating the brake pedal (with the engine turned **OFF**) 20 times.

2. Remove as much brake fluid as possible from the reservoir with a clean turkey baster or other equivalent tool.

➡**When removing brake fluid, always replace with new DOT 3 or 4 grade brake fluid**

3. Disconnect the power booster apply-rod at the brake pedal. This is done by pulling off the bayonet clip and then pulling the pin out of the piston rod.

➡**When removing or installing brake line or hoses, always use a backup wrench on the fitting to prevent twisting. Avoid bending the lines or damaging the coating.**

4. Unfasten the electrical connector and pull off the reservoir.

5. Disconnect the brake hydraulic lines at the master cylinder.

6. Unfasten the hydraulic hoses at the brake booster.

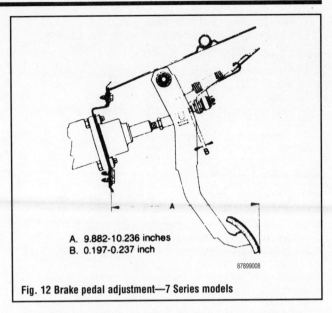

A. 9.882-10.236 inches
B. 0.197-0.237 inch

87899008

Fig. 12 Brake pedal adjustment—7 Series models

7. Remove the bolts from the driver's side of the pedal base assembly and slide the booster and master cylinder assembly out. To separate the master cylinder and booster, remove the two bolts.

8. Measure the distance from the end of the threads on the piston rod to the outer end of the forked fitting for the clevis pin. Then, transfer the fitting over to the new booster, turning it in a clockwise direction until the dimensions are the same.

To install

9. Attach the master cylinder to the booster tightening the retaining hardware to 18–21 ft. lbs. (25–29 Nm).

10. Install the booster in position securing the booster with the attaching nuts tightened to 16 ft. lbs. (22 Nm). It is helpful to keep the following points in mind:

  a. When reattaching the hydraulic fittings to the booster, make sure everything is clean and use the special tools to tighten the fittings.

  b. Check the rubber seals for the master cylinder reservoir and replace them is necessary.

  c. Bleed the brakes. Test operation and boost of the system before driving the vehicle.

Proportioning Valve

➡**Models equipped with anti-lock brakes require expensive and specialized equipment to bleed the brake system. If you do not own or have access to this equipment, it is best to have a properly equipped professional perform this procedure.**

REMOVAL & INSTALLATION

2500, 2800, Bavaria, 3000 and 3.0 Models

➡**When removing or installing brake line or hoses, always use a backup wrench on the fitting to prevent twisting. Avoid bending the lines or damaging the coating.**

1. Remove as much brake fluid from the reservoir as possible.

2. Unscrew the left rear brake hose at the control arm and brake pressure regulator. Unscrew the brake lines at the pressure regulator limiter.

3. Remove the regulator mounting bolts at the underside of the body and remove the regulator.

4. Install the regulator and reconnect the lines. Fill the reservoir with clean brake fluid and bleed the system.

318i, 325, 325e, 325i, 325iS, 325iX and M3 Models

➡**Models equipped with anti-lock brakes require expensive and specialized equipment to bleed the brake system. If you do not own or have access to this equipment, it is best to have a properly equipped professional perform this procedure.**

1. Draw off hydraulic fluid from the master cylinder.
2. Disconnect the brake lines at the top and bottom of the proportioning valve. place a container under the lines to catch any brake fluid which may drip out.
3. Remove the clamp from the valve and unfasten the pressure connection at the union.

To install:
4. Check the day/year codes, reduction factor, and switch-over pressure on the replacement valve is identical.
5. Install the valve and reconnect the brake lines.
6. Fill the reservoir and bleed the brake system.

320i Models

➡ **When removing or installing brake line or hoses, always use a backup wrench on the fitting to prevent twisting. Avoid bending the lines or damaging the coating.**

1. Remove as much brake fluid as possible from the reservoir.
2. Tag for identification, then disconnect the four brake lines at the proportioning valve.
3. Unscrew the two mounting bolts from the inner front left wheel well and remove the valve.

To install:
4. If replacing the valve, replace with a valve bearing the code **25** and an 18mm piston diameter.
5. Install the valve to the fender wall using the mounting bolts.
6. Connect the brake lines. Fill the reservoir with clean brake fluid and bleed the system.

Brake Force Regulator Valve

▸ See Figure 13

REMOVAL & INSTALLATION

➡ **Models equipped with anti-lock brakes require expensive and specialized equipment to bleed the brake system. If you do not own or have access to this equipment, it is best to have a properly equipped professional perform this procedure.**

1. Disconnect the negative battery cable.
2. Remove brake fluid from the master cylinder with a turkey baster or other suitable tool.
3. Disconnect the brake lines at the top and bottom of the proportioning valve.
4. Remove the clamp from the valve.
5. Unfasten the pressure connection at the union.
6. Check the day/year codes, reduction factor, and switch-over pressure to make sure the new valve is identical.
7. Install in reverse order. Bleed the system.

Brake Hoses and Lines

Metal lines and rubber brake hoses should be checked frequently for leaks and external damage. Metal lines are particularly prone to crushing and kinking under the vehicle. Any such deformation can restrict the proper flow of fluid and therefore impair braking at the wheels. Rubber hoses should be checked for cracking or scraping; such damage can create a weak spot in the hose and it could fail under pressure.

Any time the lines are removed or disconnected, extreme cleanliness must be observed. Clean all joints and connections before disassembly (use a stiff bristle brush and clean brake fluid); be sure to plug the lines and ports as soon as they are opened. New lines and hoses should be flushed clean with brake fluid before installation to remove any contamination.

REMOVAL & INSTALLATION

▸ See Figures 14, 15, 16 and 17

1. Disconnect the negative battery cable.
2. Raise and safely support the vehicle on jackstands.
3. Remove any wheel and tire assemblies necessary for access to the particular line you are removing.
4. Thoroughly clean the surrounding area at the joints to be disconnected.
5. Place a suitable catch pan under the joint to be disconnected.
6. Using two wrenches (one to hold the joint and one to turn the fitting), disconnect the hose or line to be replaced.
7. Disconnect the other end of the line or hose, moving the drain pan if necessary. Always use a back-up wrench to avoid damaging the fitting.
8. Disconnect any retaining clips or brackets holding the line and remove the line from the vehicle.

➡ **If the brake system is to remain open for more time than it takes to swap lines, tape or plug each remaining clip and port to keep contaminants out and fluid in.**

To install:
9. Install the new line or hose, starting with the end farthest from the master cylinder. Connect the other end, then confirm that both fittings are correctly threaded and turn smoothly using finger pressure. Make sure the new line will not rub against any other part. Brake lines must be at least 1/2 in. (13mm) from the steering column and other moving parts. Any protective shielding or insulators must be reinstalled in the original location.

✳ WARNING

Make sure the hose is NOT kinked or touching any part of the frame or suspension after installation. These conditions may cause the hose to fail prematurely.

10. Using two wrenches as before, tighten each fitting.
11. Install any retaining clips or brackets on the lines.

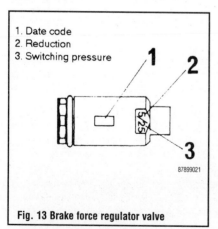

1. Date code
2. Reduction
3. Switching pressure

87899021

Fig. 13 Brake force regulator valve

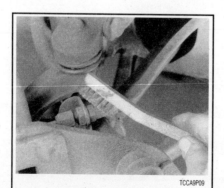

TCCA9P09

Fig. 14 Use a brush to clean the fittings of any debris

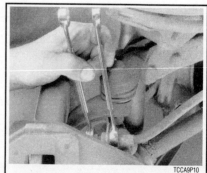

TCCA9P10

Fig. 15 Use two wrenches to loosen the fitting. If available, use flare nut type wrenches

Fig. 16 Any gaskets/crush washers should be replaced with new ones during installation

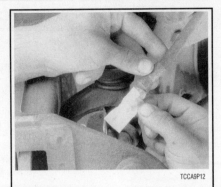

Fig. 17 Tape or plug the line to prevent contamination

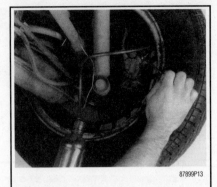

Fig. 18 Bleeding a brake caliper. Replace the bleeder cover when complete

12. If removed, install the wheel and tire assemblies, then carefully lower the vehicle to the ground.

13. Refill the brake master cylinder reservoir with clean, fresh brake fluid, meeting DOT 3 specifications. Properly bleed the brake system.

14. Connect the negative battery cable.

Brake Bleeding

➥Models equipped with anti-lock brakes require expensive and specialized equipment to bleed the brake system. If you do not own or have access to this equipment, it is best to have a properly equipped professional perform this procedure.

PROCEDURE

▶ See Figure 18

➥Whenever any hydraulic part of the brake system is removed, the entire system should be bled to remove any air which may have entered.

1. Fill the master cylinder to the maximum level with the proper brake fluid.
2. Raise and safely support the vehicle on jackstands. Remove the protective caps from the bleeder screws.
3. The proper bleeding sequence always starts with the brake farthest from the master cylinder proceeding to each wheel until you reach the brake closest to the master cylinder.

➥The proper bleeding sequence is: right rear, left rear, right front and left front.

4. Insert a tight fitting plastic tube over the bleeder screw on the caliper/wheel cylinder and the other end of the tube in a transparent container partially filled with clean brake fluid.

5. Depress the brake pedal and loosen the bleeder screw to release the brake fluid. Pump the brake pedal to the stop at least 12 times. Check the tube for air bubbles. If there are no bubbles tighten the bleeder screw.

➥On older vehicles which are not driven regularly, the master cylinder can develop "rough areas". In this case where bleeding the brakes can cause the seals in the master cylinder to tear resulting in the master cylinder needing a rebuild or replacement. As a protective measure, it is recommended that you consult a professional to pressure bleed the brake system, or use a vacuum pump with a bleeder attachment. Vacuum pumps and bleeding kits are available at most automotive parts stores.

6. Repeat this step on all 4 wheels. When complete, tighten the 7mm bleeders to 3.5 ft. lbs. (5 Nm) Replace the bleeder dust covers if cracked torn or missing. Lower the vehicle and check the brake fluid level.

1600, 2000 and 2002 Models

FRONT CALIPERS

Each front caliper must be bled in a specified sequence. Starting with the right front caliper, attach the tube to the bleed nipple at the top front portion of the caliper. Proceed to the nipple at the middle front portion of the caliper, and finally to the nipple at the rear middle portion of the caliper. It is imperative that this sequence be followed.

3 Series Models

➥Models equipped with anti-lock brakes require expensive and specialized equipment to bleed the brake system. If you do not own or have access to this equipment, it is best to have a properly equipped professional perform this procedure.

3 Series vehicles have only one bleed point on each wheel cylinder and one on each caliper. The calipers may be bled without removing the wheels.

All 6 Cylinder Models Except 528e and 733i

➥Models equipped with anti-lock brakes require expensive and specialized equipment to bleed the brake system. If you do not own or have access to this equipment, it is best to have a properly equipped professional perform this procedure.

These models have disc brakes at the rear. Bleed points for these calipers are at the top of the inside. when bleeding front calipers, follow this bleeding sequence;
1. Front top nipple.
2. Rear middle nipple.
3. Front middle nipple.

528e Models

➥Models equipped with anti-lock brakes require expensive and specialized equipment to bleed the brake system. If you do not own or have access to this equipment, it is best to have a properly equipped professional perform this procedure.

The 528e has only one bleeder screw on each caliper, front and rear. The calipers may be bled without removing the wheel.

733i Models

➥Models equipped with anti-lock brakes require expensive and specialized equipment to bleed the brake system. If you do not own or have access to this equipment, it is best to have a properly equipped professional perform this procedure.

Bleed points for these calipers are located at the top inside portion of the caliper and the top outside portion of the caliper. When bleeding the calipers, start at the inside nipple, then proceed to the outside nipple. Always install the rubber bleeder cap when finished.

FRONT DISC BRAKES

▶ See Figure 19

❈❈ CAUTION

Brake shoes and pads may contain asbestos, which has been determined to be a cancer causing agent. Never clean the brake surfaces with compressed air. Avoid inhaling any dust from any brake surface. When cleaning brake surfaces, use a commercially available brake cleaning fluid.

Brake Pads

INSPECTION

Measure the thickness of the entire pad assembly or the lining itself as specified in the "Brake Specifications Chart" and replace a pad which is at or near the wear limit. In case local inspection law specifies more lining material as a minimum requirement, the local law should take precedence.

REMOVAL & INSTALLATION

➡**Models equipped with anti-lock brakes require expensive and specialized equipment to bleed the brake system. If you do not own or have access to this equipment, it is best to have a properly equipped professional perform this procedure.**

Sliding Caliper Equipped Models

▶ See Figures 20 thru 29

➡This type of caliper is most easily identified by the retaining bolts used to secure the caliper to the brake assembly as well as a single bleeder nipple.

1. Raise the front of the vehicle and support safely with jackstands. Remove the wheel and tire.
2. Remove a sufficient quantity of brake fluid from the master cylinder reservoir to prevent the fluid from overflowing the master cylinder when the piston is pressed into the caliper bore.
3. If equipped, unfasten the electrical connector from the brake pad wear indicator and then pull the wires out of the clamp.
4. Remove the pad retaining pins and any retaining clips holding them.
5. Remove the anti-rattle and spreader springs. note the correct positioning of the springs prior to removal. Replace if necessary.
6. Force the old pads away from the brake disc (rotor) for easy withdrawal. This can be done using a pair of pliers. Lift the pads out of the caliper.

To install:

7. Check the brake disc (rotor) for excessive grooves which would indicate that the rotor(s) would need to be cut or replaced.
8. Examine the dust boot for cracks or damage. Push the piston(s) back into the cylinder bores using a C-clamp or other suitable tool. If the pistons are frozen or if the caliper is leaking hydraulic fluid, it will require overhaul or replacement.

Fig. 19 Close-up of 3 Series front disc brake assembly

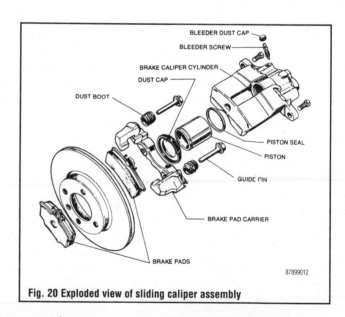

Fig. 20 Exploded view of sliding caliper assembly

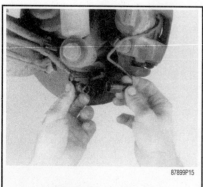

Fig. 21 If equipped, unfasten the wear sensor harness

Fig. 22 Compress the caliper using a C-clamp—this can be also done after the caliper has been removed

Fig. 23 Remove the rubber cap(s) protecting the caliper retaining hardware

Fig. 24 Use an Allen key, Torx® driver or hex wrench to remove the retainer, as needed

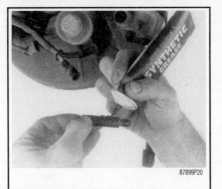

Fig. 25 . . . and grease the shaft to prevent caliper sticking

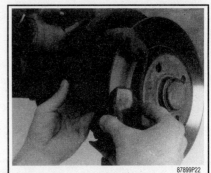

Fig. 26 Remove the front brake pads, then inspect the rotor and pads for wear or damage

Fig. 27 If the pads are equipped with wear sensors, remove and check each sensor for signs of wear

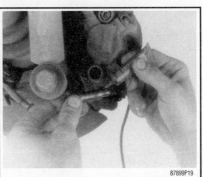

Fig. 28 Before installing the retaining hardware, apply loctite® or equivalent thread lock to the threads . . .

Fig. 29 When both retaining bolts are loosened, slide the caliper off

9. Slip the new pads into the caliper and then install one pad retaining pin and clip. Position the anti-rattle springs and/or spreader springs and then install the other pad retaining pin and clip.

10. Refill the master cylinder with the correct brake fluid.

11. Replace the wheel and lower the vehicle. Pump the brake pedal several times to bring the brakes into correct adjustment. Road test the vehicle.

➡If a firm pedal cannot be obtained, the system will require bleeding. Refer to the procedure in this section).

Fixed Caliper Equipped Models

▶ See Figures 30 and 31

➡A fixed caliper can be identified by multiple bleeder nipples and drive pins securing the brake pad in place. With this type assembly, the caliper does not have to be detached from the rotor to remove the brake pads.

1. Raise and support the front of the vehicle safely on jackstands. Remove the wheel and tire.

2. Siphon a sufficient quantity of brake fluid from the master cylinder reservoir to prevent the fluid from overflowing the master cylinder while removing the pads. This is necessary as the pistons must be forced into the cylinder bore to provide sufficient clearance to remove the pads.

3. Grasp the caliper from behind and pull it toward you. This will push the piston back into the cylinder bore.

4. Disconnect the brake pad lining wear indicator, if equipped.

5. Using a suitable punch, drive out one of the drive pins securing the brake pads in place in the caliper. as the pin is driven out, the pad tension plate will drop out.

6. Drive out the remaining brake drive pin.

7. Remove the brake pads by sliding them out the caliper opening.

To install:

8. Check the brake disc (rotor) for excessive grooves which would indicate that the rotor(s) should be cut or replaced.

9. Examine the dust boot for cracks or damage, then push the piston back into the cylinder bore. If the piston is frozen or the caliper is leaking brake fluid, it will require overhaul or replacement.

10. Slip the new pads into the mounting bracket and then install the caliper in the reverse order of removal.

11. Refill the master cylinder with the proper brake fluid.

12. Replace the wheel and lower the vehicle. Pump the brake pedal several times to bring the brakes into correct adjustment. Road test the vehicle.

➡If a firm pedal cannot be obtained, the system will require bleeding. Refer to the procedure in this section).

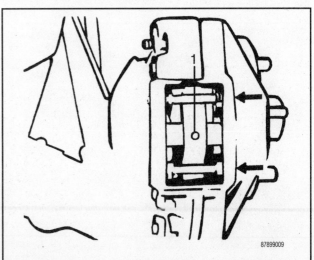

Fig. 30 Fixed caliper front brake. Notice the drive pins (arrows) and the tension plate (1)

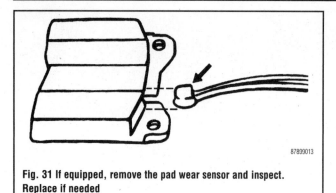

Fig. 31 If equipped, remove the pad wear sensor and inspect. Replace if needed

Front Brake Caliper

REMOVAL & INSTALLATION

Sliding Caliper

▶ See Figures 32 and 33

→Models equipped with anti-lock brakes require expensive and specialized equipment to bleed the brake system. If you do not own or have access to this equipment, it is best to have a properly equipped professional perform this procedure.

✳✳ CAUTION

Exercise extreme care in handling brake fluid near the painted surface of vehicle as fluid will destroy the pain finish if allowed to come into contact with it.

→This type of caliper is most easily identified by the retaining bolts used to secure the caliper to the brake assembly as well as a single bleeder nipple.

1. Support the front of the vehicle safely on jackstands, and remove the front wheels.
2. Remove the brake pads.

→When removing or installing brake line or hoses, always use a backup wrench on the fitting to prevent twisting. Avoid bending the lines or damaging the coating.

3. Remove as much brake fluid as possible from the reservoir, then disconnect the brake hose from the brake line, and cap the line to prevent brake fluid

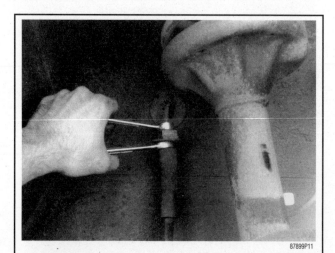

Fig. 32 Use two flare wrenches to loosen the brake hose to brake line connection

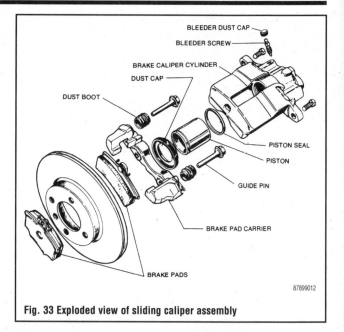

Fig. 33 Exploded view of sliding caliper assembly

from escaping or place a suitable container below the line to catch any dripping fluid.

✳✳ CAUTION

If the fluid appears to be contaminated, discolored, or otherwise unusual in appearance, viscosity, or smell, then allow the fluid to drain from the uncapped brake lines, and flush the system.

4. Remove the caliper-to-steering knuckle attaching bolts, and remove the caliper.

To install:

5. Position the caliper to the steering knuckle and install the attaching bolts and tighten the bolts to 58–70 ft. lbs (75–97 Nm).
6. Reconnect the brake lines.
7. Install the brake pads and necessary hardware.
8. Bleed the brake system.
9. Install the wheel and lower the vehicle.
10. Pump the brake pedal several times to check for pedal sloggishness.

Fixed Caliper

▶ See Figures 32 and 33

✳✳ CAUTION

Exercise extreme care in handling brake fluid near the painted surface of vehicle as fluid will destroy the pain finish if allowed to come into contact with it.

→A fixed caliper can be identified by multiple bleeder nipples and drive pins securing the brake pad in place. With this type assembly, the caliper does not have to be detached from the rotor to remove the brake pads.

1. Raise and support the front of the vehicle safely on jackstands. Remove the wheel and tire.
2. Remove as much brake fluid from the reservoir as possible.
3. Grasp the caliper from behind and pull it toward you. This will push the piston back into the cylinder bore.
4. Disconnect the brake pad lining wear indicator.
5. Remove the drive pins and brake pads.

→When removing or installing brake line or hoses, always use a backup wrench on the fitting to prevent twisting. Avoid bending the lines or damaging the coating.

6. Remove the brake line and allow any excess fluid to drip into a suitable container placed below the line.

7. Remove the retaining bolts which secure the fixed caliper to the steering knuckle.

To install:

8. Examine the dust boot for cracks or damage.

9. Install the brake line to the caliper, using a flare wrench to tighten the connection.

10. Slip the brake pads into the mounting bracket and then install the caliper in the reverse order of removal.

11. Refill the master cylinder with the proper brake fluid and bleed the brakes.

12. Replace the wheel and lower the vehicle. Pump the brake pedal several times to bring the brakes into correct adjustment. Road test the vehicle.

OVERHAUL

➡ **Models equipped with anti-lock brakes require expensive and specialized equipment to bleed the brake system. If you do not own or have access to this equipment, it is best to have a properly equipped professional perform this procedure.**

Multiple Piston Design

▶ **See Figures 34 and 35**

➡ **All fixed calipers are a multiple piston design.**

1. Raise the vehicle and support safely on jackstands.
2. Remove the wheel and tire assembly.
3. Remove the caliper from the vehicle and place on a clean surface.
4. Remove the protective dust boot snapring using a pick tool or other suitable tool.
5. Using a BMW special tool 34 1 050 or an equivalent piston pressing device, press one piston into the caliper cylinder to the fully retracted position, and lock into place. This can also be done using a C-clamp.
6. Insert a piece of hardwood, plastic, or any material of similar consistency, approximately 0.31 inches (8mm) thick, between the secured piston and the opposing piston.
7. Apply low pressure compressed air through the threaded brake line port and into the circuit which controls the locked piston, thereby forcing the opposed piston out of the cylinder.

☀ CAUTION

When using compressed air to remove a piston keep all fingers away from the piston in case it dislodges quickly.

8. Remove the piston pressing tool, and plug the open cylinder bore with an Ate sealing plate or other suitable tool.
9. Insert the protective block of wood between the remaining piston and the caliper housing, and, again, apply compressed air through the threaded brake line port and into the circuit which controls the remaining piston, thereby forcing the piston out of the cylinder.

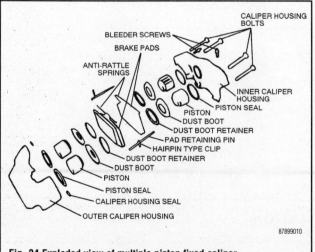

Fig. 34 Exploded view of multiple piston fixed caliper

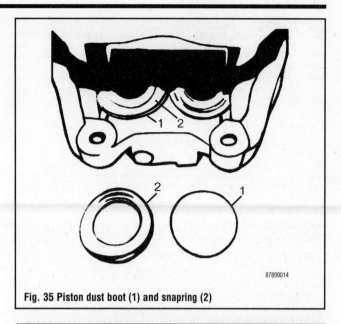

Fig. 35 Piston dust boot (1) and snapring (2)

☀ CAUTION

Apply compressed air through the circuit which corresponds with the piston to be removed. DO NOT apply compressed air to the other circuit unless the corresponding pistons are protected with the piece of wood previously mentioned.

10. Repeat Steps 2 through 6 for the remaining pistons.
11. Carefully remove the piston O-ring using a pick tool or other tool. Do not scratch the piston or bore.
12. Examine the pistons and cylinder bores for a scoring or binding condition. Replace if necessary. Minor pitting can be removed with a mild Scotchbrite® pad or other suitable product.

➡ **The manufacturer specifically advises against machining either the piston or the cylinder bore. The recommended extend of overhaul should include only the examination of parts and/or the replacement of the dust boot and piston O-ring. The caliper halves should not be separated. An exception to this would be a problem involving a piston which is jammed in the cylinder bore. In this case it may be necessary to separate the cylinder halves in order to free the piston from the cylinder bore.**

To assemble:

13. Lubricate the piston, cylinder wall, and piston O-ring with clean brake fluid prior to assembly.
14. Install the piston O-ring being careful not to tear it.
15. Position the piston into the cylinder bore and press until fully seated. If the fit is tight, do not attempt to force the piston into place. Remove clean and try again.
16. Attach the brake line to the caliper, and install on the vehicle.
17. Fill the reservoir with clean brake fluid and bleed the brake system.

733I MODELS

▶ **See Figure 35**

➡ **Because this caliper is not an isolated caliper, in that each piston is not individual of the others, two pistons will have to be removed at once.**

1. Raise the vehicle and support safely on jackstands.
2. Remove the wheel and tire assembly.
3. Remove the caliper from the vehicle and place on a clean surface.
4. Remove the protective dust boot snapring using a pick tool or other suitable tool.
5. Insert a piece of hardwood, plastic, or any material of similar consistency, approximately 0.31 inches (8mm) thick, between the pistons.
6. Apply low pressure compressed air through the threaded brake line forcing the pistons out of the cylinder.

✴✴ CAUTION

When using compressed air to remove a piston keep all fingers away from the piston in case it dislodges quickly.

7. Remove the piston and plug the open cylinder bores with a piston sealing plate or other suitable tool or device.

8. Carefully remove the piston O-ring using a pick tool or other tool. Do not scratch the piston or bore.

9. Examine the pistons and cylinder bores for a scoring or binding condition. Replace if necessary. Minor pitting can be removed with a mild Scotchbrite® pad or other suitable product.

➡**The manufacturer specifically advises against machining either the piston or the cylinder bore. The recommended extend of overhaul should include only the examination of parts and/or the replacement of the dust boot and piston O-ring.**

The caliper halves should not be separated. An exception to this would be a problem involving a piston which is jammed in the cylinder bore. In this case it may be necessary to separate the cylinder halves in order to free the piston from the cylinder bore.

To assemble:

10. Lubricate the piston, cylinder wall, and piston O-ring with clean brake fluid prior to assembly.

11. Install the piston O-ring being careful not to tear it.

12. Position the piston into the cylinder bore and press until fully seated. If the fit is tight, do not attempt to force the piston into place. Remove clean and try again.

13. Attach the brake line to the caliper, and install on the vehicle.

14. Fill the reservoir with clean brake fluid and bleed the brake system.

320I MODELS

The caliper used on the 320i is similar in construction to the standard four piston caliper, however, it is comprised of only two pistons. Proceed as though overhauling a four piston caliper.

Single Piston Design

▶ **See Figures 36, 37 and 38**

➡**All sliding calipers are a single piston design.**

1. Raise the vehicle and support safely on jackstands.

2. Remove the wheel and tire assembly.

3. Remove the caliper from the vehicle and place on a clean surface.

4. Remove the protective dust boot using a pick tool or other suitable tool.

5. Insert a piece of hardwood, plastic, or any material of similar consistency, approximately 0.31 inches (8mm) thick, between the pistons.

6. Apply low pressure compressed air through the threaded brake line forcing the pistons out of the cylinder.

✴✴ CAUTION

When using compressed air to remove a piston keep all fingers away from the piston in case it dislodges quickly.

7. Remove the piston from the cylinder bore.

8. Carefully remove the piston O-ring using a pick tool or other tool. Do not scratch the piston or bore.

9. Examine the pistons and cylinder bores for a scoring or binding condition. Replace if necessary. Minor pitting can be removed with a mild Scotchbrite® pad or other suitable product.

➡**The manufacturer specifically advises against machining either the piston or the cylinder bore. The recommended extend of overhaul should include only the examination of parts and/or the replacement of the dust boot and piston O-ring.**

To assemble:

10. Lubricate the piston, cylinder wall, and piston O-ring with clean brake fluid prior to assembly.

11. Install the piston O-ring being careful not to tear it.

12. Position the piston into the cylinder bore and press until fully seated. If the fit is tight, do not attempt to force the piston into place. Remove clean and try again.

13. Attach the brake line to the caliper, and install on the vehicle.

14. Fill the reservoir with clean brake fluid and bleed the brake system.

Brake Disc (Rotor)

REMOVAL & INSTALLATION

1600, 2000, 2002, 2500, 2800, Bavaria, 3000 and 3.0 Models

▶ **See Figure 39**

1. Raise the vehicle and support safely on jackstands.

2. Remove the wheel and tire assembly.

3. Remove the two bolts which retain the caliper to the spindle and slide the caliper off the disc. Wire the caliper up out of the way so that the flexible brake hose is not strained or kinked.

4. Remove the grease cap from the hub. Remove the cotter pin, castellated nut, and washer retaining the disc and hub assembly to the spindle. Put off the wheel and hub assembly together with the wheel bearings and grease seal.

5. Remove the Allen head bolt(s) which retain the disc to the hub and lift off the disc.

➡**If the disc is rusted or otherwise fused to the hub, loosely bolt the wheel and tire back to the hub. then, grasp the disc firmly and twist the disc back and forth, while pulling up on the disc simultaneously. This should jerk the disc loose from the hub. A little penetrating fluid on the lug nut studs will help also.**

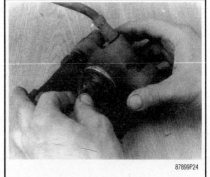

Fig. 36 Remove the protective dust boot from the piston and caliper

Fig. 37 Use compressed air to force the piston out from the cylinder bore

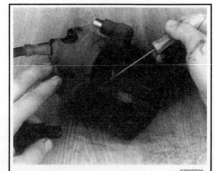

Fig. 38 With the piston removed, use a pick or other suitable tool to remove the seal within the cylinder bore

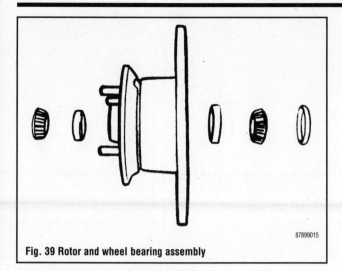

Fig. 39 Rotor and wheel bearing assembly

6. Check the disc for scoring or excessive corrosion. Minimum disc thickness is;

- 1600, 2000 and 2002 models—0.35 inches (9mm)
- 2500, 2800 and Bavaria models—0.45 inches (11.7mm)
- 3.0 models—0.81 inches (21mm)

7. If in the refinishing operation, the disc is cut to less than the minimum thickness, the disc must be replaced.

➡ **The thickness of the disc must not vary more than 0.0078 inches (0.2mm) measured at 8 points on the contact surface with a micrometer.**

To install:

8. It is good practice to remove, clean, repack and install the wheel bearings into the hub as outlined in this section.

To install:

9. Install the disc onto the hub. Tighten the Allen bolts to 43 ft. lbs. (56 Nm).

10. Install the disc and hub assembly onto the spindle. Adjust the wheel bearings as outlined in this section. Once the wheel bearings are properly adjusted, check disc run-out with a dual gauge. Maximum permissible run-out is 0.0078 inches (0.2mm).

11. Install the caliper, tightening the retaining bolts to 58 ft. lbs. (75 Nm).

12. Install the wheel and tire assembly. Lower the car and perform a road test.

3, 5, 6 and 7 Series

▶ **See Figures 40, 41 and 42**

1. Raise the vehicle and safely support on jackstands.

2. Remove the lug bolts and remove the front wheel.

3. Remove the caliper mounting bolts, and tie the caliper up out of the way (brake line still connected) using a piece of wire.

4. Remove the bolts which secure the caliper bracket to the steering knuckle.

5. Use an Allen wrench to remove the bolt retaining the disc to the hub. Then, remove the disc.

➡ **These discs are balanced. Be careful not to disturb the weights.**

6. To inspect the disc, reposition it on the hub, install the retaining bolt, and tighten to 36–42 inch lbs. (47–54 Nm). On 733i models, tighten to 23–24 ft. lbs. (30–31 Nm).

To install:

7. Adjust the wheel bearings as described below.

8. Use a dial indicator mounted at a point on the front suspension to measure the total runout of the disc. Maximum runout is 0.0078 inches (0.2mm) on all models except 733i. On 733i models, the allowable amount is 0.0058 inches (0.15mm). Use a micrometer and measure the total variation in the thickness of the disc at 8 evenly spaced points around the disc. If tolerances are greater than this, the disc must be machined.

9. Install the wheel and lower the vehicle.

Wheel Bearings

➡ **The wheel bearings for 1983–88 318i, 325, 5 and 6 Series models and 1987–88 7 Series models cannot be adjusted.**

ADJUSTMENT

1600, 2000, 2002, 320i, 630CSi, 633CSi, 635CSi and 1978–86 733i Models

▶ **See Figures 43 and 44**

1. Raise the vehicle and safely support the front wheels on jackstands.

2. Remove the end cap, washer, cotter pin and castellated nut.

3. While continuously spinning the brake disc, torque the castellated nut to 22–24 ft. lbs (29–31 Nm). Keep turning the disc making sure it turns at least two turns after the nut is torqued.

4. Loosen the nut until there is end-play and the hub rotates with the nut.

5. Finally, loosen the nut slowly just until the nut and the nearest cotter pin hole line up, then insert a new cotter pin.

6. Install the washer making sure the slotted washer is free to turn without noticeable resistance. otherwise, the end-play is not enough and the bearings will wear excessively. In this case, repeat Steps 4 and 5 again.

7. Lower the vehicle.

2500, 2800, Bavaria, 3000, 3.0, 528i and 530i Models

▶ **See Figures 43 and 44**

1. Raise the vehicle and safely support the front wheels on jackstands.

2. Remove the wheel.

3. Remove the locking cap from the hub by gripping it carefully on both sides with a pair of pliers.

4. Remove the cotter pin from the castellated nut, and loosen the nut.

5. Spin the disc constantly while torquing the nut to 7 ft. lbs (9 Nm). Continue spinning the disc after the nut is torqued and held.

Fig. 40 With the caliper safely wired aside, remove the bracket securing the caliper to the knuckle

Fig. 41 Remove the Allen bolt from the rotor face

Fig. 42 Lift the rotor off the hub assembly

6. Loosen the castellated nut $FR1/4–⅓ turn; until the slotted washer can be turned readily.

7. Fasten a dial indicator to the front suspension and rest the pin against the wheel hub. Preload the meter about 1mm to remove any play.

8. Adjust the position of the castellated nut while reading the play on the indicator. Adjust the castellation nut until the gauge reads between 0.00078–0.0039 inches (0.02–0.10mm).

9. Install the new cotter pin, then the locking cap.

10. Finally, install the wheel and lower the vehicle.

1984–88 3, 5 and 7 Series Models

1. Raise the vehicle and support it safely on jackstands. Remove the front wheels.

2. Remove the bearing cap and the locknut.

➡On these models, the wheel bearing assembly is not adjustable.

To install:

3. Install a new nut and tighten.

4. Lock the nut by hitting it with a round punch several times on the outer lip.

5. Install the bearing cap and front wheels. Lower the vehicle.

REMOVAL, PACKING & INSTALLATION

▶ **See Figures 43, 44 and 45**

1. Raise the vehicle and safely support the front wheels on jackstands.

2. Remove the wheel.

3. Remove the locking cap from the hub by gripping it carefully on both sides with a pair of pliers.

4. Remove the cotter pin from the castellated nut, if equipped.

5. Loosen and remove the castellated nut.

➡It is far easier to remove the castellated nut with an air compressor and impact gun. In the event you do not have access to this, the nut can be removed with the correct sized socket and breaker bar. Place the vehicle on the ground when removing the nut in this manner.

6. Remove the slotted washer and outer wheel bearing.

7. To access the inner wheel bearing, the caliper and rotor will have to be removed, to allow the hub assembly to be detached from the steering knuckle.

8. To remove the inner wheel bearing, with the hub removed from the vehicle and placed on a clean level surface, remove the seal from the back of the hub and press the bearing out.

9. To pack a wheel bearing;
   a. Clean the bearing using a soft rag.
   b. Place a small amount of new wheel bearing grease in the palm of your hand.
   c. Take the bearing and roll the bearing face into the wheel grease in your palm. Continue to do this until the entire bearing is well packed in grease.

➡In addition to the above method to pack wheel bearings, there are several inexpensive tools available at many automotive parts stores which will do the job with far less mess.

To install:

10. To install the inner wheel bearing, place the bearing into the hub assembly, making sure the bearing alignment is correct. Place a new seal on top of the bearing, and drive it in place using a seal installation tool or suitable socket placed over the seal and tapped in place with a hammer.

11. With the bearing inner bearing installed, place the hub on to the vehicle.

12. Place the outer bearing into position with the slotted was over the bearing.

13. Install the castellated nut, tightening finger-tight.

14. Refer to the wheel bearing adjustment section and adjust the bearing accordingly. If you are doing this procedure on a vehicle with a non-adjustable bearing, proceed as follows:
   a. Tighten the castellated nut to 210 ft. lbs. (290 Nm).
   b. Using a suitable punch, secure the nut by tapping with the punch, until an indent has been made.

15. Install any components removed earlier.

16. Finally, install the wheel and lower the vehicle.

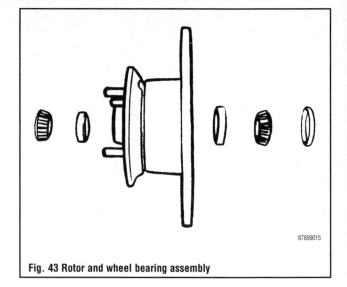

Fig. 43 Rotor and wheel bearing assembly

Fig. 44 Remove the dust cap over the nut and wheel bearing assembly

Fig. 45 Without air tools, the castellated nut can be removed with a socket and breaker bar (this is effective with the vehicle resting on the ground)

REAR DRUM BRAKES

✳✳ CAUTION

Brake shoes and pads may contain asbestos, which has been determined to be a cancer causing agent. Never clean the brake surfaces with compressed air. Avoid inhaling any dust from any brake surface. When cleaning brake surfaces, use a commercially available brake cleaning fluid.

Brake Drums

REMOVAL & INSTALLATION

▶ See Figure 46

1. Support the rear of the car securely on jackstands and remove the rear wheel. On the 320i, remove the Allen bolt from the brake drum.
2. If the drum will not come off, severe wear may have grooved the surface, causing the brake linings to prevent drum removal. To remove a drum under this situation, loosen both the brake adjuster and the hand brake cable. When loose enough, pull the drum off the axle flange.
3. Check the contact surface of the drum for scoring. Measure the inside diameter to check for ovality. Ovality must not exceed 0.02 inches (0.5mm). The drum may be machined 0.02 inches (0.5mm) at a time to a maximum oversize of 0.03 inches (1mm).

➡**If a drum needs cutting, always cut the drums in pairs.**

4. To check the drum for cracks, hang the drum by a piece of wood and tap with a small metal object. A cracked drum will sound flat.
5. To Install the drum, reverse the removal procedure, and adjust the brakes.
6. Install the wheel and lower the vehicle.

Brake Shoes

REMOVAL & INSTALLATION

1600, 2000, 2002 2500, 2800CS and 3.0 Models

1. Remove the hub cap and loosen the lug nuts a few turns. Jack up the rear of the car and install jackstands beneath the reinforced boxmember area adjacent to the rear jacking points.

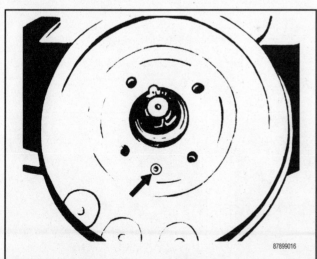

87899016

Fig. 46 If removing the rear drum on a 320i, the Allen bolt (arrow) must be removed prior to removing the drum

➡**Make sure that the parking brake is released.**

2. Remove the wheel and tire assembly.
3. Pull off the brake drum.
4. Loosen the brake shoes by turning the brake adjustment screw at each backing plate clockwise (left hand side) or counterclockwise (right hand side).
5. Remove the cotter pin and castellated nut from the axle shaft. Using a hub puller, pull off the axle shaft drive flange.
6. Disconnect the brake shoe spring at the bottom of the shoes. Leave the shoes together at the bottom end, but separate the upper ends from the wheel cylinder.
7. Disconnect the thrust rod and parking brake cable. Lift off the brake shoes, noting their placement.
8. If the shoe linings are worn down to less than 0.11 inches (3mm), the shoes must be replaced.

➡**Always replace brake shoe in pairs.**

9. Check the wheel cylinder for leakage. If any trace of brake fluid is found, remove and overhaul the wheel cylinder as outlined in this section.
   To install:
10. When installing the brake shoes, remember the following:
   a. Take care not to contaminate the brake linings with dirt, grease, or brake fluid.
   b. When installation the shoes on the backing plate, insert the long end of the spring between the parking brake lever and the brake shoe.
   c. Adjust the brakes as outlined in this section.

320I Models

▶ See Figure 46

1. Remove the brake drum as described above. Do not forget that on this model an Allen bolt must be removed in order to remove the drum.
2. With the drum removed, turn the retainers 90° and remove the retaining springs at the center of both shoes.
3. Disconnect the return springs at the bottom with a suitable return spring tool. Note the spring locations. Disconnect the bottoms of the shoes from the retainers.
4. Pull the tops of the shoes out of the brake cylinder piston rods, and pull slightly away from their mountings for clearance.
5. Then, disconnect the parking brake cable from the actuating hook, and remove the shoes.
6. Measure the brake linings. Minimum thickness is 0.11 inches (3mm). Also check the return spring for signs of heat damage and replace, if necessary.
7. Install in reverse order, making sure you connect the long end of the return spring between the parking brake lever and brake shoe.
8. Adjust the brakes as needed. Lower the vehicle.

Wheel Cylinders

REMOVAL & INSTALLATION

1. Remove the brake drum as outlined in this section.
2. Loosen the brake shoes by rotating the adjustment screw on the backing plate. (Turn the left hand screw clockwise and the right hand screw counterclockwise.)
3. Disconnect and plug the brake line to the wheel cylinder. Remove the bleed screw and mounting hardware from behind the backing plate.
4. Push the wheel cylinder from side to side and remove.
5. Reverse the above procedure to install the wheel cylinder.
6. Install the brake shoes and adjust the drum brakes as outlined in this section.
7. Bleed the brake system using clean DOT 3 or 4 brake fluid.

REAR DISC BRAKES

▶ See Figure 47

➡ Models equipped with anti-lock brakes require expensive and specialized equipment to bleed the brake system. If you do not own or have access to this equipment, it is best to have a properly equipped professional perform this procedure.

The rear disc brakes utilize sliding caliper similar to the front disc brakes. The parking brake assembly is mounted in the brake rotor hat. This is known a drum in disc design. This allows a simpler caliper design than those that incorporate the parking brake mechanism in the rear caliper. Most of the maintenance procedure are the same as the front disc brakes.

✳✳ CAUTION

Brake shoes and pads may contain asbestos, which has been determined to be a cancer causing agent. Never clean the brake surfaces with compressed air. Avoid inhaling any dust from any brake surface. When cleaning brake surfaces, use a commercially available brake cleaning fluid.

Disc Brake Pads

REMOVAL & INSTALLATION

➡ The position of the caliper piston must be checked with a special BMW gauge (or equivalent) 34 1 000 series (order by the model of your car) and, if necessary, aligned with a special tool such as 34 1 060 or equivalent. It would be best to price these tools and weigh their cost against the cost of having the repairs performed before proceeding. Do not attempt to perform the job without the special tools.

Except 1984–88 3 Series; 528e, 533i, 535i 633i, 635i and 735i Models

1. Support the rear of the vehicle safely on jackstands and remove the rear wheels.
2. Drive out the retaining pins.
3. Remove the cross springs (anti-rattle clips).
4. Using a BMW special hook, tool 34 1 010 or an equivalent tool, pull the pads out and away from the caliper.
5. Using a BMW special tool 34 10050 or equivalent, press the piston into the caliper to the fully retracted position.

To install:

➡ You may wish to drain fluid from the master cylinder first as doing this will displace fluid and raise the level there.

6. Check the 20° position of the caliper piston with a BMW special gauge 34 1 000 or an equivalent gauge. The 20° step must face the inlet or the brake disc.
7. Install the new brake pads, making sure to reinstall the anti-rattle clips.

8. Install the rear wheel.
9. Lower the vehicle.
10. Add clean brake fluid to the reservoir if removed earlier.

1977–83 630CSi, 633CSi and 1977–86 733i Models

➡ The position of the caliper piston must be checked with a special BMW gauge (or equivalent) 34 1 000 series (order by the model of your car) and, if necessary, aligned with a special tool such as 34 1 060 or equivalent. It would be best to price these tools and weigh their cost against the cost of having the repairs performed before proceeding. do not attempt to perform the job without the special tools.

1. Raise and safely support the rear of the vehicle on jackstands.
2. Remove the rear wheel. Disconnect the wear indicator harness, if equipped.
3. Drive out the retaining pins and remove the cross spring.
4. Pull the pads straight out with a tool which will grab them via the backing plate holes.

To install:

5. Install a new wear sensor with the thicker side toward the disc.
6. Use a brush and alcohol to clean the guide surface of the housing opening.
7. Force the pistons back into the caliper with BMW special tool 34 1 050 or equivalent
8. The step on the piston must face the side of the caliper where the disc enters the caliper when the vehicle is moving forward. If necessary, correct the angle of the piston with tool BMW 34 1 060 or equivalent. Measure the angle with BMW gauge 34 1 100 or equivalent.

To install:

9. Reinstall pads in reverse order. Check the cross spring and retaining pins and replace if necessary. Pump the brake pedal until all motion has been taken out of the pads and they rest at the calipers. Keep the master cylinder fluid reservoir full while doing this.
10. Lower the vehicle.

1984–88 528e Models

For rear pad removal and installation procedures, refer to the front brake pad removal and installation procedure earlier in this section.

1984–88 3 Series; 533i, 535i 633i, 635i and 735i Models

▶ See Figures 48 thru 61

1. Raise and support the vehicle safely on jackstands.
2. Remove the rear wheels.
3. Disconnect the brake pad wear sensor from the harness.
4. Carefully pry the pad retainer spring out from the hub side and remove.
5. Remove the plastic plugs from the caliper slide bolts and remove the bolts. Remove the caliper and the pads from the caliper.

To install:

6. Clean the brake caliper and all sliding surfaces. Press the caliper piston fully back into the caliper housing. Check for leaking fluid, damaged dust boots and frozen pistons.

Fig. 47 An example of a rear disc brake assembly

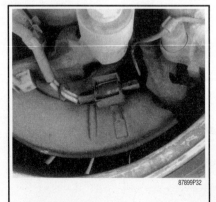

Fig. 48 Rear caliper wear sensor harness

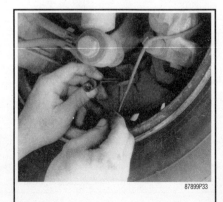

Fig. 49 Unplug the wear sensor harness

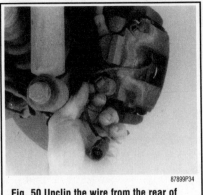

Fig. 50 Unclip the wire from the rear of the caliper

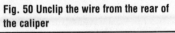

Fig. 51 Use a prytool to unfasten the brake pad clip on the caliper assembly

Fig. 52 Notice that the pad clip engages into 2 holes on the face of the caliper assembly

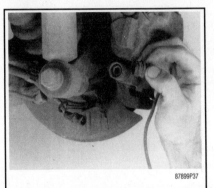

Fig. 53 Remove the plastic plug covering the caliper retaining hardware

Fig. 54 Remove the retaining bolts. Depending on model, the bolts are Allen, Torx® or standard type

Fig. 55 Slide the caliper off the rotor and bracket assembly

Fig. 56 The interior brake pad is secured to the piston via a locking clip

Fig. 57 Remove the sensor from the brake pad. Inspect the sensor for signs of wear and replace if needed

Fig. 58 Compress the piston using a cylinder compressing tool . . .

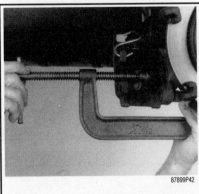

Fig. 59 . . . or use a standard C-clamp

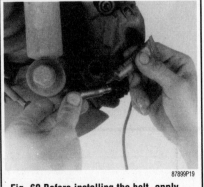

Fig. 60 Before installing the bolt, apply locktite® to the threads . . .

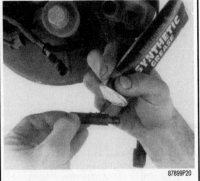

Fig. 61 . . . and grease the bolt shaft to prevent caliper sticking

7. Install a new brake pad wear sensor in the pad if the plastic part has been worn through on the old sensor. New sensors are not required unless the wire inside the plastic part has been exposed.

8. Install the brake pads in the caliper. Lower the caliper over the caliper mount. Install the bolts and torque to 18–22 ft. lbs. (25–30 Nm). Install the retainer spring.

9. Connect the brake pad wear sensor to the harness. Check for a good connection as most problems with the sensor circuit are caused by faulty connections. Check that the wire is held by the loop in the dust cover and the connector is held at the clips.

10. Install the wheels and torque to 65–79 ft. lbs. (90–110 Nm).

INSPECTION

1. Check the pad for thickness. The minimum friction material thickness allowed by BMW is 0.08 inches (2.0mm).

2. Check the condition of the friction material. If the friction material is cracking or coming loose from the backing plate, replace the pads.

3. Check the pattern of wear of the friction material. If the pads are wearing unevenly or on an angle, there may be a problem with the caliper hanging up on its slides.

4. If the inside pad is worn more than the outside pad, the caliper may not be sliding on the pins. Clean and check for free movement of the caliper.

5. If one sides set of pads wear more than the other, the caliper with the unworn pads may be frozen. Check that the piston retracts smoothly and that the dust boot is intact.

Brake Caliper

➡**Models equipped with anti-lock brakes require expensive and specialized equipment to bleed the brake system. If you do not own or have access to this equipment, it is best to have a properly equipped professional perform this procedure.**

REMOVAL & INSTALLATION

▶ **See Figures 62 and 63**

1. Raise and support the vehicle. Remove the rear wheels.

2. Disconnect the brake pad wear sensor from the harness.

3. If the caliper is to be replaced, draw off the brake fluid from the reservoir and fix the brake pedal in the depressed position. This will prevent brake fluid from draining out of the brake lines while the line is disconnected form the caliper.

4. Use flare-end wrenches to loosen the connection between the caliper brake hose and the brake line from the master cylinder.

5. Remove the caliper to knuckle mounting bolts and pull the caliper off.

6. Finish separating the hose and brake line.

7. Remove the caliper and place on a clean surface.

8. Check the condition of the brake hose. If cracked or excessively worn, replace with a new hose.

To install:

9. Install the caliper and torque the bolts to 89 ft. lbs. (123 Nm).

10. Connect the brake line to the caliper and torque to 10 ft. lbs. (14.2 Nm).

11. Connect the brake wear sensor wire to the harness. Check for a good connection as most problems with the sensor circuit are caused by faulty connections. Check that the wire is held by the loop in the dust cover and the connector is held at the clips.

12. Clip the brake line into the holder. Bleed the brake system.

13. Install the wheels and torque to 65–79 ft. lbs. (90–110 Nm).

14. Check the brake fluid level in the reservoir and add if needed.

OVERHAUL

The overhaul procedure covers replacement of the seal, dust boot and guide sleeves. If the piston or bore is found to be pitted or corroded, replacement of the caliper is recommended. Use a original manufacturer overhaul kit. Use all the parts contained in the kit. Work in a clean, dust free area. Use only alcohol and non-lubricated compressed air to clean the caliper and parts.

1977–83 630CSi, 633CSi and 1977–86 733i Models

➡**Models equipped with anti-lock brakes require expensive and specialized equipment to bleed the brake system. If you do not own or have access to this equipment, it is best to have a properly equipped professional perform this procedure.**

1. Remove the caliper as described in this section. Remove the brake pads.

2. Remove the clamp and rubber piston seal on both sides of multiple piston caliper assemblies.

3. Place a hardwood block in the caliper between the pistons.

4. Plug the brake line connecting hole and retain the piston on the connecting hole side with brake pliers or other suitable tool. Hold the piston opposite the brake line connecting hole with brake pliers or other suitable tool and apply compressed air to the connecting hole. Apply air pressure gradually until the piston pops out.

5. Lift out seals with a pick or other suitable tool.

To assemble:

6. Clean all parts in alcohol and dry with clean compressed air. Replace those calipers that have damaged bores and pistons with scored or pitted surfaces.

7. Reassemble in reverse order, using all new seals from an overhaul kit. Be careful not to cock pistons in the bores when reinstalling. Coat all parts with silicone lubricant.

8. Check the 20° position of the piston, and adjust if needed.

9. Install the calipers and pads, and bleed the system, as described above.

1984–88 528e Models

➡**Models equipped with anti-lock brakes require expensive and specialized equipment to bleed the brake system. If you do not own or have access to this equipment, it is best to have a properly equipped professional perform this procedure.**

For caliper overhaul procedures, please refer to the "Front Disc Brake" section.

1984–88 3 Series; 533i, 535i 633i, 635i and 735i Models

▶ **See Figures 64, 65, 66 and 67**

➡**Models equipped with anti-lock brakes require expensive and specialized equipment to bleed the brake system. If you do not own or have**

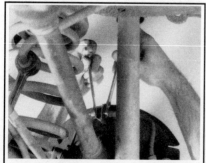

Fig. 62 Use two flare-end wrenched to loosen the brake line and brake hose connection

87899P43

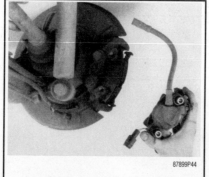

Fig. 63 Finish removing the brake hose and remove the caliper

87899P44

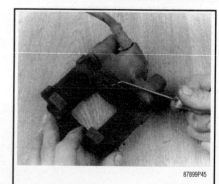

Fig. 64 Remove the metal collar around the piston dust cover

87899P45

Fig. 65 Use compressed air to force the piston out of the caliper bore

Fig. 66 Remove the piston from the bore. Do not force it out. If it is difficult to remove twist it back and forth

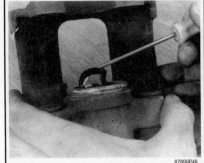

Fig. 67 Use a pick or other suitable tool to remove the seal from within the cylinder bore

access to this equipment, it is best to have a properly equipped professional perform this procedure.

1. Remove the caliper and brake pads. Remove the plastic caps and the guide bolts or slide pins.
2. Clean the exterior before further disassembly.
3. Use a pick tool or other suitable tool to remove the collar around the dust cover surrounding the caliper piston.
4. Remove the dust cover from the caliper assembly.
5. Place a piece of wood in the caliper and use compressed air at the hose connection to extend the piston out of the caliper body. Remove the piston.
6. Use a plastic pick to remove the seal from the bore.

To assemble:

7. Clean the bore and piston with alcohol and dry with non-lubricated compressed air.
8. Lubricate the parts with brake assembly paste.
9. Install the new seal in the groove.
10. Install the dust boot on the piston and slide the piston into the bore. Seat the boot into the grooves.
11. Install new guide bushing sleeves at the slides.
12. Assemble the caliper and install.

Brake Discs

REMOVAL & INSTALLATION

1977–83 Models

1. Remove the rear wheel.
2. Remove the caliper as described in this section.
3. If equipped with an Allen head bolt on the hub cap of the disc, remove the Allen bolt and remove the disc. If this is no Allen bolt present, the disc simple pulls off the shaft. Note the position of the holes in the disc and axle shaft flange.

PARKING BRAKE

Parking Brake Cable

ADJUSTMENT

Vehicles Equipped with Rear Drum Brakes

1. Support the rear of the vehicle in the raised position.
2. Fully release the handbrake.
3. While rotating the tire and wheel assembly, turn the left hand adjustment nut counterclockwise and the right hand adjustment nut clockwise until the brake shoes are tight against the drum and the wheel will no longer rotate.
4. On vehicles with self-adjusting brakes, simply operate the pedal hard several times to ensure the automatic adjusters have taken up the slack.

4. Reverse the removal procedure to install. Torque Allen bolts retaining the disc to 22–24 ft. lbs. (29–31 Nm).

1984–88 Models

1. Raise and support the vehicle. Remove the rear wheels.
2. Remove the caliper without disconnecting the brake line. Hang the caliper with a piece of wire so no tension is put on the brake line.
3. Remove the internal hex bolt from the hub and pull the rotor off the hub.
4. Check the rotor and replace as necessary.

To install:

5. Install the rotor and caliper. Install the wheels. Adjust the parking brake.
6. Burnish the rotors by making 5 full stops from 30 mph (50 kmph), then allow the brakes to cool. Make 5 additional stops from 30 mph (50 kmph) and allow the brakes to cool again. This will burnish the rotors and allow full braking efficiency.

INSPECTION

1. Mount a dial indicator on the rear caliper with the pin against the disc. It may be convenient to pull the rear brake pads out and measure between the jaws of the caliper.
2. Measure the thickness of the disc at eight points around the diameter on the worn surfaces with a micrometer. Compare the thickness readings and subtract the lowest from the highest. If this figure is greater than the maximum specification described in the specification chart at the beginning of this section, the disc must be machined. Note also the minimum thickness figures. If the disc requires machining and cannot be cleaned up before the thickness drops below the minimum figure, it must be replaced.
3. Preload the dial indicator a small amount and measure the total runout of the disc as it rotates. Compare with specifications and if runout is excessive, have the disc machined.

5. Loosen both adjustment nuts by ⅛ of a turn, so that the wheel is just able to turn, on vehicles with adjustable brakes.
6. Push up the rubber sleeve on the handbrake lever until the locknut is visible.
7. Loosen the locknut.
8. Pull up on the handbrake lever for a distance of five notches. Measure the distance between the middle of the handle and propeller shaft tunnel. This distance should be approximately 4 inches (114mm).
9. Tighten the adjustment nut until the wheels are locked, and retighten the locknut. On the 318i, the wheels must be just beginning to drag, and resistance on both sides must be equal.
10. Release the handbrake. Make sure that the wheels turn freely when the handbrake is released.
11. Lower the vehicle.

Models Equipped with Rear Disc Brakes

The procedure for adjusting the handbrake on vehicles equipped with rear disc brakes is similar to the procedure for adjusting the handbrake on vehicles equipped with rear drum brakes with one exception.

The mechanism for adjusting the brake shoes is a star wheel adjuster. Insert a screwdriver through the 15mm hole in the caliper hat, and turn the adjusting star wheel until the brake disc can no longer be moved. Proceed as though adjusting the handbrake on vehicles equipped with rear drum brakes.

3 SERIES MODELS

▶ See Figures 68 and 69

1. Remove 1 lug bolt from the wheel and turn the opening so it is positioned to the rear approximately 30 degrees from the top. This is the location of the star adjuster for the brake shoes.
2. Use a thin bladed adjustment tool or equivalent to turn the star adjuster. On the left side, turn the star up to tighten. On the right side, turn the star down to tighten.
3. Turn the star until the wheel will not turn. Loosen the star 3–4 threads. Check that the wheel can turn freely.
4. Pull the parking lever boot up in the front and pull out from the rear. Remove the rear ashtray and the underlying bolt. Pull the console back and out.

Fig. 68 With the rotor removed for explanation purposes, you can see the hand brake adjuster

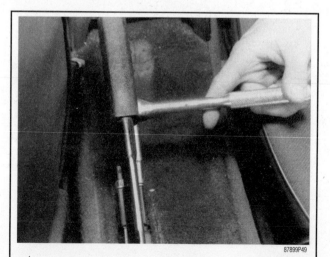

Fig. 69 With the console remove the parking brake cable can be adjusted using either an wrench or ratchet

5. Pull the parking brake lever up 5 notches. Adjust the cables with the nuts attached such that the wheels can just barely be turned. Release the lever and check that the wheels spin freely. Both sides must be adjusted evenly.
6. The parking brake indicator lamp should extinguish when the lever is released otherwise adjust the switch so it does. Install the console and the lug bolt.

5, 6 AND 7 SERIES MODELS

▶ See Figures 68 and 69

1. Remove 1 lug bolt from the wheel and turn the opening so it is positioned to the rear approximately 45 degrees from the bottom. This is the location of the star adjuster for the brake shoes.
2. Use a thin bladed adjustment tool or equivalent to turn the star adjuster. On the left side, turn the star up to tighten. On the right side, turn the star down to tighten.
3. Turn the star until the wheel will not turn. Loosen the star 18 notches: Check that the wheel turn freely.
4. Pull the parking lever dust cover trim up.
5. Pull the parking brake lever up 6 notches. Adjust the cables with the nuts so that the wheels can just barely be turned. Release the lever and check that the wheels spin freely. Both sides must be adjusted evenly.
6. The parking brake indicator lamp should extinguish when the lever is released otherwise adjust the switch so it does. Install The dust cover and the lug bolt.

BURNISHING

The parking brake is subjected to only limited wear and use. Often the friction surfaces become corroded and cause a loss of braking performance. This can often be cured by burnishing the parking brakes and the performance will return.

This procedure should also be performed whenever new shoes or rotors are installed and before the parking brake adjustment is made.

1. While driving the car at 25 mph (40 kmph) pull the parking brake lever until braking is felt. Pull the lever 1 more notch and drive the car 1300 ft. (400 m) to the working area.
2. Adjust the parking brake.
3. Check the performance of the parking brake.

REMOVAL & INSTALLATION

Models Equipped With Rear Drum Brakes

1. Remove the brake drum as in this section. Pull off the rubber boot at the handbrake lever, loosen and remove the locknuts on the appropriate side, and disconnect the cable at the handbrake lever.
2. Remove the brake shoes as described in this section.
3. From under the vehicle, Remove the cable assembly by unfastening the necessary clips. Remove the cable from the rear brake assembly.
4. On 320i models, pull the cable out of the holder toward the rear of the car. On 318i models, disconnect the cable on the rear suspension arm, compress the locking clamp, and disconnect the cable on the backing plate and pull out.
   To install:
5. Install in reverse order, making sure the cable holders are both located properly, one in the protective tube, and the other in the backing plate. On 318i models, make sure the clamp which locates the tube is properly connected. Adjust the brakes as described in this section.

Models Equipped With Rear Disc Brakes

3 SERIES MODELS

1. Raise and safely support the vehicle. Remove the rear tire and wheel assembly. Remove the rear brake rotors.
2. Pull the rubber parking brake boot up at the front and lift off at the rear. Pull out the rear ashtray and remove the bolt. Pull the console back and remove.
3. Remove the adjuster nuts from the cables. Remove the 3 bolts securing the lever and remove the lever.
4. Using brake spring pliers, disconnect the lower return spring for the parking brake shoes. Then, using the proper tool, turn the retaining springs for the parking brake shoes 90 degrees to unlock them and remove.
5. Separate the parking brake shoes at the bottom and remove from above.

6. Disconnect the spreader locks from the backing plates: first, rock the lower end of the spreader lock outward, and then pull out the pin. Press the cable connection out of the spreader lock. Pull the spreader lock out of the housing.

7. Disconnect the parking brake cable at the trailing arm and the backing plate. Remove the cable.

To install:

8. Install the support for the parking brake cable on the backing plate. Install the cable into potion and connect the housing to the trailing arm.

9. Install the cable into the tubes going to the parking brake lever. Install the parking brake lever.

10. Connect the parking brake cable to the spreader lock. Apply a light grease to the mechanism. Install the brake shoes, retainers and return spring.

11. Install the brake rotor and wheel. Adjust the shoes, the adjust the cables. Install the console and boot for the parking brake lever.

5 AND 6 SERIES MODELS

1. Raise and safely support the vehicle. Remove the rear tire and wheel assembly.

2. Remove the rear brake discs.

3. Using brake spring pliers, disconnect the upper return spring for the parking brake shoes. Then, using the proper tool, turn the retaining springs for the parking brake shoes 90 degrees to unlock them and then disconnect them.

4. Separate the parking brake shoes at the top and then remove them from below.

5. Disconnect the spreader locks from the backing plates: first, rock the lower end of the spreader lock outward, and then pull out the pin. Press the cable connection out of the spreader lock. Pull the spreader lock out of the housing. Pull the cable through the backing plate.

6. Disconnect the parking brake cable at the trailing arm.

7. Working from inside the vehicle, remove the console cover as follows:

   a. Lift out the air grille and remove the nuts underneath.

   b. Remove the cap and unscrew the mounting bolt that's located at the forward end of the console on the right side. Lift out the cover that the bolt retains.

   c. Remove the bolt on the left side of the forward end of the console. If the vehicle has power windows, disconnect the plugs. Then, lift the console and remove air ducts.

   d. Turn the retainer 90 degrees and peel the rubber cover downward. Now, unscrew the adjusting nuts on the parking brake cables and pull them out.

8. Remove the cable from the vehicle.

To install:

9. Install the support for the parking brake cable on the backing plate. Install the cable into potion and connect the housing to the trailing arm.

10. Install the cable into the tubes going to the parking brake lever. Install the parking brake lever cable nuts.

11. Connect the parking brake cable to the spreader lock. Apply a light grease to the mechanism. Install the brake shoes, retainers and return spring.

12. Install the brake rotor and wheel. Adjust the shoes, the adjust the cables. Install the console and boot for the parking brake lever.

7 SERIES MODELS

1. Lift out the cover plate that surrounds the handbrake lever. Remove the locknuts and adjusting nuts from the front ends of the brake cables.

2. Remove the rear brake discs.

3. Disconnect the spreader locks from the backing plates: first, rock the lower end of the spreader lock outward, and then pull out the pin. Press the cable connection out of the spreader lock. Pull the spreader lock out of the housing. Pull the cable through the backing plate.

4. Detach the parking brake cable at the trailing arm and remove it.

5. To install, reverse the removal procedures, giving the sliding surfaces and pin of the spreader lock a light coating of an lubricant paste. Adjust the handbrake as described in this section.

Parking Brake Shoes

REMOVAL & INSTALLATION

3 Series Models

▶ **See Figures 70 thru 79**

1. Raise and safely support the vehicle. Remove the rear tire and wheel assembly. Remove the rear brake rotors using an Allen wrench to remove the retaining bolt securing the rotor hat over the shoe assembly.

2. Spray the entire brake assembly with a suitable evaporative cleaner to control brake dust.

3. Using brake spring pliers, disconnect the upper return spring for the parking brake shoes. Then, using the proper tool, turn the retaining springs for the parking brake shoes 90 degrees to unlock them and remove.

4. Separate the parking brake shoes at the top and remove. Separate the shoes from the adjuster and spring.

5. Check the condition of the shoe retaining hardware and replace those parts excessively worn.

Fig. 70 Loosen the Allen head bolt . . .

Fig. 71 . . . and remove the bolt from the rotor . . .

Fig. 72 . . . then remove the rotor from the hub

Fig. 73 Spray the brake assembly with a suitable evaporative spray cleaner

Fig. 74 Use brake spring tools to remove one side of the upper return spring

Fig. 75 Unclip the other end of the upper spring and remove

Fig. 76 Loosen the retaining spring and pin from the middle of both brake shoes . . .

Fig. 77 . . . then remove the retaining pin and spring assembly

Fig. 78 Remove the brake shoes from the vehicle. Be careful not to loose the adjuster

Fig. 79 Exploded view of the parking brake assembly

To install:

6. Install the adjuster and spring at the shoes. Install the shoes from the top to the backing plate.

7. Install the retainer locks and the return spring. Install the rotor. Burnish and adjust the parking brake.

5, 6 and 7 Series Models

1. Raise and safely support the vehicle. Remove the rear tire and wheel assembly. Remove the rear brake rotors.

2. Using brake spring pliers, disconnect the upper return spring for the parking brake shoes. Then, using the proper tool, turn the retaining springs for the parking brake shoes 90 degrees to unlock them and remove.

3. Separate the parking brake shoes at the top and remove from below. Separate the shoes from the adjuster and spring.

To install:

4. Install the adjuster and spring at the shoes. Install the shoes from the bottom to the backing plate.

5. Install the retainer locks and the return spring. Install the rotor. Burnish and adjust the parking brake.

ANTI-LOCK BRAKE SYSTEM

Description & Operation

One of the greatest contributions to automotive safety was the advent of anti-lock braking systems. Anti-lock braking systems (ABS) allows maintaining directional control of the vehicle during braking. While benefits from ABS can be derived on dry pavement driving, the most substantial benefits are witnessed under adverse traction conditions.

Braking systems operate on the principle that motion energy is removed from the vehicle in the form of heat and dissipated. The brake calipers squeeze the brake pads against the rotors and slow the rotors. This does not stop the vehicle; the friction of the road surface against the tires is what actually slows the vehicle. The brakes merely provide the retarding force for the tires. If the tires can not maintain a level of traction with the road surface, the best braking system can not slow the vehicle.

If during braking, 1 or more tires hit a section of low traction, the braking force applied by the calipers will overwhelm the available traction at the tire contact patch. As a result the tire will slide instead of roll. If we look at the contact patch of the tire as the car rolls down the road, we would see that the tire has a relative speed of zero compared to the ground. Under braking the relative may increase so there is a slight percentage of slip between the tire and the road surface. A small percentage of slip is acceptable and friction force will rise, slowing the car. If the percentage rises too high and the tire is no longer rolling,

the friction force drops tremendously and the tire can not provide lateral or longitudinal traction.

Driving in the wet or snow, loose gravel or sand, or any other kind of low traction surface can cause the tires to lock and loose directional stability. ABS monitors the rotation of the tires and compares the speed of each. If the speed of 1 or more tires drop drastically below that of the others during braking, the ABS controller will cut hydraulic pressure to that wheel until it is rotating at the same speed as the others. This will provide the best chance of maintaining directional control of the vehicle.

In the case of the 325iX, four wheel drive vehicle, a deceleration sensor is needed to sense the relative motion of the car. Since the possibility exists that 1 or more wheels can be spinning due to acceleration, not braking, a sensor independent of the wheel speed sensors is needed.

ABS can not perform miracles. If the laws of physics are exceeded, the car can leave the roadway. ABS can only help to maintain control. Go too fast into a turn and mash the brakes, ABS or not, the tires can only do so much and control may be lost. Driving too fast in the rain or snow is a recipe for trouble. ABS is a tool to make driving safer, not a cure-all for bad driving habits.

ABS can be useful in dry ground driving in the same way it is in low traction situations. ABS, once eschewed by the racing world, has now been gladly accepted and used on vehicles ranging from rally cars, World Touring Car Championship M3's and Formula 1 cars.

COMPONENTS

Speed Sensors

▶ **See Figures 80, 81 and 82**

The speed sensors are located at each wheel and provide the speed reference to the control unit. The speed sensors are permanently magnetized inductive sensors that read pulses from a tooth wheel on each hub. A voltage signal is generated as each tooth passes through the magnetic field. The sensors are replaceable. The tooth wheels are integral with the wheel hubs and are replaced with the complete hub.

Control Unit

The control unit contains all the signal conditioning circuitry and the output circuits. The output circuits control the hydraulic unit to adjust the line pressure to each caliper. The unit is located under the dash panel on the left side in the 3 Series, and in the forward position of the electronics box in the engine compartment of the 5 Series. If a problem is sensed, the control unit will light the instrument panel warning lamp.

Hydraulic Unit

▶ **See Figures 83 and 84**

The hydraulic unit, located in the engine compartment contains valves and a pump. The valves have 3 positions; pressure build-up, pressure hold and pressure drop. As the tires locks, the control unit informs the valve to hold the pressure. If the tire remains locked, the control unit will allow the valve to drop the pressure until the tire starts to turn. The control unit will allow the valve to start building pressure to start the cycle over again.

The pump returns the brake fluid taken from the wheel cylinder while the pressure is lowered. The pump is designed to maintain separation of the 2 braking circuits.

During operation of the anti-lock system, a pulsing may be felt at the brake pedal and a clicking heard from the hydraulic unit. This is normal and informs the operator that the ABS is in the functioning mode.

SERVICING

➡ **Models equipped with anti-lock brakes require expensive and specialized equipment to bleed the brake system. If you do not own or have access to this equipment, it is best to have a properly equipped professional perform any work on the brake hydraulic system of an anti-lock brake equipped vehicle.**

While parts of the of the ABS system can be removed and replaced by the owner of the vehicle, special tool, technique and procedure are needed to check the operation and performance of the system once repairs are completed.

To bleed the hydraulic system, a necessary step after the hydraulic system has been repaired, the BMW Diagnostic Tester or equivalent must be utilized to electronically open the internal valve. Only this way can the system be completely bled.

To check the operation of the ABS system after any of the electronic portions have been replaced or disconnected, the BMW Diagnostic Tester or equivalent must be used.

It is recommended to allow a licensed and trained professional to complete repairs on the ABS system. Most repairs are straightforward, but the diagnosis and testing of the system can enter a different realm. The safety and integrity of the braking system is at stake.

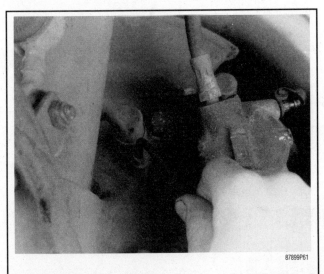

Fig. 80 Loosen the Allen head bolt . . .

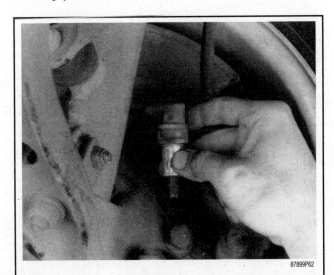

Fig. 81 . . . and slide the sensor out

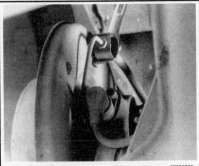

Fig. 82 Speed sensor on rear brake assembly. Removal is the same as for a front sensor

Fig. 83 Hydraulic unit of the anti-lock brake system mounted in the engine compartment

Fig. 84 With the plastic cap removed, you can see the electronic controls of the unit

Brake Specifications

All measurements in inches unless noted

Year	Model	Lug Nug Torque (ft. lbs.)	Master Cylinder Bore	Brake Disc Minimum Thickness	Brake Disc Maximum Runout	Standard Brake Drum Diameter	Minimum Lining Thickness Front	Minimum Lining Thickness Rear
1970–71	1600	53–65	.810	.354	.008	7.87	.275	.079
1970–76	2000,2002	53–65	.810 ①	.354 ②	.008	9.06	.275	.079
	2500,2800 Bavaria,3.0 3000	60–66	.874	.827F/.709R	.008	9.84 ③	.275	.275 ④
1977–81	320i	59–65	.812	.827	.008	9.84 ⑤	.301	.118
1975–81	528i,530i	59–65	.937	.827F/.335R ⑦	.008	—	—	—
1977–81	630CSi,633	59–65	.937	.827F/.709R	.008	—	—	—
1978–81	733i	60–66	.937	.827F/.354R	.006	—	—	—
1982	320i	59–65	.812	.827	0.008	10.04	—	—
	633CSi	65–79	.936	.840F/.720R	0.008	—	—	—
	733i	65–79	.874	.840F/.360R	0.008	—	—	—
1983	320i	59–65	.812	.827	0.008	10.04	—	—
	533i	65–79	—	.787	0.008	—	0.079	0.079
	633CSi	65–79	—	.960F/.315R	0.008	—	0.079	0.079
	733i	65–79	—	.906F/.315R	0.008	—	0.079	0.079
1984	318i	65–79	—	.421	0.008	9.035	0.079	0.059
	533i	65–79	—	.787	0.008	—	0.079	0.079
	633CSi	65–79	—	.906F/.315R	0.008	—	0.079	0.079
	733i	65–79	—	.906F/.315R	0.008	—	0.079	0.079
1985	318i	65–79	—	.421	0.008	9.035	0.079	0.059
	325e	65–79	—	.421	0.008	—	0.079	0.079
	528e	65–79	—	.787F/.315R	0.008	—	0.079	0.079
	524td	65–79	—	.787F/.315R	0.008	—	0.079	0.079

87899C03

Brake Specifications (cont.)

All measurements in inches unless noted

Year	Model	Lug Nug Torque (ft. lbs.)	Master Cylinder Bore	Brake Disc Minimum Thickness	Brake Disc Maximum Runout	Standard Brake Drum Diameter	Minimum Lining Thickness Front	Minimum Lining Thickness Rear
1985	535i	65–79	—	.906F/.315R	0.008	—	0.079	0.079
	635CSi	65–79	—	.906F/.315R	0.008	—	0.079	0.079
	735i	65–79	—	.906F/.315R	0.008	—	0.079	0.079
1986	325e	65–79	—	.421	0.008	—	0.079	0.079
	528e	65–79	—	.787F/.315R	0.008	—	0.079	0.079
	524td	65–79	—	.787F/.315R	0.008	—	0.079	0.079
	535i	65–79	—	.906F/.315R	0.008	—	0.079	0.079
	635CSi	65–79	—	.906F/.315R	0.008	—	0.079	0.079
	735i	65–79	—	.906F/.315R	0.008	—	0.079	0.079
1987	325i	65–79	—	.421	0.008	—	0.079	0.079
	325iS	65–79	—	.421	0.008	—	0.079	0.079
	528e	65–79	—	.787F/.315R	0.008	—	0.079	0.079
	535i	65–79	—	.906F/.315R	0.008	—	0.079	0.079
	635CSi	65–79	—	.906F/.315R	0.008	—	0.079	0.079
	735i	65–79	—	.906F/.315R	0.008	—	0.079	0.079
	M5	65–79	—	1.102F/.315R	0.008	—	0.079	0.079
	M6	65–79	—	.906F/.315R	0.008	—	0.079	0.079
1988	325 (All)	65–79	—	.787F/.315R	0.008	—	0.079	0.079
	528e	65–79	—	.787F/.315R	0.008	—	0.079	0.079
	535i	65–79	—	.787F/.315R	0.008	—	0.079	0.079
	635CSi	65–79	—	.906F/.315R	0.008	—	0.079	0.079
	M3	65–79	—	.905F/.394R	0.008	—	0.079	0.079
	M5	65–79	—	1.102F/.315R	0.008	—	0.079	0.079
	M6	65–79	—	1.024F/.315R	0.008	—	0.079	0.079
	735i	65–79	—	.906F/.315R	0.008	—	0.079	0.079
	750iL	65–79	—	NAF/.709R	0.008	—	0.079	0.079

F Front
R Rear
① 2002ti and 2002tii: .9375
② 2002ti and 2002tii: .459
③ 2800CS only
④ 2800CS: .079
⑤ '80–'82: 10.00
⑥ '80–'82: 10.04
⑦ '75–'77 530i: .461F

87899C04

10

BODY AND TRIM

EXTERIOR

Doors

ADJUSTMENT

▶ **See Figures 1, 2 and 3**

1. Check the gaps around the door. The gaps should be even.
2. Adjust the spacing by loosening the hinge mounting bolts and moving the door in the direction necessary to even out the gap. Move the door in small increments.
3. Adjust the panel height at the front edge of the door by inserting hinge shims between the hinge mount and the body. The hinges are available in 0.020 inch (0.5mm) and 0.039 inch (1.0mm) thicknesses. It is acceptable to have the front door edge set lower than the front fender by up to 0.039 inches (1.0mm). This will help prevent wind noise and stone chips.
4. Adjust the rear edge of the door by moving the door striker in or out.

HINGE BUSHING REPLACEMENT

▶ **See Figures 4, 5 and 6**

1. Remove the door from the hinge.
2. Remove the snapring and washer from the hinge pin. Press the hinge pin out of the hinge.
3. Press the hinge bushing out of the hinge.
4. Install a new hinge bushing by pressing in. Use tool 41 5 010 or equivalent to press the bushing into place.
5. Install the hinge pin and lubricate. Install the door.

Hood

ADJUSTMENT

▶ **See Figures 7, 8, 9 and 10**

The hood must be aligned for correct height and centered position. The adjustment are relatively simple.

On some older models the front grille must removed to align the hood via the hinges.

The lock stops on the side of the hood can be loosened and moved to align the height of the sides of the hood, so that it can be even with the top of the fenders.

To adjust for proper hood operation the hood latch assembly can be loosened and adjusted to the correct position. Note that the latch can also be used to adjust the rear hood height on BMW vehicles.

The final adjustment is for preload, so that the hood will open when the release is pulled. This can be done by turning the rubber stops at the corners of the hood. The hood should pop open but also close easily. It should also latch firmly.

➡**Improper latch adjustment can cause the hood to latch too loosely and may cause it to open while in motion. Check that the hood is latched firmly after each adjustment.**

1. Fully thread the rubber hood stopper(s) down on the radiator support.
2. Remove the center grille(s) and hood lock cable, if needed. This may be necessary for some older vehicles.

Fig. 1 The striker plate can be adjusted to help align the door. Start by scribing a reference mark

87890P03

Fig. 2 Use a Torx® driver to loosen the bolts and adjust the strike plate

87890P04

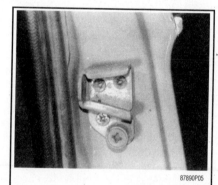

Fig. 3 This 2002 strike plate is also adjustable

87890P05

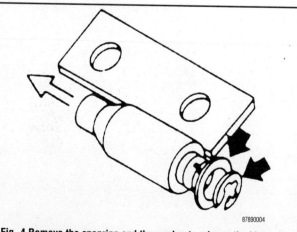

Fig. 4 Remove the snapring and the washer to release the hinge pin during bushing replacement

87890004

Fig. 5 Press the new bushing into place

87890005

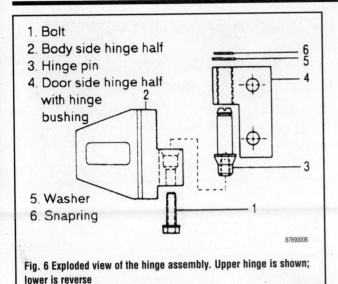

1. Bolt
2. Body side hinge half
3. Hinge pin
4. Door side hinge half with hinge bushing
5. Washer
6. Snapring

Fig. 6 Exploded view of the hinge assembly. Upper hinge is shown; lower is reverse

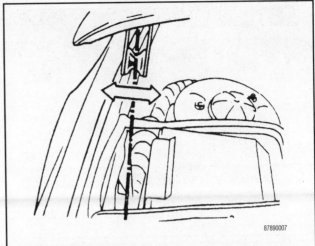

Fig. 7 On models equipped with a roller bracket, by loosening the retaining bolts, the roller can be aligned for a perfect fit

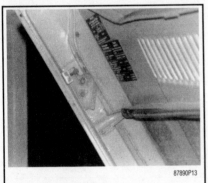

Fig. 8 To adjust the upper hood latch on a 2002, loosen the bolts

Fig. 9 To adjust the lower latch plate, loosen the bolts and adjust height and position

Fig. 10 Turn the stopper to align the hood such that it is flush with the fender

3. Adjust the side gaps between the hood and the fender by loosening the hinge mounting bolts and moving the hood from side to side. When moving the hood, move it in small increments, then tighten the bolts and check the fit.

4. Adjust the hood lock plates by loosening the adjusting bolts. Raise and lower the hood enough to align the catches.

5. Adjust the hood height at the front with the spring stopper. Loosen the bolt and adjust so the hood is equal height with the fenders.

6. If equipped, adjust the rear roller so it matches the catch and slides in with no lateral force.

7. Adjust the rear catch so the rear hood height is equal with the fenders.

8. Adjust the hood stoppers so the hood slightly presses against the stoppers while in the closed position and the hood is on the same level as the fenders.

Trunk Lid

ADJUSTMENT

▶ See Figures 11, 12, 13, 14 and 15

1. Adjust the height of the trunk lid at the hinge end by placing shims between the trunk lid and the hinge.

2. Adjust the side gaps by loosening the hinge bolts to the trunk lid and the catch bar mounting bolts. Align the lid and tighten the bolts.

Fig. 11 Early style lower trunk latch. To adjust loosen the bolts and align the latch assembly

Fig. 12 To adjust the upper trunk latch assembly on later model vehicles, scribe an orientation mark . . .

Fig. 13 . . . and loosen the bolts. Adjust the latch position and tighten the bolts

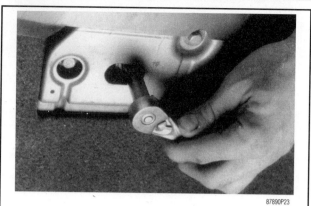

Fig. 14 The lower trunk latch can be adjusted by loosening the recessed bolts—3 Series models

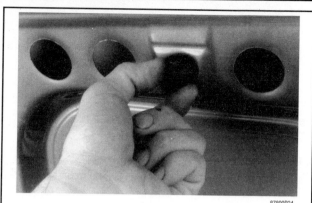

Fig. 15 To adjust the trunk lid resting height, turn the rubber stoppers

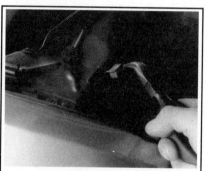

Fig. 16 Removing the clips which secure some late model grilles to the radiator support

Fig. 17 Remove the screw securing the lower portion of the headlight grille

Fig. 18 With all the hardware removed, lift the grille away from the vehicle

3. Adjust the lid height by loosening the nut on the catch and adjust the catch bar until the trunk lid sits 0.039 inches (1 Nm) below the fenders.

4. Adjust the stopper pads so the trunk lid sits flush with the fenders.

Grille

REMOVAL & INSTALLATION

♦ See Figures 16, 17 and 18

The grille is removed in 3 sections, one center and 2 side sections. The sections are held in place by screws, clips or a combination of both. If equipped with screws, remove the screws securing the section you wish to remove. A grille section can be secured with a single screw or as many as 4 screws, depending on the year and model of BMW.

If the grille is secured by clips, use a suitable prytool to remove the clips.

Note that on early 6 Series models, the center section of the grille is spring loaded, so do not loose the springs when removing it.

Outside Mirrors

REMOVAL & INSTALLATION

Depending on the year of the BMW, outside mirrors were either secured to the door panel or the window frame.

To remove a door mounted mirror, unfasten the retaining screws securing mirror to the door. If the mirror is remotely attached to the interior door panel, the bezel and control cable will also have to be removed.

To remove a mirror attached to the door window frame, proceed as follows:

➡On some later 5, 6 and 7 Series models with the speakers in the triangular panel, the speaker(s) must be unplugged. Be careful not to puncture the speaker or grille when removing the trim panel.

1. Remove the mirror mounting trim on the interior of the door by pulling it off towards the rear. On later 3 Series models, the panel is pulled off from the top after the top is pull out slightly.

2. Support the mirror and remove the retaining bolts.

3. Disconnect the harness plug and/or speaker plug, if equipped then remove the mirror.

4. To remove the mirror glass, insert a thin tool into the opening at the bottom, center of the mirror. Rotate the locking ring to the outside of the mirror to remove. Carefully pry the glass out of the mount clips at the bottom edge.

5. Install the mirror and connect the plug. Install the mounting trim.

Antenna

REMOVAL & INSTALLATION

➡Some later 5, 6 and 7 Series models came factory equipped with the antenna mounted in the rear window glass. This type antenna are not serviceable without replacing the window glass.

Post Antenna

1. Disconnect negative battery cable.

2. Unplug the antenna from the radio, this may require radio removal on some models.

3. Pull the antenna wire through the firewall.

4. Using an adjustable wrench, remove the antenna base from the fender well and remove the antenna.

5. Install in reverse order, making sure to route the antenna wire carefully through the fire wall to prevent cutting the wire.

Power Antenna

1. Disconnect the negative battery cable.
2. Open the trunk and remove the side trim panel screws and remove the panel. Remove the spare tire and jack, on some models.
3. Unplug the antenna power lead and the antenna wire.
4. Using an adjustable wrench, carefully remove the antenna mast mounting from the top of the rear fender.
5. Remove the antenna mounting bracket bolt inside the trunk and remove the antenna assembly by pulling it down and out.
6. Install the antenna in reverse order, check the operation of the antenna.

Front Fenders

The front fenders are of a bolted-on design. By removing any connecting body trim and removing the mounting bolts, the front fender can be replaced. Use only factory approved replacement panels to maintain the rust-through warranties many newer models have, as well as an original body appearance quality. Have any new panel finished using original factory methods and the work completed by a facility capable of duplicating the factory paint.

Although not a factory used method, shims may be used to install and adjust the fender. In the event you purchase a BMW vehicle with shims on the fender, chances are this vehicle has had bodywork or an aftermarket fender panel replacement.

Sunroof

REMOVAL & INSTALLATION

3, 5, 6 and 7 Series Models

▶ **See Figure 19**

1. Open the sunroof lid 2–4 inches (5–10cm).
2. Unclip the roof liner frame and push it back into the headliner opening.

3. Close the sunroof lid and loosen the retaining bolts on each end of the gates.
4. Pull in the retainers, remove the center bolts and lift off the lid.
5. Remove the cover over the control motor and gearbox. Close the sunroof, if not already closed.
6. Disconnect the wiring harness and remove the 3 mounting bolts. Remove the motor and gearbox.
7. Push the cables back evenly on both sides. Remove the rail covers and pull the cables out of their guides.
8. Place the cable in the center position of the gate and press off.

To install:

9. Install the cables into the gate. The cables are marked with the proper side of installation. Do not lubricate the fabric covered type cables.
10. Pull the cables through the guides and align the cables. Insert a hex key through the gate and cable at the 0 position on the motor or gearbox assembly.
11. Install the motor and gearbox. The motor and gearbox must be synchronized with the hole in the drivegear aligned between the centers of the 2 gears. Torque the bolts to 2.0 ft. lbs. (2.8 Nm).
12. Install the sunroof lid. Use new hardware and torque to 3 ft. lbs. (4 Nm).
13. Adjust the sunroof lid. Pull the roof liner frame into position and clip into place.

ADJUSTMENT

3, 5, 6 and 7 Series Models

1. Open the sunroof lid 2–4 inches (5–10cm).
2. Unclip the roof liner frame and push back into the opening.
3. Close the sunroof lid and loosen the screws on each end of the gates.
4. Adjust the sunroof so the front of the panel is depressed 0.039 inches (1mm) below the roof level and the rear is 1mm above the roof level.
5. Align the lid so it is centered in the opening.
6. Tighten the screws and replace the liner.

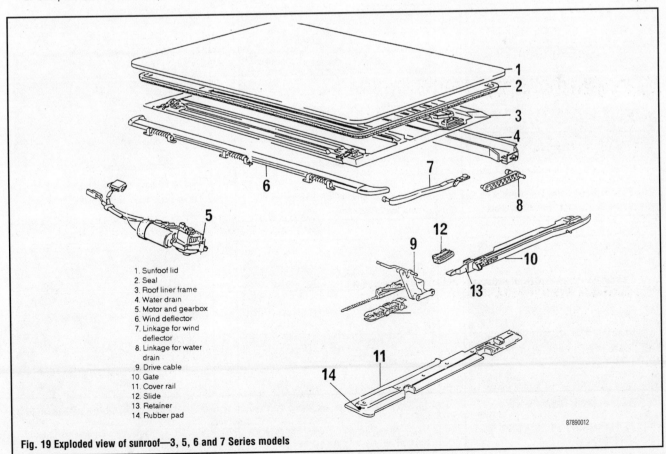

1. Sunroof lid
2. Seal
3. Roof liner frame
4. Water drain
5. Motor and gearbox
6. Wind deflector
7. Linkage for wind deflector
8. Linkage for water drain
9. Drive cable
10. Gate
11. Cover rail
12. Slide
13. Retainer
14. Rubber pad

87890012

Fig. 19 Exploded view of sunroof—3, 5, 6 and 7 Series models

INTERIOR

Dash Panel

REMOVAL & INSTALLATION

Except 3, 5, 6 and 7 Series Models

1. Disconnect the negative battery cable.
2. Remove the lower dash trim from under the steering column by removing the retaining screws. On some models the buzzer module will have to be unclipped to remove the panel from the interior of the vehicle. Unfasten the vent tubes from the circulation motor in the center of the dash.
3. Unfasten and tag the headlight switch, fog light, rear defroster, and circulation control wires. Tag prior to removal.
4. If the radio is mounted into the dash panel, remove and place aside.
5. Remove the glove box by unfastening the strap, lowering the door and removing the screws from the rear hinge.
6. Remove the steering wheel. Refer to the procedure in Section 8 for details.
7. Remove the 2 screws from the top of the instrument panel hood.
8. Remove the speaker grille and speaker from on top of the instrument panel. After the speaker has been removed, reach in and unfasten the speedometer cable from the back of the speedometer.
9. Remove the retaining screws from the lower portion of the dash panel which secure the instrument panel to the dash assembly.
10. Remove the instrument cluster and pull forward.
11. Disconnect the wire harness from the instrument cluster.
12. Remove the retaining bolts at the side of the panel securing it to the vehicle body. Working from below the panel, remove the retaining screws that run the length of the vehicle.
13. Lift the dash panel up. If all the hardware was removed, the panel will lift easily. Carefully pull the panel toward the rear of the vehicle. When the panel has cleared the retainer clips at the base of the windshield, it can be removed from the car.

To install:

14. Position the instrument panel into the vehicle and work into the retainer clips below the windshield.
15. Install the retainer screws along the the length of the panel. Attach the bolts at the side of the panel.
16. Install the remaining part in the reverse order of removal. Make sure any ground wires(brown) removed earlier are reconnected. Connect the negative battery cable. Check all cluster components and connections including the gauge lighting and speedometer cable connection.

3 Series Models

▶ See Figures 20 thru 25

1. Disconnect the negative battery cable.
2. Remove the lower dash trim from under the steering column by removing the retaining screws. On some models the buzzer module will have to be unclipped to remove the panel from the interior of the vehicle.
3. Working from under the dash panel, remove the retaining bolts at the side of the panel, as well as those above the driver;s and passenger's footwell. With all the bolts removed, proceed on to removing all the screws along the length of the panel. Make sure you remove all the screws.
4. Remove the vent tubes, headlight, fog, defroster and other switches from the panel. Tag all harness before removing.
5. Remove the steering wheel. Refer to the procedure in Section 8 for details.
6. Remove the 2 screws from the top of the instrument panel hood.
7. Remove the screws from the instrument cluster and pull forward.
8. Pull the clip off the harness plug and disconnect from the instrument cluster.
9. Remove the dash panel from the vehicle by lifting up and out. Make sure no wires are attached to the panel when removing.
10. Install in reverse order or removal. Install all retainer bolts and screws or the panel could squeak during driving. Fasten all wires and switches, including

Fig. 20 Before beginning your work, note the placement of all major components

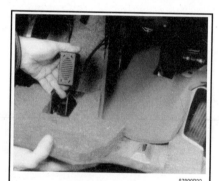

Fig. 21 If equipped with a buzzer, unclip from the lower panel

Fig. 22 Remove the retaining screws from the upper portion of the instrument panel hood

Fig. 23 Remove the instrument panel hood and place aside

Fig. 24 Bring the instrument panel forward and pull out towards you slightly . . .

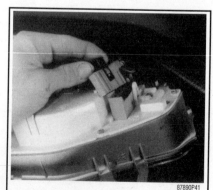

Fig. 25 . . . and unfasten the instrument panel wire harness

ground wires. Connect the negative battery cable. Check all cluster components and connections including the gauge lighting and speedometer cable connection.

5, 6 and 7 Series Models

1. Disconnect the negative battery cable.
2. Remove the lower dash trim from under the steering column by removing the retaining screws. On some models the buzzer module will have to be unclipped to remove the panel from the interior of the vehicle.
3. If equipped with wood or plastic trim panels, carefully pry them out of the panel. If a trim panel will not remove easily, look under the dash panel and check for a retainer clip.
4. Remove the steering wheel. Refer to the procedure in Section 8 for details.
5. Remove the radio from the dash.
6. Remove the screws from the top of the instrument panel hood.
7. Disconnect all switches, vent tubing and harnesses attached to the dash panel.
8. Remove the retainer bolts and screws securing the dash panel to the vehicle.
9. Remove the screws from the instrument cluster and pull forward.
10. Remove the dash panel forward and out of the vehicle.

To install:

11. Work the dash panel into position and secure with retaining hardware.
12. Connect the switches, vent tubing and harnesses removed earlier.
13. Install the remaining components in the reverse order or removal. Connect the negative battery cable. Check all cluster components and connections including the gauge lighting and speedometer cable connection.

Center Console

REMOVAL & INSTALLATION

Except 3, 5, 6 and 7 Series Models

▶ See Figure 26

1. Disconnect the negative battery cable.
2. Remove the screws or bolts depending on year and model from the driver and passenger front side of the console.
3. If equipped with radio in center console, remove. Refer to the section in Section 6 for removal details.
4. Lift out the floor section below the brake and remove the retaining screws.
5. Remove the shifter knob front the shift lever. On manual transmission equipped models, remove the shift boot around the lever.
6. On automatic equipped models, remove the retaining screws securing the shifter plate around the lever.
7. Lift the center console over the brake handle and out of the way.

To install:

8. Position the center console between the seats, and work the brake handle through the opening.
9. Install the automatic shifter plate or manual shifter boot around the shift lever.
10. Secure using the screws or bolts removed earlier.
11. Install the radio.

12. Fasten the the shifter knob to the shift lever.
13. Connect the negative battery cable.

3 Series Models

▶ See Figures 27 and 28

1. Disconnect the negative battery cable.
2. Remove the lower dash trim from under the steering column.
3. Pull out the ashtray from the rear of the console. Remove the screw underneath. Pull the console back and off the brake lever. Disconnect the wiring.
4. Pull the manual transmission shift knob off the shift lever. Pull the shifter boot up and off. On automatic equipped vehicles unclip the trim on the right side of the shifter. Remove the screws exposed.
5. Pull out and disconnect the window switches.
6. Remove the forward ashtray assembly, then remove the screws from below the forward ashtray console and lift out. Disconnect the wiring for the lighter.
7. Remove the bolts below the heater controls. Rotate the retainers on the sides of the consoles to release. Pull the console out.
8. Install in reverse order.

320i MODELS

1. Disconnect the negative battery cable.
2. Remove the screws from the driver and passenger front side of the console.
3. If equipped with a radio in the console, remove it by unfastening the knobs and retaining hardware, then sliding it out and detaching the harness from the rear. Refer to Section 6 for details.
4. If equipped with a rear ashtray, pull the ashtray out from the rear of the console. Remove the screw underneath. Disconnect any necessary wiring.
5. Pull the manual transmission shift knob off the shift lever. Pull the shifter boot up and off. On automatic transmission equipped vehicles unclip the trim on the right side of the shifter. Remove the screws exposed.
6. Pull out and disconnect the window switches, if equipped with power windows.
7. Remove the forward ashtray assembly, then remove the screws from below the forward ashtray console and lift out. Disconnect the wiring for the lighter.
8. Lift the center console over the brake handle and out of the way.

To install:

9. Position the center console between the seats, and work the brake handle through the opening.
10. Install the automatic shifter plate or manual shifter boot around the shift lever.
11. Secure using the screws or bolts removed earlier.
12. Install the radio.
13. Fasten the the shifter knob to the shift lever.
14. Connect the negative battery cable.

5, 6 and 7 Series Models

1. Disconnect the negative battery cable.
2. Remove the trim from under the steering column.
3. Remove the rear trim plate or ashtray and disconnect the wires. Remove the screws from underneath.

Fig. 26 This 2002 center console has multiple electrical items which must be detached before removal

87890P48

Fig. 27 Lift out the rear ashtray . . .

87890P42

Fig. 28 . . . and unfasten the retaining screw underneath

87890P43

4. Pull out the cassette holder, if equipped, and disconnect the wiring for the lights. Remove the retaining screws attaching the console to the floor.

5. Remove the brake lever boot and unfasten the screw in the compartment next to the lever.

6. Remove the switches and disconnect any wiring. Remove the screw. Pull off the manual gear shift knob, or remove the screw from the automatic transmission shifter and remove.

7. Slide out the rear ashtray and remove the retaining screw underneath it.

8. Remove the center cover from the console horizontal section. Remove the radio and pull out the heater controls.

9. Install in reverse order taking care to install all the screws and harness connections.

10. Connect the negative battery cable.

Door Panels

REMOVAL & INSTALLATION

1970–83 Models

➡ **All models equipped with power windows have an access plug on the door panel, which when removed will allow the window to be cranked in either direction with a suitable hex driver in the event the window fails to function.**

1. Disconnect the negative battery cable.

2. Remove the power mirror switch or remote mirror control bezel, if equipped. To remove the mirror switch, carefully pry it from the door panel. Disconnect the electrical lead from it.

➡ **The driver's door panel is the only panel to contain a mirror control switch**

3. If equipped with power windows, remove the window switch from the armrest. Disconnect the electrical wires from it.

4. If equipped with manual windows, remove the window crank by removing the center panel on the handle and removing the retaining screw.

5. Remove the screws retaining the armrest and remove the armrest from the door panel. On some models, the upper screw is hidden behind a piece of plastic. Carefully pry out the plastic piece to expose and remove the screws.

6. Remove the screw securing the door handle to the interior latch assembly.

7. Remove the screw in the plate around the inside door handle. Remove the plate from around the door handle.

8. Remove the knob around the lock rod at the top of the panel.

9. Remove the retaining screws at the bottom edge of the door panel and pull the panel off. Use care not to loose any of the retaining clips.

10. The top panel can now be removed by using the following procedures:

a. Remove the inside mirror cover, if equipped. Lift out the rear window channel slightly.

b. Remove the screws along the bottom edge of the top trim panel.

c. Remove the panel by lifting up on it and pulling out of the top of the door. Be careful not to loose any of the clips.

11. If work is to be done on the inside of the door, remove the plastic sheeting from the door. This panel must be reinstalled when finished, it serves as a water barrier for the door panel.

To install:

12. Install the top panel first, making sure the clips and screws are fully seated.

13. Install the mirror cover and reinsert the window channel in position.

14. Install the door panel, top first, by pushing in the areas where there are clips then screw the bottom in place.

15. Complete the installation by attaching the remaining components.

1984–88 Models

▸ **See Figures 29 thru 37**

➡ **All models equipped with power windows have an access plug on the door panel, which when removed will allow the window to be cranked in either direction with a suitable hex driver in the event the window fails to function.**

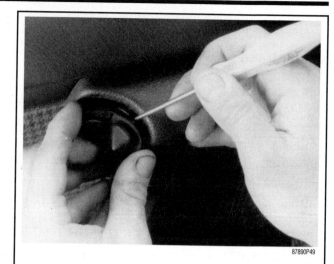

Fig. 29 If removing the mirror control switch, carefully pry out using a pick tool or small prytool

Fig. 30 Unfasten the harness and tuck inside the armrest

Fig. 31 Remove the screws from the lower portion of the armrest . .

Fig. 32 . . . and the screw from the upper part of the armrest . . .

Fig. 35 Remove the trim ring around the door handle

Fig. 33 . . . then remove the armrest

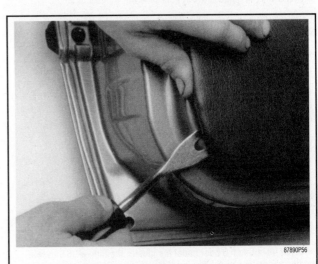
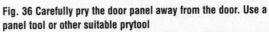

Fig. 36 Carefully pry the door panel away from the door. Use a panel tool or other suitable prytool

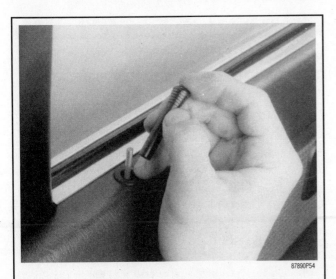

Fig. 34 Unscrew the lock knob from the top of the door panel

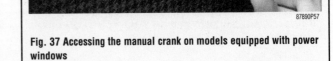

Fig. 37 Accessing the manual crank on models equipped with power windows

1. Remove the power mirror switch. Remove the screw underneath the switch and the screw(s) under the armrest. Remove the armrest.

2. Remove the door lock button. Pull the interior door handle cups out. Lower the window.

3. Pull the panel out from the bottom and unclip from the top.

4. Check the position of the clips and seals when replacing. Press down and in to seat.

Door Locks

REMOVAL & INSTALLATION

The procedure for door lock removal and installation is the same for both power and manual locks with the exception of the lock actuating switch and wiring on power lock systems.

1. Disconnect the negative battery cable.

2. Remove the front door panel.

3. Wind the window all the way up. Pull the window guide out at the bottom. This can be reached through the bottom opening in the door panel.

4. Remove the bolt retaining the lower part of the window guide rail and take the guide rail out by pulling down.

➡**Removing the guide rail will not cause the window to fall.**

5. Locate the lock assembly bracket. On power lock equipped models this will also hold the lock actuator and wiring.

6. Loosen the retaining screw and remove the bracket, then disconnect the actuator wire (if equipped with power locks).

7. Disconnect the lock rod from the lock assembly. This is the part of the lock that actually keeps the door closed.

8. Any of the other locking components can now be removed as necessary. This includes the inside release handle, the locking mechanism linkages and the key lock assembly on front doors. The key lock is removed by twisting it 90 degrees and pulling it out to the inside of the door.

To install:

9. Install any removed components then install the lock assembly bracket.

10. On models with power door locks, reconnect the wiring to the actuator.

11. Check all lock rods for binding or bent linkages. It is also a good idea to check the locking mechanism for proper operation before reinstalling the door panel.

12. After all components are in place and you are sure the locking system is working, reinstall the lower window rail and then install the door panel.

➡**When installing the door panel the plastic sheeting MUST be reinstalled as this is a water barrier. If the sheeting is damaged, use a piece of heavy plastic to replace it.**

13. Reconnect the negative battery cable and recheck the operation of the door locks.

14. On models with power door locks, be sure the entire locking system is working.

Door Lock Actuators

REMOVAL & INSTALLATION

3 Series Models

1. Disconnect the negative battery cable.

2. Remove the door panel and the water shield.

3. Disconnect the wiring from the actuator. Remove the screws and pull the actuator off the linkage.

4. When installing, move the actuator and linkage to the locked position.

5. Connect the linkage to the actuator and loosely install with the screws.

6. Compress the actuator drive to take out any play in the linkage and tighten the screws.

7. Test the locks and install the door panel.

8. Connect the negative battery cable and check the power lock functions.

5, 6 and 7 Series Models

1. Disconnect the negative battery cable.

2. Remove the door panel and the water shield.

3. Disconnect the wiring from the actuator. Remove the screws and pull the actuator off the linkage.

4. When installing, move the actuator and linkage to the locked position.

5. Connect the linkage to the actuator and loosely install with the screws.

6. Compress the actuator drive to take out any play in the linkage and tighten the screws.

7. Test the locks and install the door panel.

8. Connect the negative battery cable and check the power lock functions.

Door Glass and Regulator

REMOVAL & INSTALLATION

Models with Manual Window Controls

This procedure is good for both front and rear doors. Remember when removing window glass to use care when handling it. The glass should be placed out of the way to prevent the chance of damage.

1. Disconnect the negative battery cable.

2. Remove the door trim panel.

3. Locate the screws that hold the bottom lifting rail in place and remove them. Hold the window when doing this as it will become loose.

4. Tilt the window forward slightly and remove the lifting arm from the lifting rail.

5. Pull the window carefully out of the door.

6. The regulator can now be removed. This is done removing the bolts retaining it and pulling it out through the door.

7. Any of the window guide rails, molding or weatherstrip can now be removed.

To install:

8. Install any parts removed other than the window and regulator.

9. Install the window regulator and the lifting arm. Install the window by sliding it into the door.

10. Install the glass into the lifting arm and install the retaining screws.

11. Check the operation of the window and adjust it as necessary, using the following procedure:

   a. Put the window all the way up. Loosen the lifting rail bolts.

   b. Using special tool 51 3 150 or equivalent tool, turn the holder for the lifting rail so that both slides on the rail fit snugly. Tighten the rail bolts.

   c. Check the window travel, it should be limited by the stop on the regulator.

12. Install the door panel and check the operation of the window.

13. Connect the negative battery cable.

Window Regulator and Motor

REMOVAL & INSTALLATION

1970–83 Models

1. Disconnect the negative battery cable.

2. Remove the window glass as outlined in this section.

3. With the glass removed, the regulator assembly can now be removed. This is done by removing the bolts retaining it and pulling it out through the door.

4. The motor can be removed from the regulator assembly by pulling back the protective sleeve, turning the armature until the toothed gear is clear of the motor and removing the mounting screws. Pull the motor from the assembly.

5. Any of the window guide rails, molding or weatherstrip can now be removed. The motor control switch is also easy to remove now. To do this, disconnect the wires from it and pull it out of the door.

To install:

6. Install any parts removed other than the window and motor, and regulator assembly.

7. Install the window regulator and motor assembly, and the lifting arm. Install the window by sliding it into the door.

8. Install the glass into the lifting arm and install the retaining screws.

9. Check the operation of the window and adjust it as necessary, using the following procedure:

　　a. Put the window all the way up. Loosen the lifting rail bolts.

　　b. Using special tool 51 3 150 or equivalent tool, turn the holder for the lifting rail so that both slides on the rail fit snugly. Tighten the rail bolts.

　　c. Check the window travel, it should be limited by the stop on the motor.

10. Install the door panel and check the operation of the window, if manually controlled.

11. Connect the negative battery cable.

12. Check for proper window operation.

3 Series Models

1. Disconnect the negative battery cable.
2. Remove the door panel.
3. Remove the window glass as outlined in this section.
4. Disconnect the wiring harness from the regulator motor.
5. Remove the mounting screws from the door panel.
6. Pull the regulator out of the door cutout.
7. Install in reverse order.
8. Connect the negative battery cable, and check for proper window operation.

5, 6 and 7 Series Models

1. Disconnect the negative battery cable.
2. Remove the door panel.
3. Disconnect the window glass from the regulator and block up to support.
4. Remove the microswitch.
5. Grind out the regulator mounting rivets and remove the screw at the end of the arm.
6. Remove the regulator.
7. Install in reverse order. Replace the rivets with M6x10 bolts with 6.4mm washers and matching nuts.
8. Connect the negative battery cable and check for proper window operation.

Inside Rearview Mirror

REMOVAL & INSTALLATION

1970–83 Models

To remove the inside mirror, remove the Allen head screw that keeps it attached to its base and slide the mirror off.

On models with overhead consoles, remove the overhead console retaining screws and pull the console down. Disconnect the electrical lead and remove the console. Remove the Allen head screw and remove the mirror from its base.

1984–88 Models

The mirror is held with either a spring clip if mounted in the roof and pulls out or it mounts to a pad cemented to the windshield. If it is windshield mounted, rotate the mirror and pull off to the rear. Match the mount and press into place.

Windshield and Fixed Glass

REMOVAL & INSTALLATION

If your windshield, or other fixed window, is cracked or chipped, you may decide to replace it with a new one yourself. However, there are two main reasons why replacement windshields and other window glass should be installed only by a professional automotive glass technician: safety and cost.

The most important reason a professional should install automotive glass is for safety. The glass in the vehicle, especially the windshield, is designed with safety in mind in case of a collision. The windshield is specially manufactured from two panes of specially-tempered glass with a thin layer of transparent plastic between them. This construction allows the glass to "give" in the event that a part of your body hits the windshield during the collision, and prevents the glass from shattering, which could cause lacerations, blinding and other harm to passengers of the vehicle. The other fixed windows are designed to be tempered so that if they break during a collision, they shatter in such a way that there are no large pointed glass pieces. The professional automotive glass technician knows how to install the glass in a vehicle so that it will function optimally during a collision. Without the proper experience, knowledge and tools, installing a piece of automotive glass yourself could lead to additional harm if an accident should ever occur.

Cost is also a factor when deciding to install automotive glass yourself. Performing this could cost you much more than a professional may charge for the same job. Since the windshield is designed to break under stress, an often life saving characteristic, windshields tend to break VERY easily when an inexperienced person attempts to install one. Do-it-yourselfers buying two, three or even four windshields from a salvage yard because they have broken them during installation are common stories. Also, since the automotive glass is designed to prevent the outside elements from entering your vehicle, improper installation can lead to water and air leaks. Annoying whining noises at highway speeds from air leaks or inside body panel rusting from water leaks can add to your stress level and subtract from your wallet. After buying two or three windshields, installing them and ending up with a leak that produces a noise while driving and water damage during rainstorms, the cost of having a professional do it correctly the first time may be much more alluring. We here at Chilton, therefore, advise that you have a professional automotive glass technician service any broken glass on your vehicle.

WINDSHIELD CHIP REPAIR

▶ See Figures 38 and 39

➡**Check with your state and local authorities on the laws for state safety inspection. Some states or municipalities may not allow chip repair as a viable option for correcting stone damage to your windshield.**

Although severely cracked or damaged windshields must be replaced, there is something that you can do to prolong or even prevent the need for replacement of a chipped windshield. There are many companies which offer windshield chip repair products, such as Loctite's® Bullseye™ windshield repair kit. These kits usually consist of a syringe, pedestal and a sealing adhesive. The syringe is mounted on the pedestal and is used to create a vacuum which pulls the plastic layer against the glass. This helps make the chip transparent. The

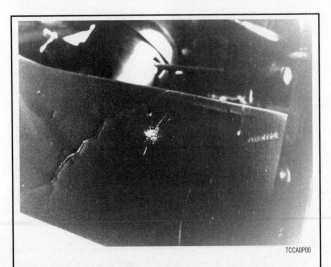

TCCA0P00

Fig. 38 Small chips on your windshield can be fixed with an aftermarket repair kit, such as the one from Loctite®

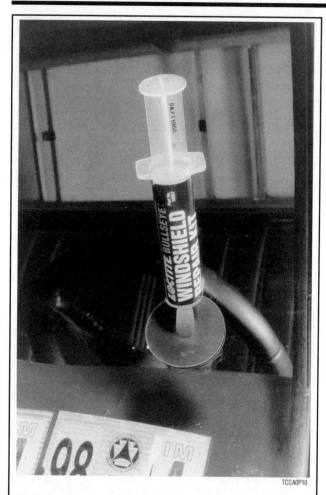

Fig. 39 Most kits use a self-stick applicator and syringe to inject the adhesive into the chip or crack

TCCA0P10

adhesive is then injected which seals the chip and helps to prevent further stress cracks from developing

➡**Always follow the specific manufacturer's instructions.**

Seats

REMOVAL & INSTALLATION

Seat removal and installation is basically the same for both manual and power seat assemblies, with the exception of wiring for power seat equipped models.

Front

➡**Depending on the year and model, some seats are secured using standard bolts, while others use Torx® or Allen head bolts. Before beginning the procedure, check the bolt head to make sure you have the correct tools for removal and installation.**

1. Disconnect the negative battery.
2. Slide the seat all the way back and locate the 2 front seat track-to-base mounting bolts.
3. Remove the front mounting bolts.
4. Slide the seat all the way forward and locate the rear seat track-to-base mounting bolts.
5. Remove the bolts and tilt the seat backward.
6. Disconnect all of the electrical wiring, if equipped and remove the seat from the vehicle.
7. The seat mounting base will still be in the vehicle, it can now be removed if desired. To do so, remove the 4 base mounting bolts and pull the assembly out of the vehicle.
8. Install the base, if it was removed. Install the seat back into the vehicle and reconnect the electrical leads.

Rear

To remove the rear seat, remove the base by pulling it up in the front and sliding it toward the front of the vehicle and out. Then remove the bolts at the bottom corners of the seat back and nuts from the center armrest, if equipped with an armrest, pull it up and out of the vehicle.

GLOSSARY

AIR/FUEL RATIO: The ratio of air-to-gasoline by weight in the fuel mixture drawn into the engine.

AIR INJECTION: One method of reducing harmful exhaust emissions by injecting air into each of the exhaust ports of an engine. The fresh air entering the hot exhaust manifold causes any remaining fuel to be burned before it can exit the tailpipe.

ALTERNATOR: A device used for converting mechanical energy into electrical energy.

AMMETER: An instrument, calibrated in amperes, used to measure the flow of an electrical current in a circuit. Ammeters are always connected in series with the circuit being tested.

AMPERE: The rate of flow of electrical current present when one volt of electrical pressure is applied against one ohm of electrical resistance.

ANALOG COMPUTER: Any microprocessor that uses similar (analogous) electrical signals to make its calculations.

ARMATURE: A laminated, soft iron core wrapped by a wire that converts electrical energy to mechanical energy as in a motor or relay. When rotated in a magnetic field, it changes mechanical energy into electrical energy as in a generator.

ATMOSPHERIC PRESSURE: The pressure on the Earth's surface caused by the weight of the air in the atmosphere. At sea level, this pressure is 14.7 psi at 32°F (101 kPa at 0°C).

ATOMIZATION: The breaking down of a liquid into a fine mist that can be suspended in air.

AXIAL PLAY: Movement parallel to a shaft or bearing bore.

BACKFIRE: The sudden combustion of gases in the intake or exhaust system that results in a loud explosion.

BACKLASH: The clearance or play between two parts, such as meshed gears.

BACKPRESSURE: Restrictions in the exhaust system that slow the exit of exhaust gases from the combustion chamber.

BAKELITE: A heat resistant, plastic insulator material commonly used in printed circuit boards and transistorized components.

BALL BEARING: A bearing made up of hardened inner and outer races between which hardened steel balls roll.

BALLAST RESISTOR: A resistor in the primary ignition circuit that lowers voltage after the engine is started to reduce wear on ignition components.

BEARING: A friction reducing, supportive device usually located between a stationary part and a moving part.

BIMETAL TEMPERATURE SENSOR: Any sensor or switch made of two dissimilar types of metal that bend when heated or cooled due to the different expansion rates of the alloys. These types of sensors usually function as an on/off switch.

BLOWBY: Combustion gases, composed of water vapor and unburned fuel, that leak past the piston rings into the crankcase during normal engine operation. These gases are removed by the PCV system to prevent the buildup of harmful acids in the crankcase.

BRAKE PAD: A brake shoe and lining assembly used with disc brakes.

BRAKE SHOE: The backing for the brake lining. The term is, however, usually applied to the assembly of the brake backing and lining.

BUSHING: A liner, usually removable, for a bearing; an anti-friction liner used in place of a bearing.

CALIPER: A hydraulically activated device in a disc brake system, which is mounted straddling the brake rotor (disc). The caliper contains at least one piston and two brake pads. Hydraulic pressure on the piston(s) forces the pads against the rotor.

CAMSHAFT: A shaft in the engine on which are the lobes (cams) which operate the valves. The camshaft is driven by the crankshaft, via a belt, chain or gears, at one half the crankshaft speed.

CAPACITOR: A device which stores an electrical charge.

CARBON MONOXIDE (CO): A colorless, odorless gas given off as a normal byproduct of combustion. It is poisonous and extremely dangerous in confined areas, building up slowly to toxic levels without warning if adequate ventilation is not available.

CARBURETOR: A device, usually mounted on the intake manifold of an engine, which mixes the air and fuel in the proper proportion to allow even combustion.

CATALYTIC CONVERTER: A device installed in the exhaust system, like a muffler, that converts harmful byproducts of combustion into carbon dioxide and water vapor by means of a heat-producing chemical reaction.

CENTRIFUGAL ADVANCE: A mechanical method of advancing the spark timing by using flyweights in the distributor that react to centrifugal force generated by the distributor shaft rotation.

CHECK VALVE: Any one-way valve installed to permit the flow of air, fuel or vacuum in one direction only.

CHOKE: A device, usually a moveable valve, placed in the intake path of a carburetor to restrict the flow of air.

CIRCUIT: Any unbroken path through which an electrical current can flow. Also used to describe fuel flow in some instances.

CIRCUIT BREAKER: A switch which protects an electrical circuit from overload by opening the circuit when the current flow exceeds a predetermined level. Some circuit breakers must be reset manually, while most reset automatically.

COIL (IGNITION): A transformer in the ignition circuit which steps up the voltage provided to the spark plugs.

COMBINATION MANIFOLD: An assembly which includes both the intake and exhaust manifolds in one casting.

COMBINATION VALVE: A device used in some fuel systems that routes fuel vapors to a charcoal storage canister instead of venting them into the atmosphere. The valve relieves fuel tank pressure and allows fresh air into the tank as the fuel level drops to prevent a vapor lock situation.

COMPRESSION RATIO: The comparison of the total volume of the cylinder and combustion chamber with the piston at BDC and the piston at TDC.

CONDENSER: 1. An electrical device which acts to store an electrical charge, preventing voltage surges. 2. A radiator-like device in the air conditioning system in which refrigerant gas condenses into a liquid, giving off heat.

CONDUCTOR: Any material through which an electrical current can be transmitted easily.

CONTINUITY: Continuous or complete circuit. Can be checked with an ohmmeter.

COUNTERSHAFT: An intermediate shaft which is rotated by a mainshaft and transmits, in turn, that rotation to a working part.

CRANKCASE: The lower part of an engine in which the crankshaft and related parts operate.

CRANKSHAFT: The main driving shaft of an engine which receives reciprocating motion from the pistons and converts it to rotary motion.

CYLINDER: In an engine, the round hole in the engine block in which the piston(s) ride.

CYLINDER BLOCK: The main structural member of an engine in which is found the cylinders, crankshaft and other principal parts.

CYLINDER HEAD: The detachable portion of the engine, usually fastened to the top of the cylinder block and containing all or most of the combustion chambers. On overhead valve engines, it contains the valves and their operating parts. On overhead cam engines, it contains the camshaft as well.

DEAD CENTER: The extreme top or bottom of the piston stroke.

DETONATION: An unwanted explosion of the air/fuel mixture in the combustion chamber caused by excess heat and compression, advanced timing, or an overly lean mixture. Also referred to as "ping".

DIAPHRAGM: A thin, flexible wall separating two cavities, such as in a vacuum advance unit.

DIESELING: A condition in which hot spots in the combustion chamber cause the engine to run on after the key is turned off.

DIFFERENTIAL: A geared assembly which allows the transmission of motion between drive axles, giving one axle the ability to turn faster than the other.

DIODE: An electrical device that will allow current to flow in one direction only.

DISC BRAKE: A hydraulic braking assembly consisting of a brake disc, or rotor, mounted on an axle, and a caliper assembly containing, usually two brake pads which are activated by hydraulic pressure. The pads are forced against the sides of the disc, creating friction which slows the vehicle.

DISTRIBUTOR: A mechanically driven device on an engine which is responsible for electrically firing the spark plug at a predetermined point of the piston stroke.

DOWEL PIN: A pin, inserted in mating holes in two different parts allowing those parts to maintain a fixed relationship.

DRUM BRAKE: A braking system which consists of two brake shoes and one or two wheel cylinders, mounted on a fixed backing plate, and a brake drum, mounted on an axle, which revolves around the assembly.

DWELL: The rate, measured in degrees of shaft rotation, at which an electrical circuit cycles on and off.

ELECTRONIC CONTROL UNIT (ECU): Ignition module, module, amplifier or igniter. See Module for definition.

ELECTRONIC IGNITION: A system in which the timing and firing of the spark plugs is controlled by an electronic control unit, usually called a module. These systems have no points or condenser.

END-PLAY: The measured amount of axial movement in a shaft.

ENGINE: A device that converts heat into mechanical energy.

EXHAUST MANIFOLD: A set of cast passages or pipes which conduct exhaust gases from the engine.

FEELER GAUGE: A blade, usually metal, or precisely predetermined thickness, used to measure the clearance between two parts.

FIRING ORDER: The order in which combustion occurs in the cylinders of an engine. Also the order in which spark is distributed to the plugs by the distributor.

FLOODING: The presence of too much fuel in the intake manifold and combustion chamber which prevents the air/fuel mixture from firing, thereby causing a no-start situation.

FLYWHEEL: A disc shaped part bolted to the rear end of the crankshaft. Around the outer perimeter is affixed the ring gear. The starter drive engages the ring gear, turning the flywheel, which rotates the crankshaft, imparting the initial starting motion to the engine.

FOOT POUND (ft. lbs. or sometimes, ft.lb.): The amount of energy or work needed to raise an item weighing one pound, a distance of one foot.

FUSE: A protective device in a circuit which prevents circuit overload by breaking the circuit when a specific amperage is present. The device is constructed around a strip or wire of a lower amperage rating than the circuit it is designed to protect. When an amperage higher than that stamped on the fuse is present in the circuit, the strip or wire melts, opening the circuit.

GEAR RATIO: The ratio between the number of teeth on meshing gears.

GENERATOR: A device which converts mechanical energy into electrical energy.

HEAT RANGE: The measure of a spark plug's ability to dissipate heat from its firing end. The higher the heat range, the hotter the plug fires.

HUB: The center part of a wheel or gear.

HYDROCARBON (HC): Any chemical compound made up of hydrogen and carbon. A major pollutant formed by the engine as a byproduct of combustion.

HYDROMETER: An instrument used to measure the specific gravity of a solution.

INCH POUND (inch lbs.; sometimes in.lb. or in. lbs.): One twelfth of a foot pound.

INDUCTION: A means of transferring electrical energy in the form of a magnetic field. Principle used in the ignition coil to increase voltage.

INJECTOR: A device which receives metered fuel under relatively low pressure and is activated to inject the fuel into the engine under relatively high pressure at a predetermined time.

INPUT SHAFT: The shaft to which torque is applied, usually carrying the driving gear or gears.

INTAKE MANIFOLD: A casting of passages or pipes used to conduct air or a fuel/air mixture to the cylinders.

JOURNAL: The bearing surface within which a shaft operates.

KEY: A small block usually fitted in a notch between a shaft and a hub to prevent slippage of the two parts.

MANIFOLD: A casting of passages or set of pipes which connect the cylinders to an inlet or outlet source.

MANIFOLD VACUUM: Low pressure in an engine intake manifold formed just below the throttle plates. Manifold vacuum is highest at idle and drops under acceleration.

MASTER CYLINDER: The primary fluid pressurizing device in a hydraulic system. In automotive use, it is found in brake and hydraulic clutch systems and is pedal activated, either directly or, in a power brake system, through the power booster.

MODULE: Electronic control unit, amplifier or igniter of solid state or integrated design which controls the current flow in the ignition primary circuit based on input from the pick-up coil. When the module opens the primary circuit, high secondary voltage is induced in the coil.

NEEDLE BEARING: A bearing which consists of a number (usually a large number) of long, thin rollers.

OHM: (Ω) The unit used to measure the resistance of conductor-to-electrical flow. One ohm is the amount of resistance that limits current flow to one ampere in a circuit with one volt of pressure.

OHMMETER: An instrument used for measuring the resistance, in ohms, in an electrical circuit.

OUTPUT SHAFT: The shaft which transmits torque from a device, such as a transmission.

OVERDRIVE: A gear assembly which produces more shaft revolutions than that transmitted to it.

OVERHEAD CAMSHAFT (OHC): An engine configuration in which the camshaft is mounted on top of the cylinder head and operates the valve either directly or by means of rocker arms.

OVERHEAD VALVE (OHV): An engine configuration in which all of the valves are located in the cylinder head and the camshaft is located in the cylinder block. The camshaft operates the valves via lifters and pushrods.

OXIDES OF NITROGEN (NOx): Chemical compounds of nitrogen produced as a byproduct of combustion. They combine with hydrocarbons to produce smog.

OXYGEN SENSOR: Use with the feedback system to sense the presence of oxygen in the exhaust gas and signal the computer which can reference the voltage signal to an air/fuel ratio.

PINION: The smaller of two meshing gears.

PISTON RING: An open-ended ring with fits into a groove on the outer diameter of the piston. Its chief function is to form a seal between the piston and cylinder wall. Most automotive pistons have three rings: two for compression sealing; one for oil sealing.

PRELOAD: A predetermined load placed on a bearing during assembly or by adjustment.

PRIMARY CIRCUIT: the low voltage side of the ignition system which consists of the ignition switch, ballast resistor or resistance wire, bypass, coil, electronic control unit and pick-up coil as well as the connecting wires and harnesses.

PRESS FIT: The mating of two parts under pressure, due to the inner diameter of one being smaller than the outer diameter of the other, or vice versa; an interference fit.

RACE: The surface on the inner or outer ring of a bearing on which the balls, needles or rollers move.

REGULATOR: A device which maintains the amperage and/or voltage levels of a circuit at predetermined values.

RELAY: A switch which automatically opens and/or closes a circuit.

RESISTANCE: The opposition to the flow of current through a circuit or electrical device, and is measured in ohms. Resistance is equal to the voltage divided by the amperage.

RESISTOR: A device, usually made of wire, which offers a preset amount of resistance in an electrical circuit.

RING GEAR: The name given to a ring-shaped gear attached to a differential case, or affixed to a flywheel or as part of a planetary gear set.

ROLLER BEARING: A bearing made up of hardened inner and outer races between which hardened steel rollers move.

ROTOR: 1. The disc-shaped part of a disc brake assembly, upon which the brake pads bear; also called, brake disc. 2. The device mounted atop the distributor shaft, which passes current to the distributor cap tower contacts.

SECONDARY CIRCUIT: The high voltage side of the ignition system, usually above 20,000 volts. The secondary includes the ignition coil, coil wire, distributor cap and rotor, spark plug wires and spark plugs.

SENDING UNIT: A mechanical, electrical, hydraulic or electro-magnetic device which transmits information to a gauge.

SENSOR: Any device designed to measure engine operating conditions or ambient pressures and temperatures. Usually electronic in nature and designed to send a voltage signal to an on-board computer, some sensors may operate as a simple on/off switch or they may provide a variable voltage signal (like a potentiometer) as conditions or measured parameters change.

SHIM: Spacers of precise, predetermined thickness used between parts to establish a proper working relationship.

SLAVE CYLINDER: In automotive use, a device in the hydraulic clutch system which is activated by hydraulic force, disengaging the clutch.

SOLENOID: A coil used to produce a magnetic field, the effect of which is to produce work.

SPARK PLUG: A device screwed into the combustion chamber of a spark ignition engine. The basic construction is a conductive core inside of a ceramic insulator, mounted in an outer conductive base. An electrical charge from the spark plug wire travels along the conductive core and jumps a preset air gap to a grounding point or points at the end of the conductive base. The resultant spark ignites the fuel/air mixture in the combustion chamber.

SPLINES: Ridges machined or cast onto the outer diameter of a shaft or inner diameter of a bore to enable parts to mate without rotation.

TACHOMETER: A device used to measure the rotary speed of an engine, shaft, gear, etc., usually in rotations per minute.

THERMOSTAT: A valve, located in the cooling system of an engine, which is closed when cold and opens gradually in response to engine heating, controlling the temperature of the coolant and rate of coolant flow.

TOP DEAD CENTER (TDC): The point at which the piston reaches the top of its travel on the compression stroke.

TORQUE: The twisting force applied to an object.

TORQUE CONVERTER: A turbine used to transmit power from a driving member to a driven member via hydraulic action, providing changes in drive ratio and torque. In automotive use, it links the driveplate at the rear of the engine to the automatic transmission.

TRANSDUCER: A device used to change a force into an electrical signal.

TRANSISTOR: A semi-conductor component which can be actuated by a small voltage to perform an electrical switching function.

TUNE-UP: A regular maintenance function, usually associated with the replacement and adjustment of parts and components in the electrical and fuel systems of a vehicle for the purpose of attaining optimum performance.

TURBOCHARGER: An exhaust driven pump which compresses intake air and forces it into the combustion chambers at higher than atmospheric pressures. The increased air pressure allows more fuel to be burned and results in increased horsepower being produced.

VACUUM ADVANCE: A device which advances the ignition timing in response to increased engine vacuum.

VACUUM GAUGE: An instrument used to measure the presence of vacuum in a chamber.

VALVE: A device which control the pressure, direction of flow or rate of flow of a liquid or gas.

VALVE CLEARANCE: The measured gap between the end of the valve stem and the rocker arm, cam lobe or follower that activates the valve.

VISCOSITY: The rating of a liquid's internal resistance to flow.

VOLTMETER: An instrument used for measuring electrical force in units called volts. Voltmeters are always connected parallel with the circuit being tested.

WHEEL CYLINDER: Found in the automotive drum brake assembly, it is a device, actuated by hydraulic pressure, which, through internal pistons, pushes the brake shoes outward against the drums.

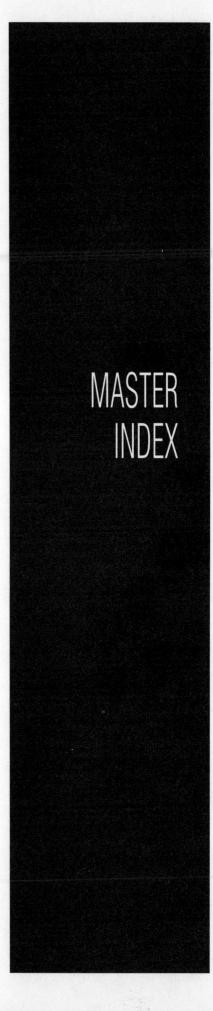

MASTER INDEX